Frommer's®
Costa Rica

My Costa Rica

by Eliot Greenspan

COSTA RICA IS AT ONCE EXOTIC AND ALLURING. ITS BIOLOGICAL

bounty is legendary; many travelers get their first taste of tropical nature here. Whether you come for adventure or rest and relaxation, this small Central American country offers a visual and sensory feast at almost every turn.

I have lived in Costa Rica for more than a decade, and the country continues to amaze me with its physical beauty—from the misty cloud forests of Monteverde to the imposing (and sometimes menacing) presence of Arenal Volcano. Its rainforests are a beguiling, dense patchwork of infinite shades of green. Hike the trails of a national park or visit one of the suspended bridge attractions to see for yourself.

Then there's the wildlife. I still get a giddy sense of awe every time I spot a troop of white-faced monkeys overhead. Or watch a newly hatched sea turtle take its first crucial dash to the sea. If you want adventure, sign up for a white-water rafting expedition. Learn to surf or ride a mountain bike along rural roads rutted by ox carts. Or strap on a harness and fly from treetop to treetop on a zip-line canopy tour. When you're tired and sore, take a soothing soak in the spectacular Tabacón hot springs.

The photos here capture some of my favorite Costa Rican images and experiences—I'm sure you'll have many more of your own.

WHITE-WATER RAFTING (right) Costa Rica's white water is wet and wild. I love taking 2-day trips on the Pacuare River, a class III–IV river that looks pretty much as pictured here for good stretches. More timid travelers can head out on gentler stretches of water, such as the Corobicí, Sarapiquí, or Reventazóon rivers.

TABACON RESORT (above) The setting at Tabacón Hot Springs Resort & Spa (www.tabacon.com), a hotel located at the foot of Arenal Volcano, is spectacular—and the waters are steamy and soothing. I like to walk the paths of the lush gardens here until I find a secluded and empty pool.

CAPUCHIN MONKEYS (above) Although these two are enjoying a quiet moment, white-faced, or capuchin, monkeys are some of the most active and acrobatic of the Costa Rican monkeys. Because they often travel in large troops, your best bet for spotting them is to listen carefully for movement in the canopy overhead.

MANUEL ANTONIO NATIONAL PARK (right) This is one of the most prized and most photographed views in Costa Rica. You don't have to stay at one of the fancier hotels in Manuel Antonio to enjoy it in person. Just head to the restaurant at La Mariposa (www.lamariposa.com) for a sunset cocktail.

NYMPAHLID BUTTERFLY (right) You'll certainly see plenty of butterflies flying free in the forests and parks of Costa Rica. But if you really want to get up close and personal with these winged beauties, be sure to visit one of the several "butterfly garden" type attractions around the country.

POAS VOLCANO NATIONAL PARK (below) Don't be fooled by the tranquil turquoise waters of the crater lake: You'll want to be upwind of the sulfuric gases rising out of the active Poás volcano. In addition to this beautiful view, there are several excellent trails through lush cloud forest here.

POISON DART FROG (above) The strawberry poison dart frog is also called the blue jean frog because its legs are the color of denim. Your best bet for seeing this guy is among tree roots and rainforest floor litter at La Selva Biological Station (www.ots.ac.cr) or in the Tortuguero area.

BASILISK LIZARD (right) Aside from looking really, really cool and somewhat prehistoric, this fellow can actually run across the surface of rivers and ponds. Hence, his more popular name: the "Jesus Christ lizard." Look for this guy along riverbeds and beside rainforest ponds across the country.

SEA TURTLE (right) You'll have to wake up very early, but you won't regret the lost sleep when you get to watch the amazing process of young hatchlings crawling toward the sea for the first time. If you're visiting Tortuguero or Playa Grande 2 to 3 months after the main nesting season, be sure to set an alarm.

CAHUITA BEACH (below) A 1991 earthquake raised the coral seabed around Cahuita by as much as 1m (3 ft.), eliminating a lot of beach but leaving a rugged and beautiful coastline. Grab a window seat at a beachside restaurant and enjoy the view.

© Kevin Schafer/Corbis

© PCL/Alamy

HAND-PAINTED OX CART (above)
Although Costa Rican commerce no
longer relies on these ox-drawn carts,
the carts remain a vibrant and popular
symbol of the country's history and
culture. You'll still see them used in
rural areas, although they're usually
more weathered and rugged than the
version pictured here.

COFFEE WORKER (right) Coffee is Costa
Rica's historic economic engine and
primary export. Although tourism currently generates more income, coffee
fields still cover most of the hillsides
around the Central Valley. If you don't
get to visit a plantation, at least be
sure to pick up some fresh beans to
bring home with you.

CAÑAS MOSAIC CHURCH If you're driving between San José and Guanacaste, make the tiny detour to visit the small city of Cañas. Hometown artist Otto Apuy is internationally known for his paintings and installations, but he returned to Cañas to make the local church perhaps the prettiest in the country. Apuy's cracked ceramic mosaics cover the entire exterior of the church, and run the gamut from abstract to representational.

ARENAL HANGING BRIDGE (above) Some 80% of a forest's biodiversity can be found in the canopy. In addition to sheltering birds, lizards, snakes, and monkeys, the canopy is home to an amazing array of epiphytic and parasitic bromeliads, orchids, vines, and lianas. Suspended bridges like this one are a great way to get a bird's-eye view of everything.

ARENAL VOLCANO (right) Folks flock to Arenal Volcano for the nighttime spectacle provided by its periodic eruptions, but the daytime views are just as impressive. Although you can't see the lava glow during the day, you can still hear earth-shaking deep rumblings and the high-pitched crackle of molten boulders crashing down its flanks.

MONTEVERDE CLOUD FOREST CANOPY TOUR Zip-line canopy tours are one of the most unique adventure options available in Costa Rica, although you're usually moving too fast to take in much scenery. The folks at The Original Canopy Tours (www.canopy tour.com) have operations at various destinations around the country.

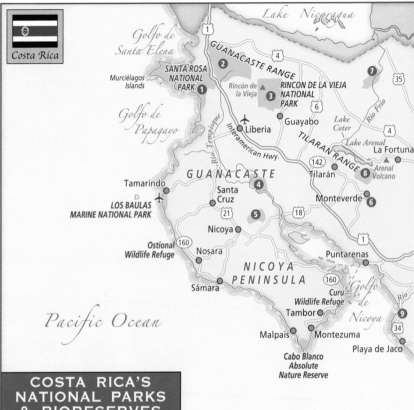

Costa Rica

Lake Nicaragua

Golfo de Santa Elena

GUANACASTE RANGE

Murciélagos Islands

SANTA ROSA NATIONAL PARK **1**

Rincón de la Vieja

RINCON DE LA VIEJA NATIONAL PARK

Golfo de Papagayo

Liberia

Interamerican Hwy.

Guayabo

Lake Coter

Rio Frio

TILARAN RANGE

Lake Arenal

La Fortuna

Arenal Volcano

GUANACASTE

Tilarán

Tamarindo

LOS BAULAS MARINE NATIONAL PARK

Santa Cruz

Monteverde **6**

Nicoya

Ostional Wildlife Refuge

Nosara

NICOYA PENINSULA

Puntarenas

Golfo de Nicoya

Curú Wildlife Refuge

Sámara

Tambor

Pacific Ocean

Malpais

Montezuma

Playa de Jaco

Cabo Blanco Absolute Nature Reserve

COSTA RICA'S NATIONAL PARKS & BIORESERVES

Arenal National Park **8**
Barra Honda National Park **5**
Braulio Carrillo National Park **11**
Cahuita National Park **17**
Caño Negro National Wildlife Refuge **7**
Carara Biological Reserve **9**
Chirripó National Park **16**
Corcovado National Park **18**
Guanacaste National Park **2**
Guayabo National Monument **13**
Irazú Volcano National Park **14**
Manuel Antonio National Park **15**
Monteverde Biological Cloud
　Forest Reserve **6**
Palo Verde National Park **4**
Poás Volcano National Park **10**
Rincón de la Vieja National Park **3**
Santa Rosa National Park **1**
Tortuguero National Park **12**

| 0 | 25 miles |
| 0 | 25 kilometers |

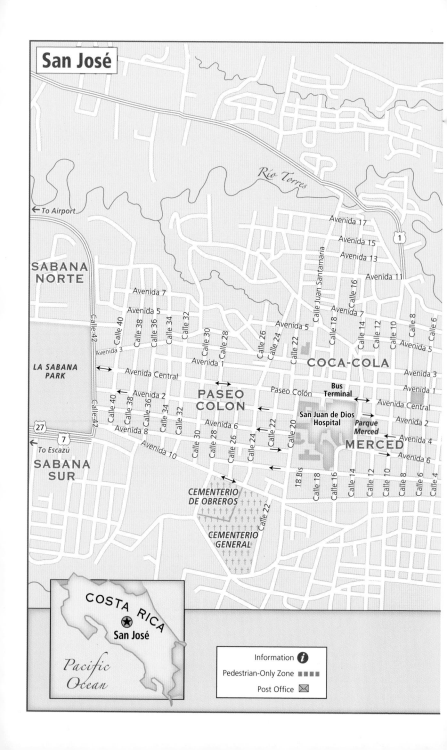

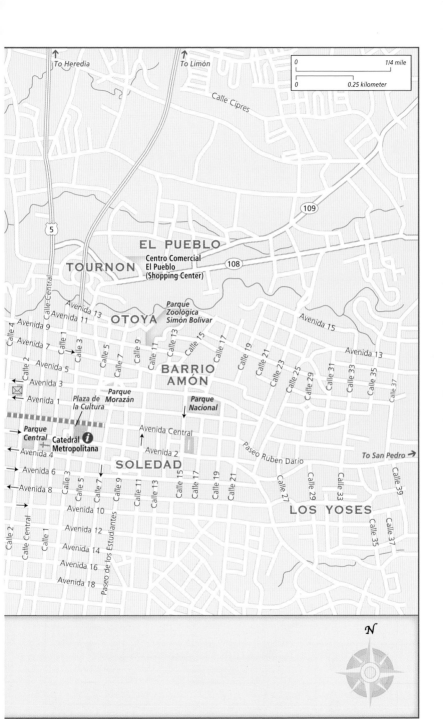

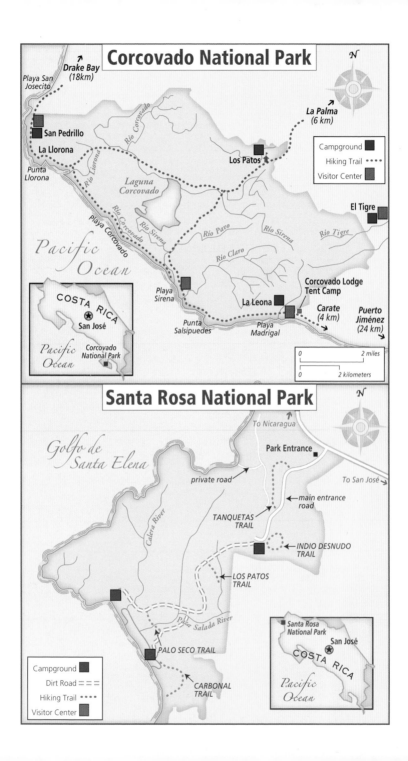

Frommer's®

Costa Rica

2009

by Eliot Greenspan

Here's what the critics say about Frommer's:

"Amazingly easy to use. Very portable, very complete."

—Booklist

"Detailed, accurate, and easy-to-read information for all price ranges."
—Glamour Magazine

"Hotel information is close to encyclopedic."

—Des Moines Sunday Register

"Frommer's Guides have a way of giving you a real feel for a place."
—Knight Ridder Newspapers

Wiley Publishing, Inc.

About the Author

Eliot Greenspan is a poet, journalist, musician, and travel writer who took his backpack and typewriter the length of Mesoamerica before settling in Costa Rica in 1992. Since then, he has worked steadily as a travel writer, freelance journalist, and translator, and continued his travels in the region. He is the author of *Frommer's Belize, Costa Rica For Dummies, Frommer's Cuba, Frommer's Ecuador, Frommer's Guatemala,* and *The Tico Times Restaurant Guide to Costa Rica,* as well as the chapter on Venezuela in *Frommer's South America.*

Published by:

Wiley Publishing, Inc.

111 River St.
Hoboken, NJ 07030-5774

ISBN 978-0-470-28553-4

Editor: Jennifer Reilly
Production Editor: M. Faunette Johnston
Cartographer: Andy Dolan
Photo Editor: Richard Fox
Production by Wiley Indianapolis Composition Services

Front cover photo: White-faced capuchin monkey on beach.
Back cover photo: Poas Volcano: Crater lake aerial view.

For information on our other products and services or to obtain technical support, please contact our Customer Care Department within the U.S. at 800/762-2974, outside the U.S. at 317/572-3993 or fax 317/572-4002.

Wiley also publishes its books in a variety of electronic formats. Some content that appears in print may not be available in electronic formats.

Manufactured in the United States of America

5 4 3 2 1

Contents

List of Maps

Acknowledgments

I say this every year, but I continue to be eternally grateful to Anne Becher and Joe Richey, who were instrumental in getting me this gig—*muchas gracias.* I'd also like to thank my parents, Marilyn and Warren Greenspan, who showed unwavering love, support, and encouragement (well, one out of three ain't bad) when I chose words and world-wandering over becoming a lawyer or a doctor. Jody and Ted Ejnes (my sister and brother-in-law) deserve a mention; they risked life and limb—literally—leading to two important tips that may help you save yours. (I now believe Ted, and he may have actually almost stepped on a crocodile.) Mayling Charpentier did some excellent phone, fax, and fact-checking work on this edition. And a big tip of my hat to Jennifer Reilly for her editorial diligence and patience.

An Invitation to the Reader

In researching this book, we discovered many wonderful places—hotels, restaurants, shops, and more. We're sure you'll find others. Please tell us about them, so we can share the information with your fellow travelers in upcoming editions. If you were disappointed with a recommendation, we'd love to know that, too. Please write to:

Frommer's Costa Rica 2009
Wiley Publishing, Inc. • 111 River St. • Hoboken, NJ 07030-5774

An Additional Note

Please be advised that travel information is subject to change at any time—and this is especially true of prices. We therefore suggest that you write or call ahead for confirmation when making your travel plans. The authors, editors, and publisher cannot be held responsible for the experiences of readers while traveling. Your safety is important to us, however, so we encourage you to stay alert and be aware of your surroundings. Keep a close eye on cameras, purses, and wallets, all favorite targets of thieves and pickpockets.

Other Great Guides for Your Trip:

Costa Rica For Dummies
Frommer's Belize
Frommer's Central America
Frommer's Guatemala
Frommer's Panama

Frommer's Star Ratings, Icons & Abbreviations

Every hotel, restaurant, and attraction listing in this guide has been ranked for quality, value, service, amenities, and special features using a **star-rating system.** In country, state, and regional guides, we also rate towns and regions to help you narrow down your choices and budget your time accordingly. Hotels and restaurants are rated on a scale of zero (recommended) to three stars (exceptional). Attractions, shopping, nightlife, towns, and regions are rated according to the following scale: zero stars (recommended), one star (highly recommended), two stars (very highly recommended), and three stars (must-see).

In addition to the star-rating system, we also use **seven feature icons** that point you to the great deals, in-the-know advice, and unique experiences that separate travelers from tourists. Throughout the book, look for:

Finds	Special finds—those places only insiders know about
Fun Fact	Fun facts—details that make travelers more informed and their trips more fun
Kids	Best bets for kids and advice for the whole family
Moments	Special moments—those experiences that memories are made of
Overrated	Places or experiences not worth your time or money
Tips	Insider tips—great ways to save time and money
Value	Great values—where to get the best deals

The following **abbreviations** are used for credit cards:

AE	American Express	DISC	Discover	V	Visa
DC	Diners Club	MC	MasterCard		

Frommers.com

Now that you have this guidebook to help you plan a great trip, visit our website at **www.frommers.com** for additional travel information on more than 4,000 destinations. We update features regularly to give you instant access to the most current trip-planning information available. At Frommers.com, you'll find scoops on the best airfares, lodging rates, and car rental bargains. You can even book your travel online through our reliable travel booking partners. Other popular features include:

- Online updates of our most popular guidebooks
- Vacation sweepstakes and contest giveaways
- Newsletters highlighting the hottest travel trends
- Podcasts, interactive maps, and up-to-the-minute events listings
- Opinionated blog entries by Arthur Frommer himself
- Online travel message boards with featured travel discussions

What's New in Costa Rica

Costa Rica hasn't been the new kid on the block for many years now—tourism here has definitely matured. Still, change and growth remain fairly constant. Here are some highlights related to new hotels and restaurants, and assorted other developments you'll find in this year's edition of the book.

PLANNING YOUR TRIP

In March 2008, Costa Rica changed from a seven-digit to an eight-digit phone numbering system. Seven-digit numbers will be changed by adding a "2" to the beginning of all land-line numbers, and an "8" to the beginning of all cellphone numbers. All of the phone numbers listed in this book are the current eight-digit numbers. However, if you come across an old seven-digit number (on a billboard or brochure, for example) here's what you do: Old cellphone numbers began either with a "3" or "8." All other numbers were land lines. Toll-free and emergency numbers were not affected.

As of February 2008, the **official exchange rate** was 500 colones to the U.S. dollar, or 1,000 colones to the British pound.

Local carrier **Sansa** (© 877/767-2672 in the U.S. and Canada, or 2290-4100 in Costa Rica; www.flysansa.com) has added four weekly flights between San José and David, Panama.

Dengue fever has become an increasing problem in Costa Rica, up some 150% in 2007, as compared to the previous year. The worst-hit areas include Limón, Liberia, and the beaches of Guanacaste.

Costa Rica is also now requiring proof of a yellow fever vaccination from all visitors who have recently been traveling in a country or region known to have yellow fever.

In 2008, the Costa Rican government raised the entrance fee to almost all national parks to $10 (£5). Chirripó National Park is one major exception, costing $15 (£7.50) per day.

Beginning February 2008, Delta (www.delta.com) began offering twice weekly (Wed and Sat) direct flights between New York's JFK and Liberia's Daniel Oduber International airports.

See chapter 3 for detailed information on planning your trip to Costa Rica.

SAN JOSE

Following the success of the recent transformation of a section of Avenida Central, Avenida 4 has been expanded as a pedestrian-only boulevard between Calle 9 and Calle 14.

If you want to take advantage of these pedestrian boulevards, check out **Tico Walks** (© 2283-8281; www.ticowalks. com), a new regularly scheduled walking tour of downtown San José.

While still a worthwhile visit, the **Museo de Jade Marco Fidel Tristán (Jade Museum)** has raised its admission fee considerably to $7 (£3.50).

In January 2008, the long-standing San José resort hotel Melia Cariari was taken over by the Hilton group and is now the **Doubletree Cariari By Hilton** (© 800/222-8733 in the U.S. and Canada; www.cariarisanjose.doubletree. com). Meanwhile, the former Tryp Corobicí is now the **Crowne Plaza Corobicí** (© 800/227-6963 in the U.S. and Canada; www.crowneplaza.com).

One of my favorite downtown restaurants, Bakea, closed its doors in 2008. Luckily, the void has been more than ably filled by **Park Café** (© 2290-6324), which serves up fine dining in a beautiful ambience.

Those looking for live music will be happy to know that the popular **Jazz Café,** in San Pedro, has opened up a sister club, **Jazz Café Escazú,** on the western side of town.

See chapter 6 for complete coverage of San José.

GUANACASTE

Nature Air (© 800/235-9272 in the U.S. and Canada or 2299-6000; www.nature air.com) now offers a 1-hour **Sky Tour** sightseeing excursion leaving from Liberia, in one of its 18-seat twin-engine planes equipped with large picture windows along the length of both sides of the fuselage.

In late 2008, the Hilton hotel group took over the former Fiesta Premier Resort and Spa. The renamed **Hilton Papagayo Resort** (© 800/445-8667; www.hilton.com) has received much-needed attention both in upkeep and remodeling, and in the realm of service.

Over in Playa del Coco, the popular restaurant and beach club Café de Playa has added five luxury rooms, the **Suites at Café de Playa** (© 2670-1553; www. merymer.com), easily the most comfortable beachfront rooms to be had in this town.

In Playa Flamingo, the long-standing and popular restaurant **Marie's** (© 2654-4136) is well-settled and thriving in its new, improved, and greatly expanded digs.

In Tamarindo, the beachfront budget hotel, **Cabinas Dolly,** has been razed as part of the sporadic enforcement of Costa Rica's strict laws regarding construction in the "maritime zone." A similar fate befell the **Zully Mar** (© 2653-0023) restaurant last year, but it has been rebuilt and reopened, just a little bit farther from the waves, but still facing the sea.

In January 2008, the Allegro Papagayo Resort was ordered shut down by the Costa Rican Ministry of Health, after having been found to be illegally dumping raw sewage directly into the ocean and clandestinely dumping more raw sewage into nearby local communities. After making some improvements, they were operating at half capacity at press time. In a more generalized, yet related issue, water samples all around Tamarindo at the end of the rainy season revealed high levels of fecal matter in prime tourist beach spots. Over-construction and shoddy waste-disposal practices are the culprit here. This is a massive problem in Costa Rica, given lax government oversight and rampant corruption.

The Marriott, Westin, and Regent resort hotel groups all have large-scale resorts in the works in this area, which should open sometime during the 2009 or 2010 seasons.

See chapter 7 for all the latest on this rapidly developing region.

PUNTARENAS & THE NICOYA PENINSULA

On the outskirts of Puntarenas, the Hilton hotel group has taken over and remodeled the former Fiesta Premier Beach Resort, and is operating it as the all-inclusive **Double Tree Resort Puntarenas** (© 800/222-8733 in the U.S. and Canada, or 2663-0808 in Costa Rica; www.puntarenas.doubletree.com).

In Montezuma, the **Mariposario Montezuma Gardens** (© 8888-4200) is a lovely new "butterfly garden" attraction, offering guided tours through its lovely gardens and butterfly breeding grounds.

Also in Montezuma, the **Ylang Ylang Beach Resort** (② 2642-0636; www.ylangylangresort.com) has added several "jungalows," semi-permanent tents with comfortable beds, ceiling fans, a small front porch, and access to shared bathrooms and showers.

You may find paparazzi hanging around just outside Playa Samara, where the actor Mel Gibson has bought the former Hacienda Dorada as a private vacation home. Whether or not you come here to catch a glimpse of the Australian-born star, the new **Samara Tree House Inn** (② 2656-0733; www.samaratreehouse.com) is a beachfront hotel that is worth considering.

For more information, see chapter 8.

THE NORTHERN ZONE

In Puerto Viejo de Sarapiquí, the **Gavilán Sarapiquí River Lodge** (② 2234-9507; www.gavilanlodge.com) has added four new superior rooms. Nearby, hotel **Sueño Azul** (② 2253-2020; www.suenoazulresort.com) has put in a trapeze setup, and now offers classes in this exhilarating circus art.

Two long-standing budget hotels in downtown La Fortuna, **Hotel La Fortuna** (② 2479-9197; www.fortunainn.com) and **Hotel Las Colinas** (② 2479-9305; www.lascolinasarenal.com), were both torn to the ground and rebuilt much bigger and better than before. Out on the outskirts of town, on the road to Tabacón, the new **Magic Mountain Hotel** (② 2479-7246; www.hotelmagicmountain.com) has brought a bit of luxury to this rustic little town.

Along the road around Lake Arenal, the **Arenal Botanical Gardens** has sadly closed, after years of delighting tourists and hummingbirds (who came to feed) alike.

Meanwhile, tourists traveling into the mists of Monteverde will be pleased to find the road in and around the central hub town of Santa Elena has been paved, although the ride up is still rough and rocky.

Also in Monteverde, the **Hotel El Sapo Dorado** (② 2645-5010; www.sapodorado.com) is remodeling all its rooms, and has built a big new restaurant and reception area down by the main road between Santa Elena and the Cloud Forest Preserve. And the folks behind the popular restaurant **Sofia** have opened a sister restaurant, **Chimera** (② 2645-6081), serving a wide range of creative tapas in a cozy, yet sophisticated, setting.

Full details on the northern zone can be found in chapter 9.

CENTRAL PACIFIC COAST

The dining scene is heating up in Playa Herradura, with the opening of several new restaurants in the marina at the Marriott Los Sueños Resort. **El Galeón** (② 2637-8536) is my top choice here for its excellent fusion cuisine, but you can also get sushi at **Bambu,** Italian fare at **La Linterna,** and American-style bar food at the **Hook Up.**

Construction is underway on a 270-slip **Marina Pez Vela,** in Quepos. In addition to the 270-slip marina, the complex will boast restaurants, shops, condominium units, and a small hotel. Work is expected to be completed in early 2009.

In Dominical, the hotel **Domilocos** (② 2787-0244; www.domilocos.com) has been expanded, remodeled, and reopened.

If you plan on climbing **Mount Chirripó,** be forewarned that rates have gone up to $15 (£7.50) per day for the national park fee, and sleeping space at the summit lodge has been limited to just 25 climbers per day.

See chapter 10 for complete coverage of this region.

THE SOUTHERN ZONE

Sansa (② 877/767-2672 in the U.S. and Canada, or 2290-4100 in Costa Rica;

www.flysansa.com) now has twice-daily flights between Drake Bay and Puerto Jiménez. This 25-minute flight leaves Drake Bay at 7 and 11:55am. The return flights leave Puerto Jiménez at 1:28 and 3:42pm. The one-way fare is $40 (£20).

Although not as fast as flying, there are now **speedboats** working as boat taxis between Puerto Jiménez and Golfito. The fare is $5 (£2.50), and the ride takes a little under 30 minutes. These boats leave several times throughout the day, beginning at around 6am.

See chapter 11 for more information on this remote region.

THE CARIBBEAN COAST

Luxury has come to Tortuguero with the opening of the **Manatus Hotel** (✆ **2239-4854;** www.manatushotel. com), an upscale boutique hotel located right on Tortuguero's main canal.

In Cahuita, the long-standing and deservedly popular restaurant, **Casa Creole,** has closed and is for sale.

Down in Puerto Viejo, the new **Banana Azul Guest House** (✆ **2750-2035;** www.bananaazul.com) is an outstanding option on an isolated section of Playa Negra, north of town. Also in Puerto Viejo, the ever popular **El Loco Natural** (✆ **2750-0263**) has a new location just south of downtown, across from the Cut Back bar.

See chapter 12 for complete coverage of this area.

1

The Best of Costa Rica

First coming to the attention of international travelers in the mid-1990s, Costa Rica is currently—and consistently—one of the hottest vacation and adventure-travel destinations in Latin America, with close to two million visitors each year. Despite the boom in vacationers, Costa Rica remains a place rich in natural wonders and biodiversity, where you can still find yourself far from the maddening crowds. The country boasts a wealth of unsullied beaches that stretch for miles, small lodgings that haven't attracted hordes of tourists, jungle rivers for rafting and kayaking, and spectacular cloud- and rainforests with ample opportunities for bird-watching and hiking. In addition to the country's trademark eco- and adventure-tourism offerings, you will also find luxury resorts and golf courses, plush spas, and some truly spectacular boutique hotels and lodges.

Having lived in Costa Rica for more than 17 years, I continue to explore and discover new spots, adventures, restaurants, and lodgings—and my "best of" experiences keep on coming. In this chapter I've selected the very best of what this unique country has to offer. These places and experiences are covered in greater detail elsewhere in the book; this chapter is merely meant to give you an overview of the highlights so that you can start planning your own adventure.

1 The Best of Natural Costa Rica

- **Rincón de la Vieja National Park** (northeast of Liberia, in Guanacaste): This is an area of rugged beauty and high volcanic activity. The Rincón de la Vieja Volcano rises to 1,848m (6,061 ft.), but the thermal activity is spread out along its flanks, where numerous geysers, vents, and fumaroles let off its heat and steam. This is a great place to hire a guide and a horse for a day of rugged exploration. There are waterfalls and mud baths, hot springs, and cool jungle swimming holes. You'll pass through pastureland, scrub savanna, and moist secondary forest; the bird-watching is excellent. See p. 161.
- **The Río Sarapiquí Region** (north of San José between Guanacaste in the west and the Caribbean coast in the east): This region is a prime place for an ecolodge experience. Protected tropical forests climb from the Caribbean coastal lowlands up into the central mountains, affording you a glimpse of a plethora of life zones and ecosystems. **Braulio Carrillo National Park** borders several other private reserves here, and a variety of ecolodges will suit any budget. See "Puerto Viejo de Sarapiquí" in chapter 9.
- **Arenal Volcano/Tabacón Hot Springs** (near La Fortuna, northwest of San José): When the skies are clear and the lava is flowing, Arenal Volcano offers a thrilling light show accompanied by an earthshaking

The Best of Costa Rica

THE BEST OF NATURAL COSTA RICA

Arenal Volcano/Tabacón Hot Springs **5**
Braulio Carrillo National Park **18**
Manuel Antonio National Park **25**
Monteverde Biological Cloud Forest Reserve **6**
Osa Peninsula & Corcovado National Park **26**
Rincón de la Vieja National Park **2**
The Río Sarapiquí Region **14**
Tortuguero Village & Jungle Canals **15**

THE BEST BEACHES

The Beaches around Playa Sámara **9**
Malpaís **11**
Manuel Antonio **25**
Playa Montezuma **12**
Punta Uva & Manzanillo **21**
Santa Rosa National Park **1**

THE BEST ADVENTURES

Battling a Billfish off the Pacific Coast **24**
Diving off Isla del Coco **10**
Hiking Mount Chirripó **22**
Kayaking Around Golfo Dulce **27**
Rafting the Upper Reventazón River **16**
Surfing & Four-Wheeling Guanacaste **8**
Surfing Pavones **28**
Windsurfing Lake Arenal **4**

THE BEST BIRD-WATCHING

Aviarios del Caribe/Cahuita National Park **20**
Caño Negro Wildlife Refuge **3**
Carara National Park **13**
Cerro de la Muerte **23**
La Selva Biological Station **17**
Parque del Este **19**
Río Tempisque Basin **7**
Wilson Botanical Gardens **29**

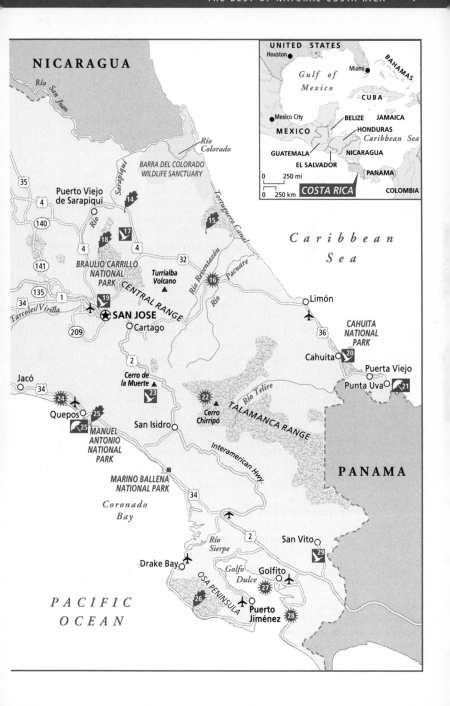

rumble that defies description. You can even see the show while soaking in a natural hot spring and having a drink at the swim-up bar at **Tabacón Grand Spa Thermal Resort** (© 2519-1900; www.tabacon.com). If the rushing torrent of volcano-heated spring water isn't therapeutic enough, you can get an incredibly inexpensive massage here. See "Arenal Volcano & La Fortuna" in chapter 9.

- **Monteverde Biological Cloud Forest Reserve** (in the mountains northwest of San José): There's something both eerie and majestic about walking around in the early morning mist surrounded by bird calls and towering trees hung heavy in broad bromeliads, flowering orchids, and hanging moss and vines. The reserve has a well-maintained network of trails, and the community is truly involved in conservation. Not only that, but in and around Monteverde and Santa Elena, you'll find a whole slew of related activities and attractions, including canopy tours that allow you to swing from treetop to treetop while hanging from a skinny cable. See p. 267.

- **Manuel Antonio** (near Quepos on the central Pacific coast): There's a reason this place is so popular and renowned: monkeys! The national park here is full of them, even the endangered squirrel monkeys. But you'll also find plenty to see and do outside the park. The road into Manuel Antonio has many lookouts that consistently offer postcard-perfect snapshots of steep jungle hills meeting the sea. Uninhabited islands lie just off the coast, and the beaches here are perfect crescents of soft, white sand. See "Manuel Antonio National Park" in chapter 10.

- **Osa Peninsula** (in southern Costa Rica): This is Costa Rica's most remote and biologically rich region. **Corcovado National Park,** the largest remaining patch of virgin lowland tropical rainforest in Central America, takes up much of the Osa Peninsula. Jaguars, crocodiles, and scarlet macaws all call this place home. Whether you stay in a luxury nature lodge in **Drake Bay** or outside of **Puerto Jiménez,** or camp in the park itself, you will be surrounded by some of the most lush and most intense jungle this country has to offer. See chapter 11.

- **Tortuguero Village & Jungle Canals** (on the Caribbean coast, north of Limón): Tortuguero Village is a small collection of rustic wooden shacks on a narrow spit of land between the Caribbean Sea and a dense maze of jungle canals. It's been called Costa Rica's Venice, but it actually has more in common with the South American Amazon. As you explore the narrow canals here, you'll see a wide variety of herons and other water birds, three types of monkeys, three-toed sloths, and caiman. If you come between June and October, you might be treated to the awe-inspiring spectacle of a green turtle nesting— the small stretch of Tortuguero beach is the last remaining major nesting site of this endangered animal. See "Tortuguero National Park" in chapter 12.

2 The Best Beaches

With more than 1,200km (750 miles) of shoreline on its Pacific and Caribbean coasts, Costa Rica offers beachgoers an embarrassment of riches.

- **Santa Rosa National Park:** If you really want to get away from it all, the beaches here in the northwest corner of Costa Rica are a good bet. You'll have to four-wheel-drive or hike 13km (8 miles) from the central ranger station to reach them. And once there, you'll find only the most basic of camping facilities: outhouse latrines and cold-water showers. But you'll probably have the place almost to yourself. In fact, the only time it gets crowded is in October, when thousands of olive ridley sea turtles nest in one of their yearly *arribadas* (arrivals). See p. 167.

- **The Beaches around Playa Sámara:** Playa Sámara itself is nice enough, but if you venture just slightly farther afield, you'll find some of the nicest and least developed beaches along the entire Guanacaste coast. **Playa Carrillo** is a long, almost always deserted crescent of palm-backed white sand located just south of Sámara, while **Playa Barrigona** and **Playa Buena Vista** are two hidden gems tucked down a couple of dirt roads to the north. The land all around Playa Barrigona was recently purchased by actor Mel Gibson, but the beach, like all beaches in Costa Rica, remains open to the public. See "Playa Sámara" in chapter 8.

- **Playa Montezuma:** This tiny beach town at the southern tip of the Nicoya Peninsula has weathered fame and infamy, but retains a funky sense of individuality. European backpackers, vegetarian yoga enthusiasts, and UFO seekers choose Montezuma's beach over any other in Costa Rica. The waterfalls are what set it apart from the competition, but the beach stretches for miles, with plenty of isolated spots to plop down your towel or mat. Nearby are the **Cabo Blanco** and **Curú** wildlife preserves. See "Playa Montezuma" in chapter 8.

- **Malpaís:** While the secret is certainly out, there's still some time to visit Costa Rica's newest hot spot before the throngs arrive. With just a smattering of luxury lodges, surf camps, and assorted hotels and *cabinas,* Malpaís is the place to come if you're looking for miles of deserted beaches and great surf. If you find Malpaís is too crowded, head farther on down the road to Santa Teresa, Playa Hermosa, and Manzanillo. See "Malpaís & Santa Teresa" in chapter 8.

- **Manuel Antonio:** The first beach destination to become popular in Costa Rica, Manuel Antonio retains its charms despite burgeoning crowds and mushrooming hotels. The beaches inside the national park are idyllic, and the views from the hills approaching the park are enchanting. This is one of the few remaining habitats for the endangered squirrel monkey. Rooms with views tend to be a bit expensive, but many a satisfied guest will tell you they're worth it. See "Manuel Antonio National Park" in chapter 10.

- **Punta Uva & Manzanillo:** Below Puerto Viejo, the beaches of Costa Rica's eastern coast take on true Caribbean splendor, with turquoise waters, coral reefs, and palm-lined stretches of nearly deserted white-sand beach. Punta Uva and Manzanillo are the two most sparkling gems of this coastline. Tall coconut palms line the shore, providing shady respite for those who like to spend a full day on the sand, and the water is usually quite calm and good for swimming. See "Puerto Viejo" in chapter 12.

3 The Best Adventures

- **Mountain-Biking the Back Roads of Costa Rica:** The lack of infrastructure and paved roads here that most folks bemoan is a huge boon for mountain bikers. There are endless back roads and cattle paths to explore. Tours of differing lengths and all difficulty levels are available. Contact **Coast to Coast Adventures** (© **2280-8054;** www.ctocadventures. com). See p. 74.

- **Swinging Through the Treetops on a Canopy Tour:** This unique adventure has become ubiquitous in Costa Rica. You'll find zip-line canopy tours all over the country. In most cases, after a strenuous climb using ascenders, you strap on a harness and zip from treetop to treetop while dangling from a cable. Check the various destination chapters to find a canopy tour operation near you.

- **Rafting the Upper Reventazón River** (near Turrialba): The Class V Guayabo section of this popular river is serious white water. Only experienced and gutsy river runners need apply. If you're not quite up to that, try a 2-day Pacuare River trip which passes through primary and secondary forests and a beautiful steep gorge. Plans to build a dam here have thankfully been rejected, or at least stalled, for the time being. **Aventuras Naturales** ✦ (© **800/514-0411** in the U.S., or 2225-3939; www.to enjoynature.com) can arrange these tours. See p. 85.

- **Surfing and Four-Wheeling Guanacaste Province:** This northwestern province has dozens of respectable beach and reef breaks, from Witch's Rock at Playa Naranjo near the Nicaraguan border to Playa Nosara more than 100km (62 miles) away. In addition to these two prime spots, try a turn at Playa Grande, Punta Langosta, and playas Negra, Avellanas, and Junquillal. Or find your own secret spot. Rent a four-by-four with a roof rack, pile on the boards, and explore. See chapter 7.

- **Battling a Billfish off the Pacific Coast:** Billfish are plentiful all along

Costa Rica's Pacific coast, and boats operate from Playa del Coco to Playa Zancudo. Costa Rican anglers hold world records for both blue marlin and Pacific sailfish. Go to Quepos (just outside Manuel Antonio) for the best après-fish scene, or head down to Drake Bay, the Osa Peninsula, or Golfo Dulce if you want some isolation. **Costa Rica Outdoors** (© **800/ 308-3394** or 2231-0306; www.costa ricaoutdoors.com) can help you find a good charter skipper or specialized fishing lodge. See chapters 7, 8, 10, 11, and 12.

- **Trying the New Adventure Sport of Canyoning:** While far from standardized, canyoning usually involves hiking along and through the rivers and creeks of steep mountain canyons, with periodic breaks to rappel down the face of a waterfall, jump off a rock into a jungle pool, or float down a small rapid. **Pure Trek Canyoning** ✦✦ (© **866/569-5723** or 2479-1313; www.puretrekcosta rica.com) in La Fortuna, and **Psycho Tours** ✦✦ (© **8353-8619;** www. psychotours.com) near Puerto Jiménez, are two of the prime operators. See chapters 9 and 11.

- **Windsurfing or Kitesurfing on Lake Arenal:** With steady gale-force winds (at certain times of the year) and stunning scenery, the northern end of Lake Arenal has become a major international windsurfing and kitesurfing hot spot. See chapter 9.

- **Diving off the Shores of Isla del Coco** (off the Pacific coast): Legendary among treasure seekers, pirate buffs, and scuba divers, this small island is consistently rated one of the 10 best dive sites in the world. A protected national park, Isla del Coco is surrounded by clear Pacific waters, and its reefs are teeming with life (divers regularly encounter large schools of hammerhead sharks, curious manta rays, and docile whale sharks). Because the island is so remote and has no overnight facilities for visitors, the most popular way to visit is on 10-day excursions on a live-aboard boat, where guests live, eat, and sleep onboard—with nights anchored in the harbor. See p. 206.

- **Hiking Mount Chirripó** (near San Isidro de El General on the central Pacific coast): The highest mountain in Costa Rica, Mount Chirripó is one of the few places in the world where (on a clear day) you can see both the Caribbean Sea and the Pacific Ocean at the same time. Hiking to Chirripó's 3,724m (12,215-ft.) summit takes you through a number of distinct bioregions, ranging from lowland pastures and a cloud forest to a high-altitude *páramo,* a tundralike landscape with stunted trees and morning frosts. See "San Isidro de El General: A Base for Exploring Chirripó National Park" in chapter 10.
- **Kayaking around the Golfo Dulce:** Slipping through the waters of the Golfo Dulce by kayak gets you intimately in touch with the raw beauty of this underdeveloped region. Spend several days poking around in mangrove swamps, fishing in estuaries, and watching dolphins frolic in the bay. **Escondido Trex** (⟨ **2735-5210;** www.escondidotrex.com) provides multiday custom kayaking trips out of Puerto Jiménez on the Osa Peninsula. See "Puerto Jiménez: Gateway to Corcovado National Park" in chapter 11.
- **Surfing Pavones** (on the southern Pacific coast): Just 13km (8 miles) from the Panamanian border at the southern reaches of Costa Rica's Pacific coast, Pavones is reputed to have one of the longest rideable waves in the world. When this left-point break is working, surfers enjoy rides of almost a mile in length. Much more can be said about this experience, but if you're a surfer, you've heard it all before. Contact **Casa Siempre Domingo** (⟨ **8820-4709;** www.casa-domingo.com), the most comfortable hotel in town, for current wave reports and other local information. See "Playa Pavones: A Surfer's Mecca" in chapter 11.

4 The Best Day Hikes & Nature Walks

- **Lankester Gardens:** If you want a really pleasant but not overly challenging day hike, consider a walk among the hundreds of distinct species of flora on display here. Lankester Gardens (⟨ **2552-3247;** www.jardinbotanicolankester.org) is just 27km (17 miles) from San José and makes a wonderful day's expedition. The trails meander from areas of well-tended open garden to shady natural forest. See p. 133.
- **Rincón de la Vieja National Park:** This park has a number of wonderful trails through a variety of ecosystems and natural wonders. My favorite hike is down to the Blue Lake and Cangrejo Falls. It's 5.1km (3¼ miles) each way, and you'll want to spend some time at the base of this amazing lake; plan on at least 5 hours for the outing, and bring along lunch and plenty of water. You can also hike up to two craters and a crater lake here, and the Las Pailas loop is ideal for those seeking a less strenuous hike. This remote volcanic national park is about an hour north of Liberia (it's only 25km/16 miles, but the road is quite rough), or about 5 hours from San José. See p. 161.

- **La Selva Biological Station:** This combination research facility and rustic nature lodge has an extensive and well-marked network of trails. You'll have to reserve in advance (© **2766-6565;** www.threepaths. co.cr) and take the guided tour if you aren't a guest at the lodge. But the hikes are led by very informed naturalists, so you might not mind the company. The Biological Station is located north-northeast on the Caribbean slope of Costa Rica's central mountain range. It'll take you about 1½ hours to drive from San José via the Guápiles Highway. See p. 240.

- **Arenal National Park and Environs:** There's great hiking all around this area. The national park itself has several excellent trails that visit a variety of ecosystems, including rainforest, secondary forest, savanna, and, my favorite, old lava flows. Most of them are on the relatively flat flanks of the volcano, so there's not too much climbing involved. There's also great hiking on the trails at the Arenal Observatory Lodge, and the trail down to the base of the La Fortuna Waterfall is a fun scramble. It's about a 3½-hour drive from San José to La Fortuna and Arenal National Park. See "Arenal Volcano & La Fortuna" in chapter 9.

- **Monteverde Biological Cloud Forest Reserve:** In the morning rush of high season, when groups and tours line up to enter the reserve, you'd think the sign said CROWD FOREST. Still, the guides here are some of the most professional and knowledgeable in the country. Take a tour in the morning to familiarize yourself with the forest, and then spend the late morning or afternoon (your entrance ticket is good for the entire day) exploring the reserve. Off the main thoroughfares, Monteverde reveals its rich mysteries with stunning regularity. Walk through the gray mist and look up at the dense tangle of epiphytes and vines. The only noises are the rustlings of birds or monkeys and the occasional distant rumble of Arenal Volcano. The trails are well marked and regularly tended. It's about 3½ hours by bus or car to Monteverde from San José. See p. 267.

- **Corcovado National Park:** This large swath of dense lowland rainforest is home to Costa Rica's second-largest population of scarlet macaws. The park has a well-designed network of trails, ranger stations, and camping facilities. Most of the lodges in Drake Bay and Puerto Jiménez offer day hikes through the park, but if you really want to experience it, you should hike in and stay at one or more of the campgrounds. This is strenuous hiking, and you will have to pack in some gear and food, but the reward is some of Costa Rica's most spectacular and unspoiled scenery. Because strict limits are placed on the number of visitors allowed into the park, you'll always be far from the crowds. See "Puerto Jiménez: Gateway to Corcovado National Park" in chapter 11.

- **Cahuita National Park:** The trails here are flat, well-maintained paths through thick lowland forest. Most of the way they parallel the beach, which is usually no more than 90m (295 ft.) away, so you can hike out on the trail and back along the beach, or vice versa. White-faced and howler monkeys are common, as are brightly colored land crabs. See p. 375.

5 The Best Bird-Watching

- **Observing Oropendola and Blue-Crowned Motmot at Parque del Este:** A boon for city bird-watchers, this San José park rambles through a collection of lawns, planted gardens, and harvested forest, but it also includes second-growth scrub and dense woodland. Oropendola and blue-crowned motmot are common species here. See p. 134.

- **Spotting Hundreds of Marsh and Stream Birds along the Río Tempisque Basin:** Hike around the Palo Verde Biological Station, or take a boat trip down the Bebedero River with **Swiss Travel Services** (© 2282-4898; www.swisstravelcr.com) or **Safaris Corobicí** (© 2669-6191; www.nicoya.com). This area is an important breeding ground for gallinules, jacanas, and limpkins, and is a common habitat for numerous heron and kingfisher species. Palo Verde is about a 3½-hour drive from San José. See p. 162.

- **Looking for 300-plus Species of Birds in La Selva Biological Station:** With an excellent trail system through a variety of habitats, from dense primary rainforest to open pasturelands and cacao plantations, this is one of the finest places for bird-watching in Costa Rica. With such a variety of habitats, the number of species spotted runs to well over 300. La Selva is located just a few miles south of Puerto Viejo. See p. 240.

- **Sizing Up a Jabiru Stork at Caño Negro National Wildlife Refuge:** Caño Negro Lake and the Río Frío that feeds it are incredibly rich in wildlife and a major nesting and gathering site for aquatic bird species. These massive birds are getting less common in Costa Rica, but this is still one of the best places to spot one. **Caño Negro Natural Lodge** (© 2265-3302; www.canonegrolodge.com) sits right on the edge of the refuge and makes a great base for exploring this region to the north of La Fortuna. See p. 250.

- **Catching a Scarlet Macaw in Flight over Carara National Park:** Home to Costa Rica's largest population of scarlet macaws, Carara Biological Reserve is a special place for devoted bird-watchers and recent converts. Macaws are noisy and colorful birds that spend their days in the park but choose to roost in the evenings near the coast. They arrive like clockwork every morning and then head for the coastal mangroves around dusk. These daily migrations give birders a great chance to see these magnificent birds in flight. The reserve is located about 2 hours from San José along the central Pacific coast. See p. 283.

- **Looking for a Resplendent Quetzal in the Cerro de la Muerte:** Don't let the name (Mountain of Death) scare you away from the opportunity to see this spectacular bird, revered by the ancient Aztecs and Mayas. Serious bird-watchers won't want to leave Costa Rica without crossing this bird off their lists, and neophytes might be hooked for life after seeing one of these iridescent green wonders fly overhead, flashing its brilliant red breast and trailing 2-foot-long tail feathers. **Trogon Lodge** (© 2293-8181; www.grupomawamba.com) can almost guarantee a sighting. The Cerro de la Muerte is a high mountain pass along the way to San Isidro de El General about 1½ hours from San José. See "En Route to San José: Three Places to See Quetzals in the Wild" in chapter 10.

- **Spotting Hundreds of Species at Wilson Botanical Gardens:** With more than 7,000 species of tropical plants and flowers, the well-tended trails and grounds of this beautiful research facility are fabulous for bird-watching. Hummingbirds and tanagers are particularly plentiful, but the bounty doesn't end there—more than 360 different species of birds have been recorded here. Wilson Gardens is located about an hour outside the town of Golfito. See "Golfito: Gateway to the Golfo Dulce" in chapter 11.

- **Taking Advantage of the Caribbean's Best Birding at Aviarios del Caribe:** In just a few short years, Aviarios del Caribe (© 2750-0775; www.sloth rescue.org) has established itself as the prime bird-watching resort on the Caribbean. If it flies along this coast, chances are good that you'll spot it here; more than 330 species of birds have been spotted so far. Located on the Caribbean coast, Aviarios del Caribe is about a 3-hour drive from San José. See p. 376.

6 The Best Destinations for Families

- **San José:** If you're spending any time in San José, you'll probably want to be outside the rough-and-tumble downtown area. The best place to experience Costa Rica's capital city (and still get a decent night's sleep) is the **Doubletree Cariari By Hilton** (© 800/222-8733 or 2239-0022; www.cariarisanjose.doubletree.com). With facilities that include several large pools, gym, casino, shuttle service to a nearby spa and 18-hole golf course, and a game room (not to mention a babysitting service), there's something here for everyone. If you're traveling with teens, they'll feel right at home at the nearby Mall Cariari, which has a multiplex theater, an indoor skating rink, and, of course, a food court. Just 15 minutes from downtown, it's well situated for exploring all of the city's sights and attractions. See p. 117.

- **La Paz Waterfall Gardens** (© 2225-0643; www.waterfallgardens.com): This multifaceted attraction features paths and suspended walkways alongside a series of impressive jungle waterfalls. Kids love the variety and vibrancy of the various attractions here, from the buzzing hummingbirds to the impressive power of the waterfalls. The rooms at the **Peace Lodge** here are some of the best in the country. See p. 133.

- **Playa Hermosa:** The protected waters of this Pacific beach make it a family favorite. However, just because the waters are calm doesn't mean it's boring here. Check in at **Aqua Sport** (© 2672-0050), where you can rent sea kayaks, sailboards, paddleboats, beach umbrellas, and bicycles. See "Playa Hermosa, Playa Panamá & Papagayo" in chapter 7.

- **Playa Tamarindo:** This lively surf town has a bit of something for everyone. This is a great spot for teens to learn how to surf or boogie-board, and there are a host of tours and activities to please the entire family. **Hotel Capitán Suizo** (© 2653-0353; www.hotelcapitansuizo.com; p. 193) has an excellent location on a calm section of beach, spacious rooms, and a great pool for kids and adults alike. See "Playa Tamarindo & Playa Grande" in chapter 7.

- **Monteverde:** Located about 160km (99 miles) northwest of San José, this area not only boasts the country's most famous cloud forest, but also sports a wide variety of related attractions and activities. After hiking through the reserve, you should be able to keep most kids happy and occupied riding horses; squirming at the local serpentarium; or visiting the butterfly farm, frog pond, bat jungle, and hummingbird gallery. More adventurous families can take a horseback ride or one of the local zip-line canopy tours. See "Monteverde" in chapter 9.

- **Playa de Jacó:** On the central Pacific coast, this is Costa Rica's liveliest and most developed beach town. The streets are lined with souvenir shops, ice-cream stands, and inexpensive eateries; there's even a miniature-golf course. Older kids can rent a surf- or boogie board, although everyone should be careful with the rough surf. The **Club del Mar Condominiums & Resort** (✆ 866/978-5669 or 2643-3194; p. 287) is situated at the calm southern end of the beach. The hotel has a large free-form pool and some shady grounds, and is accommodating to families with small children. See "Playa de Jacó, Playa Hermosa & Playa Herradura" in chapter 10.

- **Manuel Antonio:** Manuel Antonio has a little bit of everything: miles of gorgeous beaches, tons of wildlife (with almost guaranteed monkey sightings), and plenty of active-tour options. There's a load of lodging options, but **Hotel Sí Como No** (✆ 2777-0777; www.sicomono.com), with its large suites, two pools, water slide, and nightly movies, is probably your best bet. See "Manuel Antonio National Park" in chapter 10.

7 The Best Luxury Hotels & Resorts

- **Marriott Costa Rica Hotel** (San Antonio de Belén, San José area; ✆ 888/236-2427 or 2298-0844; www.marriott.com): Of all the contenders in the upscale urban market, the Marriott seems to be doing the best job. Maybe because it's the newest, but everything is in great shape, the service is bend-over-backward, the restaurants are excellent, and the hotel boasts all the facilities and amenities you could want. See p. 118.

- **Peace Lodge** (north of Varablanca; ✆ 954/727-3997 in the U.S., or 2482-2720 in Costa Rica; www.waterfallgardens.com): While the bathrooms of the deluxe units are the most luxurious and unique in the country, everything else is done in grand style as well. Each room comes with at least one custom-tiled Jacuzzi on a private balcony. The hotel adjoins the popular La Paz Waterfall Gardens. See p. 118.

- **Four Seasons Resort Costa Rica** (Papagayo Peninsula; ✆ 800/819-5053 or 2696-0000; www.fourseasons.com/costarica): This was the first major resort to really address the high-end luxury market in Costa Rica. Within its first month of operation Michael Jordan and Madonna were notable guests. A beautiful setting, wonderful installations, a world-class golf course, and stellar service continue to make this the current king of the hill in the upscale market. See p. 172.

- **Hotel Punta Islita** (on the Pacific coast in central Guanacaste; ✆ 866/446-4053 in the U.S. and Canada, or 2231-6122 in Costa Rica; www.hotelpuntaislita.com): This great getaway is perched on a high, flat bluff overlooking the Pacific Ocean. It's popular with honeymooners, and rightly so. The rooms are large and comfortable, the food is excellent, and the setting is stunning. If you venture beyond your room and the hotel's inviting hillside pool, there's a long, almost always deserted beach for you to explore, as well as a wealth of activities for the more adventurous. See p. 229.

- **Flor Blanca Resort** (Playa Santa Teresa; ✆ **2640-0232;** www.flor blanca.com): The individual villas at this intimate resort are some of the largest and most luxurious in the country. The service and food are outstanding, and the location is breathtaking, spread over a lushly planted hillside steps away from Playa Santa Teresa. See p. 221.

- **Villa Caletas** (north of Jacó; ✆ **2630-3003;** www.hotelvillacaletas.com): Spread out over a steep hillside high above the Pacific, these individual villas have a Mediterranean feel. The Greek Doric amphitheater follows the same motif. Carved into the hillside,

the theater frequently features evening concerts of jazz or classical music. The "infinity pool" here was one of the first in Costa Rica and is still my favorite. Sitting in a lounge chair at the pool's edge, you'll swear that it joins the sea beyond. See p. 290.

- **Arenas del Mar** (Manuel Antonio; ✆/fax **2777-2777;** www.arenasdel mar.com): With large and ample rooms, excellent service and amenities, a beautiful little spa, and the best beach access and location in Manuel Antonio, this hotel has a lot to offer. See p. 305.

- **Hotel Sí Como No** (Manuel Antonio; ✆ **2777-0777;** www.sicomono. com): Although there are fancier and more posh places in Costa Rica, the large modern suites and villas, spectacular views, attentive service, and first-rate facilities here earn this small resort a spot on this list. See p. 307.

8 The Best Moderately Priced Hotels

- **Hotel Grano de Oro** (San José; ✆ **2255-3322;** www.hotelgrano deoro.com): San José boasts dozens of old homes that have been converted into hotels, but few offer the luxurious accommodations or professional service found at the Grano de Oro. All the guest rooms have attractive hardwood furniture, including old-fashioned wardrobes in some rooms. When it's time to relax, you can soak in a hot tub or have a drink in the rooftop lounge while taking in San José's commanding view. See p. 112.

- **Hôtel Le Bergerac** (San José; ✆ **2234-7850;** www.bergerachotel. com): This classy little hotel has been pleasing diplomats, dignitaries, and other discerning travelers for years. Ask for one of the garden rooms or get the old master bedroom with its small private balcony. See p. 114.

- **Villa del Sueño Hotel** (Playa Hermosa; ✆ **800/378-8599** or ✆/fax 2672-0026; www.villadelsueno.com): It's not right on the beach (you'll have to walk about 90m/295 ft.), but everything else here is right on the money: clean, comfortable rooms; a nice refreshing pool; and an excellent restaurant. You can't do better in Playa Hermosa. See p. 174.

- **Amor de Mar** (Montezuma; ✆/fax **2642-0262;** www.amordemar.com): Clean, spacious, and comfortable rooms set on a sloping lawn that leads down to a rocky coastline, with a natural pool carved into the rocks, all add up to my idea of a tropical paradise. See p. 217.

- **Hotel Fonda Vela** (Monteverde; ✆ **2257-1413;** www.fondavela.com): With plush, modern rooms and an excellent restaurant, the Fonda Vela, one of the original hotels up here, is perennially a top choice in Monteverde. The hotel is located close enough to the Cloud Forest Reserve that you can even walk there. See p. 274.

- **Cariblue Bungalows** (Playa Cocles; ✆ **2750-0035;** www.cariblue.com): Try to get one of the private wooden bungalows here. If you do, you might be so happy and comfortable that you won't want to leave. Just 90m (295 ft.) or so away, however, are the warm waves of the Caribbean Sea. If this place is full, the neighboring **Azania Bungalows** (✆ **2750-0540;** www. azania-costarica.com) is just about as good. See p. 389.

9 The Best Ecolodges & Wilderness Resorts

The term "ecotourism" is now ubiquitous within the travel industry, particularly in Costa Rica. Ecolodge options in Costa Rica range from tent camps with no electricity, cold-water showers, and communal buffet-style meals to some of the most luxurious accommodations in the country. Generally, outstanding ecolodges and wilderness resorts are set apart by an ongoing commitment (financial or otherwise) to minimizing their effect on surrounding ecosystems and to supporting both conservation efforts and the residents of local communities. They should also be able to provide naturalist guides and plentiful information. All of the following do.

- **La Selva Biological Station** (south of Puerto Viejo; ✆ **2524-0607;** www.threepaths.co.cr): Sure, this place is geared more toward researchers than tourists, but that (along with the surrounding rainforest and extensive trail system) is what makes this one of the best ecotourism spots in the country. See p. 240.
- **Arenal Observatory Lodge** (near La Fortuna; ✆ **2290-7011;** www.arenal observatorylodge.com): Originally a research facility, this lodge has upgraded over the years and features comfortable rooms with impressive views of Arenal Volcano. There are excellent trails to nearby lava flows and a nice waterfall. Toucans frequent the trees near the lodge, and howler monkeys provide the wake-up calls. See p. 254.

- **Monteverde Lodge & Gardens** (Monteverde; ✆ **2257-0766;** www. monteverdelodge.com): One of the original ecolodges in Monteverde, this place has only improved over the years, with great guides, updated rooms, and lush gardens. The operation is run by the very dependable and experienced Costa Rica Expeditions. See p. 274.
- **La Paloma Lodge** (Drake Bay; ✆ **2293-7502;** www.lapalomalodge. com): If your idea of the perfect nature lodge is one where your front porch provides some prime-time viewing of flora and fauna, this place is for you. If you decide to leave the comfort of your porch, the Osa Peninsula's lowland rainforests are just outside your door. See p. 335.
- **Bosque del Cabo Rainforest Lodge** (Osa Peninsula; ✆/fax **2735-5206;** www.bosquedelcabo.com): Large, comfortable private cabins perched on the edge of a cliff overlooking the Pacific Ocean and surrounded by lush rainforest make this one of my favorite spots in the country. There's plenty to do, and there are always great guides here. See p. 344.
- **Playa Nicuesa Rainforest Lodge** (Golfo Dulce; ✆ **866/504-8116** or 2258-8250; www.nicuesalodge.com): This lodge is by far the best option on the Golfo Dulce. Set in deep forest, the individual bungalows here are a

perfect blend of rusticity and luxury. See p. 352.

- **Tortuga Lodge** (Tortuguero; © **2257-0766;** www.tortugalodge.com): The canals of Tortuguero snake through a maze of lowland primary rainforest. The beaches here are major sea-turtle nesting sites. This is not only the most comfortable option in the area, but also another of the excellent ecolodges run by Costa Rica Expeditions. See p. 370.

- **Selva Bananito Lodge** (in the Talamanca Mountains south of Limón; © **2253-8118;** www.selvabananito. com): This is one of the few lodges providing direct access to the southern Caribbean lowland rainforests. There's no electricity here, but that doesn't mean it's not plush. Hike along a riverbed, ride horses through the rainforest, climb 30m (100 ft.) up a ceiba tree, or rappel down a jungle waterfall. There's fabulous bird-watching in the area, and the Caribbean beaches are nearby. See p. 373.

10 The Best Bed & Breakfasts & Small Inns

- **Finca Rosa Blanca Country Inn** (Heredia; © **2269-9392;** www. fincarosablanca.com): If the cookie-cutter rooms of international resorts leave you cold, then perhaps the unique rooms of this unusual inn will be more your style. Square corners seem to have been prohibited here in favor of turrets and curving walls of glass, arched windows, and a semicircular built-in couch. It's set into the lush hillsides just 20 minutes from San José. See p. 117.

- **Vista del Valle Plantation Inn** (near Grecia; © **2450-0800;** www.vistadel valle.com): This is a great choice if you want something close to the airport but have no need for San José. The separate cabins are influenced by traditional Japanese architecture, with lots of polished woodwork and plenty of light. The gardens are meticulously tended, and the chef is excellent. A nice tile pool and Jacuzzi overlook a deep river canyon. See p. 119.

- **Sueño del Mar** (Playa Tamarindo; ©/fax **2653-0284;** www.sueno-del-mar.com): You might think you're dreaming here. The rooms feature African dolls on the windowsills, Kokopeli candleholders, and open-air showers with sculpted angelfish, hand-painted tiles, and lush tropical plants. The fabrics are from Bali and Guatemala. Somehow all this works well together. Add in the requisite hammocks under shade trees right on the beach and a small pool, and you really have something. The lodge's breakfasts are earning local renown; yours is included in the price of your room. See p. 194.

- **Arco Iris Lodge** (Monteverde; © **2645-5067;** www.arcoirislodge. com): This small lodge is right in Santa Elena, and it's by far the best deal in the Monteverde area. The owners are extremely knowledgeable and helpful. See p. 273.

- **Cabinas Los Cocos** (Playa Zancudo; ©/fax **2776-0012;** www.loscocos. com): If you've ever dreamed about chucking it all and setting up shop in a simple house right on the beach, give it a trial run here first. See p. 355.

- **Casa Verde Lodge** (Puerto Viejo; © **2750-0015;** www.cabinascasa verde.com): This is my favorite budget lodging along the Caribbean coast. The rooms are clean and airy and have comfortable beds with mosquito nets. The owner is friendly and is always doing some work in the gardens or around the grounds. See p. 388.

- **Tree House Lodge** (Punta Uva; ✆ **2750-0706;** www.costaricatree house. com): The collection of private houses at this small beachfront

property are the most creative and luxurious accommodations to be found on the Caribbean coast. I like the namesake Tree House, although the Beach House Suite is quite spectacular as well. See p. 389.

11 The Best Restaurants

- **Tin Jo** (San José; ✆ **2221-7605**): In a city with hundreds of Chinese restaurants, this place stands head and shoulders above the competition. In addition to an extensive selection of Szechuan and Cantonese classics, there are Japanese, Thai, Indian, and Malaysian dishes on the menu. Tin Jo has the most adventurous Asian cuisine in Costa Rica. See p. 123.

- **Grano de Oro Restaurant** (San José; ✆ **2255-3322**): This elegant little hotel has an elegant restaurant serving delicious Continental dishes and decadent desserts. The open-air seating in the lushly planted central courtyard is delightful, especially for lunch. See p. 124.

- **Bacchus** (Santa Ana; ✆ **2282-5441**): Set in a wonderfully restored and updated ancient adobe home, this restaurant serves up arguably the best Italian fare in the San José metropolitan area. See p. 127.

- **Ginger** (Playa Hermosa; ✆ **2672-0041**): Serving an eclectic mix of traditional and Pan Asian–influenced tapas, this sophisticated little joint is taking this part of Guanacaste by storm. They've got a list of creative cocktails to match the inventive dishes. See p. 174.

- **Mar y Sol** (Playa Flamingo; ✆ **2654-4151**): In a beautiful room on a high hilltop with great views, the Catalan chef here serves top-notch international fare. See p. 186.

- **Dragonfly Bar & Grill** (Tamarindo; ✆ **2653-1506**): Southwestern American and Pacific Rim fusion cuisines

are the primary culinary influences at this popular restaurant. Portions are large, service excellent, and prices fair. See p. 197.

- **Lola's** (Playa Avellanas; ✆ **2652-9097**): With a perfect setting on the sand, excellent hearty fare, and an 800-pound pet pig, this is one of the best beachfront restaurants in the country. See p. 199.

- **Nectar** (at Flor Blanca Resort, Santa Teresa; ✆ **2640-0232**): Guanacaste's best boutique resort also has one of its best restaurants. The menu changes nightly but always has a heavy Pan-Asian fusion flavor to it. The setting is romantic and subdued, in an open-air space just steps from the sand. See p. 223.

- **Playa de los Artistas** (Montezuma; ✆ **2642-0920**): This place is the perfect blend of refined cuisine and beachside funkiness. There are only a few tables, so make sure you get here early. Fresh, grilled seafood is served in oversize ceramic bowls and on large wooden slabs lined with banana leaves. See p. 219.

- **Sofia** (Monteverde; ✆ **2645-7017**): Sofia serves excellent New Latin–fusion fare at a small space about halfway along the rough dirt road between Santa Elena and the Monteverde Cloud Forest Preserve. Their new sister restaurant, **Chimera** (✆ **2645-6081**), which specializes in creative tapas, is also excellent. See p. 277.

- **Pacific Bistro** (Jacó; ✆ **2643-3771**): This place boasts a regularly changing menu of creative fusion fare with the freshest seafood and best beef available. Asian influences are prominent. See p. 291.

- **El Patio Bistro Latino** (Quepos; ℭ **2777-4982**): A casually elegant little place, El Patio Bistro Latino has made a name for itself in the Manuel Antonio area. The chef's creative concoctions take full advantage of fresh local ingredients. Its intimate setting is a welcome little oasis in Quepos. See p. 311.

- **La Pecora Nera** (Puerto Viejo; ℭ **2750-0490**): I'm not sure that a tiny surfer town on the remote Caribbean coast deserves such fine Italian food, but it's got it. Your best bet here is to allow yourself to be taken on a culinary roller-coaster ride with a mixed feast of the chef's nightly specials and suggestions. See p. 393.

12 The Best Views

- **The Summit of Irazú Volcano** (near San José): On a very clear day, you can see both the Pacific Ocean and the Caribbean Sea from this vantage point. Even if visibility is low and this experience eludes you, you can view the volcano's spectacular landscape, the Meseta Central, and the Orosi Valley. See p. 87.

- **Iguanazul Hotel** (Playa Junquillal; ℭ **2658-8123**; www.iguanazul.com): Located on a high bluff above Playa Junquillal, this hotel has a wonderful view of the Pacific and the windswept coastline in either direction. It gets best around sunset and is better yet if you can commandeer one of the hammocks set in a little palapa on the hillside itself. See p. 201.

- **Tabacón Grand Spa Thermal Resort** (near Arenal Volcano; 877/ **277-8291** or 2460-2020; www. tabacon.com): Arenal Volcano seems so close, you'll swear you can reach out and touch it. Unlike Irazú Volcano (see above), when *this* volcano rumbles and spews, you may feel the urge to seek cover. Most rooms have spectacular views from sheltered private patios or balconies. See p. 253.

- **Villa Caletas** (Playa Hermosa de Jacó; ℭ **2630-3003**): You'll have a view over the Golfo de Nicoya and the Pacific Ocean beyond. Sunsets at the hotel's outdoor amphitheater are legendary, but it's beautiful here during the day as well. See p. 290.

- **Hotel La Mariposa** (Quepos; ℭ **800/ 549-0157** or 2777-0355; www. lamariposa.com): This place has arguably the best view in Manuel Antonio, and that's saying a lot. Come for breakfast or a sunset drink because, unfortunately, I've had bad luck with dinner here. See p. 306.

- **The Summit of Mount Chirripó** (near San Isidro): What more can one say? At 3,724m (12,215 ft.), this is the highest spot in Costa Rica. On a clear day, you can see both the Pacific Ocean and the Caribbean Sea from here. Even if it isn't clear, you can catch some pretty amazing views and scenery. See "San Isidro de El General: A Base for Exploring Chirripó National Park" in chapter 10.

13 The Best After-Dark Fun

- **Night Tours** (countrywide): Most Neotropical forest dwellers are nocturnal. Animal and insect calls fill the air, and the rustling on the ground all around takes on new meaning. Night tours are offered at most rain- and cloud-forest destinations throughout the country. Many use high-powered flashlights to catch glimpses of various animals. Some of the better spots for night tours are **Monteverde, Tortuguero,** and the **Osa Peninsula.** Volcano viewing in **Arenal** is another not-to-miss nighttime activity.

- **El Cuartel de la Boca del Monte** (San José; ℭ **2221-0327**): From Wednesday to Saturday, San José's young, restless, and beautiful pack it in here. Originally a gay and bohemian hangout, it is now decidedly mixed and leaning toward yuppie. There's frequently live music. See p. 144.

- **San Pedro** (San José): This is San José's university district, and at night its streets are filled with students strolling among a variety of bars and cafes. If you'd like to join them, keep in mind that **Terra U** caters to the college crowd, **Mosaikos** is popular with young Tico rockers, **Omar Khayyam** is a great place to grab an outdoor table and watch the crowds walk by, and the **Jazz Café,** as its name indicates, is a hip live-music venue that often features local jazz and rock outfits. See "San José After Dark" in chapter 6.

- **San Clemente Bar & Grill** (Dominical; ℭ **2787-0055**): This is a quintessential surfers' joint, but whether you hang ten or not, this is where you'll want to hang out in Dominical at night. The fresh seafood and Tex-Mex specialties are hearty, tasty, and inexpensive. And there are pool, Ping-Pong, and foosball tables, as well as televised sporting events and surf videos. See "Dominical" in chapter 10.

- **Puerto Viejo:** This small beach town on the southern end of Costa Rica's Caribbean coast is one of the most active after-dark scenes in the country. **Johnny's Place** and **Stanford's** take turns as the major dance-and-party spot, but there are several other happening spots, as well as a few after-hours beach bonfires and jam sessions, to be found. See "Puerto Viejo" in chapter 12.

14 The Best Websites about Costa Rica

- **The *Tico Times*** (www.ticotimes.net): The English-language *Tico Times* makes it easy for *norteamericanos* (and other English speakers) to see what's happening in Costa Rica. It features the top story from its weekly print edition, as well as a daily update of news briefs, a business article, regional news, a fishing column, and travel reviews. There's also a link to current currency-exchange rates.

- **Latin American Network Information Center** (http://lanic.utexas.edu/la/ca/cr): This site houses a vast collection of information about Costa Rica, and is hands-down the best one-stop shop for browsing, with helpful links to a diverse range of tourism and general information sites.

- **Maptak** (www.maptak.com): This is the best site I've found for online maps. The site is still expanding and improving, and there's a tiny bit of a learning curve here, but this is overall a very valuable resource.

- **The U.S. Embassy in Costa Rica** (www.usembassy.or.cr): The official site of the U.S. Embassy in Costa Rica has a good base of information and regular updates of concern to U.S. citizens abroad, as well as about Costa Rica in general.

- **CostaRicaLiving** (http://groups.yahoo.com/group/CostaRicaLiving): This is the official home page of the best newsgroup dealing with Costa Rica. The active newsgroup deals with a wide range of issues, and its membership includes many longtime residents and bona fide experts. You have to join, but you'll find plenty of good information.

- *La Nación* **Digital** (www.nacion.com): If you can read Spanish, this is an excellent site to read regularly or simply browse. The entire content of the country's paper of record is placed online daily, and there's also an extensive searchable archive. It does maintain a small summary of major news items in English, although this section tends to run about a week behind current events.

2

Costa Rica in Depth

*P*ura Vida! (Pure Life!) is Costa Rica's unofficial national slogan, and in many ways it defines the country. You'll hear it exclaimed, proclaimed, and simply stated by Ticos from all walks of life, from children to octogenarians. It can be used as a cheer after your favorite soccer team scores a goal, or as a descriptive response when some one asks you, "How are you? (*¿Como estas?*)." It is symbolic of the easygoing and gentle nature of this country's people, politics, and personality.

Costa Rica itself is a mostly rural country with vast areas of protected tropical forests. It is one of the biologically richest places on earth, with a wealth of flora and fauna that attracts and captivates biologists, photographers, ecotourists, and casual visitors alike.

Often called the "Switzerland of Central America," Costa Rica is, and historically has been, a sea of tranquillity in a region that has been troubled by turmoil for centuries. For over 100 years, it has enjoyed a stable democracy and a relatively high standard of living for Latin America. The literacy rate is high, as are medical standards and facilities. Perhaps most significant, at least for proud and peace-loving Costa Ricans, is that this country does not have an army.

1 Costa Rica Today

Costa Rica has a population of just over four million, more than half of whom live in the Central Valley and are considered as urban. Some 94% of the population is of Spanish or otherwise European descent, and it is not at all unusual to see fair-skinned and blond Costa Ricans. This is largely because the indigenous population in place when the first Spaniards arrived was small and thereafter was quickly reduced to even more of a minority by wars and disease. There are still some remnant indigenous populations, primarily on reservations around the country; the principal tribes include the Bribri, Cabécar, Boruca, and Guaymí. In addition, on the Caribbean coast and in the big cities, there is a substantial population of English-speaking black Creoles who came over from the Antilles to work on

Where There Is a Tico, There Is Freedom

In 1989, on a visit to Costa Rica, Uruguayan President Julio María Sanguinetti famously declared: *"Donde hay un costarricense, esté donde esté, hay libertad,"* which is roughly translated in the title above.

Personally, I get a kick out of the version co-opted by a local condiment company in their advertising campaign, which states, "Where there is a Tico, there is Salsa Lizano." I find it to be equally true.

The Little Drummer Boy

Costa Rica's national hero is Juan Santamaría. The legend goes that young Juan enlisted as a drummer boy in the campaign against Walker. On April 11, 1865, when Costa Rican troops had a band of Walker's men cornered in a downtown hostel in Rivas, Nicaragua, Santamaría volunteered for a nearly certain suicide mission to set the building on fire. Although mortally wounded, Santamaría was successful in torching the building and driving Walker's men out, where they were swiftly routed. Today, April 11 is a national holiday.

the railroad and on the banana plantations. Racial tension isn't palpable, but it exists, perhaps more out of standard ignorance and fear rather than an organized or articulated prejudice.

In general, Costa Ricans are a friendly and outgoing people. In conversation and interaction with visitors, Ticos are very open and helpful. Time has relative meaning to Ticos. Although most tour companies and other establishments operate efficiently, don't expect punctuality, in general.

In a region historically plagued by internal strife and civil wars, Costa Ricans are proud of their peaceful history, political stability, and relatively high level of development. However, this can also translate into arrogance and prejudice toward immigrants from neighboring countries, particularly Nicaraguans, who make up a large percentage of the workforce on the banana and coffee plantations.

Roman Catholicism is the official religion of Costa Rica, although freedom to practice any religion is guaranteed by the country's constitution. More than 75% of the population identifies itself as Roman Catholic, while another 14% are part of a number of evangelical Christian congregations. There is a small but visible Jewish community as well. By and large, a large section of Ticos are religiously fervent. Although many city-dwellers lead quite secular lives, those in small villages and towns attend Mass regularly.

Costa Rica is the most technologically advanced and politically stable nation in Central America, and it has the largest middle class. Even the smallest towns have electricity, the water is mostly safe to drink, and the phone system is relatively good. Still, the gap between rich and poor has been widening for years. Government, banking, and social institutions are regularly embroiled in scandal. The roads, hospitals, and school systems have been in a slow but steady state of decay for decades. And there are no immediate signs that these matters will improve. Several "Free Zones" and some high-tech investments and production facilities have dramatically changed the face of Costa Rica's economy. Intel, which opened two side-by-side assembly plants in Costa Rica, currently accounts for more than 20% of the country's exports, compared with traditional exports such as coffee (3%) and bananas (8%). Although Intel and other international companies are used to trumpet a growing gross domestic product, very little of the profits actually make their way into the Costa Rican economy.

In early 2004, Costa Rican and U.S. negotiators hammered out a Free Trade Agreement, although it has still not been fully implemented. In late 2007, the agreement was approved narrowly in a national referendum, but a series of legislative changes are still needed before it can go into effect.

Still, tourism is the nation's true principal source of income, surpassing cattle ranching, textiles and exports of coffee, pineapples, bananas, and Intel microchips.

Almost two million tourists visit Costa Rica each year, and over half the working population is employed in the tourism and service industries. Increasingly, Ticos whose fathers and grandfathers were farmers and ranchers find themselves hotel owners, tour guides, and waiters. Although most have adapted gracefully and regard the industry as a source of new jobs and opportunities for economic advancement, restaurant and hotel staff can seem gruff and uninterested at times, especially in rural areas. And, unfortunately, an increase in the number of visitors has led to an increase in crime, prostitution, and drug trafficking. Common sense and street savvy are required in San José and in many of the more popular tourist destinations.

2 Looking Back at Costa Rica

EARLY HISTORY   Little is known of Costa Rica's history before its colonization by Spanish settlers. The pre-Columbian Indians who made their home in this region of Central America never developed the large cities or advanced culture that flowered farther north in what would become Guatemala, Belize, and Mexico. However, ancient artifacts indicating a strong sense of aesthetics have been unearthed from scattered excavations around the country. Beautiful gold and jade jewelry, intricately carved grinding stones, and artistically painted terra-cotta objects point to a small but highly skilled population.

SPAIN SETTLES COSTA RICA   In 1502, on his fourth and last voyage to the New World, Christopher Columbus anchored just offshore from present-day Limón. Whether he actually gave the country its name—"the rich coast"—is open to debate, but the Spaniards never did find much gold or minerals to exploit here.

The earliest Spanish settlers found that, unlike settlements to the north, the native population of Costa Rica was unwilling to submit to slavery. Despite their small numbers, scattered villages, and tribal differences, they fought back against the Spanish until they were overcome by superior firepower and European diseases. When the fighting ended, the European settlers in Costa Rica found that very few Indians were left to force into servitude. The settlers were thus forced to till their own lands, a situation unheard of in other parts of Central America. Few pioneers headed this way because they could settle in Guatemala, with its large native workforce. Costa Rica was nearly forgotten, as the Spanish crown looked elsewhere for riches to plunder and souls to convert.

It didn't take long for Costa Rica's few Spanish settlers to head for the hills, where they found rich volcanic soil and a climate that was less oppressive than in the lowlands. Cartago, the colony's first capital, was founded in 1563, but it was not until the 1700s that additional cities were established in this agriculturally rich region. In the late 18th century, the first coffee plants were introduced, and because these plants thrived in the

The Last Costa Rican Warrior

"Military victories, by themselves, are not worth much. It's what are built from them that matters."

—Jose "Pepe" Figueres

Presidential Welcome

President John F. Kennedy visited Costa Rica in March 1963. Upon his arrival, the Irazú Volcano woke up and erupted, after more than 2 decades of dormancy. Soot and ash reached as far as San José, where the soon-to-be-assassinated leader addressed students and political figures.

highlands, Costa Rica began to develop its first cash crop. Unfortunately, it was a long and difficult journey transporting the coffee to the Caribbean coast and then onward to Europe, where the demand for coffee was growing.

FROM INDEPENDENCE TO THE PRESENT In 1821, Spain granted independence to its colonies in Central America. Costa Rica joined with its neighbors to form the Central American Federation; but in 1838, it withdrew to form a new nation and pursue its own interests. By the mid-1800s, coffee was the country's main export. Free land was given to anyone willing to plant coffee on it, and plantation owners soon grew wealthy and powerful, creating Costa Rica's first elite class. Coffee plantation owners were powerful enough to elect their own representatives to the presidency.

This was a stormy period in Costa Rican history. In 1856, the country was invaded by William Walker, a soldier of fortune from Tennessee who, with the backing of U.S. President James Buchanan, was attempting to fulfill his grandiose dreams of presiding over a slave state in Central America (before his invasion of Costa Rica, he had invaded Nicaragua and Baja, California). The people of Costa Rica, led by their own president, Juan Rafael Mora, marched against Walker and chased him back to Nicaragua. Walker eventually surrendered to a U.S. warship in 1857, but, in 1860, he attacked Honduras, claiming to be the

president of that country. The Hondurans, who had had enough of Walker's shenanigans, promptly executed him.

Until 1890, coffee growers had to transport their coffee either by oxcart to the Pacific port of Puntarenas or by boat down the Río Sarapiquí to the Caribbean. In the 1870s, a progressive president proposed a railway from San José to the Caribbean coast to facilitate the transport of coffee to European markets. It took nearly 20 years for this plan to reach fruition, and more than 4,000 workers lost their lives constructing the railway, which passed through dense jungles and rugged mountains on its journey from the Central Valley to the coast. Partway through the project, as funds were dwindling, the second chief engineer, Minor Keith, proposed an idea that not only enhanced his fortunes but also changed the course of Central American history. Banana plantations would be developed along the railway right of way (land on either side of the tracks). The export of this crop would help to finance the railway, and, in exchange, Keith would get a 99-year lease on 1,976,000 hectares (800,000 acres) of land with a 20-year tax deferment. The Costa Rican government gave its consent, and in 1878 the first bananas were shipped from the country. In 1899, Keith and a partner formed the United Fruit Company, a business that eventually became the largest landholder in Central America and caused political disputes and wars throughout the region.

In 1889, Costa Rica held what is considered the first free election in Central American history. The opposition candidate won the election, and the control of the government passed from the hands of one political party to those of another without bloodshed or hostilities. Thus, Costa Rica established itself as the region's only true democracy. In 1948, this democratic process was challenged by Rafael Angel Calderón, who had served as the country's president from 1940 to 1944. After losing by a narrow margin, Calderón, who had the backing of the communist labor unions and the Catholic Church, refused to concede the country's leadership to the rightfully elected president, Otillio Ulate, and a civil war ensued. Calderón was eventually defeated by José "Pepe" Figueres. In the wake of this crisis, a new constitution was drafted; among other changes, it abolished Costa Rica's army so that such a revolution could never happen again.

In 1994, history seemed to repeat itself—peacefully this time—when José María Figueres took the reins of government from the son of his father's adversary, Rafael Angel Calderón. In 2001, Otton Solís and his new Citizen's Action Party (PAC) forced the presidential elections into a second round, opening a crack in a two-party system that had become seemingly entrenched for good. Although Solis himself finished third and didn't make it to the runoff, his upstart Citizen's Action Party won quite a few deputy slots.

The battered traditional two-party system was further threatened in 2004, when major corruption scandals became public. Two former presidents are currently under house arrest (Miguel Angel Rodríguez and Rafael Angel Calderón), and another (José María Figueres) is in Switzerland refusing a legislative call to return and testify, as well as avoiding an Interpol warrant for his capture and arrest. All are implicated, as well as a long list of high-level government employees and deputies, in various financial scandals or bribery cases. While it's unclear how these various scandals and trials will play out in the courts, they have already had a profound effect on the country's political landscape.

In 2006, former president Oscar Arias Sánchez, a Nobel Peace Prize laureate who had presided over the country during the mid-1980s, was reelected, defeating Otton Solís by an incredibly slim margin. The election was historic on two fronts. First, Arias needed to amend national law prohibiting reelection—it still prohibits consecutive terms. More importantly, spurred on by all the scandals, the traditional two-party system fractured into a multitude of smaller parties, with Solis' PAC emerging as the second political power in the country, behind Arias's PLN, with the traditional PUSC party almost disintegrating.

The most dramatic event during the early years of Arias's presidency was the October 2007 national referendum on whether or not to allow approval of a free trade agreement between Costa Rica and the United States and other Central American nations. That approval was passed by a very slim margin.

The Peace President

"Peace is the most honorable form of exhaustion, and the most exhausting form of honor."

—Oscar Arias

3 Art & Architecture

Since it's a small and provincial country, you'll find Costa Rica's culture somewhat similarly limited in size and scope. That said, there are vibrant current scenes in all the major arts—music, literature, architecture, dance, and even film.

ARCHITECTURE

Costa Rica lacks the large-scale pre-Columbian ceremonial ruins found throughout much of the rest of Mesoamerica. The only notable early archaeological site is **Guayabo** (p. 154). However, only the foundations of a few dwellings, a handful of carved petroglyphs, and some road and water infrastructure are still visible here.

Similarly, Costa Rica lacks the large and well-preserved colonial-era cities found throughout much of the rest of Latin America. The original capital of Cartago (p. 152) has some old ruins and a few colonial-era buildings, as well as the country's grandest church, **La Basílica de Nuestra Señora de los Angeles (Basilica of Our Lady of the Angels)** ⭐ (p. 152), which was built in honor of the country's patron saint, La Negrita, or the Virgin of Guadalupe.

In downtown San José, Barrio Amón and Barrio Otoya are two side-by-side upscale neighborhoods full of a stately mix of architectural stylings, with everything from colonial-era residential mansions, to Art Deco apartment buildings, and modern high-rise skyscrapers. One of the standout buildings here is the **Metal School (Escuela Metalica),** which dates to the 1880s, and was shipped over piece-by-piece from France, and erected in place.

On much of the Caribbean coast, you will find mostly wooden houses, built on raised stilts to rise above the wet ground and occasional flooding. Some of these houses feature ornate gingerbread trim.

Much of the rest of the country's architecture is pretty plain. Most residential houses are simple concrete-block affairs, with zinc roofs. A few modern architects are creating names for themselves. **Ronald Zurcher,** who designed the Four Seasons Resort (p. 172) and several other large hotel projects, is one of the shining lights of contemporary Costa Rican architecture.

ART

Unlike Guatemala, Mexico, or even Nicaragua, Costa Rica does not have a strong tradition of local or indigenous arts and crafts. The strong suit of Costa Rican art is European and Western influenced, ranging from neoclassical to modern in style.

Early painters to look out for include **Max Jimenez, Francisco Amighetti, Manuel de la Cruz,** and **Teodorico Quiros.** Recently deceased and living legends of the art world include **Rafa Fernández, Lola Fernández,** and **Cesar Valverde.** Contemporary artists making waves and names for themselves include **Fernando Carballo, Rodolfo Stanley, Lionel Gonzalez, Manuel Zumbado,** and **Karla Solano.** The last two are a husband-wife team, although they primarily work separately.

Colonial-Era Remnant or Crime Deterrent?

Most Costa Rican homes feature steel or iron grating over the doors and windows. I've heard more than one tour guide say this can be traced back to colonial-era architecture and design. However, I'm fairly convinced it is a relatively modern adaptation to the local crime scene.

Sculpture is perhaps one of the strongest aspects of the Costa Rican art scene, with the large bronze works of **Francisco "Paco" Zuñiga** among the best of the genre. Meanwhile, the artists **José Sancho, Edgar Zuñiga,** and **Jiménez Deredia** are all producing internationally acclaimed pieces, many of monumental proportions. You can see examples by all of these sculptors around the country, as well as at San José's downtown **Museo de Arte Costarricense** (p. 129). I also enjoy the whimsical works of **Leda Astorga,** who sculpts and then paints a pantheon of plump and voluptuous figures in interesting, and at times, compromising, poses.

You'll find several excellent museums and galleries in San José (p. 128), as well as in some of the larger and more popular tourist destinations.

4 The Lay of the Land

Costa Rica occupies a central spot in the isthmus that joins North and South America. For millennia, this land bridge served as a migratory thoroughfare and mating ground for species native to the once-separate continents. It was also where the Mesoamerican and Andean pre-Columbian indigenous cultures met.

The country comprises only .01% of the earth's landmass, yet it is home to 5% of the planet's biodiversity. More than 10,000 identified species of plants, 880 species of birds, 9,000 species of butterflies and moths, and 500 species of mammals, reptiles, and amphibians are found here.

The key to this biological richness lies in the many distinct life zones and ecosystems found in Costa Rica. It might all seem like one big mass of green to the untrained eye, but the differences are profound.

For more information and details on Costa Rican flora and fauna, see "Appendix C: Costa Rican Wildlife."

COSTA RICA'S ECOSYSTEMS

Costa Rica's **lowland rainforests** are true tropical jungles. Some are deluged with more than 200 inches of rainfall per year, and their climate is hot and humid. Trees grow tall and fast, fighting for sunlight in the upper reaches. In fact, life and foliage on the forest floor are surprisingly sparse. The action is typically 30m (98 ft.) up, in the canopy, where long vines stream down, lianas climb up, and bromeliads grow on the branches and trunks of towering hardwood trees. You can find these lowland rainforests along the southern Pacific coast and Osa Peninsula, as well as along the Caribbean coast. **Corcovado, Cahuita,** and **Manuel Antonio** national parks, as well as the **Manzanillo-Gandoca Wildlife Refuge,** are fine examples of lowland rainforests.

At higher altitudes you'll find Costa Rica's famed **cloud forests.** Here the steady flow of moist air meets the mountains and creates a nearly constant mist. Epiphytes—resourceful plants that live cooperatively on the branches and trunks of other trees—grow abundantly in the cloud forests, where they must extract moisture and nutrients from the air. Because cloud forests are found in generally steep, mountainous terrain, the canopy here is lower and less uniform than in lowland rainforests, providing better chances for viewing elusive fauna. Costa Rica's most spectacular cloud forest is the **Monteverde Biological Cloud Forest Reserve** in Guanacaste province (see chapter 9).

At the highest reaches, the cloud forests give way to **elfin forests** and *páramos.* More commonly associated with the South American Andes, a páramo is characterized by a variety of tundralike shrubs and grasses, with a scattering of twisted, windblown trees. Reptiles, rodents, and raptors are the most common residents here. **Mount Chirripó, Chirripó National Park,** and the **Cerro de la Muerte (Mountain of Death)** are the principal areas of páramo in Costa Rica.

In a few protected areas of Guanacaste, you will still find examples of the otherwise vanishing **tropical dry forest.** During the long and pronounced dry season (late Nov to late Apr), no rain relieves the unabated heat. In an effort to conserve much-needed water, the trees drop their leaves but bloom in a riot of color: purple jacaranda, scarlet *poró,* and brilliant orange flame-of-the-forest are just a few examples. Then during the rainy season, this deciduous forest is transformed into a lush and verdant landscape. Because the foliage is not so dense, the dry forests are excellent places to view a variety of wildlife species, especially howler monkeys and *pizotes* (coati). Dry forests are found in **Santa Rosa** and **Guanacaste** national parks.

Along the coasts, primarily where river mouths meet the ocean, you will find extensive **mangrove forests** and **swamps.** Around these seemingly monotonous tangles of roots exists one of the most diverse and rich ecosystems in the country. All sorts of fish and crustaceans live in the brackish tidal waters. Caimans and crocodiles cruise the maze of rivers and unmarked canals, and hundreds of herons, ibises, egrets, and other marsh birds nest and feed along the silted banks. Mangrove swamps are often havens for water birds: cormorants, frigate birds, pelicans, and herons. The larger birds tend to nest up high in the canopy, while the smaller ones nestle in the underbrush. The **Gulf of Nicoya** is particularly popular among frigate birds and brown pelicans, as well as all manner of terns and seagulls.

Over the last decade or so, Costa Rica has taken great strides toward protecting its rich biodiversity. Thirty years ago it was difficult to find a protected area anywhere, but now more than 11% of the country is protected within the national park system. Another 10% to 15% of the land enjoys moderately effective preservation as part of private and public reserves, Indian reserves, and wildlife refuges and corridors. Still, Costa Rica's precious tropical hardwoods continue to be harvested at an alarming rate, often illegally, while other primary forests are clear-cut for short-term agricultural gain. Many experts predict that Costa Rica's unprotected forests will be gone within the early part of this century.

This is also a land of high volcanic and seismic activity. There are three major **volcanic mountain ranges** in Costa Rica, and many of the volcanoes are still active, allowing visitors to experience the awe-inspiring sight of steaming fumaroles and intense lava flows during their stay. Two volcanoes near the capital—Poás and Irazú—are currently active, although relatively quiet. The best places to see volcanic activity are farther north in **Rincón de la Vieja National Park** and at **Arenal Volcano** (see chapters 7 and 9).

In any one spot in Costa Rica, temperatures remain relatively constant year-round. However, as seen above, they vary dramatically according to altitude, from tropically hot and steamy along the coasts to below freezing at the highest elevations.

SEARCHING FOR WILDLIFE

Animals in the forests are predominantly nocturnal. When they are active in the daytime, they are usually elusive and on the watch for predators. Birds are easier to spot in clearings or secondary forests than they are in primary forests. Unless you have lots of experience in the Tropics, your best hope for enjoying a walk through the jungle lies in employing a trained and knowledgeable guide. (By the way, if it's been raining a lot and the trails are muddy, a good pair of rubber boots comes in handy. These are usually provided by the lodges or at the sites, where necessary.)

Here are a few helpful hints:

- **Listen.** Pay attention to rustling in the leaves; whether it's monkeys up above or pizotes on the ground, you're most likely to hear an animal before seeing one.
- **Keep quiet.** Noise will scare off animals and prevent you from hearing their movements and calls.
- **Don't try too hard.** Soften your focus and allow your peripheral vision to take over. This way you can catch glimpses of motion and then focus in on the prey.
- **Bring binoculars.** It's also a good idea to practice a little first to get the hang of them. It would be a shame to be fiddling around and staring into space while everyone else in your group oohs and aahs over a quetzal.
- **Dress appropriately.** You'll have a hard time focusing your binoculars if you're busy swatting mosquitoes.

Light, long pants and long-sleeved shirts are your best bet. Comfortable hiking boots are a real boon, except where heavy rubber boots are necessary. Avoid loud colors; the better you blend in with your surroundings, the better your chances are of spotting wildlife.

- **Be patient.** The jungle isn't on a schedule. However, your best shots at seeing forest fauna are in the very early morning and late afternoon hours.
- **Read up.** Familiarize yourself with what you're most likely to see. Most lodges and hotels have a copy of *A Guide to the Birds of Costa Rica* (Cornell University Press, 1990) and other wildlife field guides, although it's always best to have your own. A good all-around book to have is Carrol Henderson's *The Field Guide to the Wildlife of Costa Rica* (University of Texas Press, 2002).

5 Costa Rica in Popular Culture: Books, Film & Music

BOOKS

Though Costa Rica's literary output is sparsely translated and little known outside of Costa Rica, there are some notable authors to look out for, especially if you can read in Spanish.

Some of the books mentioned below might be difficult to track down in U.S. bookstores, but you'll find them all in abundance in Costa Rica. A good place to check for most of these titles is **Seventh Street Books,** on Calle 7 between avenidas 1 and Central in San José (© **2256-8251**).

GENERAL INTEREST For a straightforward, albeit somewhat dry, historical overview, there's *The History of Costa Rica,* by Ivan Molina and Steven Palmer (University of Costa Rica, 2001). For a more readable look into Costa Rican society, pick up *The Ticos: Culture and Social Change* by Richard, Karen, and Mavis Biesanz (Lynne Rienner Publishers,

1999), an examination of the country's politics and culture, by the authors of the out-of-print *The Costa Ricans.* Another option worth checking out is *The Costa Rica Reader: History, Culture, Politics,* a broad selection of stories, essays, and excerpts edited by Steven Palmer and Ivan Molina, the authors of the history book mentioned above (Duke University Press, 2004).

To learn more about the life and culture of Costa Rica's Talamanca coast, an area populated by Afro-Caribbean people whose forebears emigrated from Caribbean islands in the early 19th century, look for *What Happen: A Folk-History of Costa Rica's Talamanca Coast* by Paula Palmer. This book is a collection of oral histories taken from a wide range of local characters. The newest edition was published in 2005 by Distribuidores Zona Tropical.

FICTION & POETRY *Costa Rica: A Traveler's Literary Companion*, edited by Barbara Ras and with a foreword by Oscar Arias Sánchez (Whereabouts Press, 1994), is a collection of short stories by Costa Rican writers, organized by region of the country. If you're lucky, you might find a copy of *Stories of Tatamundo* (University of Costa Rica Press, 1998), by Fabian Dobles, or *Lo Peor/The Worst* (Grupo Editorial Norma, 2006), by Fernando Contreras.

Young adults will enjoy Kristin Joy Pratt's *A Walk in the Rainforest* (Dawn Publications, 1992), while younger children will like the beautifully illustrated *The Forest in the Clouds*, by Sneed Collard and Michael Rothman (Charlesbridge Publishing, 2000), and *The Umbrella*, by Jan Brett (Putnam Juvenile, 2004), or the bilingual *Mar Azucarada/Sugar Sea* by Roberto Boccanera (Pachanga Kids, 2006), a young Costa Rican writer.

One of the most important pieces in the Costa Rican canon, Carlos Luis Fallas's 1941 tome *Mamita Yunai,* is a stark look at the impact of the large banana giant United Fruit on the country. More recently, Fernando Contreras takes up where his predecessor left off in *Unico Mirando al Mar,* which describes the conditions of the poor, predominantly children, who scavenge Costa Rica's garbage dumps.

In the field of poetry, **Eunice Odio, Juaquín Gutiérrez,** and **Jorge Debravo** are early poets who set the gold standard. Their more modern successors include **Alfonso Chase, Virginia Grutter, Laureano Alban, Ana Istaru, Osvaldo Sauma,** and **Luis Chavez.**

NATURAL HISTORY I think that everyone coming to Costa Rica should read *Tropical Nature* by Adrian Forsyth and Ken Miyata (Touchstone Books, 1987). My all-time favorite book on tropical biology, this is a wonderfully written and lively collection of tales and adventures by two Neotropical biologists who spent quite some time in the forests of Costa Rica.

Mario A. Boza's beautiful *Costa Rica National Parks* (INCAFO, 2004) has been reissued in an elegant coffee-table edition. *Wildlife of the National Parks and Reserves of Costa Rica,* by Michael and Patricia Fogden (Fundacion Neotropical, 1997), features some impressive photography by this prolific couple. *Costa Rica's National Parks and Preserves,* by Joseph Franke (The Mountaineers, 1999), is similar but with fewer photos.

For an introduction to a wide range of Costa Rican fauna, there's *The Field Guide to the Wildlife of Costa Rica,* by Carrol Henderson (University of Texas Press, 2002), or *Costa Rica: Traveller's Wildlife Guides,* by Les Beletsky (Interlink Books, 2004). Both pack a lot of useful information into a concise package and make great field guides for amateur naturalists and inquisitive tourists.

A Guide to the Birds of Costa Rica, by F. Gary Stiles and Alexander Skutch (Cornell University Press, 1989), is an invaluable guide to identifying the many birds you'll see during your stay. Most guides and nature lodges have a copy of this book on hand. This classic faces competition from the more recent *Birds of Costa Rica,* by Richard Garrigues and Robert Dean (Cornell University Press, 2007). Bird-watchers might also enjoy Dennis Rodgers's *Site Guides: Costa Rica & Panama* (Cinclus Publications, 1997), which details each country's bird-watching bounty by site and region.

Other interesting natural-history books that will give you a look at the plants and animals of Costa Rica include *Costa Rica Natural History,* by Daniel Janzen (University of Chicago Press, 1983); *A Guide to Tropical Plants of Costa Rica,* by Willow Zuchowsky (Distribuidores Zona Tropical, 2005); *The Natural History of Costa Rican Mammals,* by Mark

Wainwright (Distribuidores Zona Tropical, 2003); *A Guide to the Amphibians and Reptiles of Costa Rica,* by Twan Leenders (Distribuidores Zona Tropical, 2001); and the classic *A Neotropical Companion,* by John C. Kricher (Princeton University Press, 1999), reissued in an expanded edition with color photos.

For a rather complete list of field guides, check out www.zonatropical.net.

FILM

Costa Rica has a budding and promising young film industry. Local feature films like *Tropix, Caribe,* and *Passport* are all out on subtitled DVD. In 2008, *El Camino (The Path)* by Costa Rican filmmaker Ishtar Yasin Gutiérrez was screened at the Berlin Film Festival. And several other feature films are expected to be produced in 2009 and 2010, including *Del Amor y Otros Demonios,* based on a novel by Gabriel García Márquez.

If you want to see Costa Rica used simply as a backdrop, the major motion picture productions of *1492* by Ridley Scott and starring Gerard Depardieu and Sigourney Weaver; *Congo,* featuring Laura Linney and Ernie Hudson, and *The Blue Butterfly* with William Hurt, all feature sets and scenery from around the country.

There's a small **Costa Rican Film and Video festival** (www.centrodecine.go.cr) each November in San José.

MUSIC

Several musical traditions and styles meet and mingle in Costa Rica. The northern Guanacaste region is a hotbed of folk music that is strongly influenced by the *marimba* (wooden xylophone) traditions of Guatemala and Nicaragua, while also featuring guitars, maracas, and the occasional harp. On the Caribbean coast you can hear traditional calypso sung by descendants of the original black workers brought over to build the railroads and tend the banana plantations. Roving bands play a mix of guitar, banjo, washtub bass, and percussion in the bars and restaurants of Cahuita and Puerto Viejo.

There's also a healthy contemporary music scene. The jazz-fusion trio **Editus** has won two Grammy awards for its work with Panamanian salsa giant (and movie star and Tourism minister) **Rubén Blades.** Meanwhile, **Malpaís,** the closest thing Costa Rica has to a super-group, is a pop-rock outfit that is tearing it up in Costa Rica and around Central America.

You should also seek out discs by **Cantoamérica,** which plays upbeat dance music ranging from salsa to calypso to merengue. Jazz pianist **Manuel Obregón** (a member of Malpaís) has several excellent solo albums out, including *Simbiosis,* on which he improvises along with the sounds of Costa Rica's wildlife, waterfalls, and weather; as well as his work with the *Papaya Orchestra,* a collaboration and gathering of musicians from around Central America.

Local label **Papaya Music** (www.papayamusic.com) has done an excellent job promoting and producing albums by Costa Rican musicians in a range of styles and genres. Their offerings range from the Guanacasteca folk songs of **Max Goldemberg,** to the boleros of **Ray Tico,** to the original calypso of **Walter "Gavitt" Ferguson.** You can find their discs at gift shops and record stores around the country, as well as at airport souvenir stores.

Classical music lovers will want to head to San José, where there's a symphony orchestra, youth symphony, opera company, and choir. The local symphony sometimes features the works of local composers like **Benjamin Guitiérrez** and **Eddie Mora.** On occasion, small-scale music festivals will bring classical offerings to some of the beach and inland tourist destinations around the country.

Bars and discos around the country spin salsa, merengue, and cumbia, as well as more modern grooves that include house, electronic, trip-hop, and reggaeton.

6 Eating & Drinking in Costa Rica

Costa Rican food is not especially memorable. Perhaps that's why there's so much international food available here. San José remains the unquestioned gastronomic capital of the country, and here you can find many of the cuisines of the world served at moderate prices. At even the more expensive restaurants, it's hard to spend more than $50 (£25) per person unless you really splurge on drinks and wine. It gets even cheaper outside the city. You can find several excellent French, Italian and contemporary fusion restaurants around the San José area, as well as Peruvian, Japanese, Swiss, and Spanish establishments.

However, if you really want to save money, Costa Rican, or *típico*, food is always the cheapest nourishment available. It's primarily served in *sodas*, Costa Rica's equivalent of diners.

Outside the capital and major tourist destinations, your options get very limited very fast. In fact, many beach destinations are so remote that you have no choice but to eat in the hotel's dining room. Even on the more accessible beaches, the only choices aside from the hotel dining rooms are often cheap local places or overpriced tourist traps serving indifferent meals. At remote jungle lodges, the food is usually served buffet- or family-style and can range from bland to inspired, depending on who's doing the cooking, and turnover is high.

If you see a restaurant billing itself as a **mirador**, it means it has a view. If you are driving around the country, don't miss an opportunity to dine with a view at some little roadside restaurant. The food might not be fantastic, but the scenery will be.

I have separated restaurant listings throughout this book into three price categories, based on the average cost of a meal per person, including tax and service charge. The categories are **Expensive,** more than $25 (£13); **Moderate,** $10 to $25 (£5–£13); and **Inexpensive,** less than $10 (£5). (Note, however, that individual items in the listings—entrees, for instance—do not include the sales or service taxes.) Keep in mind that there is an additional 13% sales tax, as well as a 10% service charge. Ticos rarely tip, but that doesn't mean that you shouldn't. If the service was particularly good and attentive, you should probably leave a little extra.

MEALS & DINING CUSTOMS

Rice and beans are the bases of Costa Rican meals—all three of them. At breakfast, they're called *gallo pinto* and come with everything from eggs to steak to seafood. At lunch or dinner, rice and beans are an integral part of a *casado* (which translates as "married" and is the name for the local version of a blue-plate special). A *casado* usually consists of cabbage-and-tomato salad, fried plantains (a starchy, banana-like fruit), and a chicken, fish, or meat dish of some sort. On the Caribbean coast, rice and beans are called *rice 'n' beans,* and are cooked in coconut milk.

Dining hours in Costa Rica are flexible but generally follow North American customs. Some downtown restaurants in San José are open 24 hours; however, expensive restaurants tend to be open for lunch between 11am and 3pm and for dinner between 6 and 11pm.

APPETIZERS Known as *bocas* in Costa Rica, appetizers are served with drinks in most bars. Often the *bocas* are free, but even if they aren't, they're very inexpensive. Popular *bocas* include *gallos* (tortillas piled with meat, chicken, cheese, or beans), ceviche (a marinated seafood salad), tamales (stuffed cornmeal patties wrapped and steamed inside banana leaves), *patacones* (fried green plantain chips), and fried yuca.

SANDWICHES & SNACKS Ticos love to snack, and there's a large variety of tasty little sandwiches and snacks available on the street, at snack bars, and in *sodas*. *Arreglados* are little meat-filled sandwiches, as are *tortas*, which are served on little rolls with a bit of salad tucked into them. Tacos, tamales, *gallos* (see above), and *empanadas* (turnovers) also are quite common.

MEAT Costa Rica is beef country, having converted much of its rainforest land to pastures for raising beef cattle. Consequently, beef is cheap and plentiful, although it might be a bit tougher—and cut and served thinner—than it is back home. One typical local dish is called *olla de carne*, a bowl of beef broth with large chunks of meat, local tubers, and corn. Spit-roasted chicken is also very popular here and is surprisingly tender.

SEAFOOD Costa Rica has two coasts, and, as you'd expect, plenty of seafood is available everywhere in the country. Corvina (sea bass) is the most commonly served fish and is prepared innumerable ways, including as ceviche. (*Be careful:* In many cheaper restaurants, particularly in San José, shark meat is often sold as corvina.) You should also come across *pargo* (red snapper), *dorado* (mahimahi), and tuna on some menus, especially along the coasts. Although Costa Rica is a major exporter of shrimp and lobster, both are relatively expensive and in short supply here.

VEGETABLES On the whole, you'll find vegetables surprisingly lacking in the meals you're served in Costa Rica—usually nothing more than a little pile of shredded cabbage topped with a slice or two of tomato. For a much more satisfying and filling salad, order *palmito* (hearts of palm salad). The heart (actually the stalk or trunk of these small palms) is first boiled and then chopped into circular pieces and served with other fresh vegetables, with a salad dressing on top. If you want something more than this, you'll have to order a side dish such as *picadillo*, a stew or purée of vegetables with a bit of meat in it.

Though they are giant relatives of bananas and are technically considered a fruit, *plátanos* (plantains) are really more like vegetables and require cooking before they can be eaten. Green plantains have a very starchy flavor and consistency, but they become as sweet as candy as they ripen. Fried *plátanos* are one of my favorite dishes. Yuca (manioc root or cassava in English) is another starchy staple root vegetable in Costa Rica.

One more vegetable worth mentioning is the *pejibaye*, a form of palm fruit that looks like a miniature orange coconut. Boiled *pejibayes* are frequently sold from carts on the streets of San José. When cut in half, a *pejibaye* reveals a large seed surrounded by soft, fibrous flesh. You can eat it plain, but it's usually topped with a dollop of mayonnaise.

FRUITS Costa Rica has a wealth of delicious tropical fruits. The most common are mangoes (the season begins in May), papayas, pineapples, melons, and bananas. Other fruits include *marañón*, which is the fruit of the cashew tree and has orange or yellow glossy skin; *granadilla* or *maracuyá* (passion fruit); *mamón chino*, which Asian travelers will immediately recognize as rambutan; and *carambola* (star fruit).

DESSERTS *Queque seco*, literally "dry cake," is the same as pound cake. *Tres leches* cake, on the other hand, is so moist that you almost need to eat it with a spoon. Flan is a typical custard dessert. It often comes as either *flan de caramelo* (caramel) or *flan de coco* (coconut). Numerous other sweets are available, many of which are made with condensed milk and raw sugar. *Cajetas* are popular handmade candies, made from sugar and

Coconut, Straight Up

Throughout Costa Rica (particularly on the coastal road between Limón and Cahuita), keep your eye out for roadside stands selling fresh, green coconuts, or *pipas* in Spanish. Green coconuts have very little meat, but are filled with copious amounts of a slightly sweet, clear liquid that is amazingly refreshing. According to local legend, this liquid is pure enough to be used as plasma in an emergency situation. Armed with a machete, the *pipa* seller will cut out the top and stick in a straw. In the best of cases, the *pipa* will have been cooled over ice. The entire thing should cost around $1 (50p).

various mixes of evaporated, condensed, and powdered milk. They are sold in differing-size bits and chunks at most *pulperías* (general stores) and streetside food stands.

BEVERAGES

Frescos, refrescos, and *jugos naturales* are my favorite drinks in Costa Rica. They are usually made with fresh fruit and milk or water. Among the more common fruits used are mangoes, papayas, blackberries *(mora),* and pineapples. You'll also come across passion fruit *(maracuyá)* and *carambola.* Some of the more unusual frescos are *horchata* (made with rice flour and a lot of cinnamon) and *chan* (made with the seed of a plant found mostly in Guanacaste—definitely an acquired taste). The former is wonderful; the latter requires an open mind (it's reputed to be good for the digestive system). Order *un fresco con leche sin hielo* (a *fresco* with milk but without ice) if you're avoiding untreated water.

If you're a coffee drinker, you might be disappointed here. Most of the best coffee has traditionally been targeted for export, and Ticos tend to prefer theirs weak and sugary. Better hotels and restaurants are starting to cater to gringo and European tastes and are serving up superior blends. If you want black coffee, ask for *café negro;* if you want it with milk, order *café con leche.*

For something different for your morning beverage, ask for *agua dulce,* a warm drink made from melted sugar cane and served either with milk or lemon, or straight.

See "Where to Dine" on p. 120 in chapter 6 for more info on drinks.

WATER   Although water in most of Costa Rica is safe to drink, bottled water is readily available and is a good option if you're worried about an upset stomach. *Agua mineral,* or simply soda, is sparkling water in Costa Rica. If you like your water without bubbles, request *aqua mineral sin gas,* or *agua en botella.*

BEER, WINE & LIQUOR   The German presence in Costa Rica over the years has produced several fine beers, which are fairly inexpensive. Most Costa Rican beers are light pilsners. The most popular brands are Bavaria, Imperial, and Pilsen. I personally can't tell much of a difference between any of them. Licensed local versions of Heineken and Rock Ice are also available.

You can find imported wines at reasonable prices in the better restaurants throughout the country. You can usually save money by ordering a Chilean wine over a Californian or European one.

Costa Rica distills a wide variety of liquors, and you'll save money by ordering these over imported brands. The national liquor is *guaro,* a crude cane liquor that's often combined with a soft drink or tonic. If you want to try *guaro,* stick to the Cacique brand. The Café Britt and Salicsa brands produce a couple of types of coffee-based liqueurs. Café Rica is similar to Kahlúa and quite good.

3

Planning Your Trip to Costa Rica

Costa Rica is beginning to be old hat. It seems like almost everybody's already been, or knows someone who's been. As Costa Rica matures as a tourist destination, things are getting easier and easier for international travelers. There are more and more hotels and rental car agencies to choose from, and services are expanding and improving across the board. That said, most travelers—even experienced travelers and repeat visitors—will want to do some serious pretrip planning.

Some basic questions need to be addressed right from the get-go. When is the best time to go to Costa Rica? Should you rent a car (or will you need 4WD), and what will it cost? What are the hotels like? How much should you budget for your trip? How can you save money? How does the local currency work, and should you use cash or credit cards? These are just a few of the important questions that this chapter answers so that you can be prepared when you arrive in Costa Rica.

The question of where to go is actually addressed elsewhere—in fact, throughout the book. For a start in narrowing down your choices, see the "Suggested Itineraries" and "Active Vacation Planner" chapters 4 and 5, as well as my "Best Of" selections in chapter 1 and individual destination chapters, to see what most strikes your fancy.

For additional help in planning your trip and for more on-the-ground resources in Costa Rica, please turn to the "Fast Facts, Toll-Free Numbers & Websites" appendix A on p. 395.

1 Visitor Information

In the United States or Canada, you can get basic information on Costa Rica by contacting the **Costa Rican Tourist Board (ICT,** or Instituto Costarricense de Turismo) (© **866/COSTA RICA;** www. visitcostarica.com). Travelers from the United Kingdom, Australia, and New Zealand will have to rely primarily on this website because the ICT does not have toll-free access in these countries.

In addition to this official site, you'll be able to find a wealth of Web-based information on Costa Rica with a few clicks of your mouse. In fact you'll be better off surfing, as the ICT site is rather limited and clunky. See "The Best Websites about Costa Rica" in chapter 1 for some helpful suggestions about where to begin your online search.

You can pick up a map when you arrive at the ICT's information desk at the airport, or at their downtown San José offices (although the map included with this book is generally better). Other sources in San José for detailed maps include **Seventh Street Books,** Calle 7 between avenidas Central and 1 (© **2256-8251**); **Librería Lehmann,** Avenida Central between calles 1 and 3 (© **2223-1212**); and **Librería Universal,** Avenida Central between calles Central and 1 (© **2222-2222**).

Perhaps the best map to have is the waterproof country map of Costa Rica put out by **International Travel Maps** (www.itmb.com), which can be ordered directly from their website, or any major online bookseller, like Amazon.com.

2 Entry Requirements

PASSPORTS

Citizens of the United States, Canada, Great Britain, and most European nations may visit Costa Rica for a maximum of 90 days. No visa is necessary, but you must have a valid passport, which you should carry with you at all times while you're in Costa Rica. Citizens of Australia, Ireland, and New Zealand can enter the country without a visa and stay for 30 days, although once in the country, visitors can apply for an extension.

If you overstay your visa or entry stamp, you will have to pay around US$45 (£23) for an exit visa. If you need to get an exit visa, a travel agent in San José can usually obtain one for a small fee and save you the hassle of dealing with Immigration. If you want to stay longer than the validity of your entry stamp or visa, the easiest thing to do is cross the border into Panama or Nicaragua for 72 hours and then reenter Costa Rica on a new entry stamp or visa. However, be careful: Periodically the Costa Rican government has cracked down on "perpetual tourists"; if it notices a continued pattern of exits and entries designed simply to support an extended stay, it might deny you reentry.

If you need a visa or have other questions about Costa Rica, you can contact any of the following Costa Rican embassies or consulates: in the **United States,** 2114 S St. NW, Washington, DC 20008 (© **202/234-2945;** www.costarica-embassy.org for consulate locations around the country); in **Canada,** 325 Dalhousie St., Ste. 407, Ottawa, Ontario K1N 5TA (© **613/562-2855**); and in **Great Britain,** 14 Lancaster Gate, London, England W2 3LH (© **020/7706-8844**). There are no Costa Rican embassies in Australia or New Zealand, but you could try contacting the honorary consul in Sydney, Australia, at Level 11, De La Sala House, 30 Clarence St., Sydney NSW 2000 (© **02/9261-1177**).

For information on how to obtain a passport, go to **"Passports"** in the **"Fast Facts"** appendix A (p. 399).

MEDICAL REQUIREMENTS

No shots or inoculations are required to enter Costa Rica. The exception to this is for those who have recently been traveling in a country or region known to have yellow fever. In this case, proof of a yellow fever vaccination is required.

For more on medical concerns and recommendations, see "Health," p. 49.

CUSTOMS
WHAT YOU CAN TAKE HOME FROM COSTA RICA:

U.S. Citizens: For specifics on what you can bring back and the corresponding fees, download the invaluable free pamphlet *Know Before You Go* online at www.cbp.gov. (Click on "Travel," and then click on "Know Before You Go! Online Brochure") Or contact the U.S. Customs & Border Protection (CBP), 1300 Pennsylvania Ave., NW, Washington, DC 20229 (© **877/287-8667**) and request the pamphlet.

Canadian Citizens: For a clear summary of Canadian rules, write for the booklet *I Declare,* issued by the Canada Border Services Agency (℃ 800/461-9999 in Canada, or 204/983-3500; www.cbsa-asfc.gc.ca).

U.K. Citizens: For information, contact **HM Customs & Excise** at ℃ 0845/010-9000 (from outside the U.K., 020/8929-0152), or consult their website at **www.hmce.gov.uk**.

Australian Citizens: A helpful brochure available from Australian consulates or Customs offices is *Know Before You Go.* For more information, call the **Australian Customs Service** at ℃ 1300/363-263, or log on to **www.customs.gov.au**.

New Zealand Citizens: Most questions are answered in a free pamphlet available at New Zealand consulates and Customs offices: *New Zealand Customs Guide for Travellers, Notice no. 4.* For more information, contact **New Zealand Customs,** The Customhouse, 17–21 Whitmore St., Box 2218, Wellington (℃ 04/473-6099 or 0800/428-786; **www.customs.govt.nz**).

3 When to Go

Costa Rica's high season for tourism runs from late November to late April, which coincides almost perfectly with the chill of winter in the United States, Canada, and Great Britain. The high season is also the dry season. If you want some unadulterated time on a tropical beach and a little less rain during your rainforest experience, this is the time to come. During this period (and especially around the Christmas holiday), the tourism industry operates at full tilt—prices are higher, attractions are more crowded, and reservations need to be made in advance.

Local tourism operators often call the tropical rainy season (May through mid-Nov) the "green season." The adjective is appropriate. At this time of year, even brown and barren Guanacaste province becomes lush and verdant. I personally love traveling around Costa Rica during the rainy season (but then again, I'm not trying to flee cold snaps in Canada). It's easy to find or at least negotiate reduced rates, there are far fewer fellow travelers, and the rain is often limited to a few hours each afternoon (although you can occasionally get socked in for a week at a time). *A drawback:* Some of the country's rugged roads become downright impassable without four-wheel-drive during the rainy season.

CLIMATE

Costa Rica is a tropical country and has distinct wet and dry seasons. However, some regions are rainy all year, and others are very dry and sunny for most of the year. Temperatures vary primarily with elevations, not with seasons: On the coasts it's hot all year; in the mountains it can be cool at night any time of year. Frost is common at the highest elevations (3,000–3,600m/9,840–11,808 ft.).

Average Daytime Temperatures & Rainfall in San José

	Jan	Feb	Mar	Apr	May	June	July	Aug	Sept	Oct	Nov	Dec
Temp (°F)	73	75	77	78	78	78	77	77	76	77	75	73
Temp (°C)	23	24	25	26	26	26	25	25	24	25	24	23
Days of rain	1	0	1	4	17	20	18	19	20	22	14	4

Generally, the **rainy season** (or "green season") is from May to mid-November. Costa Ricans call this wet time of year their winter. The **dry season,** considered summer by Costa Ricans, is from mid-November to April. In Guanacaste, the dry northwestern province, the dry season lasts several weeks longer than in other places. Even in the rainy season, days often start sunny, with rain falling in the afternoon and evening. On the Caribbean coast, especially south of Limón, you can count on rain year-round, although this area gets less rain in September and October than the rest of the country.

In general, the best time of year to visit weather-wise is in December and January, when everything is still green from the rains, but the sky is clear.

HOLIDAYS

Because Costa Rica is a Roman Catholic country, most of its holidays are church-related. The biggies are Christmas, New Year's, and Easter, which are all celebrated for several days. Keep in mind that Holy Week (Easter week) is the biggest holiday time in Costa Rica, and many families head for the beach. (This is the last holiday before school starts.) Also, there is no public transportation on Holy Thursday or Good Friday. Government offices and banks are closed on official holidays, transportation services are reduced, and stores and markets might also close.

Official holidays in Costa Rica include **January 1** (New Year's Day), **March 19** (St. Joseph's Day), Thursday and Friday of Holy Week, **April 11** (Juan Santamaría's Day), **May 1** (Labor Day), **June 29** (St. Peter and St. Paul Day), **July 25** (annexation of the province of Guanacaste), **August 2** (Virgin of Los Angeles's Day), **August 15** (Mother's Day), **September 15** (Independence Day), **October 12** (Discovery of America/Día de la Raza), **December 8** (Immaculate Conception of

the Virgin Mary), **December 24** and **25** (Christmas), and **December 31** (New Year's Eve).

CALENDAR OF EVENTS

Some of the events listed here might be considered more of a *happening* than an event—there's not, for instance, a Virgin of Los Angeles PR Committee that readily dispenses information. If I haven't listed a contact number, your best bet is to call the **Costa Rican Tourist Board (ICT)** at © **866/COSTA RICA** in the U.S. and Canada, or 2223-1733 in Costa Rica, or visit **www.visitcostarica.com**.

For an exhaustive list of events beyond those listed here, check http://events.frommers.com, where you'll find a searchable, up-to-the-minute roster of what's happening in cities all over the world.

January

Copa del Café (Coffee Cup), San José. Matches for this international event on the junior tennis tour are held at the Costa Rica Country Club (© **2228-9333**). First week in January.

Fiesta of Palmares, Palmares. Perhaps the largest and best organized of the traditional *fiestas,* it includes bullfights, a horseback parade *(tope),* and many concerts, carnival rides, and food booths. First 2 weeks in January.

Fiesta of Santa Cruz, Santa Cruz, Guanacaste. This religious celebration honors the Black Christ of Esquipulas (a famous Guatemalan statue), featuring folk dancing, marimba music, and bullfights. Mid-January.

Fiesta of the Diablitos, Rey Curré village near San Isidro de El General. Boruca Indians wearing wooden devil and bull masks perform dances representative of the Spanish conquest of Central America; there are fireworks displays and an Indian handicrafts market. Late January.

March

Día del Boyero (Oxcart Drivers' Day), San Antonio de Escazú. Colorfully painted oxcarts parade through this suburb of San José, and local priests bless the oxen. Second Sunday in March.

National Orchid Show, San José. Orchid growers throughout the world gather to show their wares, trade tales and secrets, and admire the hundreds of species on display. Contact the Costa Rican Tourist Board for location and dates in 2007. Mid-March.

April

Holy Week. Religious processions are held in cities and towns throughout the country. Week before Easter.

Juan Santamaría Day, Alajuela. Costa Rica's national hero is honored with parades, concerts, and dances. April 11.

May

Carrera de San Juan. The country's biggest marathon runs through the mountains, from the outskirts of Cartago to the outskirts of San José. May 17.

July

Fiesta of the Virgin of the Sea, Puntarenas. A regatta of colorfully decorated boats carrying a statue of Puntarenas's patron saint marks this festival. A similar event is held at Playa de Coco. Saturday closest to July 16.

Annexation of Guanacaste Day, Liberia. Tico-style bullfights, folk dancing, horseback parades, rodeos, concerts, and other events celebrate the day when this region became part of Costa Rica. July 25.

August

Fiesta of the Virgin of Los Angeles, Cartago. This is the annual pilgrimage day of the patron saint of Costa Rica. Many people walk from San José 24km (15 miles) to the basilica in Cartago. August 2.

Día de San Ramón, San Ramón. More than two dozen statues of saints from various towns are brought to San Ramón, where they are paraded through the streets. August 31.

September

Costa Rica's Independence Day, celebrated all over the country. One of the most distinctive aspects of this festival is the nighttime marching band parades of children in their school uniforms, who play the national anthem on steel xylophones. September 15.

International Beach Clean-Up Day. This is a good excuse to chip in and help clean up the beleaguered shoreline of your favorite beach. Third Saturday in September.

October

Fiesta del Maíz, Upala. At this celebration of corn, local beauty queens wear outfits made from corn plants. October 12.

Limón Carnival/Día de la Raza, Limón. A smaller version of Mardi Gras, complete with floats and dancing in the streets, commemorates Columbus's discovery of Costa Rica. Week of October 12.

November

All Souls' Day/Día de los Muertos, celebrated countrywide. Although it is not as elaborate or ritualized as in Mexico, most Costa Ricans take some time this day to remember the dead with flowers and trips to cemeteries. November 2.

December

Día de la Pólvora, San Antonio de Belén and Jesús María de San Mateo. Fireworks honor Our Lady of the Immaculate Conception. December 8.

Fiesta de los Negritos, Boruca. Boruca Indians celebrate the feast day of their patron saint, the Virgin of the Immaculate Conception, with costumed dances and traditional music. December 8.

Fiesta de la Yeguita, Nicoya. A statue of the Virgin of Guadalupe is paraded through the streets, accompanied by traditional music and dancing. December 12.

Las Posadas. Countrywide, children and carolers go door-to-door seeking lodging in a reenactment of Joseph and Mary's search for a place to stay. Begins December 15.

El Tope and Carnival, San José. The streets of downtown belong to horses and their riders in a proud recognition of the country's important agricultural heritage. The next day, those same streets are taken over by carnival floats, marching bands, and street dancers. December 26 and 27.

Festejos Populares, San José. Bullfights and a pretty respectable bunch of carnival rides, games of chance, and fast-food stands are set up at the fairgrounds in Zapote. Last week of December.

4 Getting There & Getting Around

GETTING THERE
BY PLANE

It takes between 3 and 7 hours to fly to Costa Rica from most U.S. cities. Most international flights still land in San José's **Juan Santamaría International Airport** (airport code SJO). However, more and more direct international flights are touching down in Liberia's **Daniel Oduber International Airport** (airport code LIR).

Liberia is the gateway to the beaches of the Guanacaste region and the Nicoya Peninsula, and a direct flight here eliminates the need for a separate commuter flight in a small aircraft or roughly 5 hours in a car or bus. If you are planning to spend all, or most, of your vacation time in the Guanacaste region, you'll want to fly in and out of Liberia. However, San José is a much more convenient gateway if you are planning to head to Manuel Antonio, the Central Pacific coast, the Caribbean coast, or the Southern zone.

Numerous airlines fly into Costa Rica. Be warned that the smaller Latin American carriers tend to make several stops (sometimes unscheduled) en route to San José, thus increasing flying time.

From North America, **Air Canada, American Airlines, Continental, Delta, Frontier, Grupo Taca, Mexicana, Spirit Air,** and **US Airways** all have regular direct flights to Costa Rica.

From Europe, **Iberia** and **Martin Air** have established routes to San José, some direct and others with one connection. Alternately, you can fly to any major U.S. hub city and make connections to one of the airlines mentioned above.

For additional help in booking your air travel to Costa Rica, please turn to the "Fast Facts, Toll-Free Numbers & Websites" appendix A on p. 395.

BY CAR

It's possible to travel to Costa Rica by car, but it can be difficult, especially for U.S. citizens. After leaving Mexico, the Interamerican Highway (Carretera Interamericana, also known as the Pan-American Hwy.) passes through Guatemala, El Salvador, Honduras, and Nicaragua before reaching Costa Rica. All of these countries can be problematic for travelers for a variety of reasons, including internal violence, crime, corrupt border crossings, and visa formalities. If you do decide to undertake this adventure, take the **Gulf Coast route** from the border crossing at Brownsville, Texas, because it involves traveling the fewest miles through Mexico. Those planning to travel this route should purchase a copy of *You Can Drive to Costa Rica in 8 Days!,* by Dawn Rae Lessler (Harmony Gardens Publishing, 1998), which is available from the major online bookstores. You might also try to find a copy of *Driving the Pan-Am Highway to Mexico and Central America,* by Audrey and Raymond Pritchard (Costa Rica Books, 1997), which is harder to find. There is also a wealth of information online at **www.sanbornsinsurance. com** and **www.drivemeloco.com**.

CAR DOCUMENTS   You will need a current driver's license, as well as your vehicle's registration and the original title (no photocopies), to enter the country.

CENTRAL   AMERICAN   AUTO INSURANCE   Contact   **Sanborn's Insurance   Company** (© **800/222-0158** or 956/686-0711; www.sanborns insurance.com), which has agents at various border towns in the United States. These folks have been servicing this niche for more than 50 years. They can supply you with trip insurance for Mexico and Central America (you won't be able to buy insurance after you've left the U.S.), driving tips, and an itinerary.

CAR SAFETY   Be sure your car is in excellent working order. It's advisable not to drive at night because of the danger of being robbed by bandits, especially in Mexico, Guatemala, El Salvador, and Honduras.

For listings of the major car-rental agencies in Costa Rica, please see the "Fast Facts, Toll-Free Numbers & Websites" appendix A (p. 399).

GETTING AROUND COSTA RICA
BY PLANE

Flying is one of the best ways to get around Costa Rica. Because the country is quite small, flights are short and not too expensive. The domestic airlines of Costa Rica are Sansa and Nature Air.

Sansa (© **877/767-2672** in the U.S. and Canada, or 2290-4100 in Costa Rica; www.flysansa.com) operates from a separate terminal at San José's **Juan Santamaría International Airport,** and offers a free shuttle bus from its downtown San José office to the airport.

Nature Air (© **800/235-9272** in the U.S. and Canada or 2299-6000; www. natureair.com) operates from **Tobías Bolaños International Airport** (SYQ) in Pavas, 6.4km (4 miles) from San José. The ride from downtown to Pavas takes about 10 minutes, and a metered taxi fare should cost $10 to $20 (£5–£10). The ride from the airport to downtown is a different story: Most taxis refuse to use their meter, and the standard fee is set at double the metered rate, around $12 to $18 (£6–£9).

In the high season (late Nov to late Apr), be sure to book reservations well in advance. Both companies have online booking systems via their websites.

BY BUS

This is by far the most economical way to get around Costa Rica. Buses are inexpensive and relatively well maintained, and they go nearly everywhere. There are two types: **Local buses** are the cheapest and slowest; they stop frequently and are generally a bit dilapidated. **Express buses** run between San José and most beach towns and major cities; these tend to be newer units and more comfortable, although very few are so new or modern as to have bathroom facilities, and they sometimes operate only on weekends and holidays.

Two companies run regular, fixed-schedule departures in passenger vans and small buses to most of the major tourist destinations in the country. **Gray Line** (© **2220-2126;** www.graylinecostarica. com) is run by Fantasy Tours, and has about 10 departures leaving San José each morning and heading or connecting to Jacó, Manuel Antonio, Liberia, Playa Hermosa, La Fortuna, Tamarindo, and playas Conchal and Flamingo. There are return trips to San José every day from these destinations and a variety of interconnecting routes. A similar service, **Interbus** (© **2283-5573;** www.interbus online.com) has a slightly more extensive route map and more connections. Fares run between $25 and $45 (£13–£23) depending upon the destination. ***Beware:*** Both of these companies offer pickup and drop-off at a wide range of hotels. This means that if you are the first picked up or last dropped off, you might have to sit through a long period of subsequent stops before finally hitting the road or reaching your destination. Moreover, I've heard some horror stories about both lines, concerning missed or severely delayed connections and rude drivers. For details on how to get to various destinations from San José, see the "Getting There" sections in the chapters that follow.

BY CAR

Renting a car in Costa Rica is no idle proposition. The roads are riddled with potholes, most rural intersections are unmarked, and, for some reason, sitting behind the wheel of a car seems to turn peaceful Ticos into homicidal maniacs. But unless you want to see the country from the window of a bus or pay exorbitant amounts for private transfers, renting a car might be your best option for independent exploring. (That said, if you don't want to put up with any stress on your vacation, it might be worthwhile springing for a driver.)

Be forewarned, however: Although rental cars no longer bear special license plates, they are still readily identifiable to thieves and are frequently targeted. (Nothing is ever safe in a car in Costa Rica, although parking in guarded parking lots helps.) Transit police also seem to target tourists; never pay money directly to a police officer who stops you for any traffic violation.

Before driving off with a rental car, be sure that you inspect the exterior and point out to the rental-company representative every tiny scratch, dent, tear, or any other damage. It's a common practice with many Costa Rican car-rental companies to claim that you owe payment for minor dings and dents that the company finds when you return the car. Also, if you get into an accident, be sure that the rental company doesn't try to bill you for a higher amount than the deductible on your rental contract.

These caveats aren't meant to scare you off from driving in Costa Rica. Thousands of tourists rent cars here every year, and the large majority of them encounter no problems. Just keep your wits about you and guard against car theft (see p. 45 for info) and you'll do fine. Also keep in mind that four-wheel-drives are particularly useful in the rainy season (May to mid-Nov) and for navigating the bumpy, poorly paved roads year-round.

Note: It's sometimes cheaper to reserve a car in your home country rather than book when you arrive in Costa Rica. If you know you'll be renting a car, it's always wise to reserve it well in advance for the high season because the rental fleet still can't match demand.

Among the major international agencies operating in Costa Rica are **Alamo, Avis, Budget, Hertz, National, Payless,** and **Thrifty.** For a complete list of car-rental agencies and their contact information, see "Appendix A: Fast Facts, Toll-Free Numbers & Websites," p. 395, as well as the "Getting Around" sections of other major tourist destinations.

GASOLINE   Gasoline is sold as "regular" and "super." Both are unleaded; super is just higher octane. Diesel is available at almost every gas station as well. Most rental cars run on super, but always ask your rental agent what type of gas your car takes. When going off to remote places, try to leave with a full tank of gas because gas stations can be hard to find. If you need to gas up in a small town, you can sometimes get gasoline from enterprising families who sell it by the liter from their houses. Look for hand-lettered signs that say GASOLINA. At press time a liter of super cost 573 colones, or roughly $4.35 (£2.15) per gallon.

ROAD CONDITIONS The awful road conditions throughout Costa Rica are legendary, and deservedly so. Despite constant promises to fix the problem, the hot sun, hard rain, and rampant corruption outpace any progress made toward improving the condition. Even paved roads are often badly potholed, so stay alert. Road conditions get especially tricky during the rainy season, when heavy rains and runoff can destroy a stretch of pavement in the blink of an eye.

Note: Estimated driving times are listed throughout this book, but bear in mind that it might take longer than estimated to reach your destination during the rainy season or if roads have deteriorated.

Route numbers are very rarely used on road signs in Costa Rica, although there are frequent signs listing the number of kilometers to various towns or cities. Your best bets for on-road directions are billboards and advertisements for hotels. It's always a good idea to know the names of a few hotels at your destination, just in case your specific hotel hasn't put up any billboards or signs.

RENTER'S INSURANCE Even if you hold **your own car-insurance policy** at home, coverage doesn't always extend abroad. Be sure to find out whether you'll be covered in Costa Rica, whether your policy extends to all persons who will be driving the rental car, how much liability is covered in case an outside party is injured in an accident, and whether the *type* of vehicle you are renting is included under your contract.

DRIVING RULES A current foreign driver's license is valid for the first 3 months you are in Costa Rica. Seat belts are required for the driver and front-seat passengers. Motorcyclists must wear helmets. Highway police use radar, so keep to the speed limit (usually 60–90kmph/37–56 mph) if you don't want to get pulled over. Speeding tickets can be charged to your credit card for up to a year after you leave the country if they are not paid before departure.

To reduce congestion and fuel consumption, a rotating ban on rush-hour traffic takes place in the central core of San José Monday through Friday from 7 to 8:30am and from 4 to 5:30pm. The ban affects cars with licenses ending in the digits 1 or 2 on Monday; 3 or 4 on Tuesday; 5 or 6 on Wednesday; 7 or 8 on Thursday; and 9 or 0 on Friday. If you are caught driving a car with the banned license plate during these hours on a specified day, you will be ticketed.

BREAKDOWNS Be warned that emergency services, both vehicular and medical, are extremely limited outside San José, and their availability is directly related to the remoteness of your location at the time of breakdown. You'll find service stations spread over the entire length of the Interamerican Highway, and most of these have tow trucks and mechanics. The major towns of Puntarenas, Liberia, Quepos, San Isidro, Palmar, and Golfito all have hospitals, and most other moderately sized cities and tourist destinations have some sort of clinic or health-services provider.

If you're involved in an accident, you should contact the **National Insurance Institute (INS)** at ℂ **800/800-8000.** You should probably also call the **Transit Police** (ℂ **2222-9330** or 2222-9245); if they have a unit close by, they'll send one. An official transit police report will greatly facilitate any insurance claim. If you can't get help from any of these, try to get written statements from any witnesses. Finally, you can also call ℂ **911,** and they should be able to redirect your call to the appropriate agency.

If the police do show up, you've got a 50-50 chance of finding them helpful or downright antagonistic. Many officers are unsympathetic to the problems of what they perceive to be rich tourists running around in fancy cars with lots of expensive toys and trinkets. Success and happy endings run about equal with horror stories.

If you don't speak Spanish, expect added difficulty in any emergency or stressful situation. Don't expect that rural (or urban) police officers, hospital personnel, service-station personnel, or mechanics will speak English.

If your car breaks down and you're unable to get well off the road, check your trunk for reflecting triangles. If you find some, place them as a warning for approaching traffic, arranged in a wedge that starts at the shoulder about 30m (98 ft.) back and nudges gradually toward your car. If your car has no triangles, try to create a similar warning marker using a pile of leaves or branches.

Finally, although not endemic, there have been reports of folks being robbed by seemingly friendly Ticos who stop to give assistance. To add insult to injury, there have even been reports of organized gangs who puncture tires of rental cars at rest stops or busy intersections, only to follow them, offer assistance, and make off with belongings and valuables. If you find yourself with a flat tire, try to ride it to the nearest gas station. If that's not possible, try to pull over into a well-lit public spot. Keep the doors of the car locked and an eye on your belongings while changing the tire, by yourself.

BY FERRY

Three different ferries operate across the Gulf of Nicoya. Two are car ferries: one from Puntarenas to Playa Naranjo, and one from Puntarenas to Paquera. The third is a passenger ferry that runs between Puntarenas and Paquera. There's also regular passenger ferry service between the southern cities of Golfito and Puerto Jiménez. See the destination chapters for details. *Note:* Be careful while waiting in line for the ferry and on board any ferry. Thieves prey on the hefty bounty carried in most tourist rental cars.

BY THUMB

Although buses serve most towns in Costa Rica, service can be infrequent in the remote regions, so local people often hitchhike to get to their destinations sooner. If you're driving a car, people will frequently ask you for a ride. In remote rural areas, a hitchhiker carrying a machete is not necessarily a great danger, but use your judgment. Hitchhiking is not recommended on major roadways or in urban areas. In rural areas it's usually pretty safe. (However, women should be extremely cautious about hitchhiking anywhere in Costa Rica.) If you choose to hitchhike, keep in mind that if a bus doesn't go to your destination, there probably aren't too many cars going there, either. Good luck.

5 Money & Costs

It's always advisable to bring money in a variety of forms on a vacation: a mix of cash, credit cards, debit cards, and, occasionally, traveler's checks. In many international destinations, including Costa Rica, ATMs often offer the best exchange rates. Avoid exchanging money at commercial exchange bureaus and hotels, which often have the highest transaction fees.

CURRENCY

The unit of currency in Costa Rica is the **colón.** In March 2008, there were approximately 500 colones to the American dollar. In late 2006, the Costa Rican government eliminated decades of programmed regular devaluations of the colón. Since then, the exchange rate has stayed remarkably stable at somewhere between 490 and 515 colones to the dollar. Still, because of past devaluation and accompanying inflation, *this book generally lists prices in U.S. dollars and British pounds only.* To check the very latest exchange rates before you leave home, point your browser to **www.xe.com/ucc**.

The colón is divided into 100 **céntimos.** Currently, two types of coins are in circulation. The older and larger nickel-alloy coins come in denominations of 10, 25, and 50 céntimos and 1, 2, 5, 10, and 20 colones; however, because of their evaporating value, you will probably never see or have to handle céntimos, or anything lower than a 5-colón coin. In 1997 the government introduced gold-hued 5-, 10-, 25-, 50-, 100-, and 500-colón coins. They are smaller and heavier than the older coins, and while the plan was to have them eventually phase out the other currency, this hasn't happened yet.

There are paper notes in denominations of 1,000, 2,000, 5,000, and 10,000 colones. You might also encounter a special-issue 5-colón bill that is a popular gift and souvenir. It is valid currency, although it sells for much more than its face value. You might hear people refer to a *rojo* or *tucán,* which are slang terms for the 1,000- and 5,000-colón bills, respectively. One-hundred-colón denominations are called *tejas,* so *cinco tejas* is 500 colones. The 2,000 and 10,000 bills are relatively new, and I've yet to encounter a slang equivalent.

Forged bills are not entirely uncommon. When receiving change in colones, it's a good idea to check the larger-denomination bills, which should have protective bands or hidden images that appear when held up to the light.

If your ATM card doesn't work and you need cash in a hurry, **Western Union** (© 800/777-7777 in Costa Rica or 2283-6336; www.westernunion.com) has numerous offices around San José and in several major towns and cities around the country. It offers a secure and rapid,

although pricey, money-wire service. A $100 (£50) wire costs around $20 (£10), and a $1,000 (£500) wire costs around $80 (£40).

You can change money at all banks in Costa Rica. However, be forewarned that service at state banks can be slow and tedious. The principal state banks are Banco Nacional and Banco de Costa Rica. You're almost always better off finding a private bank. Luckily, there are hosts of private banks around San José and in most major tourist destinations.

Since banks handle money exchanges, there are very, very few exchange houses in Costa Rica. One major exception to this is the **Global Exchange** office at the airport. However, be forewarned they exchange at more than 10% below the official exchange rate.

Hotels will often exchange money and cash traveler's checks as well; there usually isn't much of a line, but they might shave a few colones off the exchange rate. Be very careful about exchanging money on the streets; it's extremely risky. In addition to forged bills and short counts, street money-changers frequently work in teams that can leave you holding neither colones nor dollars. Also be very careful when leaving a bank. Criminals are often looking for foreigners who have just withdrawn or exchanged cash.

ATMs

The easiest and best way to get cash away from home is from an ATM (automated teller machine). The **Cirrus** (© 800/424-7787; www.mastercard.com) and **PLUS** (© 800/843-7587; www.visa.com) networks span the globe. Go to your bank card's website to find ATM locations at your destination. Be sure you know your daily withdrawal limit before you depart. *Note:* Many banks impose a fee every time you use a card at another bank's ATM, and that fee can be higher for international transactions (up to $5/£2.50 or

What Things Cost in Costa Rica	US$	UK£
Taxi from the airport to the city center	22.30	13.51
Taxi from the airport to downtown San José	15.00	7.50
Double room, expensive	200.00	100.00
Double room, moderate	100.00	50.00
Double room, inexpensive	35.00	18.00
Three-course dinner for one without wine, moderate	15.00–25.00	7.50–13.00
Bottle of Imperial beer	1.00–1.50	50p–75p
Bottle of Coca-Cola	1.00	50p
Cup of coffee	1.00–1.50	50p–75p
Gallon of premium gas	4.35	2.20
Admission to most museums	2.00–5.00	1.00–2.50
Admission to most national parks	10.00	5.00

more) than for domestic ones (where they're rarely more than $2/£1). In addition, the bank from which you withdraw cash may charge its own fee. For international withdrawal fees, ask your bank.

Note: Banks that are members of the **Global ATM Alliance** charge no transaction fees for cash withdrawals at other Alliance member ATMs; these include Bank of America, Scotiabank (Canada, Caribbean, and Mexico), Barclays (U.K. and parts of Africa), Deutsche Bank (Germany, Poland, Spain, and Italy), and BNP Paribas (France). Scotiabank has branches in Costa Rica.

It's probably a good idea to change your PIN to a four-digit PIN. While many ATMs in Costa Rica will accept five- and six-digit PINs, some will only accept four-digit PINs.

CREDIT CARDS

Credit cards are another safe way to carry money in Costa Rica. You can withdraw cash advances from your credit cards at banks or ATMs but high fees make credit card cash advances a pricey way to get cash. Keep in mind that you'll pay interest from the moment of your withdrawal, even if you pay your monthly bills on time. Also, note that many banks now assess a 1% to 3% "transaction fee" on **all** charges you incur abroad (whether you're using the local currency or your native currency).

MasterCard and Visa are the most widely accepted credit cards in Costa Rica, followed by American Express. Most hotels and restaurants accept all of these, especially in tourist destination areas. Discover and Diners Club are far less commonly accepted.

TRAVELER'S CHECKS

Given widespread acceptance of credit cards and growing prevalence of ATMs, traveler's checks are becoming pretty anachronistic in Costa Rica. Still, they do provide a level of built-in insurance, and are accepted by most major tourist hotels and some restaurants around the country. You can buy traveler's checks at most banks. They are offered in denominations of $20, $50, $100, $500, and sometimes $1,000. Generally, you'll pay a service charge ranging from 1% to 4%.

The most popular traveler's checks are offered by **American Express** (© **800/ 807-6233** or © **800/221-7282** for cardholders—this number accepts collect calls, offers service in several foreign languages, and exempts AmEx gold and platinum cardholders from the 1% fee); **Visa** (℮ **800/732-1322**)—AAA members can obtain Visa checks for a $9.95 fee (for checks up to $1,500) at most AAA offices or by calling ℮ **866/339-3378;** and **MasterCard** (℮ **800/223-9920**).

Be sure to keep a record of the traveler's checks serial numbers separate from your checks in the event that they are stolen or lost. You'll get a refund faster if you know the numbers.

6 Health

STAYING HEALTHY

Staying healthy on a trip to Costa Rica is predominantly a matter of being a little cautious about what you eat and drink, and using common sense. Know your physical limits, and don't overexert yourself in the ocean, on hikes, or in athletic activities. Respect the tropical sun and protect yourself from it. Limit your exposure to the sun, especially during the first few days of your trip and, thereafter, from 11am to 2pm. Use sunscreen with a high protection factor, and apply it liberally. Remember that children need more protection than adults. I recommend buying and drinking bottled water or soft drinks, but the water in San José and in most of the heavily visited spots is safe to drink.

If you suffer from a chronic illness, consult your doctor before leaving. For conditions such as epilepsy, diabetes, or heart problems, wear a **MedicAlert identification tag** (℮ **800/825-3785;** www. medicalert.org), which will immediately alert doctors to your condition and give them access to your records through MedicAlert's 24-hour hot line.

Pack **prescription medications** in your carry-on luggage, and carry prescription medications in their original containers. Also bring along copies of your prescriptions in case you lose your pills or run out, and carry the generic name of prescription medicines in case a local pharmacist is unfamiliar with the brand name. And don't forget an extra pair of contact lenses or prescription glasses.

Contact the **International Association for Medical Assistance to Travelers (IAMAT)** (℮ **716/754-4883** or, in Canada, 416/652-0137; www.iamat.org) for tips on travel and health concerns in the countries you're visiting, and for lists of local, English-speaking doctors. The United States **Centers for Disease Control and Prevention** (℮ **800/311-3435;** www.cdc.gov) provides up-to-date information on health hazards by region or country and offers tips on food safety. **Travel Health Online** (www.tripprep. com), sponsored by a consortium of travel medicine practitioners, may also offer helpful advice on traveling abroad. You can find listings of reliable medical clinics overseas at the **International Society of Travel Medicine** (www.istm.org).

GENERAL AVAILABILITY OF HEALTHCARE

Any local consulate in Costa Rica can provide a list of area doctors who speak English. The local English-language newspaper, the *Tico Times,* is another good resource. I've listed the best hospitals in San José in "Fast Facts: San José," in chapter 6; these have the most modern facilities in the country. Most state-run hospitals and walk-in clinics around the country have emergency rooms that can treat most conditions, although I highly recommend the private hospitals in San José if your condition is not life-threatening and can wait for treatment until you reach one of them.

I list **additional emergency numbers** in the "Fast Facts" in appendix A.

COMMON AILMENTS

TROPICAL DISEASES   Your chance of contracting any serious tropical disease in Costa Rica is slim, especially if you stick to the beaches or traditional spots for visitors. However, malaria, dengue fever, and leptospirosis all exist in Costa Rica, so it's a good idea to know what they are.

Malaria is found in the lowlands on both coasts and in the northern zone. Although it's rarely found in urban areas, it's still a problem in remote wooded regions and along the Caribbean coast. Malaria prophylaxes are available, but several have side effects, and others are of questionable effectiveness. Consult your doctor regarding what is currently considered the best preventive treatment for malaria. Be sure to ask whether a recommended drug will cause you to be hypersensitive to the sun; it would be a shame to come down here for the beaches and then have to hide under an umbrella the whole time. Because malaria-carrying mosquitoes usually come out at night, you should do as much as possible to avoid being bitten after dark. If you are in a malaria-prone area, wear long pants and long sleeves, use insect repellent, and either sleep under a mosquito net or burn mosquito coils (similar to incense, but with a pesticide).

Of greater concern is **dengue fever,** which has had periodic outbreaks in Latin America since the mid-1990s. Dengue fever is similar to malaria and is spread by an aggressive daytime mosquito. This mosquito seems to be most common in lowland urban areas, and Puntarenas, Liberia, and Limón have been the worst-hit cities in Costa Rica. Dengue is also known as "bone-break fever" because it is usually accompanied by severe body aches. The first infection with dengue fever will make you very sick but should cause no serious damage. However, a second infection with a different strain of the dengue virus can lead to internal hemorrhaging and could be life threatening.

Many people are convinced that taking B-complex vitamins daily will help prevent mosquitoes from biting you. I don't think the American Medical Association has endorsed this idea yet, but I've run across it in enough places to think that there might be something to it.

One final tropical fever that I think you should know about (because I got it myself) is **leptospirosis.** There are more than 200 strains of leptospires, which are animal-borne bacteria transmitted to humans via contact with drinking, swimming, or bathing water. This bacterial infection is easily treated with antibiotics; however, it can quickly cause very high fever and chills, and should be treated promptly.

If you develop a high fever accompanied by severe body aches, nausea, diarrhea, or vomiting during or shortly after a visit to Costa Rica, consult a physician as soon as possible.

Costa Rica has been relatively free of the cholera epidemic that has spread through much of Latin America in recent years. This is largely due to an extensive public-awareness campaign that has promoted good hygiene and increased sanitation. Your chances of contracting cholera while you're here are very slight.

AMOEBAS, PARASITES, DIARRHEA & OTHER INTESTINAL WOES

Even though the water in San José and most popular destinations in Costa Rica is generally safe, and even though you've been careful to buy bottled water, order *frescos en leche* (fruit shakes made with milk rather than water), and drink your soft drink warm (without ice cubes—which are made from water, after all), you still might encounter some intestinal difficulties. Most of this is just due to tender northern stomachs coming into contact with slightly more aggressive Latin American intestinal flora. In extreme cases of diarrhea or intestinal discomfort, it's worth taking a stool sample to a lab for analysis.

The results will usually pinpoint the amoe-bic or parasitic culprit, which can then be readily treated with available over-the-counter medicines.

Except in the most established and hygienic of restaurants, it's also advisable to avoid ceviche, a raw seafood salad, especially if it has any shellfish in it. It could be home to any number of bacter-ial critters.

TROPICAL SUN   Limit your exposure to the sun, especially during the first few days of your trip and, thereafter, from 11am to 2pm. Use a sunscreen with a high protection factor, and apply it liber-ally. Remember that children need more protection than adults.

RIPTIDES   Many of Costa Rica's beaches have riptides: strong currents that can drag swimmers out to sea. A riptide occurs when water that has been dumped on the shore by strong waves forms a channel back out to open water. These channels have strong currents. If you get caught in a riptide, you can't escape the current by swimming toward shore; it's like trying to swim upstream in a river. To break free of the current, swim parallel to shore and use the energy of the waves to help you get back to the beach.

BEES, SNAKES & BUGS   Although Costa Rica has Africanized bees (the notorious "killer bees" of fact and fable) and several species of venomous snakes, your chances of being bitten are minimal, especially if you refrain from sticking your hands into hives or under rocks in the forest. If you know that you're allergic to bee stings, consult your doctor before traveling.

Snake sightings, much less snakebites, are very rare. Moreover, the majority of snakes in Costa Rica are nonpoisonous. If you do encounter a snake, stay calm, don't make any sudden movements, and do not try to handle it. As recommended above, avoid sticking your hands under rocks, branches, and fallen trees.

Scorpions, black widow spiders, taran-tulas, bullet ants, and biting insects of many types can all be found in Costa Rica. In general, they are not nearly the danger or nuisance most visitors fear. Watch where you stick your hands; in addition, you might want to shake out your clothes and shoes before putting them on to avoid any unpleasant and painful surprises.

WHAT TO DO IF YOU GET SICK AWAY FROM HOME

For travel abroad, you may have to pay all medical costs upfront and be reimbursed later. Medicare and Medicaid do not pro-vide coverage for medical costs outside the U.S. Before leaving home, find out what medical services your health insurance covers. To protect yourself, consider buy-ing medical travel insurance (see "Insur-ance," under "Appendix A: Fast Facts, Toll-Free Numbers & Websites," p. 397).

Very few health insurance plans pay for medical evacuation back to the U.S. (which can cost $10,000 and up). A number of companies offer medical evac-uation services anywhere in the world. If you're ever hospitalized more than 150 miles from home, **MedjetAssist** (© **800/527-7478;** www.medjetassistance.com) will pick you up and fly you to the hospi-tal of your choice virtually anywhere in the world in a medically equipped and staffed aircraft 24 hours day, 7 days a week. Annual memberships are $225 individual, $350 family; you can also purchase short-term memberships.

7 Safety

Although most of Costa Rica is safe, petty crime and robberies committed against tourists are endemic. San José is known for its pickpockets, so never carry a wallet in your back pocket. A woman should keep a tight grip on her purse (keep it tucked under your arm). Thieves also target gold chains, cameras and video cameras, prominent jewelry, and nice sunglasses. Be sure not to leave valuables unsecured in your hotel room. Given the high rate of stolen passports in Costa Rica, mostly as collateral damage in a typical pickpocketing or room robbery, it is recommended that, whenever possible, leave your passport in a hotel safe, and travel with a photocopy of the pertinent pages. Don't park a car on the street in Costa Rica, especially in San José; plenty of public parking lots are around the city.

Rental cars generally stick out and are easily spotted by thieves. Don't leave anything of value in a car parked on the street, not even for a moment. Be wary of solicitous strangers who stop to help you change a tire or take you to a service station. Although most are truly good Samaritans, there have been reports of thieves preying on roadside breakdowns. See p. 45 for more info.

Public inter-city buses are also frequent targets of stealthy thieves. Never check your bags into the hold of a bus. If this can't be avoided, keep your eye on what leaves the hold. If you put your bags in an overhead rack, be sure you can see the bags at all times. Try not to fall asleep.

Single women should use common sense and take precaution, especially after dark. I don't recommend that single women walk alone anywhere at night, especially on seemingly deserted beaches, or dark uncrowded streets.

8 Specialized Travel Resources

TRAVELERS WITH DISABILITIES

Most disabilities shouldn't stop anyone from traveling. There are more options and resources out there than ever before.

Still, although Costa Rica does have a law mandating Equality of Opportunities for People with Disabilities, and facilities are beginning to be adapted, in general, there are relatively few buildings for travelers with disabilities in the country. In San José, sidewalks are particularly crowded and uneven, and they are nonexistent in most of the rest of the country. Few hotels offer wheelchair-accessible accommodations, and there are no public buses thus equipped. In short, it can be difficult for a person with disabilities to get around San José and Costa Rica.

However, one local agency specializes in tours for travelers with disabilities and restricted ability. **Vaya Con Silla de Ruedas** (©/fax 2454-2810; www.gowith wheelchairs.com) has a ramp- and elevator-equipped van and knowledgeable, bilingual guides. It charges very reasonable prices and can provide anything from simple airport transfers to complete multi-day tours.

Organizations that offer a vast range of resources and assistance to travelers with disabilities include **MossRehab** (© 800/ CALL-MOSS [2255-6677]; www.moss resourcenet.org); the **American Foundation for the Blind (AFB)** (© 800/ 232-5463; www.afb.org); and **SATH** (Society for Accessible Travel & Hospitality) (© 212/447-7284; www.sath.org).

For more on organizations that offer resources to travelers with disabilities, go to frommers.com.

GAY & LESBIAN TRAVELERS

Costa Rica is a Catholic, conservative, macho country where public displays of same-sex affection are rare and considered somewhat shocking. Public figures, politicians, and religious leaders regularly denounce homosexuality. However, gay and lesbian tourism to Costa Rica is quite robust, and gay and lesbian travelers are generally treated with respect and should not experience any harassment.

For a general overview of the current situation, news of any special events or meetings, and up-to-date information, the website **www.gaycostarica.com** is your best bet, especially for gay men, and to a much lesser extent for lesbian women.

The **International Gay and Lesbian Travel Association (IGLTA)** (© **800/448-8550** or 954/776-2626; www.iglta.org) is the trade association for the gay and lesbian travel industry, and offers an online directory of gay- and lesbian-friendly travel businesses and tour operators.

For more gay and lesbian travel resources visit frommers.com.

SENIOR TRAVEL

Be sure to mention that you're a senior when you make your travel reservations. Although it's not common policy in Costa Rica to offer senior discounts, don't be shy about asking for one anyway. You never know. Always carry some kind of identification, such as a driver's license, that shows your date of birth, especially if you've kept your youthful glow.

Members of **AARP** (formerly known as the American Association of Retired Persons), 601 E St. NW, Washington, DC 20049 (© **888/687-2277;** www.aarp.org), get discounts on hotels, airfares, and car rentals. AARP offers members a wide range of benefits, including *AARP The Magazine* and a monthly newsletter. Anyone over 50 can join.

Many reliable agencies and organizations target the 50-plus market. **Elderhostel** (© **800/454-5768;** www.elderhostel.org) arranges Costa Rica study programs for those ages 55 and older. **ElderTreks** (© **800/741-7956** or 416/558-5000 outside North America; www.eldertreks.com) offers small-group tours to Costa Rica, restricted to travelers 50 and older.

Frommers.com offers more information and resources on travel for seniors.

FAMILY TRAVEL

To locate accommodations, restaurants, and attractions that are particularly kid-friendly, refer to the "Kids" icon throughout this guide.

Hotels in Costa Rica often give discounts for children 11 and under, and children under 3 or 4 are usually allowed to stay for free. Discounts for children and the cutoff ages vary according to the hotel, but in general, don't assume that your kids can stay in your room for free.

Many hotels, villas, and cabinas come equipped with kitchenettes or full kitchen facilities. These can be a real money-saver for those traveling with children, and I've listed many of these accommodations in the destination chapters in this book.

Hotels offering regular, dependable babysitting service are few and far between. If you will need babysitting, make sure that your hotel offers it, and be sure to ask whether the babysitters are bilingual. In many cases they are not. This is usually not a problem with infants and toddlers, but it can cause problems with older children.

Recommended family travel websites include **Family Travel Forum** (www.familytravelforum.com), a comprehensive site with customized trip planning; **Family Travel Network** (www.familytravelnetwork.com), an online magazine providing travel tips; and **TravelWith YourKids.com** (www.travelwithyourkids.com), a site written by parents for parents offering comprehensive advice for long-distance and international travel with children.

For a list of more family-friendly travel resources, turn to the experts at frommers.com.

WOMEN TRAVELERS

For lack of better phrasing, Costa Rica is a typically "macho" Latin American nation. Single women can expect a nearly constant stream of catcalls, hisses, whistles, and car horns, especially in San José. Women should be careful walking alone at night throughout the country.

For general travel resources for women, go to frommers.com.

STUDENT TRAVEL

Check out the **International Student Travel Confederation (ISTC)** (www. istc.org) website for comprehensive travel services information and details on how to get an **International Student Identity Card (ISIC),** which qualifies students for substantial savings on rail passes, plane tickets, entrance fees, and more. It also provides students with basic health and life insurance and a 24-hour help line. The card is valid for a maximum of 18 months. You can apply for the card online or in person at **STA Travel** (© **800/781-4040** in North America, 132-782 in Australia, 0871/230-0040 in the U.K.; www.statravel.com), the biggest

student travel agency in the world; check out the website to locate STA Travel offices worldwide. If you're no longer a student but are still under 26, you can get an **International Youth Travel Card (IYTC)** from the same people, which entitles you to some discounts. **Travel CUTS** (© **800/592-2887;** www.travel cuts.com) offers similar services for both Canadians and U.S. residents. Irish students may prefer to turn to **USIT** (© **01/602-1904;** www.usit.ie), an Ireland-based specialist in student, youth, and independent travel.

In Costa Rica, there is one travel agency specializing in student and youth travel: **OTEC** (© **2256-0633;** www.otectours. com). These folks have three offices in San José, located in downtown, Escazu, and the university district of San Pedro.

Although you won't find any discounts at the national parks, most museums and other attractions around Costa Rica do offer discounts for students. It always pays to ask.

9 Sustainable Tourism

Sustainable tourism is conscientious travel. It means being careful with the environments you explore, and respecting the communities you visit. Two overlapping components of sustainable travel are **ecotourism** and **ethical tourism.** The **International Ecotourism Society** (TIES) defines ecotourism as responsible travel to natural areas that conserves the environment and improves the well-being of local people. TIES suggests that ecotourists follow these principles:

- Minimize environmental impact.
- Build environmental and cultural awareness and respect.
- Provide positive experiences for both visitors and hosts.
- Provide direct financial benefits for conservation and for local people.

- Raise sensitivity to host countries' political, environmental, and social climates.
- Support international human rights and labor agreements.

You can find some ecofriendly travel tips and statistics, as well as touring companies and associations—listed by destination under "Travel Choice"—at the **TIES** website, www.ecotourism.org. Also check out **Ecotravel.com**, which lets you search for sustainable touring companies in several categories (water-based, landbased, spiritually oriented, and so on).

While much of the focus of ecotourism is about reducing impacts on the natural environment, ethical tourism concentrates on ways to preserve and enhance local economies and communities, regardless of

(Tips It's Easy Being Green

Here are a few simple ways you can help conserve fuel and energy when you travel:

- Each time you take a flight or drive a car greenhouse gases release into the atmosphere. You can help neutralize this danger to the planet through "carbon offsetting"—paying someone to invest your money in programs that reduce your greenhouse gas emissions by the same amount you've added. Before buying carbon offset credits, just make sure that you're using a reputable company, one with a proven program that invests in renewable energy. Reliable carbon offset companies include **Carbonfund** (www.carbonfund.org), **TerraPass** (www.terrapass.org), and **Carbon Neutral** (www.carbonneutral.org).

- Whenever possible, choose nonstop flights; they generally require less fuel than indirect flights that stop and take off again. Try to fly during the day—some scientists estimate that nighttime flights are twice as harmful to the environment. And pack light—each 15 pounds of luggage on a 5,000-mile flight adds up to 50 pounds of carbon dioxide emitted.

- Where you stay during your travels can have a major environmental impact. To determine the green credentials of a property, ask about trash disposal and recycling, water conservation, and energy use; also question if sustainable materials were used in the construction of the property. The website **www.greenhotels.com** recommends green-rated member hotels around the world that fulfill the company's stringent environmental requirements. Also consult **www.environmentallyfriendlyhotels.com** for more green accommodations ratings.

- At hotels, request that your sheets and towels not be changed daily. (Many hotels already have programs like this in place.) Turn off the lights and air conditioner (or heater) when you leave your room.

- Use public transport where possible—trains, buses and even taxis are more energy-efficient forms of transport than driving. Even better is to walk or cycle; you'll produce zero emissions and stay fit and healthy on your travels.

- If renting a car is necessary, ask the rental agent for a hybrid, or rent the most fuel-efficient car available. You'll use less gas and save money at the tank.

- Eat at locally owned and operated restaurants that use produce grown in the area. This contributes to the local economy and cuts down on greenhouse gas emissions by supporting restaurants where the food is not flown or trucked in across long distances.

location. You can embrace ethical tourism by staying at a locally owned hotel or shopping at a store that employs local workers and sells locally produced goods.

Responsible Travel (www.responsible travel.com) is a great source of sustainable travel ideas; the site is run by a spokesperson for ethical tourism in the travel industry. **Sustainable Travel International** (www.sustainabletravel international.org) promotes ethical tourism practices, and manages an extensive directory of sustainable properties and tour operators around the world.

In the U.K., **Tourism Concern** (www. tourismconcern.org.uk) works to reduce social and environmental problems connected to tourism. The **Association of Independent Tour Operators (AITO)** (www.aito.co.uk) is a group of specialist operators leading the field in making holidays sustainable.

Costa Rica is one of the planet's prime ecotourism destinations. Many of the isolated nature lodges and tour operators around the country are pioneers and dedicated professionals in the ecotourism and sustainable tourism field. Many other hotels, lodges, and tour operators are simply "green-washing," using the terms "eco" and "sustainable" in their promo materials, but doing little real good in their daily operations. The government-run tourism institute (ICT) provides a sustainability rating of a host of hotels, called the Certificate of Sustainable Tourism Program (CST). You can look up hotel ratings at the website **www.turismo-sostenible. co.cr**; however, the list is far from comprehensive, and die-hard ecologists find some of these listings somewhat suspect. Still, this list and rating system is a good start, and is evolving constantly.

Volunteer travel has become increasingly popular among those who want to venture beyond the standard group-tour experience to learn languages, interact with locals, and make a positive difference while on vacation. Volunteer travel usually doesn't require special skills—just a willingness to work hard—and programs vary in length from a few days to a number of weeks. Some programs provide free housing and food, but many require volunteers to pay for travel expenses, which can add up quickly.

For general info on volunteer travel, visit **www.volunteerabroad.org** and **www.idealist.org**. Specific volunteer options in Costa Rica are listed under "Volunteer & Study Programs," in chapter 5, "The Active Vacation Planner."

Before you commit to a volunteer program, it's important to make sure any money you're giving is truly going back to the local community, and that the work you'll be doing will be a good fit for you. **Volunteer International** (www.volunteer international.org) has a helpful list of questions to ask to determine the intentions and the nature of a volunteer program.

For information on animal-friendly issues throughout the world, visit **Tread Lightly** (www.treadlightly.org). For information about the ethics of swimming with dolphins, visit the **Whale and Dolphin Conservation Society** (www.wdcs.org).

10 Packages for the Independent Traveler

Package tours are simply a way to buy the airfare, accommodations, and other elements of your trip (such as car rentals, airport transfers, and sometimes even activities) at the same time and often at discounted prices.

One good source of package deals is the airlines themselves. Most major airlines offer air/land packages, including **American Airlines Vacations** (© 800/321-2121; www.aavacations.com), **Delta Vacations**

(© 800/654-6559; www.deltavacations. com), **Continental Airlines Vacations** (© 800/301-3800; www.covacations. com), and **United Vacations** (© 888/854-3899; www.unitedvacations.com). Several big **online travel agencies**—Expedia, Travelocity, Orbitz, and Lastminute .com—also do a brisk business in packages.

Travel packages are also listed in the travel section of your local Sunday newspaper. Or check ads in national

> ### ⟮Tips⟯ Ask Before You Go
>
> Before you invest in a package deal or an escorted tour:
>
> - Always ask about the **cancellation policy.** Can you get your money back? Is a deposit required?
> - Ask about the **accommodations choices and prices** for each. Then look up the hotels' reviews in a Frommer's guide and check their rates online for your specific dates of travel. Also find out what types of rooms are offered.
> - Request a complete **schedule.** (Escorted tours only)
> - Ask about the **size** and demographics of the group. (Escorted tours only)
> - Discuss what is included in the **price** (transportation, meals, tips, airport transfers, and the like). (Escorted tours only)
> - Finally, look for **hidden expenses.** Ask whether airport departure fees and taxes, for example, are included in the total cost—they rarely are.

travel magazines such as *Arthur Frommer's Budget Travel Magazine, Travel + Leisure, National Geographic Traveler,* and *Condé Nast Traveler.*

For more information on Package Tours and for tips on booking your trip, see frommers.com.

11 Escorted & Special-Interest Tours

Escorted tours are structured group tours with a group leader. The price usually includes everything from airfare to hotels, meals, tours, admission costs, and local transportation.

Despite the fact that escorted tours require big deposits and predetermine hotels, restaurants, and itineraries, many people derive security and peace of mind from the structure they offer. Escorted tours—whether they're navigated by bus, motorcoach, train, or boat—let travelers sit back and enjoy the trip without having to drive or worry about details. They take you to the maximum number of sights in the minimum amount of time with the least amount of hassle. They're particularly convenient for people with limited

mobility, and they can be a great way to make new friends.

On the downside, you'll have little opportunity for serendipitous interactions with locals. The tours can be jam-packed with activities, leaving little room for individual sightseeing, whim, or adventure—plus they often focus on the heavily touristed sites, so you miss out on many a lesser-known gem.

You'll find a list of reputable escorted general interest and "soft adventure" tour operators in chapter 5, "The Active Vacation Planner." For more information on escorted and special interest tours, including questions to ask before booking your trip, see frommers.com.

12 Staying Connected

TELEPHONES

Costa Rica has an excellent phone system, with a dial tone similar to that heard in the United States.

A phone call within Costa Rica costs around 10 colones (2¢/1p) per minute. Pay phones take a calling card or 5-, 10-, or 20-colón coins. Calling cards are much more practical, and coin-operated phones are getting harder to find. You can purchase calling cards in a host of gift shops and pharmacies. However, there are several competing calling-card companies, and certain cards work only with certain phones. **CHIP** calling cards work with a computer chip and just slide into specific phones, although these phones aren't widely available. Better bets are the **197** and **199** calling cards, which are sold in varying denominations. These have a scratch-off PIN and can be used from any phone in the country. Generally, the 197 cards are sold in smaller denominations and are used for local calling, while the 199 cards are deemed international and are easier to find in larger denominations. Either card can be used to make any call, however, provided that the card can cover the costs. Another perk of the 199 cards is the fact that you can get the instructions in English. For local calls, it is often easiest to call from your hotel, although you will likely be charged around 150 to 300 colones (30¢–60¢/15p–30p) per call.

To call Costa Rica from abroad:

1. Dial the international access code: 011 from the U.S.; 00 from the U.K., Ireland, or New Zealand; or 0011 from Australia.
2. Dial the country code 506.
3. Dial the number.

To make international calls: To make international calls from Costa Rica, first dial 00 and then the country code (U.S. or Canada 1, U.K. 44, Ireland 353, Australia 61, New Zealand 64). Next you dial the area code and number. For example, if you wanted to call the British Embassy in Washington, D.C., you would dial 00-1-202-588-7800.

For directory assistance: Dial 113 if you're looking for a number inside Costa Rica, and dial 124 for numbers to all other countries.

For operator assistance: If you need operator assistance in making a call, dial

116 if you're trying to make an international call and 0 if you want to call a number in Costa Rica.

Toll-free numbers: Numbers beginning with 0800 or 800 within Costa Rica are toll-free, but calling a 1-800 number in the States from Costa Rica is not toll-free. In fact, it costs the same as an overseas call.

CELLPHONES

The three letters that define much of the world's wireless capabilities are **GSM (Global System for Mobile Communications),** a big, seamless network that makes for easy cross-border cellphone use. If your cellphone is on a GSM system, and you have a world-capable multiband phone such as many Sony Ericsson, Motorola, or Samsung models, you can make and receive calls across civilized areas around much of the globe. Just call your wireless operator and ask for "international roaming" to be activated on your account. Per-minute charges can be high, though—up to $5 (£2.50) in Costa Rica, depending upon your plan.

Unfortunately, those with unlocked triband GSM phones cannot simply buy a local SIM card in Costa Rica. **Renting** a phone in Costa Rica can be problematic, too. Due to a state monopoly on telecommunications, the entire cellphone rental industry exists in an area of legal limbo. Several local firms are renting cellphones to visiting tourists and businessmen, but this may be illegal, and the Costa Rican telecommunications institute could theoretically crack down on them at any time. However, to date, they've been able to go about their business, albeit discreetly.

None of the rental companies has a booth or office at the airport, so you'll have to contact them either beforehand or from your hotel. Most will deliver the phone to your hotel. **Cell Service** (© **2296-5553;** www.cellservicecr.com) and **GSM Rent A Cell** (© **2231-5410;** www.gsmrentacell.com) both rent cellphones. Rates run

New Numbers

In March 2008, Costa Rica changed all of its phone numbers from seven to eight digits. The change involved adding a "2" to the beginning of all existing land line numbers, and an "8" to all existing cellphone numbers. All of the phone numbers listed in this book are the current eight-digit numbers. However, if you come across an old seven-digit number (on a billboard or brochure, for example) here's what you do: Old cellphone numbers began either with a "3" or "8." All other numbers were land lines. Toll-free and emergency numbers were not affected.

around $5 (£2.50) per day or $35 (£18) per week for the rental, with charges of 70¢ to $1.50 (35p–75p) per minute for local calls and $1.50 to $3 (75p–£1.50) per minute for international calls.

An alternative to the above companies are some of the car-rental agencies. Currently, most of the major car-rental agencies are offering cellphone rentals, for rates similar to those listed above.

VOICE-OVER INTERNET PROTOCOL (VOIP)

If you have Web access while traveling, consider a broadband-based telephone service (in technical terms, **Voice over Internet protocol,** or **VoIP**) such as Skype (www.skype.com) or Vonage (www. vonage.com), which allow you to make free international calls from your laptop or in a cybercafe. Neither service requires the people you're calling to also have that service (though there are fees if they do not). Check the websites for details.

INTERNET/E-MAIL
WITHOUT YOUR OWN COMPUTER

Cybercafes can be found all over Costa Rica, especially in the more popular tourist destinations. To find cybercafes before you travel check **www.cybercaptive.com** and **www.cybercafe.com**. Juan Santamaría International Airport has free Wi-Fi, as well as a makeshift Internet cafe.

For help locating cybercafes and other establishments where you can go for Internet access, please see the destination chapters throughout this book.

WITH YOUR OWN COMPUTER

More and more hotels, resorts, cafes, and retailers around Costa Rica are becoming "hotspots" that offer free high-speed Wi-Fi access or charge a small fee for usage. Most laptops sold today have built-in wireless capability. To find public Wi-Fi hotspots before you travel, go to **www.jiwire.com**; its Hotspot Finder holds the world's largest directory of public wireless hotspots.

Costa Rica uses standard U.S.-style two- and three-prong electric outlets with 110-volt AC current, and standard U.S.-style phone jacks. Wherever you go, bring a **connection kit** with power and phone adapters, a spare phone cord, and a spare Ethernet network cable—or find out whether your hotel supplies them to guests.

13 Tips on Accommodations

When the Costa Rican tourist boom began in the late 1980s, hotels popped up like mushrooms after a heavy rain. By the 1990s the country's first true megaresorts opened, more followed, and still more are under construction or in the planning phase. Except during the few busiest weeks of the year, there's a relative glut of rooms in Costa Rica. That said, most hotels are small to midsize, and the best ones fill up fast most of the year. You'll generally have to reserve well in advance if you want to land a room at any of the hotels on my "Best of" lists in chapter 1. Still, in broader terms, the glut of rooms is good news for travelers and bargain hunters. Less popular hotels that want to survive are being forced to reduce their rates and provide better service.

Your best bet in Costa Rica is negotiating directly with the hotels themselves, especially the smaller hotels. Almost every hotel in Costa Rica has e-mail, if not its own website, and you'll find the contact information in this book. However, be aware that response times might be slower than you'd like, and many of the smaller hotels might have some trouble communicating back and forth in English.

Throughout this book, I separate hotel listings into several broad categories: **Very Expensive,** $200 (£100) and up; **Expensive,** $126 to $199 (£63–£100); **Moderate,** $60 to $125 (£30–£63); and **Inexpensive,** under $60 (£30) for a double. *Rates given in this book do not include the 16.3% room taxes, unless otherwise specified.* These taxes will add considerably to the cost of your room.

HOTEL OPTIONS

Upscale travelers are finally starting to get their due in Costa Rica. It has taken time, but spurred on by the example and standards of several international chains, service and amenities have been improving across the board, particularly in the upscale market. While the Four Seasons remains the only large resort guaranteed to please the exceedingly demanding luxury traveler, there are several wonderful high-end boutique hotels, both in San José and the Central Valley and around the country, that are geared toward this niche.

The country's strong suit is its **moderately priced hotels.** In the $60-to-$125 (£30–£63) price range, you'll find comfortable and sometimes outstanding accommodations almost anywhere in the country. However, room size and quality vary quite a bit within this price range, so don't expect the kind of uniformity that you may find at home.

If you're even more budget- or bohemian-minded, you can find quite a few good deals for less than $50 (£25) double. *But beware:* Budget-oriented lodgings often feature shared bathrooms and either cold-water showers or showers heated by electrical heat-coil units mounted at the shower head, affectionately known as "suicide showers." If your hotel has one, do not adjust it while the water is running. Unless specifically noted, all rooms listed in this guide have a private bathroom.

Online Traveler's Toolbox

Veteran travelers usually carry some essential items to make their trips easier. Following is a selection of handy online tools to bookmark and use.

- **Airplane Food** (www.airlinemeals.net)
- **Airplane Seating** (www.seatguru.com and www.airlinequality.com)
- **Foreign Languages for Travelers** (www.travlang.com)
- **Maps** (www.mapquest.com)
- **Time and Date** (www.timeanddate.com)
- **Travel Warnings** (http://travel.state.gov, www.fco.gov.uk/travel, www. voyage.gc.ca, www.smartraveller.gov.au)
- **Universal Currency Converter** (www.oanda.com)
- **Weather** (www.intellicast.com and www.weather.com)

Tips **Skip the Motel**

You'll want to avoid motels in Costa Rica. To a fault, these are cut-rate affairs geared toward lovers consummating their affairs—usually illicit. Most rent out rooms by the hour, and most have private garages with roll-down doors outside each room, so that snoopy spouses or ex-lovers can't check for cars or license plates.

Note: Air-conditioning is not necessarily a given in many midrange hotels and even some upscale joints. In general, this is not a problem. Cooler nights and a well-placed ceiling fan are often more than enough to keep things pleasant, unless I mention otherwise in the hotel reviews.

Bed-and-breakfasts are now also abundant. Although the majority are in the San José area, you'll also find B&Bs (often gringo-owned and operated) throughout the country. Another welcome hotel trend in the San José area is the renovation and conversion of old homes into **small hotels.** Most are in the Barrio Amón district of downtown San José, which means that you'll sometimes have to put up with noise and exhaust fumes, but these establishments have more character than any other hotels in the country. You'll find similar hotels in the Paseo Colón and Los Yoses districts.

Costa Rica is still riding the ecotourism wave, and you'll find small nature-oriented **ecolodges** throughout the country. These lodges offer opportunities to see wildlife (including sloths, monkeys, and hundreds of species of birds) and learn about tropical forests. They range from spartan facilities catering primarily to scientific researchers, to luxury accommodations that are among the finest in the country. Keep in mind that although the nightly room rates at these lodges are often quite moderate, prices start to climb when you throw in transportation (often on chartered planes), guided excursions, and meals. Also, just because you can book a reservation at most of these lodges doesn't mean that they're not remote. Be sure to find out how you get to and from the ecolodge, and what tours and services are included in your stay. Then think long and hard about whether you really want to put up with hot, humid weather (cool and wet in the cloud forests); biting insects; rugged transportation; and strenuous hikes to see wildlife.

A couple of uniquely Costa Rican accommodations types that you might encounter are the *apartotel* and the *cabina.* An apartotel is just what it sounds like: an apartment hotel where you'll get a full kitchen and one or two bedrooms, along with daily maid service. *Cabinas* are Costa Rica's version of cheap vacation lodging. They're very inexpensive and very basic—often just cinder-block buildings divided into small rooms. Occasionally, you'll find a cabina in which the units are actually cabins, but these are a rarity. Cabinas often have clothes-washing sinks *(pilas),* and some come with kitchenettes; they cater primarily to Tico families on vacation.

For tips on surfing for hotel deals online, visit frommers.com.

4

Suggested Costa Rica Itineraries

Costa Rica is a compact, yet varied, destination with numerous natural attractions and a broad selection of exciting sights, scenery, adventure activities, and ecosystems. On a trip to Costa Rica you can visit rainforests, cloud forests, and active volcanoes, and walk along miles of beautiful beaches on both the Pacific and Caribbean coasts. Adventure hounds will have their fill choosing from an exciting array of activities, and those looking for some rest and relaxation can grab a chaise longue and a good book. Costa Rica is also a relatively compact country, which makes visiting several destinations during a single vacation both easy and enjoyable.

The fastest and easiest way to get around the country is by small commuter aircraft. Most major destinations are serviced by reasonably priced regular commuter or charter airline companies. However, this does imply using San José or Liberia as periodic transfer hubs. If your connections don't line up, you may end up having to tack on nights in either of these cities in the middle of your trip.

Luckily, there are sufficient flights and internal connections to make this an infrequent inconvenience.

Getting around Costa Rica by car is another excellent option (especially if you pay for a driver). Most major destinations are between 3 and 5 hours from San José by car, and many can be linked together in a well-planned and convenient loop. For example, one popular loop links Arenal Volcano, Monteverde, and Manuel Antonio. However, be forewarned that the roads here are often in terrible shape, many major roads and intersections are unmarked, and Tico drivers can be reckless and rude. See "By Car" under "Getting Around Costa Rica," in chapter 3 for more information on driving in Costa Rica.

The following itineraries are specific blueprints for fabulous vacations, and you can follow them to the letter. You might also decide to use one or more of them as an outline and then fill in some blanks with other destinations, activities, and attractions that strike your fancy from the rest of this book.

1 Costa Rica Regions in Brief

Costa Rica rightfully should be called "Costas Ricas" because it has two coasts: one on the Pacific Ocean and one on the Caribbean Sea. These two coasts are as different from each other as are the Atlantic and Pacific coasts of North America.

Costa Rica's **Pacific coast** is characterized by a rugged (although mostly accessible) coastline where forested mountains often meet the sea. It can be divided into four distinct regions—Guanacaste, the Nicoya Peninsula, the Central Coast, and the Southern Coast. There are some spectacular stretches of coastline, and most of the country's top beaches are here. This coast varies from the dry, sunny climate of the northwest to the hot, humid rainforests of the south.

The **Caribbean coast** can be divided into two roughly equal stretches. The remote northeast coastline is a vast flat plain laced with rivers and covered with rainforest; it is accessible only by boat or small plane. Farther south, along the stretch of coast accessible by car, there are uncrowded beaches and even a bit of coral reef.

Bordered by Nicaragua in the north and Panama in the southeast, Costa Rica is only slightly larger than Vermont and New Hampshire combined. Much of the country is mountainous, with three major ranges running northwest to southeast. Among these mountains are several volcanic peaks, some of which are still active. Between the mountain ranges are fertile valleys, the largest and most populated of which is the Central Valley. With the exception of the dry Guanacaste region, much of Costa Rica's coastal area is hot and humid and covered with dense rainforests.

See the map on the inside back cover of this book for a visual of the regions detailed below.

SAN JOSE & THE CENTRAL VALLEY
The Central Valley is characterized by rolling green hills that rise to heights between 900 and 1,200m (2,952–3,936 ft.) above sea level. The climate here is mild and springlike year-round. It's Costa Rica's primary agricultural region, with coffee farms making up the majority of landholdings. The rich volcanic soil of this region makes it ideal for farming. The country's earliest settlements were in this area, and today the Central Valley (which includes San José) is densely populated, crisscrossed by decent roads, and dotted with small towns. Surrounding the Central Valley are high mountains, among

which are four volcanic peaks. Two of these, **Poás** and **Irazú,** are still active and have caused extensive damage during cycles of activity in the past 2 centuries. Many of the mountainous regions to the north and to the south of the capital of San José have been declared national parks (Tapantí, Juan Castro, and Braulio Carrillo) to protect their virgin rainforests against logging.

GUANACASTE
The northwestern corner of the country near the Nicaraguan border is the site of many of Costa Rica's sunniest and most popular **beaches.** There are literally scores of popular beach destinations, towns, and resorts along this long string of coastline. Because many foreigners have chosen to build beach houses and retirement homes here, Guanacaste is experiencing quite a bit of development. Don't expect a glut of Cancún-style high-rise hotels, but condos, luxury resorts, and golf courses are springing up like mushrooms. That's not to say you'll be towel-to-towel with thousands of strangers. On the contrary, you can still find long stretches of deserted sands. That might not be true for long, however: The international airport in Liberia receives a steady stream of daily direct flights from a variety of hub cities and the number of these flights is steadily increasing. More and more travelers are using Liberia as their gateway to Costa Rica, bypassing San José and the central and southern parts of the country entirely.

With about 65 inches of rain a year, this region is by far the driest in the country and has been likened to west Texas. Guanacaste province is named after the shady trees that still shelter the herds of cattle roaming the dusty savanna here. In addition to cattle ranches, Guanacaste boasts semiactive volcanoes, several lakes, and one of the last remnants of tropical dry forest left in Central America. (Dry forest once stretched all the way from Costa Rica up to the Mexican state of Chiapas.)

PUNTARENAS & THE NICOYA PENINSULA Just south of Guanacaste lies the Nicoya peninsula. Similar to Guanacaste in many ways, the Nicoya peninsula is nonetheless somewhat more inaccessible, and thus much less developed and crowded. However, this is already starting to change. The neighboring beaches of **Malpaís** and **Santa Teresa** are perhaps the fastest growing new hot spots anywhere along the Costa Rican coast.

While similar in terms of geography, climate, and ecosystems, as you head south from Guanacaste, the region begins to get more humid and moist. The forests are taller and lusher than those found in Guanacaste. The Nicoya peninsula itself juts out to form the Golfo de Nicoya (Nicoya Gulf), a large, protected body of water. **Puntarenas,** a small fishing town, is the main port found inside this gulf, and one of the main commercial ports in all of Costa Rica. Puntarenas is also the departure point for the regular ferries that connect the Nicoya peninsula to San José and most of mainland Costa Rica.

THE NORTHERN ZONE This inland region lies to the north of San José and includes rainforests, cloud forests, hot springs, the country's two most active volcanoes (**Arenal** and **Rincón de la Vieja**), **Braulio Carrillo National Park,** and numerous remote lodges. Because this is one of the few regions of Costa Rica without any beaches, it primarily attracts people interested in nature and active sports. **Lake Arenal** boasts some of the best windsurfing in the world, as well as several good mountain-biking trails along its shores. The **Monteverde Cloud Forest,** perhaps Costa Rica's most internationally recognized attraction, is another top draw in this region.

THE CENTRAL PACIFIC COAST Because it's the most easily accessible coastline in Costa Rica, the central Pacific coast boasts the greatest number of beach resorts and hotels. **Playa de Jacó** is the most popular destination here, a beach within a few hours' drive of San José that attracts many Canadian and German charter groups and plenty of Tico tourists on weekends. **Manuel Antonio,** a popular coastal national park, as well as the resort area that surrounds it, caters to people seeking a bit more tranquillity and beauty. This region is also home to the highest peak in Costa Rica—**Mount Chirripó**—where frost is common.

THE SOUTHERN ZONE This hot, humid region is one of Costa Rica's most remote and undeveloped. It is characterized by dense rainforests, large national parks and protected areas, and rugged coastlines. Much of the area is protected in **Corcovado** and **La Amistad** national parks. A number of wonderful nature lodges are spread around the shores of the **Golfo Dulce** and along the **Osa Peninsula.** There's a lot of solitude to be found here, due in no small part to the fact that it's hard to get here and hard to get around. But if you like your ecotourism authentic and challenging, you'll find the southern zone to your liking.

THE CARIBBEAN COAST Most of the Caribbean coast is a wide, steamy lowland laced with rivers and blanketed with rainforests and banana plantations. The culture here is predominantly Afro-Caribbean, with many residents speaking an English or Caribbean patois. The northern section of this coast is accessible only by boat or small plane and is the site of **Tortuguero National Park,** which is known for its nesting sea turtles and riverboat trips. The towns of **Cahuita, Puerto Viejo,** and **Manzanillo,** on the southern half of the Caribbean coast, are increasingly popular destinations. The coastline here boasts many beautiful beaches and, as yet, few large hotels. However, this area can be rainy, especially between December and April.

2 Costa Rica in 1 Week

The timing is tight, but this itinerary packs a lot into a weeklong vacation. This route takes you to a trifecta of Costa Rica's primary tourist attractions: Arenal Volcano, Monteverde, and Manuel Antonio. You can explore and enjoy tropical nature, take in some beach time, and experience a few high-adrenaline adventures to boot.

Day ❶: Arrive & Settle into San José

Arrive and get settled in **San José.** If your flight gets in early enough and you have time, head downtown and tour the **Museos del Banco Central de Costa Rica (Gold Museum)** ✿✿ (p. 131).

FRESH FRUIT
As you walk around town, stop at one of the roadside stands or kiosks selling small bags of pre-cut and prepared fruit. Depending on the season, you might find mango, pineapple, or papaya on offer. If you're lucky they'll have *mamon chino,* an odd-looking golf ball–size fruit you might also know as rambutan or litchi nut, if you've been to Asia.

Head over to the **Teatro Nacional (National Theater;** p. 142). If anything is playing that night, buy tickets for the show. For an elegant and delicious dinner, I recommend **Grano de Oro Restaurant** ✿✿✿ (p. 124), which is an elegant restaurant with seating in and around an open-air central courtyard in a beautiful downtown hotel.

Day ❷: Hot Rocks ✿✿

Rent a car and head to the Arenal National Park to see **Arenal Volcano** ✿✿. Settle into your hotel and spend the afternoon at the **Tabacón Grand Spa Thermal Resort** ✿✿✿ (p. 248) working out the kinks from the road. In the evening either sign up for a volcano-watching tour or take one on your own by driving the road to **Arenal National Park** and finding a quiet spot to pull over and wait for the sparks to fly.

Day ❸: Adventures Around Arenal, Ending Up in Monteverde ✿✿

Spend the morning doing something adventurous around Arenal National Park. Your options range from white-water rafting to mountain biking to horseback riding and then hiking to the Río Fortuna Waterfall. My favorite is the **canyoning** adventure offered by **Pure Trek Canyoning** ✿✿ (p. 247). Allow at least 4 hours of daylight to drive around **Lake Arenal** to **Monteverde.** Stop for a break at **Toad Hall** ✿✿ (p. 260) and the **Lucky Bug Gallery** ✿✿ (p. 260); both are along the road between Tabacón and Nuevo Arenal, and are excellent places to shop for gifts, artwork, and souvenirs. Once you get to Monteverde, settle into your hotel and head for a drink and dinner at **Chimera** ✿✿ (p. 276).

Day ❹: Monteverde Cloud Forest Reserve ✿✿✿

Wake up early and take a guided tour of the **Monteverde Cloud Forest Reserve** ✿✿✿ (p. 267). Be sure to stop in at the **Hummingbird Gallery** ✿ (p. 272) next door to the entrance after your tour. There's great shopping, and the scores of brilliant hummingbirds buzzing around your head are always fascinating. Spend the afternoon visiting several of the area's attractions, which might include any combination of the following: the **Butterfly Garden** ✿, **Orchid Garden** ✿, **Monteverde Serpentarium, Frog Pond of Monteverde** ✿, the **Bat Jungle,** and the **World of Insects** (p. 271).

Costa Rica in 1 Week

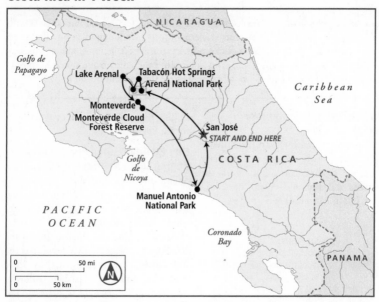

Day ❺: From the Treetops to the Coast ⭐⭐⭐

Use the morning to take one of the **zip-line canopy tours** here. I recommend **Selvatura Park** ⭐⭐ (p. 269), which has a wonderful canopy tour, as well as other interesting exhibits. Be sure to schedule the tour early enough so that you can hit the road by noon for your drive to **Manuel Antonio National Park.** Settle into your hotel and head for a **sunset drink** at one of the several roadside restaurants with spectacular views over the rainforest to the sea. You can drop your car off at any point now and just rely on taxis and tours.

Day ❻: Manuel Antonio ⭐⭐

In the morning take a boat tour of the **Damas Island estuary** (p. 302) with

Jorge Cruz, and then reward yourself for all the hard touring so far with an afternoon lazing on one of the beautiful beaches inside **Manuel Antonio National Park** ⭐⭐ (p. 296). If you just can't lie still, be sure to hike the loop trail through the rainforest here and around **Cathedral Point** ⭐⭐. Make reservations at the **Sunspot Bar & Grill** ⭐⭐ (p. 311) for an elegant and intimate final dinner in Costa Rica.

Day ❼: Saying *Adiós*

Fly back to **San José** in time to connect with your departing flight home. If you have extra time, feel free to head back into Manuel Antonio National Park, do some souvenir shopping, or simply laze around your hotel pool. You've earned it.

3 Costa Rica in 2 Weeks

If you have 2 weeks, you'll be able to hit all the highlights mentioned above, as well as some others, and at a slightly more relaxed pace to boot. The first part of this itinerary is very similar to the 1-week itinerary laid out above. It's a real judgment call,

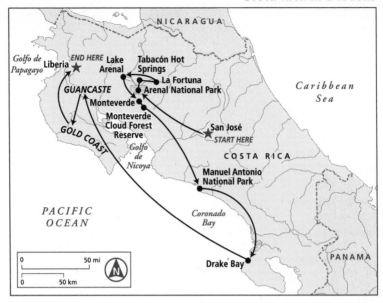

NICARAGUA

Golfo de Papagayo

Liberia

END HERE

Lake Arenal

Tabacón Hot Springs

La Fortuna

Arenal National Park

Caribbean Sea

GUANCASTE

Monteverde

Monteverde Cloud Forest Reserve

San José

START HERE

COSTA RICA

GOLD COAST

Golfo de Nicoya

Manuel Antonio National Park

PACIFIC OCEAN

Coronado Bay

PANAMA

Drake Bay

0   50 mi

0   50 km

N

but you might want to substitute a 2- to 3-day trip to Tortuguero for either the Guanacaste or the southern zone section listed below, or whittle down a day here or there along the way in order to squeeze in Tortuguero.

Days ❶ & ❷: San José

Follow the option listed under **Days 1 and 2** in "Costa Rica in 1 Week," above. Another option for dinner on your second night is **Café Mundo** ✷ (p. 122), a lively restaurant and nightspot set in a wonderfully restored old colonial home in the heart of downtown.

Day ❸: Active in Arenal

Spend the morning doing something adventurous in **Arenal National Park,** as recommended in **Day 3** in "Costa Rica in 1 Week," above. If you're really active, you can schedule a second adventure for the afternoon or take time to visit the town of **La Fortuna.** In the evening return to the **Tabacón Grand Spa Thermal Resort.** If you were smart, you'll have already booked yourself a **spa treatment.**

Day ❹: Driving (& Shopping) Your Way Around the Lake to Monteverde

Give yourself at least 4 hours of daylight to drive around **Lake Arenal** to **Monteverde.** But you can take even longer. During your drive, be sure to stop at both **Toad Hall** ✷✷ (p. 260) and the **Lucky Bug Gallery** ✷✷ (p. 260), where you can shop for gifts, artwork, and souvenirs. Once you're in Monteverde, settle into your hotel and head for a drink and dinner at **Chimera** ✷✷ (p. 276).

Day ❺: Monteverde Cloud Forest Reserve

Spend **Day 5** as described for **Day 4** of "Costa Rica in 1 Week," above; however, head to **Sofia** ✷✷ (p. 277) for dinner and grab a window table fronting its well-lighted and lush gardens.

Day ⑥: More Monteverde

There's just no way you can hit all the local **Monteverde** attractions in a day. Use today to visit a few that you missed. Also be sure to stop in at several of the local **art galleries** and **crafts shops.** Monteverde has one of the country's most vibrant arts scenes, and there are several worthwhile galleries, including Casa de Arte (p. 272). In the evening, be sure to try **El Sapo Dorado** ⭐ (p. 276) a long-standing and deservedly popular restaurant serving eclectic international fare.

Day ⑦: Monteverde to Manuel Antonio

Spend this day as in **Day 5** of "Costa Rica in 1 Week," above. However, after your sunset drink, head down into the town of Quepos for dinner at **El Patio Bistro Latino** ⭐⭐⭐ (p. 311), a cozy little spot serving some of the best food in the area.

Day ⑧: Manuel Antonio ⭐⭐

Spend this day as in **Day 6** of "Costa Rica in 1 Week," above.

Days ⑨, ⑩ & ⑪: Southern Costa Rica

Fly from Quepos and Manuel Antonio to **Drake Bay** and settle into a remote ecolodge, such as **La Paloma Lodge** ⭐⭐⭐ (p. 335). You'll need 3 days to experience the many natural wonders of this southern zone. Aside from hiking in the rainforest, you'll be able to take scuba or snorkel outings, sportfishing trips, kayak adventures, and surfing lessons.

Days ⑫, ⑬ & ⑭: Guanacaste's Gold Coast

You've had enough nature and adventure; it's time to enjoy some pure R & R. From the southern zone, fly up to **Guanacaste** and spend your final days enjoying the pleasures of one of Costa Rica's **Gold Coast** beaches. If you can afford it and rooms are available, I recommend the **Four Seasons Resort** ⭐⭐⭐ (p. 172). Alternatively, you might enjoy a smaller boutique hotel such as **Sueño del Mar** ⭐ (p. 194).

If just lying on the beach or poolside is too mellow, there are scores of tour and activity options. If you're not feeling that active or adventurous, simply break out that novel you've been too busy to open and enjoy. On your last day, fly home from **Liberia.**

4 Costa Rica for Families

While Costa Rica is not a particularly kid-friendly destination, it isn't especially unfriendly either. So far, there are few attractions or activities geared for the very young and few resorts with well-developed children's programs. However, youngsters and teens, especially those with strong adventurous and inquisitive traits, will do great here. The biggest challenges to families traveling with children are travel distances and the logistical challenges of moving around within the country, which is why I recommend flying in and out of Liberia and basing yourself in Guanacaste.

Day ①: Arrive in Guanacaste

Fly directly into **Liberia.** From here it's a drive of 30 to 45 minutes to any of the area's many beach resorts, especially around the **Papagayo Peninsula.** I recommend either the **Four Seasons Resort** ⭐⭐⭐ (p. 172) or the **Hilton Papagayo Resort** ⭐ (p. 172). Both have excellent children's programs and tons of activity and tour options.

Day ②: Get Your Bearings & Enjoy Your Resort

Get to know and enjoy the facilities and activities offered up at your hotel or resort. Spend some time on the beach or

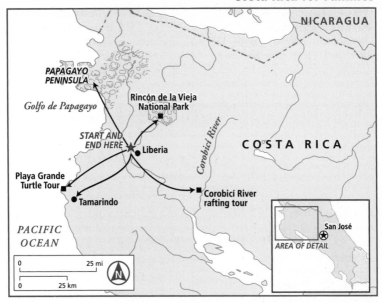

at the pool. Enjoy the resort's on-hand watersports equipment and activities. Check out the **children's program** and any scheduled **activities** or **tours** that particularly appeal to anyone in the family. Feel free to adapt the following days' suggestions accordingly.

Day ❸: Rafting on the Corobicí River

The whole family will enjoy a **rafting tour** on the gentle Corobicí River. **Safaris Corobicí** (p. 163) offers leisurely trips that are appropriate for all ages, except infants. In addition to the slow float and occasional mellow rapids, there'll be plenty of opportunities to watch birds and other wildlife along the way. If you're here between late September and late February, book a **turtle tour** (p. 191) at nearby **Playa Grande** for the evening. The whole family will be awe-struck by the amazing spectacle of a giant leatherback turtle digging a nest and laying its eggs.

Day ❹: Parent's Day Off

Drop the kids off with the children's program for at least 1 full day and treat yourselves to a **sailboat cruise.** You'll spend some time cruising the coast, take a break or two to snorkel, and probably stop for lunch at a deserted beach. If you really want to pamper yourself, also schedule in some **spa services.**

Day ❺: Hacienda Guachipelín ✦

It's time to head for the hills, which are mostly volcanoes in this neck of the woods. Book a full-day outing to **Hacienda Guachipelín** ✦ (p. 165), near the Rincón de la Vieja National Park. Older and more adventurous children can sign up for a **horseback ride** or **canopy tour.** Younger children should get a kick out of visiting this working farm and cattle ranch.

Day ❻: Learn to Surf

Head to **Tamarindo** ✦ (p. 186) and arrange for the whole family to take **surf** or **boogie-board lessons.** Hopefully you will have already booked a class with **Tamarindo Surf School** or **Witch's Rock Surf Camp** (p. 192). Be sure to rent your boards for a full day, so that you can practice after the lesson is over.

Day ❼: Leaving Liberia

Use any spare time you have before your flight out of **Liberia** to buy last-minute souvenirs and gifts, or just laze on the beach or by the pool.

5 A High-Octane Week of Adventures

Costa Rica is a major adventure-tourism destination. The following basic itinerary packs a lot of adventure into a single week; if you want to do more mountain biking or kayaking, just schedule that time in. If you're into windsurfing or kiteboarding, you'll definitely want to visit Lake Arenal between December and March.

Day ❶: Arrive & Settle into San José

Arrive and get settled in **San José.** If your flight gets in early enough and you have time, head downtown and tour the **Museos del Banco Central de Costa Rica** ✹✹ (p. 131) and the **Teatro Nacional** (p. 142). Take a break for an afternoon coffee at the **Cafeteria 1830** (p. 122). Be sure to grab an outdoor table and enjoy some people-watching. For a delicious dinner with a spectacular view, head to **La Cava Grill** ✹ (p. 128), which is located in the hills above Escazú.

Days ❷ & ❸: Get Wet & Wild

Take a 2-day white-water rafting expedition on the **Pacuare River** with **Exploradores Outdoors** ✹ (p. 151). Camp out at their rustic tent camp on the river's edge. When you finish running the Pacuare, have them arrange for a transfer to **La Fortuna** at the end of your rafting trip. Settle into your hotel and head to the **Tabacón Grand Spa Thermal Resort** (p. 248) to have a soothing soak and to watch the volcano.

Day ❹: Waterfalls Two Ways

Go canyoning with **Pure Trek Canyoning** ✹✹ (p. 247) in the morning, and then hop on a horse or a mountain bike in the afternoon and be sure to stop at the **Río Fortuna Waterfall** ✹ (p. 250). Take the short hike down to the base of the

falls and take a dip in one of the pools there. In the evening check out the **Eco Termales** ✹✹ (p. 249) hot springs.

Day ❺: Getting There Is Part of the Fun & Adventure

Arrange a **taxi-to-boat-to-horse** transfer over to **Monteverde** with **Desafío Expeditions** ✹✹ (p. 245). Settle in quickly at your hotel and take a zip-line **canopy tour** in the afternoon. I recommend the **Original Canopy Tour** ✹ (p. 270) in Monteverde. Finally, if you've got the energy, take a **night tour** through the Monteverde Cloud Forest Reserve.

Day ❻: Monteverde Cloud Forest Reserve ✹✹✹

Wake up early and head back to take a daytime guided tour of the **Monteverde Cloud Forest Reserve** ✹✹✹. Be sure to bring a packed lunch. After the guided tour, spend the next few hours continuing to explore the trails through the cloud forest here. See if you can spot a **quetzal** (p. 264) on your own. Then transfer back to San José.

Day ❼: Squeeze in a Soccer Game before Splitting

Unfortunately, you'll most likely be on an early flight home from **San José.** If you have a few hours to kill, head for a **hike** or **jog** around Parque La Sabana or, better yet, try to join a **pickup soccer game** (p. 134) here.

A High-Octane Week of Adventures

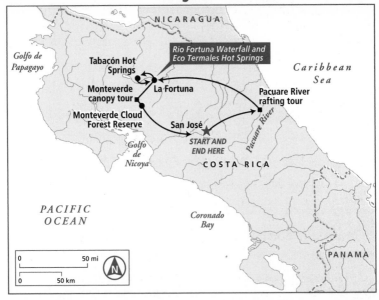

6 San José in 3 Days

While most tourists seek to almost immediately get out of San José for greener pastures, there's still plenty to see and do in Costa Rica's vibrant capital. If you have even more days, take a white-water rafting trip on the Pacuare River, or head out to the Irazú Volcano, Orosi Valley, and Cartago area.

Day ❶: Getting to Know the City

Start your day on the **Plaza de la Cultura.** Visit the **Museos del Banco Central de Costa Rica** ⚜⚜ (p. 131), and see if you can get tickets for a performance that night at the **Teatro Nacional** (p. 142). From the Plaza de la Cultura, stroll up Avenida Central to the **Museo Nacional de Costa Rica (National Museum)** ⚜ (p. 130). After touring the museum, have lunch at one of the neighborhood restaurants. Then, head over to the neighboring **Centro Nacional de Arte y Cultura (National Center of Art and Culture)** ⚜ (p. 129). After you're finished taking in all this culture, some shopping at the open-air stalls at the **Plaza de la Democracia** (p. 138) is in order.

CAFE MUNDO ⚜
Try dinner at the popular local hangout **Café Mundo,** at Calle 15 and Avenida 9, 200m (656 ft.) east and 100m (328 ft.) north of the INS building. See p. 122.

After dinner, head to the Teatro Nacional for the night's performance.

Day ❷: Enjoying Some Nearby Attractions

Get an early start for the **Poás Volcano** ⚜⚜ (p. 151), before the clouds sock the main crater in. After visiting the volcano, head to the **La Paz Waterfall Gardens** ⚜⚜ (p. 133). Take a walk on the waterfall trail, and also enjoy the

San José in 3 Days

1 Plaza de la Cultura
2 Museos del Banco Central de Costa Rica
3 Museo Nacional de Costa Rica
4 Centro Nacional de Arte y Cultura
5 Plaza de la Democracia
☕ Café Mundo

6 Teatro Nacional
7 Museo de Arte Costarricense
8 Parque La Sabana
9 Spirogyra Butterfly Garden
10 Mercado Central
☕ La Cocina de Leña

immense butterfly garden and lively hummingbird garden. This is a good place to have lunch. On your way back to San José, you'll be making a loop through the hills of **Heredia,** with a stop at **INBio Park** 🐾🐾 (p. 155). In addition to being a fascinating natural-history museum, INBio Park also has a wonderful collection of intriguing animal sculptures by Costa Rican artist José Sancho.

Day ❸: More City Sights & Shopping

Spend your third day further exploring the capital. Start by heading out on Paseo Colón to the **Museo de Arte Costarricense (Costa Rican Art Museum)** 🐾🐾 (p. 129) and **Parque La Sabana** (p. 134). Tour the museum and its growing sculpture garden, but also take a stroll around the beautiful and expansive downtown park. If you've brought kids along, you'll definitely want to visit the **Spirogyra Butterfly Garden** (p. 131). Intrepid travelers can also do some shopping at the **Mercado Central** (p. 137).

LA COCINA DE LEÑA
For a final taste of local culture, head to the El Pueblo entertainment center for dinner at **La Cocina de Leña,** Centro Comercial El Pueblo. See p. 122.

5

The Active Vacation Planner

Active and adventure travelers will have their hands full in Costa Rica. While it's possible to stay clean and dry, most visitors want to spend at least some time getting their hair wet, their feet muddy, and their adrenaline pumping. Opportunities for such action range from bird-watching to scuba diving to kiteboarding, and beyond.

There are myriad approaches to planning an active vacation in Costa Rica. This chapter lays out your options, from tour operators who run multiactivity package tours that often include stays at ecolodges, to the best places in Costa Rica to pursue active endeavors (with listings of tour operators, guides, and outfitters that specialize in each), to an overview of the country's national parks and bioreserves. I also list some educational and volunteer travel options for those of you with a little more time on your hands and a desire to actively contribute to the country's social welfare, or assist Costa Rica in the maintenance and preservation of its natural wonders.

1 Organized Adventure Trips

Because many travelers have limited time and resources, organized ecotourism or adventure-travel packages, arranged by tour operators in either Costa Rica or the United States, are a popular way of combining several activities. Bird-watching, horseback riding, rafting, and hiking can be teamed with, say, visits to Monteverde Biological Cloud Forest Reserve and Manuel Antonio National Park.

Traveling with a group has several advantages over traveling independently: Your accommodations and transportation are arranged, and most (if not all) of your meals are included in the cost of a package. If your tour operator has a reasonable amount of experience and a decent track record, you should proceed to each of your destinations quickly without the snags and long delays that those traveling on their own can occasionally face. You'll also have the opportunity to meet like-minded souls who are interested in nature and active sports. Of course, you'll pay more for the convenience of having all your arrangements handled in advance.

In the best cases, group size is kept small (10–20 people), and tours are escorted by knowledgeable guides who are either naturalists or biologists. Be sure to ask about difficulty levels when you're choosing a tour. Most companies offer "soft adventure" packages that those in moderately good, but not phenomenal, shape can handle; others focus on more hard-core activities geared toward only seasoned athletes or adventure travelers.

COSTA RICAN TOUR AGENCIES

Because many U.S.-based companies subcontract portions of their tours to established Costa Rican companies, some travelers like to cut out the middleman and set up their tours directly with these companies. That means that these packages are often less expensive than those offered by U.S. companies, but it doesn't mean they are cheap. You're still paying for the convenience of having your arrangements handled for you.

Scores of agencies in San José offer a plethora of adventure options. These agencies can arrange everything from white-water rafting to sightseeing at one of the nearby volcanoes or a visit to a butterfly farm. Although it's generally quite easy to arrange a day trip at the last minute, other tours are offered only on set dates or when enough people are interested. It pays to contact a few of the companies before you leave the United States and find out what they might be doing when you arrive. These local operators tend to be a fair share less expensive than their international counterparts, with 10-day tours generally costing in the neighborhood of $1,500 to $3,000 (£750–£1,500) per person, not including airfare to Costa Rica.

Coast to Coast Adventures ✦ (© **2280-8054;** www.ctocadventures.com) has a unique excursion involving no motor vehicles. The company's namesake 2-week trip spans the country, with participants traveling on horses and rafts, by mountain bike, and on foot. Custom-designed trips (with a minimum of motorized transport) of shorter duration are also available.

Costa Rica Expeditions ✦✦ (© **2257-0766;** www.costaricaexpeditions.com) offers everything from 10-day tours covering the entire country to 3-day/2-night and 2-day/1-night tours of Monteverde Biological Cloud Forest Reserve, Tortuguero National Park, and Corcovado National Park, where they run their own lodges. It also offers 1- to 2-day white-water rafting trips and other excursions. All excursions include transportation, meals, and lodging. Its tours are some of the most expensive in the country, but it is the most consistently reliable outfitter as well (and its customer service is excellent). If you want to go out on your own, Costa Rica Expeditions can supply you with just transportation from place to place.

Costa Rica Sun Tours ✦ (© **2296-7757;** www.crsuntours.com) offers a wide range of tours and adventures and specializes in multiday tours that include stays at small country lodges for travelers interested in experiencing nature.

Horizontes ✦✦ (© **2222-2022;** www.horizontes.com) is not a specifically adventure-oriented operator, but it offers a wide range of individual, group, and package tours, including those geared toward active and adventure travelers. The company generally hires responsible and knowledgeable guides.

Serendipity Adventures ✦ (© **877/507-1358** in the U.S. and Canada, or 2558-1000; www.serendipityadventures.com), an adventure-travel operator, offers everything from ballooning to mountain biking, and sea kayaking to canyoning, as well as most of the popular white-water rafting trips.

U.S.-BASED ADVENTURE TOUR OPERATORS

These agencies and operators specialize in well-organized and coordinated tours that cover your entire stay. Many travelers prefer to have everything arranged and confirmed before arriving in Costa Rica, and this is a good idea for first-timers and during the high season. *Be warned:* Most of these operators are not cheap, with 10-day tours generally costing in the neighborhood of $2,500 to $4,000 (£1,250–£2,000) per person, not including airfare to Costa Rica.

Abercrombie & Kent ✦✦ (© **800/554-7016;** www.abercrombiekent.com) is a luxury-tour company that offers upscale trips around the globe, and it has several tours of Costa Rica on its menu. It specializes in a 9-day highlight tours hitting Monteverde, Arenal, and Tortuguero. Service is personalized and the guides are top-notch.

Butterfield & Robinson ✸✸ (© **866/551-9090;** www.butterfield.com) is another company specializing in the very high-end market. One of its most interesting options is a trip designed for families with children over 8 years old. The trip provides a wealth of activities and adventures for parents and children to enjoy both together and apart.

Costa Rica Experts ✸ (© **800/827-9046** or 773/935-1009; www.costaricaexperts. com) offers a large menu of a la carte and scheduled departures, as well as day trips and adventure packages.

Overseas Adventure Travel ✸✸ (© **800/493-6824;** www.oattravel.com) offers good-value natural-history and "soft adventure" itineraries with optional add-on excursions. Tours are limited to 16 people and are guided by naturalists. All accommodations are in small hotels, lodges, or tent camps.

Nature Expeditions International ✸ (© **800/869-0639;** www.naturexp.com) specializes in educational and "low intensity adventure" trips tailored to independent travelers and small groups. These folks have a steady stream of programmed departures, or can customize a trip to your needs.

Tico Travel (© **800/493-8426;** www.ticotravel.com) has offices in both the United States and Costa Rica. It specializes in surfing and sportfishing packages, but it can put together a wide range of tours.

In addition to these companies, many environmental organizations, including the **Sierra Club** (© **415/977-5522;** www.sierraclub.org), and the **Smithsonian Institute** (© **877/338-8687;** www.smithsonianjourneys.org), regularly offer organized trips to Costa Rica.

2 Activities A to Z

Each listing in this section describes the best places to practice a particular sport or activity and lists tour operators and outfitters. If you want to focus on only one active sport during your Costa Rican stay, these companies are your best bets for quality equipment and knowledgeable service.

Adventure activities and tourism, by their very nature, carry certain risks and dangers. Over the years, there have been several deaths and dozens of minor injuries in activities ranging from mountain biking to white-water rafting to canopy tours. I've tried to list only the most reputable and safest of companies. However, if you ever have any doubt as to the safety of the guide, equipment, or activity, it's better to be safe than sorry. Moreover, know your limits and abilities, and don't try to exceed them.

See "A High-Octane Week of Adventures" in chapter 4 for additional tour ideas.

BIKING

There are several significant regional and international touring races in Costa Rica each year, but as a general rule the major roads are dangerous and inhospitable for cyclists. Roads are narrow, there's usually no shoulder, and most drivers show little care or consideration for those on two wheels. The options are much more appealing for mountain bikers and off-track riders. Fat-tire explorations are still relatively new to Costa Rica, but options are growing fast. If you plan to do a lot of biking and are very attached to your rig, bring your own. However, several companies in San José and elsewhere rent bikes, and the quality of the equipment is improving all the time. I've listed rental shops in each of the regional chapters that follow.

The area around **Lake Arenal** and **Arenal Volcano** wins my vote as the best place for mountain biking in Costa Rica. The scenery's great, with primary forests, waterfalls,

Ruta de los Conquistadores

Each year, Costa Rica hosts what many consider to be the most challenging and grueling mountain-bike race on the planet. La Ruta de los Conquistadores (the Route of the Conquerors; www.adventurerace.com) retraces the path of the 16th-century Spanish conquistadores from the Pacific Coast to the Caribbean Sea—all in 4 days. The race usually takes place in mid-November, and draws hundreds of competitors from around the world.

and plenty of trails. And the hot springs at nearby Tabacón Grand Spa Thermal Resort is a perfect place for those with aching muscles to unwind at the end of the day. See chapter 9 for full details.

TOUR OPERATORS & OUTFITTERS

Bike Arenal ✦ (✆ **866/465-4114** in U.S. and Canada, or 2479-9454; www.bike arenal.com) is based in La Fortuna and specializes in 1-day and multiday trips around the Arenal area.

Coast to Coast Adventures ✦ (✆ **2280-8054;** www.ctocadventures.com) offers mountain-biking itineraries among its many tour options.

Costa Rica Biking Adventures (✆ **2235-4982;** www.bikingincostarica.com) is a local outfit offering day trips and multiday excursions around the country using high-quality Trek and Cannondale bikes.

ExperiencePlus! Specialty Tours ✦✦ (✆ **800/685-4565** or 970/484-8489 in the U.S.; www.experienceplus.com) offers guided group and assisted individual bike tours around the country. This is the only company I know of that uses touring bikes. It also offers guided group hiking tours.

Lava Tours (✆ **888/862-2424** in the U.S. and Canada, or 2278-2558; www.lava-tours.com) conducts a variety of fixed-date-departure and custom mountain-bike tours all over Costa Rica.

Serendipity Adventures ✦ (✆ **877/507-1358** in the U.S. and Canada, or 2558-1030; www.serendipityadventures.com) offers several mountain-biking trips among its many other expeditions.

BIRD-WATCHING

With more than 850 species of resident and migrant birds identified throughout the country, Costa Rica abounds with great bird-watching sites. Lodges with the best bird-watching include **Savegre Lodge,** in Cerro de la Muerte, off the road to San Isidro de El General (quetzal sightings are almost guaranteed); **La Paloma Lodge** in Drake Bay, where you can sit on the porch of your cabin as the avian parade goes by; **Arenal Observatory Lodge,** on the flanks of Arenal Volcano; **La Selva Biological Station,** in Puerto Viejo de Sarapiquí; **Aviarios del Caribe** and **Selva Bananito Lodge,** both just north of Cahuita; **Lapa Ríos** and **Bosque del Cabo,** on the Osa Peninsula; **Playa Nicuesa Rainforest Lodge,** along the Golfo Dulce; **La Laguna del Lagarto Lodge,** up by the Nicaraguan border; and **Tiskita Lodge,** down by the Panamanian border.

Some of the best parks and preserves for serious birders are **Monteverde Biological Cloud Forest Reserve** (for resplendent quetzals and hummingbirds); **Corcovado National Park** (for scarlet macaws); **Caño Negro Wildlife Refuge** (for wading birds, including jabiru storks); **Wilson Botanical Gardens** and the **Las Cruces Biological**

Station, near San Vito (the thousands of flowering plants here are bird magnets); **Guayabo, Negritos,** and **Pájaros Islands biological reserves** in the Gulf of Nicoya (for magnificent frigate birds and brown boobies); **Palo Verde National Park** (for ibises, jacanas, storks, and roseate spoonbills); **Tortuguero National Park** (for great green macaws); and **Rincón de la Vieja National Park** (for parakeets and curassows). Rafting trips down the Corobicí and Bebedero rivers near Liberia, boat trips to or at Tortuguero National Park, and hikes in any cloud forest also provide good bird-watching opportunities.

In San José your best bets are to head toward the lush grounds and gardens of the University of Costa Rica, or to Parque del Este, a little farther east in the foothills just outside of town.

COSTA RICAN TOUR AGENCIES

In addition to the agencies listed below, check in with the **Birding Club of Costa Rica** ✺✺ (© 2282-5365; costaricabirding@hotmail.com), which runs monthly outings and provides you with the opportunity to connect with local birders. These are also the folks to contact if you want to participate in the annual Christmas bird count. This event is part of a worldwide network of bird counts loosely coordinated by the Audubon Society.

Costa Rica Expeditions ✺✺ (© 2257-0766; www.costaricaexpeditions.com) and **Costa Rica Sun Tours** ✺✺ (© 2296-7757; www.crsuntours.com) are well-established companies with very competent and experienced guides who offer a variety of tours to some of the better birding spots in Costa Rica.

U.S.-BASED TOUR OPERATORS

Field Guides (© 800/728-4953 or 512/263-7295; www.fieldguides.com) is a specialty bird-watching travel operator. Its 16-day tour of Costa Rica costs $4,575 (£2,288), not including airfare. Group size is limited to 14 participants.

Victor Emanuel Nature Tours ✺✺ (© 800/328-8368, or 512/328-5221 in the U.S.; www.ventbird.com) is a well-respected small-group tour operator specializing in bird-watching trips. Their 12-day "Best of Costa Rica" trip costs $3,975 (£1,988).

WINGS (© 888/293-6443 or 520/320-9868; www.wingsbirds.com) is a specialty bird-watching travel operator with 30 years of experience in the field. Its 14-day Costa Rica trip covers the major bird-watching zones in the country and costs around $4,460 (£2,230), not including airfare. Group size is usually between 6 and 14 people.

BUNGEE JUMPING

Tropical Bungee (© 2248-2212; www.bungee.co.cr) will let you jump off an 80m (262-ft.) bridge over the Río Colorado for $65 (£33), including transportation from San José and a video of your jump. A second jump will cost you another $30 (£15). The jump site is located on a small bridge over the Río Colorado about 37km (23 miles) northwest of San José, just off the Pan-American Highway. There are obvious and well-placed signs on the highway. Someone should be there from 9am to 3pm every day. They prefer for you to have a reservation, but if you show up on your own, they'll probably let you jump, unless huge groups are booked ahead of you.

CAMPING

Heavy rains, difficult access, and limited facilities make camping a challenge in Costa Rica. Nevertheless, a backpack and tent will get you far from the crowds and into

Where to See the Resplendent Quetzal

Revered by pre-Columbian cultures throughout Central America, the resplendent quetzal has been called the most beautiful bird on earth. Ancient Aztec and Maya Indians believed that the robin-size quetzal protected them in battle. The males of this species have brilliant red breasts; iridescent emerald green heads, backs, and wings; and white tail feathers complemented by a pair of iridescent green tail feathers that are more than .5m (1¾ ft.) long.

The belief that these endangered birds live only in the dense cloud forests cloaking the higher slopes of Central America's mountains was instrumental in bringing many areas of cloud forest under protection as quetzal habitats. (Since then, researchers have discovered that the birds do not, in fact, spend their entire lives here.) After nesting between March and July, resplendent quetzals migrate down to lower slopes in search of food. These lower slopes have not been preserved in most cases, and now conservationists are trying to salvage enough lower-elevation forests to help the quetzals survive.

Although for many years **Monteverde Biological Cloud Forest Reserve** was *the* place to see quetzals, throngs of people crowding the reserve's trails now make the pursuit more difficult. Other places where you can see quetzals are in the **Los Angeles Cloud Forest Reserve** near San Ramón, in **Tapantí National Wildlife Refuge,** and in **Chirripó National Park.** Perhaps the best place to spot a quetzal is at one of the specialized lodges located along the Cerro de la Muerte between San José and San Isidro de El General.

some of the most pristine and undeveloped nooks and crannies of the country. Those who relish sleeping out on a beach but wouldn't mind a bit more luxury (beds, someone to prepare meals for you, and running water) might want to consider staying at the **Corcovado Lodge Tent Camp** on the Osa Peninsula (p. 346). Camping is forbidden in some national parks, so read the descriptions for each park carefully before you pack a tent.

If you'd like to participate in an organized camping trip, contact **Coast to Coast Adventures** (© 2280-8054; www.ctocadventures.com) or **Serendipity Adventures** (© 877/507-1358 in the U.S. and Canada, or 2558-1030; www.serendipity adventures.com).

In my opinion, the best place to pop up a tent on the beach is in **Santa Rosa National Park** or at the Puerto Vargas campsite in **Cahuita National Park.** The best camping trek is, without a doubt, a hike through **Corcovado National Park** or a climb up **Mount Chirripó.**

CANOPY & CANYONING TOURS

Canopy tours are all the rage in Costa Rica, largely because they are such an exciting and unique way to experience tropical rainforests. It's estimated that some two-thirds of a typical rainforest's species live in the canopy (the uppermost, branching layer of the forest). From the relative luxury of Rain Forest Aerial Tram's high-tech funicular to the rope-and-climbing-gear rigs of more basic operations, a trip into the canopy will give you a bird's-eye view of a Neotropical forest. There are now canopy-tour operations in or close to nearly every major tourist destination in the country, including Monteverde, Manuel Antonio, La Fortuna, Tabacón, Montezuma, Punta Islita, Villablanca, and Rincón de la Vieja, as well as on Tortuga Island and around Guanacaste and the Osa Peninsula. There's even a small canopy tour in the La Sabana Park in downtown San José.

Most canopy tours involve strapping yourself into a climbing harness and being winched up to a platform some 30m (100 ft.) above the forest floor, or doing the work yourself. Many of these operations have a series of treetop platforms connected by taut cables. Once up on the first platform, you click your harness into a pulley and glide across the cable to the next (slightly lower) platform, using your hand (protected by a thick leather glove) as a brake. When you reach the last platform, you usually rappel down to the ground. (Don't worry—they'll teach even the most nervous neophyte.)

Although this can be a lot of fun, do be careful because these tours are popping up all over the place and there is precious little regulation of the activity. Some of the tours are set up by fly-by-night operators (obviously, I haven't listed any of those). Be especially sure that you feel comfortable and confident with the safety standards, guides, and equipment before embarking. Before you sign on to any tour, ask whether you have to hoist yourself to the top under your own steam, and then make your decision accordingly.

One of the country's more reputable operators is the **Original Canopy Tours** 𝕬 (𝒞 **2291-4465;** www.canopytour.com), which has sites in Monteverde and Mahogany Park, about an hour outside of San José. The operation in **Monteverde** features an ascent up the hollow interior of a giant strangler fig tree.

Another option is to try one of the tram or gondola tours through the canopy. The folks at Rain Forest Aerial Tram (see below) currently have two such operations, and there's a ski-lift-style gondola ride at **Turu BaRi Tropical Park** (𝒞 **2428-6070;** www. turubari.com) outside of San José. See "Side Trips from San José" in chapter 6 for more information.

Canyoning tours are even more adventurous. Hardly standardized, most involve hiking down along a mountain stream, river, and/or canyon, with periodic breaks to rappel down the face of a waterfall, or swim in a jungle pool. The best canyoning operations in Costa Rica are offered by **Pure Trek Canyoning** 𝕬𝕬 (𝒞 **866/569-5723** in the U.S. and Canada, or 2479-1313; www.puretrekcostarica.com) and **Desafío Expeditions** 𝕬𝕬 (𝒞 **2479-9464;** www.desafiocostarica.com), both in La Fortuna; and **Psycho Tours** 𝕬𝕬 (𝒞 **8353-8619;** www.psychotours.com), which operates outside of Puerto Jimenez.

Rain Forest Aerial Tram Caribbean 𝕬 (𝒞 **2257-5961;** www.rainforesttram.com) is located some 50 minutes from San José. For $55 (£28; transportation extra), this modern tram takes you on a 90-minute trip through the rainforest canopy in the comfort and safety of an enclosed cab. The entrance fee includes an additional guided hike and access to its trail system, butterfly garden, and other attractions. The best thing here isn't necessarily the tram ride, which I find somewhat disappointing, but the fact that this makes a good spot for a full-day excursion relatively close to San José. The outfit has a sister project on the central Pacific coast just outside of Jacó. See "Side Trips from San José" in chapter 6 and "Playa de Jacó, Playa Hermosa & Playa Herradura" in chapter 10 for more information.

> ⸨ *Tips* ⸩ **Beach Blanket Bingo**
>
> If you plan to spend time at the beach, it's often a good idea to pack your own beach towel or mat. Many of the midrange and budget hotels in Costa Rica do not provide them.

CRUISING

Cruising options in Costa Rica range from transient cruisers setting up a quick charter business to converted fishing boats taking a few guests out to see the sunset.

The most popular cruise option is a day trip from San José (the boats actually leave from Puntarenas) to **Tortuga Island** in the Nicoya Gulf (see "Side Trips from San José" in chapter 6). Alternatively, you can book a cruise to Tortuga from Playa Montezuma at the tip of the Nicoya Peninsula (see chapter 10 for details). It's much cheaper from here (around $40–$50/£20–£25 per person), but the excursion doesn't include the gourmet lunch that's usually featured on cruises leaving from San José.

If diesel fumes and engine noise bother you, the best places to charter a sailboat are in Playa del Coco, Playa Hermosa, and Playa Flamingo in Guanacaste province (see chapter 7); Playa Herradura and Quepos along the central Pacific coast (see chapter 10); and Golfito along the southern Pacific coast (see chapter 11). You can get information about sailboat rides and charters at any one of the larger lodgings in these areas. My favorite place to charter a sailboat is **Golfito.** From here, it's a pleasant, peaceful day's sail around the Golfo Dulce (see chapter 11).

DIVING & SNORKELING

Many islands, reefs, caves, and rocks lie off the coast of Costa Rica, providing excellent spots for underwater exploration. Visibility varies with season and location. Generally, heavy rainfall tends to swell the rivers and muddy the waters, even well offshore. Banana plantations and their runoff have destroyed most of the Caribbean reefs, although there's still good diving at **Isla Uvita,** just off the coast of Limón, and in **Manzanillo,** down near the Panamanian border. Most divers choose Pacific dive spots such as **Isla del Caño, Bat Island,** and the **Catalina Islands,** where you're likely to spot manta rays, moray eels, white-tipped sharks, and plenty of smaller fish and coral species. But the ultimate in Costa Rican dive experiences is 7 to 10 days on a chartered boat, diving off the coast of **Isla del Coco** (see "Diving Trips to Isla del Coco [Cocos Island]" on p. 206).

Snorkeling is not incredibly common or rewarding in Costa Rica. The rain, runoff, and wave conditions that drive scuba divers well offshore tend to make coastal and shallow-water conditions less than optimal. If the weather is calm and the water is clear, you might just get lucky. Ask at your hotel or check the different beach listings in this book to find snorkeling options and operators up and down Costa Rica's coasts. The best snorkeling experience to be had in Costa Rica is on the reefs off **Manzanillo Beach** in the southern Caribbean coast, particularly in the calm months of September and October.

DIVING OUTFITTERS & OPERATORS

In addition to the companies listed below, check the listings at specific beach and port destinations in the regional chapters.

Aggressor Fleet Limited ❀❀ (© **800/348-2628** in the U.S., or 2257-0191; www. aggressor.com) runs the 36m (118-ft.) *Okeanos Aggressor* on regular trips out to Isla del Coco.

Diving Mania (© **2291-2936;** www.divingmania.net) is a San José–based outfit that offers equipment rental, certification classes, and tours.

Diving Safaris de Costa Rica ❀❀ (© **2672-1260;** www.costaricadiving.net) is perhaps the largest, most professional, and best-established dive operation in the country. Based out of the Sol Playa Hermosa Hotel in Playa Hermosa, this outfitter is also a local pioneer in nitrox diving.

Undersea Hunter ❀❀ (© **800/203-2120** in the U.S., or 2228-6613; www.undersea hunter.com) offers the *Undersea Hunter* and its sister ship, the *Sea Hunter,* two pioneers of the live-aboard diving excursions to Isla del Coco.

FISHING

Anglers in Costa Rican waters have landed over 100 world-record catches, including blue marlin, Pacific sailfish, dolphin, wahoo, yellowfin tuna, guapote, and snook. Whether you want to head offshore looking for a big sail, wrestle a tarpon near a Caribbean river mouth, or choose a quiet spot on Arenal Lake to cast for guapote, you'll find it here. You can raise a marlin anywhere along the Pacific coast.

Many of the Pacific port and beach towns—Quepos, Puntarenas, Playa del Coco, Tamarindo, Flamingo, Golfito, Drake Bay, Zancudo—support large charter fleets and have hotels that cater to anglers; see chapters 7, 9, 10, and 11 for recommended boats, captains, and lodges. Costs for fishing trips usually range between $400 and $1,600 (£200–£800) per day (depending on the size of the boat) for boat, captain, tackle, drinks, and lunch, so the cost per person depends on the size of the group.

Costa Rica Outdoors ❀❀ (© **800/308-3394** in the U.S. or 2231-0306; www. costaricaoutdoors.com) is a well-established operation founded by longtime resident, fisherman, and outdoor writer Jerry Ruhlow, specializing in booking fishing trips around the country.

FISHING LODGES

Aguila de Osa Inn ❀ (© **866/924-8452** in the U.S. and Canada, or 2296-2190; www.aguiladeosainn.com) is a luxury lodge in Drake Bay. See p. 334.

The **Río Colorado Lodge** (© **800/243-9777** in the U.S. and Canada, or 2232-4063; www.riocoloradolodge.com) is located at the Barra del Colorado National Wildlife Refuge. See p. 362.

The **Zancudo Lodge** ❀❀ (© **800/854-8791** in the U.S., or 2776-0008; www. thezancudolodge.com) is located in Playa Zancudo. See p. 354.

Silver King Lodge ❀❀ (© **800/847-3474** in the U.S., or 2711-0708; www. silverkinglodge.net) is a luxury lodge at Barra del Colorado. See p. 362.

GOLF

Costa Rica is not one of the world's great golfing destinations—at least not yet, anyway. There are currently seven regulation 18-hole courses open to the public and visitors, but several others are either under construction or in the planning stages, with a potential boom shaping up in Guanacaste.

Currently, the best option for golfers staying in and around San José is **Parque Valle del Sol** ❀ (© **2282-9222;** www.vallesol.com), an 18-hole course in the western suburb of Santa Ana. Greens fees are $90 (£45), including a cart. The **Cariari Country**

Club ★★ (✆ 2293-3211), just outside of San José, is a private course and not open to the public. However, guests at the **Marriott Costa Rica** and some neighboring hotels can play. If you can wrangle an invitation, or are staying at a hotel with an agreement with the club, greens fees are $80 (£40), including a mandatory caddy. You should expect to tip your caddy around $10 (£5), and pay an extra $25 (£13) for a cart.

The Meliá chain also runs the **Garra de León course** ★★ at the **Paradisus Playa Conchal** resort (✆ 2654-4123; www.solmelia.com) up in Guanacaste. Greens fees here are $180 (£90), including a cart. With advance notice and depending on available tee times, this course is currently open to guests at other hotels in the region.

Another major resort course is at the **Los Sueños Marriott Ocean & Golf Resort** ★★ in Playa Herradura (✆ 800/228-9290 in the U.S., or 2630-9028; www.marriott.com). Greens fees, including a cart, run around $155 (£78) for the general public, and guests pay slightly less.

Hacienda Pinilla ★ (✆ 2680-7000; www.haciendapinilla.com) is an 18-hole links-style course located south of Tamarindo. This might just be the most challenging course in the country, and the facilities, though limited, are top-notch. Currently, the course is open to golfers staying at hotels around the area, with advance reservations. Greens fees run around $165 (£83) for 18 holes, including a cart.

The new **Papagayo Golf & Country Club** (✆ 2697-1313; www.papagayo-golf.com), on the outskirts of Playa del Coco, offers up a full 18-hole course, with a pro shop, driving range, and rental equipment. It costs $80 (£40) in greens fees, including a cart.

The most spectacular course in Costa Rica is at **Four Seasons Resort** ★★★ (✆ 212/688-2440 in the U.S., or 2696-0871; www.fourseasons.com), but it is open only to hotel guests. Greens fees run around $215 (£108).

Golfers who want the most up-to-date information, or those who are interested in a package deal that includes play on a variety of courses, should contact **Costa Rica Golf Adventures** ★ (✆ 877/258-2688; www.golfcr.com).

HANG GLIDING, PARAGLIDING & BALLOONING

Paragliding with a pilot in a tandem rig is taking off (pardon the pun) in the cliff areas around Caldera, just south of Puntarenas, as well as other spots around Costa Rica. If you're looking to paraglide, check in with the folks at the **Costa Rican Association of Free Flying** (call Miguel Dib at ✆ 8842-9644; www.parapente-costa-rica.org).

Serendipity Adventures (✆ 877/507-1358 in the U.S. and Canada, or 2558-1000; www.serendipityadventures.com) will take you up, up, and away in a hot-air balloon on a variety of single- or multiday tours, either in Turrialba, in Naranjo, or near Arenal Volcano. A basic flight costs around $345 (£173) per passenger, with a two-person minimum, and a five-person or 800-pound maximum.

Hang Glide Costa Rica (✆ 8353-5514; www.hangglidecr.com) offers about a half-hour of gentle hang gliding in a tandem rig, which begins with a tow by an ultra-light, for $99 to $150 (£50–£75) per person.

HORSEBACK RIDING

Costa Rica's rural roots are evident in the continued use of horses for real work and transportation throughout the country. Visitors will find that horses are easily available for riding, whether you want to take a sunset trot along the beach, ride through the cloud forest, or take a multiday trek through the northern zone.

Tips Tai Chi in Paradise

For the past 19 years, tai chi master and two-time U.S. national champion Chris Luth has been leading weeklong retreats to Costa Rica, combining intensive classes in this ancient Chinese martial art with rainforest hikes, river rafting, and just enough beach time. For more information, contact **T'ai Chi in Paradise** (© 858/259-1396; www.taichiinparadise.com).

Most travelers simply saddle up for a couple of hours, but those looking for a more specifically equestrian-based visit should check in with the following folks.

Coast to Coast Adventures (© 2280-8054; www.ctocadventures.com) specializes in 2-week trips spanning the country via horseback, raft, or mountain bike, as well as on foot, with no motor vehicles involved. Other trips are also available.

Nature Lodge Finca Los Caballos ✪ (©/fax 642-0124; www.naturelodge.net) specializes in horse tours, and has the healthiest horses in the Montezuma area.

Serendipity Adventures (© 877/507-1358 in the U.S. and Canada, or 2558-1030; www.serendipityadventures.com) offers horseback treks and tours.

MOTORCYCLES

Visiting bikers can either cruise the highways or try some off-road biking around Costa Rica. All the caveats about driving conditions and driving customs in Costa Rica apply equally for bikers. If you want to rent a Harley-Davidson for cruising around the country, **María Alexandra Tours** (© 2289-5552; www.mariaalexandra.com) conducts guided bike tours, and rents well-equipped late-model Harleys by the day or the week. If your tastes run to off-road riding, **MotoAdventures** (© 440/256-8508 in the U.S., or 2228-8494 in Costa Rica; www.motoadventuring.com) runs guided multiday tours on Honda dirt bikes. Bike rental rates run between $70 and $150 (£35–£75) per day.

ROCK CLIMBING

Although this is a nascent sport in Costa Rica, the possibilities are promising. There are several challenging rock formations close to San José and along the Cerro de la Muerte, as well as great climbing opportunities on Mount Chirripó. The folks at **Tropical Bungee** (© 2248-2212; www.bungee.co.cr) are the most dependable operators in this field, and they regularly organize climbing outings. Alternatively, you could visit **Mundo Aventura** (© 2221-6934; www.maventura.com), an adventure- and climbing-gear store with an indoor climbing wall and in-house tour company.

SPAS & YOGA RETREATS

In addition to the places listed below, the bar just may be getting raised, as **Miraval Resorts** (© 800/232-3969 in the U.S. and Canada; www.miravalresort.com) is slated to open a destination spa in Guanacaste by early 2010.

Hotel Borinquen Mountain Resort, Cañas Dulces (© 2690-1900; www.borinquen resort.com; p. 165), on the flanks of the Rincón de la Vieja volcano, has the setting, natural hot springs, volcanic mud pots, and luxurious accommodations to be a world-class destination spa. But, despite being in operation for several years, they've so far been unable to get the spa operation up to snuff.

The **Four Seasons Resort** ✪✪✪ (© 800/819-5053 in the U.S., or 2696-0000; www.fourseasons.com/costarica; p. 172) on the Papagayo Peninsula has ample and luxurious facilities and treatment options, as well as scheduled classes in yoga, aerobics, and other disciplines.

Samasati ⭐, Puerto Viejo de Talamanca (© **800/563-9643** in the U.S., or 2750-0315; www.samasati.com), is a lovely yoga retreat in some dense forest on a hillside above the Caribbean. Accommodations here range from budget to rustically luxurious. See "Puerto Viejo" in chapter 12.

Serenity Spa ⭐ (© **2643-4094;** www.serenityspacr.com) started out with a little storefront spa in Jacó but now contracts out the spa services at several large resorts up and down the Pacific coast. At last count, it was running the spas at Villas Caletas, Hotel Sí Como No, Villablanca, in San José.

Sueño Azul Resort ⭐⭐, Las Horquetas de Sarapiquí (© **2764-1048;** www.suenoazulresort.com; p. 241), is a nature lodge and retreat center with regular programs and retreats in a wonderful setting at the juncture of two rivers.

Tabacón Grand Spa Thermal Resort ⭐⭐⭐, Tabacón (© **877/277-8291** in the U.S. and Canada, or 2519-1900; www.tabacon.com; p. 248), is a top-notch spa with spectacular hot springs, lush gardens, and a volcano view. A complete range of spa services and treatments is available at reasonable prices.

Xandari Resort & Spa ⭐⭐, Alajuela (© **866/363-3212** in the U.S., or 2443-2020; www.xandari.com; p. 118), is a unique and distinctive little luxury hotel that has some top-notch spa facilities and services. This is a good choice if you're looking for a day or two of pampering, or for day treatments while staying in San José. Xandari has also opened a sister resort on the Central Pacific coast, for those looking for a beach spa retreat (p. 294).

SURFING

When *Endless Summer II,* the sequel to the all-time surf classic, was filmed, the production crew brought its boards and cameras to Costa Rica. Point and beach breaks that work year-round are located all along Costa Rica's immense coastline. **Playas Hermosa, Jacó,** and **Dominical,** on the central Pacific coast, and **Tamarindo** and **Playa Guiones,** in Guanacaste, are becoming mini surf meccas. **Salsa Brava** in Puerto Viejo is a steep and fast wave that peels off both right and left over shallow coral. It has a habit of breaking boards, but the daredevils keep coming back for more. Beginners and folks looking to learn should stick to the mellower sections of **Jacó** and **Tamarindo**—surf lessons are offered at both beaches. Crowds are starting to gather at the more popular breaks, but you can still stumble onto secret spots on the **Osa** and **Nicoya peninsulas** and along the northern Guanacaste coast. Costa Rica's signature wave is still found at **Playa Pavones,** which is reputed to have one of the longest lefts in the world. The cognoscenti, however, also swear by places such as **Playa Grande, Playa Negra, Matapalo, Malpaís,** and **Witch's Rock.** An avid surfer's best bet is to rent a dependable four-wheel-drive vehicle with a rack and take a surfin' safari around the breaks of Guanacaste.

If you're looking for an organized surf vacation, contact **Tico Travel** (© **800/493-8426** in the U.S.; www.ticotravel.com), or check out **www.crsurf.com**. For swell reports, general surf information, live wave-cams, and great links pages, point your browser to **www.surfline.com**. Although killer sets are possible at any particular spot at any time of the year, depending upon swell direction, local winds, and distant storms, in broad terms, the northern coast of Guanacaste works best from December to April; the central and southern Pacific coasts work best from April to November; and the Caribbean coast's short big-wave season is December through March.

WHITE-WATER RAFTING, KAYAKING & CANOEING

Whether you're a first-time rafter or a world-class kayaker, Costa Rica's got some white water suited to your abilities. Rivers rise and fall with the rainfall, but you can get wet and wild here even in the dry season. The best white-water rafting ride is still the scenic **Pacuare River;** although there has been talk about damming it to build a hydroelectric plant, the project has thankfully failed to materialize. If you're just experimenting with river rafting, stick to Class II and III rivers, such as **Reventazón, Sarapiquí, Peñas Blancas,** and **Savegre.** If you already know which end of the paddle goes in the water, there are plenty of Class IV and V sections to run.

Die-hard river rats should get *Chasing Jaguars: The Complete Guide to Costa Rican Whitewater,* by Lee Eudy (Earthbound Sports Inc., 2003), a book loaded with photos, technical data, and route tips on almost every rideable river in the country.

Aventuras Naturales ★★ (© **800/321-8410** in the U.S., or 2225-3939; www. toenjoynature.com) is a major rafting operator that runs daily trips on the most popular rivers in Costa Rica. Its Pacuare Jungle Lodge is pretty plush, and a great place to spend the night on one of its 2-day rafting trips.

Canoe Costa Rica (©/fax **732/736-6586** in the U.S., or 2282-3579; www.canoe costarica.com) is the only outfit I know of that specializes in canoe trips; it works

---

In Search of Turtles

Few places in the world have as many sea-turtle nesting sites as Costa Rica. Along both coasts, five species of these huge marine reptiles come ashore at specific times of the year to dig nests in the sand and lay their eggs. Sea turtles are endangered throughout the world due to over-hunting, accidental deaths in fishing nets, development on beaches that once served as nesting areas, and the collection and sale (often illegally) of their eggs. International trade in sea-turtle products is already prohibited by most countries (including the U.S.), but sea-turtle numbers continue to dwindle.

Among the species of sea turtles that nest on Costa Rica's beaches are the **olive ridley** (known for their mass egg-laying migrations, or *arribadas*), **leatherback, hawksbill, green,** and **Pacific green turtle.** Excursions to see nesting turtles have become common, and they are fascinating, but please make sure that you and/or your guide do not disturb the turtles. Any light source (other than red-tinted flashlights) can confuse female turtles and cause them to return to the sea without laying their eggs. In fact, as more development takes place on the Costa Rican coast, hotel lighting may cause the number of nesting turtles to drop. Luckily, many of the nesting beaches have been protected as national parks.

Here are the main places to see nesting sea turtles: **Santa Rosa National Park** (near Liberia), **Las Baulas National Marine Park** (near Tamarindo), **Ostional National Wildlife Refuge** (near Playa Nosara), and **Tortuguero National Park** (on the northern Caribbean coast).

See the regional chapters for descriptions of the resident turtles and their respective nesting seasons, as well as listings of local tour operators and companies that arrange trips to see sea turtles nesting.

primarily with custom-designed tours and itineraries, although it does have several set departure trips each year.

Exploradores Outdoors ✦ (© **2222-6262;** www.exploradoresoutdoors.com) is another good company run by a longtime and well-respected river guide. They run the Pacuare, Reventazón, and Sarapiquí rivers, and even combine a 1-day river trip with onward transportation to or from the Caribbean coast, or the Arenal volcano area, for no extra cost.

If you're out on the Osa Peninsula, hook up with **Escondido Trex** ✦ (©/fax **2735-5210;** www.escondidotrex.com).

Ríos Tropicales ✦ (© **866/722-8273** in the U.S. and Canada, or 2233-6455 in Costa Rica; www.riostropicales.com) is one of the major operators in Costa Rica, operating on most of the popular rivers. Lodgings include a very comfortable lodge on the banks of the Río Pacuare for the 2-day trips.

WINDSURFING & KITEBOARDING

Windsurfing is not very popular on the high seas here, where winds are fickle and rental options are limited, even at beach hotels. However, **Lake Arenal** is considered one of the top spots in the world for high-wind boardsailing. During the winter months, many of the regulars from Washington's Columbia River Gorge take up residence around the nearby town of Tilarán. Small boards, water starts, and fancy gibes are the norm. The best time for windsurfing on Lake Arenal is between December and March. The same winds that buffet Lake Arenal make their way down to **Bahía Salinas** (also known as Bolaños Bay), near La Cruz, Guanacaste, where you can get in some good windsurfing. Both spots have also recently seen the opening of operations offering lessons and equipment rentals in the new high-action sport of kiteboarding. See "La Cruz & Bahía Salinas" in chapter 7 and "Along the Shores of Lake Arenal" in chapter 9 for details.

3 Costa Rica's Top National Parks & Bioreserves

Costa Rica has 28 national parks, protecting more than 12% of the country. They range in size from the 212-hectare (524-acre) Guayabo National Monument to the 189,696-hectare (468,549-acre) La Amistad National Park. Many of these national parks are undeveloped tropical forests, with few services or facilities available for visitors. Others, however, offer easier access to their wealth of natural wonders.

Most of the national parks charge a $10 (£5) per-person per-day fee for any foreigner, although Chirripó National Park costs $15 (£7.50) per day. Costa Ricans and foreign residents continue to pay just $1 (50p). At parks where camping is allowed, there is usually an additional charge of around $2 (£1) per person per day.

This section is not a complete listing of all of Costa Rica's national parks and protected areas, but rather a selective list of those parks that are of greatest interest and accessibility. They're popular, but they're also among the best. You'll find detailed information about food and lodging options near some of the individual parks in the regional chapters that follow. As you'll see from the descriptions, Costa Rica's national parks vary greatly in terms of attractions, facilities, and accessibility. For a map of the country's key parks, see the color insert at the front of this book.

If you're looking for a camping adventure or an extended stay in one of the national parks, I recommend **Santa Rosa, Rincón de la Vieja, Chirripó, Corcovado,** or **Cahuita.** Any of the others are better suited for day trips or guided hikes, or in combination with your travels around the country.

For more information, call the national parks information line at ℭ **192,** or the main office at ℭ **2283-8004.** You can also stop by the **National Parks Foundation office** (ℭ 2257-2239) in San José, located between Calle 23 and Avenida 15. Both offices are open Monday through Friday from 9am to 5pm.

SAN JOSE/CENTRAL VALLEY AREA

GUAYABO NATIONAL MONUMENT   This is the country's only significant pre-Columbian archaeological site. It's believed that Guayabo supported a population of about 10,000 people some 3,000 years ago. The park is set in a forested area rich in flora and fauna, although the ruins are quite small and limited when compared to sites in Mexico, Guatemala, and South America. **Location:** 19km (12 miles) northeast of Turrialba, which is 53km (33 miles) east of San José. See "Side Trips from San José" in chapter 6.

IRAZU VOLCANO NATIONAL PARK ✮   Irazú Volcano is the highest (3,378m/11,080 ft.) of Costa Rica's four active volcanoes and a popular day trip from San José. A paved road leads right up to the crater, and the lookout also has a view of both the Pacific and the Caribbean on a clear day. The volcano last erupted in 1963 on the same day U.S. President John F. Kennedy visited the country. There are an information center, picnic tables, restrooms, and a parking area here. **Location:** 55km (34 miles) east of San José. See "Holy Smoke! Choosing the Volcano Trip That's Right for You" in chapter 6.

POAS VOLCANO NATIONAL PARK ✮✮   Poás is the other active volcano close to San José. The main crater is more than 1.6km (1 mile) wide, and it is constantly active with fumaroles and hot geysers. I slightly prefer Poás to Irazú because it is sur-rounded by dense cloud forests, and there are some nice gentle trails to hike here. Although the area around the volcano is lush, much of the growth is stunted due to the gases and acid rain. The park sometimes closes when the gases get too feisty. There are nature trails, picnic tables, restrooms, and an information center. **Location:** 37km (23 miles) northwest of San José. See "Holy Smoke! Choosing the Volcano Trip That's Right for You" in chapter 6.

GUANACASTE & THE NICOYA PENINSULA

BARRA HONDA NATIONAL PARK   Costa Rica's only underground national park, Barra Honda features a series of limestone caves that were once part of a coral reef some 60 million years ago. Today the caves are home to millions of bats and impressive stalactite and stalagmite formations. Only Terciopelo Cave is open to the public. A camping area, restrooms, and an information center are here, as well as trails through the surrounding tropical dry forest. **Location:** 335km (208 miles) northwest of San José. See "Playa Sámara" in chapter 8.

PALO VERDE NATIONAL PARK   A must for bird-watchers, Palo Verde National Park is one of Costa Rica's best-kept secrets. This part of the Tempisque River low-lands supports a population of more than 50,000 waterfowl and forest bird species. Various ecosystems here include mangroves, savanna brush lands, and evergreen forests. There are camping facilities, an information center, and some nice, fairly new accommodations at the Organization for Tropical Studies (OTS) research station here. **Location:** 200km (124 miles) northwest of San José. Be warned that the park entrance is 28km (17 miles) off the highway down a very rugged dirt road; it's another 9km (5½ miles) to the OTS station and campsites. For more information, call the OTS (ℭ **240-6696;** reservas@cro.ots.ac.cr). See "Liberia" in chapter 7.

RINCON DE LA VIEJA NATIONAL PARK 🎯🎯   This large tract of parkland experiences high volcanic activity, with numerous fumaroles and geysers, as well as hot springs, cold pools, and mud pots. You'll find excellent hikes to the upper craters and to several waterfalls. You should hire a guide for any hot-spring or mud-bath expeditions as inexperienced visitors have been burned. Camping is permitted at two sites, each of which has an information center, a picnic area, and restrooms. **Location:** 266km (165 miles) northwest of San José. See "Liberia" in chapter 7.

SANTA ROSA NATIONAL PARK 🎯   Occupying a large section of Costa Rica's northwestern Guanacaste province, Santa Rosa has the country's largest area of tropical dry forest, important turtle-nesting sites, and the historically significant La Casona monument. There are also caves for exploring. The beaches are pristine and have basic camping facilities, and the waves make them quite popular with surfers. An information center, a picnic area, and restrooms are at the main campsite and entrance. **Location:** 258km (160 miles) northwest of San José. For more information, you can call the park office at © **666-5051.** See "La Cruz & Bahía Salinas" in chapter 7.

THE NORTHERN ZONE

ARENAL NATIONAL PARK 🎯🎯   This park, created to protect the ecosystem that surrounds Arenal Volcano, has few services or attractions. Basically, the government has set up a tollbooth on the access road leading to an up-close view of the volcano's lava flows. Most travelers and tour operators choose to forgo the entrance fee and watch the volcano from spots along the dirt road leading to the Arenal Observatory Lodge, or from the road to Tabacón, where the view is just as good as it is inside the park. However, there are several excellent hiking trails inside the park that explore cooled-off lava flows and the neighboring rainforest. **Location:** 129km (80 miles) northwest of San José. See "Arenal Volcano & La Fortuna" in chapter 8.

BRAULIO CARRILLO NATIONAL PARK   Braulio Carillo, which occupies a large area of the nation's central mountain range, is the park you pass through on your way from San José to the Caribbean coast. A deep rainforest, Braulio Carrillo receives an average of 177 inches of rain per year. There are beautiful rivers, majestic waterfalls, and more than 6,500 species of plants and animals. The park has an information center, picnic tables, restrooms, and hiking trails. Camping is allowed but is not common or recommended. Be careful here. Make sure you park your car in and base your explorations from the park's main entrance, not just anywhere along the highway. There have been several robberies and attacks against visitors reported at trails leading into the park from the highway. This park also seems to have the highest incidence of lost hikers. **Location:** 22km (14 miles) north of San José. See "Puerto Viejo de Sarapiquí" in chapter 9.

CAÑO NEGRO NATIONAL WILDLIFE REFUGE 🎯   A lowland swamp and drainage basin for several northern rivers, Caño Negro is excellent for bird-watching. There are a few basic cabinas and lodges in this area, but the most popular way to visit is on a combined van and boat trip from the La Fortuna/Arenal area. **Location:** 20km (12 miles) south of Los Chiles, near the Nicaraguan border. See "Arenal Volcano & La Fortuna" in chapter 9.

MONTEVERDE BIOLOGICAL CLOUD FOREST RESERVE 🎯🎯🎯   This private reserve might be the most famous patch of forest in Costa Rica. It covers some 26,000 acres of primary forest, mostly mid-elevation cloud forest, with a rich variety of flora and fauna. Epiphytes thrive in the cool, misty climate. The most famous resident is the spectacular resplendent quetzal. There is a well-maintained trail system, as well as some of the best-trained and most experienced guides in the country. Nearby you can visit both the Santa Elena and Sendero Tranquilo reserves. **Location:** 167km (104 miles) northwest of San José. See "Monteverde" in chapter 9.

CENTRAL PACIFIC COAST

CARARA NATIONAL PARK Located just off the highway near the Pacific coast, on the road to Jacó, this is one of the best places in Costa Rica to see scarlet macaws. Several trails run through the park, including one that is wheelchair accessible. The park is comprised of various ecosystems, ranging from rainforests to transitional forests to mangroves. **Location:** 102km (63 miles) west of San José. See "Playa de Jacó, Playa Hermosa & Playa Herradura" in chapter 10.

CHIRRIPO NATIONAL PARK Home to Costa Rica's tallest peak, 3,761m (12,336-ft.) Mount Chirripó, Chirripó National Park is a hike, but on a clear day you can see both the Pacific Ocean and the Caribbean Sea from its summit. There are a number of interesting climbing trails here, and camping is allowed. **Location:** 151km (94 miles) southeast of San José. See "San Isidro de El General: A Base for Exploring Chirripó National Park" in chapter 10.

MANUEL ANTONIO NATIONAL PARK Though relatively small, Manuel Antonio is the most popular national park and supports the largest number of hotels and resorts. This lowland rainforest is home to a healthy monkey population, including the endangered squirrel monkey. The park is best known for its splendid beaches. **Location:** 129km (80 miles) south of San José. See "Manuel Antonio National Park" in chapter 10.

THE SOUTHERN ZONE

CORCOVADO NATIONAL PARK The largest single block of virgin lowland rainforest in Central America, Corcovado National Park receives more than 200 inches of rain per year. It's increasingly popular but still very remote. (It has no roads; only dirt tracks lead into it.) Scarlet macaws live here, as do countless other Neotropical species, including two of the country's largest cats, the puma and the endangered jaguar. There are camping facilities and trails throughout the park. **Location:** 335km (208 miles) south of San José, on the Osa Peninsula. See "Puerto Jiménez: Gateway to Corcovado National Park" in chapter 11.

THE CARIBBEAN COAST

CAHUITA NATIONAL PARK A combination land and marine park, Cahuita National Park protects one of the few remaining living coral reefs in the country. The topography here is lush lowland tropical rainforest. Monkeys and numerous bird species are common. Camping is permitted, and there are basic facilities at the Puerto Vargas entrance to the park. If you want to visit for only the day, however, enter from Cahuita village because the local community has taken over that entrance and is asking for only a voluntary donation, in lieu of the normal $6 (£3) fee. **Location:** On the Caribbean coast, 42km (26 miles) south of Limón. See "Cahuita" in chapter 12.

TORTUGUERO NATIONAL PARK Tortuguero National Park has been called the Venice of Costa Rica due to its maze of jungle canals that meander through a dense lowland rainforest. Small boats, launches, and canoes carry visitors through these waterways, where caimans, manatees, and numerous bird and mammal species are common. The extremely endangered great green macaw lives here. On the beaches green sea turtles nest here every year between June and October. The park has a small but helpful information office and some well-marked trails. **Location:** 258km (160 miles) northeast of San José. See "Tortuguero National Park" in chapter 12.

4 Tips on Health, Safety & Etiquette in the Wilderness

Much of what is discussed here is common sense. For more detailed information, see "Health" in chapter 3. Although most tours and activities are safe, there are risks involved in any adventure activity. Know and respect your own physical limits before undertaking any strenuous activity. Be prepared for extremes in temperature and rainfall and for wide fluctuations in weather. A sunny morning hike can quickly become a cold and wet ordeal, so it's usually a good idea to carry along some form of rain gear when hiking in the rainforest, or to have a dry change of clothing waiting at the end of the trail. Be sure to bring along plenty of sunscreen when you're not going to be covered by the forest canopy.

If you do any backcountry packing or camping, remember that it really *is* a jungle out there. Don't go poking under rocks or fallen branches. Snakebites are very rare, but don't do anything to increase the odds. If you encounter a snake, stay calm, don't make any sudden movements, and *do not* try to handle it. Also avoid swimming in major rivers unless a guide or local operator can vouch for their safety. Although white-water sections and stretches in mountainous areas are generally safe, most mangrove canals and river mouths in Costa Rica support healthy crocodile and caiman populations.

Bugs and bug bites will probably be your greatest health concern in the Costa Rican wilderness, and even they aren't as big of a problem as you might expect. Mostly, bugs are an inconvenience, although mosquitoes can carry malaria or dengue (see "Health," in chapter 3, for more information). A strong repellent and proper clothing minimize both the danger and the inconvenience; you might also want to bring along some cortisone or Benadryl cream to soothe itching. At the beaches, you'll probably be bitten by *pirujas* (sand fleas). These nearly invisible insects leave an irritating welt. Try not to scratch because this can lead to open sores and infections. Pirujas are most active at sunrise and sunset, so you might want to cover up or avoid the beaches at these times.

And remember: Whenever you enter and enjoy nature, you should tread lightly and try not to disturb the natural environment. There's a popular slogan well known to most campers that certainly applies here: "Leave nothing but footprints; take nothing but memories." If you must take home a souvenir, take photos. Do not cut or uproot plants or flowers. Pack out everything you pack in, and *please* do not litter.

5 Volunteer & Study Programs
LANGUAGE IMMERSION

As more people travel to Costa Rica with the intention of learning Spanish, the number of options for Spanish immersion vacations increases. You can find courses of varying lengths and degrees of intensiveness, and many that include cultural activities and day excursions. Many of these schools have reciprocal relationships with U.S. universities, so, in some cases, you can even arrange for college credit. Most Spanish schools can arrange for home stays with a middle-class Tico family for a total-immersion

Monkey Business

No trip to Costa Rica would be complete without at least one monkey sighting. Home to four distinct species of primates, Costa Rica offers the opportunity for one of the world's most gratifying wildlife-viewing experiences. Just listen for the deep guttural call of a howler or the rustling of leaves overhead—telltale signs that monkeys are in your vicinity.

Costa Rica's most commonly spotted monkey is the white-faced or **capuchin monkey** (*mono cara blanca* in Spanish), which you might recognize as the infamous culprit from the film *Outbreak*. Contrary to that film's plot, however, capuchins are native to the New World tropics and do not exist in Africa. Capuchins are agile, medium-size monkeys that make good use of their long, prehensile tails. They inhabit a diverse collection of habitats, ranging from the high-altitude cloud forests of the central region to the lowland mangroves of the Osa Peninsula. It's almost impossible not to spot capuchins at Manuel Antonio (see chapter 10), where they have become a little too dependent on fruit and junk-food feedings by tourists. Please do not feed wild monkeys (and try to keep your food away from them—they're notorious thieves), and boycott establishments that try to attract both monkeys and tourists with daily feedings.

Howler monkeys (*mono congo* in Spanish) are named for their distinct and eerie call. Large and mostly black, these monkeys can seem ferocious because of their physical appearance and deep, resonant howls that can carry for more than a mile, even in dense rainforest. Biologists believe that male howlers mark the bounds of their territories with these deep, guttural sounds. In the presence of humans, however, howlers are actually a little timid and tend to stay higher up in the canopy than their white-faced cousins. Howlers are fairly common and easy to spot in the dry tropical forests of coastal Guanacaste and the Nicoya Peninsula (see chapter 7).

Even more elusive are **spider monkeys** (*mono araña* in Spanish). These long, slender monkeys are dark brown to black and prefer the high canopies of primary rainforests. Spiders are very adept with their prehensile tails but actually travel through the canopy with a hand-over-hand motion frequently imitated by their less graceful human cousins on playground monkey bars around the world. I've had my best luck spotting spider monkeys along the edges of Tortuguero's jungle canals (see chapter 12), where howlers are also quite common.

The rarest and most endangered of Costa Rica's monkeys is the tiny **squirrel monkey** (*mono tití* in Spanish). These small, brown monkeys have dark eyes surrounded by large white rings, white ears, white chests, and very long tails. In Costa Rica, squirrel monkeys can be found only at Manuel Antonio (see chapter 10) and the Osa Peninsula (see chapter 11). These seemingly hyperactive monkeys are predominantly fruit eaters and often feed on bananas and other fruit trees near hotels in both of the above-mentioned regions. Squirrel monkeys usually travel in large bands, so if you do see them, you'll likely see quite a few.

experience. Classes are often small, or even one-on-one, and can last anywhere from 2 to 8 hours a day. Listed below are some of the larger and more established Spanish-language schools, with approximate costs. Most are located in San José, but there are also schools in Monteverde, Manuel Antonio, Playa Flamingo, Malpaís, Playa Nosara, and Tamarindo. (I'd certainly rather spend 2 weeks or a month in one of these spots than in San José.) Contact the schools for the most current price information.

Adventure Education Center (AEC) Spanish Institute ⚡ (© 800/237-2730 in the U.S. and Canada, or 2248-0147; www.adventurespanishschool.com) has branches in La Fortuna, Dominical, and Turrialba, and specializes in combining language learning with adventure activities. A 1-week course here with 4 hours of classes each day, including room and board with a Costa Rican family, costs $400 (£200).

Centro Lingüístico Conversa ⚡ (© 888/669-1664 in the U.S. and Canada, or 2221-7649; www.conversa.net) has classes in both San José and Santa Ana (a suburb of the capital city). A 1-week course here with 4 hours of classes each day, including room and board with a Costa Rican family, costs between $500 and $715 (£250–£358), depending on which campus you choose.

Centro Panamericano de Idiomas (CPI) ⚡ (© 877/373-3116 in the U.S., or 2265-6306; www.cpi-edu.com) has three campuses: one in the quiet suburban town of Heredia, another in Monteverde, and one at the beach in Playa Flamingo. A 1-week program, with 4 hours of class per day and a home stay with a Costa Rican family, costs $465 (£233).

Costa Rican Language Academy ⚡ in San José (© 866/230-6361 in the U.S., or 2280-5164; www.spanishandmore.com) has intensive programs with classes held Monday to Thursday to give students a chance for longer weekend excursions. The academy also integrates Latin dance and Costa Rican cooking classes into the program. A 1-week class with 4 hours of class per day, plus a home stay, costs $321 (£161).

Costa Rica Spanish Institute (COSI) (© 2234-1001; www.cosi.co.cr) offers small classes in the San Pedro neighborhood of San José, as well as a program at Manuel Antonio. The weekly cost of $450 (£225) includes a home stay.

Forester Instituto Internacional ⚡ (© 2225-3155 or 2225-0135; www.fores.com), is 75m (246 ft.) south of the Automercado in the Los Yoses district of San José. I've received glowing reports from satisfied customers here. The cost of a 1-week language course with a home stay and excursions is approximately $570 (£285).

Institute for Central American Development Studies (ICADS) ⚡⚡ near San Pedro (© 2225-0508; www.icads.org) has one of the best and most extensive field-work and volunteer programs in Costa Rica, as well as quality Spanish-language immersion programs. A 4-week course with home stay costs $1,900 (£950).

International House Costa Rica ⚡ (© 2234-9054; www.institutobritanico.co.cr), formerly the Instituto Britanico, is a venerable institution with installations in the Los Yoses neighborhood of San José. A bit more attention seems to be paid to teacher training and selection here than at other institutions around town. A 2-week course with 40 hours of classes and a home stay costs $810 (£405).

Escuela D'Amore ⚡ (© 800/261-3203 in the U.S. and Canada, or ©/fax 2777-1143; www.escueladamore.com) is situated in the lush surroundings of Manuel Antonio National Park. A 2-week conversational Spanish course, including a home stay and two meals daily, costs $995 (£498). This is a much nicer environment than San José for learning Spanish (for most everything else too, in fact).

Wayra Instituto de Español (℗/fax **2653-0359;** www.spanish-wayra.co.cr) is located in the beach town of Tamarindo. A week of classes, 4 hours per day, will run you $250 (£125). Home stays and apartment rentals can be arranged.

SUSTAINABLE VOLUNTEER PROJECTS

Below are some institutions and organizations that are working on ecology and sustainable development projects.

APREFLOFAS (Association for the Preservation of the Wild Flora and Fauna) (℗ **2574-6816;** www.preserveplanet.org) is a pioneering local conservation organization that accepts volunteers and runs environmentally sound educational tours around the country.

Asociación de Voluntarios para el Servicio en las Areas Protegidas (ASVO) ✿ (℗ **2258-4430;** www.asvocr.org) organizes volunteers to work in Costa Rican national parks. A 2-week minimum commitment is required, as is a basic ability to converse in Spanish. Housing is provided at a basic ranger station, and there is a $15 (£7.50) daily fee to cover food, which is basic Tico fare.

Caribbean Conservation Corporation (℗ **800/676-2018** in the U.S., or 2278-6058; www.cccturtle.org) is a nonprofit organization dedicated to sea turtle research, protection, and advocacy. Their main operation in Costa Rica is headquartered in Tortuguero, where volunteers can aid in various scientific studies, as well as nightly patrols of the beach during nesting seasons to prevent poaching.

Costa Rica Rainforest Outward Bound School (℗ **800/676-2018** in the U.S., or 2278-6058; www.crrobs.org) is the local branch of this well-respected international adventure-based outdoor-education organization. Courses range from 2 weeks to a full semester, and offerings include surfing, kayaking, tree climbing, and learning Spanish.

Earthwatch Institute (℗ **800/776-0188** in the U.S.; www.earthwatch.org) organizes volunteers to go on research trips to help scientists collect data and conduct field experiments in a number of scientific fields and a wide range of settings. Expeditions to Costa Rica range from studies of the nesting habits of leatherback sea turtles to research into sustainable coffee-growing methods. Fees for food and lodging average around $2,750 (£1,375) for a 2-week expedition, excluding airfare.

Eco Teach (℗ **800/626-8992** in the U.S.; www.ecoteach.com) works primarily in facilitating educational trips for high school and college student groups. Trips focus on Costa Rican ecology and culture. Costs run around $1,445 to $1,595 (£723–£798) per person for a 10-day trip, including lodging, meals, classes, and travel within the country. Airfare to Costa Rica is extra.

Global Volunteers (℗ **800/487-1074** in the U.S.; www.globalvolunteers.org) is a U.S.-based organization that offers a unique opportunity to travelers who've always wanted a Peace Corps–like experience but can't make a 2-year commitment. For 2 to 3 weeks, you can join one of its working vacations in Costa Rica. A certain set of skills, such as engineering or agricultural knowledge, is helpful but by no means necessary. Each trip is undertaken at a particular community's request, to complete a specific project. However, be warned: These "volunteer" experiences do not come cheap. You must pay for your transportation as well as a hefty program fee, around $2,495 (£1,248) for a 2-week program.

Habitat for Humanity International (℗ **2296-3436;** www.habitatcostarica.org) has several chapters in Costa Rica and sometimes runs organized Global Village programs here.

The **Institute for Central American Development Studies** ✱ (© 2225-0508; www.icads.org) offers internship and research opportunities in the areas of environment, agriculture, human rights, and women's studies. An intensive Spanish-language program can be combined with work-study or volunteer opportunities.

The **Monteverde Institute** (© 2645-5053; www.mvinstitute.org) offers study programs in Monteverde and also has a volunteer center that helps in placement and training of volunteers.

The **Organization for Tropical Studies** ✱ (© 2524-0607; www.threepaths.co.cr) represents several Costa Rican and U.S. universities. This organization's mission is to promote research, education, and the wise use of natural resources in the Tropics. Research facilities include La Selva Biological Station near Braulio Carrillo National Park and Palo Verde, and the Wilson Botanical Gardens near San Vito. Housing is provided at one of the research facilities. There's a wide variety of programs, ranging from full-semester undergraduate programs to specific graduate courses (of varying duration) to its tourist programs. (These are generally being sponsored/run by established operators such as Costa Rica Expeditions and Elderhostel.) These range in duration from 3 to 10 days, and costs vary greatly. Entrance requirements and competition for some of these courses can be demanding.

Vida (© 2221-8367; www.vida.org) is a local nongovernmental organization working on sustainable development and conservation issues; it can often place volunteers. However, their website is entirely in Spanish, and some reasonable Spanish language skills are recommended for working with them.

6

San José

Gone are the days when all international tourists to Costa Rica had to spend at least some time in San José. With the increasing number of direct flights into Liberia, San José is no longer the de facto transportation hub for all arriving travelers, but most do still fly in and out of the country's capital. For as long as I've written this book, my stock advice to tourists in terms of San José has been to get in and out as quickly as possible. In most cases, this remains good counsel. But San José is the country's only major metropolitan city, with varied and active restaurant and nightlife scenes, several museums and galleries worth visiting, and a steady stream of theater, concerts, and other cultural events that you won't find elsewhere in the country.

At first blush, San José seems little more than a chaotic jumble of cars, buses, buildings, and people. The central downtown section of San José exists in a near-constant state of gridlock. Antiquated buses spewing diesel fumes and a lack of emission controls have created a brown cloud over the city's sky. Sidewalks are poorly maintained and claustrophobic, and street crime is a serious problem. Most visitors quickly seek the sanctuary of their hotel room and the first chance to escape the city.

Still, things have been improving in recent years. Mayor Johnny Araya has led ambitious and controversial campaigns to rid the narrow sidewalks of impromptu and illegal vendors, to reduce the clutter of billboards and overhead signs, and to bury a good share of the city's electrical and phone cables.

This chapter helps you plan whatever time you intend for the capital and ease your way through the pitfalls inherent in such a rough-and-tumble little city.

IT'S IN THE BEANS San José was built on the profits of the coffee-export business. Between the airport and downtown, you'll pass working coffee farms. Glance up from almost any street in the city and on the surrounding volcanic mountains you'll see a patchwork quilt of farm fields, most of which are planted with the *grano de oro* (golden bean), as it's known here. San José was a forgotten backwater of the Spanish empire until the first shipments of the local beans made their way to sleepy souls in Europe late in the 19th century. Soon San José was riding high. Coffee planters, newly rich and craving culture, imposed a tax on themselves to build the Teatro Nacional (National Theater), San José's most beautiful building. Coffee profits also built the city a university. Today you can wake up and smell the coffee roasting as you wander the streets near the Central Market (Mercado Central), and in any cafe or restaurant you can get a hot cup of sweet, milky *café con leche* to taste the bean that built San José.

Part of the reason the coffee grows so well is the climate. The Central Valley, in which the city sits, has what's often been described as a perfect climate. At 1,125m (3,690 ft.) above sea level, San José enjoys springlike temperatures year-round. The pleasant climate, along with the beautiful views of lush green mountainsides, makes

San José a memorable city to visit. All you have to do is glance up at those mountains to know that this is one of the most beautifully situated capitals in Central America. And if a glance isn't enough for you, you'll find that it's extremely easy to get out into the countryside. Within an hour or two, you can climb a volcano, go white-water rafting, hike through a cloud forest, and stroll through a butterfly garden—among many other activities.

1 Orientation

ARRIVING
BY PLANE

Juan Santamaría International Airport (© **2437-2626** for 24-hr. airport information; airport code SJO) is near the city of Alajuela, about 20 minutes from downtown San José. A taxi into town costs between $12 and $18 (£6–£9), and a bus is only 75¢ (35p). The Alajuela–San José buses run frequently and will drop you off anywhere along Paseo Colón or at a station near the Parque de la Merced (downtown, btw. calles 12 and 14 and avs. 2 and 4). There are two separate lines: **Tuasa** (© **2442-6900**) buses are red; **Station Wagon** (© **8388-9263**) buses are beige/yellow. At the airport you'll find the bus stop directly in front of the main terminal, beyond the parking structure. Be sure to ask whether the bus is going to San José, or you'll end up in Alajuela. If you have a lot of luggage, you should probably take a cab.

Quite a few car-rental agencies have desks and offices at the airport, although if you're planning to spend a few days in San José itself, a car is a liability. (If you're heading off immediately to the beach, though, it's much easier to pick up your car here than at a downtown office.) Several car-rental agencies already have desks inside the new terminal, right where passengers exit Customs and Immigration; others are still awaiting completion of an airport remodeling (see below), so be sure to contact them first to confirm that they will have an agent or an office at the airport when you arrive.

At press time the airport was still in the midst of a major renovation and expansion, a process that has been plagued by work stoppages, delays, and bickering between the government and international company in charge of the work. So far, the first phase of the new terminal has been completed, and all of the major airlines have moved their desks into the terminal. Unfortunately, the new baggage claim and Customs and Immigration areas, which are modern and spacious, are not necessarily fast and efficient. Moreover, despite the major remodeling, chaos and confusion continue to greet arriving passengers the second they step out of the terminal. You must abandon your luggage carts just before exiting the building and then face a gauntlet of aggressive taxi drivers and people offering to carry your bags. Fortunately, the official airport taxi service (see below) has a booth inside the terminal after you clear Customs. Most porters or skycaps wear a uniform identifying them as such, but sometimes "improvised" porters will try to earn a few dollars here. (Moreover, there's often really nowhere for them to have to carry your bags because the line of waiting taxis and shuttles is just steps away.) The entire airport renovation and expansion should be completed sometime in mid-2009. There is hope that things will improve once the work is done and new facilities are opened.

In terms of taxis, you should stick with the official airport taxi service, **Taxis Unidos Aeropuerto** (© **2221-6865**), which operates a fleet of orange vans and sedans, charging fixed prices according to your destination. Head to its kiosk in the no man's land just outside the exit door for arriving passengers. Here you can buy a prepaid voucher to the hotel or destination of your choice. Despite the fact that Taxis Unidos has an official monopoly at the airport, you will usually find a handful of regular cabs (in traditional red sedans) and "pirate" cabs, freelance drivers using their own vehicles. You could use either of these latter options, and they tend to charge a dollar or two less, but I recommend using the official service for safety and standardized prices. Keep a very watchful eye on your bags: Thieves have historically preyed on newly arrived passengers and their luggage. You should tip porters about 50¢ (25p) per bag.

You have several options for **exchanging money** when you arrive at the airport. There's an ATM in the baggage claim area, which is connected to both the PLUS and Cirrus networks. There's also a **Global Exchange** money exchange booth just as you clear Customs and Immigration. It's open whenever there are arriving flights; however, these folks exchange at more than 10% below the official rate. There's a branch of the **Banco de San José** inside the main terminal, on the second floor across from the airline check-in counters, as well as a couple more ATMs up there. The taxi company and rental-car agencies accept U.S. dollars. See "Money & Costs," in chapter 3, for more details.

Tip: There's really no pressing need to exchange money the minute you arrive. Taxis Unidos accepts dollars. You can wait until after you settle into your hotel, and see if the hotel will give you a good rate of exchange, or use one of the many downtown banks or ATMs.

If you arrive in San José via Nature Air, private aircraft, or another small commuter or charter airline, you might find yourself at the **Tobías Bolaños International Airport** in Pavas. This small airport is located on the western side of downtown San José, about 10 minutes by car from the center. There are no car-rental desks here, so unless you have a car or a driver waiting for you here, you will have to take a cab into town, which should cost between $10 and $20 (£5–£10).

BY BUS

If you're coming to San José by bus, where you disembark depends on where you're coming from. (The different bus companies have their offices, and thus their drop-off points, all over downtown San José. When you buy your ticket, ask where you'll be let off.) Buses arriving from Panama pass first through Cartago and San Pedro before letting passengers off in downtown San José; buses arriving from Nicaragua generally enter the city on the west end of town, on Paseo Colón. If you're staying here, you can ask to be let off before the final stop.

BY CAR

For those of you intrepid readers arriving by car, you'll enter San José via the Interamerican Highway. If you arrive **from Nicaragua and the north,** the highway brings you first past the airport and the city of Alajuela, to the western edge of downtown, right at the end of Paseo Colón, where it hits Parque La Sabana (La Sabana Park). The area is well marked with large road signs that direct you either to downtown (CENTRO) or to the western suburbs of Rohrmoser, Pavas, and Escazú. If you're heading toward downtown, follow the flow of traffic and turn left on Paseo Colón.

For those of you entering **from Panama and the south,** things get a little more complicated. The Interamerican Highway first passes through the city of Cartago and then through the San José suburbs of Curridabat and San Pedro before reaching downtown. This route is relatively well marked, and if you stick with the major flow of traffic, you should find San José without any problem.

"I Know There's Got to Be a Number Here Somewhere . . . ": The Arcane Art of Finding an Address in San José

This is one of the most confusing aspects of visiting Costa Rica in general, and San José in particular. Although there are often street addresses and building numbers for locations in downtown San José, they are almost never used. Addresses are given as a set of coordinates such as "Calle 3 between avenidas Central and 1." It's then up to you to locate the building within that block, keeping in mind that the building could be on either side of the street. Many addresses include additional information, such as the number of meters from a specified intersection or some other well-known landmark. (These "meter measurements" are not precise but are a good way to give directions to a taxi driver. In basic terms, 100m = 1 block, 200m = 2 blocks, and so on.) These landmarks are what become truly confusing for visitors to the city because they are often simply restaurants, bars, and shops that would be familiar only to locals.

Things get even more confusing when the landmark in question no longer exists. The classic example of this is "the Coca-Cola," one of the most common landmarks used in addresses in the blocks surrounding San José's main market. The trouble is, the Coca-Cola bottling plant that it refers to is no longer there; the edifice is long gone, and one of the principal downtown bus depots stands in its place. Old habits die hard, though, and the address description remains. You might also try to find someplace near the antiguo higuerón ("old fig tree") in San Pedro. This tree was felled years ago. In outlying neighborhoods, addresses can become long directions such as "50m (½ block) south of the old church, then 100m (1 block) east, then 20m (two buildings) south." Luckily for the visitor, most downtown addresses are more straightforward.

Oh, and if you're wondering how letter carriers manage, well, welcome to the club. Some folks actually get their mail delivered this way, but most people and businesses in San José use a post office box. This is called an apartado and is abbreviated "Apdo." or "A.P." in mailing addresses.

VISITOR INFORMATION

There's an **Instituto Costarricense de Turismo (ICT)** (© **2443-1535;** www.visit costarica.com) desk at the Juan Santamaría International Airport, located in the baggage claims area, just before Customs. You can pick up maps and browse brochures, and they might even lend you a phone to make or confirm a reservation. It's open daily from 9am to 10pm. If you're looking for the **main ICT visitor information center** in San José, it's located below the Plaza de la Cultura, at the entrance to the Gold Museum, on Calle 5 between avenidas Central and 2 (© **2222-1090**). The people here are helpful, although the information they have to offer is rather limited. This office is also open Monday through Saturday from 9am to 5pm.

CITY LAYOUT

Downtown San José is laid out on a grid. *Avenidas* (avenues) run east and west, while *calles* (streets) run north and south. The center of the city is at **Avenida Central** and **Calle Central.** To the north of Avenida Central, the avenidas have odd numbers beginning with Avenida 1; to the south, they have even numbers beginning with Avenida 2. Likewise, calles to the east of Calle Central have odd numbers, and those to the west have even numbers. The main downtown artery is **Avenida 2,** which merges with Avenida Central on either side of the downtown area. West of downtown, Avenida Central becomes **Paseo Colón,** which ends at Parque La Sabana and feeds into the highway to Alajuela, the airport, Guanacaste, and the Pacific coast. East of downtown, Avenida Central leads to San Pedro and then to Cartago and the Interamerican Highway heading south. **Calle 3** takes you out of town to the north, onto the Guápiles Highway that leads to the Caribbean coast.

THE NEIGHBORHOODS IN BRIEF

San José is divided into dozens of neighborhoods known as *barrios*. Most of the listings in this chapter fall within the main downtown area, but there are a few outlying neighborhoods you'll need to know about.

Downtown In San José's busy downtown, you'll find most of the city's museums, as well as a handful of small urban parks and open-air plazas, and the city's main cathedral. There are also many tour companies, restaurants, and hotels here. Unfortunately, traffic noise and exhaust fumes make this one of the least pleasant parts of the city. Streets and avenues are usually bustling and crowded with pedestrians and vehicular traffic, and street crime is most rampant here. Still, the sections of Avenida Central between Calle Central and Calle 7, as well as Avenida 4 between Calle 9 and Calle 14 have been converted into a pedestrian malls, slightly improving things on these stretches.

Barrio Amón/Barrio Otoya These two picturesque neighborhoods, just north and east of downtown, are the site of the greatest concentration of historic buildings in San José. Some of these have been renovated and turned into boutique hotels and atmospheric restaurants. If you're looking for character and don't mind the noise and exhaust fumes from passing cars and buses, this neighborhood makes a good base for exploring the city.

La Sabana/Paseo Colón Paseo Colón, a wide boulevard west of downtown, is an extension of Avenida Central and ends at Parque La Sabana. It has several good, small hotels and numerous restaurants. This is also where several of the city's car-rental agencies have their in-town offices. Once the site of the city's main airport, the Parque La Sabana is San José's largest public park, with ample green areas, an urban "canopy tour," sport facilities, and the Costa Rican Art Museum.

San Pedro/Los Yoses Located east of downtown San José, Los Yoses is an upper-middle-class neighborhood that is home to many diplomatic missions and embassies. San Pedro is a little farther east and is the site of the University of Costa Rica. Numerous college-type bars and restaurants are all around the edge of the campus, and several good restaurants and small hotels are in both neighborhoods.

San José

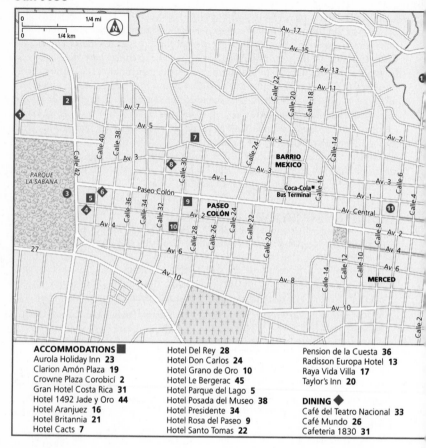

ACCOMMODATIONS ■
Aurola Holiday Inn **23**
Clarion Amón Plaza **19**
Crowne Plaza Corobicí **2**
Gran Hotel Costa Rica **31**
Hotel 1492 Jade y Oro **44**
Hotel Aranjuez **16**
Hotel Britannia **21**
Hotel Cacts **7**
Hotel Del Rey **28**
Hotel Don Carlos **24**
Hotel Grano de Oro **10**
Hotel Le Bergerac **45**
Hotel Parque del Lago **5**
Hotel Posada del Museo **38**
Hotel Presidente **34**
Hotel Rosa del Paseo **9**
Hotel Santo Tomas **22**
Pension de la Cuesta **36**
Radisson Europa Hotel **13**
Raya Vida Villa **17**
Taylor's Inn **20**

DINING ◆
Café del Teatro Nacional **33**
Café Mundo **26**
Cafeteria 1830 **31**

Escazú/Santa Ana Located in the hills west of San José, Escazú and Santa Ana are two fast-growing suburbs. Although the area is only 15 minutes from San José by car or taxi, it feels much farther away because of its relaxed and suburban atmosphere. This area also has a large expatriate community with many bed-and-breakfast establishments and excellent restaurants.

Heredia/Alajuela/Airport Area Heredia and Alajuela are two colonial-era cities that lie closer to the airport than San José. Alajuela is closest to the airport; Heredia is about midway between Alajuela and the capital. For more information on Heredia, see "Side Trips from San José," later in this chapter. Several quite nice high-end boutique hotels are in this area, and several large hotels and one chain hotel are located on, or just off, the Interamerican Highway close to the airport.

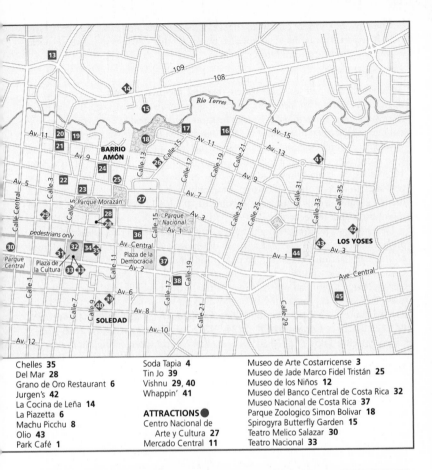

2 Getting Around

BY BUS

Bus transportation around San José is cheap—the fare is usually somewhere around 10¢ to 45¢ (5p–20p)—although the Alajuela/San José buses that run in from the airport cost 75¢ (40p). The most important buses are those running east along Avenida 2 and west along Avenida 3. The **Sabana/Cementerio** bus runs from Parque La Sabana to downtown and is one of the most convenient buses to use. You'll find a bus stop for the outbound Sabana/Cementerio bus near the main post office on Avenida 3 near the corner of Calle 2, and another one on Calle 11 between avenidas Central and 1. This bus also has stops all along Avenida 2. **San Pedro** buses leave from Avenida Central between calles 9 and 11, in front of the Cine Capri, and take you out of downtown heading east. **Escazú-** and **Santa Ana**–bound buses leave from the Coca-Cola bus station, as well as from Avenida 1 between calles 24 and 28. Alternatively, you can pick up both the Escazú and Santa Ana buses from the busy bus stop on Calle 42, just north of Gimnasio Nacional.

The city's bus drivers can make change, although they don't like to receive large bills. Be especially mindful of your wallet, purse, or other valuables, because pickpockets often work the crowded buses.

BY TAXI

Although taxis in San José have meters *(marías)*, the drivers sometimes refuse to use them, particularly with foreigners, so you'll occasionally have to negotiate the price. Always try to get them to use the meter first (say *"ponga la maría, por favor"*). The official rate at press time is around 90¢ (45p) for the first kilometer (½ mile) and around 70¢ (35p) for each additional kilometer. If you have a rough idea of how far it is to your destination, you can estimate how much it should cost from these figures. After 10pm taxis are legally allowed to add a 20% surcharge. Some of the meters are programmed to include the extra charge automatically, but be careful: Some drivers will use the evening setting during the daytime or (at night) to charge an extra 20% on top of the higher meter setting.

Depending on your location, the time of day, and the weather (rain places taxis at a premium), it's relatively easy to hail a cab downtown. You'll always find taxis in front of the Teatro Nacional (albeit at high prices) and around the Parque Central at Avenida Central and Calle Central. Taxis in front of hotels and the El Pueblo tourist complex usually charge more than others, although this is technically illegal. Most hotels will gladly call you a cab, either for a downtown excursion or for a trip back out to the airport. You can also get a cab by calling **Coopetaxi** (© **2235-9966**), **Coopeirazu** (© **2254-3211**), **Coopetico** (© **2224-7979**), or **Coopeguaria** (© **2226-1366**). **Cinco Estrellas Taxi** (© **2228-3159**) is another company that is based in Escazú but services the entire metropolitan area and airport, and claims to always have an English-speaking operator on call.

ON FOOT

Downtown San José is very compact. Nearly every place you might want to go is within a 15-by-4-block area. Because of traffic congestion, you'll often find it faster to walk than to take a bus or taxi. Be careful when walking the streets any time of day or night. Flashy jewelry, loosely held handbags or backpacks, and expensive camera equipment tend to attract thieves. **Avenida Central** is a pedestrian-only street for the blocks from Calle Central toward the Cultural Plaza and a little bit beyond. It has been redone with interesting paving stones and the occasional fountain in an attempt to create a comfortable pedestrian mall. A similar pedestrian-only walkway has recently been created on Avenida 4, between the Parque La Merced and the Iglesia La Soledad.

BY TRAIN

In mid-2005, urban commuter train service was reopened in downtown San José. A single line connecting the western neighborhood of Pavas with the eastern suburb of San Pedro passes right through the downtown, with prominent stops at, or near, the U.S. Embassy, Parque La Sabana, the downtown court area, and the Universidad de Costa Rica (University of Costa Rica) and Universidad Latina (Latin University). The train runs in each direction roughly every 2 hours between 5am and 6pm. The fare ranges from 20¢ to 70¢ (10p–35p) depending on the length of your ride.

Tips **Car-Rental Advice**

If you plan to rent a car, I recommend reserving it in advance from home. All the major international agencies and many local companies have toll-free numbers and websites. Sometimes you can even save a bit on the cost by reserving in advance. Costa Rica's car-rental fleet is not sufficient to meet demand during the high season when rental cars run at a premium. Sometimes this allows agencies here to gouge last-minute car-rental shoppers.

BY CAR

It will cost you between $45 and $140 (£23–£70) per day to rent a car in Costa Rica (the higher prices are for 4WD vehicles). Many car-rental agencies have offices at the airport. If not, they will usually either pick you up or deliver the car to any San José hotel. If you decide to pick up your rental car in downtown San José, be prepared for some very congested streets.

The following companies have desks at Juan Santamaría International Airport, as well as offices downtown: **Alamo** (© 800/462-5266 toll-free within Costa Rica, or 2242-7733 for central reservations; www.alamocostarica.com), **Adobe Rent A Car** (© 2442-2422 at the airport, or 2258-4242 in downtown San José; www.adobecar. com), **Avis** (© 800/331-1084 in the U.S., or 2293-2222 central reservation number in Costa Rica; www.avis.com), **Budget** (© 800/527-0700 in the U.S., 2436-2000 at the airport, or 2255-4750 in downtown San José; www.budget.co.cr), **Dollar** (© 2443-2950 at the airport, or 257-1585 in downtown San José; www.dollarcosta rica.com), **Hertz** (© 800/654-3001 in the U.S., 2443-4645 at the airport, or 2221-1818 in downtown San José; www.hertz.com), **National Car Rental** (© 877/862-8227 toll-free in the U.S. and Canada; 2440-0085 at the airport, or 2290-8787 in downtown San José; www.natcar.com), **Payless Rent A Car** (© 2257-0026 main reservations office in downtown San José, 2441-9366 at the airport; www.payless cr.com), **Thrifty** (© 800/847-4389 in the U.S., 2442-8585 at the airport, or 2257-3434 in downtown San José; www.thrifty.com), and **Toyota Rent A Car** (© 2441-1411 at the airport, or 2258-5797 in downtown San José; www.toyotarent.com).

There are dozens of other car-rental agencies in San José, and most will arrange for airport or hotel pickup or delivery. One of the more dependable agencies is **Hola! Rent A Car,** across the street (west) of Denny's, La Uruca, San José (© 2520-0100; www.hola.net). For more advice on renting cars, see "Getting There & Getting Around," in chapter 3.

FAST FACTS: **San José**

American Express American Express Travel Services is represented in Costa Rica by **ASV Olympia**, Oficentro La Sabana, Sabana Sur (© 2242-8585; www.asv olympia.com), which can issue traveler's checks and replacement cards and provide other standard services. To report lost or stolen Amex traveler's checks within Costa Rica, call the number above or call © 2295-9000, or call collect to 336/393-1111 in the United States.

Bookstores **Seventh Street Books,** Calle 7 between avenidas 1 and Central (© 2256-8251), has a wide range of new and used books in English, with an excellent selection of tropical biology, bird, and flora books; it's open daily from 9am to 7pm. For a wide selection of new books in English and Spanish, check out **Librería Internacional** (© 2257-2563; www.libreriainternacional.com), which has stores in downtown San José, Santa Ana, Zapote, Alajuela, Rohrmoser, Heredia, Barrio Escalante, and inside most major malls around the metropolitan area.

Camera Repair **Dima,** Avenida Central between calles 3 and 5 (© 2222-3969), is your best bet for any equipment or repair needs.

Car Rentals See "Getting Around," above.

Dentists Call your embassy, which will have a list of recommended dentists. Many bilingual dentists also advertise in the *Tico Times*. Because treatments are so inexpensive in Costa Rica, dental tourism has become a popular option for people needing extensive work.

Doctors Contact your embassy for information on doctors in San José, or see "Hospitals," below.

Drugstores There are countless pharmacies and drugstores in San José. Many of them deliver at little or no extra cost. The pharmacy at the **Hospital Clínica Bíblica,** Avenida 14 between calles Central and 1 (© 2522-1000), is open 24 hours every day. The pharmacy (© 2208-1080) at the **Hospital CIMA** in Escazú is also open 24 hours daily. **Farmacia Fischel** (© 2295-7555; www.fischel.co.cr) has numerous branches around the metropolitan area.

Embassies & Consulates See "Appendix A: Fast Facts, Toll-Free Numbers & Websites."

Emergencies In case of any emergency, dial © **911** (which should have an English-speaking operator); for an ambulance, call © **128;** and to report a fire, call © **118.**

Express Mail Services Many international courier and express-mail services have offices in San José, including **DHL,** on Paseo Colón between calles 30 and 32 (© 2209-0000; www.dhl.com); **EMS Courier,** with desks at the principal metropolitan post offices (© **800/900-2000** in Costa Rica; www.correos.go.cr); **FedEx,** which is based in Heredia but will arrange pickup anywhere in the metropolitan area (© **800/463-3339;** www.fedex.com); and **United Parcel Service,** in Pavas (© 2290-2828; www.ups.com). *Beware:* Despite what you might be told, packages sent overnight to U.S. addresses tend to take 3 to 4 days to reach their destination.

Eyeglasses Look for the word *óptica*. **Optica Vision** (© 2255-2266) is a widespread and dependable chain with stores all around San José and the rest of the country. They can do everything from eye exams to eyeglass repairs.

Hospitals **Clínica Bíblica,** Avenida 14 between calles Central and 1 (© 2522-1000; www.clinicabiblica.com), is conveniently located close to downtown and has several English-speaking doctors. The **Hospital CIMA** (© 2208-1000; www.hospitalsanjose.net), located in Escazú on the Próspero Fernández Highway, which connects San José and the western suburb of Santa Ana, has the most modern facilities in the country.

Internet Access   Internet cafes are all over San José. Rates run between 50¢ and $2 per hour (25p–£1). Many hotels have their own Internet cafe or allow guests to send and receive e-mail. And many have added wireless access, either for free or a small charge. You can also try **Racsa**, Avenida 5 and Calle 1 (© **2287-0087**; www.racsa.co.cr), the state Internet monopoly, which sells prepaid cards in 5-, 10-, and 15-hour denominations for connecting your laptop to the Web via a local phone call. Some knowledge of configuring your computer's dial-up connection is necessary, and you'll want to factor in the phone call charge if calling from a hotel.

Laundry & Dry Cleaning   Self-service laundromats are uncommon in Costa Rica, and hotel services can be expensive. **Aqua Matic** (© **2291-2847**) and **Tyson** (© **2215-2362**) are two dependable laundry and dry-cleaning chains with outlets all over town. The latter will even pick up and deliver your clothes free of charge.

Maps   The Costa Rican Tourist Board (ICT; see "Visitor Information," earlier in this chapter) can usually provide you with decent maps of both Costa Rica and San José. Also try **Seventh Street Books,** Calle 7 between avenidas Central and 1 (© **2256-8251**); **Librería Lehmann,** Avenida Central between calles 1 and 3 (© **2522-4848**); and **Librería Universal,** Avenida Central and calles Central and 1 (© **2222-2222**).

Newspapers & Magazines   See "Appendix A: Fast Facts, Toll-Free Numbers & Websites."

Photographic Needs   Film is generally more expensive in Costa Rica, so bring from home what you need. You should also have your film processed at home, but if you must develop your prints here, try **Rapi Foto** (© **2223-7640**) or **IFSA-Kodak** (© **2223-1444**), both of which have several storefronts around downtown. For more serious photographic needs (equipment, repairs, and so on), try **Dima,** Avenida Central between calles 3 and 5 (© **2222-3969**).

Police   Dial © **911** or 2222-1365 for the police. They should have someone available who speaks English.

Post Office   The main post office *(correo)* is on Calle 2 between avenidas 1 and 3 (© **800/900-2000** toll-free in Costa Rica, or 2202-2900; www.correos.go.cr). See "Mail" in appendix A for more information.

Restrooms   These are known as *sanitarios* or *servicios sanitarios*. You might also hear them called *baños*. They are marked *damas* (women) and *hombres* or *caballeros* (men). Public restrooms are rare to nonexistent, but most big hotels and public restaurants will let you use their restrooms. Downtown, you can find public restrooms at the entrance to the Museos del Banco Central de Costa Rica (p. 131).

Safety   Pickpockets and purse slashers are rife in San José, especially on public buses, in the markets, on crowded sidewalks, near hospitals, and lurking outside of bank offices and ATMs. Leave most of your money and other valuables in your hotel safe, and carry only as much as you really need when you go out. If you do carry anything valuable with you, keep it in a money belt or special passport bag around your neck. Day packs are a prime target of brazen pickpockets throughout the city. One common scam involves someone dousing you or your pack with mustard or ice cream. Another scamster (or two) will then quickly come to your aid—they are usually much more interested in cleaning you out than cleaning you up.

Stay away from the red-light district northwest of the Central Market. Also be advised that the Parque Nacional is not a safe place for a late-night stroll. Other precautions include walking around corner vendors, not between the vendor and the building. The tight space between the vendor and the building is a favorite spot for pickpockets. Never park a car on the street, and never leave anything of value in a car, even if it's in a guarded parking lot. Don't even leave your car unattended by the curb in front of a hotel while you dash in to check on your reservation. With these precautions in mind, you should have a safe visit to San José. Also, see "Safety" in chapter 3.

Taxes All hotels charge 16.39% tax. Restaurants charge 13% tax and also add on a 10% service charge, for a total of 23% more on your bill. There is an airport departure tax of $26 (£13).

Taxis See "Getting Around," above.

Telegrams & Faxes With the spread of Internet communications, faxes and telegrams are becoming somewhat obsolete. Most hotels can send a fax for you. You can send telegrams and faxes from either the **ICE office** on Avenida 2 between calles 1 and 3 (www.grupoice.com; daily 7am–10pm), or **Racsa** (Av. 5 and Calle 1; © **2287-0087**; www.racsa.co.cr; Mon–Fri 7:30am–5pm, Sat 9am–1pm), as well as from most **post office** branches (© **800/900-2000** toll-free in Costa Rica; www.correos.go.cr).

Telephones See "Staying Connected" in chapter 3. There are no city or area codes to dial from within Costa Rica; use the country code, 506, only when dialing a San José number from outside Costa Rica. (To call San José from the U.S., dial the international access code [011], then 506, and then the eight-digit number.)

Time Zone San José is on Central Standard Time (same as Chicago and St. Louis), 6 hours behind Greenwich Mean Time.

Useful Telephone Numbers For directory assistance, call © **113**; for international directory assistance, call © **124**; and for the exact time (in Spanish), call © **112**.

Water The water in San José is perfectly fine to drink. Nonetheless, some travelers experience stomach discomfort during their first few days in Costa Rica. If you want to be cautious, drink bottled water and *frescos* made with milk instead of water. *Sin hielo* means "no ice," and this is what you'll want to say if you're nervous about the water—just because it's frozen doesn't mean it's not water.

Weather The weather in San José (including the Central Valley) is usually temperate, never getting extremely hot or cold. May through November is the rainy season, although the rain usually falls only in the afternoon and evening.

3 Where to Stay

In San José, your hotel choices range from expensive luxury resorts to budget pensions charging only a few dollars a night. However, these two extremes are the exceptions, not the norm. The vast number of accommodations, and the best deals, are in the $90-to-$160 (£45–£80) price range. Within this relatively moderate bracket, you'll find restored homes that have been turned into small hotels and bed-and-breakfasts, modern hotels with pools and exercise rooms, and older downtown business hotels.

While, in general, there are plenty of rooms to go around in San José, the small boutique hotels and better-run establishments (including those recommended here) are often booked well in advance during the high season.

CHOOSING WHERE TO STAY   **Downtown hotels,** many of which are in beautifully restored homes, are convenient to museums, restaurants, and shopping, but they can be noisy. Many people are also bothered by the exhaust fumes that permeate downtown streets. Moreover, because the streets of downtown are not especially safe, particularly at night, you should plan on taking taxis whether you stay downtown or in a nearby neighborhood or suburb. **Barrio Amón** is the downtown neighborhood with the most character and remnants of colonial architecture. If you want clean air and a peaceful night's sleep, consider staying out in the suburbs. **Escazú** and **Santa Ana** are both quiet yet modern suburbs, and many of the hotels there have great views. Heading east from downtown, **Los Yoses** is fairly close to the center of the action yet is still quiet. If you've rented a car, make sure your hotel provides secure parking or you'll have to find (and pay for) a nearby lot. If you plan to take some day tours, you can just as easily arrange these from a hotel situated outside the downtown area.

If you're heading out to Guanacaste, the central Pacific, or the northern zone, you might consider a hotel or bed-and-breakfast either near or beyond the airport. Sure, you give up proximity to downtown, but you can cut as much as an hour off your travel time to any of these destinations. Many car-rental companies will even deliver to or pick up cars from these establishments.

ALTERNATIVES TO HOTELS   If you plan to be in town for a while or are traveling with family or several friends, you might want to consider staying in an *aparto-tel,* a cross between an apartment complex and a hotel. You can rent by the day, week, or month, and you get a furnished apartment with a full kitchen, plus housekeeping and laundry service. Options include **Apartotel El Sesteo** ⋒ (② 877/623-3198 in the U.S. and Canada, or 2296-1805; fax 2296-1865; www.sesteo.com), **Apartotel La Sabana** ⋒ (② 877/722-2621 in the U.S. and Canada, or 2220-2422; fax 2231-7386; www.apartotel-lasabana.com), **Apartotel María Alexandra** (② 2228-1507; fax 2289-5192; www.mariaalexandra.com), and **Apartotel Los Yoses** (② 888/790-5264 in the U.S. and Canada, or 2225-0033; fax 2225-5595; www.apartotel.com).

DOWNTOWN SAN JOSE/BARRIO AMON
EXPENSIVE
Aurola Holiday Inn   Situated directly across the street from the attractive downtown Parque Morazán, this is San José's only high-rise business-class hotel. The rooms are everything you might expect from a prominent international chain in this price range—but nothing more. Service can be somewhat hit-or-miss, and the restaurants here leave lots to be desired. Still, the location is great for exploring downtown on

foot, and if you get one of the upper-floor rooms on the north side, you'll have one of the best views in the city.

Av. 5 and Calle 5 (A.P. 7802-1000), San José. ✆ **800/465-4329** in the U.S. and Canada, or 2523-1000. Fax 2248-3101. www.holiday-inn.com. 200 units. $128–$148 (£64–£74) double; $168 (£84) junior suite; $228–$298 (£114–£149) suite. Rates lower in the off season. Internet rates available. AE, DC, MC, V. Free parking. **Amenities:** 2 restaurants; bar; poolside snack bar; indoor pool; exercise room; Jacuzzi; sauna; tour desk; car-rental desk; well-appointed business center; limited room service; laundry service; nonsmoking rooms. *In room:* A/C, TV, dataport, free Wi-Fi, minibar, coffeemaker, hair dryer, iron, safe.

Clarion Amón Plaza ⊛

On the north edge of the historic Barrio Amón neighborhood, this hotel is a pretty dependable business-class option. There's nothing particularly distinctive about the property or rooms here; however, in terms of service, location, and price, this hotel gets my nod over the nearby Holiday Inn. The rooms are all spacious, well kept, and come with plenty of amenities. And you are close to all the downtown action. I recommend paying the extra $30 (£15) for the executive-floor rooms, which get you free happy hour food and drinks, a separate lounge area, and more recently upgraded and furnished rooms. While the food is merely average, the ambience of their little outdoor, sidewalk cafe, El Cafetal de la Luz, is delightful. There's also a fairly swank casino on-site. You can usually do a bit better than the rack rates listed below if you book through www.choicehotels.com.

Av. 11 and Calle 3 bis (A.P. 4192-1000), San José. ✆ **877/424-6423** in the U.S. and Canada, or 2523-4600 in Costa Rica. Fax 2523-4614. www.hotelamonplaza.com. 87 units. $130–$160 (£65–£80) double; $220 (£110) suite. AE, DC, MC, V. Free parking. **Amenities:** Restaurant; bar; lounge; casino; small exercise room; Jacuzzi; sauna; tour desk; modest business center; babysitting; laundry service; nonsmoking rooms. *In room:* A/C, TV, free Wi-Fi, coffeemaker, hair dryer, safe.

Radisson Europa Hotel ⊛⊛

This hotel is geared primarily to business travelers, but it's a good choice for anyone looking for a big, dependable hotel near downtown San José. Wooden headboards, angular window nooks, and other small architectural details give these rooms an edge over those in the Aurola Holiday Inn and Clarion Amón Plaza, although it's not as convenient for walking around downtown. For a modest price increase, you can opt for an executive room, which is basically a standard room with a coffeemaker, a scale, terry-cloth bathrobes, and an extra telephone in the bathroom. The junior suites come with all the above amenities, as well as a desk and chair, in-room fax machine, and small balcony. Both the executive rooms and suites have wireless Internet access. This hotel is particularly well-located if you are driving to or from the Caribbean coast, as it is set right off the main downtown entrance to the highway to Guapiles.

Calle Blancos, behind La República building (A.P. 538-2120), San José. ✆ **888/201-1718** in the U.S., or 2257-3257. Fax 2257-8221. www.radisson.com. 107 units. $140–$160 (£70–£80) double; $200–$280 (£100–£140) junior suite. Rates include continental breakfast. AE, DC, MC, V. Free parking. **Amenities:** 2 restaurants; bar; lounge; casino; pool; gym; tour desk; car-rental agency; full-service business center; small shopping arcade; limited room service; massage; laundry service; nonsmoking rooms. *In room:* A/C, TV, free Wi-Fi, dataport, minibar, hair dryer, iron, safe.

MODERATE

In addition to the hotels listed below, the **Sleep Inn** (Av. 3 btw. calles 9 and 11; ✆ **2222-0101;** www.choicehotels.com) is a modern, American-style chain hotel in the heart of downtown, while **Hotel Doña Inés** (✆ **2222-7443;** www.donaines.com) on Calle 11 between avenidas 2 and 6, and **Hotel Rincón de San José** (✆ **2221-9702;** www.hotel rincondesanjose.com) on the corner of Avenida 9 and Calle 15, are two little boutique hotels, that are also good options.

Gran Hotel Costa Rica   The Gran Hotel Costa Rica has arguably the best location of any downtown hotel (bordering the Teatro Nacional and the Plaza de la Cultura), and a major remodeling has finally brought the rooms and amenities almost up to snuff. Most of the rooms here are fairly large, and they sport fresh carpets, paint, and furnishings. However, they still feel a bit spartan and dated, and hot water seems to be in seriously short supply. Although it's set a half-block from busy Avenida 2, some find the street noise a problem here. The Cafeteria 1830, reviewed separately later in this chapter, is perhaps the hotel's greatest attribute. It's memorable not so much for its food as for its atmosphere—it's an open-air patio that overlooks the Teatro Nacional, street musicians, and all the activity of the Plaza de la Cultura.

Av. 2, btw. calles 1 and 3, San José. © **800/949-0592** in the U.S., or 2221-4000. Fax 2221-3501. www.grandhotel costarica.com. 104 units. $81–$97 (£41–£49) double; $135–$179 (£68–£90) suite. Rates include breakfast buffet. AE, DC, MC, V. Free parking. **Amenities:** 2 restaurants; bar; small casino; small gym; tour desk; 24-hr. room service; laundry service. *In room:* TV, free Wi-Fi, minibar, safe.

Hotel Britannia ⭐ *Value*   This is the most elegant of the many small hotels that have been created from restored old houses in downtown San José. Built in 1910, the large, low building, with its wraparound veranda, is certainly one of the most attractive in the neighborhood. In the lobby, tile floors, large stained-glass picture windows, a brass chandelier, and reproduction Victorian decor all help set a tone of tropical luxury. Along with restoring the old home, the owners have built a four-story addition, which is separated from the original building by a narrow atrium. Rooms in the original home have hardwood floors and furniture; high ceilings and fans help keep them cool. Although the streetside rooms have double glass, light sleepers will still want to avoid them. The quietest rooms are those toward the back of the addition. The hotel's buffet breakfast, along with afternoon tea and happy-hour drinks, is served in a skylit room adjacent to the restaurant.

Calle 3 and Av. 11 (A.P. 3742-1000), San José. © **800/263-2618** in the U.S. or 2223-6667. Fax 2223-6411. www. hotelbritanniacostarica.com. 23 units. $89–$105 (£44–£52) double; $117 (£59) junior suite. AE, MC, V. Parking nearby. **Amenities:** Restaurant; bar; tour desk; limited room service; laundry service; all rooms nonsmoking. *In room:* A/C (in suites), TV, free Wi-Fi, minibar (in suites), coffeemaker, hair dryer, safe.

Hotel Del Rey   You can't miss the Del Rey: It's a massive pink corner building with vaguely colonial styling. The lobby continues the facade's theme with pink-tile floors and stone columns. Inside, a carved hardwood door marks every guest room. The rooms vary in size and comfort: There are quiet interior rooms that have no windows, and larger rooms with windows (but also street noise). Try for a sixth-floor room with a balcony. The hotel's main restaurant is across the street in an old restored home, with plenty of stained glass. The hotel's 24-hour lobby bar and cafe serves respectable U.S.-style deli sandwiches, seafood, steaks, and pasta dishes. Much of the first floor is taken up with a bustling casino and the neighboring Blue Marlin Bar, which is very popular with tourists, expatriates, and prostitutes. The hotel's owners also manage the popular Key Largo Bar, just across the street.

Av. 1 and Calle 9 (A.P. 6241-1000), San José. © **866/765-8037** in the U.S. and Canada, or 2257-7800. Fax 2221-0096. www.hoteldelrey.com. 104 units. $95–$120 (£48–£60) double. AE, MC, V. Parking nearby. **Amenities:** Restaurant; bar; tour desk; 24-hr. room service; laundry service. *In room:* A/C, TV, Wi-Fi, minibar, hair dryer, safe.

Hotel Don Carlos ⭐⭐ *Finds*   If you're looking for a small downtown hotel that is unmistakably Costa Rican and hints at the days of the planters and coffee barons, this is the place for you. Located in an old residential neighborhood, only blocks from the business district, the Don Carlos was a former president's mansion. Inside you'll find a slew of arts-and-crafts works and archaeological reproductions, as well as orchids, ferns, palms, and parrots. The rooms are distinct and vary greatly in size, so be specific when you reserve, or ask if it's possible to see a few when you check in. Breakfast is served in an outdoor orchid garden and atrium. The gift shop here is one of the largest in the country, and guests get unlimited free local calls, one free international call, and free Internet access with the hotel's computer; if you brought your own laptop, you can use the hotel's Wi-Fi network.

779 Calle 9, btw. avs. 7 and 9, San José. © **2221-6707.** Fax 2258-1152. www.doncarloshotel.com. 33 units. $75–$95 (£38–£48) double. Rates include continental breakfast. AE, MC, V. Free parking. **Amenities:** Restaurant; bar; Jacuzzi; tour desk; limited room service; laundry service. *In room:* TV, free Wi-Fi, hair dryer, iron, safe.

Hotel Presidente   This modern business-class hotel is a good midrange option in the heart of downtown. Although the hotel's eight stories practically qualify it for skyscraper status, very few of the rooms have any view to speak of; those with north-facing windows are your best bet. Rooms are all well-kept and feature the basic amenities you'd expect; recent upgrades have added more contemporary furnishings and decor. If you want more space, opt for one of the junior suites. Rooms and suites with a "spa" designation come with a private Jacuzzi. The master suite is a massive two-bedroom affair, featuring a widescreen TV in the living room and a private eight-person Jacuzzi. There's a very popular casual cafe-style restaurant just off the street. While similar in style and vibe, the Presidente is a bit more tranquil and subdued than the Del Rey (see above), especially after dark.

Av. Central and Calle 7 (A.P. 2922-1000), San José. © **2222-3022.** Fax 2221-1205. www.hotel-presidente.com. 100 units. $89 (£45) double; $125–$145 (£63–£73) junior or spa suite; $325 (£162) master suite. Rates include full breakfast buffet. AE, MC, V. Free parking. **Amenities:** Restaurant; bar; casino; small gym; rooftop Jacuzzi and sauna; tour desk; limited room service; babysitting; laundry service. *In room:* A/C, TV, free Wi-Fi, minifridge, hair dryer, safe.

Hotel Santo Tomás (Value   Even though it's on a busy downtown street, this converted mansion is a quiet oasis inside. Built more than 100 years ago by a coffee baron, the house has been lovingly restored and maintained by its owner, Thomas Douglas. Throughout the hotel you'll enjoy the deep, dark tones of well-aged and well-worked wood. The rooms vary in size, but most are fairly spacious and have a small table and chairs. Skylights in some bathrooms will brighten your morning, and firm beds provide a good night's sleep. There's also a small outdoor pool with a Jacuzzi above it; the two are solar heated and connected by a tiny water slide. The staff and management are extremely helpful, and the restaurant here is excellent. This neighborhood is a little bit sketchy after dark, so you'd be advised to take a taxi to and from the hotel for any evening excursions.

Av. 7, btw. calles 3 and 5, San José. © **877/446-0658** in the U.S. or 2255-0448. Fax 2222-3950. www.hotelsanto tomas.com. 20 units. $80–$110 (£40–£55) double. Rates include breakfast buffet. MC, V. Parking nearby. **Amenities:** Restaurant; bar; lounge; small pool; exercise room; Jacuzzi; tour desk; laundry service; all rooms nonsmoking. *In room:* TV, free Wi-Fi, hair dryer, safe.

Raya Vida Villa   Located behind a big iron gate at the end of a narrow, dead-end lane, this little bed-and-breakfast is so secluded that it seems to be in a world all its own, yet it's in downtown San José. Behind the gate, in a shady old garden, is a miniature villa. The restored old stucco home is furnished with the owners' eclectic collection of crafts from around the world, and in the living room you'll find a grand piano and fireplace. Guest rooms are all different in style and decor. One features a four-poster bed with carved pineapples on the top of each post. The upstairs rooms have the largest bathrooms, and one even has a Jacuzzi tub. However, I like the downstairs room that opens onto a small open-air patio with a fountain.

Barrio Amón (A.P. 2209-2100), San José. ℭ **2223-4168.** Fax 2223-4157. www.rayavida.com. 4 units. $95 (£48) double. Rates include full breakfast. MC, V. Free parking. *In room:* TV, no phone.

INEXPENSIVE

In addition to the places listed below, **Kap's Place** (ℭ **2221-1169;** www.kaps place.com), across from the Hotel Aranjuez on Calle 19 between avenidas 11 and 13, is another good choice, while real budget hounds might want to try either **Tranquilo Backpackers** (ℭ **2222-2493;** www.tranquilobackpackers.com), on Calle 7 between avenidas 9 and 11, or **Costa Rica Backpackers** (ℭ **2221-6191;** www.costa ricabackpackers.com), on Avenida 6 between calles 21 and 23.

Hotel Colonial ⍟ (Calle 11 btw. avs. 4 and 6; ℭ **2223-0109;** www.hotelcolonialcr. com) is a good boutique hotel in a restored Victorian-style home a couple of blocks south of the city center, with rooms that fall into the upper end of this price range.

Hotel Aranjuez *Value*   This is probably the best and deservedly most popular budget option close to downtown. On a quiet and safe street in the Barrio Amón neighborhood, this humble hotel is made up of five contiguous houses. All rooms are simple and clean, although some are a little dark. Rooms and bathrooms vary greatly in size, so ask when reserving, or try to see a few rooms when you arrive. The nicest features here, aside from the convivial hostel-like atmosphere, are the lush and shady gardens; the hanging orchids, bromeliads, and ferns decorating the hallways and nooks; and the numerous open lounge areas furnished with chairs, tables, and couches—great for lazing around and sharing travel tales with your fellow guests. The hotel has a couple of computers, as well as a free Wi-Fi network, and provides free local calling.

Calle 19, btw. avs. 11 and 13 (A.P. 457-2070), San José. ℭ **877/898-8663** in the U.S. or 2256-1825. Fax 2223-3528. www.hotelaranjuez.com. 36 units, 6 with shared bathroom. $25 (£13) double with shared bathroom; $40–$47 (£20–£24) double with private bathroom. Rates include breakfast buffet. V. Free parking. **Amenities:** Restaurant; bar; several lounge areas; tour desk; laundry service. *In room:* TV, free Wi-Fi, safe.

Hotel Posada del Museo   Located just across busy Avenida 2 from the Museo Nacional, this place offers up clean and cheerful rooms in the heart of downtown. The Victorian-style building dates to 1928 and has been immaculately restored. Rooms are spacious and feature either varnished wood or original ornate tile floors. The small restaurant here is set on a small pedestrian mall that leads to the Costa Rican Court complex, and features a few outdoor tables perfect for people-watching. The only downside here is the fact that Avenida 2 is one of the city's busiest and loudest, with a steady stream of bus, truck, and even train traffic struggling up the steep hill that crests right at this hotel. Even the rooms farthest from the street are susceptible to street noise.

Av. 2 and Calle 17, San José. ℭ **2258-1027.** ℭ/fax 2257-9414. www.hotelposadadelmuseo.com. 10 units. $55–$80 (£28–£40) double. Rates include full breakfast. Rates lower in off season. AE, DC, MC, V. Free parking. **Amenities:** Restaurant; lounge; tour desk; laundry service. *In room:* TV, free Wi-Fi.

Pensión de la Cuesta *Value*   If you don't mind a clean communal bathroom down the hall from your room, this little bed-and-breakfast on the hill leading up to the Parque Nacional is a real bargain and definitely worth considering. It was once the home of Otto Apuy, a well-known Costa Rican artist, and original artwork abounds. The building itself is a classic example of a tropical wood-frame home and has been painted an eye-catching pink with blue and white trim. Some rooms are a bit dark and very simply furnished, but there's a sunny and cheery sunken lounge/courtyard area in the center of the house. Most rooms have one double and a set of bunk beds. Overall, the place feels a lot like a hostel. The owners give you free run of the kitchen and offer free use of their Internet connection. They also rent out a fully furnished apartment.

1332 Cuesta de Núñez, Av. 1 btw. calles 11 and 15, San José. © 2256-7946 or ©/fax 2255-2896. www.pension delacuesta.com. 15 units, none with private bathroom. $28 (£14) double. Rates include continental breakfast. Children 11 and under stay free in parent's room. AE, MC, V. Parking nearby. **Amenities:** Lounge w/cable TV; tour desk; laundry service. *In room:* Free Wi-Fi, no phone.

LA SABANA/PASEO COLON
EXPENSIVE
Crowne Plaza Corobicí ⚜   Just past the end of Paseo Colón and on the edge of Parque La Sabana, the Corobicí offers all the amenities you would expect at a large business-class hotel. The lobby is a vast expanse of marble floor faced by blank walls, although the Art Deco furnishings lend a bit of character. Guest rooms are contemporary and comfortable, with firm beds and walls of glass through which, on most floors, you get good views of the valley and surrounding mountains. Joggers will enjoy the nearby Parque La Sabana. The Corobicí has a large, modern spa, where you will find a well-equipped gym featuring a large exercise room, on-staff trainers, and regular classes. The Fuji restaurant here is one of the better Japanese and sushi restaurants in San José.

Autopista General Cañas, Sabana Norte (A.P. 2443-1000), San José. © 800/227-6963 in the U.S. or 2232-8122. Fax 2231-5698. www.crowneplaza.com. 213 units. $150–$200 (£75–£100) double; $201–$400 (£101–£200) suite; $600 (£300) presidential suite. AE, MC, V. Free parking. **Amenities:** 2 restaurants; bar; lounge; casino; midsize pool; health club and spa; Jacuzzi; sauna; tour desk; car-rental desk; business center; shopping arcade; salon; 24-hr. room service; in-room massage; babysitting; laundry service; all rooms nonsmoking. *In room:* A/C, TV, free Wi-Fi, minibar, coffeemaker, hair dryer, safe.

MODERATE
Hotel Grano de Oro ⚜⚜ *(Finds*   San José boasts dozens of old homes that have been converted into hotels, but the Grano de Oro tops them all in terms of design, comfort, and service. On a quiet side street off Paseo Colón, it offers a variety of room types to fit a range of budgets and tastes. I favor the patio rooms, which have French doors opening onto private patios. Throughout all the guest rooms, you'll find attractive hardwood furniture, including old-fashioned wardrobes in some. The Vista de Oro suite is the hotel's crown jewel, with its own private staircase and wonderful views of the city and surrounding mountains. If you don't grab one of the suites (which have whirlpool tubs), you still have access to the hotel's two rooftop Jacuzzis. The restaurant serves excellent international cuisine and some of the city's best desserts. The hotel owners support a noble shelter for young, unwed mothers, Casa Luz. Feel free to inquire as to how you can help.

Calle 30, no. 251, btw. avs. 2 and 4, 150m (1½ blocks) south of Paseo Colón, San José (mailing address: SJO 36, P.O. Box 025216, Miami, FL 33102). © 2255-3322. Fax 2221-2782. www.hotelgranodeoro.com. 40 units. $105–$140 (£53–£70) double; $160–$275 (£80–£138) suite. AE, MC, V. Free parking. **Amenities:** Restaurant; bar; lounge; 2 rooftop Jacuzzis; concierge; tour desk; limited room service; laundry service; all rooms nonsmoking. *In room:* TV, dataport, free Wi-Fi, minibar, safe.

Hotel Parque del Lago ⭐ This midsize business-class hotel is located on the west-ern edge of busy Paseo Colón, right near the Costa Rican Art Museum and Parque La Sabana. Rooms are large and modern, but have a rather sober decor. The junior suites are especially spacious, with a comfortable couch, sitting area, wet bar, and microwave oven. The best room here is the rooftop penthouse, and it's not that much more expensive than the suites and worth the slight splurge if available. There's wireless Internet throughout the hotel, and an elegant little restaurant and bar area just off the lobby. This hotel is convenient to both downtown and the western suburbs of Escazú and Santa, with easy access to the country's major highways.

Calle 40, btw. Av. 2 and Paseo Colón, San José. ℭ **2257-8787.** Fax 2223-1617. www.parquedellago.com. 40 units. $114 (£57) double; $144 (£72) junior suite; $194 (£97) penthouse. Rates include buffet breakfast. AE, MC, V. Free parking. **Amenities:** Restaurant; bar; lounge; small gym; spa; Jacuzzi; sauna; tour desk; car-rental desk; business center; limited room service; laundry service; nonsmoking rooms. *In room:* A/C, TV, free Wi-Fi, minibar, coffeemaker, hair dryer, safe.

Hotel Rosa del Paseo ⭐ This hotel is housed in one of San José's most beautiful old stucco homes, right on busy Paseo Colón. However, the rooms are all located away from the street and are pretty well insulated against the noise. Built more than 115 years ago, this old home has received regular upkeep and upgrading, yet is neverthe-less richly appointed and surprisingly evocative of 19th-century Costa Rica. The rooms are all very comfortable. I'd definitely try to grab one of the rooms on the sec-ond floor, which feature wooden floors and front doors that open onto the open-air central courtyard. The master suite comes with its own balcony and Jacuzzi. Beautiful details are spread throughout the hotel, including transoms, ornate stucco door frames, and polished hardwood floors.

2862 Paseo Colón, btw. calles 28 and 30 (A.P. 287-1007, Centro Colón), San José. ℭ **2257-3225.** Fax 2223-2776. www.rosadelpaseo.com. 19 units. $75 (£38) double; $90–$120 (£45–£60) suite. Rates include continental breakfast. AE, DC, MC, V. Limited free parking. **Amenities:** Bar; lounge; tour desk; babysitting; laundry service; nonsmoking rooms. *In room:* A/C, TV, safe.

Taylor's Inn Here's yet another lovely converted old downtown home turned bed-and-breakfast. The rooms are all arranged around the interior courtyard, which fea-tures flowering ginger and other tropical flora—a perfect place for breakfast. Most rooms have one single and one double bed, although a few have sleeping lofts and are good for families. All are very clean and feature artwork from prominent Costa Rican artists. The suite is a bit bigger. Don't expect a sense of hermetic privacy here, though—most of the rooms open onto the courtyard, and the old wooden construc-tion guarantees that you hear every footfall and conversation of other guests passing by your door. The hotel has a helpful tour desk.

Av. 13, btw. calles 3 and 3 bis (A.P. 531-1000), San José. ℭ **2257-4333.** Fax 2221-1475. www.taylorinn.com. 12 units. $60 (£30) double. Rates include continental breakfast. Rates slightly lower in the off season. AE, MC, V. **Ameni-ties:** Lounge; tour desk; laundry service; nonsmoking rooms. *In room:* TV, safe.

INEXPENSIVE

Hotel Cacts *(Finds* Housed in an attractive tropical contemporary home on a business and residential street, this is one of the more interesting and unusual budget hotels in San José. The seemingly constantly expanding complex is a maze of rooms and hall-ways on several levels. Rooms vary considerably in size, so it's always best to check out a few first if possible. The deluxe rooms here come with televisions and telephones, whereas the standard rooms lack both of these amenities. The newest additions are a small pool and separate Jacuzzi, in a lush garden patio. The third-floor open terrace serves as the breakfast area. The staff here is very helpful, and the hotel will receive mail and faxes, change money, and store baggage for guests.

Av. 3 bis, no. 2845, btw. calles 28 and 30 (A.P. 379-1005), San José. ✆ **2221-2928** or 2221-6546. Fax 2221-8616. www.hotelcacts.com. 26 units. $45–$60 (£23–£30) double. Rates include breakfast buffet. MC, V. Free parking. **Amenities:** Lounge; small outdoor pool; Jacuzzi; tour desk; laundry service; all rooms nonsmoking. *In room:* Free Wi-Fi, no phone in some rooms.

SAN PEDRO/LOS YOSES
MODERATE

In addition to the places listed below, the **Hotel Boutique Jade** (✆ **2224-2455;** www. hotelboutiquejade.com) is a modern business-class hotel with an excellent restaurant, while the **Hotel Don Fadrique** (✆ **2225-8186;** www.hoteldonfadrique.com) is another good option in a converted home, bedecked in interesting artwork.

Hotel 1492 Jade y Oro   Housed in a restored old home on a quiet street in the heart of the Barrio Escalante neighborhood just east of the city center, this little bed-and-breakfast makes a good base for exploring the city or this side of town. The rooms are simple and tastefully done with locally crafted wooden furniture, plenty of light, local art on the walls, and a homey feel, but some are pretty small. All rooms have showers only. Breakfast is served in an open-air rancho overlooking a lovely little garden. The hotel is run by a Costa Rican family, and you really get the feel that you are staying in a typical Tico home here.

Av. 1, no. 2985, btw. calles 31 and 33, Barrio Escalante. ✆ **2256-5913.** Fax 2280-6206. www.hotel1492.com. 10 units. $70–$80 (£35–£40) double; $90 (£45) suite. Rates include full breakfast. AE, MC, V. Free parking. **Amenities:** Laundry service; nonsmoking rooms. *In room:* TV, free Wi-Fi, hair dryer, safe.

Hôtel Le Bergerac ★★ *Finds*   With all the sophistication and charm of a small French inn, the Hotel Le Bergerac has ingratiated itself over the years with business travelers and members of various diplomatic missions. These visitors have found a tranquil environment in a quiet suburban neighborhood, spacious and comfortable accommodations, personal service, and gourmet meals. Still, you don't have to be a diplomat or business traveler to enjoy this hotel's charms. Le Bergerac is composed of three houses with courtyard gardens in between. Almost all the rooms are fairly large, and each is a little different. I favor those with private patio gardens. In the evenings candlelight and classical music set a relaxing and romantic mood. The hotel's long-standing L'Ile de France restaurant serves gourmet French and continental dinners for guests and the public by reservation only.

Calle 35 no. 50 (A.P. 1107-1002), San José. ✆ **2234-7850.** Fax 2225-9103. www.bergerachotel.com. 26 units. $85–$140 (£43–£70) double. Rates include full breakfast. AE, DC, MC, V. Free parking. **Amenities:** Restaurant; lounge; concierge; tour desk; business and secretarial services; laundry service. *In room:* TV, hair dryer, safe.

Hotel Milvia ★ *Finds*   Art lovers should definitely look into this offbeat little hotel. This old converted home is chock-full of paintings and sculptures by a wide range of contemporary Costa Rican artists. One of the owners, Florencia Urbina, happens to be one of these artists. Other artists represented include Mario Maffioli and Fabio Herrera. My favorite pieces are the large-scale sculptures by Leda Astorga, including two functional and funny chairs. The rooms are bright and airy, and most are plenty spacious. The hotel has a mix of courtyards and gardens that seem to beckon one to linger with a book or sketch pad in hand.

1 block north and 2 blocks east of the Muñoz y Nanne Supermarket, San Pedro. ℂ **2225-4543**. Fax 2225-7801. www.hotelmilvia.com. 9 units. $80 (£40) double. Rates include continental breakfast. AE, MC, V. **Amenities:** Restaurant; lounge; tour desk; laundry service. *In room:* TV, free Wi-Fi.

ESCAZÚ & SANTA ANA

Located about 15 minutes west of San José and about the same distance from the international airport, these affluent suburbs have experienced rapid growth in recent years, as the metropolitan area continues its urban sprawl. Both Escazú and Santa Ana are popular with the Costa Rican professional class and North American retirees and expatriates, and quite a few hotels have sprung up to cater to their needs. It's relatively easy to commute between Escazú or Santa Ana and downtown via bus or taxi. Taxi fare should run around $8 to $12 (£4–£6), each way. A bus costs around 35¢ (15p).

EXPENSIVE

Alta Hotel 🏨🏨 This small boutique hotel is infused with old-world charm. Curves and high arches abound. My favorite touch is the winding interior alleyway that snakes down from the reception through the hotel. Most of the rooms here have wonderful views of the Central Valley from private balconies; the others have pleasant garden patios. The rooms are all up to modern resort standards, although some have slightly cramped bathrooms. The suites are considerably larger, each with a separate sitting room with its own television, as well as large Jacuzzi-style tubs in spacious bathrooms. The master suite has a steam bath as well. If you opt to rent the entire upper floor, the penthouse becomes a three-bedroom, full-floor extravaganza, with a massive living room and open-air rooftop patio. The hotel's La Luz restaurant (p. 128) is one of the more elegant and creative dining spots in the Central Valley.

Alto de las Palomas, old road to Santa Ana. ℂ **888/388-2582** in the U.S. and Canada or 2282-4160. Fax 2282-4162. www.thealtahotel.com. 23 units. $167 (£84) double; $197 (£99) junior suite; $390 (£195) master suite; $820 (£410) penthouse. Rates include continental breakfast and round-trip airport transfers. AE, DC, MC, V. Free parking. **Amenities:** Restaurant; bar; midsize pool; exercise room; Jacuzzi; sauna; concierge; tour desk; secretarial services; limited room service; in-room massage; laundry service. *In room:* A/C, TV, dataport, free Wi-Fi, minibar, coffeemaker, hair dryer, iron, safe.

Corteza Amarilla Art Lodge & Spa 🏨 *Finds* Artistic touches abound in this whimsical hotel. Most of the rooms are classified as junior suites, although they really are just good-size rooms, with no separate sitting area, or other distinguishing factor that I usually associate with a junior. These are found in a series of individual and duplex buildings spread around the hotel's lush grounds. All come with wood floors, stone showers, and artsy tile work on the bathroom sinks and counters. I prefer no. 4 through no. 7, which have higher ceilings. The two master suites are in the main building, and are larger, and come with massive flatscreen television sets and a good-size private patio garden. A variety of treatments and therapies are offered at the small spa here, and the in-house restaurant is excellent. This hotel is located just outside of Santa Ana, on the main road to Ciudad Colón.

Prospero Fernández Hwy., just outside of Santa Ana. ℂ **800/961-0419** in the U.S. and Canada, or 2203-7503 in Costa Rica. Fax 2282-6641. www.cortezaamarillalodge.com. 12 units. $140 (£70) double junior suite; $170 (£85) master suite. Rates include full breakfast. AE, MC, V. **Amenities:** Restaurant; bar; small spa; Jacuzzi; tour desk; laundry service. *In room:* A/C, TV, minibar, coffeemaker, hair dryer.

Real InterContinental San José 🏨 This is a modern and luxurious large-scale business-class hotel, with three five-story wings. The large, open lobby has a beautiful flagstone-and-mosaic floor. The rooms are all well-appointed, with either one king-size or two double beds, a working desk, a sitting chair and ottoman, and a large armoire housing a 25-inch television. For a little extra, you can stay on the Club InterContinental floor and enjoy personalized concierge and butler services, a separate check-in area, an on-floor buffet breakfast, and an assortment of refreshments and snacks throughout the day. The hotel is just across from a large, modern shopping-mall complex, which is nice if you want access to shopping, restaurants, and a six-plex movie theater. Overall, the InterContinental offers many of the same features and amenities as the Marriott (p. 118), although the latter gets my nod in terms of service, restaurants, and ambience.

Autopista Próspero Fernández, across from the Multiplaza mall, Escazú. ℂ **2208-2100.** Fax 2208-2101. www.grupo real.com. 261 units. $190–$380 (£95–£190) double; $600–$1,200 (£300–£600) suite. AE, MC, V. Free parking. **Amenities:** 3 restaurants; 2 bars; lounge; large free-form pool; tennis court; modest health club and spa; Jacuzzi; concierge; tour desk; car-rental desk; well-appointed business center; small shopping arcade; salon; 24-hr. room service; in-room massage; laundry service; nonsmoking rooms. *In room:* A/C, TV, Wi-Fi, minibar, coffeemaker, hair dryer, safe.

MODERATE

In addition to the hotels listed below, the **Courtyard San José** (ℂ **888/236-2427** in the U.S. and Canada, or 2208-3000; www.marriott.com) and **Quality Hotel Santa Ana** (ℂ **877/424-6423** in the U.S. and Canada, or 2204-6700; www.choicehotels. com) are both modern business-class hotels a few miles of each other, right on the western Próspero Fernández Highway connecting Santa Ana and Escazú with San José.

Casa de las Tías *(Finds)*   This old Victorian-style home is comfortable and brimming with local character. The rooms are homey and simply decorated in a sort of Costa Rican country motif. The hotel has a wonderful covered veranda for sitting and admiring the well-tended gardens, as well as a TV room and common areas inside the house. The owners live on-site and are extremely helpful and friendly—you really get the sense of staying in someone's home here. Though it's on a quiet side street, Casa de las Tías is nonetheless just a block away from a busy section of Escazú, where you'll find scores of restaurants and shops, and easy access to public transportation. The hotel is 100m (1 block) south and 150m (1½ blocks) east of El Cruce de San Rafael de Escazú.

San Rafael de Escazú. ℂ **2289-5517.** Fax 2289-7353. www.hotels.co.cr/casatias.html. 5 units. $72–$82 (£36–£41) double. Rates include full breakfast. AE, MC, V. **Amenities:** Tour desk; laundry service. *In room:* Free Wi-Fi.

Hotel Casa Alegre *(Finds)*   Housed in a converted home on a residential side street just a couple of blocks from Santa Ana's central square and church, this hotel offers spacious, comfortable rooms. The decor leans heavily on Southwest American artwork and design touches, combined with Guatemalan textiles and locally made heavy wooden furniture. My favorite rooms are the upstairs units. Room nos. 3 and 4 even have skylights in their bathrooms. A midsize outdoor pool, which is good for lap swimming, takes up much of the backyard, but there's also a shady lounge area out back as well.

Santa Ana. ℂ/fax **2203-7467.** www.hotelcasaalegre.com. 8 units. $65–$79 (£33–£40) double. Rates include full breakfast. AE, MC, V. **Amenities:** Tour desk; laundry service. *In room:* TV, free Wi-Fi.

INEXPENSIVE

Hotel Mirador Pico Blanco   There's nothing fancy about the rooms here, but most offer absolutely fabulous views, at a good value. Some rooms have high ceilings, creating an appearance of spaciousness, and almost all of them have balconies (albeit

small ones) with good views. Most are pretty spartan in decor. The restaurant and bar also have stunning views. A few resident macaws fly around the hillsides during the day but come home here each evening.

1km (½ mile) south of the church in San Antonio de Escazú (A.P. 900), Escazú. ℂ **2228-1908.** Fax 2289-5189. www.hotelpicoblanco.com. 25 units. $50–$70 (£25–£35) double. Rates lower in the off season. MC, V. Free parking. **Amenities:** Restaurant; bar; tour desk; limited room service; babysitting; laundry service. *In room:* TV, no phone.

HEREDIA & ALAJUELA (AIRPORT AREA)

Alajuela and Heredia, two colonial-era cities that lie much closer to the airport than San José, are two great places to find small, distinct, and charming hotels. To learn more about Heredia, see "Side Trips from San José," later in this chapter. If you plan to get yourself to a remote beach or rainforest lodge as quickly as possible and to use San José and the Central Valley purely as a transportation hub, or if you just detest urban clutter, noise, and pollution, you might do well to choose one of the hotels listed below.

VERY EXPENSIVE

Doubletree Cariari By Hilton *Kids*   The Hilton company took over this historic resort hotel in 2008. With its use of stone walls, an open-air lobby, and lush garden plantings, the Cariari has always had a warm tropical feel and it still does after recent upgrades and renovations. The rooms, which are done in subdued tones, have either one king-size bed or two double beds, although I find most of the bathrooms a bit small. The suites are similarly appointed, but more spacious and with larger bathrooms. The Royal Service rooms come with extra perks, including personalized butler service. There's a full complement of facilities and services here, and families can take advantage of the dependable babysitting, game room, children's menus, and easy access to the modern mall nearby.

Autopista General Cañas, Ciudad Cariari (A.P. 737-1007, Centro Colón), San José. ℂ **800/222-8733** in the U.S. and Canada or 2239-0022. Fax 2239-2803. www.cariarisanjose.doubletree.com. 222 units. $179–$209 (£90–£105) double; $359–$559 (£180–£280) suite; $1,000 (£500) presidential suite. Rates include airport and downtown shuttle. Rates lower in the off season. AE, DC, MC, V. Free valet parking. **Amenities:** 2 restaurants; 2 bars; lounge; casino; large pool w/swim-up bar; small exercise room and spa; game room; concierge; tour desk; car-rental desk; business center; salon; 24-hr. room service; in-room massage; babysitting; laundry service; nonsmoking rooms. *In room:* A/C, TV, dataport, Wi-Fi, minibar, coffeemaker, hair dryer, iron, safe.

Finca Rosa Blanca Country Inn *Finds*   Finca Rosa Blanca is an eclectic architectural confection set amid the lush, green hillsides of a coffee plantation. There are turrets and curving walls of glass, arched windows, and a semicircular built-in couch. Everywhere the glow of polished hardwood blends with blindingly white stucco walls and brightly painted murals. If breathtaking bathrooms are your idea of ultimate luxury, consider splurging on the master suite, which has a stone waterfall that cascades into a tub in front of a huge picture window. This suite also has a spiral staircase that leads to the top of the turret. Still, all of the suites and villas have the same sense of eclectic luxury, with beautiful tile work, fabulous views, and creative design touches at every turn. Each decidedly unique room also comes with a private Jacuzzi tub. A brand-new restaurant with beautiful indoor and outdoor seating, as well as a full-service spa, were inaugurated in 2008.

Santa Bárbara de Heredia (mailing address: SJO 3475, P.O. Box 25369, Miami, FL 33102). ℂ **2269-9392.** Fax 2269-9555. www.fincarosablanca.com. 13 units. $270–$425 (£135–£213) double. Rates include breakfast. AE, MC, V. Free parking. **Amenities:** Restaurant; bar; lounge; small free-form pool set in the hillside; full-service spa; small exercise room; Jacuzzi; concierge; tour desk; limited room service; in-room massage; babysitting; laundry service; all rooms nonsmoking. *In room:* Free Wi-Fi, minibar, safe.

Marriott Costa Rica Hotel ★★★ For my money, the Marriott remains the best large luxury resort hotel in the San José area. Amenities are plentiful, and service is excellent. The hotel is designed in a mixed colonial style, with hand-painted Mexican tiles, antique red-clay roof tiles, weathered columns, and heavy wooden doors, lintels, and trim. The centerpiece is a large open-air interior patio that somewhat replicates Old Havana's Plaza de Armas. All rooms are cozy and well-appointed, with either a king-size or two double beds, a working desk, an elegant wooden armoire, plenty of closet space, a comfortable sitting chair and ottoman, and a small "Juliet" balcony. The bathrooms are up to par but seem slightly small for this price. The casual Antigua restaurant serves well-prepared Costa Rican and international dishes, and there's a more upscale Spanish restaurant and tapas bar. The large lobby-level bar features daily piano music and weekend jazz nights, with both indoor and patio seating.

San Antonio de Belén (A.P. 502-4005). © **888/236-2427** in the U.S. and Canada or 2298-0844 in Costa Rica. Fax 2298-0033. www.marriott.com. 299 units. $249 (£126) double; $299 (£149) executive level; $550 (£275) master suite; $1,000 (£500) presidential suite. Rates lower in off season. AE, DC, MC, V. Free valet parking. **Amenities:** 3 restaurants; bar; lounge; 2 pools; golf driving range; 3 tennis courts; small but well-appointed health club; Jacuzzi; sauna; concierge; tour desk; car-rental desk; free airport shuttle; business center and secretarial services; small shopping arcade; salon; 24-hr. room service; in-room massage; babysitting; laundry service; nonsmoking rooms. *In room:* A/C, TV, dataport, Wi-Fi, minibar, coffeemaker, hair dryer, iron, safe.

Peace Lodge ★★ *Finds* Nearby the popular La Paz Waterfall Gardens, the rooms here just might be some of the most impressive in the country. All are quite large and feature sparkling wood floors, handcrafted four-poster beds, beautiful stone fireplaces, intricately sculpted steel light fixtures, and a host of other creative details—along with a private balcony fitted with a mosaic-tiled Jacuzzi. The deluxe bathrooms come with a second oversize Jacuzzi set under a skylight in the middle of an immense room that features a full interior wall planted with ferns, orchids, and bromeliads and fed by a functioning waterfall system. Guests here have full access to all the tours and attractions of the La Paz Waterfall Gardens (p. 133) during normal operating hours and beyond. The lodge is located about 45 minutes from the airport and makes a good first stop if your itinerary takes you next to La Fortuna and Arenal Volcano, or to the Puerto Viejo de Sarapiquí region.

6km (3¾ miles) north of Varablanca on the road to San Miguel. © **954/727-3997** in the U.S., or 2482-2720 or 2225-0643 in Costa Rica. www.waterfallgardens.com. 17 units. $245–$305 (£123–£153) double; $395 (£198) villa. Rates include breakfast and entrance to La Paz Waterfall Gardens. Rates lower in off season; higher during peak weeks. AE, MC, V. **Amenities:** Restaurant; bar; 2 outdoor swimming pools; Jacuzzi; tour desk; laundry service. *In room:* A/C, TV, free Wi-Fi, minibar, coffeemaker, safe.

Xandari Resort & Spa ★★ *Finds* Xandari is yet another architecturally stunning small hotel not far from the airport. Set on a high hilltop above the city of Alajuela, Xandari commands wonderful views of the surrounding coffee farms and the Central Valley below. The owners are artists, and their original works and innovative design touches abound. The villas are huge private affairs with high-curved ceilings, stained-glass windows, living rooms with rattan sofas and chairs, as well as small kitchenettes. All come with both an outdoor patio with a view and a private covered palapa, as well as a smaller interior terrace with chaise longues. Most have king-size beds; the rest have two queen-size. The hotel grounds contain several miles of trails that pass by at least five jungle waterfalls, as well as lush gardens and fruit orchards. The adjacent "spa village" features a series of private thatch-roofed treatment rooms; a wide range of fitness classes is offered, too.

Alajuela (A.P. 1485-4050). © **866/363-3212** in the U.S. or 2443-2020. Fax 2442-4847. www.xandari.com. 22 villas. $230–$315 (£115–£158) villa for 2. Rates include continental breakfast. $25 (£13) for extra person; children 3 and under stay free in parent's room. Rates lower in off season; higher during peak periods. AE, DC, MC, V. **Amenities:** Restaurant; bar; lounge; 2 lap pools; spa; several Jacuzzis; in-room massage; laundry service. *In room:* Kitchenette, minibar, safe.

EXPENSIVE

Vista del Valle Plantation Inn ★★ *Finds*   Several individual and duplex villas are spread around the grounds here, which command an impressive view over the Río Grande and its steep-walled canyon. The architecture has a strong Japanese influence, from the open and airy villas to the comfortable wraparound decks. My favorite rooms are the Mona Lisa and Ilan-Ilan suites, which are octagonal affairs set on the edge of the bluff with great views and private outdoor showers. The grounds are wonderfully landscaped, with several inviting seating areas among a wealth of flowering tropical plants. There are stunning views from the restaurant, which features a regularly changing menu of fine international cuisine prepared with local ingredients. The hotel is 20 minutes north of the Juan Santamaría Airport, and staying here can cut as much as an hour off your travel time if you're heading out to the Pacific coast beaches, Arenal Volcano, and the Monteverde Cloud Forest.

A.P. 185-4003, Alajuela (mailing address: SJO 1994, P.O. Box 025216, Miami, FL 33102). © **2450-0800.** ©/fax 2451-1165. www.vistadelvalle.com. 11 units. $100 (£50) double; $155–$170 (£78–£85) villa. Rates include full breakfast. Rates lower in off season. AE, MC, V. **Amenities:** Restaurant; midsize tile pool w/interesting little fountain/waterfall; tennis court; Jacuzzi; limited room service; laundry service; horseback riding. *In room:* Free Wi-Fi, kitchenettes (in some), minibar, no phone.

MODERATE

In addition to the places listed below, **Viña Romantica** (© **2430-7621;** www.vina romantica.com) is a cozy new bed-and-breakfast in the hills just above Alajuela, which is earning strong praise for its amiable hosts and excellent restaurant, while **Pura Vida Hotel** (© **2441-1157;** www.puravidahotel.com) is a popular Alajuela inn that's also convenient to the airport.

El Rodeo Country Inn ★   Located around the "backside" of the airport, in San Antonio de Belén, this long-standing hotel got a major makeover and face-lift in 2007. All of the rooms are spacious and feature updated furnishings and decor, including sturdy beds with artistic wood-and-metal headboards adorned with sculpted cala lilies. Most have wood floors and large bathrooms. I'd ask for one either in the new section, or on the second floor of the older building. The suites have a Jacuzzi tub and sitting area. There are several lounge areas spread around the rambling structure, as well as a pool table on a large open second-floor veranda. The namesake El Rodeo steakhouse restaurant here is excellent.

San Antonio de Belén. © **2293-3909.** Fax 2293-3464. www.elrodeohotel.com. 29 units. $115 (£58) double; $175 (£88) suite. Rates include buffet breakfast. AE, DC, MC, V. Free parking. **Amenities:** 2 restaurants; bar; midsize pool; unlit outdoor tennis court; Jacuzzi; tour desk; limited room service; laundry service. *In room:* A/C, TV, free Wi-Fi, minibar, coffeemaker, hair dryer, safe.

Hampton Inn & Suites   If familiarity, comfort, and proximity to the airport are important to you, then the Hampton Inn is your best bet. The rooms are what you'd expect from a well-known chain, and because the hotel is relatively new, they don't show much wear and tear. The hotel has both standard rooms and suites. Breakfast is served, but no other dining options are on-site; a Denny's and a separate Costa Rican fast-food chicken joint are just across the parking lot, as is a large swank casino, with a popular bar. This is a good choice if your plane arrives very late or leaves very early and you don't plan to spend any time in San José. Free local calls, high-speed Internet access in all rooms, and Wi-Fi in public areas are all perks that will appeal to business travelers and vacationers alike. Those staying in the suites get free international calls.

Autopista General Cañas, by the airport (A.P. 195-4003), San José. © 800/426-7866 in the U.S. or 2436-0000. Fax 2442-2781. www.hamptoninn.com. 100 units. $156 (£78) double; $183 (£92) suite. Rates include buffet breakfast and airport shuttle. AE, DC, MC, V. Free parking. **Amenities:** Bar; small pool; small exercise room; tour desk; business center; babysitting; laundry service; nonsmoking rooms. *In room:* A/C, TV, dataport, free Wi-Fi, minifridge and microwave (in suites), coffeemaker, hair dryer, iron.

Hotel Bougainvillea (★ (*Value*)   The Hotel Bougainvillea is an excellent choice—a great value if you're looking for a hotel in a quiet residential neighborhood not far from downtown. It offers most of the amenities of the more expensive resort hotels around the Central Valley, but it charges considerably less. The views across the valley from this hillside location are wonderful, and the gardens are beautifully designed and well tended. In fact, the bird-watching is pretty good in the hotel's relatively expansive gardens. Rooms are carpeted and have small triangular balconies oriented to the views. Free Wi-Fi connections are offered throughout most of the hotel. A complimentary hourly downtown shuttle bus will take you in and out of town.

In Santo Tomás de Santo Domingo de Heredia, 100m (1 block) west of the Escuela de Santo Tomás (A.P. 69-2120), San José. © 2244-1414. Fax 2244-1313. www.hb.co.cr. 81 units. $100–$115 (£50–£58) double; $123–$135 (£62–£67) suite. Rates include hourly free downtown shuttle bus. AE, DC, MC, V. Free parking. **Amenities:** Restaurant; bar; midsize pool in attractive garden; 2 lighted tennis courts; Jacuzzi; sauna; tour desk; business center; limited room service; babysitting; laundry service; nonsmoking rooms. *In room:* TV, free Wi-Fi, coffeemaker, hair dryer.

Orquídeas Inn   This boutique inn is just 10 minutes from the airport on the road heading out of Alajuela to Grecia and the Poás Volcano. The rooms are all spacious and comfortable, with tile floors, private bathrooms, and colorful Guatemalan bedspreads. The deluxe rooms are in a separate building up on a hill, and most of these offer wonderful views, particularly those with balconies facing one of the nearby volcanoes. There are a few larger minisuites located around the small pool, as well as a separate geodesic dome with a king-size bed in a loft reached by a spiral staircase, a large sunken tub in the bathroom, and a full kitchen and living-room area. The entire grounds are lush and tropical. The Marilyn Monroe bar serves up good drinks, *bocas* (appetizers), and some seriously spicy Buffalo wings. The hotel provides free local calls and Internet access to guests.

A.P. 394, Alajuela. © 2433-7128. Fax 2433-9740. www.orquideasinn.com. 27 units. $69–$99 (£34–£49) double; $119–$160 (£60–£80) suite. Rates include breakfast buffet. AE, MC, V. Free parking. **Amenities:** Restaurant; bar; pool; Jacuzzi; concierge; tour desk; laundry service. *In room:* A/C, TV (in some), coffeemaker, hair dryer, safe.

4 Where to Dine

In broad terms, Costa Rican cuisine is easily disparaged and dismissed. Rice and beans are served at nearly every meal, the selection of other dishes is minimal, and Ticos generally don't go for spicy food. In recent years, though, some contemporary and creative chefs have been trying to educate and enlighten the Costa Rican palate, particularly in San José, and the results are promising. Still, most visitors to the capital city quickly tire of Tico fare, even in its more chichi incarnations, and start seeking out the many local restaurants serving international cuisines. They are richly rewarded.

San José has a rather amazing variety of restaurants serving cuisines from all over the world. Most restaurants fall into the moderate price range, although prices have crept up in recent years, and unless you stick to simple local joints, you probably won't find many true bargains. Service can be indifferent at many restaurants because the gratuity is already tacked on to the check, and tipping is not common among locals.

LOCAL CUISINE   If you'd really like to sample the local flavor, head to a *soda,* the equivalent of a diner in the United States, where you can get good, cheap, filling Tico food. Rice and beans are the staples and show up at breakfast, lunch, and dinner (when mixed together, they're called *gallo pinto*). For breakfast, they're garnished with everything from fried eggs to steak. At lunch and dinner, rice and beans are the main components of a *casado* (which means "married"), the Costa Rican equivalent of a "blue-plate special." A *casado* generally is served with a salad of cabbage and tomatoes; fried plantains; and steak, chicken, or fish. A plate of *gallo pinto* might cost $2 (£1), and a *casado* might cost $2.50 to $4 (£1.25–£2), usually with a *fresco* (a fresh-fruit drink) thrown into the bargain.

While in Costa Rica, be sure to taste a few *frescos.* They're a bit like a fresh-fruit milkshake without the ice cream, and when made with mangoes, papayas, bananas, or any of the other delicious tropical fruits of Costa Rica, they're pure ambrosia. *Frescos* can be made with water *(con agua)* or with milk *(con leche),* and preferences vary. Certain fruits such as carambola (star fruit), *maracuyá* (a type of passion fruit), and *cas* (you'll just have to try it) are used only with water. But remember, although the water in Costa Rica is generally very safe to drink, those with tender stomachs or intestinal tracts should stick to *frescos* made with milk because it's pasteurized.

FRUIT VENDORS   There's a fruit vendor on almost every street corner in downtown San José. If you're lucky enough to be in town between April and June, you can sample more varieties of mangoes than you ever knew existed. I like buying them already cut up in a little bag; they cost a little more this way, but you don't get nearly as messy. Be sure to try a green mango with salt and chili peppers—it's guaranteed to wake up your taste buds. Another common street food that you might be wondering about is called *pejibaye,* a bright orange palm nut about the size of a plum. They're boiled in big pots on carts, you eat them in much the same way you eat an avocado, and they taste a bit like squash.

LATE-NIGHT BITES   San José has quite a few **24-hour restaurants.** The best of these is **Cafeteria 1830,** which is described below. Another popular place, which is definitely a bit seedier, is **Chelles,** on Avenida Central and Calle 9 (see "San José After Dark," later in this chapter, for more information). Then there's **Del Mar,** which belongs to and is across from the Hotel Del Rey (p. 109); with stained-glass windows and efficient service, this is a good option, although the food is rather pedestrian and uninspired. Finally, you'll find a **Denny's** (② 2231-3500), at the Best Western Irazú, on the highway out to the airport (there's another beside the Hampton Inn at the airport).

DOWNTOWN SAN JOSE
MODERATE

Café Mundo *Finds* INTERNATIONAL   This popular place mixes creative cuisine with an ambience of casual elegance. Wood tables and Art Deco wrought-iron chairs are spread spaciously around several rooms in this former colonial mansion. Additional seating can be had on the open-air front veranda and in the small gardens both front and back. The appetizers include vegetable tempura, crab cakes, and chicken satay alongside more traditional Tico standards such as *patacones* (fried plantain chips) and fried yuca. There's a long list of pastas and pizzas, as well as more substantial main courses, nightly specials, and delicious desserts. One room here boasts colorful wall murals by Costa Rican artist Miguel Cassafont. This place is almost always filled with a broad mix of San José's gay, bohemian, theater, arts, and university crowds.

Calle 15 and Av. 9, 200m (2 blocks) east and 100m (1 block) north of the INS building. ② 2222-6190. Reservations recommended. Main courses $5.50–$18 (£2.75–£9). AE, MC, V. Mon–Thurs 11am–11pm; Fri 11am–midnight; Sat 5pm–midnight.

Cafeteria 1830 *Finds* INTERNATIONAL   With veranda and patio seating directly fronting the Plaza de la Cultura, this is one of the most atmospheric spots for a casual bite and some good people-watching. A wrought-iron railing, white columns, and arches create an old-world atmosphere; on the plaza in front of the cafe, a marimba band performs and vendors sell handicrafts. Stop by for the breakfast and watch the plaza vendors set up their booths, or peruse the *Tico Times* over coffee while you have your shoes polished. The menu is basic and the food is respectable, if unspectacular, but there isn't a better place downtown to bask in the tropical sunshine while you sip a beer or have a light lunch, and it's a great place to come before or after a show at the Teatro Nacional.

At the Gran Hotel Costa Rica, Av. 2, btw. calles 1 and 3. ② 2221-4011. Sandwiches $5.50–$8 (£2.75–£4); main courses $7–$35 (£3.50–£18). AE, DC, MC, V. Daily 24 hr.

La Cocina de Leña COSTA RICAN   Located in the El Pueblo shopping, dining, and entertainment center, La Cocina de Leña ("The Wood Stove") is designed to invoke the ambience and vibe of a rustic rural Costa Rican home. There are stacks of firewood on shelves above the booths, long stalks of bananas hanging from pillars, tables suspended from the ceiling by heavy ropes, and, most unusual of all, menus printed on paper bags. If you're adventurous, you could try some of the more unusual dishes—perhaps oxtail stew served with yuca and *plátano* might appeal to you. If not, there are plenty of steaks and seafood dishes on the menu. *Chilasuilas* are delicious tortillas filled with fried meat. Black-bean soup with egg is a Costa Rican standard and is mighty fine here; the corn soup with pork is equally satisfying. For dessert, there's *tres leches* cake as well as the more unusual sweetened *chiverre*, which is a type of squash that looks remarkably like a watermelon.

Centro Comercial El Pueblo. ② 2255-1360 or 2223-3704. Reservations recommended. Main courses $6–$25 (£3–£13). AE, MC, V. Daily 11:30am–11pm.

La Piazzetta *Finds* ITALIAN   With a long menu and formal service, this restaurant reminds me of the Italian restaurants of old in New York's Little Italy. The menu includes quite a few risotto dishes, as well as several lobster offerings and some Sicilian fare. The veal scaloppini in a truffle sauce is excellent. Salads are colorful and artistically arranged. For dessert, sample a classic chocolate mousse or tiramisu. The wine list is quite extensive, with good and reasonably priced offerings from Italy, and most other prominent wine producing regions around the world.

Paseo Colón near Calle 40 (opposite Banco de Costa Rica). ⑦ 2221-8451. Reservations recommended. Main courses $6–$28 (£2.90–£14). AE, MC, V. Mon–Sat 11:30–3pm and 6:30–11pm.

Tin Jo 🍴🍴 *Finds* CHINESE/PAN-ASIAN   San José has hundreds of Chinese restaurants, but most simply serve up tired takes on chop suey, chow mein, and fried rice. In contrast, Tin Jo has a wide and varied menu, with an assortment of Cantonese and Szechuan staples, as well as a range of Thai, Japanese, and Malaysian dishes, and even some Indian food. This is San José's only true Pan-Asian restaurant. It's also a restaurant that pays attention to the details. Some of the dishes are served in edible rice-noodle bowls, and the pineapple shrimp in coconut-milk curry is served in the hollowed-out half of a fresh pineapple. Dishes not to miss include the salt-and-pepper shrimp, beef teriyaki, and Thai curries. For dessert, try the sticky rice with mango, or banana tempura. The waiters here are some of the most attentive in Costa Rica. The decor features artwork and textiles from across Asia, and you'll have real tablecloths and cloth napkins. Tin Jo is also a great option for vegetarians, and even vegans.

Calle 11, btw. avs. 6 and 8. ⑦ 2221-7605 or 2257-3622. Main courses $8–$22 (£4–£11). AE, MC, V. Mon–Sat 11:30am–3pm and 5:30–10pm (Fri–Sat kitchen open 'til 11pm); Sun 11:30am–10pm.

INEXPENSIVE

In addition to the places listed below, the **Q'Café** (⑦ 2221-0707) is a delightful little European-style cafe with a pretty perch above the busy corner of Avenida Central and Calle 2. Try to grab a seat overlooking the action on the street below.

Café del Teatro Nacional 🍴 CAFE/COFFEE SHOP   Even if there's no show on during your visit, you can enjoy a light meal, sandwich, dessert, or a cup of coffee here, while soaking up the neoclassical atmosphere. The theater was built in the 1890s from the designs of European architects, and the Art Nouveau chandeliers, ceiling murals, and marble floors and tables are pure Parisian. The ambience is French-cafe chic, but the marimba music drifting in from outside the open window and the changing art exhibits by local artists will remind you that you're still in Costa Rica. On sunny days, there's outdoor seating at wrought-iron tables on the side of the theater. In addition to the regular hours of operation listed below, the cafe is open until 8pm any evening that there is a performance in the theater.

In the Teatro Nacional, Av. 2 btw. calles 3 and 5. ⑦ 2221-1329. Sandwiches $3–$7 (£1.50–£3.50); main courses $5–$12 (£2.50–£6). AE, MC, V. Mon–Sat 9am–4:30pm.

Vishnu VEGETARIAN   Vegetarians will likely find their way to this Vishnu restaurant or one of its many sister outlets around the city. The vibe's a little too plastic, too loud, and too brightly lit for my tastes in a vegetarian joint. However, most people just come for the filling *plato del día* that includes soup, salad, veggies, an entree, and dessert for under $4 (£2). The menu also offers bean burgers and cheese sandwiches on whole-wheat bread. At the cashier's counter you can buy natural cosmetics, honey, and bags of granola. There's another Vishnu (⑦ 2223-3095) on the north side of Avenida 8, between calles 11 and 9.

Av. 1, btw. calles 1 and 3. ⑦ 2256-6063. Main courses $3.50–$10 (£1.75–£5). MC, V. Daily 7am–9:30pm.

> (*Moments*   **Only in the Central Valley: Dining Under the Stars on a Mountain's Edge**
>
> Although there are myriad unique experiences to be had in Costa Rica, one of my favorites is dining on the side of a volcano with the lights of San José shimmering below. These hanging restaurants, called *miradores,* are a resourceful response to the city's topography. Because San José is set in a broad valley surrounded on all sides by volcanic mountains, people who live in these mountainous areas have no place to go but up—so they do, building roadside cafes vertically up the sides of the volcanoes.
>
> The food at most of these establishments is not spectacular, but the views often are, particularly at night, when the wide valley sparkles in a wash of lights. The town of **Aserrí,** 10km (6¼ miles) south of downtown San José, is the king of *miradores,* and **Mirador Ram Luna** (© 2230-3060) is the king of Aserri. Grab a window seat and, if you've got the fortitude, order a plate of *chicharrones* (fried pork rinds). There's often live music. You can hire a cab for around $10 (£5) or take the Aserri bus at Avenida 6 between calles Central and 2. Just ask the driver where to get off.
>
> There are also *miradores* in the hills above Escazú and in San Ramón de Tres Ríos and Heredia. The most popular is **Le Monestère** (© 2289-4404; closed Sun), an elegant converted church serving somewhat overrated French and Belgian cuisine in a spectacular setting above the hills of Escazú. I recommend coming here just for the less formal **La Cava Grill** ⊕, which often features live music, mostly folk-pop but sometimes jazz. I also like **Mirador Tiquicia** (© 2289-5839), which occupies several rooms in a sprawling old Costa Rican home and has live folkloric dance shows on Thursday.

LA SABANA/PASEO COLON
EXPENSIVE

Grano de Oro Restaurant ⊛⊛⊛ *Finds* INTERNATIONAL   Following a major remodel, this restaurant is even larger and more ornate, but still set around the lovely interior courtyard of the wonderful Hotel Grano de Oro (p. 112). The atmosphere here is intimate, relaxed, and refined, all at the same time. The menu features a wide range of meat and fish dishes. The *lomito piemontes* is two medallions of filet mignon stuffed with Gorgonzola cheese in a sherry sauce, while the *pernil de conejo* is a rabbit thigh stuffed with a mushroom pâté and served with a Dijon mustard sauce. If you opt for fish, I recommend the macadamia-encrusted corvina, which is served with a light and tangy orange sauce. Be sure to save room for the "Grano de Oro pie," a decadent dessert with various layers of chocolate and coffee mousses and creams. This place also has a good wine list, including a range of options by the glass.

Calle 30, no. 251, btw. avs. 2 and 4, 150m (1½ blocks) south of Paseo Colón. © 2255-3322. Reservations recommended. Main courses $8.50–$30 (£4.25–£15). AE, MC, V. Daily 6am–10pm.

Park Café ⊛⊛⊛ *Finds* INTERNATIONAL   Having opened and run a Michelin two-star restaurant in London and another one-star joint in Cannes, Richard Neat now finds himself turning out his impressive fusion cuisine in an intimate space spread around the interior patio courtyard of a stately old downtown mansion, which also doubles as an antiques and imported furniture store. The menu changes regularly but might feature some roasted scallops with ricotta tortellini in a pumpkin jus, or some expertly grilled quail on a vegetable purée bed, topped with poached quail egg. Presentations are artfully done, and often served in such a way as to encourage sharing. The well-thought-out and fairly priced wine list is a perfect complement to the cuisine.

Sabana Norte, 1 block north of Rostipollos. (✆ **2290-6324**. Reservations recommended. Main courses $12–$25 (£6–£13). V. Tues–Sat noon–2pm and 7–9:30pm.

MODERATE

El Chicote ✿ COSTA RICAN/STEAK   This is one of San José's most venerable and popular steakhouses. The large room is divided by half-walls planted with tropical flora and a bevy of hanging ferns, and heavy wooden beams and plenty of varnished-wood accents are used throughout. True meat aficionados should order the imported rib-eye or pound-and-a-half T-bone. There's an extensive selection of fish and poultry dishes as well. Everything comes with a choice of baked or mashed potatoes, black beans, and fresh tortillas. The wine list features a broad range of Italian, Spanish, French, and Californian wines. Waiters wear black jackets, white shirts, and black bow ties—typical of the unusually formal (for Costa Rica) service.

Av. Las Américas, 400m (4 blocks) west of the ICE building, Sabana Norte. (✆ **2232-0936** or 2232-3777. Reservations recommended. Main courses $8–$22 (£4–£11). AE, MC, V. Mon–Fri 11am–3pm and 6–11pm; Sat–Sun 11am–11pm.

Machu Picchu ✿ PERUVIAN/INTERNATIONAL   Machu Picchu is an unpretentious little restaurant that is perennially one of the most popular places in San José. The menu is classic Peruvian. One of my favorite entrees is the *causa limeña,* lemon-flavored mashed potatoes stuffed with shrimp. The ceviche here is excellent, as is the *ají de gallina,* a dish of shredded chicken in a fragrant cream sauce, and octopus with garlic butter. For main dishes, I recommend *corvina a lo macho,* sea bass in a slightly spicy tomato-based seafood sauce. Be sure to ask for a pisco sour, a classic Peruvian drink made from pisco, a grape liquor. These folks have a sister restaurant over in San Pedro (✆ **2283-3679**), and another in Santa Ana (✆ **2203-7657**), set on a hillside with a great view over the valley below.

Calle 32, btw. avs. 1 and 3, 150m (1½ blocks) north of the KFC on Paseo Colón. (✆ **2222-7384**. Reservations recommended. Main courses $4–$16 (£2–£8). AE, DC, MC, V. Mon–Sat 11am–3pm and 6–10pm.

INEXPENSIVE

Soda Tapia COSTA RICAN   The food is unspectacular, dependable, and quite inexpensive at this very popular local diner. There's seating inside the brightly lit dining room, as well as on the sidewalk-style patio fronting the parking area. Dour but efficient waitstaff take the order you mark down on your combination menu/bill. This is a great place for late-night eats or for before or after a visit to Parque La Sabana or Museo de Arte Costarricense. These folks also have another site in a small strip mall in Santa Ana (✆ **2203-7174**).

Calle 42 and Av. 2, across from the Museo de Arte Costarricense. (✆ **2222-6734**. Sandwiches $2–$4 (£1–£2); main dishes $4–$8 (£2–£4). MC, V. Sun–Thurs 6am–2am; Fri–Sat 24 hr.

SAN PEDRO/LOS YOSES

In addition to the restaurants listed below, local and visiting vegetarians swear by the little **Comida Para Sentir Restaurante Vegetariano San Pedro** (© 2224-1163), located 125m (1¼ blocks) north of the San Pedro Church. Despite the massive size and popularity of the nearby **Il Pomodoro,** I prefer **Pane E Vino** (© 2280-2869), an excellent pasta-and-pizza joint on the eastern edge of San Pedro.

For Peruvian cuisine try **Bohemia** ✸ (© 2253-6348) in Barrio Escalante, or the branch of **Machu Picchu** (© 2283-3679; see above for a review) in San Pedro. Finally, if you're hankering for sushi, try **Ichiban** ✸ (© 2253-8012) in San Pedro, or **Matsuri** ✸ (© 2280-5522), a little farther east in Curridabat.

MODERATE

Donde Carlos ✸✸ ARGENTINE/STEAK   Bold architectural touches abound in this stylish restaurant, yet the food is built primarily around simple, perfectly grilled meats and fresh fish. You pass the wood-burning Argentine-style charcoal grill as you enter. I like the outdoor tables on the second-floor balcony when the weather permits. Most folks stick to the hearty steak options, but you can also order a wide range of sausages and offal meats, as well as fresh tuna. Don't pass on the apple pancake dessert, since it's delicious. All portions are huge, and this place has a good and reasonably priced wine list to boot.

1 block north of the Fatima Church in Los Yoses. © 2225-0819. Main courses $8–$24 (£4–£12). AE, MC, V. Mon–Fri noon–3pm; Mon–Thurs 6:30–10:30pm; Fri 6:30–11pm; Sat noon–11pm; Sun noon–7pm.

Jurgen's ✸✸ INTERNATIONAL   Housed in a boutique business-class hotel, this elegant little restaurant serves excellent European-style continental fare in a refined atmosphere. The lighting is low and service extremely professional. You'll find poached salmon with a dill sauce, and grilled tilapia with a Dijon mustard sauce. The steaks are top cuts of beef, perfectly prepared. This place has one of the more extensive wine lists in town. The owner, Jurgen Mormel, also has several gourmet specialty food shops around San José and in Playa Herradura.

Inside Hotel Jade, 2½ blocks north of the Subaru dealership, Los Yoses. © 2283-2239. Main courses $8–$24 (£4–£12). AE, MC, V. Mon–Fri noon–2:30pm and 6–10pm; Sat 6–10:30pm.

Olio ✸ *Value* MEDITERRANEAN   The exposed brick walls, dark wood wainscoting, and stained-glass lamps imbue this place with character and romance. Couples might want to grab a table in a quiet nook, while groups tend to dominate the large main room or crowd the bar. There are even a few outdoor tables on a narrow sidewalk beside some train tracks, and nonsmokers might want these, as the main bar and dining areas are often tightly packed and smoke-filled. The extensive tapas menu features traditional Spanish fare, as well as bruschetta, antipasti, and a Greek *mezza* plate. For a main dish, I recommend the chicken Vesuvio, which is marinated first in a balsamic vinegar reduction and finished with a creamy herb sauce; or the *arrollado siciliano,* which is a thin filet of steak rolled around spinach, sun-dried tomatoes, and mozzarella cheese and topped with a pomodoro sauce. The midsize wine list features very reasonably priced wines from Italy, France, Spain, Germany, Chile, Greece, and even Bulgaria.

Barrio California, 200m (2 blocks) north of Bagelman's. © 2281-0541. Main courses $5–$14 (£2.50–£7). AE, DC, MC, V. Mon–Fri 11:30am–1am; Sat 4pm–midnight.

INEXPENSIVE

Whappin' ✿ *Finds* COSTA RICAN/CARIBBEAN   You don't have to go to Limón or Cahuita to get good home-cooked Caribbean food. In addition to *rondon,* a coconut milk–based stew or soup (see "That Rundown Feeling" on p. 392), you can also get the classic rice and beans cooked in coconut milk, as well as a range of fish and chicken dishes from the coastal region. I like the whole red snapper covered in a spicy sauce of sautéed onions. There's a small bar at the entrance and some simple tables spread around the restaurant, with an alcove here and there. Everything is very simple, and prices are quite reasonable. After a dinner of fresh fish, with rice, beans, and *patacones,* the only letdown is that the beach is some 4 hours away.

Barrio Escalante, 200m (2 blocks) east of El Farolito. ✆ **2283-1480.** Main courses $8–$12 (£4–£6). AE, MC, V. Mon–Sat 11:30am–2:30pm and 6–10pm.

ESCAZU & SANTA ANA

These two suburbs on the western side of town have the most vibrant restaurant scene in San José. Although there's high turnover and sudden closings, this remains a good area to check out for a variety of dining experiences. In addition to the places mentioned below, **Il Panino** ✿ (✆ 2228-3126) is an upscale sandwich shop and cafe, located in the Centro Comercial El Paco. **Santa Ana Tex Mex** (✆ 2282-6342) is one of the most popular places on this side of town. Located a half-block north of the main church in Santa Ana, it serves up Tex-Mex cuisine in a lively atmosphere. Located just outside of Santa Ana, **Essentia** ✿ (✆ 2203-7503) is another excellent fusion restaurant, located inside the hotel **Corteza Amarilla** (p. 115).

Finally, a good one-stop option to consider is the Plaza Itskatzu shopping center, just off the highway and sharing a parking lot with the Courtyard San José. Here you'll find a wide variety of moderately priced restaurant options, including **Tutti Li** (✆ 2289-8768), a good Italian restaurant and pizzeria; **Chancay** (✆ 2289-6964), which serves Peruvian and Peruvian/Chinese cuisine; **La Guagua** (✆ 2288-5112), serving up tasty Cuban food; **Las Tapas de Manuel** ✿ (✆ 2288-5700), a Spanish-style tapas restaurant; and franchise outlets of both **Hooters** (✆ 2289-3498) and **Outback Steakhouse** (✆ 2288-0511).

EXPENSIVE

Bacchus ✿✿✿ *Finds* ITALIAN   Easily my favorite Italian restaurant in San José, this place is housed in a historic home that is over a century old. You'd never know it following the massive restoration and remodel. Nevertheless, this place somehow seamlessly blends the old with the new in an elegant atmosphere. The best tables are on the covered back patio, where you can watch the open kitchen and wood-burning pizza oven in action. The menu features a range of antipasti, pastas, pizzas, and main dishes. Everything is perfectly prepared and beautifully presented. The desserts are also excellent, and the wine list is extensive and fairly priced.

Downtown Santa Ana. ✆ **2282-5441.** Reservations required. Main courses $8–$24 (£4–£12). AE, MC, V. Tues–Sat noon–3pm and 6–11pm; Sun noon–9pm.

Barbecue Los Anonos ✿ COSTA RICAN/STEAK   Good steaks and well-prepared Costa Rican cuisine have made this simple restaurant something of an institution. Most of the seating is at rustic wooden tables covered with red-and-white checkered tablecloths, and long and rustic booths set under the shelter of low interior red-tile roofs. Aged Angus beef is served, and this is *the* place to come if you're craving a 16-ounce T-bone on the west side of town. There are also a host of chicken, pork, and fish options; I recommend the mixed-grill plate for two, which comes with a little bit of everything.

600m (6 blocks) west of the Los Anonos bridge in San Rafael de Escazú, next to the Sarretto Market. ✆ **2228-0180**. Reservations recommended. Main courses $10–$28 (£5–£14). AE, MC, V. Tues–Sat noon–3pm; Tues–Thurs 6–10pm; Fri–Sat 6–11pm; Sun 11:30–9pm.

La Luz ✿✿ CALIFORNIAN/FUSION   La Luz was one of the first fusion restaurants in Costa Rica, and it continues to serves up some of the better prepared and more adventurous food in Costa Rica. I keep coming back for the fiery garlic prawns, which are sautéed in ancho-chili oil and sage and served over a roasted-garlic potato mash. The whole thing is served with a garnish of fried leeks and a tequila-lime butter and cilantro-oil sauce. I also enjoy the passion fruit–glazed duck breast. On top of an extensive menu, there are nightly specials and a wide selection of inventive appetizers and desserts. The glass-walled dining room is one of the most elegant in town, with a view of the city lights. The waitstaff is attentive and knowledgeable.

In the Alta Hotel (p. 115), on the old road to Santa Ana. ✆ **2282-4160**. Reservations recommended. Main courses $14–$21 (£7–£11). AE, DC, MC, V. Daily 6:30am–10pm.

MODERATE

La Cava Grill ✿ *Finds* COSTA RICAN/STEAK   This place is a cozy and warm spot built underneath the popular yet overpriced and overrated Le Monestère restaurant. While the decor is much less ornate, the service much less formal, and the menu much less French, the view is just as spectacular. Grab a window seat on a clear night and enjoy the sparkle of the lights below. The menu features a range of simply prepared meat, poultry, and fish. More adventurous diners can try the *tepezquintle* (a large rodent, also called a *paca*), which is actually quite tasty. There's live music and a festive party most weekend nights in the attached bar. My big complaint here is that the wine list is borrowed from the upstairs restaurant, and is pretentious and expensive.

1.5km (1 mile) south of Centro Comercial Paco; follow the signs to Le Monestère. ✆ **2289-4404**. Reservations recommended. Main courses $6–$20 (£3–£10). AE, MC, V. Mon–Sat 6pm–1:30am.

Taj Mahal ✿ *Finds* INDIAN   The only true and dedicated Indian restaurant in the country, this place does a good, but not great, job. The menu is quite extensive and covers most of the traditional bases with *biryanis, vindaloos, tikka masalas,* and a variety of curries. They have an authentic tandoor oven, and the tandoori meats are excellently prepared. The restaurant is spread out through several rooms in a converted home. The decorations and furniture are mostly imported from India. I like the few outdoor tables in the backyard, especially for lunch. As at Tin Jo, this is a great choice for vegetarians.

On the old road to Santa Ana, 1km (½ mile) west of Centro Comercial Paco. ✆ **2228-0980**. Reservations recommended. Main courses $7–$15 (£3.50–£7.50). AE, MC, V. Tues–Sun noon–3pm and 6–11pm.

5 What to See & Do

Most visitors to Costa Rica try to get out of the city as fast as possible so they can spend more time on the beach or off in the rainforests. But there are a few attractions in San José to keep you busy. Some of the best and most modern museums in Central America are here, with a wealth of fascinating pre-Columbian artifacts. Standouts include the remodeled Museo de Jade Marco Fidel Tristán (Jade Museum) and the centrally located Centro Nacional de Arte y Cultura (National Center of Arts and Culture), featuring yet another museum and several performing-arts spaces.

There are also several great things to see and do just outside San José in the Central Valley. If you start doing day trips out of the city, you can spend quite a few days in this region. See "San José in 3 Days" in chapter 4 for additional touring ideas.

ORGANIZED TOURS   There really isn't much reason to take a tour of San José. It's so compact that you can easily visit all the major sights on your own, as described below. However, if you want to take a city tour, which will run you between $15 and $40 (£7.50–£20), here are some companies you can use: **Horizontes Travel** ✪✪, Calle 32 between avenidas 3 and 5 (✆ 2222-2022; www.horizontes.com); **Gray Line Tours,** Avenida 7 between calles 6 and 8, with additional offices at the Hampton Inn and Best Western Irazú (✆ 2220-2126; www.graylinecostarica.com); and **Swiss Travel Service** (✆ 2282-4898; www.swisstravelcr.com). These same companies also offer a complete range of day trips out of San José (see "Side Trips from San José," later in this chapter). Almost all of the major hotels have tour desks, and most of the smaller hotels will also help arrange tours and day trips.

One interesting alternative to the standard tour bus–based city tours is **Tico Walks'** (✆ 2283-8281; www.ticowalks.com) guided 2½-hour walking tour of the downtown center, which takes in many of the city's top architectural sites and urban attractions. The tour runs every Tuesday, Thursday, Saturday, and Sunday at 10am, and costs $10 (£5) per person. Private tours are also available.

THE TOP ATTRACTIONS

In addition to the attractions listed below, you might consider a quick stop at San José's main **cathedral.** The church and its interior are largely unspectacular. However, you'll see a pretty garden, as well as a massive marble statue of Pope Juan Pablo II, with a woman and child, carved by celebrated Costa Rican sculptor Jorge Jiménez Deredia. Deredia also has a work at the Vatican. The cathedral is located at the corner of Avenida 2 and Calle Central.

Centro Nacional de Arte y Cultura (National Center of Art and Culture) ✪ *Finds*
Occupying a full city block, this was once the National Liquor Factory (FANAL). Now it houses the offices of the Cultural Ministry, several performing-arts centers, and the Museum of Contemporary Art and Design. The latter has done an excellent job of promoting cutting-edge Costa Rican and Central American artists, while also featuring impressive traveling international exhibits, including large retrospectives by Mexican painter José Cuevas and Ecuadorian painter Oswaldo Guayasamín. If you're looking for modern dance, experimental theater, or a lecture on Costa Rican video, this a good place to check out. Allow around 2 hours to take in all the exhibits here.

Calle 13 btw. avs. 3 and 5. (✆ 2257-7202 or 2257-9370. Admission $2 (£1), 80¢ (40p) for students with valid ID, free for seniors and children 11 and under, free for everyone on Mon. Museum Mon–Sat 10:30am–5:30pm.

Museo de Arte Costarricense (Costa Rican Art Museum) ✪✪
This small museum at the end of Paseo Colón in Parque La Sabana was formerly the country's principal airport terminal. Today it houses a collection of works in all media by Costa Rica's most celebrated artists. On display are some exceptionally beautiful pieces in a wide range of styles, demonstrating how Costa Rican artists have interpreted and imitated the major European movements over the years. In addition to the permanent

collection of sculptures, paintings, and prints, there are regular temporary exhibits. If the second floor is open during your visit, have a look at the conference room's bas-relief walls, which chronicle the history of Costa Rica from pre-Columbian times to the present with evocative images of its people. Be sure to visit the outdoor sculpture garden. So far, the collection is small, but it does include at least one representative work each by José Sancho, Jorge Jiménez Deredia, Max Jiménez, and Francisco Zuñiga. Moreover, the outdoor setting is lovely. You can easily spend an hour or two at this museum—more if you take a stroll through the neighboring park.

Calle 42 and Paseo Colón, Parque La Sabana Este. © 2222-7155. www.musarco.go.cr. Admission $5 (£2.50) adults, $3 (£1.50) for students with valid ID, free for children and seniors, free for everyone Sun. Tues–Fri 9am–5pm; Sat–Sun 10am–4pm.

Museo de Jade Marco Fidel Tristán (Jade Museum) 🏛   Jade was the most valu-able commodity among the pre-Columbian cultures of Mexico and Central America, worth more than gold. Located on the first floor of the INS (National Insurance Company) building, this popular museum houses a huge collection of jade artifacts dating from 500 B.C. to A.D. 800. Most are large pendants that were parts of necklaces and are primarily human and animal figures. A fascinating display illustrates how the primitive peoples of this region carved this extremely hard stone.

The museum also possesses an extensive collection of pre-Columbian polychrome terra-cotta vases, bowls, and figurines. Some of these pieces are amazingly modern in design and exhibit a surprisingly advanced technique. Particularly fascinating is a vase that incorporates real human teeth, and a display that shows how jade was embedded in human teeth merely for decorative reasons. All of the explanations are in English and Spanish. Allot at least an hour to tour this museum.

Av. 7 btw. calles 9 and 9B, INS Building. © 2287-6034. Admission $7 (£3.50), free for children 11 and under. Mon–Fri 8:30am–3:30pm; Sat 9am–1pm.

Museo de Los Niños (Children's Museum) *Kids*   If you're traveling with children, you'll definitely want to come here, and you might want to visit even if you aren't. A former barracks and then a prison, this museum houses an extensive collection of exhibits designed to edify and entertain children of all ages. Experience a simulated earthquake or make music by dancing across the floor. Many exhibits encourage hands-on play. The museum sometimes features limited shows of "serious" art and is also the home of the National Auditorium. You can spend anywhere from 1 to 4 hours here, depending on how long your children linger at each exhibit. Be careful, though: The museum is large and spread out; it's easy to lose track of a family member or friend.

This museum is a few blocks north of downtown, on Calle 4. It's within easy walk-ing distance, but you might want to take a cab because you'll have to walk right through the worst part of the red-light district.

Calle 4 and Av. 9. © 2258-4929. www.museocr.com. Admission $2 (£1) adults, $1.20 (60p) students and children 17 and under. Tues–Fri 8am–4:30pm; Sat–Sun 10am–5pm.

Museo Nacional de Costa Rica (National Museum) 🏛   Costa Rica's most important historical museum is housed in a former army barracks that was the scene of fighting during the civil war of 1948. As you approach the building, or walk around it, you can still see hundreds of bullet holes on the turrets at its corners. Inside this traditional Spanish-style courtyard building, you will find displays on Costa Rican history and culture from pre-Columbian times to the present. In the pre-Columbian rooms, you'll see a 2,500-year-old jade carving that is shaped like a seashell and etched with an image of a hand holding a small animal.

Among the most fascinating objects unearthed at Costa Rica's numerous archaeological sites are many *metates,* or grinding stones. This type of grinding stone is still in use today throughout Central America; however, the ones on display here are more ornately decorated than those that you will see anywhere else. Some of the *metates* are the size of a small bed and are believed to have been part of funeral rites. A separate vault houses the museum's collection of pre-Columbian gold jewelry and figurines. In the courtyard you'll be treated to a wonderful view of the city and see some of Costa Rica's mysterious stone spheres. It takes about 2 hours to take in the lion's share of the collection here.

Calle 17, btw. avs. Central and 2, on the Plaza de la Democracia. © 2257-1433. www.museocostarica.go.cr. Admission $4 (£2) adults, $2 (£1) students and children 11 and under. Tues–Sat 8:30am–4:30pm; Sun 9am–4:30pm. Closed Dec 25 and Dec 31.

Museos del Banco Central de Costa Rica (Gold Museum) ★★ Located

directly beneath the Plaza de la Cultura, this unusual underground museum houses one of the largest collections of pre-Columbian gold in the Americas. On display are more than 20,000 troy ounces of gold in more than 2,000 objects. The sheer number of pieces can be overwhelming and seem redundant, but the unusual display cases and complex lighting systems show off every piece to its utmost. This complex also includes a gallery for temporary art exhibits, separate numismatic and philatelic museums (coins and stamps, for us regular folks), a modest gift shop, and a branch of the Costa Rican Tourist Institute's info center. Plan to spend an hour or two here.

Calle 5, btw. avs. Central and 2, underneath the Plaza de la Cultura. © 2243-4202. www.museosdelbanco central.org. Admission $6 (£3) adults, $4 (£2) students, 80¢ (40p) children 11 and under. Daily 9:30am–5pm.

Parque Zoológico Simón Bolívar *Kids* This zoo no longer suffers from the over-

whelming sense of neglect and despair that once plagued it, though it's still pretty lackluster and depressing. Why spend time here when you could head out into the forests and jungles? You won't see the great concentrations of wildlife available in one stop here at the zoo, but you'll see the animals in their natural habitats, not yours. The zoo is really geared toward locals and school groups, with a collection that includes Asian, African, and Costa Rican animals. There's a children's discovery area, a snake-and-reptile house, and a gift shop. You can easily spend a couple of hours here.

Av. 11 and Calle 7, in Barrio Amón. © 2256-0012. Admission $2 (£1) adults, $1 (50p) children, free for children 2 and under. Mon–Fri 8am–4pm; Sat–Sun 9am–4:30pm.

Spirogyra Butterfly Garden This butterfly garden is smaller and less elaborate

than the Butterfly Farm (see below), but it provides a good introduction to the life cycle of butterflies. It's also a calm and quiet oasis in a noisy and crowded city, quite close to downtown. Plan on a half-hour to several hours here, depending on whether they have lunch or refreshments at the small coffee shop and gallery. You'll be given a self-guided-tour booklet when you arrive, and an 18-minute video show runs continuously throughout the day. You'll find Spirogyra near El Pueblo, a short taxi ride from the center of San José. This is a convenient place to visit in combination with some shopping and a meal at El Pueblo.

100m (1 block) east and 150m (1½ blocks) south of El Pueblo Shopping Center. ©/fax 2222-2937. www.infocosta rica.com/butterfly. Admission $6 (£3). Daily 8am–4pm (cafe 'til 7:30pm).

OUTSIDE SAN JOSE

The **Museo Historico Cultural Juan Santamaría,** Avenida 3 between calles Central and 2 (© **2441-4775**), isn't worth a trip of its own, but if you're planning an afternoon in Alajuela, you may want to stop here before or after Zoo Ave. (p. 134). The museum commemorates Costa Rica's national hero, Juan Santamaría, who gave his life defending the country against a small army led by William Walker, a U.S. citizen who invaded Costa Rica in 1856, attempting to set up a slave state. The museum is open Tuesday through Sunday from 10am to 6pm; admission is free.

To locate the attractions below, see "The Central Valley" map on p. 147.

Butterfly Farm 🐦   At any given time, you might see around 30 of the 80 species of butterflies raised at this butterfly farm south of Alajuela. The butterflies live in a large enclosed garden similar to an aviary and flutter about the heads of visitors during tours of the gardens. You should be certain to spot glittering blue morphos and a large butterfly that mimics the eyes of an owl. Admission includes a 2-hour guided tour. In the demonstration room you'll see butterfly eggs, caterpillars, and pupae. There are cocoons trimmed in a shimmering gold color and cocoons that mimic a snake's head to frighten away predators. The last guided tour of the day begins at 3pm.

If you reserve in advance, the Butterfly Farm has three daily bus tours that run from many major San José hotels. The cost, including round-trip transportation and admission to the garden, is $25 (£13) for adults, $20 (£10) for students, and $12 (£6) for children 11 and under. Buses pick up passengers at more than 20 different hotels in the San José area.

In front of Los Reyes Country Club, La Guácima de Alajuela. © **2438-0400**. www.butterflyfarm.co.cr. Admission $15 (£7.50) adults, $10 (£5) students, $7 (£3.50) children 5–11, free for children 4 and under. Daily 8:30am–5pm.

Café Britt Farm 🐦   Although bananas are the main export of Costa Rica, most people are far more interested in the country's second-most-important export crop: coffee. Café Britt is one of the leading brands here, and the company has put together an interesting tour and stage production at its farm, which is 20 minutes outside of San José. Here, you'll see how coffee is grown. You'll also visit the roasting and processing plant to learn how a coffee "cherry" is turned into a delicious roasted bean. Tasting sessions are offered for visitors to experience the different qualities of coffee. There are also a restaurant and a store where you can buy coffee and coffee-related gift items. The entire tour, including transportation, takes about 3 to 4 hours. Allow some extra time and an extra $10 (£5) for a visit to their nearby working plantation and mill. You can even strap on a basket and go out coffee picking during harvest time.

The folks here offer several full-day options that combine a visit to the Britt Farm with a stop at Poás Volcano, the Butterfly Farm (see above), or the Rain Forest Aerial Tram Caribbean. They also offer mountain bike tours in the Heredia hills above their farm, ending with lunch or refreshments at their restaurant.

North of Heredia on the road to Barva. © **2277-1600**. www.coffeetour.com. Admission $20 (£10) adults, $16 (£8) children 6–11; $37 (£19) adults and $33 (£17) children, including transportation from downtown San José and a coffee drink; add $15 (£7.50) for full buffet lunch. 3 tours daily: 9 and 11am, and 3pm during the high season; reduced schedule in the off season. Store and restaurant daily 8:30am–5pm year-round.

Else Kientzler Botanical Garden 🐦🐦 *Kids*   Located on the grounds of an ornamental flower farm, on the outskirts of the tourist town Sarchí, these are extensive, impressive, and lovingly laid out botanical gardens. Over 2.5km (1½ miles) of trails run through a collection of more than 2,000 species of flora. All of the plants are labeled with their Latin names, with some further explanations around the grounds in both English and Spanish. There's a topiary labyrinth, as well as a variety of lookouts, gazebos, and shady benches on the grounds. A children's play area features some water games, jungle gym setups, and a child-friendly little zip-line canopy tour. Over 40% of the gardens are wheelchair accessible.

Tuan (© 2258-2004) buses leave San José about five times throughout the day for Sarchí from Calle 18 between avenidas 5 and 7. The fare is $1.20 (60p). Alternatively, you can take any Grecia bus from this same station. In Grecia they connect with the Alajuela-Sarchí buses, leaving every 30 minutes from Calle 8 between avenidas Central and 1 in Alajuela.

Sarchí, Alajuela. © 2454-2070. www.elsegarden.com. Admission $14 (£7), $8 (£4) students with valid ID and children 5–12. A guided tour costs an extra $15 (£7.50) per guide per hour, for a group of up to 15 persons. Advance reservations are necessary for guided tours. Daily 8am–4pm. About 6 blocks north of the central football (soccer) stadium in the town of Sarchí.

INBio Park (Kids) Run by the National Biodiversity Institute (Instituto Nacional de Biodiversidad, or INBio), this place is part museum, part educational center, and part nature park. In addition to watching a 15-minute informational video, visitors can tour two large pavilions explaining Costa Rica's biodiversity and natural wonders, and hike on trails that re-create the ecosystems of a tropical rainforest, dry forest, and premontane forest. A 2-hour guided hike is included in the entrance fee, and self-guided-tour booklets are also available. There's a good-size butterfly garden, as well as a Plexiglas viewing window into the small lagoon. One of my favorite attractions here is the series of wonderful animal sculptures donated by one of Costa Rica's premiere artists, José Sancho. There's a simple cafeteria-style restaurant here for lunch, as well as a coffee shop and gift shop. You can easily spend 2 to 3 hours here.

400m (4 blocks) north and 250m (2½ blocks) west of the Shell station in Santo Domingo de Heredia. © 2507-8107. www.inbio.ac.cr. Admission $23 (£12) adults, $13 (£6.50) children 12 and under. Daily 8am–6pm (admission closes at 4pm). INBio Park can arrange round-trip transportation from downtown for $18 (£9) per person.

Lankester Gardens Costa Rica has more than 1,400 varieties of orchids, and almost 800 species are cultivated and on display at this botanical garden in Cartago province. Created in the 1940s by English naturalist Charles Lankester, the gardens are now administered by the University of Costa Rica. The primary goal is to preserve the local flora, with an emphasis on orchids and bromeliads. Paved trails meander from open, sunny gardens into shady forests. In each environment different species of orchids are in bloom. There's an information center and a gift shop, and the trails are well tended and well marked. Plan to spend between 1 and 3 hours here if you're interested in flowers and gardening; you could run through it more quickly if you're not. You can easily combine a visit here with a tour at Cartago and/or the Orosi Valley and Irazú Volcano. See "Side Trips from San José," later in this chapter.

Paraíso de Cartago. © 2552-3247. www.jardinbotanicolankester.org Admission $5 (£2.50) adults, $3.50 (£1.75) children 6–16. Daily 8:30am–4:30pm. Closed all national holidays. Take the Cartago bus from San José, and then the Paraíso bus from a stop 1 block south and ¾ block west of the Catholic church ruins in Cartago (ride takes 30–40 min.).

La Paz Waterfall Gardens (Kids) The main attraction here consists of a series of trails through primary and secondary forests alongside the La Paz River, with lookouts over a series of powerful falls, including the namesake La Paz Fall. In addition to an orchid garden and a hummingbird garden, you must visit their huge butterfly garden, which is easily the largest in Costa Rica. A small serpentarium, featuring a mix of venomous and non-venomous native snakes, and several terrariums containing various frogs and lizards, are added attractions. There's also a man-made trout pond where you can cast for trout, or just take a swim with them. While the admission fee is a little steep, everything is wonderfully done and the trails and waterfalls are beautiful. A buffet lunch at the large cafeteria-style restaurant costs an extra $12 (£6) for adults, or $6 (£3) for kids. This is a good stop after a morning visit to the Poás Volcano. Plan to spend 2 to 4 hours here. The hotel rooms (Peace Lodge; p. 118) are some of the nicest in the country.

6km (3¾ miles) north of Varablanca on the road to San Miguel. ℂ 2225-0643. www.waterfallgardens.com. Admission $32 (£16) adults, $20 (£10) children and students with valid ID. Daily 8:30am–5:30pm. Take a Puerto Viejo de Sarapiquí bus from Calle 12 and Av. 9 (make sure it passes through Varablanca and La Virgen), and ask to be let off at the entrance. Buses are infrequent, and coordinating your return can be difficult, so it's best to come in a rental car or arrange transport.

Zoo Ave. 😾 Dozens of scarlet macaws, reclusive owls, majestic raptors, several different species of toucans, and a host of brilliantly colored birds from Costa Rica and around the world make this one exciting place to visit. In total, over 115 species of birds are on display, including some 80 species found in Costa Rica. Bird-watching enthusiasts will be able to get a closer look at birds they might have seen in the wild. There are also large iguana, deer, tapir, ocelot, puma, and monkey exhibits—and look out for the 3.6m (12-ft.) crocodile. Zoo Ave. houses only injured, donated, or confiscated animals. It takes about 2 hours to walk the paths and visit all the exhibits here.

La Garita, Alajuela. ℂ 2433-8989. www.zooave.org. Admission $15 (£7.50), $13 (£6.50) students with valid ID. Daily 9am–5pm. Catch a bus to Alajuela on Av. 2 btw. calles 12 and 14. In Alajuela, transfer to a bus to Atenas and get off at Zoo Ave. before you get to La Garita. Fare is 60¢ (30p).

6 Outdoor Activities & Spectator Sports

Due to the chaos and pollution, you'll probably want to get out of the city before undertaking anything too strenuous. But if you want to brave the elements, there are a few outdoor activities in and around San José.

Parque La Sabana (at the western end of Paseo Colón), formerly San José's international airport, is the city's center for active sports and recreation. Here you'll find everything from jogging trails, soccer fields, and a few public tennis courts to the National Stadium. All the facilities are free and open to the public. Families gather for picnics, people fly kites, and there's even an outdoor sculpture garden. If you really want to experience the local culture, try getting into a pickup soccer game here. However, be careful in this park, especially at dusk or after dark, when it becomes a favorite haunt for youth gangs and muggers.

For information on horseback riding, hiking, and white-water rafting trips from San José, see "Side Trips from San José," later in this chapter.

BIRD-WATCHING   Serious birders will certainly want to head out of San José, but it is still possible to see quite a few species in the metropolitan area. Two of the best spots for urban bird-watching are the campus at the **University of Costa Rica,** in the eastern suburb of San Pedro, and **Parque del Este** 😾, located a little farther east on the road to San Ramón de Tres Ríos. You'll see a mix of urban species, and if you're lucky, you might spy a couple of hummingbirds or even a blue-crowned motmot. To get to the university campus, take any San Pedro bus from Avenida Central between calles 9 and 11. To get to Parque del Este, take the San Ramón/Parque del Este bus from Calle 9 between avenidas Central and 1. To hook up with fellow birders, e-mail the **Birding Club of Costa Rica** 🐾🐾 (© **2282-5365;** costaricabirding@hotmail.com), which frequently organizes expeditions around the Central Valley and beyond.

BULLFIGHTING   Although I hesitate to call it a sport, **Las Corridas a la Tica (Costa Rican bullfighting)** is a popular and frequently comic stadium event. Instead of the blood-and-gore/life-and-death confrontation of traditional bullfighting, Ticos just like to tease the bull. In a typical *corrida,* anywhere from 50 to 150 *toreadores improvisados* (literally, "improvised bullfighters") stand in the ring waiting for the bull. What follows is a slapstick scramble to safety whenever the bull heads toward a crowd of bullfighters. The braver bullfighters try to slap the bull's backside as the beast chases down one of his buddies.

You can see a bullfight during the various Festejos Populares (City Fairs) around the country. The country's largest Festejos Populares are held in Zapote, a suburb east of San José during Christmas week and the first week in January. Admission is $2 to $5 (£1–£2.50). This is a purely seasonal activity and occurs in San José only during the Festejos. However, there are yearly *festejos* in nearly every little town around the country. These are spread out throughout the year. Ask at your hotel; if your timing's right, you might be able to take in one of these.

GOLF & TENNIS   If you want to play tennis or golf in San José, your options are limited. If you're looking for a real local experience on some rough concrete courts, you can take a racket and some balls down to **Parque La Sabana.** However, the best facilities for visiting golfers and tennis players are found at **Parque Valle del Sol** 🐾 (© **2282-9222;** www.vallesol.com), in the western suburb of Santa Ana. The 18-hole course here is open to the general public. Greens fees are $90 (£45) per golfer per day, including the cart and unlimited playing both on the course and driving range. The tennis courts here cost around $8 (£4) per hour. Reservations are essential. The golf course at the Cariari Country Club is not open to the general public.

HOTEL SPAS & WORKOUT FACILITIES   Most of the city's higher-end hotels have some sort of pool and exercise facilities. You'll find the best of these at the Marriott Costa Rica Hotel (p. 118) and Crowne Plaza Corobicí (p. 112). If you're looking for a good, serious workout, I recommend the **Multispa** 🐾 (© **2231-5542**), located in the Tryp Corobicí. Even if you're not a guest at the hotel, you can use the facilities here and join in any class for $15 (£7.50) per day. Multispa has five other locations around the Central Valley.

JOGGING   Try **Parque La Sabana,** mentioned above, or head to **Parque del Este,** which is east of town in the foothills above San Pedro. Take the San Ramón/Parque del Este bus from Calle 9 between avenidas Central and 1. It's never a good idea to jog at night, on busy streets, or alone. Women should be particularly careful about jogging alone. And remember, Tico drivers are not accustomed to joggers on residential streets, so don't expect drivers to give you much berth.

SOCCER *(FUTBOL)*   Ticos take their *fútbol* seriously. Costa Rican professional soccer is some of the best in Central America, and the national team, or *Sele (selección nacional),* qualified for the World Cup in 2002 and 2006, although they made early exits both times. The soccer season runs from September to June, with the finals spread out over several weeks in late June and early July.

You don't need to buy tickets in advance. Tickets generally run between $2 and $15 (£1–£7.50). It's worth paying a little extra for *sombra numerado* (reserved seats in the shade). This will protect you from both the sun and the more rowdy aficionados. Costa Rican soccer fans take the sport seriously, and several violent incidents, both inside and outside the stadiums, have marred the sport in recent years, so be careful. Other options include *sombra* (general admission in the shade), *palco* and *palco numerado* (general admission and reserved mezzanine), and *sol general* (general admission in full sun).

The main San José team is Saprissa (affectionately called El Monstruo, or "The Monster"). **Saprissa's stadium** is in Tibás (*©* **2240-0002;** take any Tibás bus from Calle 2 and Av. 5). Games are often held on Sunday at 11am, but occasionally they are scheduled for Saturday afternoon or Wednesday evening. Check the local newspapers for game times and locations.

SWIMMING   If you aren't going to get to the beach anytime soon and your hotel doesn't have a pool, you can use the pool at the Multispa facility at the hotel **Crowne Plaza Corobicí** (*©* **2231-5542**) for $15 (£7.50). Alternatively, for a real Tico experience, head to **Ojo de Agua** (*©* **2441-2808**), on the road between the airport and San Antonio de Belén. The spring-fed waters are cool and refreshing, and even if it seems a bit chilly in San José, it's always several degrees warmer out here. This place is very popular with Ticos and can get quite crowded on weekends. Unfortunately, the place is perennially run-down and you have to keep an eye on your valuables here. Admission is $2 (£1). Buses leave almost hourly for Ojo de Agua from Avenida 2 and Calle 12.

7 Shopping

Serious shoppers will be disappointed in Costa Rica. Aside from coffee and oxcarts, there isn't much that's distinctly Costa Rican. To compensate for its own relative lack of goods, Costa Rica does a brisk business in selling crafts and clothes imported from Guatemala, Panama, and Ecuador.

THE SHOPPING SCENE   San José's central shopping corridor is bounded by avenidas 1 and 2, from about Calle 14 in the west to Calle 13 in the east. For several blocks west of the Plaza de la Cultura, **Avenida Central** is a pedestrian-only street mall where you'll find store after store of inexpensive clothes for men, women, and children. Depending on the mood of the police that day, you might find a lot of street vendors as well. Most shops in the downtown district are open Monday through Saturday from about 8am to 6pm. Some shops close for lunch, while others remain open (it's just the luck of the draw for shoppers). You'll be happy to find that the sales and import taxes have already been figured into the display price.

International laws prohibit trade in endangered wildlife, so don't buy any plants or animals, even if they're readily for sale. Do not buy any kind of sea-turtle products (including jewelry); wild birds; lizards, snakes, or cat skins; corals; or orchids (except those grown commercially). No matter how unique, beautiful, insignificant, or inexpensive it might seem, your purchase will directly contribute to the further hunting of these species.

It's especially hard to capture the subtle shades and colors of the rainforests and cloud forests, and many a traveler has gone home thinking that his or her undeveloped film contained the full beauty of the jungle, only to return from the photo developer with 36 bright-green blurs. To avoid this heartache, you might want to pick

Tips Joe to Go

Two words of advice: Buy coffee. Lots of it.

Coffee is the best shopping deal in all of Costa Rica. Although the best Costa Rican coffee is allegedly shipped off to North American and European markets, it's hard to beat the coffee that's roasted right in front of you here. Best of all is the price: One pound of coffee sells for around $3 to $6 (£1.50–£3). It makes a great gift and truly is a local product.

Café Britt is the big name in Costa Rican coffee. These folks have the largest export business in the country, and, although high-priced, its blends are very dependable. Café Britt is widely available at gift shops around the country, and at the souvenir concessions at both international airports. My favorites, however, are the coffees roasted and packaged in Manuel Antonio and Monteverde, by **Café Milagro** and **Café Monteverde**, respectively. If you visit either of these places, definitely pick up their beans.

In general, the best place to buy coffee is in any supermarket. Why pay more at a gift or specialty shop? You can also try **Café Trébol,** on Calle 8 between avenidas Central and 1 (on the western side of the Central Market; © **2221-8363**). It's open Monday through Saturday from 7am to 6:30pm and Sunday from 8:30am to 12:30pm.

Be sure to ask for whole beans; Costa Rican grinds are often too fine for standard coffee filters. The store will pack beans for you in whatever size bag you want. If you buy prepackaged coffee in a supermarket in Costa Rica, the whole beans will be marked either *grano* (grain) or *grano entero* (whole bean). If you opt for ground varieties *(molido),* be sure the package is marked *puro;* otherwise, it will likely be mixed with a good amount of sugar, the way Ticos like it.

One good coffee-related gift to bring home is a coffee sock and stand. This is the most common mechanism for brewing coffee beans in Costa Rica. It consists of a simple circular stand, made out of wood or wire, which holds a sock. Put the ground beans in the sock, place a pot or cup below it, and pour boiling water through. You can find the socks and stands at most supermarkets and in the Mercado Central. In fancier crafts shops, you'll find them made out of ceramic. Depending on its construction, a stand will cost you between $1.50 and $15 (75p–£7.50); socks run around 30¢ (15p), so buy a few spares.

up some postcards of the sights you want to remember forever and send them to yourself.

MARKETS   There are several markets near downtown, but by far the largest is the **Mercado Central,** located between avenidas Central and 1 and calles 6 and 8. Although this dark maze of stalls is primarily a food market, inside you'll find all manner of vendors, including a few selling Costa Rican souvenirs, crude leather goods, and musical instruments. Be especially careful about your wallet or purse and any prominent jewelry because very skilled pickpockets frequent this area. All the streets surrounding the

Mercado Central are jammed with produce vendors selling from small carts or loading and unloading trucks. It's always a hive of activity, with crowds of people jostling for space on the streets. Your best bet is to visit on Sunday or on weekdays; Saturday is particularly busy. In the hot days of the dry season, the aromas can get quite heady.

There is also a daily street market on the west side of the **Plaza de la Democracia.** Here you'll find two long rows of outdoor stalls selling T-shirts, Guatemalan and Ecuadorian handicrafts and clothing, small ceramic *ocarinas* (a small musical wind instrument), and handmade jewelry. The atmosphere here is much more open than at the Mercado Central, which I find just a bit too claustrophobic. You might be able to bargain prices down a little bit, but bargaining is not a traditional part of the vendor culture here, so you'll have to work hard to save a few dollars.

Finally, two other similar options downtown are **La Casona,** Calle Central between avenidas Central and 1 (© 2222-7999), a three-story warren of crafts and souvenir shops; and **El Pueblo,** a tourism complex built in the style of a mock colonial-era village, with a wide range of restaurants, gift shops, art galleries, bars, and discos.

MODERN MALLS   With globalization and modernization taking hold in Costa Rica, much of the local shopping scene has shifted to large megamalls. Modern multilevel affairs with cineplexes, food courts, and international brand-name stores are becoming more ubiquitous. The biggest and most modern of these malls include the **Mall San Pedro, Multiplaza, Terra Mall,** and **Mall Real Cariari.** Although they lack the charm of small shops found around San José, they are a reasonable option for one-stop shopping; most contain at least one or two local galleries and crafts shops, along with a large supermarket, which is always the best place to stock up on local coffee, hot sauces, liquors, and other non-perishable foodstuffs.

SHOPPING A TO Z
ART GALLERIES

Art lovers should check out Molly Keeler's 1-day **Art Tour** ⍟ (© 8359-5571 or 2288-0896; www.costaricaarttour.com), which includes scheduled visits to the studios and personal shops of prominent local artists working in a wide range of media.

Arte Latino   This gallery carries original artwork in a variety of media, featuring predominantly Central American themes. Some of it is pretty gaudy, but this is generally a good place to find Nicaraguan and Costa Rican "primitive" paintings. The gallery also has storefronts in the Multiplaza Mall in Escazú and at the Mall Cariari, which is on the Interamerican Highway, about halfway between the airport and downtown, across from the Hotel Herradura. Calle 5 and Av. 1. © 2258-3306.

Galería Amón ⍟   Located in a stylish old house in the historic Barrio Amón district, this gallery features contemporary artists from Central and South America. Feature exhibits are mixed with a regularly rotating collection of works from a stable of artists. The spaces are ample and well-lit, giving this place almost a museum-like feel. No. 937 Calle 7 btw. Av. 7 and 9. © 2223-9725. www.amon937.com.

Galería 11–12 ⍟⍟⍟   This outstanding gallery deals mainly in high-end Costa Rican art, from neoclassical painters such as Teodorico Quirós to modern masters such as Francisco Amighetti and Paco Zuñiga, to current stars such as Rafa Fernández, Rodolfo Stanley, Fernando Carballo, and Fabio Herrera. Plaza Itzkatzu, off the Prospero Fernández Hwy., Escazú. © 2288-1975. www.galeria11-12.com.

Galería Jacobo Karpio   This excellent gallery handles some of the more adventurous modern art to be found in Costa Rica. Karpio has a steady stable of prominent Mexican, Cuban, and Argentine artists, as well as some local talent. Av. 1, casa no. 1352, btw. calles 13 and 15. ℂ 2257-7963.

Galería Kandinsky   Owned by the daughter of one of Costa Rica's most prominent modern painters, Rafa Fernández, this small gallery usually has a good selection of high-end contemporary Costa Rican paintings, be it the house collection or a specific temporary exhibit. Centro Comercial Calle Real, San Pedro. ℂ 2234-0478.

TEORetica ✦✦   This small downtown gallery is run by one of the more adventurous and internationally respected collectors and curators in Costa Rica, Virginia Pérez-Ratton. You'll often find very interesting and cutting-edge exhibitions here. Calle 7 btw. Av. 9 and 11. ℂ 2233-4881. www.teoretica.org.

BOOKS
For English-language novels, field guides and general guidebooks, and natural history books, head to either **Seventh Street Books** (ℂ 2256-8251; Calle 7 btw. avs. 1 and Central), or **Librería Internacional** (ℂ 2253-9553; www.libreriainternacional.com). Librería Internacional has several outlets around San José, including storefronts in most of the major modern malls.

HANDICRAFTS
The quality of Costa Rican handicrafts is generally very low, and the offerings are limited. The most typical items you'll find are hand-painted wooden **oxcarts.** These come in a variety of sizes, and you can ship the big ones to your home for a very reasonable price. If you want to stick to downtown San José, try the outdoor market on the **Plaza de la Democracia,** although prices here tend to be high and bargaining can be difficult. If you prefer to do your crafts shopping in a flea-market atmosphere, head over to **La Casona** on Calle Central between avenidas Central and 1.

Notable exceptions to the generally meager crafts offerings include the fine wooden creations of **Barry Biesanz** ✦✦ (ℂ 2289-4337; www.biesanz.com). His work is sold in many of the finer gift shops around and at his own shop (see below), but beware: Biesanz's work is often imitated, so make sure that what you buy is the real deal (he generally burns his signature into the bottom of the piece). **Lil Mena** is a local artist who specializes in working with and painting on handmade papers and rough fibers. You'll find her work in a number of shops around San José.

You might also run across **carved masks** made by the indigenous Boruca people of southern Costa Rica. These full-size balsa-wood masks come in a variety of styles, both painted and unpainted, and run anywhere from $15 to $80 (£7.50–£40), depending on the quality of workmanship. **Cecilia "Pefi" Figueres** ✦✦ makes practical ceramic wares that are lively and fun. Look for her brightly colored abstract and figurative bowls, pitchers, coffee mugs, and more at some of the better gift shops around the city.

Scores of shops around San José sell a wide variety of crafts, from the truly tacky to the divinely inspired. Here are some that sell more of the latter and fewer of the former.

Biesanz Woodworks ✦ *(Finds*   Biesanz makes a wide range of high-quality items, including bowls, jewelry boxes, humidors, and some wonderful sets of wooden chopsticks. Biesanz Woodworks is actively involved in local reforestation. Bello Horizonte, Escazú. ℂ 2289-4337. www.biesanz.com. Call for directions and off-hour appointments.

Boutique Annemarie ⭐ Occupying two floors at the Hotel Don Carlos (p. 109), this shop has an amazing array of wood products, leather goods, papier-mâché figurines, paintings, books, cards, posters, and jewelry. You'll see most of this stuff at the other shops, but not in such quantities or in such a relaxed and pressure-free environment. At the Hotel Don Carlos, Calle 9, btw. avs. 7 and 9. ✆ **2221-6063.**

Galería Namu ⭐⭐ Galeria Namu has some very high-quality arts and crafts, specializing in truly high-end indigenous works, including excellent Boruca and Huetar carved masks and "primitive" paintings. It also carries a good selection of more modern arts and craft pieces, including the ceramic work of Cecilia "Pefi" Figueres. This place organizes tours to visit various indigenous tribes and artisans as well. Av. 7 btw. calles 5 and 7. ✆ **2256-3412.** www.galerianamu.com.

Green Turtle This large shop has a vast selection of handicrafts and souvenirs. Most of it is of very standard to poor quality, but this does make a particularly convenient stop for some last-minute shopping on your way to the airport. In fact, if you call, they will provide free round-trip transport from and to the airport. 4 blocks north of Denny's, near the airport. ✆ **2430-0211.** www.greenturtlesouvenirs.com.

Las Garzas Handicraft Market This is an appealing collection of artisans' shops in a suburb on the outskirts of San José. It includes more than 25 shops selling wood, metal, and ceramic crafts, among a large variety of other items. There's a huge selection, and you can get some good buys here. In Moravia, 100m (1 block) south and 50m (1/2 block) east of the Red Cross Station. ✆ **2236-0037.** Ask a taxi driver to take you to Las Garzas Mercado de Artesanía in Moravia.

Orinoco Arts & Crafts Gallery ⭐⭐ With a stellar and varied collection from Costa Rica and around Latin America, particularly Venezuela and Guatemala, this shop has some of the best high-quality arts and craft pieces you'll find in the country. The selection ranges from paintings and sculptures, to baskets, woodcarvings, textiles, and ceramic works. Plaza Itzkatzu, off the Prospero Fernández Highway, Escazú. ✆ **2288-2949.** www.orinocoarts.com.

Suraska Among the selections here are ceramics, mobiles, and jewelry. This store tends to carry higher-quality items than most gift shops downtown. However, be warned that prices are accordingly more expensive. Calle 5 and Av. 3. ✆ **2222-0129.**

JEWELRY

Plaza Esmeralda Part working jewelry factory, part shopping center, part tourist trap, this is still a good place to come to buy replicas of pre-Columbian jewelry. The several shops here carry a wide range of typical tourist souvenirs and locally produced arts and craftworks at fair prices. Visitors are treated to a 15-minute guided tour where you can see some of the jewelry being manufactured. Sabana Norte. 800m (8 blocks) north of Jack's in Pavas. ✆ **2296-0312.**

Studio Metallo ⭐⭐ The outgrowth of a jewelry-making school and studio, this shop has some excellent handcrafted jewelry made in a range of styles, using everything from 18-karat white and yellow gold and pure silver, to some less exotic and expensive alloys. Some works integrate gemstones, while many others focus on the metalwork. 61/2 blocks east of the Iglesia Santa Teresita, Barrio Escalante. ✆ **2281-3207.** www.studiometallo.com.

LEATHER GOODS

In general, Costa Rican leather products are not of the highest grade or quality, and prices are not particularly low. In addition to the shop listed below, **Del Río** (② 2262-1415) is a local leather goods manufacturer, with stores in most of the city's modern malls. It also offers free hotel pickup and transfer to its factory outlet in Heredia.

Malety   At this outlet in San José, you can shop for locally produced leather bags, briefcases, purses, wallets, and other such items. A second store is located on Calle 1 between avenidas Central and 2. Av. 1 btw. calles 1 and 3. ② 2221-1670.

LIQUOR

The national drink here is *guaro,* a relatively unrefined, clear liquor made from sugar cane. The most popular brand is **Cacique,** available at every liquor store and most supermarkets. Costa Ricans drink their *guaro* straight or mixed with club soda or Fresca. When drinking it straight, it's customary to follow a shot with a bite into a fresh lime covered in salt.

Costa Ricans also drink a lot of rum. The premier Costa Rican rum is **Centenario,** but I recommend that you opt for the Nicaraguan **Flor de Caña** ✪ or Cuban **Havana Club** ✪, both of which are far superior rums. *Note:* Because of the trade embargo, it is illegal to bring Havana Club into the United States.

Several brands and styles of coffee-based liqueurs are also produced in Costa Rica. **Café Rica** is similar to Kahlúa, and you can also find several types of coffee cream liqueurs. The folks at **Café Britt** produce their own line of coffee liqueurs which are quite good and available in most supermarkets, liquor stores, and tourist shops; the best prices I've seen are at the supermarket chain **Más × Menos.** There is a Más × Menos store on Paseo Colón and another on Avenida Central at the east end of town, just below the Museo Nacional de Costa Rica.

8 San José After Dark

Catering to a mix of tourists, college students, and just generally party-loving Ticos, San José has a host of options to meet the nocturnal needs of visitors and residents alike. You'll find plenty of interesting clubs and bars, a wide range of theaters, and some very lively discos and dance salons.

To find out what's going on in San José while you're in town, pick up a copy of the *Tico Times* (English) or *La Nación* (Spanish). The former is a good place to find out where local expatriates are hanging out; the latter's "Viva" and "Tiempo Libre" sections have extensive listings of discos, movie theaters, and live music.

THE PERFORMING ARTS

Theater is very popular in Costa Rica, and downtown San José is studded with small theaters. However, tastes tend toward the burlesque, and the crowd pleasers are almost always simplistic sexual comedies. The **National Theater Company** (② 2221-1273) is an exception, tackling works from Lope de Vega to Lorca to Mamet. Similarly, the small independent group **Abya Yala** (② 2240-6071) also puts on several cutting-edge avant-garde shows each year. Almost all of the theater offerings are in Spanish, although the **Little Theater Group** (www.littletheatregroup.org) is a long-standing amateur group that periodically stages works in English. Finally, **Britt Expresivo** (② 2277-1600; www.brittexpresivo.com) has been staging regular works ranging from original pieces to Shakespeare to Beckett, in both English and Spanish, at the small theater up at Café Britt (p. 132) in the hills above Heredia. Check the *Tico Times* to see if anything is running during your stay.

Costa Rica has a strong modern-dance scene. Both the **University of Costa Rica** and the **National University** have modern-dance companies that perform regularly in various venues in San José. In addition to the university-sponsored companies, there's a host of smaller independent companies worth catching; check local papers for details.

The **National Symphony Orchestra** is respectable by regional standards, although its repertoire tends to be rather conservative. Symphony season runs March through November, with concerts roughly every other weekend at the **Teatro Nacional,** Avenida 2 between calles 3 and 5 (𝄢 **2221-5341;** www.teatronacional.go.cr), and the **Auditorio Nacional** (𝄢 **2256-5876**) at the Museo de Los Niños (p. 130). Tickets cost between $3 and $25 (£1.50–£13) and can be purchased at the box office.

Visiting artists stop in Costa Rica on a regular basis. Recent concerts have featured hard rockers Smashing Pumpkins and Iron Maiden, pop phenom the Black Eyed Peas, Brazilian maestro Caetano Veloso, reggaeton giant Daddy Yankee, and Mexican singing sensations Ricky Martin and Chayanne. Many of these performances take place in San José's two historic theaters, the **Teatro Nacional** (see above) and the **Teatro Melico Salazar,** Avenida 2 between calles Central and 2 (𝄢 **2221-4952**), as well as at the **Auditorio Nacional** (see above). Really large shows are usually held at soccer stadiums or large, natural amphitheaters.

Costa Rica's cultural panorama changes drastically every November when the country hosts large arts festivals. In odd-numbered years, **El Festival Nacional de las Artes** reigns supreme, featuring purely local talent. In even-numbered years, the month-long fete is **El Festival Internacional de las Artes,** with a nightly smorgasbord of dance, theater, music, and monologues from around the world. Most nights of the festival offer between 4 and 10 shows. Many are free, and the most expensive ticket is usually around $5 (£2.50). For exact dates and details, you can contact the Ministry of Youth, Culture, and Sports (𝄢 **2255-3188;** www.mcjdcr.go.cr), although you might have trouble getting any information if you don't speak Spanish.

THE CLUB, MUSIC & DANCE SCENE

You'll find plenty of places to hit the dance floor in San José. Salsa and merengue are the main beats that move people here, and many of the dance clubs, discos, and salons feature live music on the weekends. You'll find a pretty limited selection, though, if you're looking to catch some small-club jazz, rock, or blues.

The daily "Viva" and Friday's "Tiempo Libre" sections of *La Nación* newspaper have weekly performance schedules. Some dance bands to watch for are Cantoamérica, Kalua, Chocolate, Timbaleo, and Los Brillanticos. While Ghandi, Evolución, and Malpaís are popular local rock groups, Marfil is a good cover band, and both Harmony Roads and the Blind Pig Blues Band are outfits that play American-style rock, blues, and folk music. If you're looking for jazz, check out Editus, El Sexteto de Jazz Latino, or pianist Manuel Obregón. For a taste of something eclectic, look for Santos y Zurdo; Peregrino Gris; or Amarillo, Cyan y Magenta.

A good place to sample a range of San José's nightlife is in **El Pueblo,** a shopping, dining, and entertainment complex done up like an old Spanish village. It's just across the river to the north of town. The best way to get there is by taxi; all the drivers know El Pueblo well. Within the alleyways that wind through El Pueblo are a dozen or more bars, clubs, and discos—there's even an indoor soccer playing field. **Fiesta Latina**

(℃ 2222-8782), **Twister** (℃ 2222-5746), and **Friends** (℃ 2233-5283) are happening party spots. Across the street, **Copacabana** (℃ 2233-5516) is a popular dance spot. For a mellower option, inside El Pueblo, try **Café Art Boruca** (℃ 2221-3615).

Most of the places listed below charge a nominal cover charge; sometimes it includes a drink or two.

Castro's ✸ *(Finds* This is a classic Costa Rican dance club. The music varies throughout the night, from salsa and merengue to reggaeton and occasionally electronic trance. There are several rooms and various types of environments, including some intimate and quiet corners, spread over a couple of floors. It's open daily from noon to anytime between 3 and 6am. Avenida 13 and Calle 22, Barrio Mexico. ℃ 2256-8789.

Copacabana ✸ This large, open, upscale disco has long been a favored dance venue for the young and beautiful of San José. The interior is designed to resemble a colonial plaza. Tunes come in sets that can range from salsa to merengue to reggae to electronic. This place pulls a younger crowd than many of the other spots around town; the party here is Wednesday through Saturday nights 'til around 4am. Admission is around $3 (£1.50). Across from the El Pueblo shopping center. ℃ 2233-5516.

El Tobogán ✸✸ *(Finds* The dance floor in this place is about the size of a football field, yet it still fills up. This is a place where Ticos come with their loved ones and dance partners. The music is a mix of classic Latin dance rhythms—salsa, cumbia, and merengue. It's open only on the weekends ('til about 2am), but there's always a live band here, and sometimes it's very good. 200m (2 blocks) north and 100m (1 block) east of the La República main office, off the Guápiles Hwy. ℃ 2223-8920.

Salsa 54 This is the place to go to watch expert salsa dancers and to try some yourself. You can take formal Latin dance classes here, or you might learn something just by watching. This place is popular with Ticos, and tourists are a rare commodity here—tourists who can really dance salsa, even more so. It's open daily 'til 4am. Calle 3 btw. avs. 1 and 3. ℃ 2233-3814.

Utopia In a modern strip mall on the road between the western suburbs of Santa Ana and San Antonio de Belén, this new club is one of the hippest places to see and be seen. In fact, bouncers out front often screen the incoming clientele, admitting only the prettiest and best connected. Music is loud and modern, and the decor is minimal. It's open daily 'til 4am. Radial San Antonio de Beleén-Santa Ana. ℃2221-6655.

Vértigo Tucked inside a nondescript office building and commercial center on Paseo Colón, this new club remains one of the more popular places for rave-style late-night dancing and partying. The dance floor is huge and the ceilings are high, and electronic music rules the roost. It's open daily 'til 4am. Edificio Colón, Paseo Colón. ℃ 2257-8424.

THE BAR SCENE

There seems to be something for every taste here. Lounge lizards will be happy in most hotel bars in the downtown area, while students and the young at heart will have no problem mixing in at the livelier spots around town. Sports fans can find plenty of places to catch the most important games of the day, and there are even a couple of brewpubs that are drastically improving the quality and selection of the local suds.

The best part of the varied bar scene in San José is something called a *boca,* the equivalent of a tapa in Spain: a little dish of snacks that arrives at your table when you order a drink. Although this is a somewhat dying tradition, especially in the younger, hipper bars, you will still find *bocas* alive and well in the older, more traditional Costa Rican drinking establishments. In most, the *bocas* are free, but in some, where the dishes are more sophisticated, you'll have to pay for the treats. You'll find drinks reasonably priced, with beer costing around $2 (£1) a bottle, and mixed drinks costing $2 to $5 (£1–£2.50).

Café Expresivo ☆   Laid-back and funky, this cafe, restaurant, and gallery often features occasional DJs spinning dance beats. When there's no act, this is a mellow place to have a drink and good conversation. It's open Tuesday through Friday from noon to midnight, and Saturday and Sunday from 5pm to midnight. 4 blocks east of the Santa Teresita Church, Barrio Escalante. ℭ **2224-1202.**

Chelles *(Finds)*   This classic downtown bar and restaurant makes up for its lack of ambience with plenty of tradition and a diverse and colorful clientele. The lights are bright, the chairs surround simple Formica-topped card tables, and mirrors adorn most of the walls. Simple sandwiches and meals are served, and pretty good *bocas* come with the drinks. It's open daily, round-the-clock. Av. Central and Calle 9. ℭ **2221-1369.**

El Cuartel de la Boca del Monte ☆☆   This popular bar, one of San José's best, began life as an artist-and-bohemian hangout, and has evolved into the leading meat market for the young and well-heeled. However, artists still come, as do foreign exchange students, visitors, and a broad cross section of San José's youth, so there's always a diverse mix. There's usually live music here on Monday, Wednesday, and Friday nights, and when there is, the place is packed shoulder to shoulder. From Monday to Friday it's open for lunch and again in the evenings; on weekends it opens at 4pm. On most nights it's open 'til about 1am, although the revelry might continue 'til about 3am on Friday or Saturday. One corner has been separated into a more bohemian-style bar or pub called La Esquina, or "The Corner." Av. 1 btw. calles 21 and 23 (50m/1/2 block west of the Cine Magaly). ℭ **2221-0327.**

El Observatorio ☆☆ *(Finds)*   It's easy to miss the narrow entrance to this hot spot across from the Cine Magaly. Owned by a local filmmaker, its decor includes a heavy dose of cinema motifs. The space is large, with high ceilings, and one of the best (perhaps only) smoke extraction systems of any popular bar, making the place bearable, even though most of the clientele are chain-smoking. There's occasional live music and movie screenings and a decent menu of appetizers and main dishes drawn from various world cuisines. It's open noon to 2am daily. Calle 23 btw. avs. Central and 1. ℭ **2223-0725.**

Key Largo ☆ *(Finds)*   This meticulously restored downtown mansion is also one of San José's top prostitute pickup bars. Housed in a beautiful old building just off Parque Morazán in the heart of downtown, Key Largo is worth a visit if only to take in the scene and admire the dark-stained carved wood ceilings. There are a couple of pool tables, there's usually a live band, and there are always working women—however, this is still an acceptable place for visiting couples and those not actively shopping the wares. It's open 11am to 3am daily. Calle 7 btw. avs. 1 and 3. ℭ **2221-0277.**

Shakespeare Bar   Located next to, and somewhat underneath, the Sala Garbo movie theater, this quiet little spot is a good place to meet after a movie or a show at the Sala Garbo or Laurence Olivier Theater next door. Intimate and reserved, it's open daily 'til midnight. Av. 2 and Calle 28. ℭ **2258-6787.**

Terra U Set on a busy corner in the heart of the university district, this two-story joint is one of the most popular bars in the area. Part of this is due to the inviting open-air street-front patio area, which provides a nice alternative to the all-too-common smoke-filled rooms found at most other trendy spots. It's open Monday through Saturday evenings 'til 2am. 200m (2 blocks) east and 150m (11/2 blocks) north of the church in San Pedro. ☎ 2225-4261.

HANGING OUT IN SAN PEDRO

The funky 2-block stretch of **San Pedro** ★★ just south of the University of Costa Rica has been dubbed La Calle de Amargura, or the "Street of Bitterness," and it's the heart and soul of this eastern suburb and college town. Bars and cafes are mixed in with bookstores and copy shops. After dark the streets are packed with teens, punks, students, and professors barhopping and just hanging around. You can walk the strip until someplace strikes your fancy—you don't need a travel guide to find **Omar Khayyam** (☎ 2253-8455), **Marrakech Pool & Pizza** (☎ 253-2049), **Tavarua Surf & Skate Bar** (☎ 2225-7249), or **Caccio's** (☎ 2224-3261), which lie at the heart of this district—or you can try one of the places listed below. *Note:* La Calle de Amargura attracts a certain unsavory element. Use caution here. Try to visit with a group, and try not to carry large amounts of cash or wear flashy jewelry.

You can get here by heading out (east) on Avenida 2, and following the flow of traffic. You will first pass through the neighborhood of Los Yoses before you reach a large traffic circle with a big fountain in the center (La Fuente de la Hispanidad). The Mall San Pedro is located on this traffic circle. Heading straight through the circle (well, going around it and continuing on what would have been a straight path), you'll come to the Church of San Pedro, about 4 blocks east of the circle. The church is the major landmark in San Pedro. You can also take a bus here from downtown.

Jazz Café ★ The Jazz Café is consistently a great spot to find live music and one of the more happening spots in San Pedro. It remains one of my favorites, although low ceilings and poor air circulation make it almost unbearably smoky most nights. Wrought-iron chairs, sculpted busts of famous jazz artists, and creative lighting give the place ambience. There's live music here most nights. It's open daily 'til about 2am. These folks recently opened a sister Jazz Café Escazu on the western end of town. The new spot is much larger and should get some bigger acts. Next to the Banco Popular on Av. Central. ☎ 2253-8933. www.jazzcafecostarica.com.

Mosaikos The entrance to this popular nightspot is a long, narrow corridor/bar that is generally packed solid. A larger room in the back has another bar, some tables, and some funky art. The crowd here is young and can get quite rowdy. They often have live DJs playing a mix of house, techno, and trance-style dance music, although you're also just as likely to hear reggae, ska, or hip-hop tunes blasting. It's open Monday through Saturday from 11am to 2am, Sunday from 5pm to 2am. 200m (2 blocks) east and 150m (11/2 blocks) north of the Church in San Pedro. ☎ 2280-9541.

THE GAY & LESBIAN SCENE

Because Costa Rica is such a conservative Catholic country, the gay and lesbian communities here are rather discreet. Homosexuality is not generally under attack, but many gay and lesbian organizations guard their privacy, and the club scene is changeable and not well publicized.

The most established and happening gay and lesbian bar and dance club in San José is **La Avispa** ✦, Calle 1 between avenidas 8 and 10 (℃ **2223-5343;** www.laavispa. co.cr). It is popular with both men and women, although it sometimes sets aside certain nights of the week or month for specific persuasions. There's also **Buenas Vibraciones** (℃ **2223-4573**), out on Paseo de los Estudiantes; **Club Oh** (℃ **2248-1500**), on Calle 2 between avenidas 14 and 16; **Pucho's Bar** (℃ **2256-1147**), on Calle 11 and Avenida 8; **El Bochinche** (℃ **2221-0500**), on Calle 11 between avenidas 10 and 12; and **Punto G** (℃ **2280-3726**) in San Pedro, half a block southwest of the Higuerón. Out in the suburb of San Antonio de Belén is the new **Kashmir Cocktail Lounge** (℃ **2293-0162**) located inside the La Ribera shopping center.

CASINOS

Gambling is legal in Costa Rica, with casinos at virtually every major hotel. However, as with Tico bullfighting, there are some idiosyncrasies involved in gambling *a la Tica*.

If blackjack is your game, you'll want to play "rummy." The rules are almost identical, except that the house doesn't pay 1½ times on blackjack—instead, it pays double on any three of a kind or three-card straight flush.

If you're looking for roulette, what you'll find here is a bingolike spinning cage of numbered balls. The betting is the same, but some of the glamour is lost.

You'll also find a version of five-card-draw poker, but the rule differences are so complex that I advise you to sit down and watch for a while and then ask questions before joining in. That's about all you'll find. There are no craps tables or baccarat.

There's some controversy over slot machines—one-armed bandits are currently outlawed—but you will be able to play electronic slots and poker games. Most casinos here are casual and small by international standards. You may have to dress up slightly at some of the fancier hotels, but most are accustomed to tropical vacation attire.

9 Side Trips from San José

San José makes an excellent base for exploring the beautiful Central Valley and the surrounding mountains. For first-time visitors, the best way to make the most of these excursions is usually to take a guided tour, but if you rent a car, you'll have greater independence. Some day trips also can be done by public bus.

GUIDED TOURS & ADVENTURES

A number of companies offer a wide variety of primarily nature-related day tours out of San José. The most reputable include **Costa Rica Expeditions** ✦✦ (℃ 2257-0766; www.costaricaexpeditions.com), **Costa Rica Sun Tours** ✦ (℃ 2296-7757; www. crsuntours.com), **Horizontes Tours** ✦✦ (℃ 2222-2022; www.horizontes.com), and **Swiss Travel Service** (℃ 2282-4898; www.swisstravelcr.com).

Before signing on for a tour of any sort, find out how many fellow travelers will be accompanying you, how much time will be spent in transit and eating lunch, and how much time will actually be spent doing the primary activity. I've had complaints about tours that were rushed, that spent too much time in a bus or on secondary activities, or that had a cattle-car, assembly-line feel to them. The tours below are arranged by type of activity. In addition to these, you'll find many other tours that combine two or three different activities or destinations.

BUNGEE JUMPING There's nothing unique about bungee jumping in Costa Rica, but the site here is quite beautiful. If you've always had the bug, **Tropical**

The Central Valley

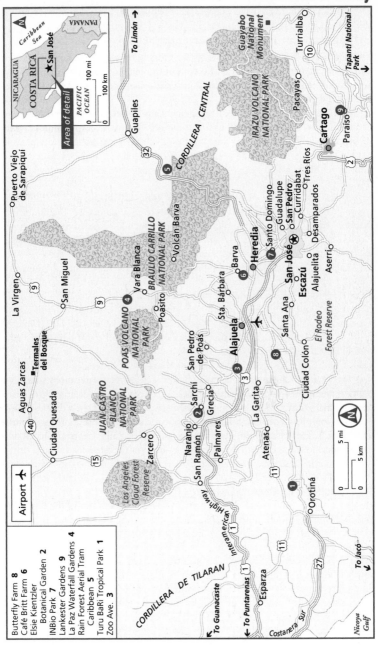

Butterfly Farm **8**
Café Britt Farm **6**
Elsie Kientzler
   Botanical Garden **2**
INBio Park **7**
Lankester Gardens **9**
La Paz Waterfall Gardens **4**
Rain Forest Aerial Tram
   Caribbean **5**
Turu BaRi Tropical Park **1**
Zoo Ave. **3**

Airport ✈

Bungee (© **2248-2212;** www.bungee.co.cr) will let you jump off an 80m (262-ft.) bridge for $65 (£33); two jumps cost $95 (£48). Transportation is provided free from San José twice daily. These folks also offer paragliding tours.

CANOPY TOURS & AERIAL TRAMS   Getting off the ground and up into the treetops is the latest fad in Costa Rican tourism, and there are scores of such tours around the country. You have several options relatively close to San José, and one actually in the city center.

The quickest and easiest way to experience a zip-line canopy tour from San José is to head to the La Sabana park and take the new **Urban Canopy Tour** (© **2215-2544**). Given the fact that this tour is set on a relatively flat patch of city park, it is neither as extensive nor exciting as the other options listed in this section. Still, the tour has eight zip-line cables, with the longest being some 200m (650 ft.) long. The tour costs $20 (£10).

Another option is the **Rain Forest Aerial Tram Caribbean** (© **2257-5961;** www.rainforesttram.com), built on a private reserve bordering Braulio Carrillo National Park. This pioneering tramway is the brainchild of rainforest researcher Dr. Donald Perry, whose cable-car system through the forest canopy at Rara Avis helped establish him as an early expert on rainforest canopies. The tramway takes visitors on a 90-minute ride through the treetops, where they have the chance to glimpse the complex web of life that makes these forests unique. Additional attractions include a butterfly garden, serpentarium, and frog collection. They also have their own zip-line canopy tour, and the grounds feature well-groomed trails through the rainforest and a restaurant—with all this on offer, a trip here can easily take up a full day. If you want to spend the night, there are 10 simple but clean and comfortable bungalows, which cost $110 (£55) per person per day (double occupancy), including three meals, three guided tours, taxes, two tram rides, and unlimited use of the rest of the facilities.

The cost for a full-day tour, including both the aerial tram and canopy tour, all the park's other attractions, and transportation from San José and either breakfast or lunch, is $105 (£52). Alternatively, you can drive or take one of the frequent Guápiles buses—they leave every half-hour throughout the day and cost $2 (£1)—from the Caribbean bus terminal (Gran Terminal del Caribe) on Calle Central, 1 block north of Avenida 11. Ask the driver to let you off in front of the *teleférico*. If you're driving, head out on the Guápiles Highway as if driving to the Caribbean coast. Watch for the tram's roadside welcome center—it's hard to miss. For walk-ins, the entrance fee is $55 (£28); students and anyone under 18 pay $28 (£14). Because this is a popular tour for groups, I highly recommend that you get an advance reservation in the high season and, if possible, a ticket; otherwise you could wait a long time for your tram ride or even be shut out. The tram handles only about 80 passengers per hour, so scheduling is tight; the folks here try to schedule as much as possible in advance.

Turu BaRi Tropical Park (© **2250-0705** or 2428-6070; www.turubari.com) is another similar attraction that aims to cover as many bases as possible. Located about 90 minutes outside San José, this park features a series of gardens, trails, and exhibits set in a deep valley that you can reach by means of a gondola-style ski lift, by cable and zip-line canopy tour, or on horseback. Down in the valley, you can wander around the botanical gardens, orchid gardens, and butterfly gardens, or grab a bite at the typical Costa Rican restaurant. The gondola ride here actually features enclosed cabin cars (with windows that open) and doesn't provide nearly the sense of intimacy or contact with the forest that the Aerial Tram does. Admission is $60 (£30) for adults, $55 (£28) for students, and $40 (£20) for children; all the various adventure tour options cost extra. However, various combination package tours, with or without transportation and meals, are available.

Finally, the folks at **Original Canopy Tours** ⊕ (© 2291-4465; www.canopy tour.com) have their **Mahogany Park** operation, located about 1 hour outside of San José. The tour here features 10 platforms, and at the end you have the choice of taking a cable to a ground station or doing an 18m (60-ft.) rappel down to finish off. The tour takes about 2 hours and costs $45 (£23). Package tours with transportation from San José are also available.

DAY CRUISES   Several companies offer cruises to lovely Tortuga Island in the Gulf of Nicoya. These full-day tours generally entail an early departure for the 2½-hour chartered bus ride to Puntarenas, where you board your vessel for a 1½-hour cruise to Tortuga Island. Then you get several hours on the uninhabited island, where you can swim, lie on the beach, play volleyball, or try a canopy tour, followed by the return journey.

The original and most dependable company running these trips is **Calypso Tours** ⊕ (© 2256-2727; www.calypsotours.com). The tour costs $99 (£49) per person and includes round-trip transportation from San José, a basic continental breakfast during the bus ride to the boat, all drinks on the cruise, and an excellent buffet lunch on the beach at the island. The Calypso Tours main vessel is a massive motor-powered catamaran. A second runs a separate tour to a private nature reserve at **Punta Coral** ⊕. The beach is much nicer at Tortuga Island, but the tour to Punta Coral is more intimate, and the restaurant, hiking, and kayaking are all superior here.

EXPLORING PRE-COLUMBIAN RUINS   Although Costa Rica lacks the kind of massive pre-Columbian archaeological sites found in Mexico, Guatemala, or Honduras, it does have **Guayabo National Monument** ⊕, a small excavated town that today is just a small collection of building foundations, cobbled streets, aqueducts, and a small plaza. **Costa Rica Sun Tours** (© 2296-7757; www.crsuntours.com) offers a day trip here for around $130 (£65) per person. If you have a car or are an intrepid bus hound, you can do this tour on your own. Admission to the park is $10 (£5), and you can usually find a guide at the entrance for around $5 (£2.50). See the below section on Turrialba for more information on Guayabo.

HIKING   Most of the tour agencies listed above offer 1-day guided hikes to a variety of destinations. In general, I recommend taking guided hikes to really see and learn about the local flora and fauna.

HORSEBACK RIDING   Options are nearly endless outside of San José, but it's more difficult to find a place to saddle up in the metropolitan area. The **La Caraña Riding Academy** (© 2282-6106; www.lacarana.com) and **Centro Ecuestre Valle Yos Oy** (© 2282-6934) are both in Santa Ana, and offer riding classes as well as some guided trail rides.

MOUNTAIN BIKING   The best bicycle riding is well outside of San José—on dirt roads where you're not likely to be run off the highway by a semi, or run head-on into someone coming around a blind curve in the wrong lane. Several companies run a variety of 1-day and multiday tours out of San José. The 1-day tours usually involve a round-trip bus or van ride out of downtown to the primary destination, such as the towns of Sarchí and Turrialba, and the Irazú and Poás volcanoes. Several of these tours are entirely or primarily descents. **Costa Rica Biking Adventure** (©2225-6591;

Holy Smoke! Choosing the Volcano Trip That's Right for You

Poás, Irazú, and Arenal volcanoes are three of Costa Rica's most popular destinations, and the first two are easy day trips from San José (see below). Although numerous companies offer day trips to Arenal, I don't recommend them because there's at least 3½ hours of travel time in each direction. You usually arrive when the volcano is hidden by clouds and leave before the night's darkness shows off its glowing eruptions. For more information on Arenal Volcano, see chapter 9.

Tour companies offering trips to Poás and Irazú include **Costa Rica Expeditions** 𝕲𝕲 (© 2257-0766), **Costa Rica Sun Tours** 𝕲 (© 2296-7757), **Horizontes** 𝕲𝕲 (© 2222-2022), and **Swiss Travel Service** (© 2282-4898). Prices range from $30 to $50 (£15–£25) for a half-day trip, and from $50 to $110 (£25–£55) for a full-day trip.

The 3,378m (11,080-ft.) **Irazú Volcano** 𝕲 (© 2551-9398) is historically one of Costa Rica's more active volcanoes, although it's relatively quiet these days. It last erupted on March 19, 1963, the day that President John F. Kennedy arrived in Costa Rica. There's a good paved road right to the rim of the crater, where a desolate expanse of gray sand nurtures few plants and the air smells of sulfur. The landscape here is often compared to that of the moon. There are magnificent views of the fertile Meseta Central and Orosi Valley as you drive up from Cartago, and if you're very lucky, you might be able to see both the Pacific Ocean and the Caribbean Sea. Clouds usually descend by noon, so get here as early in the day as possible.

The visitor center up here has information on the volcano and natural history. A short trail leads to the rim of the volcano's two craters, their walls a maze of eroded gullies feeding onto the flat floor far below. This is a national park, with an admission fee of $10 (£5) charged at the gate. Dress in layers; this might be the Tropics, but it can be cold up at the top if the sun's not out. The park restaurant, at an elevation of 3,022m (9,912 ft.), with walls of windows looking out over the valley far below, claims to be the highest restaurant in Central America.

If you don't want an organized tour, buses leave for Irazú Volcano daily at 8am from Avenida 2 between calles 1 and 3 (across the street from the entrance to the Gran Hotel Costa Rica). The fare is $7 (£3.50) round-trip,

www.bikingincostarica.com) offers a variety of mountain-biking tours using high-end bikes and gear. A 1-day trip costs between $80 and $160 (£40–£80) per person.

Another company offering mountain-biking trips is **Coast to Coast Adventures** 𝕲 (© 2280-8054; www.ctoadventures.com), which, in addition to its 2-week namesake adventure, also designs customized mountain-biking trips of shorter durations.

A unique new option is to take a **Railbike Tour** (© 8303-3300; www.railbike. com). This tour involves a mountain bike rigged to a contraption that fits over abandoned railroad tracks, running through the countryside outside San José. The full-day tour costs $75 (£38) and includes all equipment, plus a light breakfast and full lunch.

with the bus leaving the volcano at 12:30pm. This company is particularly fickle; to make sure that the buses are running, call © **2530-1064,** although that might not help much, since they often don't answer their phone, and speak only Spanish. If you're driving, head northeast out of Cartago toward San Rafael, and then continue driving uphill toward the volcano, passing the turnoffs for Cot and Tierra Blanca en route.

Poás Volcano ⋒⋒ (© **2482-2424**) is 37km (23 miles) from San José on narrow roads that wind through a landscape of fertile farms and dark forests. As at Irazú, there's a paved road right to the top, although you'll have to hike in about 1km (½ mile) to reach the crater. The volcano stands 2,640m (8,659 ft.) tall and is located within a national park, which preserves not only the volcano but also dense stands of virgin forest. Poás's crater, said to be the second largest in the world, is more than a mile across. Geysers in the crater sometimes spew steam and muddy water 180m (590 ft.) into the air, making this the largest geyser in the world. There's an information center where you can see a slide show about the volcano, and there are well-groomed and marked hiking trails through the cloud forest that rings the crater. About 15 minutes from the parking area, along a forest trail, is an overlook onto beautiful Botos Lake, which has formed in one of the volcano's extinct craters.

Be prepared when you come to Poás: This volcano is often enveloped in dense clouds. If you want to see the crater, it's best to come early and during the dry season. Moreover, it can get cool up here, especially when the sun isn't shining, so dress appropriately. Admission to the national park is $10 (£5).

In case you don't want to go on a tour, there's a daily bus (© **2442-6900** or 2222-5325) from Avenida 2 between calles 12 and 14 that leaves at 8am and returns at 2pm. The fare is $5 (£2.50) round-trip. The bus is often crowded, so arrive early. If you're driving, head for Alajuela and continue on the main road through town and follow signs for Fraijanes. Just beyond Fraijanes you will connect with the road between San Pedro de Poás and Poasito; turn right toward Poasito and continue to the rim of the volcano.

RAFTING, KAYAKING & RIVER TRIPS   Cascading down Costa Rica's mountain ranges are dozens of tumultuous rivers, several of which are very popular for white-water rafting and kayaking. If I had to choose just one day trip out of San José, it would be a white-water rafting trip. For between $75 and $110 (£38–£55), you can spend a day rafting through lush tropical forests; multiday trips are also available. Some of the most reliable rafting companies are **Aventuras Naturales** ⋒ (© 800/ **514-0411** in the U.S., or 2225-3939), **Exploradores Outdoors** ⋒ (© **2222-6262**), and **Ríos Tropicales** ⋒ (© **2233-6455**). These companies all ply a number of rivers of varying difficulties, including the popular Pacuare and Reventazón rivers. For details, see "White-Water Rafting, Kayaking & Canoeing," in chapter 5.

The Sarapiquí River is also a popular waterway for day trips outside of San José. **Ecoscapes Highlights Tour** (© 2297-0664; www.ecoscapetours.com) runs a jam-packed trip here that combines a stop at the La Paz waterfall, a visit to a banana plantation, a rainforest hike, and a boat ride on the river for $83 (£41) per person, including round-trip transportation, breakfast, and lunch.

Perhaps the best-known river tours are those that go up to **Tortuguero National Park** ✦✦. It's possible to do this tour as a day trip out of San José, but it's a long, tiring, and expensive day. You're much better off doing it as a 1- or 2-night trip. See chapter 12 for details.

CARTAGO & THE OROSI VALLEY

These two regions southeast of San José can easily be combined into a day trip. You might also squeeze in a visit to the Irazú Volcano (see box above, for details).

CARTAGO

Located about 24km (15 miles) southeast of San José, **Cartago** ✦ is the former capital of Costa Rica. Founded in 1563, it was Costa Rica's first city—and was, in fact, its *only* city for almost 150 years. Irazú Volcano rises up from the edge of town, and although it's quiet these days, it has not always been so peaceful. Earthquakes have damaged Cartago repeatedly over the years, so today few of the old colonial buildings are left standing. In the center of the city, a public park winds through the ruins of a large church that was destroyed in 1910 before it could be finished. Construction was abandoned after the quake, and today the ruins sit at the heart of a neatly manicured park, with quiet paths and plenty of benches. The ruins themselves are closed off, but the park itself is lovely. (The park is a free Wi-Fi hotspot, as well.)

Cartago's most famous building is the **Basílica de Nuestra Señora de los Angeles (Basilica of Our Lady of the Angels)** ✦, which is dedicated to the patron saint of Costa Rica and stands on the east side of town. Within the walls of this Byzantine-style church is a shrine containing the tiny carved figure of **La Negrita**, the Black Virgin, which is nearly lost amid its ornate altar. Legend has it that La Negrita first revealed herself on this site to a peasant girl in 1635. The walls of the shrine are covered with a fascinating array of tiny silver images left as thanks for cures affected by La Negrita. Amid the plethora of diminutive silver arms and legs, there are also hands, feet, hearts, lungs, kidneys, eyes, torsos, breasts, and—peculiarly—guns, trucks, beds, and planes. There are even dozens of sports trophies that I assume were left as thanks for helping teams win big games. Outside the church, vendors sell a wide selection of these trinkets, as well as little candle replicas of La Negrita.

More than 1km (½ mile) east of Cartago, on the road to Paraíso, you'll find **Lankester Gardens** ✦✦ (© 2552-3247; p. 133), a botanical garden known for its orchid collection.

GETTING THERE   Lumaca buses (© 2537-0347) for Cartago leave San José every 3 to 5 minutes between 5am and 9pm, with slightly less frequent service until midnight, from Calle 3 and Avenida 2. You can also pick up one en route at any of the little covered bus stops along Avenida Central in Los Yoses and San Pedro. The length of the trip is 45 minutes; the fare is about 60¢ (30p).

OROSI VALLEY

The Orosi Valley, southeast of Cartago and visible from the top of Irazú on a clear day, is generally considered one of the most beautiful valleys in Costa Rica. The Reventazón

Fun Fact **La Negrita**

Legend has it that Juana Pereira stumbled upon the statue of La Negrita sitting atop a rock, while gathering wood. Juana took it home, but the next morning it was gone. She went back to the rock, and there it was again. This was repeated three times, until Juana took her find to a local priest. The priest took the statue to his church for safekeeping, but the next morning it was gone, only to be found sitting upon the same rock later that day. The priest eventually decided that the strange occurrences were a sign that the Virgin wanted a temple or shrine built to her upon the spot. And so work was begun on what would eventually become today's impressive basilica.

Miraculous healing powers have been attributed to La Negrita, and, over the years, a parade of pilgrims have come to the shrine seeking cures for their illnesses and difficulties. August 2 is her patron saint's day. Each year, on this date, tens of thousands of Costa Ricans and foreign pilgrims walk to Cartago from San José and elsewhere in the country in devotion to this powerful statue.

River meanders through this steep-sided valley until it collects in the lake formed by the Cachí Dam. There are scenic overlooks near the town of Orosi, which is at the head of the valley, and in Ujarrás, which is on the banks of the lake. Near **Ujarrás** are the ruins of Costa Rica's oldest church (built in 1693), whose tranquil gardens are a great place to sit and gaze at the surrounding mountains. In the town of Orosi itself, there is yet another colonial church and convent, built in 1743. A small museum here displays religious artifacts. Near the town of Cachí, you'll find **La Casa del Soñador** (the **House of the Dreamer;** ℂ **2577-1983**), the home and gallery of the late sculptor Macedonio Quesada and his sons, who carry on the family tradition.

From the Orosi Valley, it's a quick shot to the entrance to the **Tapantí National Park** ⊛ (ℂ **2552-4823**), where you'll find some gentle and beautiful hiking trails, as well as riverside picnic areas. The park is open daily from 8am to 4pm; admission is $10 (£5).

If you're interested in staying out here, check out the charming little **Orosi Lodge** (ℂ **2533-3578;** www.orosilodge.com), which is located right next to some simple hot spring pools.

GETTING THERE If you're driving, take the road to Paraíso from Cartago, head toward Ujarrás, continue around the lake, and then pass through Cachí and on to Orosi. From Orosi, the road leads back to Paraíso. It is difficult to explore this whole area by public bus because this is not a densely populated region and connections are often infrequent or unreliable. However, there are regular buses from Cartago to the town of Orosi. These buses run roughly every half-hour and leave the main bus terminal in Cartago. The trip takes 30 minutes, and the fare is 60¢ (30p). There are also guided day tours of this area from San José (call any of the companies listed under "Guided Tours & Adventures," earlier in this section).

TURRIALBA

This attractive little town 53km (33 miles) east of San José is best known as the starting point and home base for many popular white-water rafting trips. However, it's also worth a visit if you have an interest in pre-Columbian history or tropical botany.

Guayabo National Monument ✦ (© **2559-1220**) is one of Costa Rica's only pre-Columbian sites that has been excavated and is open to the public. It's 19km (12 miles) northeast of Turrialba and preserves a town site that dates from between 1000 B.C. and A.D. 1400. Archaeologists believe that Guayabo might have supported a population of as many as 10,000 people, but there is no clue yet to why the city was eventually abandoned only shortly before the Spanish arrived in the New World. Excavated ruins at Guayabo consist of paved roads, aqueducts, stone bridges, and house and temple foundations. There are also gravesites and petroglyphs. The monument is open daily from 8am to 4pm. This is a national park, and admission is $10 (£5) at the gate. For information about other parks in this area, see "Costa Rica's Top National Parks & Bioreserves," in chapter 5.

Botanists and gardeners will want to pay a visit to the **Center for Agronomy Research and Development** (**CATIE;** www.catie.ac.cr), which is located 5km (3 miles) southeast of Turrialba on the road to Siquirres. This center is one of the world's foremost facilities for research into tropical agriculture. Among the plants on CATIE's 2,000 acres are hundreds of varieties of cacao and thousands of varieties of coffee. The plants here have been collected from all over the world. In addition to trees used for food and other purposes, there are plants grown strictly for ornamental purposes. CATIE is open Monday through Friday from 7am to 4pm. Guided tours are available with advance notice for $10 to $25 (£5–£13) per person, depending upon the size of your group, and how extensive a tour you decide to take. Call © **2556-2700** for reservations.

While you're in Turrialba, you might want to spend a little time at **Turrialtico** (© **2538-1111;** www.turrialtico.com), a rustic yet beautiful open-air restaurant and small hotel high on a hill overlooking the Turrialba Valley. The view from here is one of the finest in the country, with lush greenery far below and volcanoes in the distance. Meals are quite inexpensive; a double room will cost you around $62 to $66 (£31–£32) including breakfast and taxes. This place is popular with rafting companies that bring groups here for meals and for overnights before, during, and after multiday rafting trips. You'll find Turrialtico about 10km (6¼ miles) outside of Turrialba on the road to Siquirres.

If you're looking for more luxury in this area, check out **Casa Turire** ✦✦ (© **2531-1111;** www.hotelcasaturire.com), where well-appointed rooms and suites in an elegant country mansion run between $135 and $330 (£68–£165). The hotel is set on the banks of the lake formed by the Angostura dam project, and you can take a kayak or paddleboat out on the lake here.

Since Turrialba is a main base for several rafting trips and rafting operators, the town has a healthy population of rafting guides living here, and as a result, it actually has a pretty active nightlife.

GETTING THERE **Transtusa** buses (© **2222-4464** or 2556-4233) leave San José hourly for Turrialba between 5am and 10pm from Calle 13 between avenidas 6 and 8. The fare is $1.80 (90p). If you're driving, take the road from Cartago to Paraíso, then through Juan Viñas, and on to Turrialba. It's pretty well marked. (Alternatively you can head toward the small town of Cot, on the road to Irazú Volcano, and then through the town of Pacayas on to Turrialba, another well-marked route.)

Turrialba itself is a bit of a jumble, and you will probably have to ask directions to get to locations outside of town. Guayabo is about 20km (12 miles) beyond Turrialba on a road that is paved the entire way except for the last 3km (1¾ miles). Around three buses also head to Guayabo daily from the main bus terminal in Turrialba.

HEREDIA, GRECIA, SARCHÍ & ZARCERO

All of these cities and towns are northwest of San José and can be combined into a long day trip (if you have a car), perhaps in conjunction with a visit to Poás Volcano and/or the Waterfall Gardens. The scenery here is rich and verdant, and the small towns and scattered farming communities are truly representative of Costa Rica's agricultural heartland and *campesino* tradition. This is a great area to explore on your own in a rental car, if you don't mind getting lost a bit (roads are narrow, winding, and poorly marked). If you're relying on buses, you'll be able to visit any of the towns listed below, but probably just one or two per day.

The road to Heredia turns north off the highway from San José to the airport. If you're going to Sarchí, take the highway west toward Puntarenas. Turn north to Grecia and then west to Sarchí. There'll be plenty of signs.

HEREDIA

Set on the flanks of the impressive Barva Volcano, this city was founded in 1706. Heredia is affectionately known as "The City of Flowers." A colonial church inaugurated in 1763 stands in the central park—the stone facade leaves no questions as to the age of the church. The altar inside is decorated with neon stars and a crescent moon surrounding a statue of the Virgin Mary. In the middle of the palm-shaded park is a music temple, and across the street, beside several tile-roofed municipal buildings, is the tower of an old Spanish fort. Of all the cities in the Meseta Central, Heredia has the most colonial feel to it—you'll still see adobe buildings with Spanish tile roofs along narrow streets. Heredia is also the site of the **National Autonomous University,** so you'll find some nice coffee shops and bookstores near the school.

Surrounding Heredia is an intricate maze of picturesque villages and towns, including Santa Bárbara, Santo Domingo, Barva, and San Joaquín de Flores. San Isidro de Heredia has a lovely, large church with an ornate facade. However, the biggest attraction up here is **INBio Park** ✦✦ (✆ **2507-8107;** p. 133). Located on 5 hectares (12 acres) in Santo Domingo de Heredia, this place is part museum, part educational center, and part nature park. This is also where you'll find the **Café Britt Farm** ✦ (✆ **2277-1600;** p. 132). On the road to Barva, you'll find the small **Museo de Cultura Popular** (✆ **2260-1619**), which is open Monday through Friday from 8am to 4pm and Saturday and Sunday from 10am to 5pm; admission is $2 (£1). Anyone with an interest in medicinal herbs should plan a visit to the **Ark Herb Farm** ✦ (✆ **8846-2694** or 2269-4847; www.arkherbfarm.com). These folks offer guided tours of their gardens, which feature more than 300 types of medicinal plants. The tour costs $12 (£6) per person, and includes a light snack and refreshments. Reservations are required.

If you make your way to San Pedro de Barva de Heredia, stop in at **La Lluna de Valencia** (✆ **2269-6665**), a delightful rustic Spanish restaurant with amazing paella, delicious sangria, and a very amiable host.

Buses leave for Heredia every 5 minutes between 5am and 11pm from Calle 1 between avenidas 7 and 9, or from Avenida 2 between calles 12 and 14. Bus fare is 45¢ (25p).

GRECIA

The picturesque little town of Grecia is noteworthy for its unusual metal church, which is painted a deep red and has white gingerbread trim. Just off the central park, next to the Palacio Municipal, you'll find the humble **Grecia Regional Museum**

(© **2494-6767**), which has some simple exhibits and information about the town's history. About 1km (½ mile) outside of Grecia, on the old road to Alajuela, you will find the **World of Snakes** (© **2494-3700**). Open daily from 8am to 4pm, this serpentarium has more than 150 snakes representing more than 50 species. Admission, which includes a guided tour, is $11 (£5.50) for adults, and $6 (£3) for children 7 to 14.

Tuan (© **2258-2004**) buses leave San José every half-hour for Grecia from Calle 18 between avenidas 5 and 7 (on the east side of the Abonos Agros building). The fare is $1.20 (60p). The road to Sarchí is to the left as you face the church in Grecia, but due to all the one-way streets, you'll have to drive around it.

SARCHÍ ⍟

Sarchí is Costa Rica's main artisan town. The colorfully painted miniature **oxcarts** that you see all over the country are made here. Oxcarts such as these were once used to haul coffee beans to market. Today, although you might occasionally see oxcarts in use, most are purely decorative. However, they remain a well-known symbol of Costa Rica. In addition to miniature oxcarts, many carved wooden souvenirs are made here with rare hardwoods from the nation's forests. There are dozens of shops in town, and all have similar prices. Perhaps your best one-stop shop in Sarchí is the large and long-standing **Chaverri Oxcart Factory** ⍟ (© **2454-4411**), which is right in the center of things, but it never hurts to shop around and visit several of the stores.

Aside from handicrafts, there are other reasons to visit Sarchí. Built between 1950 and 1958, the town's main **church** ⍟ is painted pink with aquamarine trim and looks strangely like a child's birthday cake. But my favorite attraction in Sarchí is the **Else Kientzler Botanical Garden** ⍟⍟ (© **2454-2070**; p. 132), which features an extensive collection of several thousand types of plants, flowers, and trees.

While there are no noteworthy accommodations in Sarchí itself, the plush new **El Silencio Lodge & Spa** (© **2291-3044**; www.elsilenciolodge.com; p. 257) is about a 35-minute drive away in a beautiful mountain setting. **Tuan** (© **2258-2004**) buses leave San José about five times throughout the day for Sarchí from Calle 18 between avenidas 5 and 7. The fare is $1.20 (60p). Alternatively, you can take any Grecia bus from this same station. In Grecia they connect with the Alajuela-Sarchí buses, leaving every 30 minutes from Calle 8 between avenidas Central and 1 in Alajuela.

ZARCERO

Beyond Sarchí, on picturesque roads lined with cedar trees, you'll find the town of Zarcero. In a small park in the middle of town is a **menagerie of sculpted shrubs** that includes a monkey on a motorcycle, people and animals dancing, an ox pulling a cart, a man wearing a top hat, and a large elephant. Behind all the topiary is a wonderful rural **church.** It's not really worth the drive just to see this park, but it's a good idea to take a break in Zarcero to walk the gardens, on the way to La Fortuna and Arenal Volcano.

Daily buses (© **2255-0567**) for Zarcero leave from San José hourly from the Atlántico del Norte bus station at Avenida 9 and Calle 12. This is actually the Ciudad Quesada–San Carlos bus. Just tell the driver that you want to get off in Zarcero, and keep an eye out for the topiary. The ride takes around 1½ hours, and the fare is around $1.60 (80p).

7

Guanacaste: The Gold Coast

Guanacaste is known as Costa Rica's "Gold Coast." And it's not because this is where the Spaniards found vast quantities of the shiny soft metal ore. Instead, it's because more and more visitors to Costa Rica are choosing Guanacaste as their first—and often only—stop. Beautiful beaches abound along this coastline. Some are still pristine and deserted, some are packed with a mix of hotels and resorts, and others are backed by small fishing villages. Choices range from long, broad stretches of sand to tiny pocket coves bordered by rocky headlands.

This is Costa Rica's most coveted vacation destination and the site of its greatest tourism development. Change here is fast and ongoing. Several large resorts have sprung up, and more are in the works. The international airport in Liberia receives daily direct flights from several major U.S. and Canadian hub cities, allowing tourists to visit some of Costa Rica's prime destinations without having to go through San José.

This is also Costa Rica's driest region. The rainy season starts later and ends earlier here, and overall it's more dependably sunny here than in other parts of the country. Combine this climate with a coastline that stretches south for hundreds of miles, from the Nicaraguan border, all the way to the southern tip of the Nicoya Peninsula, and you have an equation that yields beach bliss.

There is one caveat: During the dry season (mid-Nov to Apr), when sunshine is most reliable, the hillsides in Guanacaste turn browner than the chaparral of Southern California. Dust from dirt roads blankets the trees in many areas, and the vistas are far from tropical. Driving these dirt roads without air-conditioning and the windows rolled up tight can be extremely unpleasant.

On the other hand, if you happen to visit this area in the rainy season (particularly from May–Aug), the hillsides are a beautiful, rich green, and the sun usually shines all morning, giving way to an afternoon shower—just in time for a nice siesta.

Inland from the beaches, Guanacaste remains Costa Rica's "Wild West," a land of dry plains populated with cattle ranches and cowboys, who are known here as *sabaneros,* a name that derives from the Spanish word for "savanna" or "grassland." If it weren't for those rainforest-clad volcanoes in the distance, you might swear you were in Texas.

Guanacaste is home to several active volcanoes and some beautiful national parks, including **Santa Rosa National Park** ⊛, the home to massive sea turtle nestings and the site of a major battle to maintain independence, and **Rincón de la Vieja National Park** ⊛⊛, which features hot springs and bubbling mud pots, pristine waterfalls, and an active volcanic crater.

1 Liberia

217km (135 miles) NW of San José; 132km (82 miles) NW of Puntarenas

Founded in 1769, Liberia is the capital of Guanacaste province, and although it can hardly be considered a bustling metropolis, it is growing rapidly, in large part as a business center to feed the growing coastal boom. Hardware stores, warehouses, malls, and shipping companies are setting up shop in Liberia, and the city is serving as a housing hub for the many workers needed to man the construction and tourism boom along the coast here.

Still, Liberia does boast more colonial atmosphere than almost any other city in the country. Its narrow streets are lined with charming old adobe homes, many of which have ornate stone accents on their facades, carved wooden doors, and aged red-tile roofs. Many have beautiful large, shuttered windows (some don't even have iron bars for protection) opening onto the narrow streets. The central plaza, which occupies 2 square blocks in front of the church, is still the city's social hub and principal gathering spot.

Liberia works well as a base for exploring this region or as an overnight stop as part of a longer itinerary. You'll find several moderately priced hotels in the city and its outskirts. Still, all things considered, it's usually preferable to base yourself either at the beach or at one of the mountain lodges in the area, and to visit the city on a day trip.

ESSENTIALS

GETTING THERE & DEPARTING **By Plane** The **Daniel Oduber International Airport** (℗ 2668-1010; airport code LIR) in Liberia receives a steady stream of scheduled commercial and charter flights throughout the year. **Delta** (℗ 800/241-4141; www.delta.com) has daily direct flights between its Atlanta hub and Liberia, twice-weekly direct flights from New York's JFK to Liberia; and a once-weekly direct flight between Los Angeles and Liberia; **American Airlines** (℗ 800/433-7300; www.aa.com) offers daily direct flights between Miami and Liberia, and twice-weekly flights between Dallas–Ft. Worth and Liberia; **Continental** (℗ 800/231-0856; www.continental.com) has daily direct flights between Houston and Liberia; and twice-weekly flights between Newark and Liberia; and **US Airways** (℗ 800/622-1015; www.usairways.com) has one weekly direct flight between Charlotte and Liberia. In addition, there are numerous commercial charter flights from various North American cities throughout the high season. Check with your travel agent.

Sansa (℗ 877/767-2672 in the U.S. and Canada, or 2290-4100 in Costa Rica; www.flysansa.com) has five daily flights to Liberia leaving between 6am and 11:40am from San José's Juan Santamaría International Airport. Return flights depart for San José between 7:40am and 12:40pm. During the high season, one late-afternoon flight is added. The fare for the 50-minute flight is $102 (£51) each way.

Nature Air (℗ 800/235-9272 in the U.S. and Canada or 2299-6000; www.natureair.com) has three flights daily to Liberia at 6:30 and 10:10am, and 12:25 and 4:30pm from Tobías Bolaños International Airport in Pavas. Return flights leave Liberia at 7, 11, and 11:30am, and 5:10pm. Fares are $108 (£54) each way. Nature Air also has direct flights between Liberia and Arenal, Quepos, Tamarindo, and Tambor, as well as connections to just about every major destination in Costa Rica, and a daily tourist flight that cruises over several active volcanoes and the Santa Elena peninsula. See p. 163 for more details.

Guanacaste

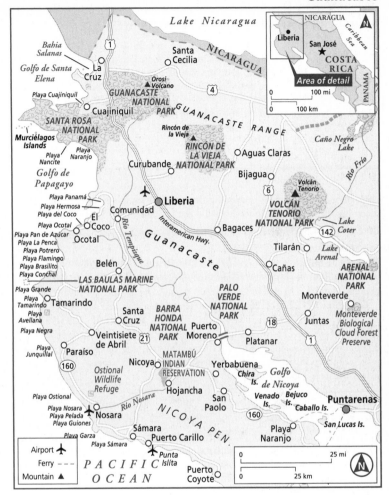

If you plan to fly here and rent a car to continue on to one of the nearby beaches and explore the region, the following companies all have local agencies: **Adobe** (📞 2667-0608), **Alamo** (📞 2668-1111), **Avis** (📞 2668-1138), **Budget** (📞 2668-1118), **Dollar** (📞 2668-1061), **Economy** (📞 2666-2816), **Hertz** (📞 2668-1048), **Payless** (📞 2667-0511), **Sol** (📞 2666-2222), **Thrifty** (📞 2665-0787), and **Toyota** (📞 2668-1212). You can also reserve with these and most major international car-rental companies via their San José and international offices (see "Getting Around," in chapter 6).

Note: The official word is that the cramped, inefficient, and overcrowded terminals, for both arriving and departing passengers, at the Daniel Oduber International Airport will be replaced with a major, modern new facility by mid-2009. If experience is any guide, I wouldn't start holding my breath for a couple years beyond that date, but

---

Finds An Interesting Stop on Your Way to Liberia

If you're driving to or from Guanacaste, be sure to take a brief break to check out the **Iglesia de Cañas (Cañas Church)** ✦✦ in Cañas. Well-known painter, installation artist, and local prodigal son Otto Apuy has designed and directed the envelopment of the entire church in colorful mosaic. The work uses whole and broken tiles in glossy, vibrant colors to depict both religious and abstract themes. The church's central tower, which is entirely covered in mosaic, is nearly 30m (100 ft.) tall. It is estimated that more than a million pieces of ceramic were used in the work. The church is located in the center of town, just a few blocks off the highway.

---

don't be surprised if there is ongoing construction when you arrive. Taxis await all incoming flights; a taxi into town should cost around $10 (£5).

By Car   Take the Interamerican Highway west from San José, and follow the signs for Nicaragua and the Guanacaste beaches. Liberia is about a 3½- to 4-hour drive.

By Bus   **Pulmitan** express buses (© **2222-1650** in San José, or 2666-0458 in Liberia) leave **San José** roughly every hour between 6am and 8pm from Calle 24 between avenidas 5 and 7. The ride to Liberia takes 4 hours. A one-way fare costs $5 (£2.50).

   Gray Line (© **2220-2126;** www.graylinecostarica.com) has a daily bus that leaves San José for Liberia at 8am. The fare is $33 (£16). **Interbus** (© **2283-5573;** www.interbusonline.com) has two daily buses that leave San José for Liberia at 7:45am and 2:30pm; the fare is $35 (£17) to Liberia. The morning bus (for either company) makes connections to Rincón de la Vieja and Santa Rosa national parks. Both companies will pick you up at most San José–area hotels.

   Buses depart for San José and most of the area beaches and national parks from the Liberia bus station on the edge of town, 200m (2 blocks) north and 100m (1 block) east of the main intersection on the Interamerican Highway. Express buses for San José leave roughly every hour between 4am and 8pm.

FAST FACTS   There are several state and private bank offices clustered around downtown Liberia, as well as a branch of the **Banco de Costa Rica** inside the airport. The local **police** number is © **2690-0129,** and the **Liberia Hospital** number is © **2666-0011.** If you need a taxi, dial © **2666-3330.** There are a host of Internet cafes on the blocks surrounding and just off of the central plaza.

   On the southern outskirts of the city is a modern shopping mall, the place to come for a food court fix or to catch a semi-late-run movie at the local multiplex. Another similar complex should be completed near the airport by late 2009.

EXPLORING THE TOWN

The central plaza in Liberia is a great place to people-watch, especially in the early evenings and on weekends. Grab a seat on one of the many concrete benches, or join the families and young lovers as they leisurely stroll around. If you venture off for a few blocks down **Calle Real** ✦, you'll see fine examples of the classic Spanish colonial architecture—adobe buildings with ornate wooden doors, heavy beams, central courtyards, and faded, sagging, red-tile roofs.

While the Catholic church that anchors the central plaza is unspectacular, if you head several blocks east of the plaza, you will come to **Iglesia La Ermita de la Agonía** ★, which was built in 1865, and is still in pretty decent shape. The church is open daily for visits from 2:30 to 3:30pm.

It's not much, but you might want to check out the tiny **Sabanero Museum** (✆ 2665-0135), which has a small collection of photos and exhibits depicting the life and times and tools of the trade of the colonial and post-colonial residents of this horse-and-cattle country. The museum is housed in a small space off the south side of the main church. It's ostensibly open Monday through Saturday from 8am to 5pm, with an hour-long break for lunch; admission is 50¢ (25p). However, because demand is so low, this place is often closed without warning or according to the staff's whims.

OUTDOOR ADVENTURES NEAR LIBERIA
EXPLORING RINCON DE LA VIEJA NATIONAL PARK ★★

This national park begins on the flanks of the Rincón de la Vieja Volcano and includes this volcano's active crater. Down lower you'll find an area of geothermal activity similar to that of Yellowstone National Park in the United States. Fumaroles, geysers, and hot pools cover this small area, creating a bizarre, otherworldly landscape. In addition to hot springs and mud pots, you can explore waterfalls, a lake, and volcanic craters. The bird-watching here is excellent, and the views across the pasturelands to the Pacific Ocean are stunning.

The main entrance is 25km (16 miles) northeast of Liberia, down a badly rutted dirt road. The park entrance fee is $10 (£5) per person per day, and the park is open daily from 7am to 3pm.

Camping will cost you an extra $2 (£1) per person per day. There are actually two entrances and camping areas here: **Santa María** and **Las Pailas** (also called Las Espuelas; ✆ 2661-8139) ranger stations. The latter is by far the more popular and accessible, and it's closer to the action. These small camping areas are near each other. I recommend the one closer to the river, although the bathroom and shower facilities are about 90m (295 ft.) away, at the other site. For those seeking a less rugged tour of the park, there are several lodges located around the perimeter of the park; all offer guided hikes and horseback rides into the park.

GETTING THERE   To reach the Las Pailas (Las Espuelas) entrance, drive about 5km (3 miles) north of Liberia and turn right on the dirt road to the park. The turnoff is well marked. In about 12km (7½ miles), you'll pass through the small village of Curubandé. Continue on this road for another 6km (3¾ miles) until you reach the Hacienda Guachipelin. The lodge is private property, and the owners charge vehicles a $2 (£1) toll to pass through their gate and continue on to the park. I'm not sure if this is legal or mandatory, but it's not worth the hassle to protest. Pay the toll, pass through the gate, and continue for another 4km (2½ miles) until you reach the park entrance.

There are two routes to the **Santa María entrance.** The principal route heads out of the northeastern end of Liberia toward the small village of San Jorge. This route is about 25km (16 miles) long and takes about 45 minutes. A four-wheel-drive vehicle is required. Alternatively, you can reach the entrance on a turnoff from the Interamerican Highway at Bagaces. From here, head north through Guayabo, Aguas Claras, and Colonia Blanca. The road is paved up to Colonia Blanca, but again a four-wheel-drive vehicle is required for the final, very rough 10km (6¼ miles) of gravel road.

HIKING IN THE PARK   There are several excellent trails inside the Rincón de la Vieja National Park. More energetic hikers can tackle the 8km (5 miles) up to the **summit** and explore the several craters and beautiful lakes up here. On a clear day you'll be rewarded with a fabulous view of the plains of Guanacaste and the Pacific Ocean below. The easiest hiking is the gentle **Las Pailas loop** ⚐. This 3km (1.75-mile) trail is just off the Las Espuelas park entrance and passes by several bubbling mud pots and steaming fumaroles. This trail crosses a river, so you'll have to either take off your shoes or get them wet. The whole loop takes around 2 hours.

My favorite hike here is to the **Blue Lake** and **La Cangrejo Waterfall** ⚐⚐. This 5km (3-mile) trail passes through several different life zones, including dry forest, transitional moist forest, and open savanna. A variety of birds and mammals are commonly sighted. Pack a lunch; at the end of your 2-hour hike in, you can picnic at the aptly named Blue Lake, where a 30m (98-ft.) waterfall empties into the small pond whose crystal-blue hues are amazing.

LLANO DE CORTES WATERFALL ⚐

Located about 25km (16 miles) south of Liberia, the Llano de Cortes Waterfall is a beautiful and wide jungle waterfall with an excellent pool at the base for cooling off and swimming. At roughly 12m (40 ft.) wide, the falls are actually slightly wider than they are tall. This is a great spot for a picnic. The turnoff for the dirt road to the falls is well marked and located about 3km (1¾ miles) north of the crossroads for Bagaces. From the turnoff, you must drive a rough dirt road to the parking area and then hike down a short steep trail to the falls. Admission is free.

BACK TO AFRICA

Since the landscape is postcard-perfect, especially in the dry season, you shouldn't be too surprised to see antelope, zebra, giraffe, and elands roaming the grassy plains of Guanacaste. **Africa Mia (My Africa)** (© 8357-5555; www.africamia.net) offers safari-style open-jeep tours through its 100-hectare (247-acre) private reserve, which is populated with a wide range of nonnative (predominantly African) species. All of the animals are herbivores, so don't expect to see any lions, hyenas, or cheetahs. Still, the trip does provide some of the sense of being on the Serengeti or some other African plain. The animals have plenty of room to roam. Admission, which is $15 (£7.50) for adults, and $10 (£5) for children 11 and under, includes a 90-minute guided tour. Other more extensive tours are offered, including those that get you closer to the animals. Africa Mia is located just of the Interamerican Highway, 8km (5 miles) south of Liberia. The park is open daily from 8am to 6pm.

BIRDING

The **Río Tempisque Basin** ⚐, southwest of town, is one of the best places in the country to spot marsh and stream birds by the hundreds. This area is an important breeding ground for gallinules, jacanas, and limpkins, as well as a common habitat for numerous heron and kingfisher species. Several tour operators offer excursions and a wide range of tours in the region from Liberia. **Swiss Travel Services** (© 2282-4898; www.swisstravelcr.com) is the largest and most reliable of the major operators here.

One of the most popular tours is a boat tour down the Bebedero River to **Palo Verde National Park** ⚐, which is south of Cañas and is best known for its migratory bird populations. Some of the best bird-watching requires no more than a little walking around the Biological Station in the park.

RAFTING TRIPS
Leisurely raft trips (with little white water) are offered by **Safaris Corobicí** (Ⓒ/fax **2669-6191;** www.nicoya.com), about 40km (25 miles) south of Liberia. It has 2-hour ($37/£18), 3-hour ($45/£22), and half-day ($60/£30) trips that are great for families (children 13 and under are half-price) and bird-watchers. Along the way you may see many of the area's more exotic animal residents: howler monkeys, iguanas, caimans, coatimundis, otters, toucans, parrots, motmots, trogons, and many other species of birds. Aside from your binoculars and camera, a bathing suit and sunscreen are the only things you'll need. Safaris Corobicí is based on the main highway, just before the Restaurant Rincón Corobicí (p. 166). For a much wetter and wilder ride, the folks at **Hacienda Guachipelin** (see below) offer white-water inner-tube trips on the narrow Río Negro.

ONE STOP ADVENTURE SHOP
Hacienda Guachipelin (see below) offers up a range of adventure tour options, including horseback riding, hiking, white-water river inner-tubing, a waterfall canyoning and rappel tour, and a more traditional zip-line canopy tour. The most popular is the hacienda's **1-Day Adventure pass** ★★, which allows you to choose as many of the hotel's different tour options as you want and fit them into 1 adventure-packed day. The price for this is $80 (£40), including a buffet lunch. Almost all of the beach hotels and resorts of Guanacaste offer day trips here, or you can book directly with the lodge, including transportation. Be forewarned: During the high season, there's a bit of a cattle-car feel to the whole operation, with busloads of day-trippers coming in from the beach. Also, I have found the inner-tube adventure to be extremely dangerous and somewhat carelessly run, especially during or just after the rainy season.

HOT SPRINGS & MUD BATHS
Even if you're not staying at the Hacienda Guachipelin, you can take advantage of the hot spring pools, and hot mud pools at their **Simbiosis Spa** (Ⓒ **2666-8075;** www.simbiosis-spa.com). A $15 (£7.50) entrance fee gets you a stint in a sauna, self-application of the hot volcanic mud, and free run of the pools. *Be forewarned:* The pools are better described as warm, not hot, mud pools, and mud is the operative word here. A wide range of massages, mud wraps, facials and other treatments are available at very reasonable prices.

BIRD'S-EYE VIEWING
For an alternative means of taking in a massive amount of Costa Rican sightseeing in a short period of time, **Nature Air** (Ⓒ **800/235-9272** in the U.S. and Canada or 2299-6000; www.natureair.com) offers a 1-hour **Sky Tour** sightseeing excursion leaving from Liberia, in one of its 18-seat twin-engine planes equipped with large picture windows along the length of both sides of the fuselage. The exact route is flexible and might change according to group dynamics and weather conditions, but you can usually count on an overflight of several volcanoes—Arenal, Tenorio, Miravalles, and Rincon de la Vieja—and/or such prominent landmarks as Lake Arenal, Santa Elena National Park, and the Tempisque river basin. The cost is $200 (£100) per person, with an eight-person minimum. Departures can be arranged to suit the group needs.

SHOPPING
On the road to the beaches, just west of the airport, are several large souvenir shops. These are popular stopping points on organized tours throughout this region. The

best of the bunch for a one-stop shop is **Kaltak Arts & Craft Market** (© 2667-0696). However, you might find better selection and prices, especially for Guaitíl pottery, at some of the smaller makeshift roadside kiosks that line the road between Liberia and the Guanacaste beaches.

WHERE TO STAY IN TOWN
MODERATE
Best Western El Sitio Hotel & Casino   Located just out of town, about 75m (¾ block) west of the main intersection on the road to Santa Cruz and the beaches, this hotel has definitely seen better days. This hotel is primarily used by Costa Ricans as both a conference center and a weekend getaway. At present it's the closest thing to a modern, midrange resort hotel in Liberia, although upkeep and service are pretty spotty, and competition should be arriving in the relatively near future. The hotel is actually pretty from the outside, with a Spanish-influenced hacienda style, and an open, modern feel. However, the rooms are worn and dated. There's a rancho-style bar/restaurant beside the large, shady pool, as well as a fairly well equipped little gym.

Liberia (A.P. 134-5000), Guanacaste. © **800/780-7234** in the U.S. and Canada, or 2666-1211 in Costa Rica. Fax 2666-2059. www.bestwestern.com. 52 units. $70–$80 (£35–£40) double. Rates include full breakfast. AE, MC, V. **Amenities:** 2 restaurants; 2 bars; large pool; exercise room; Jacuzzi; tour desk; car-rental desk; room service; laundry service. *In room:* A/C, TV, dataport, free Wi-Fi, safe.

Hotel Boyeros *(Value*   Although it doesn't have the brand name, extensive facilities, or casino found at the Best Western El Sitio, I still prefer this place for a night in Liberia. Arches with turned wooden railings and a red-tile roof give this two-story motel-style building a Spanish feel. The best and coolest rooms are on the second floor of the east wing. There's a large central courtyard with two swimming pools, some basic playground equipment, and a massive shade tree.

Liberia (A.P. 85-5000), Guanacaste. © **2666-0722** or 2666-0809. Fax 2666-2529. www.hotelboyeros.com. 70 units. $65 (£33) double. AE, MC, V. **Amenities:** Restaurant; bar; midsize pool and children's pool; game room; limited room service; laundry service. *In room:* A/C, TV, free Wi-Fi, safe.

INEXPENSIVE
Hotel Guanacaste   This basic, economical choice is primarily a hostel catering to young travelers on a tight budget. In addition to the small and simply furnished rooms—almost all of which have bunk beds with thin foam mattresses—there's a basic *soda* (diner) serving inexpensive meals. The management here can help arrange trips to nearby national parks and tell you about other budget accommodations around the country. The best rooms here have double beds, private bathrooms, and air-conditioning, and these cost slightly more. Camping is also allowed, for $6 (£3) per person.

A.P. 251-5000 (1 block north and 2 blocks east of the intersection of the Interamerican Hwy. and the beach highway), Liberia, Guanacaste. © **2666-0085**. Fax 2666-2287. www.higuanacaste.com. 27 units. $20–$30 (£10–£15) double. Discounts for students and those holding a valid hostel ID. AE, MC, V. **Amenities:** Restaurant; bike rental; tour desk; laundry service. *In room:* No phone.

Posada del Tope   This rustic little pension is nothing fancy, but the rooms and shared bathrooms are clean, the owners are friendly and helpful, and it's a real bargain. Only a couple of rooms have double beds; the rest have one, two, or three single beds. The nicest thing about Posada del Tope is that it's housed in a wonderfully restored traditional colonial home with high ceilings, big shuttered windows facing the street, and hefty wooden trim all around. There's safe parking and Internet access, and every room comes with a television. These folks also run another simple hotel in another old home, Casa Real, located directly across the street. This annex has more rooms and a basic restaurant serving inexpensive Tico cuisine.

Calle Real (1½ blocks south of the central park), Liberia, Guanacaste. ©/fax **2666-3876**. 22 units, 13 with shared bathroom. $15 (£7.50) double with shared bathroom; $20 (£10) double with private bathroom. AE, MC, V. Free parking. **Amenities:** Restaurant; bike rental; tour desk; laundry service. *In room:* TV, no phone.

WHERE TO STAY NEAR RINCON DE LA VIEJA NATIONAL PARK

In addition to the hotels listed below, there are a couple of other good choices by the park. On Cañas Dulces road, **Buena Vista Lodge** ★ (© **2690-1414;** www.buenavista lodgecr.com) is set on the edge of the national park and offers a wide range of activities and attractions. The delightful **La Carolina Lodge** ★ (© **8380-1656;** www. lacarolinalodge.com) is on a working farm, next to a clear flowing river. This place is located on the road between the Interamerican Highway and Upala, and it affords excellent access to the Tenorio Volcano and Río Celeste Falls.

Hacienda Guachipelin ★   Located right on the edge of Rincón de la Vieja National Park, this lodge is centered on a 19th-century ranch house and a still-operational cattle-and-horse ranch. The best rooms here are located a short walk away from the old ranch house and lobby. These are in long rows of rooms enclosing a large lawn and garden area. They are all quite spacious and modern and come with a wide shared veranda. The older rooms are still clean and comfortable, but much more rustic in feel. In addition to the lodge's good-size pool, nearby creeks and rivers feature a couple of natural swimming holes. It isn't easy to get to the lodge, so plan to take all your meals here. Meals are buffet affairs, although you can opt out of the meal plan and go a la carte. This place does a brisk business as a day-tour destination for a variety of hotels and resorts around Guanacaste, and there's a cattle-car feel to the operation at times. See above for a description of their many tour offerings.

Rincón de la Vieja (23km/14 miles northeast of Liberia). © **2665-3303** for reservations, or 2666-8075 at the lodge. Fax 2665-2178. www.guachipelin.com. 52 units. $133 (£67) standard double; $143 (£72) superior double. Rates include 3 meals and taxes. Rates higher during peak periods. AE, MC, V. Follow the directions/signs to Curubandé and Rincón de la Vieja National Park. A 4WD vehicle is required in the rainy season (May to mid-Nov) and strongly recommended at other times. **Amenities:** Restaurant; pool; small spa; tour desk; laundry service. *In room:* Free Wi-Fi, no phone.

Hotel Borinquen Mountain Resort ★   This the fanciest resort in the Rincón de la Vieja area. Individual and duplex bungalows are set on a hillside above the main lodge, restaurants, and hot springs. While the individual bungalow units are slightly larger, every room is very spacious and comes with two queen-size beds, high ceilings, heavy wooden furniture, a large TV, and a plush bathroom. Each has an ample wooden deck with a view over the valley and surrounding forests. In the foot of the valley are several natural hot-spring pools of varying temperatures, a natural sauna, and an area for full-body mud baths given with hot volcanic mud; a good-size free-form man-made swimming pool is on-site as well. There are good hiking and horseback riding here and some nice waterfalls nearby, and golf carts are available to shuttle you around. Despite the amazing facilities, the hotel's service and food have always been lacking, and the spa has yet to be fully developed.

Cañas Dulces (A.P. 108-5000), Liberia. © **2690-1900.** Fax 2690-1903. www.borinquenresort.com. 33 units. $204 (£102) double villa; $254–$290 (£127–£145) double bungalow; $356 (£178) junior suite. Rates include breakfast and unlimited use of the hot springs, sauna, and mud baths. Rates lower in off season; higher during peak weeks. AE, MC, V. Drive 26km (16 miles) north of Liberia along the Interamerican Hwy., take the turnoff toward Cañas Dulces, and follow the signs. The hotel is approximately 18km (11 miles) from the highway and 3.5km (2¼ miles) beyond Cañas Dulces. **Amenities:** Restaurant; bar; large swimming pool; small spa; tour desk; laundry service. *In room:* A/C, TV, free Wi-Fi, minibar, safe.

Rincón de la Vieja Mountain Lodge   This is the closest lodge to the Las Pailas mud pots and the Azufrale hot springs. Rooms vary in size, and the best are the individual cabins, which come with hammocks on their private balconies. In all rooms, the furnishings and decor are simple, rustic, and feel pretty dated. Quite a few come with one queen-size and one set of bunk beds. Meals are served in a large open-air rancho in the middle of the complex. The lodge offers numerous daylong tours either on foot, by mountain bike, or on horseback. It also runs an extensive canopy tour, which takes you on a high-wire ride over a couple dozen different treetop platforms, beginning with a manual ascent up a towering ceiba tree. This place is geared toward backpackers, students, and nature enthusiasts.

Rincón de la Vieja (A.P. 164-5000, Liberia), Guanacaste. ✆ 2200-0238. Fax 2666-2441. www.rincondelaviejalodge. net. 40 units. $70–$80 (£35–£40) double. Student discounts and off-season rates available. AE, MC, V. If you're driving, follow the directions to the Hacienda Lodge Guachipelin and continue driving on this dirt road for another 7km (4⅓ miles), bearing right at the turnoff for the park entrance. **Amenities:** Restaurant; bar; small pool; laundry service. *In room:* No phone.

WHERE TO DINE

There are plenty of standard Tico dining choices in Liberia. In town the most popular alternatives are **Pizzería Pronto** (✆ 2666-2098), which is 100m (1 block) north of the visitor information center, and **Pizzería da Beppe** (✆ 2666-1111), near the highway on the road that leads into central Liberia. Both serve a wide range of pizzas and assorted pasta dishes. A favorite of mine is **Café Liberia** ⋇ (✆ 2665-1660), a little French-style coffee shop and bistro that morphs into a sort of European-style hip lounge and bar at night. Another alternative is to choose one of the *sodas* around the central park. The best of these is **Restaurante Paseo Real** (✆ 2666-3455). If you want fast food, you can find both **Burger King** and **Papa John's** in a small shopping complex on the northwest corner of the main intersection of the Interamerican Highway and the road to the beaches, as well as an even bigger food court with more fastfood options at the mall on the southern outskirts of town.

Restaurant Rincón Corobicí COSTA RICAN/INTERNATIONAL   This roadside tourist restaurant can be packed with tour groups, and the food is far from memorable. But the setting on the banks of the Corobicí River is wonderful. Although plenty of covered seating is available in the main open-air dining room, try to get a table on the wooden deck overlooking the river. The sound of rushing water tumbling over the rocks in the riverbed is a soothing accompaniment to the simple but filling meals. The whole fried fish is your best choice here, although you can also have steaks, lobster, shrimp, sandwiches, and even a couple of lamb dishes. This restaurant makes an ideal lunch stop if you're heading to or coming from Liberia, or if you have just done a rafting trip on the Corobicí River. Be sure to try the fried yuca chips; they're excellent.

Interamerican Hwy., 5km (3 miles) north of Cañas. ✆ 2669-6262. Main courses $5.50–$16 (£2.75–£8). AE, DC, MC, V. Daily 8am–5pm.

2 La Cruz & Bahía Salinas

277km (172 miles) NW of San José; 59km (37 miles) NW of Liberia; 20km (12 miles) S of Peñas Blancas

Near the Nicaraguan border, La Cruz is a tiny hilltop town that has little to offer beyond a fabulous view of Bahía Salinas (Salinas Bay), but it does serve as a gateway to the nearly deserted beaches down below, a few mountain lodges bordering the nearby Santa Rosa and Guanacaste national parks, and the Nicaraguan border crossing at Peñas Blancas.

There's little reason to stay in La Cruz, but if you must, check out either **Amalia's Inn** (℃/fax **2679-9681**) or **Hotel Bella Vista** (℃ **2679-8060**). Both are simple hotels, and both have small pools and good views of the bay. (Instead of staying in town, check out the listings below for places to stay on the shores of the beaches below.)

ESSENTIALS

GETTING THERE & DEPARTING   By Plane   The nearest airport with regular service is in Liberia (see "Liberia," earlier in this chapter).

By Car   Take the Interamerican Highway west from San José and follow the signs for Nicaragua and the Guanacaste beaches. When you reach Liberia, head straight through the major intersection, following signs to Peñas Blancas and the Nicaraguan border. Allow approximately 5 hours to get from San José to La Cruz.

By Bus   **Transportes Deldú** buses (℃ **2256-9072** in San José, or 2677-0091 in La Cruz) leave San José at least every 2 hours (often more frequently) between 5am and 6pm for **Peñas Blancas** from Calle 20 and Avenida 1. These buses stop in La Cruz and will also let you off at the entrance to Santa Rosa National Park. The ride to La Cruz takes 6 hours; a one-way fare costs $6.30 (£3.15). Additional buses are often added on weekends.

Local buses leave Liberia for Peñas Blancas periodically throughout the day. The ride to La Cruz takes about 1 hour and costs $2 (£1). Buses depart for San José from Peñas Blancas daily between 5am and 5:30pm, passing through La Cruz about 20 minutes later. Buses leave Liberia for San José roughly every hour between 5am and 7pm.

ORIENTATION   The highway passes slightly to the east of town. You'll pass the turnoffs to Santa Rosa National Park and Playa Caujiniquil before you reach the town. To reach the beaches of Bahía Salinas, head into La Cruz and take the road that runs along the north side of the small central park and then follow the signs down to the water and Bahía Salinas.

EXPLORING SANTA ROSA NATIONAL PARK

Known for its remote, pristine beaches (reached by several kilometers of hiking trails or a 4WD vehicle), **Santa Rosa National Park** ⚘ (℃ **2666-5051**) is a great place to camp on the beach, surf, or (if you're lucky) watch sea turtles nest. Located 30km (19 miles) north of Liberia and 21km (13 miles) south of La Cruz on the Interamerican Highway, Costa Rica's first national park blankets the Santa Elena Peninsula. Unlike other national parks, it was founded not to preserve the land but to save a building, known as **La Casona,** that played an important role in Costa Rican independence. It was here, in 1856, that Costa Rican forces fought the decisive Battle of Santa Rosa, forcing the U.S.-backed soldier of fortune William Walker and his men to flee into Nicaragua. La Casona was completely destroyed by arson in 2001, but it has been rebuilt, very accurately mimicking the original building, and houses a small museum.

It costs $10 (£5) per person to enter the park. Camping is allowed at several sites within the park. A campsite costs $2 (£1) per person per day. There's camping near the entrance and principal ranger station, as well as near La Casona and down by playas Naranjo and Nancite. For trail information, see the "Santa Rosa National Park" map in the color insert at the front of this book.

THE BEACHES ★★   Eight kilometers (5 miles) west of La Casona, down a rugged road that's impassable during the rainy season (it's rough on 4WD vehicles even in the dry season), is **Playa Naranjo.** Four kilometers (2½ miles) north of Playa Naranjo, along a hiking trail that follows the beach, you'll find **Playa Nancite. Playa Blanca** is 21km (13 miles) down a dirt road from Caujiniquil, which itself is 20km (12 miles) north of the park entrance. None of these three beaches has shower or restroom facilities. (Playa Nancite does have some facilities, but they're in a reservation-only camping area.) Bring along your own water, food, and anything else you'll need, and expect to find things relatively quiet and deserted.

Playa Nancite is known for its *arribadas* ("arrivals," grouped egg-layings) of olive ridley sea turtles, which come ashore to nest by the tens of thousands each year in October. Playa Naranjo is legendary for its perfect surfing waves. In fact, this spot is quite popular with day-trippers who come in by boat from the Playa del Coco area to ride the waves that break around **Witch's Rock,** which lies just offshore.

On the northern side of the peninsula is **Playa Blanca,** a beautiful, remote white-sand beach with calm waters. This beach is reached by way of the small village of Caujiniquil and is accessible only during the dry season.

If you reach Caujiniquil and then head north for a few kilometers, you'll come to a small annex to the national park system at **Playa Junquillal** (© 2679-9692), not to be confused with the more-developed beach of the same name farther south in Guanacaste. This is a lovely little beach that is also often good for swimming. You'll have to pay the park entrance fee ($10/£5) to use the beach, and $2 (£1) more to camp here. There are basic bathroom and shower facilities.

FUN ON & OVER THE WAVES

The waters of Bahía Salinas are buffeted by serious winds from mid-November through mid-May, and this area is a prime spot for windsurfing and kiteboarding. The folks at **Ecoplaya Beach Resort** (see below) have the best windsurfing operation and rental equipment in the area. If you want to try your hand at the sport of kiteboarding, check in with the folks at the **Kitesurfing Center,** who operate out of the **Blue Dream Hotel** (© **2676-1042** or 8826-5221; www.bluedreamhotel.com) in Playa Copal.

Note: If you're coming to this area and aren't interested in windsurfing or kitesurfing, the winds can make your beach time rather unpleasant during the peak wind months. If you're just looking for a beach-resort vacation, I recommend heading to one of the beaches farther south in Guanacaste.

WHERE TO STAY NEAR LA CRUZ

Ecoplaya Beach Resort ★   This is by far the most comfortable, dare I say luxurious, beach hotel in the area. (However, aside from a facile attempt to cash in on a trend, I see no reason to use "eco" in the name.) The rooms are classified as either studios or junior, master, or luxury suites. Definitely opt for one of the suites because the studios are a bit cramped. The wide range in prices here reflects the wide range of room sizes. Inside they all have high ceilings, tile floors, and plenty of varnished wood accents. The beach here is calm and attractive, although the winter winds really howl. To take advantage of this, the hotel features a fully equipped windsurf center, offering rentals and classes. This is also a good option if you're looking to combine some beach time with excursions to Santa Rosa National Park and/or neighboring Nicaragua.

La Coyotera Beach, Salinas Bay. (𝐂) **2228-7146.** Fax 2289-4536. www.ecoplaya.com. 35 units. $98–$120 (£49–£60) double; $150–$245 (£75–£122) suite. Rates include taxes. Rates lower in the off season, higher during peak weeks. AE, MC, V. From La Cruz, take the dirt road that passes to the right of El Mirador Ehecatl restaurant (as you face the water), and then follow signs to the hotel. **Amenities:** Restaurant; bar; midsize pool; 2 Jacuzzis; watersports equipment rental; tour desk; laundry service. *In room:* A/C, TV, kitchenette, fridge, coffeemaker.

3 Playa Hermosa, Playa Panamá & Papagayo ⟨★⟩

258km (160 miles) NW of San José; 40km (25 miles) SW of Liberia

While most of Costa Rica's coast is highly coveted by surfers, the beaches here are mostly protected and calm. A good destination for families with kids, **Playa Hermosa** ★ means "beautiful beach," which is an appropriate name for this crescent of sand. Surrounded by steep forested hills, this curving gray-sand beach is long and wide and the surf is usually quite gentle. Fringing the beach is a swath of trees that stays surprisingly green even during the dry season. The shade provided by these trees, along with the calm protected waters, is a big part of the beach's appeal. Rocky headlands jut out into the surf at both ends of the beach, and at the base of these rocks, you'll find fun tide pools to explore.

Beyond Playa Hermosa you'll find **Playa Panamá** ★ and, farther on, the calm waters of **Bahía Culebra** ★, a large protected bay dotted with small, private patches of beach and ringed with mostly intact dry forest. Around the north end of Bahía Culebra is the rapidly developing **Papagayo Peninsula** ★, which is currently the home to two large all-inclusive resorts and one championship golf course. This peninsula has a half-dozen or so small to midsize beaches, the nicest of which might just be **Playa Nacascolo** ★★, which is inside the domain of the Four Seasons Resort here—but all beaches in Costa Rica are public, so you can still visit, albeit after passing through security and parking at the public parking lot.

This area is in the midst of a major boom. Condos, beach homes, and hotels are sprouting up all over the once forested hills here, and throughout the day you can often hear the sound of construction all around.

ESSENTIALS

GETTING THERE & DEPARTING   By Plane   The nearest airport with regularly scheduled service is in Liberia. From there you can arrange a taxi to bring you the rest of the way. The ride takes about 25 minutes and should cost $40 to $50 (£20–£25).

By Car   Follow the directions for getting to Liberia (described earlier in this chapter), and then head west toward Santa Cruz. The turnoff for the Papagayo Peninsula is prominently marked 8km (5 miles) south of the Liberia airport. At the corner here you'll see a massive Do It Center hardware store and lumber yard. If you're going on to Playa Hermosa, continue on a little farther and, just past the village of Comunidad, turn right. In about 11km (6¾ miles) you'll come to a fork in the road; take the right fork. The drive takes about 4½ hours from San José.

If you are going to the Papagayo Peninsula, turn at the Do It Center and follow the paved road out and around the peninsula. If you are going to Playa Panamá, you can either take the paved roads all the way, by heading first to Playa Hermosa, and continuing on to Playa Panamá. Or, you can take a dirt road shortcut that leads from a turnoff on the Papagayo Peninsula road, just beyond the Do It Center, directly to the beach here.

These roads are all relatively well marked, and a host of prominent hotel billboards should make it easy enough to find the beach or resort you are looking for.

By Bus   A **Tralapa** express bus (© 2221-7202) leaves San José daily at 3pm from Calle 20 and Avenida 3, stopping at Playa Hermosa and Playa Panamá, 3km (1¾ miles) farther north. One-way fare for the 5-hour trip is $6.50 (£3.25).

Gray Line (© 2220-2126; www.graylinecostarica.com) has a daily bus that leaves San José at 8am for all beaches in this area. The fare is $33 (£17). **Interbus** (© 2283-5573; www.interbusonline.com) has two daily buses that leave San José at 7:45am and 2:30pm for all beaches in this area. The fare is $35 (£18). Both companies will pick you up at most San José–area hotels.

You can take a bus from San José to Liberia (see "Essentials," earlier in this chapter) and then take a bus from Liberia to Playa Hermosa and Playa Panamá. Buses (© 2666-0042) leave Liberia for Playa Hermosa and Playa Panamá at 4:45, 7:30 and 11:30am, and 1, 3:30 and 5:30pm. The trip lasts 40 minutes because the bus stops frequently to drop off and pick up passengers. The one-way fare costs $1.75 (85p). These bus schedules change from time to time, so it's always best to check in advance. During the high season and on weekends, extra buses from Liberia are sometimes added. You can also take a bus to Playa del Coco, from which playas Hermosa and Panamá are a relatively quick taxi ride away. Taxi fare should run between $5 and $8 (£2.50–£4).

One direct bus departs for San José daily at 5am from Playa Panamá, with a stop in Playa Hermosa along the way. Buses to Liberia leave Playa Panamá at 6, 7, and 10am and 2, 5, and 7pm, stopping in Playa Hermosa a few minutes later. Ask at your hotel where to catch the bus.

ORIENTATION   From the well-marked turnoff for the Papagayo Peninsula (near the prominent Do It Center hardware store), a paved road leads around to the Allegro Papagayo and Four Seasons resorts. If you are heading to the beaches a little farther south, continue on to the well-marked turnoff for Playa del Coco and Playa Hermosa. The road forks before reaching Playa del Coco. You'll come to Playa Hermosa first, followed by Playa Panamá a few kilometers farther along the same road. The road ends at the Hilton Papagayo Resort. There is also a connecting road between the Papagayo Peninsula road and Playa Panamá. This 11km (6¾-mile) stretch of road is unpaved but well maintained and it's definitely your quickest route to Playa Panamá.

Playa Hermosa is about a 450m (1,476-ft.) stretch of beach, with all the hotels laid out along this stretch. From the main road, which continues on to Playa Panamá, three access roads head off toward the beach. All the hotels are well marked, with signs pointing guests down the right access road. Playa Panamá is the least developed of the beaches out here. Somewhat longer than Playa Hermosa, it also has several access roads heading in toward the beach from the main road, which is slightly inland.

FUN ON & UNDER THE WATER
Most of the beaches up here are usually quite calm and good for swimming.

If you want to do some diving, check in with **Diving Safaris de Costa Rica** ❀ (© 2672-1259; www.costaricadiving.net), which is headquartered on the principal access road into Playa Hermosa, about 137m (450 ft.) before you hit the beach. This is a long-established and respected dive operation. It has a large shop and offers a wide range of trips to numerous dive spots, and it also offers night dives, multiday packages, certification classes, and Nitrox dives. These folks also offer multiday liveaboard and dive trips on their 14m (48 ft.) yacht.

Alternatively, you can check out **Resort Divers** (© 2672-0106; www.resortdivers-cr.com), which has set up shop at the Hilton Resort in Playa Panama.

Both of the above-mentioned companies will accept divers from any of the hotels in the area, and can arrange transport. A two-tank dive should run between $70 and $140 (£35–£70) per person, depending primarily on the distance traveled to the dive sites.

In the middle of Playa Hermosa, **Aqua Sport** (© 2672-0050) is where to go for watersports equipment rental in Playa Hermosa. Kayaks, sailboards, canoes, bicycles, beach umbrellas, snorkel gear, and parasails are available for rental at fairly reasonable rates. You'll also find here a small supermarket, public phones, and a restaurant.

Because the beaches in this area are relatively protected and generally flat, surfers should look into boat trips to nearby **Witch's Rock** ✸✸ and **Ollie's Point** ✸. **Diving Safaris de Costa Rica** (© 2672-1259), **Hotel Finisterra** (© 2670-0293), and **Aqua Sport** (© 2672-0050) all offer trips for up to six surfers for around $250 to $350 (£125–£175), including lunch. All of these companies also offer fishing trips for between $250 and $1,500 (£125–£750) for groups of two to four anglers.

If you're interested in wind power, check in with the folks at the hotel **El Velero Hotel** (see below), or **Tahini Yacht Tours** (© 2672-1037). Both offer a range of full- and half-day tours, with snorkel stops, as well as sunset cruises.

OTHER OPTIONS

Other activities in the area include horseback riding, all-terrain quad tours, canopy tours, and trips to other major attractions in the Guanacaste region. **Swiss Travel Service** (© 2668-1020) has operations in the area and offers a wide range of activities and tours, including trips to Santa Rosa or Rincón de la Vieja national parks, and rafting on the Corobicí River. These folks have desks at many of the hotels around here and will pick you up at any hotel in the area.

The best zip-line canopy tour in this area is the **Witch's Rock Canopy Tour** (© 2667-0661), just before the Allegro Papagayo Resort. The 2½-hour tour covers 3km (1¾ miles) of cables touching down on 24 platforms and costs $65 (£33).

Finally, the Arnold Palmer–designed championship course at the Four Seasons Resort is hands down the most beautiful and challenging **golf course** in the country. However, it is open only to guests at the Four Seasons.

WHERE TO STAY

In January 2008, the Allegro Papagayo Resort was ordered shut down by the Costa Rican Ministry of Health, after having been found to be illegally dumping raw sewage directly into the ocean and clandestinely trucking more raw sewage to be dumped illegally into nearby local communities. In March 2008, after making some improvements, they were allowed to operate at half capacity, but their crimes were so egregious that I cannot recommend them. *Note:* The Grand Papagayo resort listed below is run by the same parent company. Moreover, this is a massive problem in Costa Rica, given lax government oversight and rampant corruption. I highly doubt that the Allegro Papagayo is the only party guilty of such sins.

In mid-2008, **Hotel Playa Hermosa Bosque Mar** (© 2672-0046; www.hotel playahermosa.com) was closed for a major remodel and expansion. It is expected to open in early 2009. Although it's too early to be sure, I expect the hotel to be one of the better options in Playa Hermosa, with a fabulous beachfront location.

Both the Westin and Regent resort hotel groups have large-scale resorts in the works in this area, which should open sometime during the 2009 or 2010 seasons.

VERY EXPENSIVE

Four Seasons Resort Costa Rica ★★★ *(Kids)*   On a narrow spit of land between two white-sand beaches, this is the most luxurious and impressive large-scale resort in Costa Rica. The architecture is stunning, with most buildings featuring flowing roof designs and other touches imitating the forms of turtles, armadillos, and butterflies. All the rooms are very spacious, with wood floors, rich wood furnishings, tasteful fixtures and decorations from around the world, and marble bathrooms with deep tubs and separate showers. The rooms on the third and fourth floors have the best views and are priced accordingly. Each has a large private balcony with a sofa, a table, and a couple of chairs. On the rocky hill at the very end of the peninsula are the resort's suites and villas. These have even more space and often either a private pool, a Jacuzzi, or an open-air gazebo for soaking in the views. The resort also features the Four Seasons' renowned service (including family-friendly amenities such as kid-size bathrobes and childproof rooms), one of the best-equipped full-service spas in the country, and a spectacular golf course that offers ocean views from 15 of its 18 holes.

Papagayo Peninsula, Guanacaste. © 800/819-5053 in the U.S. or 2696-0000. Fax 2696-0500. www.fourseasons.com/costarica. 153 units. $735–$950 (£368–£475) double; $1,670–$10,000 (£835–£5,000) suites and villas. Children stay free in parent's room. AE, DC, DISC, MC, V. **Amenities:** 4 restaurants; 2 bars; lounge; 3 free-form pools; championship 18-hole golf course; 2 tennis courts; modern, full-service spa; watersports equipment; children's programs; tour desk; concierge; 24-hr. room service; massage; babysitting; laundry service; nonsmoking rooms. *In room:* A/C, TV/DVD, dataport, Wi-Fi, hair dryer, safe.

Grand Papagayo ★★   The Grand Papagayo is the highest-end all-inclusive resort of the Occidental Hotel chain in Costa Rica. The rooms are spread over a broad and contoured hillside overlooking the ocean, but not all rooms come with an ocean view. At the center of the complex is a large, free-form pool. The beach here is very protected and calm, although it almost entirely disappears at peak high tide. The resort is geared toward couples, and the vast majority of the rooms come with just one king-size bed, although there are some with two queen-size. I like the Grand Concierge rooms, which are close to the pool and restaurants, and feature marble floors. However, the Royal Club rooms and suites are the best rooms here, and they come with beefed up concierge services, separate check-in and checkout, as well as daily refills of the minibar—as opposed to every other day with the other rooms. A host of scheduled activities and entertainment options are offered, and a wide range of additional tours and activities can be added on.

Papagayo Peninsula, Guanacaste. © 800/858-2258 in the U.S. and Canada, 2672-0191 for reservations inside Costa Rica. Fax 2672-0057. www.occidentalhotels.com. 169 units. $250–$550 (£125–£275) per person double occupancy; $600–$1,200 (£300–£600) Royal Club room double. Rates include food, drinks, a range of activities, and taxes. AE, DC, MC, V. **Amenities:** 4 restaurants; 2 bars; lounge; 2 large free-form pools; 1 lighted tennis court; gym; spa; watersports equipment; tour desk; massage; babysitting; laundry service; nonsmoking rooms. *In room:* A/C, TV, stocked minibar, coffeemaker, hair dryer, safe.

Hilton Papagayo Resort ★ *(Kids)*   This was the very first all-inclusive resort in the Guanacaste region. It has changed its name and management at least four times, most recently in 2008, being taken over by the Hilton group. Most of the duplex villas can be separated into two rooms or shared by a family or two couples. Inside, one room is equipped with a king-size bed; the other has two queen-size beds. All rooms have marble floors, large bathrooms, and small private patios or balconies. The resort is quite spread out, so if you don't want to do a lot of walking or wait for the minivan shuttles, ask for a room near the main pool and restaurants. If you want a good view, ask for one on the hill overlooking the bay. For those seeking more isolation, there are rooms located in the dry forest behind the resort. The hotel has a large, modern, and plush spa facility. It also has its own small crescent-shape swath of beach, which is very calm and protected for swimming.

Playa Panamá, Guanacaste. © 800/445-8667 in the U.S. and Canada, or 2672-0000 in Costa Rica. Fax 2672-0181. www.hilton.com. 202 units. $359–$750 (£180–£375) double; $2,500 (£1,250) presidential suite. Rates include food, drinks, activities, and taxes. Rates lower in the off season. AE, DC, DISC, MC, V. **Amenities:** 3 restaurants; 2 bars; 3-tiered main pool, small lap pool, and resistance lap pool; tennis court; well-equipped fitness center and spa; Jacuzzi; sauna; watersports equipment; children's programs; tour desk; car-rental desk; shopping arcade; salon; babysitting; laundry service. *In room:* A/C, TV, free Wi-Fi, minibar, coffeemaker, hair dryer, safe.

Villas Sol Hotel & Beach Resort

Set on a steep hillside at the north end of the beach, the Villas Sol is part of a long-standing project that has changed hands several times, divided, and grown over the years. The hotel is at the top of the hill, inland from the beach. You'll need to be in good shape to stay here, or you'll spend some time waiting for the sporadic jitney service. Luckily, the two pools are both at the top of the hill if you want to opt out of the trip to and from the beach. The hotel rooms are all well maintained and most have excellent views. (Given their placement just off the entrance, though, not all of the villas have spectacular views.) All rooms have kitchens, satellite TVs, and modern furnishings. About a third of them have their own small swimming pool or Jacuzzi.

Playa Hermosa, Guanacaste. © 800/572-9934 in the U.S. and Canada, or 2258-5883 reservations in San José, or 2672-0001 at the hotel. Fax 2223-3086. www.villassol.com. 54 units, 106 villas. $450–$600 (£225–£300) double; $600–$1,400 (£300–£700) villa. Rates include food, drinks, activities, and taxes. Rates lower during off season; higher during peak weeks. AE, DC, MC, V. **Amenities:** 3 restaurants; 2 bars; 2 pools; 2 lighted tennis courts; small spa; limited watersports equipment rental; tour desk; laundry service. *In room:* A/C, TV, free Wi-Fi, minifridge, coffeemaker, hair dryer, safe.

MODERATE

El Velero Hotel ⚓

This place is one of my top choices right on the beach in Playa Hermosa. White walls and polished tile floors give El Velero a Mediterranean flavor. The guest rooms are large, and those on the second floor have high ceilings. The furnishings are simple, though, and some of the bathrooms are a bit small. The hotel has its own popular little restaurant, which offers a good selection of meat, fish, and shrimp dishes, as well as weekly barbecue fests. Various tours, horseback riding, and fishing trips can be arranged through the hotel; however, the most popular excursions are the full-day and sunset cruises on the hotel's namesake sailboat.

Playa Hermosa (A.P. 49-5019), Guanacaste. © 2672-1017. Fax 2672-0016. www.costaricahotel.net. 22 units. $79 (£39) double. Rates lower in off season; higher during peak periods. AE, MC, V. **Amenities:** Restaurant; bar; small pool by the beach; tour desk; laundry service. *In room:* A/C, TV, free Wi-Fi, coffeemaker, hair dryer, safe.

Hotel Finisterra

This hillside hotel offers neat, spacious accommodations on the southern end of Playa Hermosa. All rooms are located on the second floor and come with either one queen-size bed or two double beds. Large picture windows face either a forested hillside or the Pacific Ocean. A large open-air restaurant and lounge takes up most of the first floor, and a refreshing little pool has good views. The beach is about 270m (886 ft.) away, down the steep driveway. The restaurant serves a nightly mix of fresh seafood, steaks, and chicken prepared with fusion flare. The folks here can arrange a wide variety of tours, including sportfishing and surf trips to Witch's Rock.

Playa Hermosa, Guanacaste. ©/fax 2672-0227. www.lafinisterra.com. 10 units. $100 (£50) double. Rates include full breakfast. Rates lower in off season; higher during peak periods. AE, MC, V. **Amenities:** Restaurant; bar; small pool; tour desk; babysitting; laundry service. *In room:* A/C, free Wi-Fi, no phone.

Villa del Sueño Hotel ⭐ Villa del Sueño offers clean and comfortable rooms at a good price, and the restaurant here is one of the best in Playa Hermosa (see below). All the rooms have cool tile floors, high hardwood ceilings, ceiling fans, and well-placed windows for cross ventilation. The second-floor superior rooms have more space and larger windows. The more expensive rooms come with air-conditioning and televisions. Although this hotel isn't right on the beach (it's about 1 block inland), its well-groomed lawns and gardens feel like an oasis in the dust and heat of a Guanacaste dry season. There's a small pool and open-air bar in the center courtyard. In addition to fine meals, the restaurant features live music, by a variety of local acts, during much of the high season. Also under this hotel's management is the neighboring "El Oasis" condominium development, which has additional apartment and efficiency units available for nightly and weekly rentals, as well as its own pool.

Playa Hermosa, Guanacaste. ℂ **800/378-8599** in the U.S. and Canada, or 2672-0026. Fax 2672-0021. www.villadel sueno.com. 45 units. $75–$105 (£38–£52) double; $130–$255 (£115–£128) condo. Rates lower in off season; higher during peak periods. AE, MC, V. **Amenities:** Restaurant; bar; small pool; tour desk; laundry service. *In room:* A/C, free Wi-Fi.

DINING & AFTER-DARK DIVERSIONS

For nightlife, find out whether the **Villa del Sueño Restaurant** (see below) has live music. Two Saturdays a month, Villa del Sueño hosts larger concerts, featuring prominent Costa Rican acts, in its spiffy open-air amphitheater.

In addition to the places listed below, you'll find good restaurants at both the **El Velero Hotel** and the **Hotel Finisterra** (see "Where to Stay," above). For U.S.-style bar food and entertainment, also try the new **Upper Deck Sports Bar** (ℂ 2672-1276), just off the main road.

Ginger ⭐⭐ *Finds* INTERNATIONAL/TAPAS In this most creative restaurant in the area, the architecture and decor are stylish and modern, with sharp angles and loads of chrome and glass. The food is an eclectic mix of modern takes on wide-ranging international fare, all served as tapas, meant to be shared while sampling some of the many cocktails and wines served here. Still, it's easy to make a full meal. Order the house special ginger-glazed chicken wings, along with some spring rolls, and a plate of fresh mahimahi marinated in vodka and Asian spices. There are also more traditional Mediterranean and Spanish-style tapas, as well as delicious desserts.

On the main road, Playa Hermosa. ℂ **2672-0041.** Tapas $4–$8 (£2–£4). AE, MC, V. Tues–Sun 11:30am–10pm.

Villa del Sueño Restaurant ⭐ INTERNATIONAL A mellow yet refined atmosphere presides under slow-turning ceiling fans at this simple open-air restaurant. In addition to lots of fresh fish, there are well-prepared pasta dishes, as well as meat and poultry options. A small selection of specials is offered nightly. Live music is available many nights during high season.

At the Villa del Sueño Hotel. ℂ **2672-0026.** Main courses $8–$16 (£4–£8). AE, MC, V. Daily 7am–10pm.

4 Playa del Coco & Playa Ocotal

253km (157 miles) NW of San José; 35km (22 miles) W of Liberia

In the midst of an ongoing and major construction boom, **Playa del Coco** is one of the busiest and most built-up beaches in this area. With a large modern mall and shopping center anchoring the eastern edge of town, you'll pass through a tight jumble of restaurants, hotels, and souvenir shops for several blocks before you hit the sand

and sea, while homes, condos, and hotels are sprouting up along the beach in either direction. This has long been, and remains, a popular destination with middle-class Ticos and weekend revelers from San José. It's also a prime jumping-off point for some of Costa Rica's best scuba diving. The beach, which has grayish-brown sand and gentle surf, is quite wide at low tide and almost nonexistent at high tide. The crowds that come here like their music loud and constant, so if you're in search of a quiet retreat, stay away from the center of town. Still, if you're looking for a beach with a wide range of inexpensive hotels, lively nightlife, and plenty of cheap food and beer close at hand, you'll enjoy Playa del Coco.

Better still, in my opinion, is **Playa Ocotal** 𝒦, which is a couple of kilometers to the south. This tiny pocket cove features a small salt-and-pepper beach bordered by high bluffs and is quite beautiful. When it's calm there's good snorkeling around some rocky islands close to shore here.

ESSENTIALS

GETTING THERE & DEPARTING   By Plane   The nearest airport with regularly scheduled flights is in Liberia. From there you can arrange for a taxi to take you to Playa del Coco or Playa Ocotal, which is about a 25-minute drive, for $30 to $40 (£15–£20).

By Car   From Liberia, head west toward Santa Cruz. Just past the village of Comunidad, turn right. In about 11km (6¾ miles) you'll come to a fork in the road. Take the left fork. It takes about 4½ hours from San José.

By Bus   Pulmitan express buses (𝐶 2222-1650) leave San José for Playa del Coco at 8am and 2 and 4pm daily from Calle 24 between avenidas 5 and 7. Allow 5 hours for the trip. A one-way ticket is $6 (£3). From Liberia, buses (𝐶 2666-0458) to Playa del Coco leave regularly throughout the day between 5am and 7pm. A one-way ticket for the 40-minute trip costs $1.75 (85p). These bus schedules change frequently, so it's always best to check in advance. During the high season and on weekends, extra buses from Liberia are sometimes added. The direct bus for San José leaves Playa del Coco daily at 4 and 8am and 2pm. Local buses for Liberia leave between 5am and 7pm.

Gray Line (𝐶 2220-2126; www.graylinecostarica.com) has a daily bus that leaves San José at 8am for Playa del Coco. The fare is $33 (£17). **Interbus** (𝐶 2283-5573; www.interbusonline.com) has two daily buses that leave San José at 7:45am and 2:30pm. The fare is $35 (£18). Both companies will pick you up at most San José–area hotels.

Depending on demand, the Playa del Coco buses sometimes go as far as Playa Ocotal; it's worth checking beforehand if possible. Otherwise, a taxi should cost around $5 (£2.50).

ORIENTATION   Playa del Coco is a compact and busy beach town. Most of its hotels and restaurants are either on the water, on the road leading into town, or on the road that heads north, about 100m (328 ft.) inland from and parallel to the beach.

Playa Ocotal, which is south of Playa del Coco on a paved road that leaves the main road about 183m (600 ft.) before the beach, is a small collection of vacation homes, condos, and a couple of hotels. It has one bar and one restaurant on the beach.

GETTING AROUND   You can rent cars from any number of rental companies. Most are based in Liberia, or at the airport. See "Essentials" under "Liberia" for details and contact information.

If you can't flag down a **taxi** easily on the street, call 𝐶 2670-0408.

FAST FACTS The nearest major hospital is in Liberia (© **2666-0011**). For the local **health clinic,** call © **2670-0987;** and for the local **pharmacy** call © **2670-1186.** For the local **police,** dial © **2670-0258.**

There's a branch of the state-run **Banco Nacional** (© **2670-0801**) on the main road into town, about 3 blocks before you hit the beach.

FUN ON & OFF THE BEACH

Plenty of boats are anchored here at Playa del Coco, and that means plenty of opportunities to go fishing, diving, or sailing. Still, the most popular activities, especially among the hordes of Ticos who come here, are hanging out on the beach, hanging out in the *sodas,* and cruising the bars and discos at night. If you're interested, you might be able to join a soccer match. (The soccer field is in the middle of town.) You can also arrange horseback rides; ask at your hotel.

BEACH CLUB If you're staying at a hotel without a pool, or just want a sense of exclusivity on the beach, you might check out **Café de Playa Beach & Dining Club** (© **2670-1621;** www.cafedeplaya.com). In addition to having an excellent restaurant (see below), this place offers up day passes for $15 (£7.50) that allow you access to their pool and private grassy lawn fronting the beach, and spread with comfortable teak chaise longues. They also have a host of watersports equipment rental and tour options, and a small spa on-site, offering a broad range of massages and treatments.

GOLF Located about 10km (6¼ miles) outside Playa del Coco, the new **Papagayo Golf & Country Club** (© **2697-1313;** www.papagayo-golf.com) offers up a full 18-hole course, with a pro shop, driving range, and rental equipment. It costs $80 (£40) in greens fees, including a cart.

SAILING Several cruising sailboats and longtime local salts offer daily sailing excursions. The 50-foot *Drums of Bora* (© **2670-1033** or 8845-9448) is a large motor-sailer plying the waters off Playa del Coco. A full-day cruise with lunch and drinks runs $65 (£33) per person. The trip includes a couple of snorkel stops and an open bar. You could also book a ride on the *Don Bosco* (© **2670-0181**), a 65-foot ketch, that includes a beach barbecue and party as part of its daily cruise itinerary ($90–$120/£45–£60 per person, full day). Both of the above boats also offer half-day cruises and sunset sails.

SCUBA DIVING Scuba diving is the most popular watersport in the area, and dive shops abound. **Ocotal Diving** (© **2670-0321;** www.ocotaldiving.com), **Summer Salt** (© **2670-0308;** www.summer-salt.com) and **Rich Coast Diving** (© **800/434-8464** in the U.S. and Canada, or 2670-0176 in Costa Rica; www.richcoastdiving.com) are the most established and offer equipment rentals and dive trips. A two-tank dive, with equipment, should cost between $70 and $140 (£35–£70) per person, depending on the distance to the dive site. The more distant dive sites visited include the Catalina Islands and Bat Island. All of these operators also offer PADI certification courses.

SPA If you're looking for some pampering, whether it be a massage, facial, or body scrub, check out **Spa Mariposa** (© **2670-1886**), which has a wide range of treatment options.

SPORTFISHING Full- and half-day sportfishing excursions can be arranged through any of the hotel tour desks, or with **Tranquilamar** (©/fax **2670-0400** or 8814-0994; www.tranquilamar.com). A half-day of fishing, with boat, captain, food,

> ### *Fun Fact* Charlie Don't Surf, But Ollie Does
>
> Ollie's Point is named after Oliver North, the famous and felonious former lieu-
> tenant colonel at the center of the Iran-Contra scandal. The beaches and ports
> of northern Guanacaste were a staging ground for supplying the Nicaraguan
> Contra rebels. Legend has it that during a news broadcast of an interview with
> North, some surfers noticed a fabulous point break going off in the back-
> ground. Hence, the discovery and naming of Ollie's Point.

and tackle, should cost between $250 and $600 (£125–£300) for two to four passengers; a full day should run between $600 and $1,600 (£300–£800).

SURFING There's no surf whatsoever in Playa del Coco. But this is a popular
jumping-off point for daily boat trips to Witch's Rock or Roca Bruja, and Ollie's Point
up in Santa Rosa National Park. Most of the above-mentioned sportfishing and dive
operations also offer trips to ferry surfers up to these two isolated surf breaks. Alternatively, you can contact **Roca Bruja Surf Operations** (© **2670-1020**). A boat that
carries six surfers for a full day, including lunch and beer, should run around $250 to
$375 (£125–£188). *Tip:* Both Witch's Rock and Ollie's Point are technically within
Santa Rosa National Park. Permits are sometimes required, and boats without permits
are sometimes turned away. If you decide to go, be sure your boat captain is licensed
and has cleared access to the park. You may also have to pay the park's $10 (£5)
entrance fee.

WHERE TO STAY
EXPENSIVE
El Ocotal Beach Resort ✎ This is the most luxurious and complete resort hotel
in the Playa del Coco area. The guest rooms vary in size and styling. Spread up a steep
hillside are six large duplex bungalows. Each of these bungalows shares a small oceanview plunge pool. The rooms with the best views are at the top of the hill, overlooking a dramatic stretch of rocky coastline, although if you want quick access to the
beach, choose one of the lower units. The third-floor suite, no. 520, is the best room
in the whole joint, with a large wraparound balcony and private Jacuzzi. Scuba diving
and sportfishing are the main draws here, and package tours are available. El Ocotal's
hilltop restaurant is also one of its greatest assets. The large open-air dining room
opens onto an expansive, multilevel deck that has more seating, as well as a stunning
view of Playa Ocotal and miles of coastline. This is a great place to come for sunset
and a drink. There's also another restaurant down by the beach. *Note:* It's a steep, vigorous hike from bottom to top at this resort.

Playa del Coco (A.P. 1), Guanacaste. © **877/862-6825** in U.S. and Canada, or 2670-0321 in Costa Rica. Fax 2670-
1122. www.ocotalresort.com. 42 units, 12 bungalows, 5 suites. $172 (£86) double; $265 (£133) bungalow; $325
(£163) suite. Rates include full breakfast. Rates lower in off season; higher during peak weeks. AE, DC, MC, V. **Amenities:** 2 restaurants; 3 outdoor swimming pools and 3 plunge pools; lighted tennis court; exercise room; Jacuzzi; tour
desk; babysitting; laundry service. *In room:* A/C, TV, free Wi-Fi, minifridge, coffeemaker, hair dryer, safe.

The Suites at Café de Playa ✎ While simple and understated, the five rooms
here are the plushest you'll find right in Playa del Coco. The design and decor are
sleek, with contemporary fixtures, furnishings, and art. Rooms are arranged around a
central pool area and come with either one or two queen-size beds. The best thing

about these rooms is the fact that they are just a few steps from the sand, and allow you access to the facilities and services available at Café de Playa.

Playa del Coco, Guanacaste. (C) **2670-1553** or 2670-1554. www.merymer.com. 5 units. $197 (£99) double. Rates lower in off season; higher during peak weeks. AE, DC, MC, V. **Amenities:** Restaurant; outdoor pool; small spa; tour desk; laundry service. *In room:* A/C, TV, safe.

MODERATE

Coco Bay Hotel & Casino   This two-story hotel is the biggest thing in Playa del Coco and is an acceptable choice if you're looking for cookie-cutter-style room close to the beach, restaurants, and action. The very bland rooms are identical in size but have a variety of bedding options for singles, couples, and families. They all share a common veranda, which gets blasted by the hot afternoon sun. The casino here is the best in Playa del Coco. You can't miss this large building on your right, on the main road into Playa del Coco—about 200m (656 ft.) before you hit the beach.

Playa del Coco, Guanacaste. (C) **2670-0494.** Fax 2670-0555. 33 units. $80 (£40) double. Rates lower in off season. V. **Amenities:** Restaurant; bar; casino; small pool; small spa; tour desk; laundry service. *In room:* A/C, TV, coffeemaker, hair dryer, safe.

Hotel Villa Casa Blanca ✦   With friendly owners, beautiful gardens, and attractive rooms, this bed-and-breakfast inn is one of my favorite options in the area. Located about 500m (1,640 ft.) inland from the beach at Playa Ocotal, it's built in the style of a Spanish villa. All the guest rooms feature fine furnishings and are well kept. Some are a tad small, but others are quite roomy and even have kitchenettes. The suites are higher up and have ocean views. My favorite has a secluded patio with lush flowering plants all around. A little rancho serves as an open-air bar and breakfast area, and beside this is a pretty little lap pool with a bridge over it. Another separate rancho serves as a sort of lounge/recreation area and has a satellite television.

Playa Ocotal (A.P. 176-5019), Playa del Coco, Guanacaste. (C) **2670-0518.** Fax 2670-0448. www.hotelvillacasa blanca.com. 10 units. $105 (£53) double; $125 (£63) double suite. Rates include breakfast buffet. Rates lower in off season; higher during peak periods. AE, MC, V. **Amenities:** Outdoor lounge and bar; small pool; Jacuzzi; tour desk; laundry service. *In room:* A/C, free Wi-Fi.

Villa del Sol B&B   This small bed-and-breakfast, located 1km (½ mile) north of Playa del Coco village, is a friendly family-run joint. There are seven rooms in the original building here. All are spacious and clean and receive plenty of light. The most interesting room has a round queen-size bed, high ceilings, and views of the gardens. Still, the nicest rooms here are the six studios, each with a small kitchenette, private bathroom, television, and telephone. Those on the second floor even have a bit of an ocean view from their shared veranda. There's an inviting small pool with a covered barbecue area. Tasty dinners from a small menu of European-influenced dishes are prepared nightly for guests.

Playa del Coco, (A.P. 52-5019) Guanacaste. (C) **866/793-9523** in the U.S. or (C)/fax 2670-0085 in Costa Rica. www.villadelsol.com. 13 units, 11 with private bathroom. $70 (£35) double; $87 (£44) studio apt. Rates include taxes, and full breakfast (for rooms only, not studio apts). Rates lower in off season; higher during peak periods. AE, MC, V. **Amenities:** Restaurant; small pool; tour desk. *In room:* A/C, free Wi-Fi, no phone.

WHERE TO DINE

There are dozens of basic open-air *sodas* at the traffic circle in the center of El Coco village. These restaurants serve Tico standards, with an emphasis on fried fish. Prices are quite low—and so is the quality, for the most part.

In addition to the places listed below, you can get excellent Italian food at **Sol y Luna,** at the Hotel La Puerta del Sol (📞 **2670-0195**), 200m (2 blocks) north and 100m (1 block) east of the main road at the turnoff just beyond the Coco Beach Hotel, before you hit the beach, and at **La Dolce Vita** (📞 **2670-1384;** www.ladolce vitacostarica.com), in the little El Pueblito strip mall on the road running north and parallel to the beach.

Right on the main strip, you'll also find the neighboring Papagayo and Louisiana operations. Growing out of the success of their seafood restaurant, **Papagayo Seafood** (📞 **2670-0298**), has recently opened **Papagayo Steak House** (📞 **2670-0605**), while the **Louisiana Bar & Grill** (📞 **2670-0315**), which serves Cajun cuisine and seafood, has added on the **Louisiana Sport Bar Café & Pizza,** in an attempt to cover all possible bases.

For something a little different, try **Coco Sushi** (📞 **2670-0153**), at the Coco Palms hotel, right across from the soccer field.

Café de Playa ★★ *Finds* INTERNATIONAL/FUSION

This hip restaurant is the most elegant and enjoyable spot in Playa del Coco. The creative menu covers a lot of ground, with influences from Italy and across Asia quite prevalent. Appetizers range from an octopus carpaccio to a cold Thai beef salad. There's a range of pasta choices, and a very tasty oriental rice salad with smoked tuna, caviar, and avocado. Lobster is served several ways, as are tender filets of sirloin. For dessert be sure to try the passion-fruit ice cream. Heavy teak tables and chairs are spread around the ample open-air dining room, or out under the open sky (either sun or stars, depending upon the hour). These folks have an excellent wine list, with plenty of Italian and French choices, in addition to the more common Chilean and Argentine fare. The bar—which is made from thick bamboo—and lounge are dimly lit, chic, and very inviting.

On the beach, Playa del Coco. 📞 **2670-1621.** Reservations recommended. Main courses $6–$17 (£3–£8.50). MC, V. Daily 7am–11pm.

Picante ★ INTERNATIONAL

This is a large, open-air, poolside restaurant at Bahía Pez Vela resort and condominium project. Beyond the pool and down a steep little hill, you can see the Pacific Ocean. The menu is pretty simple and straightforward, with a selection of fresh fish and seafood dishes, big burgers, excellent fish sandwiches, and large creative salads. There are also daily chalkboard specials, which are usually more creative and eclectic, ranging from sesame-seared tuna to mahimahi topped with a homemade curry sauce.

At Bahía Pez Vela resort, Playa Ocotal. 📞 **2670-0901.** Reservations recommended. Main courses $5–$18 (£2.50–£9). MC, V. Daily 9am–10pm.

Tequila Bar & Grill ★ MEXICAN

This is a simple and rustic joint that serves good Mexican food and magnificent margaritas—in fact, there are 20 different types of margaritas on the menu here. Because this is a fishing town, I recommend the seafood tacos and fajitas, which are excellent, although they both come in chicken and beef varieties. Main-course meals include pork chops in a chipotle barbecue sauce and grilled chicken with tomatillo and lime. Definitely grab one of the open-air streetside tables if you get here early enough to snag one.

On the main road, 150m (1½ blocks) before the beach. 📞 **2670-0741.** Reservations not necessary. Main courses $4–$14 (£2–£7). V. Thurs–Tues noon–10pm.

PLAYA DEL COCO AFTER DARK

Playa del Coco is one of Costa Rica's liveliest beach towns after dark. On the road into town, you'll find the **Lizard Lounge** ⊛, which has a popular pool table and a laid-back tropical vibe. For a more European style, check out **Zouk Santana** ⊛, which often has a DJ spinning electronic dance and lounge music. Finally, for a Middle Eastern–inspired mellow lounge scene, head to the new **Kashbar,** in the Pueblito shopping center. On the south end of the beach, you'll find **La Vida Loca** a lively beachfront bar, with a pool table, Ping-Pong table, and foosball table, as well as occasional live bands.

Cocomar is the main disco in town. It's just off the little park fronting the beach. (If these directions don't get you there, just follow the loud music.) The **Café de Playa** often has live music and concerts, with major acts from San José, as well as local talent filling the bills. Finally, if you want to test your luck, head to the casino at the **Coco Bay Hotel & Casino** (see above).

5 Playas Flamingo ⊛⊛, Potrero, Brasilito & Conchal ⊛⊛

280km (174 miles) NW of San José; 66km (41 miles) SW of Liberia

For a time this was the epicenter of Costa Rica's beach tourism. The heart of Guanacaste's "Gold Coast." Then Tamarindo to the south and the Papagayo peninsula to the north stole much of its thunder, and things were dormant here for a long while. However, this is area is booming once again, and major construction and development are going on all over the place.

Playa Conchal ⊛⊛ is the first in a string of beaches stretching north along this coast. This beach is almost entirely backed by the massive Paradisus Playa Conchal resort complex. The unique beach here was once made up primarily of soft crushed shells. Nearly every place you could walk, turn, or lay down your towel was shell-collectors' heaven. Unfortunately, as Conchal has developed and its popularity spread, unscrupulous builders have brought in dump trucks to haul away the namesake seashells for landscaping and construction, and the impact is noticeable.

Just beyond Playa Conchal to the north, you'll come to **Playa Brasilito,** a tiny beach town and one of the few real villages in the area. The soccer field is the center of the village, and around its edges you'll find a couple of little *pulperías* (general stores). There's a long stretch of beach, and though it's of gray sand, it still has a quiet, undiscovered feel—this is about to change, though, as the **Hyatt** hotel group has broken ground on a massive project here (expected to be completed in mid-2009).

Playa Flamingo ⊛⊛ is a long, broad stretch of pinkish white sand, located on a long spit of land that forms part of Potrero Bay. At the northern end of the beach is a high rock outcropping upon which most of Playa Flamingo's hotels and vacation homes are built. There are great views from this rocky hill.

If you continue along the road from Brasilito without taking the turn for Playa Flamingo, you'll come to **Playa Potrero.** The sand here is a brownish gray, but the beach is long, clean, deserted, and very calm for swimming. You can see the hotels of Playa Flamingo across the bay. Drive a little farther north and you'll find the still-underdeveloped beaches of **Playa La Penca** ⊛ and, finally, **Playa Pan de Azúcar** ⊛, or **Sugar Beach.**

ESSENTIALS

GETTING THERE & DEPARTING   By Plane   The nearest airport with regularly scheduled flights is in Tamarindo (see "Essentials," in section 6 of this chapter), although it is also possible to fly into Liberia (p. 158). From either of these places, you can arrange for a taxi to drive you to any of these beaches. Playas Brasilito and Conchal are about 25 minutes from Tamarindo and 40 minutes from Liberia (add about 5 min. for Flamingo and 10 min. for Potrero). A taxi from Tamarindo should cost around $30 to $40 (£15–£20), and between $40 and $60 (£20–£30) from Liberia.

By Car   There are two major routes to the beaches. The most direct is by way of the La Amistad Bridge over the Tempisque River. Take the Interamerican Highway west from San José. Forty-seven kilometers (29 miles) past the turnoff for Puntarenas, you'll see signs for the turnoff to the bridge. After crossing the Tempisque River, follow the signs for Nicoya, continuing north to Santa Cruz. About 16km (10 miles) north of Santa Cruz, just before the village of Belén, take the turnoff for playas Flamingo, Brasilito, and Potrero. After another 20km (12 miles), at the town of Huacas, take the right fork to reach these beaches. The drive takes about 4½ hours.

Alternatively, you can drive here via Liberia. When you reach Liberia, turn west and follow the signs for Santa Cruz and the various beaches. Just beyond the town of Belén, take the turnoff for playas Flamingo, Brasilito, and Potrero, and continue following the directions given above. This route takes around 5 hours.

By Bus   **Tralapa** express buses (© **2221-7202** in San José, or **2654-4203** in Flamingo) leave San José daily at 8 and 10:30am and 3pm from Calle 20 between avenidas 3 and 5, stopping at playas Brasilito, Flamingo, and Potrero, in that order. The ride takes around 5½ hours. A one-way ticket costs $7 (£3.50).

Alternatively, the same company's buses to Santa Cruz (© **2680-0392**) connect with one of the several buses from Santa Cruz to Playa Potrero. Buses depart San José for Santa Cruz roughly every 2 hours between 7am and 6pm from Calle 20 between avenidas 3 and 5. Trip duration is around 4 hours; the fare is $4.20 (£2.10). From Santa Cruz, the ride is about 90 minutes; the fare is $1.50 (75p).

Gray Line (© **2220-2126;** www.graylinecostarica.com) has a daily bus that leaves San José for Playa Flamingo at 8am. The fare is $33 (£17). **Interbus** (© **2283-5573;** www.interbusonline.com) has two daily buses that leave San José for Playa Flamingo at 7:45am and 2:30pm. The fare is $35 (£18). Both companies will pick you up at most San José–area hotels.

Express buses depart **Playa Potrero** for San José at 3 and 9am and 2pm, stopping a few minutes later in playas Flamingo and Brasilito. Ask at your hotel where to catch the bus. Buses to **Santa Cruz** leave Potrero at regular intervals throughout the day and take about 90 minutes. If you're heading north toward Liberia, get off the bus at Belén and wait for a bus going north. Buses leave Santa Cruz for San José roughly every hour between 6am and 6pm.

GETTING AROUND   **Economy Rent A Car** (© **2654-4543**) has an office in Playa Flamingo.

ORIENTATION   The pavement ends just beyond Playa Conchal as you leave the small village of Brasilito. The rest of these beaches are strung out over several kilometers of rough dirt roads. Playa Flamingo is by far the most developed town in this region. There's a small collection of shops, in a couple of minimalls at the crossroads in the center of Playa Flamingo. Here you'll find a branch of the **Banco de Costa Rica,** as well as the **Santa Fe Pharmacy and Medical Center** (© **2654-9000**).

FUN ON & OFF THE BEACH

Playa Flamingo 🐦🐦 is a long and beautiful stretch of soft white sand, although the surf can sometimes get a bit rough here. There isn't much shade on the beach, so be sure to use plenty of sunscreen and bring an umbrella if you can. If you're not staying here, there are parking spots all along the beach road where you can park your car for the day—although remember not to leave anything of value inside.

Playa Potrero has the gentlest surf and, therefore, is the best swimming beach. However, the beach is made up of hard-packed dark sand that is much less appealing than that found at other spots mentioned here. The water at **Playa Brasilito** is often fairly calm, which makes it another good swimming choice.

Playa Conchal 🐦🐦, which is legendary for its crushed seashells, is also stunningly beautiful, but the drop-off is quite steep, making it notorious for its strong riptides. My favorites for a full day of swimming and sunbathing are **Playa La Penca** 🐦🐦 and **Playa Pan de Azúcar** 🐦🐦, both of which are north of Playa Potrero.

Tip: All beaches in Costa Rica are public property. But the land behind the beaches is not, and the Meliá company owns almost all of it in Playa Conchal, so the only public access is along the soft-sand road that follows the beach south from Brasilito (see below). Before the road reaches Conchal, you'll have to ford a small river and then climb a steep, rocky hill, so four-wheel-drive is recommended.

GOLF The **Paradisus Playa Conchal** 🐦🐦 (② 2654-4123) is home to an excellent golf course featuring a few wonderful views of the ocean. This Robert Trent Jones–designed resort course is open to the walk-in public from neighboring hotels and resorts. It costs $180 (£87) in greens fees for as many rounds as you can squeeze into 1 day, including a cart. If you tee off after 1pm, it's just $120 (£58).

HORSEBACK RIDING You can arrange a horseback ride with the **Flamingo Equestrian Center** (② 2654-4089), **Casagua Horses** (② 2653-8041), or **Brasilito Excursions** (② 2654-4237). This latter place works out of the Hotel Brasilito. Depending on the size of your group, it should cost between $10 and $20 (£5–£10) per person per hour.

LEARN THE LANGUAGE The **Centro Panamericano de Idiomas** (② 2654-5002; www.cpi-edu.com), which has schools in San José and Monteverde, has a branch in Flamingo, across from the Flamingo Marina, facing Potrero Bay. A 1-week course with 4 hours of classes per day, including a home stay, costs $465 (£233). Longer course options are available.

SCUBA DIVING Scuba diving is quite popular here. The **Edge Adventure Company** (② 2654-4946) and **Costa Rica Diving** (②/fax 2654-4148; www.costarica-diving.com) both have shops in Flamingo and offer trips to the Catalina and Bat islands for between $75 and $150 (£38–£75). Both also offer PADI certification courses, as well as multiday packages. Alternatively, you can check in at the **Flamingo Marina Resort Hotel and Club** (p. 184).

SPORTFISHING & SAILBOAT CHARTERS Although the Flamingo Marina remains in a state of legal limbo and turmoil, you still have plenty of sportfishing and sailboat charter options here. Jim McKee, the former force behind the Flamingo Marina, manages a fleet of boats. Contact him via his company, **Oso Viejo** (② 8827-5533; www.flamingobeachcr.com). A full-day fishing excursion costs between $500 and $1,600 (£250–£800), depending on the size and quality of the boat, and distance traveled to the fishing grounds. Half-day trips cost between $200 and $700 (£100–£350).

If you're looking for a full- or half-day sail or sunset cruise, check in with **Oso Viejo** (see above) to see what boats are available, or ask about the 52-foot cutter *Shannon.* The 52-foot ketch *Samonique III* (© 8388-7870; www.costarica-sailing.com) and the 43-foot catamaran **Seabird Sailing** (© 8381-1060; www.seabirdsailing.com) are two other good options. Prices range from around $50 to $120 (£25–£60) per person, depending on the length of the cruise. Multiday trips are also available.

Alternatively, you can contact the **Edge Adventure Company** or the **Flamingo Marina Resort Hotel and Club.**

OTHER ADVENTURE TOURS   You can sign up for a **sea kayaking or surf trip** with the **Edge Adventure Company.** Alternatively, check in with the tour desk at the **Flamingo Marina Resort Hotel and Club,** which offers a host of tours to other nearby destinations, as well as hiking and rafting trips.

WHERE TO STAY

If you plan to be here for a while or are coming down with friends or a large family, you might want to consider renting a condo or house. For information and reservations, contact the folks at **Emerald Shores Realty** (© 2654-4554; www.emeraldshores realty.net) or **Century 21 Marina Trading Post** (© 2654-4004; www.century21 costarica.net).

VERY EXPENSIVE

Paradisus Playa Conchal ✪✪   This sprawling all-inclusive resort is the largest in Costa Rica. From the massive open-air reception building down to the free-form swimming pool, everything here is on a grand scale; still, there's a small-village feel to the layout. All rooms are suites and come with either one king-size bed or two double beds in a raised bedroom nook. The bathrooms feature marble tiles, full tubs, bidets, and a telephone. Each unit has a garden patio or a small balcony. Although the rooms are almost exactly the same, the Royal level suites come with butler service and access to a private, adults-only pool. Very few rooms here have ocean views. Unlike most all-inclusives, most of the restaurants are sit-down a la carte affairs, although they are decidedly mediocre. The golf course, with its ponds and wetlands, allows for healthy populations of parrots, roseate spoonbills, and wood storks. Because the hotel owns so much land behind Playa Conchal, guests have almost exclusive access to this crushed-seashell beach.

Playa Conchal (A.P. 499-4005, San Antonio de Belén), Guanacaste. © 888/336-3542 in the U.S. or 2654-4123. Fax 2654-4181. www.solmelia.com. 406 suites. $420–$650 (£210–£325) double; $650–$850 (£325–£425) Royal suites; $1,150 (£575) Presidential suite. Rates include all meals, drinks, taxes, a wide range of activities, and use of nonmotorized land and watersports equipment. Golf and spa services extra. AE, MC, V. **Amenities:** 8 restaurants; 3 bars; 2 lounges; casino, dance club, massive free-form pool w/several Jacuzzis, and another large outdoor pool for Royal Level suites; Robert Trent Jones II–designed 18-hole golf course and pro shop; 4 lighted tennis courts; exercise room; modest exercise facilities and spa; watersports equipment rental; bike rental; children's programs; concierge; tour desk; car-rental desk; modest business center; shopping arcade; 24-hr. room service; in-room massage; babysitting; laundry service; nonsmoking rooms. *In room:* A/C, TV, free Wi-Fi, minibar, fridge, coffeemaker, hair dryer, safe.

EXPENSIVE

Bahía del Sol ✪   This small-scale resort sits right on the water's edge at the heart of Playa Potrero. The rooms are all large and feature contemporary decor with bright primary colors at every turn, although the furnishings are rather sparse. All have either a private balcony or shared veranda, and most of these are strung with hammocks. They also have fully equipped studio and two-bedroom apartments that are a good bet for longer stays. The midsize pool is set in a small grassy lawn, just beyond the beach. The pool features a Jacuzzi above it, whose water cascades down a faux-waterfall into it. The large open-air restaurant serves fresh seafood and international fare, and offers wonderful views of Potrero Bay.

Playa Potrero, Guanacaste. ✆ 866/223-2463 in the U.S. and Canada, or 2654-4671 in Costa Rica. Fax 2654-5182. www.bahiadelsolhotel.com. 28 units. $140–$155 (£70–£78) double; $195–$310 (£98–£155) suite. Rates include full breakfast. Rates lower in off season; higher during peak periods. AE, MC, V. **Amenities:** Restaurant; bar; large pool; Jacuzzi; small spa; tour desk; room service 7am–9pm; laundry service; all rooms nonsmoking. *In room:* A/C, TV, coffeemaker, hair dryer, safe.

Flamingo Beach Resort ✪ Located right across the road from the best section of beach at Playa Flamingo, this large resort is the best full-service hotel in Flamingo, with an enviable location fronting a gorgeous section of beach. The hotel is constructed in a horseshoe shape around a large pool and opens out onto the ocean. Half of the rooms have clear views of the ocean across a narrow dirt road. I definitely prefer the pool and oceanview rooms. Others, which are termed "mountain view" rooms, aren't quite as desirable. All the rooms are clean and cool, with tile floors and comfortable bathrooms. The suites are larger and better equipped, with full-size refrigerators, kitchenettes, and 27-inch television sets.

Playa Flamingo, Guanacaste. ✆ 2654-4444. Fax 2654-4060. www.resortflamingobeach.com. 130 units. $149–$169 (£75–£85) double; $209–$269 (£105–£135) suite. Rates include full breakfast. Rates lower in off season; higher during peak periods. AE, MC, V. **Amenities:** 2 restaurants; 2 bars; casino; large pool; outdoor lighted tennis court; exercise room; game room; tour desk; limited room service; laundry service. *In room:* A/C, TV, minifridge, coffeemaker, hair dryer, safe.

MODERATE
Flamingo Marina Resort Hotel and Club ✪ Uphill from the beach, the Flamingo Marina Hotel is a midsize resort with a good mix of facilities and amenities. This place was built in several phases, and there's not much overall sense of coherence or grand plan here. Still, the entire complex has received steady upkeep and makeovers over the years. The rooms have white tile floors, bright bedspreads, and lots of light. The suites have leather couches and a wet bar in the seating area, as well as private whirlpool tubs. Condo units have full kitchenettes. All the rooms have patios or balconies, and most have pretty good bay views. This place caters to fishermen and scuba divers, and a host of tours and adventures are offered. While not directly on the beach (like Sugar Beach, see below), the hotel is very close to Flamingo's principal beach, as well as all of the town's restaurants and nightlife options.

Playa Flamingo (A.P. 321-1002, San José), Guanacaste. ✆ 800/276-7501 in the U.S. and Canada, or 2654-4141. Fax 2654-4035. www.flamingomarina.com. 45 units, 44 apts. $119 (£60) double; $169–$180 (£85–£90) suite; $180–$280 (£90–£140) apt. Rates lower in the off season, slightly higher during peak periods. AE, DC, MC, V. **Amenities:** Restaurant; snack bar; bar; 4 small pools; tennis court; exercise room; Jacuzzi; watersports equipment rental; tour desk; laundry service. *In room:* A/C, TV, free Wi-Fi, safe.

Hotel Sugar Beach ✪✪ Hotel Sugar Beach is on a beautiful, semiprivate salt-and-pepper beach about a 10-minute drive north of Playa Potrero along a rough dirt road. It's one of the only hotels in the area, and that's what gives it most of its charm, in my opinion—lots of seclusion and privacy. The beach is on a small cove surrounded by rocky hills. The hotel itself is perched above the water. Nature lovers will be thrilled to find howler monkeys and iguanas almost on their doorsteps. Snorkelers should be happy here too; this cove has some good snorkeling in the dry season. My favorite rooms are the oceanfront standard rooms, which have great views and easy access to the beach. However, the deluxe rooms and suites are larger and more luxurious, and some have excellent ocean views from their private balconies. If you don't land one of the rooms with a sea view, the main lodge and restaurant have commanding views from a hillside perch.

Playa Pan de Azúcar (A.P. 90, Santa Cruz), Guanacaste. ℂ **2654-4242**. Fax 2654-4239. www.sugar-beach.com. 30 units. $125–$155 (£63–£78) double; $195 (£98) suite. Rates include breakfast. Rates lower in off season. AE, MC, V. **Amenities:** Restaurant; bar; small kidney-shape pool set on the hillside; watersports equipment rental; tour desk; laundry service. *In room:* A/C, TV, minifridge, safe.

INEXPENSIVE

There is a string of inexpensive *cabinas* on the main road leading into Brasilito, just before you hit the beach. It's also possible to camp on playas Potrero and Brasilito. At the former, contact **Maiyra's** (ℂ **2654-4213**); at the latter, try **Camping Brasilito** (ℂ **2654-4452**). Both of these places offer some budget rooms as well. Each charges around $4 to $8 (£2–£4) per person to make camp and use the basic bathroom facilities, or around $10 to $15 (£5–£7.50) per person to stay in a rustic room.

Hotel Brasilito *(Value)* This hotel, just across a sand road from the beach, offers pretty basic and small rooms that are nonetheless quite clean and well maintained. There's also a bar and a big open-air restaurant that is excellent. Even with Playa Brasilito's glut of budget options, this is one of the best values in town and is the closest to the water. The best rooms have nice balconies with ocean views, and air-conditioning. The hotel rents snorkeling equipment, kayaks, body boards, and horses and can arrange a variety of tours.

Playa Brasilito, Santa Cruz, Guanacaste. ℂ **2654-4237**. Fax 2654-4247. www.brasilito.com. 15 units. $40–$76 (£20–£38) double. Rates include taxes. Rates lower in the off season; higher during peak periods. V. **Amenities:** Restaurant; watersports equipment rental; tour desk; laundry service. *In room:* Free Wi-Fi, no phone.

WHERE TO DINE

In addition to the places listed below, you'll find good fresh seafood and international fare at the **Happy Snapper** (ℂ **2654-4413**) in Brasilito, and high-end, fancy French fare at **Les Arcades** (ℂ **2654-5713**), on the main road into Flamingo. Out in Playa Potrero, **El Castillo** (ℂ **2654-4271**) is the most happening spot, with a wide-ranging menu of bar food and main courses.

Camarón Dorado *(Finds)* SEAFOOD With a series of tables and kerosene torches set right in the sand just steps from the crashing surf, this is one of the most perfectly placed beach restaurants in the country. There are more tables in a simple, open-air dining room, for those who don't want sand in their shoes. The service is semiformal, and at times can be anything from lax to rude. The seafood is fresh, excellently prepared, and reasonably priced. When I asked to see the wine list, two waiters came over carrying about 12 different bottles between them.

Playa Brasilito ℂ **2654-4028**. Reservations recommended in high season. Main courses $6–$23 (£3–£12). MC, V. Daily 11am–10pm.

Marie's *(★)* COSTA RICAN/SEAFOOD In large, new digs, this long-standing local restaurant is still a great place for a quick bite or a leisurely sit-down meal (it's also now a free Wi-Fi hotspot). The new building is an open-air affair, with a soaring thatch roof and tall, thick columns all around. The menu has grown steadily over the years, although the best option here is always some simply prepared fresh fish, chicken, or meat. Check the blackboard for the daily specials, which usually highlight the freshest catch, such as mahimahi *(dorado),* marlin, and red snapper. You'll also find such Tico favorites as *casados* (rice-and-bean dish), rotisserie chicken, and ceviche, as well as burritos and quesadillas.

Playa Flamingo. © 2654-4136. Reservations recommended for dinner during the high season. Sandwiches $4–$8 (£2–£4); main courses $6.50–$21 (£3.25–£11). V. Daily 6:30am–10pm.

Mar y Sol ★★ *Finds* INTERNATIONAL/SEAFOOD   Seventh-generation Catalan chef Alain Taulere has prepared food for regular folk and royalty. For visitors to his hilltop restaurant in Flamingo Beach, he offers a small, well-executed, and pricey selection of fresh seafood and meats. The ambience is casually formal, with the open-air main dining room dimly lit by old-fashioned lamp posts and covered by a thatched roof. Along with a surf-and-turf combo featuring filet mignon and either lobster tails or jumbo shrimp, menu highlights include rich and creamy lobster bisque, and a hearty bouillabaisse. I enjoyed the tender duck served with passion-fruit-cognac sauce. For starters, try the escargot in puff pastry. Call in advance for free transportation from and back to your hotel.

Playa Flamingo. © 2654-4151. Reservations recommended for dinner in high season. Main courses $14–$32 (£7–£16). AE, DC, MC, V. Nov–Apr daily 10am–3:30pm and 5–10pm; May–Aug daily 2–10pm. Closed Sept–Oct.

Outback Jack's Australian Roadkill Grill & Beach Bar *Kids* INTERNATIONAL The menu here is almost as long, eclectic, and varied as the name. Still, at heart, this is just a simple beachside bar and grill. You can get nachos, quesadillas, and spicy wings, as well as fresh fish and seafood in a variety of preparations. For something more adventurous, try the fresh grilled tuna with an eggplant *caponata,* served over some spaghetti with pesto. There's even a full children's menu, which is hard to come by in these parts. A few tables are set in the sand in front of the joint, facing the beach and Brasilito bay. Inside, there's a thatched Tiki-style bar and some large-screen televisions for sporting events, and a host of heavy wooden tables set on a polished concrete floor. The whole restaurant is a free Wi-Fi hotspot.

Playa Brasilito. © 2654-5463. Main courses $8–$16 (£4–£8). AE, MC, V. Daily 11am–11pm.

PLAYA FLAMINGO AFTER DARK

With both a disco and casino, **Amberes** is the undisputed hot spot in this area; however, there's also now a casino at the **Flamingo Beach Resort.** You might also see if there's any live music or sports events on the televisions at the **Happy Snapper** or **Outback Jack's Australian Road Kill Grill & Beach Bar.** In Playa Potrero, locals and tourists alike gather at **El Castillo,** which sometimes has live bands. All of the other beaches and towns here are rather quiet.

6 Playa Tamarindo ★ & Playa Grande ★★

295km (183 miles) NW of San José; 73km (45 miles) SW of Liberia

Tamarindo is the biggest boomtown in Guanacaste—and personally, I think the boom has gone a bit too far, a bit too fast. The main road into Tamarindo has turned into a seemingly helter-skelter jumble of strip malls, surf shops, hotels and random restaurants. Ongoing development is spreading up the hills inland from the beach and south beyond Punta Langosta. None of it seems regulated or particularly planned out.

Tamarindo

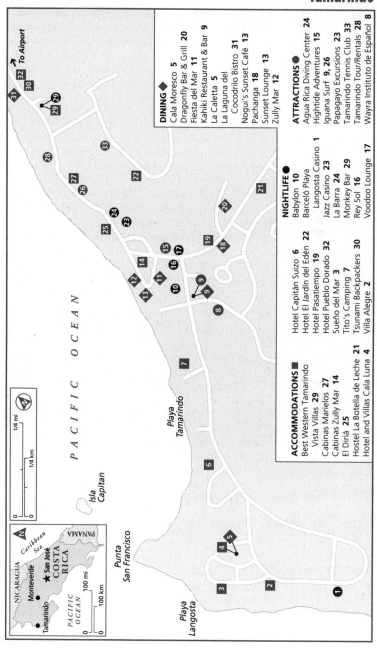

ACCOMMODATIONS ■
Best Western Tamarindo
Vista Villas **29**
Cabinas Marielos **27**
Cabinas Zully Mar **14**
El Diriá **25**
Hostel La Botella de Leche **21**
Hotel and Villas Cala Luna **4**

Hotel Capitán Suizo **6**
Hotel El Jardín del Edén **22**
Hotel Pasatiempo **19**
Hotel Pueblo Dorado **32**
Sueño del Mar **3**
Tito's Camping **7**
Tsunami Backpackers **30**
Villa Alegre **2**

DINING ◆
Cala Moresco **5**
Dragonfly Bar & Grill **20**
Fiesta del Mar **11**
Kahiki Restaurant & Bar **9**
La Caletta **5**
La Laguna del
   Cocodrilo Bistro **31**
Nogui's Sunset Café **13**
Pachanga **18**
Sunset Lounge **13**
Zully Mar **12**

ATTRACTIONS ●
Agua Rica Diving Center **24**
Hightide Adventures **15**
Iguana Surf **9, 26**
Papagayo Excursions **23**
Tamarindo Tennis Club **33**
Tamarindo Tour/Rentals **28**
Wayra Instituto de Español **8**

NIGHTLIFE ●
Babylon **10**
Barceló Playa
Langosta Casino **1**
Jazz Casino **23**
La Barra **24**
Monkey Bar **29**
Rey Sol **16**
Voodoo Lounge **17**

In fact, Tamarindo was thrust into the local headlines in late 2007, when it was discovered that much of this development was undertaken without adequate sewage or water treatment. Tests all around the beach revealed very high levels of fecal waste in the ocean, particularly during the rainy season.

Still, the wide range of accommodations, abundant restaurants, and active nightlife, along with very dependable surf have established Tamarindo as one of the most popular beaches on this coast. The beach itself is a long, wide swath of white sand that curves gently from one rocky headland to another. Fishing boats bob at their moorings and brown pelicans fish just beyond the breakers. A sandy islet off the southern end of the beach makes a great destination if you're a strong swimmer; if you're not, it makes a great foreground for sunsets. Tamarindo is also popular with surfers, who ply the break right here or use the town as a jumping-off place for playas Grande, Langosta, Avellanas, and Negra.

Just to the north of Tamarindo lies **Playa Grande,** one of the principal nesting sites for the giant leatherback turtle, the largest turtle in the world. This beach is often too rough for swimming, but the well-formed and consistent beach break is very popular with surfers. I almost hate to mention places to stay in Playa Grande because the steady influx of tourists and development has apparently doomed it as a turtle-nesting site.

Behind all the beaches in this area are low, dry hills that can be a dreary brown in the dry season but that instantly turn green with the first brief showers of the rainy season.

ESSENTIALS

GETTING THERE & DEPARTING   **By Plane**   **Sansa** (© 877/767-2672 in the U.S. and Canada, or 2290-4100 in Costa Rica; www.flysansa.com) has seven daily flights to Tamarindo from San José's Juan Santamaría International Airport, with the first flight leaving at 6am and the last flight departing at 1:50pm. The flight takes 55 minutes. The fare is $102 (£51) each way. During the high season, a later afternoon flight is added.

Nature Air (© 800/235-9272 in the U.S. and Canada, or 2299-6000; www.natureair.com) flies to Tamarindo daily at 6:30, 10, and 10:10am, and 12:25 and 4:30pm from Tobías Bolaños International Airport in Pavas. The fare is $108 (£54) each way. The flight takes 55 minutes. Nature Air also has connections between Tamarindo and Arenal, Liberia, and Quepos.

Whether you arrive on Sansa or Nature Air, a couple of cabs or minivans are always waiting for arriving flights. It costs $3 to $6 (£1.50–£3) for the ride into town.

Sansa flights leave Tamarindo for San José between 7am and 3pm. Nature Air flights leave for San José at 7:25 and 11:25am, and 2:25 and 4:35pm.

If you're flying into Liberia, a taxi should cost around $50 to $70 (£25–£35). Alternately, you can use **Tamarindo Shuttle** (© 2653-1326; www.tamarindoshuttle.com), which charges $18 (£9) per person.

By Car   The most direct route is by way of the La Amistad bridge. Take the Interamerican Highway west from San José. Forty-seven kilometers (29 miles) past the turnoff for Puntarenas, you'll see signs for the turnoff to the bridge. After crossing the river, follow the signs for Nicoya and Santa Cruz. Continue north out of Santa Cruz, until just before the village of Belén, where you will find the turnoff for Tamarindo. In another 20km (12 miles) take the left fork for Playa Tamarindo at Huacas and continue on until the village of Villareal, where you make your final turn into Tamarindo. The trip should take around 4½ hours.

You can save a little time, especially in the dry season, by taking a more direct but rougher route: You turn left just after passing the main intersection for Santa Cruz at the turnoff for playas Junquillal and Ostional. The road is paved until the tiny village of Veintesiete de Abril. From here, it's about 20km (12 miles) on a rough dirt road until the village of Villareal, where you make your final turn into Tamarindo.

Alternatively, you can drive here via Liberia. When you reach Liberia, turn west and follow the signs for Santa Cruz and the various beaches. Just beyond the town of Belén, take the turnoff for playas Flamingo, Brasilito, and Tamarindo, and then follow the directions for the second option above. This route takes around 5½ hours.

By Bus   **Tracopa-Alfaro** express buses (© 2222-2160) leave San José daily for Tamarindo at 8:30 and 11:30am and 3:30pm, departing from Calle 14 between avenidas 3 and 5. **Tralapa** (© 2221-7202) also has one daily direct bus to Tamarindo leaving at 4pm from their main terminal at Calle 20 between avenidas 3 and 5. The trip takes 5 hours, and the one-way fare is around $6.50 (£3.25).

Alternatively, you can catch a bus to Santa Cruz from the either of the above bus companies. Buses leave both stations for Santa Cruz roughly every hour between 6am and 6pm. The trip's duration is 4 hours; the one-way fare is around $5.50 (£2.25). Buses leave Santa Cruz (© 2680-0392) for Tamarindo roughly every 1½ hours between 6am and 6pm; the one-way fare is $1.60 (80p).

Gray Line (© 2220-2126; www.graylinecostarica.com) has a daily bus that leaves San José for Tamarindo at 8am. The fare is $33 (£17). **Interbus** (© 2283-5573; www.interbusonline.com) has two daily buses that leave San José for Tamarindo at 7:45am and 2:30pm. The fare is $35 (£18). Both companies will pick you up at most San José–area hotels.

Direct buses leave Tamarindo for San José daily at 3:30 and 5:45am and 2 and 4pm. Buses to Santa Cruz leave roughly every 1½ hours between 6am and 6pm. In Santa Cruz you can transfer to one of the frequent San José buses.

ORIENTATION   The road leading into town runs parallel to the beach and ends in a small cul-de-sac just past Zully Mar. A couple of side roads off this main road lead farther on, to playa Langosta. You'll find several of the newer hotels mentioned below off these side roads. To reach playas Avellanas, Negra, and Junquillal, you have to first head out of town and take the road toward Santa Cruz.

FAST FACTS   The local **police** can be reached at © 2653-0283. In the event of a medical emergency, call **Pacific Emergencies** (© 8378-8265).

There's a **Banco Nacional** branch at the little mall across from El Diria, and a branch of the **Banco de Costa Rica** in the Plaza Conchal mall. There are also several Internet cafes and a couple of pharmacies in town. You'll find the **Mariposa Laundry** (no phone) just past the turnoff for Playa Langosta.

GETTING AROUND   For a rental car, **Adobe** (© 2653-0031), **Alamo** (© 2653-0727), **Budget** (© 2436-2000), **Economy** (© 2653-0752), **Europcar** (© 2653-1809), **Hertz** (© 2653-1358), **Payless** (© 2653-0015), and **Thrifty** (© 2653-0829) have offices in Tamarindo.

The town itself is very compact and you should be able to walk most places. Aside from that, a large fleet of taxis are usually cruising around town, or hanging out at principal intersections and meeting points. If you need to, you can call a **taxi** at © 2653-0751, 8836-7783, or 2653-0586.

FUN ON & OFF THE BEACH

Tamarindo is a long, white-sand beach. Still, you have to be careful when and where you swim. The calmest water and best swimming are always down at the far southern end of the beach, toward Punta Langosta. Much of the sea in just off the busiest part of the town is best for surfing. When there's any swell, you'll find scores of surfers in the water here. Be careful: There are rocks just offshore in several places, some of which are exposed only at low tide. An encounter with one of these rocks could be nasty, especially if you're bodysurfing. I also advise that you avoid swimming near the estuary mouth, where the currents can carry you out away from the beach.

BIKING   Bikes are available for rent at several locations in Tamarindo. Check around; you'll probably find your best bikes at the **Blue Trax Bike Shop** ✆ (© 2653-1705; www.bluetraxcr.com), which rents everything from single-gear beach cruisers for $10 (£5) per day, to high-end Trek and Specialized mountain bikes for between $20 and $50 per day (£10–£25). These folks also offer guided mountain-bike tours and excursions.

FOUR-WHEELING   **Hightide Adventures** (© 2653-0108; www.tamarindo adventures.net) has a fleet of four-wheel-drive all-terrain vehicles. They're available for the day ($110/£55) and half-day ($65/£33). A variety of guided ATV tours range in duration from 1 to 8 hours and in price from $45 to $150 (£23–£75) per person. This company also rents dirt bikes, snorkel equipment, surf and boogie boards, and jet skis and offers a full menu of other guided tours around the region.

Another alternative is to sign up for a tour with **Off Road Costa Rica** (© 2653-1969; www.offroadcostarica.com), which employs a fleet of open-air restored Toyota Land Cruisers, and head into the backcountry and hinterlands. A wide range of outings are offered, from a couple of hours to several days. The jeeps are taken through rivers, mud, and forests and over deserted stretches of beach.

GOLF   **Hacienda Pinilla** ✆✆ (© 2680-7000; www.haciendapinilla.com) is a beautiful 18-hole links-style course located south of Tamarindo. Hotel and residential development here is still in its infancy, although a JW Marriott should be finished by 2010. The course is currently accepting golfers staying at hotels around the area, with advance reservation. Greens fees run around $165 (£83) for 18 holes, including a cart. Many folks staying in Tamarindo also play at the **Paradisus Playa Conchal** ✆✆, an excellent resort course (p. 182).

HORSEBACK RIDING   Although some will be disappointed, I think it's a very good thing that horses are no longer allowed on the beach. Fortunately, you'll find plenty of opportunities to ride in the hills and forests around Tamarindo. You can go riding with **Casagua Horses** ✆ (© 2653-8041), **Hightide Adventures** (© 2653-0108; www.tamarindoadventures.net), **Iguana Surf** (© 2653-0148; www.iguana surf.net), or **Papagayo Excursions** (© 2653-0254). Rates for horse rental, with a guide, are around $15 to $30 (£7.50–£15) per hour.

SAILBOAT CHARTERS   There are several boats offering cruises offshore from Tamarindo; the 50-foot schooner *Lemuria* (© 8831-8875; www.tamarindosailing. com), and the 40-foot catamaran *Blue Dolphin* (© 2653-0446; www.sailblue dolphin.com) are both good choices. Options range from sunset cruises to weeklong trips out to Isla del Coco. A half-day snorkel or shorter sunset cruise should cost $50 to $70 (£25–£35) per person, and a full day should run between $75 and $130

Tips Yo Quiero Hablar Español

If you want to try an intensive immersion program or just brush up on your rusty high school Spanish, check in with the folks at **Wayra Instituto de Español** (© /fax **2653-0359;** www.spanish-wayra.co.cr). This place is located up a side street from Iguana Surf.

(£38–£65) per person. This usually includes an open bar and snacks on the half-day and sunset cruises, and all of that plus lunch on the full-day trip.

SCUBA DIVING   If you want to do any scuba diving or snorkeling while you're here, check in with **Agua Rica Diving Center** ✦ (© **2653-0094;** www.aguarica.net). These folks are the best and longest running operators in Tamarindo, and have a full-service dive shop. They offer day trips, multiday dive cruises, and the standard resort and full-certification courses.

SPORTFISHING   A host of captains offer anglers a chance to go after the "big ones" that abound in the waters offshore here. From the Tamarindo estuary, it takes only 20 minutes to reach the edge of the continental shelf, where the waters are filled with mostly marlin and sailfish. Although fishing is good all year, the peak season for billfish is between mid-April and August. You can contact **Tamarindo Sportfishing** (© **2653-0090;** www.tamarindosportfishing.com), **Capullo Sportfishing** (© **2653-0048;** www.capullo.com), or **Osprey Sportfishing** (© **2653-0162;** www.osprey-sportfishing.com).

TENNIS   You can rent court time and equipment at the **Tamarindo Tennis Club** (© **2653-0898**), which features two lighted outdoor courts located on the back road on the way to the Hotel El Jardín del Edén. It is open daily from 7am to 9pm, and court time runs $10 (£5) per hour. You can also play out at **Hacienda Pinilla** (see above) for $5 (£2.50) per hour during the day, and $10 (£5) per hour at night.

TOURS GALORE   **Hightide Adventures, Papagayo Excursions,** and **Iguana Surf** (see above for all) all offer a host of tour and activity options. Papagayo Excursions probably offers the widest selection of full- and multiday trips, including outboard or kayak tours through the nearby estuary and mangroves, excursions to Santa Cruz and Guaitíl, raft floats on the Corobicí River, and tours to Palo Verde and Rincón de la Vieja national parks. Rates run between $30 and $140 (£15–£70), depending on the length of the tour and group size.

There's no longer a canopy tour available right in Tamarindo, but the **Santa Rosa Canopy Tour** (© **2653-0926**) and **Cartagena Canopy Tour** (© **2675-0801**) are nearby. Both charge $40 (£20) per person and include transportation from Tamarindo. Of these two, I recommend the Cartagena tour, which has a much more lush forest setting, but I think your best bet is to take a day trip to Hacienda Guachipelin (p. 165) and do the "Canyon Tour" there.

WATCHING NESTING SEA TURTLES   On nearby **Playa Grande,** leatherback sea turtles nest between early October and mid-February. The turtles come ashore to lay their eggs only at night. During the nesting season, you'll be inundated with opportunities to sign up for nightly tours, which usually cost $35 to $50 (£18–£25) per person. No flash photography or flashlights are allowed because any sort of light can confuse the turtles and prevent them from laying their eggs; guides must use red-tinted flashlights.

Note: Turtle nesting is a natural, unpredictable, and increasingly rare event. Moreover, things have gotten worse here in recent years. The number of nesting turtles was down severely in 2007 and 2008. All indications are that excessive building and lighting close to the beach are the culprits. Even during heavy nesting years you sometimes have to wait your turn for hours, hike quite a way, and even accept the possibility that no nesting mothers will be spotted that evening.

If your hotel can't set it up for you, you'll see signs all over town offering tours. Make sure you go with someone licensed and reputable. Do-it-yourselfers can drive over to Playa Grande and book a tour directly with the **National Parks Service** (© 2653-0470; $15/£7.50). The Parks Service operates out of a small shack just before the beach, across from the hotel Las Tortugas. It opens each evening at around 6pm to begin taking reservations. They sometimes answer their phone during the day, and it's best to make a reservation in advance because only a limited number of people are allowed on the beach at one time. Spots fill up fast, and if you don't have a reservation, you may have to wait until really late, or you may not be able to go out onto the beach.

WATERSPORTS If you want to try snorkeling, surfing, or sea kayaking while in Tamarindo, **Iguana Surf** and **Hightide Adventures** (see above) both rent snorkeling equipment, boogie boards, sea kayaks, and surfboards. They have half-day and hourly rates for many of these items.

If you want to learn to catch a wave while in Tamarindo, check in with the **Tamarindo Surf School** (© 2653-0923; www.tamarindosurfschool.com), **Banana Surf Club** (© 2653-1270; www.bananasurfclub.com), or **Witch's Rock Surf Camp** (© 2653-1262; www.witchsrocksurfcamp.com).

PAMPER ME PLEASE Several of the higher-end hotels have their own spas, and most hotels can call you a massage therapist. But if you're looking for a local day spa experience, try **Domaniti's Day Spa** (© 2653-0995), which has a wide range of treatments and packages, from facials and pedicures to two-therapist Balinese-style massages.

SHOPPING

Tamarindo is awash in souvenir stands, art galleries, jewelry stores, and clothing boutiques. The new **Garden Plaza** shopping center is located near the entrance to town, and has several high-end shops, as well as a massive and modern **Automercado** supermarket.

Tips Pretty Pots

The lack of any long-standing local arts and craft tradition across Costa Rica is often lamented. One of the outstanding exceptions to this rule is the small village of Guaitíl, located on the outskirts of the provincial capital of Santa Cruz. The small central plaza—actually a soccer field—of this village is ringed with craft shops and artisan stands selling a wide range of ceramic wares. Most are low-fired relatively soft clay pieces, with traditional Chorotega indigenous design motifs. All of the local tour agencies offer day trips to Guaitíl, or you can drive there yourself, by heading first to Santa Cruz, and they taking the well-marked turnoff for Guaitíl, just south of the city, on the road to Nicoya.

WHERE TO STAY IN TOWN

In addition to the hotels listed below, Tamarindo and Playa Grande have a wide range of beach houses and condos for rent by the night, the week, or the month. For more information on this option, check out **Remax Tamarindo** (✆ **2653-0073;** www.remax-oceansurf-cr.com) or **Century 21** (✆ **866/978-4492** in the U.S. and Canada, or 2653-0030 in Costa Rica; www.costarica1realestate.com).

VERY EXPENSIVE

Hotel and Villas Cala Luna ✿✿   If you're looking for serious luxury in Tamarindo, stay in one of the two- or three-bedroom villas here, which are the size of a small home and just as well equipped. The living rooms are huge, with high-peaked ceilings, couches, tables and chairs, satellite televisions, and complete sound systems. The full kitchens come with top-end appliances, including fancy cappuccino machines, and you also get a washer-dryer. If this isn't enough, each villa has its own private swimming pool. The bedrooms are spacious and elegant, with either a king-size bed or two double beds. Everything is done in soft pastels with hand-painted accents, and the red-tile roofs and Mexican tile floors add elegance while keeping things cool. Rooms in the hotel are similarly well done, with their own terraces, but you'll have to share the hotel's main swimming pool with the rest of the guests. The hotel isn't right on the beach; you have to cross the street and walk a short path to reach the ocean.

Playa Langosta, Guanacaste. ✆ **800/503-5202** in the U.S. and Canada, or 2653-0214 in Costa Rica. Fax 2653-0213. www.calaluna.com. 20 units, 18 villas. $205 (£102) double; $410–$520 (£205–£260) villa. Rates for rooms, but not villas, include continental breakfast. Rates lower in off season; slightly higher during peak weeks. AE, MC, V. **Amenities:** 2 restaurants; bar; large free-form pool w/poolside bar; watersports equipment rental; bike rental; tour desk; limited room service; in-room massage; babysitting; laundry service. *In room:* A/C, TV, free Wi-Fi, minibar, hair dryer, safe.

EXPENSIVE

El Diriá ✿   This is Tamarindo's largest beachfront resort. Wedged into a narrow piece of land planted with tropical gardens and palm trees, the Diriá has an enviable spot, smack-dab in the middle of Tamarindo's long beach. The rooms in the main building are done in pastel colors with red-tile floors. Some have separate seating areas, and all come with a small bathroom. I especially recommend the second- and third-floor "sunset deluxe" rooms, which feature oceanview private balconies. However, some rooms are across the street from the beach, so be sure you know what type of room you are booking when you reserve. The central location and modern rooms make this an excellent choice in town, although service here can be spotty. The hotel has several swimming pools, as well as a lighted outdoor tennis court. They also have a large, open-air amphitheater that they use for weddings, private parties, and the occasional public concert, as well as a golf driving range on the outskirts of town.

Playa Tamarindo (A.P. 476-1007, San José), Guanacaste. ✆ **866/603-4742** in the U.S. and Canada, or 2653-0031 in Costa Rica. Fax 2653-0848. www.tamarindodiria.com. 182 units. $140–$220 (£70–£110) double. Rates include breakfast buffet. Rates lower in off season. AE, MC, V. **Amenities:** 2 restaurants; 2 bars; 3 pools; watersports equipment rental; game room; tour desk; car-rental desk; laundry service. *In room:* A/C, TV, Wi-Fi, minibar (in some units), fridge, hair dryer, safe.

Hotel Capitán Suizo ✿✿ *(Kids)*   This well-appointed beachfront hotel sits on the quiet southern end of Tamarindo. The rooms are housed in a series of two-story buildings. The lower rooms have air-conditioning and private patios; the upper units have plenty of cross ventilation, ceiling fans, and cozy balconies. All have large bathrooms and sitting rooms with fold-down futon couches. In effect, all the rooms are really suites, with separate sitting/living room areas. The spacious bungalows are spread around the shady grounds; these all come with a tub in the bathroom and an inviting outdoor shower among the trees. The hotel's free-form pool is very pretty, with tall shade trees all around. The shallow end slopes in gradually, imitating a beach, and there's also a separate children's pool. Perhaps the greatest attribute here is that it's just steps from one of the calmer and more isolated sections of Playa Tamarindo, making it a good family pick.

Playa Tamarindo, Guanacaste. ℭ 2653-0353 or 2653-0075. Fax 2653-0292. www.hotelcapitansuizo.com. 22 units, 8 bungalows. $175–$195 (£88–£98) double; $235–$275 (£118–£123) bungalow; $360 (£180) suite. Rates include breakfast buffet. Rates lower in off season; higher during peak periods. AE, MC, V. **Amenities:** Restaurant; bar; mid-size pool and children's pool; small exercise room; tour desk; babysitting; laundry service. *In room:* Minifridge, coffeemaker, safe.

Hotel El Jardín del Edén ⚘

It isn't right on the beach, but this is one of the more luxurious and stylish hotels in Tamarindo, with a sense of sophistication that's often lacking at beach hotels in Costa Rica. There are splendid views from many of the guest rooms, which are in Mediterranean-style buildings on a hill 136m (446 ft.) from and high above the beach. Almost all have balconies or private terraces with views of the Pacific. Those with large stone-tiled terraces, in particular, give you the sense that you're staying at your own private villa. Steady upkeep and remodeling continue to keep this place a top choice in town.

Playa Tamarindo, Guanacaste. ℭ 2653-0137. Fax 2653-0111. www.jardindeleden.com. 36 units, 2 apts. $135–$185 (£68–£93) double; $165–$220 (£83–£110) apt or suite. Rates include full breakfast. Rates lower in off season; higher during peak weeks. AE, MC, V. **Amenities:** Restaurant; bar; 2 small adjoining pools; small exercise room; Jacuzzi; tour desk; limited room service; laundry service. *In room:* A/C, TV, minibar, hair dryer, safe.

Sueño del Mar ⚘ *(Finds*

On Playa Langosta, Sueño del Mar has charming little touches and innovative design: four-poster beds made from driftwood; African dolls on the windowsills; Kokopeli candleholders; and open-air showers with sculpted angelfish, hand-painted tiles, and lush tropical plants. Fabrics are from Bali and Guatemala. Somehow all of this works well together, and the requisite chairs, hammocks, and lounges nestled under shade trees right on the beach add the crowning touch. The two casitas have their own kitchens, veranda, and sleeping loft. The honeymoon suite is a spacious second-floor room, with wraparound screened-in windows, a delightful open-air bathtub and shower, and an ocean view. The beach right out front is rocky and a bit rough, but it does reveal some nice, quiet tidal pools at low tide; it's one of the better sunset-viewing spots in Costa Rica. Breakfasts are huge, elaborate, and delicious.

Playa Langosta, Guanacaste. ℭ/fax 2653-0284. www.sueno-del-mar.com. 4 units, 2 casitas. $195 (£98) double; $220–$295 (£110–£148) suite or casita. Rates include full breakfast. Rates lower in off season; higher during peak periods. No children 11 and under. MC, V. **Amenities:** Small pool; free use of snorkel equipment and boogie boards; tour desk; laundry service. *In room:* A/C, free Wi-Fi, hair dryer, safe.

Villa Alegre

This small bed-and-breakfast on Playa Langosta is a well-located and homey option. The owners' years of globetrotting have inspired them to decorate each room in the theme of a different country. In the main house, Guatemala, Mexico, and the United States are all represented. Of these, Mexico is the most spacious, with a large open-air bathroom and shower. The smallest are Guatemala and the California casita. The latter room is quite small, in fact. Every room has its own private patio, courtyard, or balcony. The villas are spacious and luxurious, with kitchenettes. My favorite is the Japanese unit, with its subtle design touches and great woodwork. The

Russian villa and the United States rooms are truly wheelchair accessible and equipped, with ramps and modified bathrooms with handrails. The beach is just a short stroll away through the trees. Breakfasts are delicious and abundant.

Playa Langosta, Guanacaste. © **2653-0270.** Fax 2653-0287. www.villaalegrecostarica.com. 5 units, 2 villas. $170–$185 (£85–£93) double; $230 (£115) villa. Rates include full breakfast. AE, MC, V. **Amenities:** Small pool. *In room:* A/C, free Wi-Fi, safe, no phone.

MODERATE

In addition to the places listed here, **Hotel Pueblo Dorado** (© 2653-0008; www.pueblodorado.com) is a well-located option just across from the beach; it's under new management, and showing the positive effects of some care and remodeling.

Best Western Tamarindo Vista Villas   This place was originally conceived as a condo project and then was converted into a hotel and taken over by a local surfer and businessman and now is marketed as part of the Best Western chain. This mixed breeding shows in the wide range of accommodations here, from the simple garden-view rooms to the Tropical and Corona suites. The former are basic budget motel-like affairs. The latter are split-level one-bedroom affairs with full kitchens, large living rooms (with two couches that can double as single beds), and either a private patio or a balcony with fabulous views of the Pacific Ocean. This hotel really caters to surfers, and there is often a lively, beach-party at spring break–like atmosphere around the pool and at the bar here—in fact, scenes from MTV's "Wild On" were shot here.

Playa Tamarindo, Guanacaste. © **800/536-3241** in the U.S. and Canada, or 2653-0114 in Costa Rica. Fax 2653-0115. www.tamarindovistavillas.com. 29 units. $89–$119 (£45–£60) double; $159–$229 (£80–£115) suite. Rates lower in off season; higher during peak periods. AE, DC, MC, V. **Amenities:** Restaurant; bar; midsize free-form pool w/swim-up bar and a waterfall; tour desk; laundry service. *In room:* A/C, TV, free Wi-Fi, safe.

Cabinas Zully Mar   The Zully Mar has long been a favorite of budget travelers, although they've definitely upgraded their rooms and upped their prices over the years. The best rooms here are in a two-story white-stucco building with a wide, curving staircase on the outside. They have air-conditioning, tile floors, long verandas or balconies, overhead or standing fans, large bathrooms, and doors that are hand-carved with pre-Columbian motifs. The less expensive rooms are smaller and darker and just have ceiling fans. There is a small free-form pool that's refreshing if you don't want to walk across the street to the beach. This place is set on the busiest intersection in Tamarindo, smack-dab in the center of things, and noise can be a problem at times.

Playa Tamarindo, Guanacaste. ©/fax **2653-0140.** Fax 2653-0028. www.zullymar.com. 25 units. $46–$79 (£23–£39) double. Rates higher during peak periods. AE, MC, V. **Amenities:** Restaurant; small pool; laundry service. *In room:* Minifridge, no phone.

Hotel Pasatiempo ✪   A long-standing and highly dependable option, this hotel is set back from the beach a couple of hundred meters in a grove of shady trees. Most rooms are housed in duplex buildings, but each room has its own private patio with a hammock or chairs. Every room has plenty of space, and all have received regular upkeep and remodeling over the years. The two suites are very comfortable and well equipped. Each room bears the name of a different beach, and the bedroom walls feature hand-painted murals. A small yet very inviting pool sits in the center of the complex. The restaurant serves excellent fresh fish, as well as pizza and Tex-Mex specialties. This popular rancho-style affair also has a pool table, a nightly happy hour, cable TV with live sporting events, good snacks, and occasional live music.

Playa Tamarindo, Santa Cruz, Guanacaste. ✆ 2653-0096. Fax 2653-0275. www.hotelpasatiempo.com. 17 units. $99–$129 (£50–£65) double. Rates lower in off season; higher during peak periods. AE, MC, V. **Amenities:** Restaurant; bar; midsize pool; tour desk; laundry service. *In room:* A/C, free Wi-Fi, safe, no phone.

INEXPENSIVE

In addition to the *cabinas* listed below, **Hostal La Botella de Leche** (✆ 2653-0189; www.labotelladeleche.com) and **Tsunami Backpackers** (✆ 2653-0956) are two popular budget options, and the latter also allows camping. Just off the beach, out toward Hotel Capitán Suizo, **Tito's Camping** (no phone) charges $4 to $6 (£2–£3) per person for camping.

Cabinas Marielos ✪ This place is located up a palm-shaded driveway across the road from the beach just before the center of town. Rooms are clean and well maintained, although most are small and simply furnished. Most have air-conditioning. Some of the bathrooms are quite small, but they're clean. There's a kitchen that guests can use, and the lush gardens are beautiful and provide some welcome shade. Common verandas and balconies are cool places to sit and read a book. The staff and owners are incredibly helpful and will make you feel like part of the family—in fact many of them are already family to each other.

Playa Tamarindo, Guanacaste. ✆/fax **2653-0141**. www.cabinasmarieloscr.com. 20 units. $40–$55 (£20–£28) double. Rates include taxes. Rates lower in off season. AE, MC, V. **Amenities:** Tour desk; surfboard rentals. *In room:* No phone.

WHERE TO STAY IN PLAYA GRANDE

In addition to the places listed below, **Hotel Bula Bula** ✪ (✆ 877/658-2880 in the U.S. and Canada, or 2653-0975 in Costa Rica; www.hotelbulabula.com) is another excellent inland option, while the **Playa Grande Surf Camp** (✆ 2653-1074; www.playagrandesurfcamp.com) is geared toward surfers and budget travelers.

Hotel Las Tortugas ✪ *Finds* Playa Grande is best known for the leatherback turtles that nest here, and much of the beach is now part of Las Baulas National Park, which was created to protect the turtles. However, this beach is also very popular with surfers, who make up a large percentage of the clientele at this beachfront hotel. Several of the rooms are quite large, and most have interesting stone floors and shower stalls. The upper suite has a curving staircase that leads to its second room. A few canoes on the nearby estuary are available for gentle paddling among the mangroves.

The owners here led the fight to have the area declared a national park and continue to do everything possible to protect the turtles. As part of the hotel's turtle-friendly design, a natural wall of shrubs and trees shields the beach from the restaurant's light and noise, and the swimming pool is shaped like a turtle. These folks also have a collection of fully equipped apartments located a few blocks inland from the water, and available for weekly or monthly rental.

Playa Grande (A.P. 164, Santa Cruz), Guanacaste. ✆ **2653-0423** or ✆/fax 2653-0458. www.lastortugashotel.com. 11 units. $50–$80 (£25–£40) double; $120 (£60) suite. Rates lower in off season; slightly higher during peak weeks. MC, V. **Amenities:** Restaurant; bar; small pool; Jacuzzi. *In room:* A/C, no phone.

Ripjack Inn ✪ This hotel is located about 100m (328 ft.) inland from the beach, which is reached via a short path. The rooms are all clean and cool, with tile floors, air-conditioning, and private bathrooms. The rooms come in several sizes and a mix of bed arrangements. They feature various Indonesian-inspired and imported design touches. The hotel's restaurant and bar, which is located on the second floor of the octagonal main building, is one of the best restaurants in Playa Grande. The hotel has a large yoga studio, with regular classes for guests and the local community.

Playa Grande, Guanacaste. ℂ **800/808-4605** in the U.S. and Canada, or 2653-0480 in Costa Rica. Fax 2652-9272. www.ripjackinn.com. 8 units. $75–$95 (£38–£48) double. Rates lower in off season; slightly higher during peak weeks. MC, V. **Amenities:** Restaurant; bar; laundry service. *In room:* A/C, free Wi-Fi, coffeemaker, no phone.

WHERE TO DINE

Tamarindo has a glut of stylish and creative restaurants. **Nogui's Café** (ℂ **2653-0029**) is one of the more popular places in town—and rightly so. This simple open-air cafe just off the beach on the small traffic circle serves hearty breakfasts and well-prepared salads, sandwiches, burgers, and casual meals. In the evenings—actually, beginning a bit before sunset—the second floor here becomes the **Sunset Lounge** ⭐, serving up a regularly changing menu of international tapas, small entrees, and sunset views. The **Cala Moresco** ⭐ (ℂ **2653-0214**) restaurant, at the Hotel and Villas Cala Luna (p. 193), is the place to go if you're looking for some good Italian and Mediterranean cuisine served up in an elegant open-air atmosphere. The folks at Cala Luna also have a sushi bar, **La Caletta** (ℂ **2653-0214**).

Finally, I haven't been able to sample it yet, but I'm hearing good things about the Pacific Rim fusion cuisine and general ambience and bar scene at the new **Kahiki Restaurant & Bar** (ℂ **2653-3816**), at the main Iguana Surf outlet on the road to Playa Langosta.

Meanwhile, over on Playa Grande, try **Upstairs** ⭐, the restaurant at the Ripjack Inn (see above), or the **Great Waltini's** ⭐, at the Hotel Bula Bula (see above). Both are excellent restaurants serving fresh seafood and prime meats, cooked with care and creativity.

Dragonfly Bar & Grill ⭐⭐ INTERNATIONAL/FUSION Tucked away on a back street, this restaurant has garnered fast praise and a loyal following with its excellent food and cozy ambience. The menu mixes and matches several cuisines, with the Southwestern United States and Pacific Rim fusion as the strongest influences. There are daily fish and seafood specials, which might range from seared tuna to wood-fired red snapper. If you're in the mood for meat, try the thick-cut pork chop with chipotle apple chutney. The restaurant space itself is a simple open-air affair, with a concrete floor and rough wood tree trunks as support columns. There's an open wood-fired grill and oven on one side, and a popular bar toward the back. They even offer free Wi-Fi throughout the restaurant.

Down a dirt road behind the Hotel Pasatiempo. ℂ 2653-1506. Reservations recommended. Main courses $11–$16 (£6–£8). AE, MC, V. Mon–Sat 6–10pm.

Fiesta del Mar SEAFOOD/COSTA RICAN A popular local spot, just across from the beach, on the popular traffic circle near the center of town, Fiesta del Mar specializes in seafood, steaks, and chicken cooked over a raging wood fire and coals. Try the grilled steak or whole fish in garlic sauce. They also have typical Costa Rican–style roast chicken. The open-air dining area is edged with greenery and has a thatch roof, so it feels very tropical. There's live music by a local marimba band most nights. This is also a good place for an inexpensive Costa Rican breakfast.

On the traffic circle, at the end of the main road. ℂ 2653-0914. Reservations not necessary. Main courses $4–$20 (£2–£10). MC, V. Daily 8am–11pm.

La Laguna del Cocodrilo Bistro ⭐⭐⭐ INTERNATIONAL/FUSION Yet another option for fine dining and fusion cuisine, this small open-air restaurant has impressed me every time I've eaten here. When weather permits, more tables are set up under the trees in their beachfront garden area. Beautiful presentations and creative use of ingredients are the norm. The menu changes regularly, but the chefs always focus on using on the freshest and best ingredients available. One of the best options is the nightly tasting menu, which will feature anywhere from 5 to 7 courses, including dessert (which is always excellent here). The restaurant also has a good wine list, and they keep their bottles properly cool, to compensate for the often unforgiving heat of Guanacaste.

On the main road, toward the north end of Tamarindo. ℂ 2653-3897. Reservations recommended. Main courses $14–$26 (£7–£13). MC, V. Mon–Sat 7:30am–9pm.

Pachanga ★★ INTERNATIONAL   This is another of Tamarindo's standout restaurants. Chef and owner Slomy Koren has earned a fond following for both his consistency and creativity. The open-air dining room is cramped and rustic, and it's a wonder the tiny kitchen can handle the nightly crowds. The contemporary cuisine carries a heavy Mediterranean influence: The seared tuna in a honey chili marinade is always a favorite, as is the seafood pasta with an unexpected lemon vinaigrette sauce. Desserts often feature homemade ice creams and sorbets.

Across from Hotel Pasatiempo. ℂ 8368-6983. Reservations recommended. Main courses $12–$16 (£6–£8). No credit cards. Mon–Sat 6–10pm.

Zully Mar COSTA RICAN/SEAFOOD   This place has one of the most enviable locations, right on the beach and facing the bay, in the center of Tamarindo. The food and menu are not fancy, nor extensive, but the fresh fish and seafood specials are all well prepared and reasonably priced. You can also get a range of Costa Rican standards, as well as decent pizzas. The restaurant is a simple, open-air affair, but there are quite a few tables with good views of the sea.

On the beach, across from the Hotel Zully Mar. ℂ 2653-0023. Main courses $5–$16 (£2.50–£8). MC, V. Daily 7am–10pm.

TAMARINDO AFTER DARK

As a popular surfer destination, Tamarindo has a sometimes raging nightlife. The most happening bars in town are **Babylon** and **La Barra** ★. Other popular spots that go on throughout the week include the **Monkey Bar** at the Best Western Tamarindo Vista Villas (p. 195), and the bar at the **Hotel Pasatiempo** (p. 195). Both of these places have televisions for sporting events and sometimes feature live music. For a chill-out dance scene try the new **Voodoo Lounge,** and for late-night action, head to the local hangout **Rey Sol.**

For those looking for some gaming, there are two casinos in town: the **Jazz Casino,** across from the El Diriá hotel, and the casino at the **Barceló Playa Langosta** resort.

EN ROUTE SOUTH: PLAYA AVELLANAS & PLAYA NEGRA

Heading south from Tamarindo are several as-yet-undeveloped beaches, most of which are quite popular with surfers. Beyond Tamarindo and Playa Langosta are **Playa Avellanas** and **Playa Negra,** both with a few basic *cabinas* catering to surfers.

While these are currently relatively undeveloped, that will all change in the next couple of years. The large golf, residential, and vacation resort complex of **Hacienda Pinilla** (www.haciendapinilla.com) sits above Playa Avellanas. Today, they only have residential units and one small hotel. However, a large JW Marriott is under construction and expected to open by 2010.

WHERE TO STAY

In addition to the places listed below, the **Mono Congo Lodge** (② 2658-8261; www.monocongolodge.com), located just outside of Playa Negra, is a rustically plush option in a lush, forested setting a few hundred yards from the water.

About a 15- to 20-minute drive inland is **Los Altos de Eros** ⭐⭐ (② 8850-4222; www.losaltosdeeros.com) a small, adults-only, luxury hotel and spa.

Cabinas Las Olas   This collection of duplex cabins is a popular surf lodge set in the shade of some tall trees, a couple hundred meters inland from the beach and bordering a mangrove reserve. The rooms are simple but clean and are a good value. Each comes with a private little veranda with a table and some chairs and a hammock. The beach is a long stretch of almost always uncrowded white sand. There are good beach breaks for surfers up and down the shoreline, especially toward the northern end and the Langosta estuary. Mountain bikes and sea kayaks are available for rent.

Playa Avellanas, Santa Cruz, Guanacaste. ② 2658-9315. Fax 2658-9331. www.cabinaslasolas.co.cr. 10 units. $80 (£40) double. Rates lower in off season. MC, V. **Amenities:** Restaurant; bar; laundry service. *In room:* No phone.

Hotel Playa Negra   This collection of thatch-roofed bungalows is right in front of the famous Playa Negra point break. Even if you're not a surfer, you'll appreciate the beautiful beach and coast with its coral and rock outcroppings and calm tide pools. The round bungalows each have one queen-size and two single beds, two desks, a ceiling fan, and a private bathroom. Although they have concrete floors, everything is painted in contrasting pastels and feels quite comfortable. Still, they're a bit pricey for what you get, unless all you're after is proximity to the wave. The restaurant is close to the ocean in a large open-air rancho and serves as a social hub for guests and surfers staying at more basic *cabinas* inland from the beach.

Playa Negra (A.P. 31-5150, Santa Cruz), Guanacaste. ② 2652-9134. Fax 2652-9035. www.playanegra.com. 10 units. $95 (£48) double. Rates lower in off season; higher during peak periods. AE, MC, V. **Amenities:** Restaurant; bar; midsize oval pool; laundry service. *In room:* No phone.

WHERE TO DINE

Lola's ⭐⭐⭐ *Finds* INTERNATIONAL/SEAFOOD   Long loved by locals, the secret is out on Lola's. Named after the owner's 800-pound pet pig—Lola will never be made into bacon—this place serves up top-notch fresh fare in a beautiful open-air beachfront setting. Most of the heavy, homemade wooden tables and chairs are set in the sand, under the intermittent shade of palm trees and large canvas umbrellas. The fresh seared tuna, big healthy salads, and Belgian french fries are the favorites here, alongside the fresh fruit smoothies and delicious sandwiches on just-baked bread. You'll have to come early on weekends to get a good seat.

On the beach, Playa Avellanas. ② 2652-9097. Reservations not accepted. Main courses $6–$18 (£3–£9). No credit cards. Tues–Sun 8am–sunset.

7 Playa Junquillal ⭐

30km (19 miles) W of Santa Cruz; 20km (12 miles) S of Tamarindo

A long, windswept beach that, for most of its length, is backed by grasslands, Playa Junquillal remains a nearly undiscovered gem on an increasingly crowded coast—although this could change at any time. There's really no village to speak of here and the road is rough, so it's a good place to get away from it all and enjoy some unfettered time on a nearly deserted beach. The long stretch of white sand is great for strolling, and the sunsets are superb. When the waves are big, this beach is great for surfing, but can be a little dangerous for swimming. When it's calm, jump right in.

ESSENTIALS

GETTING THERE & DEPARTING   By Plane   The nearest airport with regularly scheduled flights is in Tamarindo (see earlier in this chapter). You can arrange a taxi from the airport to Playa Junquillal. The ride should take around 40 minutes and cost about $40 to $50 (£20–£25).

By Car   Take the Interamerican Highway from San José. Forty-seven kilometers (29 miles) past the turnoff for Puntarenas, you'll see signs and the turnoff for the La Amistad Bridge. After crossing the river, follow the signs for Nicoya and Santa Cruz. Just after leaving the main intersection for Santa Cruz, you'll see a marked turnoff for Playa Junquillal, Ostional, and Tamarindo. The road is paved for 14km (8½ miles), until the tiny village of Veintesiete de Abril. From here, it's another rough 18km (11 miles) to Playa Junquillal.

From Liberia, head south to Santa Cruz on the main road to all the beach towns, passing through Filadelfia and Belén. Then follow the directions above from Santa Cruz.

By Bus   To get here by bus, you must first head to Santa Cruz and, from there, take another bus to Playa Junquillal. Buses depart San José for Santa Cruz roughly every hour between 6am and 6pm from the **Tralapa** bus station (© **2221-7202**) at Calle 20 between avenidas 3 and 5, and from the **Tracopa-Alfaro** bus station (© **2222-2666**) at Calle 14 between avenidas 3 and 5. Trip duration is around 4 hours; the fare is $5.50 (£2.75). Buses leave Santa Cruz for Junquillal at 5 and 10am, and 2:30 and 5:30pm from the town's central plaza. The ride takes about 1 hour, and the one-way fare is $1.80 (90p). Buses depart Playa Junquillal for Santa Cruz daily at 6 and 9am, and 12:30 and 4:30pm.

Always check with your hotel in advance as the schedule of buses between Junquillal and Santa Cruz is notoriously fickle. If you miss the connection, or there's no bus running, you can hire a taxi for the trip to Junquillal for $25 to $40 (£13–£20). From Tamarindo, a taxi should cost $40 to $50 (£20–£25).

WHAT TO DO IN JUNQUILLAL

Other than walking on the beach, surfing, swimming when the surf isn't too strong, and exploring tide pools, there isn't much to do here—which is just fine with me. This beach is ideal for anyone who wants to relax without any distractions. Bring a few good books. You can rent bikes at the Iguanazul Hotel (see below), which is a good way to get up and down to the beach; horseback-riding tours are also popular. If you have a car you explore the coastline just north and south of here, as well.

For surfers, the beach break right in Junquillal is often pretty good. I've also heard that if you look hard enough, there are a few hidden reef and point breaks around.

Several sportfishing boats operate out of Playa Junquillal. Inquire at your hotel or ask at the Iguanazul Hotel. If you want to rent a mountain bike, you can also check in at the Iguanazul. If you want to ride a horse on the beach, call **Paradise Riding** (© **2658-8162**).

Finally, if you want to do some diving, check in with Micke and Maarten at **El Lugarcito** (©/fax **2658-8436**). With advance notice, these folks offer day trips to the Catalina Islands, as well as resort and full-certification courses.

WHERE TO STAY & DINE

All of the hotels listed below have their own restaurants. You can get good pizza, homemade pasta, and fresh seafood at **Pizzería Tatanka** (✆ 2658-8426), which also offers simple rooms at very reasonable rates. It's near the Iguanazul Hotel on your left as you come into Junquillal, and also has good ocean and sunset views. For a more elegant dining experience, also featuring Italian cuisine, try **La Puesta del Sol** (✆ 2658-8442), which is on a hillside overlooking the sea. This is a great place for sunsets. For a change of pace, try **Lak Ampu** (✆ 2658-8339), which serves up Peruvian fare.

MODERATE

Iguanazul Hotel 🌟 Set on a windswept, grassy bluff above a rocky beach, Iguanazul is the biggest, best-equipped, and most happening hotel in Junquillal. The pool—which features a tiny island with a palm tree growing on it—is large, as is the surrounding patio area, and there's also a volleyball court. If you're feeling mellow, head down to one of the quiet coves or grab a hammock set in a covered palapa on the hillside. Guest rooms are spacious and nicely decorated with basket lampshades, wicker furniture, red-tile floors, high ceilings, and blue-and-white-tile bathrooms. Even if you're not staying here, it's a good place to dine; the food is excellent and the sunset views are phenomenal. These folks can also rent out fully equipped houses and condos for longer stays at their neighboring residential project.

Playa Junquillal (A.P. 130-5150, Santa Cruz), Guanacaste. ✆ 2658-8123 or ✆/fax 2658-8235. www.iguanazul.com. 24 units. $70–$110 (£35–£55) double. Rates include continental breakfast. Rates lower in off season. AE, MC, V. **Amenities:** Restaurant; bar; pool; small spa; watersports equipment rental; bike rental; game room; tour desk; laundry service. *In room:* A/C, TV, free Wi-Fi.

INEXPENSIVE

In addition to the lodgings listed below, **Camping Los Malinches** (✆ 2658-8429) has wonderful campsites on fluffy grass amid manicured gardens set on a bluff above the beach. Camping costs $6 (£3) per person, and includes bathroom and shower privileges. You'll see a sign on the right as you drive toward Playa Junquillal, a little bit beyond the Iguanazul Hotel. The campground is located about 1km (½ mile) down this dirt road. These folks also have some simple, rustic rooms.

Hotel El Castillo Divertido This fanciful hotel is a tropical rendition of a classic medieval castle (well, sort of). Ramparts and a turret with a rooftop bar certainly grab the attention of passersby. Guest rooms are fairly small, although rates are fair. Ask for an upstairs room with a balcony. If you don't get one of these, you'll still have a good view from the hotel's rooftop bar, which sometimes features live music, from Latin folk to reggae. The hotel is on a hillside, about 500m (1,640 ft.) from the beach.

Playa Junquillal, Santa Cruz, Guanacaste. ✆/fax 2658-8428. www.costarica-adventureholidays.com. 6 units. $40–$55 (£20–£28) double. Rates lower in off season. AE, MC, V. **Amenities:** Restaurant; bar. *In room:* No phone.

Hotel Hibiscus *Value* Although the accommodations here are simple, the friendly German owner makes sure that everything is always in top shape. The grounds are pleasantly shady, with plenty of flowering tropical flora, and the beach is just across the road. The rooms have cool Mexican-tile floors and firm beds. The service and ambience are excellent for the price range. The restaurant serves very well-prepared international cuisine and fresh seafood at reasonable prices.

Playa Junquillal (A.P. 163-5150, Santa Cruz), Guanacaste. ✆/fax 2658-8437. www.adventure-costarica.com/hibiscus. 4 units. $55 (£28) double. Rates include full breakfast and taxes. MC, V. **Amenities:** Restaurant; laundry service. *In room:* No phone.

8

Puntarenas & the Nicoya Peninsula

The beaches of the Nicoya peninsula don't get nearly as much attention or traffic as those to the north in Guanacaste. However, they are just as stunning, varied, and rewarding. **Montezuma,** with its jungle waterfalls and gentle surf, is the original beach destination out this way. However, it's getting a concerted run for its money from the up-and-coming hot spots of **Malpaís** and **Santa Teresa.**

Farther up the peninsula lie the beaches of **Playa Samara** and **Playa Nosara.** With easy access via paved roads and the time-saving La Amistad River bridge, Playa Samara is one of the coastline's more popular destinations, especially with Ticos looking for a quick and easy weekend getaway. Just north of Samara, Nosara and its neighboring beaches remain remote and sparsely visited, thanks in large part to the horrendous dirt road that separates these distinctly different destinations. However, Nosara is widely known and coveted as one of the country's top **surf spots,** with a host of different beach and point breaks from which to choose.

Nearby **Puntarenas** was once Costa Rica's principal Pacific port. The town bustled and hummed with commerce, fishermen, coffee brokers, and a weekend rush of urban dwellers enjoying some sun and fun at one of the closest beaches to San José. Today, Puntarenas is a run-down shell of its former self. Still, it remains a major fishing port, and the main gateway to the isolated and coveted beaches of the Nicoya Peninsula.

1 Puntarenas

115km (71 miles) W of San José; 191km (118 miles) S of Liberia; 75km (47 miles) N of Playa de Jacó

They say you can't put lipstick on a pig, and this has proven true for Puntarenas. Despite serious investment and the steady influx of cruise ship passengers, Puntarenas has yet to shed its image as a rough-and-tumble, perennially run-down port town. While the seafront **Paseo de los Turistas (Tourist Walk)** has a string of restaurants and souvenir stands, there's really little in this town to interest visitors, and the beach here pales in comparison to almost any other beach destination in the country.

A 16km (10-mile) spit of land jutting into the Gulf of Nicoya, Puntarenas was once Costa Rica's busiest port, but that changed drastically when the government inaugurated nearby Puerto Caldera, a modern container port facility. After losing its shipping business, the city has survived primarily on commercial fishing.

There's a good highway leading all the way from San José, so you can reach Puntarenas (on a good day, with little traffic) in a little more than 2 hours by car, which makes it one of the closest beaches to San José(at least in elapsed time, if not in distance. A

The Nicoya Peninsula

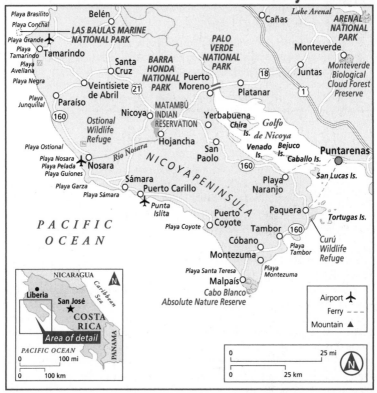

long, straight stretch of sand with gentle surf, the beach is backed for most of its length by the Paseo de los Turistas. Across a wide boulevard from the Paseo de los Turistas are hotels, restaurants, bars, discos, and shops. The sunsets and the views across the Gulf of Nicoya are quite beautiful, and there's usually a cooling breeze blowing in off the water. All around town you'll find unusual old buildings, reminders of the important role that Puntarenas once played in Costa Rican history. It was from here that much of the Central Valley's coffee crop was once shipped, and while the coffee barons in the highlands were getting rich, so were the merchants of Puntarenas.

Puntarenas is primarily popular as a weekend holiday spot for Ticos from San José and is at its liveliest on weekends. Puntarenas is also where you must pick up the ferries to the southern Nicoya Peninsula, and some folks like to arrive the night before and get an early start.

ESSENTIALS

GETTING THERE & DEPARTING   By Car   Head west out of San José on the Interamerican Highway, passing the airport and Alajuela, and follow the signs to Puntarenas. The drive takes between 2 and 2½ hours. To reach Puntarenas from Liberia, just take the Interamerican Highway south, to the well-marked exit for Puntarenas.

Moments   A Colorful Festival

If you're in Puntarenas on the Saturday closest to July 16, you can witness the **Fiesta of the Virgin of the Sea**. During this festival a regatta of colorfully decorated boats carries a statue of Puntarenas's patron saint. Boats run all along the waterfront, but the Paseo de los Turistas makes for a good place to catch the action.

By Bus   **Empresarios Unidos** express buses (© 2222-0064) leave San José daily every hour between 6am and 8pm from Calle 16 and Avenida 12. Trip duration is 2½ hours; the fare is $2.80 (£1.40). The main Puntarenas bus station is cater-cornered to the main pier on the Paseo de los Turistas. Buses to **San José** leave daily every hour between 5am and 8pm. The bus to **Santa Elena** leaves daily at 2pm from a stop across the railroad tracks from the main bus station. Buses to **Quepos** (Manuel Antonio) leave daily at 5 and 11am and 2:30 and 4:30pm.

By Ferry   See "Playa Tambor" or "Playa Montezuma" below for information on crossing and returning from Puntarenas from Paquera or Naranjo on the Nicoya Peninsula.

By Train   One unique option for getting here is to take the train. Although Costa Rica's train system is for the most part nonoperational, the **Tico Train Tour** (© 2233-3300; www.americatravelcr.com) runs the 87km (54-mile) stretch between San José and the nearby port city of Caldera. The train runs very infrequently, and only when there's sufficient demand, but it usually runs most weekends, especially in the high season. The 4-hour ride, including a snack and refreshments, costs $12 (£6).

ORIENTATION   Puntarenas is built on a long, narrow sand spit that stretches 16km (10 miles) out into the Gulf of Nicoya and is marked by only five streets at its widest. The ferry docks for the Nicoya Peninsula are near the far end of town, as are the bus station and market. The north side of town faces an estuary, and the south side faces the mouth of the gulf. The Paseo de los Turistas is on the south side of town, beginning at the pier and extending out to the point.

FAST FACTS   There are several banks, Internet cafes, and general markets all located within a 2-block radius of the town's small church and central park. If you need a taxi, call **Coopetico** (© 2663-2020).

WHAT TO SEE & DO

Take a walk along the **Paseo de los Turistas,** which feels rather like a Florida beach town out of the 1950s. The hotels across the street range in style from converted old wooden homes with bright gingerbread trim to modern concrete monstrosities to tasteful Art Deco relics that need a new coat of paint.

If you venture into the center of the city, be sure to check out the **central plaza around the Catholic church.** The large, stone church itself is interesting because it has portholes for windows, reflecting the city's maritime tradition. It's also one of the few churches in the country with a front entry facing east, as most face west. Here you'll also find the city's cultural center, **La Casa de la Cultura** (© 2661-1394), and the **Museo Histórico Marino** (© 2661-5036), a small museum on the city's maritime history, with exhibits in both English and Spanish. Admission is free, and it's open Monday to Saturday from 8am to 4pm. If you're looking for a shady spot to take a break, there are some inviting benches in a little park off the north side of the church.

The biggest attraction in town is the **Parque Marino del Pacífico (Pacific Marine Park)** (© 2661-5272; www.parquemarino.org), a modest collection of saltwater aquariums highlighting the sea life of Costa Rica. There are 22 separate tanks, with the largest dedicated to re-creating the undersea environment of Isla del Coco. Despite only being a few years old, this park already has a rather neglected and run-down feel to it. This place is located 2 blocks east of the main cruise ship terminal and is open Tuesday through Sunday from 9am to 5pm. Admission is $4 (£2) for adults, and $2 (£1) for children 13 and under.

If you want to go swimming, the ocean waters are now said to be perfectly safe (pollution was a problem for many years), although the beach is still not very attractive. Your best bet is to head back down the spit; just a few kilometers out of town, you'll find **Playa Doña Aña,** a popular beach with picnic tables, restrooms and changing rooms, and a couple of *sodas* (diners). If you head a little farther south, you will come to **Playa Tivives,** which is virtually unvisited by tourists but quite popular with Ticos, many of whom have beach houses up and down this long, brown-sand beach. Surfers can check out the beach break here or head to the mouth of the Barranca River, which boasts an amazingly long left break. Still, surfers and swimmers should be careful; there are crocodiles in both the Barranca and Tivives river mouths, and I'd be wary of pollution in the waters emptying out of the rivers here.

Puntarenas isn't known as one of Costa Rica's prime sportfishing ports, but a few charter boats are usually available. Check at your hotel or head to the docks and ask around. Rates (for up to six people) are usually between $400 and $600 (£200–£300) for a half-day and between $800 and $1,600 (£400–£800) for a full day.

You can also take a yacht cruise through the tiny, uninhabited islands of the Guayabo, Negritos, and Pájaros Islands Biological Reserve. These cruises include a lunch buffet and a relaxing stop on beautiful and undeveloped **Tortuga Island** (★, where you can swim, snorkel, and sunbathe. The water is clear blue, and the sand is bright white. However, this trip has surged in popularity, and many of the tours here have a cattle-car feel. Several San José–based companies offer these excursions, with round-trip transportation from San José, but if you're already in Puntarenas, you might receive a slight discount by boarding here.

Calypso Tours (★ (© 2256-8585; www.calypsotours.com) is the most reputable company that cruises out of Puntarenas. In addition to **Tortuga Island** trips, Calypso Tours takes folks to its own private nature reserve at **Punta Coral** and even on a sunset cruise that includes dinner and some guided stargazing. The Tortuga Island cruise costs $99 (£49) per person, and the Punta Coral trip costs $119 (£60). These prices are the same whether you join them in San José or Puntarenas. If you ask around at the docks, you might find some other boats that ply the waters of the Nicoya Gulf. Some of these companies also offer sunset cruises with live music, snacks, and a bar.

WHERE TO STAY

In addition to the places mentioned below, the former Fiesta Premier Beach Resort has been taken over, remodeled, and rechristened as the **Double Tree Resort Puntarenas** (© 800/222-8733 in the U.S. and Canada, or 2663-0808 in Costa Rica; www.puntarenas.doubletree.com). The all-inclusive resort sits on a decidedly unspectacular

Diving Trips to Isla del Coco (Cocos Island)

This little speck of land located some 480km (300 miles) off the Pacific coast was a prime pirate hide-out and refueling station. Robert Louis Stevenson most likely modeled *Treasure Island* on Cocos. Sir Francis Drake, Captain Edward Davis, William Dampier, and Mary Welch are just some of the famous corsairs who dropped anchor in the calm harbors of this Pacific pearl. They allegedly left troves of buried loot, although scores of treasure hunters over several centuries have failed to unearth more than a smattering of the purported bounty. The Costa Rican flag was first raised here on September 15, 1869. Throughout its history, Isla del Coco has provided anchorage and fresh water to hundreds of ships and has entertained divers and dignitaries. (Franklin Delano Roosevelt visited it three times.) In 1978 it was declared a national park and protected area.

The clear, warm waters around Cocos are widely regarded as one of the most rewarding **dive destinations** ☆☆☆ on this planet. This is a prime place to see schooling herds of scalloped hammerhead sharks. On a recent shallow-water checkout dive—normally, a perfunctory and uninspiring affair—I spotted my first hammerhead lurking just 4.5m (15 ft.) below me within 15 seconds of flipping into the water. Soon there were more, and soon they came much, much closer.

Other denizens of the waters around Isla del Coco include white- and silver-tipped reef sharks; marbled, manta, eagle, and mobula rays; moray and spotted eels; octopi; spiny and slipper lobsters; hawksbill turtles; squirrel

patch of sand, just south of the Puntarenas peninsula. I never much cared for it in its previous incarnation, and while accommodations and service have definitely improved, it's still not a top beach resort pick in my book.

MODERATE

Hotel Alamar ☆   This hotel is easily the most contemporary and luxurious option in town. Located toward the end of the Paseo de los Turistas, more than half of its units are one- or two-bedroom apartments, with fully equipped kitchens. All the rooms are roomy, clean, and modern. Walls are painted in bright primary colors and pastels. The furniture and decor are contemporary. In the center of the hotel complex are a refreshing pool and Jacuzzi. Ample breakfast buffets are served poolside. The best rooms here feature water-facing balconies and Jacuzzi tubs.

Paseo de los Turistas (A.P. 195-5400), Puntarenas. ✆ **2661-4343.** Fax 2661-2726. www.alamarcr.com. 34 units. $105–$128 (£52–£64) double. Rates include buffet breakfast. Rates lower in off season. AE, DC, MC, V. **Amenities:** Restaurant; bar; small pool; Jacuzzi; tour desk; laundry service. *In room:* A/C, TV, free Wi-Fi, minifridge, coffeemaker, hair dryer, iron, safe.

Hotel Las Brisas   Out near the end of the Paseo de los Turistas, you'll find this older, yet well-kept hotel with large air-conditioned rooms, a small pool out front, and the beach right across the street. All the rooms have tile floors, double or twin beds, and small televisions and tables. Large picture windows keep the rooms sunny and fish, trigger fish, and angelfish; surgeon fish, trumpet fish, grouper, grunts, snapper, jack, and tangs; and more. Two of the more spectacular underwater residents here include the red-lipped batfish and the frogfish.

Most diving at Cocos is relatively deep (26–35m/85–115 ft.), and there are often strong currents and choppy swells to deal with—not to mention all those sharks. This is not a trip for novice divers.

The perimeter of Isla del Coco is ringed by steep, forested cliffs punctuated by dozens of majestic waterfalls cascading down in stages or steady streams for hundreds of feet. The island itself has a series of trails that climb its steep hills and wind through its rainforested interior. There are several endemic bird, reptile, and plant species here, including the ubiquitous Cocos finch, which I spotted soon after landing onshore, and the wild Isla del Coco pig.

With just a small ranger station housing a handful of national park guards, Isla del Coco is essentially uninhabited. Visitors these days come on private or charter yachts, fishing boats, or one of the few live-aboard dive vessels that make regular voyages out here. It's a long trip: Most dive vessels take 30 to 36 hours to reach Cocos. Sailboats are even slower.

Both **Aggressor Fleet Limited** (© **800/348-2628** in the U.S. and Canada, or 2257-0191 in Costa Rica; www.aggressor.com) and **Undersea Hunter** (© **800/ 203-2120** in the U.S., or 2228-6613 in Costa Rica; www.underseahunter.com) regularly run dive trips to Isla del Coco from Puntarenas.

bright during the day. There's complimentary coffee and a secure parking lot. The hotel's small open-air restaurant serves Greek specialties, fresh seafood, and other international fare. Personally, I find the rooms here a little more cheery and better maintained than those at the Tioga. But it's a close call.

Paseo de los Turistas (A.P. 83-5400), Puntarenas. © **2661-4040**. Fax 2661-2120. www.lasbrisashotelcr.com. 27 units. $69 (£34) double. Rates lower in off season. AE, DC, MC, V. **Amenities:** Restaurant; bar; small pool; small gym; Jacuzzi; laundry service. *In room:* A/C, TV, free Wi-Fi, safe.

Hotel Tioga This 1950s-style hotel was once the standard-bearer beachfront accommodations in Puntarenas. It's still dependable, but it's showing its age. There's a courtyard with a pool that's been painted bright blue, yet feels slightly claustrophobic. Rooms vary in size and view. The larger, most expensive rooms are attractive, with huge closets, modern bathrooms, and private balconies with a view of the ocean. The smaller, less expensive rooms have louvered, frosted-glass windows to let in lots of light and air while maintaining some privacy. The hotel runs a small casino next door. The beach is across the street, and plenty of restaurants are nearby.

Paseo de los Turistas (A.P. 96-5400), Puntarenas. © **2661-0271** or 2255-3115. Fax 2661-0127. www.hoteltioga.com. 52 units. $64–$126 (£32–£63) double. Rates include breakfast. Rates lower in off season and for extended stays. AE, DC, MC, V. **Amenities:** Restaurant; bar; casino; small pool; tour desk; room service; laundry service. *In room:* A/C, TV, free Wi-Fi, safe.

INEXPENSIVE

Hotel La Punta   Most budget lodgings in Puntarenas are real port-town dives. This place isn't for rock-bottom backpackers, but it's the most appealing and comfortable hotel I've found here for those looking for a relatively inexpensive room. The rooms are spread around the two-story building here. Some are a bit small and spartan. You have to pay a little more for air-conditioning, but you'll almost definitely need it. There's a small pool for cooling off in the day, as well as safe parking and easy access to the ferry terminal and docks.

A.P. 228, Puntarenas (50m/164 ft. south of the ferry terminal). © 2661-0696. 11 units. $40–$60 (£20–£30) double. MC, V. **Amenities:** Restaurant; bar; small pool; laundry service. *In room:* A/C (extra fee), no phone.

WHERE TO DINE

You're in a seaport, so try some of the local catch. *Corvina* (sea bass) is the most popular offering, and it's served in various forms and preparations. My favorite dish on a hot afternoon is ceviche, and you'll find that just about every restaurant in town serves this savory marinated seafood concoction.

The most economical option is to pull up a table at one of the many open-air *sodas* along the Paseo de los Turistas, serving everything from sandwiches, drinks, and ice cream to ceviche and fish meals. Sandwiches are priced at around $2 (£1), and a fish filet with rice and beans should cost around $4 (£2). If you want some seafood in a slightly more formal atmosphere, try the **Jardin Cervecero** or **Casa de los Mariscos,** or the open-air **Restaurant Aloha,** all located on the Paseo de los Turistas.

La Yunta Steakhouse 🐾 *Finds* STEAK/SEAFOOD   This airy place bills itself as a steakhouse, but it has an ample menu of seafood dishes as well. Most of the tables are located on a two-tiered covered veranda at the front of the restaurant, overlooking the street and the ocean just beyond. Overall, this restaurant has the nicest ambience in town. The portions are immense, and the meat is tender and well prepared.

Paseo de los Turistas. © 2661-3216. Reservations recommended in high season and on weekends. Main courses $6–$19 (£3–£10). AE, MC, V. Daily 24 hr.

2 Playa Tambor

150–168km (93–104 miles) W of San José (not including ferry ride); 20km (12 miles) S of Paquera; 38km (24 miles) S of Naranjo

Playa Tambor is home to Costa Rica's first large-scale all-inclusive resort, the Barceló Playa Tambor Beach Resort. Despite big plans, the resort and surrounding area have never really taken off. Though this beach and the two hotels listed below were chosen as the prime locations for the TV show *Temptation Island 2* and got lots of international television exposure, Tambor still has a forgotten, isolated feel to it.

Playa Tambor itself is a long, gently curving stretch of beach protected on either end by rocky headlands. These headlands give the waters ample protection from Pacific swells, making this a good beach for swimming. However, the sand is a rather hard-packed, dull gray-brown color, which often receives a large amount of flotsam and jetsam brought in by the sea. I find the whole beach much less attractive than those located farther south along the Nicoya Peninsula.

Tambor is the site of the only major commuter airport on the southern Nicoya peninsula, and it is here you will be arriving and departing if you choose to visit Montezuma or Malpaís by air.

ESSENTIALS

GETTING THERE & DEPARTING   By Plane   Sansa (© 877/767-2672 in the U.S. and Canada, or 2290-4100 in Costa Rica; www.flysansa.com) flies three times daily to Tambor from San José's Juan Santamaría International Airport, at 8:25 and 11:30am and 12:55pm. These flights depart for San José at 9:05am and 12:10 and 1:40pm. Flight duration is 30 minutes; the fare is $76 (£38) each way.

Nature Air (© 800/235-9272 in the U.S. and Canada, or 2299-6000; www.natureair.com) flies to Tambor daily at 8:10 and 9:40am from Tobías Bolaños International Airport in Pavas. Flight duration is 30 minutes; the fare is $81 (£41) each way. Return flights for San José leave at 8:50 and 10:20am, and 2:50pm. Nature Air also has either direct flights or connecting flights between Tambor and Liberia, Tamarindo, Quepos, Palmar Sur, and Puerto Jiménez.

Taxis are generally waiting to meet most regularly scheduled planes, but if they aren't, you can call Gilberto (© 2642-0241) or Ronald (© 8822-0610) for a cab. The short ride into Tambor should cost around $4 (£2).

By Car   The traditional route here is to take the Interamerican Highway from San José to Puntarenas and catch the ferry to either Naranjo or Paquera. Tambor is about 30 minutes south of Paquera and about an hour and 20 minutes south of Naranjo. The road from Paquera to Tambor is paved and usually in pretty good shape, and taking the Paquera ferry will save you time and some rough, dusty driving. The road from Naranjo to Paquera is all dirt and gravel and often in very bad shape.

Car ferries to Paquera leave Puntarenas roughly every 2 hours between 5am and 8:30pm. The trip takes 1½ hours. **ADIP Ferry Peninsular** (© 2641-0515) and **Naviera Tambor** (© 2661-2084) are two competing ferry companies, which more or less alternate departures. The fare is around $9 to $12 (£4.50–£6) per car; $1 to $2 (50p–£1) per adult, and 70¢ to $1 (35p–50p) for children. The ADIP ferries are less expensive than those run by Naviera Tambor. I recommend arriving early during the peak season and on weekends because lines can be long; if you miss the ferry, you'll have to wait around 2 hours or more for the next one. Moreover, the ferry schedule changes frequently, with fewer ferries during the low season, and the occasional extra ferry added during the high season to meet demand. It's always best to check in advance.

The **Naranjo ferry** (© 2661-1069) leaves daily at 6:30 and 10am and 2:30 and 7pm. The trip takes 1½ hours. Return ferries leave Naranjo for Puntarenas daily at 8am and 12:30, 5:30, and 9pm. The fare is $9 (£4.50) for cars, $1.80 (90p) for adults, and 80¢ (40p) for children.

Another option is to drive via the La Amistad Bridge over the Tempisque River. I only recommend this route when the ferries are on the fritz, or when the wait for the next ferry that your car will fit on is over 2 hours. (When the lines are long, you may not find room on the next departing ferry.) Although heading farther north and crossing the bridge is more circuitous, you will be driving the whole time, which beats waiting around in the midday heat of Puntarenas. To go this route, take the Interamerican Highway west from San José. Forty-seven kilometers (29 miles) past the turnoff for Puntarenas, turn left for the La Amistad Bridge. After you cross the Tempisque River, head to Quebrada Honda and then south to Route 21, following signs for San Pablo, Jicaral, Lepanto, Playa Naranjo, and Paquera.

The car ferry from Paquera to Puntarenas leaves roughly every 2 hours between 8am and 9pm. *Note:* If you have to wait for the ferry, do not leave your car unattended, since break-ins are common.

To drive to Tambor from Liberia, head out of town on the main road to the Guanacaste beaches, passing through Filadelfia, Santa Cruz, and Nicoya on your way toward the turnoff for the La Amistad Bridge. Continue straight at this turnoff, and follow the directions for this route as listed above.

By Bus & Ferry   **Transportes Rodriguez Hermanos** (℗ 2642-0219) runs three daily direct buses between San José and Cobano, dropping passengers off in Tambor en route. The buses leave from the Coca Cola bus terminal at Calle 12 and Avenida 5 at 7:30 and 11:30am and 3:30pm. The fare is around $10 (£5), including the ferry ride, and the trip takes a little over 4 hours.

Alternately, it takes two buses and a ferry ride to get to Tambor. **Empresarios Unidos** express buses (℗ 2222-0064) for Puntarenas leave San José daily every hour between 6am and 8pm from Calle 16 and Avenida 12. Trip duration is 2½ hours; the fare is $2.80 (£1.40).

From Puntarenas, you can take one of the car ferries mentioned above or the passenger launch *Don Bernardiono* or **Paquereña** (℗ 2641-0515), which leaves from the pier behind the market at 11:30am and 4pm. Ferry-trip duration is 1½ hours; the fare is 80¢ (40p). A bus south to Montezuma (this will drop you off in Tambor) will be waiting to meet the ferry when it arrives in Paquera. The bus ride takes about 35 minutes; the fare is $2 (£1). Be careful not to take the Naranjo ferry because it does not meet with regular onward bus transportation to Tambor.

When you're ready to head back, buses originating in Montezuma, Cobano, or Malpaís pass through Tambor at least every 2 hours between 6am and 4:30pm. The Paquereña ferry returns for Puntarenas at 7:30am and 2pm, but you can also hop any of the car ferries listed above. Total trip duration is 3½ hours. Buses to San José leave Puntarenas daily every hour between 5am and 8pm.

ORIENTATION   Although there's a tiny village of Tambor, through which the main road passes, the hotels themselves are scattered along several kilometers, with Tango Mar (see below), definitively outside of Tambor proper. You'll see signs for all these hotels as the road passes through and beyond Playa Tambor.

If you need a bank, pharmacy, or post office, you'll have to head to nearby Cóbano.

FUN ON & OFF THE BEACH

Curú Wildlife Refuge ☆ (℗ 2641-0004; www.curuwildliferefuge.com), 16km (10 miles) north of Tambor, is a private reserve that has several pretty, secluded beaches, as well as forests and mangrove swamps. This area is extremely rich in wildlife. Howler and white-faced monkeys are often spotted here, as are quite a few species of birds. You can usually spot scarlet macaws, and the refuge is actively involved in a macaw protection and repopulation effort. Admission for the day is $8 (£4) per person. Horses are available to rent for $10 (£5) per hour. There are also some rustic cabins available with advance notice for $30 (£15) per person per day, including the entrance and three square meals. If you don't have a car, you should arrange pickup with the folks who manage this refuge. Or you could hire a taxi in Paquera to take you there for around $7 (£3.50).

Both the hotels listed below offer horseback riding and various tours around this part of the peninsula and can arrange fishing and dive trips. If you want to rent an ATV for some land exploration, or a jet ski for some on-the-water fun, head to **Free Willy Tours** (℗ 8857-4857), which is on the beach right in the center of town.

WHERE TO STAY & DINE

Aside from the hotels listed here, there are a few inexpensive *cabinas* available near the town of Tambor, at the southern end of the beach. Of these, your best bet is **Hotel Dos Largatos** (𝄞/fax **2683-0236**), located right on the beach next to Tambor Tropical. Another option is **Costa Coral** 𝄞 (𝄞 **2683-0105;** www.costacoral.com), a very attractive place with a good restaurant. This place would be my top choice in Tambor, except it's unfortunately set right off the busy main road here, several hundred meters from the beach.

The **Barceló Playa Tambor Beach Resort** (𝄞 **2683-0303;** www.barcelo.com) was Costa Rica's first all-inclusive resort, but its beach is mediocre at best, and the Barceló company has been accused of violating Costa Rica's environmental laws, ignoring zoning regulations, and mistreating workers. So although this resort is a major presence here, I don't recommend it; there are much better all-inclusive options available farther north in Guanacaste.

Tambor Tropical 𝄞   This is one of the more architecturally interesting hotels around. The rooms here are located in five two-story octagonal cabins, and the whole place is an orgy of varnished hardwoods, with purple heart and cocobolo offsetting each other at every turn. The rooms are enormous and come with large, complete kitchens and a spacious sitting area. The walls are, in effect, nothing but shuttered picture windows, which give you the choice of gazing out at the ocean or shutting in for a bit of privacy. The upstairs rooms have large wraparound verandas, and the lower rooms have garden-level decks. The beach is only steps away. Plenty of coconut palms and flowering plants provide a very tropical feel.

Tambor, Puntarenas (mailing address: 867 Liberty St. NE, Salem, OR 97301). 𝄞 **866/890-2537** in the U.S., or 2683-0011 in Costa Rica. Fax 2683-0013. www.tambortropical.com. 12 units. $165–$190 (£83–£95) double. Rates include continental breakfast. AE, MC, V. No children 15 and under. **Amenities:** Restaurant; bar; small free-form tile pool and Jacuzzi; small spa; tour desk; laundry service. *In room:* Free Wi-Fi, kitchenette, fridge, coffeemaker, iron, no phone.

Tango Mar Resort 𝄞𝄞   Tango Mar was *the* original luxury resort in this neck of the woods, and it's still a great place to get away from it all. With only 18 rooms and scattered suites and villas, there are never any crowds. If you choose to go exploring, you'll find seaside cliffs and a beautiful nearby waterfall that pours into a tide pool. The rooms have big balconies and glass walls to soak up ocean views; some even have their own Jacuzzis. The suites are set back among shade trees and flowering vegetation. Most come with carved four-poster canopy beds and indoor Jacuzzis. The villas are all different, spacious, and relatively secluded. Some suites and villas are a bit far from the beach and main hotel, so you'll need either your own car or one of the hotel's gas-powered golf carts. In addition to a 9-hole par-3 golf course and two lighted tennis courts, the hotel has a small spa and yoga space to keep you fit and busy.

Playa Tambor, Puntarenas. 𝄞 **866/770-7383** in the U.S., or 2683-0001 in Costa Rica. Fax 2683-0003. www.tangomar. com. 18 units, 17 suites, 3 villas. $180 (£90) double; $230 (£115) suite; $450–$1,000 (£225–£500) villa. Rates include breakfast. Rates slightly lower during the off season, higher during peak weeks. AE, DC, MC, V. **Amenities:** Restaurant; bar; 3 small pools; small spa; 9-hole par-3 golf course ($20/£10 full-day greens fee) w/wonderful sea views; 2 lighted tennis courts; limited watersports equipment rental; bike rental; tour desk; limited room service; in-room massage; laundry service. *In room:* A/C, TV, minibar, safe.

3 Playa Montezuma ★★

166–184km (103–114 miles) W of San José (not including the ferry ride); 36km (22 miles) SE of Paquera; 54km (33 miles) S of Naranjo

Montezuma still feels worlds apart from most other beach destinations in Guanacaste and Nicoya. For years, this remote village and its surrounding beaches, forests, and waterfalls have enjoyed near-legendary status among backpackers, UFO seekers, hippie expatriates, and European budget travelers. Although it maintains its alternative vibe, Montezuma is a great destination for all manner of travelers looking for a beach retreat surrounded by some stunning scenery. As with the rest of Guanacaste and Nicoya, the town is booming, and there are lodgings of value and quality in all price ranges. Active pursuits abound, from hiking in the Cabo Blanco Absolute Nature Reserve to horseback riding to a beachside waterfall. The natural beauty, miles of almost abandoned beaches, rich wildlife, and jungle waterfalls here are what first made Montezuma famous, and they continue to make this one of my favorite beach towns in Costa Rica.

ESSENTIALS

GETTING THERE & DEPARTING   By Plane   The nearest airport is in Tambor, 17km (11 miles) away (see "Playa Tambor," above, for details). Some of the hotels listed below might pick you up in Tambor for a reasonable fee. If not, you'll have to hire a taxi, which could cost anywhere between $20 and $30 (£10–£15). **Taxis** are generally waiting to meet most regularly scheduled planes, but if they aren't, you can call Gilberto (© **2642-0241**) or Ronald (© **8822-0610**) for one.

By Car   The traditional route here is to take the Interamerican Highway from San José to Puntarenas and catch the ferry to either Naranjo or Paquera. Montezuma is about 30 minutes south of Tambor, 1 hour south of Paquera, and about 2 hours south of Naranjo. The road from Paquera to Tambor is paved and usually in pretty good shape, and taking the Paquera ferry will save you time and some rough, dusty driving. The road from Naranjo to Paquera is all dirt and gravel and often in very bad shape.

Ferries to Paquera leave Puntarenas roughly every 2 hours between 5am and 8:30pm. The trip takes 1½ hours. **ADIP Ferry Peninsular** (© **2641-0515**) and **Naviera Tambor** (© **2661-2084**) are two competing ferry companies, who more or less alternate departures. The fare is around $9 to $12 (£4.50–£6) per car; $1 to $2 (50p–£1) per adult, and 70¢ to $1 (35p–50p) for children. The ADIP ferries are less expensive than those run by Naviera Tambor. I recommend arriving early during the peak season and on weekends because lines can be long; if you miss the ferry, you'll have to wait around 2 hours or more for the next one. Moreover, the ferry schedule changes frequently, with fewer ferries during the low season, and the occasional extra ferry added during the high season to meet demand. It's always best to check in advance.

The **Naranjo ferry** (© **2661-1069**) leaves daily at 6:30 and 10am and 2:30 and 7pm. The trip takes 1½ hours. Return ferries leave Naranjo for Puntarenas daily at 8am and 12:30, 5:30, and 9pm. The fare is $9 (£4.50) for cars, $1.80 (90p) for adults, and 80¢ (40p) for children.

Another option is to drive via the La Amistad bridge. I only recommend this route when the ferries are on the fritz, or when the wait for the next ferry is over 2 hours. (Note that, when the lines are long, you may not find room on the next departing ferry.) Although heading farther north and crossing the bridge is more circuitous, you will be driving the whole time, which beats waiting around in the midday heat of Puntarenas. To go this route, take the Interamerican Highway west from San José. Forty-seven kilometers (29 miles) past the turnoff for Puntarenas, turn left for the La Amistad bridge. After you cross the Tempisque River, head to Quebrada Honda and then south to Route 21, following signs for San Pablo, Jicaral, Lepanto, Playa Naranjo, and Paquera.

The car ferry from Paquera to Puntarenas leaves roughly every 2 hours between 8am and 9pm. *Note:* If you have to wait for the ferry, do not leave your car unattended, since break-ins are common.

To drive to Montezuma from Liberia, head out of town on the main road to the Guanacaste beaches, passing through Filadelfia, Santa Cruz, and Nicoya on your way toward the turnoff for the La Amistad bridge. Continue straight at this turnoff, and follow the directions for this route as listed above.

By Bus & Ferry   Transportes Rodriguez Hermanos (© **2642-0219**) runs three daily direct buses between San José and Montezuma. The buses leave from the Coca Cola bus terminal at Calle 12 and Avenida 5 at 7:30 and 11:30am and 3:30pm. The fare is around $10 (£5), including the ferry ride, and the trip takes a little over 4 hours.

Alternately, it takes two buses and a ferry ride to get to Montezuma. **Empresarios Unidos** express buses (© **2222-0064**) for Puntarenas leave San José daily every hour between 6am and 8pm from Calle 16 and Avenida 12. Trip duration is 2½ hours; the fare is $2.80 (£1.40).

From Puntarenas, you can take one of the car ferries mentioned above or the passenger launch *Don Bernardino* or *Paquereña* (© **2641-0515**), which leaves from the pier behind the market at 11:30am and 4pm. Ferry-trip duration is 1½ hours; the fare is 80¢ (40p). A bus south to Montezuma will be waiting to meet the ferry when it arrives in Paquera. The bus ride takes about 55 minutes; the fare is $2.50 (£1.25). Be careful not to take the Naranjo ferry because it does not meet with regular onward bus transportation to Montezuma.

Buses are met by hordes of locals trying to corral you to one of the many budget hotels. Remember, they are getting a commission for everybody they bring in, so their information is biased. Not only that, they are often flat-out lying when they tell you the hotel you wanted to stay in is full.

When you're ready to head back, direct buses leave Montezuma at 4:30 and 8:30am, and 2:30pm. Regular local buses to Paquera leave Cóbano roughly every 2 hours throughout the day starting around 4am. The Paquereña ferry returns for Puntarenas at 7:30am and 2pm. Total trip duration is 3½ hours. Buses to San José leave Puntarenas daily every hour between 5am and 8pm.

ORIENTATION   As the winding mountain road that descends into Montezuma bottoms out, you turn left onto a small dirt road that defines the village proper. On this 1-block road, you will find El Sano Banano Village Cafe and, across from it, a small shady park with plenty of tall trees, as well as a basketball court and children's playground. The bus stops at the end of this road. From here, hotels are scattered up and down the beach and around the village's few sand streets.

There are several tour agencies and Internet cafes clustered among the restaurants and souvenir stores around the center of town.

FUN ON & OFF THE BEACH

The ocean here is a gorgeous royal blue, and beautiful beaches stretch out along the coast on either side of town. Be careful, though: The waves can occasionally be too rough for casual swimming, and you need to be aware of stray rocks at your feet. Be sure you know where the rocks and tide are before doing any bodysurfing. The best places to swim are a couple hundred meters north of town in front of **El Rincón de los Monos,** or several kilometers farther north at Playa Grande.

If you're interested in more than simple beach time, head for the **Montezuma waterfall** *✦* just south of town—it's one of those tropical fantasies where water comes pouring down into a deep pool. It's a popular spot, and it's a bit of a hike up the stream. There are actually a couple of waterfalls up this stream, but the upper falls are by far the more spectacular. You'll find the trail to the falls just over the bridge south of the village (on your right just past Las Cascadas restaurant). At the first major outcropping of rocks, the trail disappears and you have to scramble up the rocks and river for a bit. A trail occasionally reappears for short stretches. Just stick close to the stream and you'll eventually hit the falls.

Note: Be very careful when climbing close to the rushing water, and also if you plan on taking any dives into the pools below. The rocks are quite slippery, and several people each year get very scraped up, break bones, and otherwise hurt themselves here.

Another popular local waterfall is **El Chorro** *✦*, located 8km (5 miles) north of Montezuma. This waterfall cascades down into a tide pool at the edge of the ocean. The pool here is a delightful mix of fresh- and seawater, and you can bathe while gazing out over the sea and rocky coastline. When the water is clear and calm, this is one of my favorite swimming holes in all of Costa Rica. However, a massive landslide in 2004 filled in much of this pool and also somewhat lessened the drama and beauty of the falls. Moreover, the pool here is dependent upon the tides—it disappears entirely at very high tide. It's about a 2-hour hike along the beach to reach El Chorro. Alternatively you can take a horseback tour here (see below).

ON THE WING   For an intimate look at the life cycle and acrobatic flights-of-fancy of butterflies, head to the new **Mariposario Montezuma Gardens** (*✆* 8888-4200). This is perhaps the most wild and natural feeling of all the butterfly gardens in Costa Rica. Wooden walkways wind through thick vegetation under black screen meshing. Most of the butterflies in the enclosure are self-reproducing, and there are trails through open forested areas outside the enclosure, where you can also see butterflies and other wildlife. Located along the dirt road heading up hill just beyond the entrance to the waterfall trail, this place is open daily from 8am to 4pm. Admission is $8 (£4), and includes a guided tour. These folks also have a few pretty rooms they rent out, or give to volunteers in exchange for work around the gardens.

Tips **Buy the Book . . . or Just Borrow It**

If you came unprepared or ran out of reading material, check in at **Librería Topsy** (*✆* 2642-0576), which, in addition to selling books, runs a lending library and serves as the local post office. These folks have also opened a branch up in Cabuya.

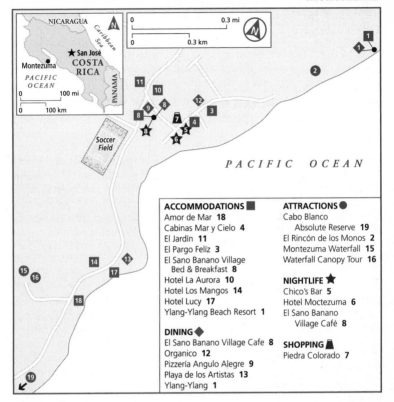

HORSEBACK RIDING Several people around the village will rent you horses for around $8 to $12 (£4–£6) an hour, although most people choose to do a guided 4-hour horseback tour for $30 to $40 (£15–£20). Any of the hotels or tour agencies in town can arrange it for you, or you can look for "Roger, the horse guy"—any local can direct you to him. However, you'll find the best-cared-for and best-kept horses at **Finca Los Caballos** ⚲ (✆ **2642-0124**), which is up the hill on the road leading into Montezuma.

OTHER ACTIVITIES There are some shops in the center of the village where you can rent a bicycle by the day or hour, as well as boogie boards and snorkeling equipment (although the water must be very calm for snorkeling).

A range of guided tour and adventure options is available in Montezuma. **CocoZuma Traveller** (✆ **2642-0911;** www.cocozuma.com) and **Montezuma Travel Adventures** (✆ **2642-0808;** www.montezumatraveladventures.com) can both arrange horseback riding, boat excursions, scuba-dive and snorkel tours, ATV outings, and rafting trips; car and motorcycle rentals; airport transfers; international phone, fax, and Internet service; and currency exchange.

One popular tour option here is the **Waterfall Canopy Tour** ⚲ (✆ **8823-6111** or 2642-0808), which is built right alongside Montezuma's famous falls. The tour, which features 9 cables connecting 11 platforms, includes a swim at the foot of the falls and costs $40 (£20) per person.

There are plenty of simple souvenir stores, as well as itinerant artisans selling their wares on the street, but it's worth stopping in at **Piedra Colorado** (© 8841-5855) to check out their impressive silver, stone, and polished-shell creations. This place is located in the tiny strip mall in the center of Montezuma.

AN EXCURSION TO CABO BLANCO NATURE RESERVE

As beautiful as the beaches around Montezuma are, the beaches at **Cabo Blanco Absolute Nature Reserve** ★★, 11km (6¾ miles) south of the village, are even more stunning. Located at the southernmost tip of the Nicoya Peninsula, Cabo Blanco is a national park that preserves a nesting site for brown pelicans, magnificent frigate birds, and brown boobies. The beaches are backed by a lush tropical forest that is home to howler monkeys. You can hike through the preserve's lush forest right down to the deserted, pristine beach, which is 4km (2½ miles) away. Or you can take a shorter 2km (1¼-mile) loop trail through the primary forest here. This is Costa Rica's oldest official bioreserve and was set up thanks to the pioneering efforts of conservationists Karen Mogensen and Nicholas Wessberg. Admission is $10 (£4.85); the reserve is closed on Monday and Tuesday.

On your way out to Cabo Blanco, you'll pass through the tiny village of **Cabuya.** Some very basic *cabinas* and hotels have sprung up out here, and there are a couple of hidden patches of beach to discover if you poke around some of the deserted dirt roads.

Shuttle buses head from Montezuma to Cabo Blanco roughly every 2 hours beginning at 8am, and then turn around and bring folks from Cabo Blanco to Montezuma; the last one leaves Cabo Blanco around 5pm. The fare is $2 (£1) each way. These shuttles often don't run during the off season. Alternatively, you can share a taxi: The fare is around $15 to $20 (£7.50–£10) per taxi, which can hold four or five passengers. Taxis tend to hang around Montezuma center. One dependable *taxista* is **Gilberto Rodríguez** (© 2642-0241).

WHERE TO STAY
VERY EXPENSIVE

Ylang Ylang Beach Resort ★★ *(Finds)*   Set in a lush patch of forest just steps away from the sand, this hotel boasts rooms and cabins in a variety of shapes and sizes. Coco Joe's Rancho is the largest cabin and features a luscious wraparound balcony and a small sleeping loft. But I also like the smaller cabins, which are ferroconcrete geodesic domes that look like igloos. These have both indoor and outdoor garden showers that match the surroundings perfectly. There are also spacious suites with private balconies and sleeping lofts in a separate building, with standard rooms on the ground floor below them. The newest rooms are the "jungalows," large tents set up on a wooden platform, featuring an indoor sink, small fridge, ceiling fan, either one king-size or two twin beds, and a private deck. These units share nearby bathrooms and showers. A beautiful swimming pool with a sculpted waterfall is on-site, and the whole operation is set amid lush gardens. You cannot drive in and out of the hotel, so arrival and check-in are handled at the downtown El Sano Banano Village Cafe (see below).

Montezuma, Cóbano de Puntarenas. © **2642-0636.** Fax 2642-0068. www.ylangylangresort.com. 26 units. $210–$315 (£105–£158) double. Rates include breakfast and dinner. Rates lower in off season. AE, MC, V. **Amenities:** Restaurant; bar; midsize outdoor pool; tour desk; in-room massage; laundry service. *In room:* Free Wi-Fi, fridge, coffeemaker, hair dryer, safe, no phone.

MODERATE

The El Sano Banano folks also run an in-town B&B (© **2642-0636;** www.el banano.com), just off the popular restaurant (see below). The rooms here feature air-conditioning and satellite televisions; because of the design, you are basically forced to use the air-conditioning. Rooms here go for $75 (£38) double, including breakfast.

El Jardin   Set on a steep hill, right on the crossroads leading into "downtown," this is a good choice if you're looking for a comfortable and well-equipped room close to the action. The rooms are located in a series of different buildings spread across the hillside. Number 9 is my favorite, with pretty stone work in the bathroom, a greater sense of privacy than some of the others, and a good view from its private terrace. There's a two-level pool and Jacuzzi in a relaxing little garden area. Although the hotel doesn't have a restaurant, the town and its many dining options are just steps away.

Montezuma. ©/fax **2642-0074.** © 2642-0548. www.hoteleljardin.com. 15 units. $80–$95 (£40–£48) double. Rates lower in off season. MC, V. **Amenities:** Small pool; Jacuzzi; tour desk; laundry service. *In room:* A/C, minifridge, safe, no phone.

Nature Lodge Finca Los Caballos ⭐   This lodge is on a high ridge about 3km (1¾ miles) above Montezuma. The rooms are simple, yet elegant. Spanish-style tile roofs, hardwood trim, stone floors, and some pretty paintings and craft works add decorative accents. Every room has a private patio or balcony with either a garden, jungle, or ocean view. The best rooms are the Superior Pacific Rooms, which feature ocean views out across the forested hills below. There's a small pool here, and plenty of hammocks strung around for relaxing. The restaurant serves creative, well-prepared meals using fresh and natural ingredients.

Finca Los Caballos translates to "horse ranch," and riding is taken seriously by the hotel. The owners have 16 hectares (40 acres) of land and access to many neighboring ranches and trail systems. Standard trips to Montezuma's waterfalls are available, as well as a host of other adventure-tour options. Be forewarned: If you stay here, it's a quick car ride, but very hefty hike, especially on the way back, to the beach.

Montezuma, (A.P. 22, Cóbano de Puntarenas). © **2642-0124.** ©/fax 2642-0664. www.naturelodge.net. 12 units. $86–$138 (£43–£69) double. Rates include breakfast. Rates lower in off season. MC, V. **Amenities:** Restaurant; small pool; horse rental and tours; tour desk; laundry service. *In room:* Minifridge, safe, no phone.

INEXPENSIVE

Now that camping on the beach is discouraged (although many folks still get away with it), most campers make do at **El Rincón de los Monos** (© 2642-0048), which is about 90m (295 ft.) north of town along the beach. It charges about $3 (£1.50) per tent and provides showers and bathrooms. Others head south toward Cabuya and Cabo Blanco. **El Pargo Feliz** (© 2642-0065) and **Cabinas Mar y Cielo** (© 2642-0261) are two good budget options right in the center of town.

Amor de Mar ⭐ *Value*   This hotel has a wonderful setting overlooking the ocean. With its wide expanse of neatly trimmed grass sloping down to the sea, tide pools (one of which is as big as a small swimming pool), and hammocks slung from the mango trees, this is the perfect place for anyone who wants to do some serious relaxing. The rooms are housed in a beautifully appointed two-story building, which abounds in varnished hardwoods. Although simply appointed, most rooms have plenty of space and receive lots of sunlight. Five of them have air-conditioning. My favorite room is no. 5, which now has exclusive access to a long second-floor balcony with a superb ocean view. Breakfast and lunch only are served here on a beautiful open-air patio overlooking the sea. The breakfast specialties include big banana pancakes and fresh homemade whole-wheat French bread. These folks also rent out a large fully equipped two-story, four-bedroom house next to the hotel.

Montezuma, (A.P. 22, Cóbano de Puntarenas). ℭ/fax **2642-0262**. www.amordemar.com. 11 units, 9 with private bathroom. $45–$55 (£23–£28) double with shared bathroom; $70–$90 (£35–£45) double with private bathroom; $170 (£85) house. Rates lower in off season. V. **Amenities:** Restaurant; laundry service. *In room:* No phone.

Hotel La Aurora   Just to the left as you enter the village of Montezuma, you'll find this long-standing hotel. The rooms are spread out over three floors in two neighboring buildings fronting the village's small park and playground. All rooms are clean and well-kept. There's a two-room apartment on the third floor here, with a private balcony and a bit of an ocean view through the treetops. The hotel also features a couple of common sitting areas, a small lending library, some hammocks and comfortable chairs for chilling out in, a communal kitchen, and flowering vines growing up the walls. In fact, there are plants and vines all over La Aurora, which keeps things cool and gives the place a fitting tropical feel. Fresh coffee, tea, and hearty breakfasts are served each morning.

Montezuma (A.P. 2), Cóbano de Puntarenas. ℭ/fax **2642-0051**. www.playamontezuma.net. 18 units. $45–$70 (£23–£35) double. Rates include taxes. Rates lower in off season. AE, MC, V. **Amenities:** Laundry service. *In room:* A/C, TV, minifridge, no phone.

Hotel Los Mangos   Across the road from the water, a bit before the waterfall on the road toward Cabo Blanco, this place takes its name from the many mango trees under which the bungalows are built. (If mango is your passion, come in May, when it's in season.) The shared-bathroom budget rooms are very basic, but they are a decent value and you get access to the pool to boot. However, the octagonal bungalows built of Costa Rican hardwoods are the better accommodations here. Each has a small porch with rocking chairs, a thatched roof, a good amount of space, and ceiling fans. The swimming pool is built to resemble a natural pond—there's even an artificial waterfall flowing into it—and there's a separate Jacuzzi. The former restaurant here has been converted into a yoga studio, and daily yoga classes are offered.

Montezuma, Cóbano de Puntarenas. ℭ **2642-0076**. Fax 2642-0259. www.hotellosmangos.com. 10 units, 6 with private bathroom; 9 bungalows. $35 (£18) double with shared bathroom; $70 (£35) double with private bathroom; $82 (£41) bungalow. Rates lower in off season. AE, DC, MC, V. **Amenities:** Small pool; yoga studio, Jacuzzi; laundry service. *In room:* Safe, no phone.

Hotel Lucy *Value*   Situated on a pretty section of beach a bit south of town, in front of Los Mangos, this converted two-story wooden home has the best location of any budget lodging in Montezuma. If you can snag a second-floor room with an ocean view, like room no. 19, you'll be in budget heaven. While basic, the rooms are kept clean. The beach here is a bit rough and rocky for swimming, but the sunbathing and sunsets are beautiful.

Montezuma, Cóbano de Puntarenas. ℭ **2642-0273**. 17 units, 6 with bathroom. $16 (£8) double with shared bathroom; $20 (£10) double with private bathroom. No credit cards. **Amenities:** Restaurant; laundry service. *In room:* No phone.

WHERE TO DINE

In addition to the places listed below, you'll find several basic *sodas* and casual restaurants right in the village. My favorite of these is the **Pizzería Angulo Al** (ℭ **2642-0489**), which is at the crossroads into town and serves good thin-crust pizzas, calzones, and pastas. You might also want to check out the Spanish cuisine and fabulous setting at the downtown **Hotel Moctezuma** (© 2642-0657), or the varied international fare at **Cocolores** (© 2642-0348). For breakfast, coffee, and light meals, the new **Organico** (© 8359-4197) is a good option, with a range of healthy sandwiches, daily specials, and fresh baked goods.

El Sano Banano Village Cafe ☆☆ VEGETARIAN/INTERNATIONAL   Delicious vegetarian meals, including nightly specials, sandwiches, and salads, are the specialty of this perennially popular Montezuma restaurant, although there's also a variety of fish and chicken dishes. Lunches feature hefty sandwiches on whole-wheat bread and filling fish and vegetarian *casados.* The natural yogurt fruit shakes are fabulous, but I like to get a little more decadent and have one of the mocha chill shakes.

El Sano Banano also doubles as the local movie house. Nightly DVD releases are projected on a large screen; the selection ranges from first-run to quite artsy, and there's a constantly growing library of more than 800 movies. The movies begin at 7:30pm and require a minimum purchase of $6 (£3).

On the main road into the village. © 2642-0944. Main courses $5–$16 (£2.50–£8). AE, MC, V. Daily 7am–9:30pm.

Playa de los Artistas ☆☆☆ *Finds* ITALIAN/MEDITERRANEAN   This popular open-air restaurant is beside an old house fronting the beach, and there are only a few tables, so arrive early. If you don't get a seat and you feel hearty, try the low wooden table surrounded by tatami mats on the sand. Meals are served in large classy and creative plates, in broad wooden bowls set on ceramic-ringed coasters, or on large wooden planks lined with banana leaves. The menu changes nightly but always features several fish and seafood dishes. The fresh grouper in a black-pepper sauce is phenomenal, as is the *moscardini* polenta, a tasty appetizer of polenta pieces topped with grilled calamari tentacles and pecorino cheese. The outdoor brick oven and grill turns out consistently spectacular grilled fish and seafood. All meals come with plenty of fresh bread for soaking up the delicious sauces.

Across from Hotel Los Mangos. © 2642-0920. Reservations recommended. Main courses $6.50–$14 (£3.25–£7). No credit cards. Mon–Sat noon–4pm and 5:30–9:30pm.

Ylang-Ylang ☆☆ INTERNATIONAL   Located at the Ylang Ylang Beach Resort, this pretty, open-air affair features a sculpted bar with indigenous and wildlife motifs. The menu is broad, with a prominent Asian influence, ranging from sushi to vegetarian teriyaki stir-fry. There are also several crepe and pasta options and plenty of fresh seafood dishes. For lunch you can have a bruschetta or some cool gazpacho and be just a few steps from the sand when you're done.

At the Ylang Ylang Beach Resort. © 2642-0402 or 8833-4106. Reservations recommended. Main courses $7–$21 (£3.50–£11). AE, MC, V. Daily 7am–10pm.

MONTEZUMA AFTER DARK

Montezuma has had a tough time coming to terms with its nightlife. For years, local businesses banded together to force most of the loud, late-night activity out of town. This has eased somewhat, and there's currently quite an active nightlife in Montezuma proper. The local action seems to base itself either at **Chico's Bar** ☆ or at the bar at the **Hotel Montezuma.** Both are located on the main strip in town facing the water. If your evening tastes are mellower, **El Sano Banano Village Cafe** (p. 219) doubles as the local movie house, with nightly late-run features projected on a large screen.

4 Malpaís & Santa Teresa ★★

150km (93 miles) W of San José; 12km (7½ miles) S of Cóbano

Malpaís (or Mal País) means "badlands," and, while this may have been an apt moniker several years ago, it no longer accurately describes this booming beach area. Malpaís is a bucket term often used to refer to a string of neighboring beaches running from south to north, and including Malpaís, Playa Carmen, Santa Teresa, Playa Hermosa, and Playa Manzanillo. To a fault, these beaches are long, wide expanses of light sand dotted with rocky outcroppings. Currently, this area is one of Costa Rica's hottest spots, and hotels and restaurants are opening at a dizzying pace. Still, it will take some time before this place is anything like more developed destinations like Tamarindo or Manuel Antonio. In Malpaís and Santa Teresa today, you'll find a mix of beach hotels and resorts, restaurants, shops, and private houses, as well as miles of nearly deserted beach, and easy access to some nice jungle and the nearby **Cabo Blanco Nature Reserve** (p. 216).

ESSENTIALS

GETTING THERE & DEPARTING   By Plane   The nearest airport is in Tambor (see "Playa Tambor," p. 208, for flight details). Some of the hotels listed below might be willing to pick you up in Tambor for a reasonable fee. If not, you'll have to hire a taxi, which could cost anywhere between $30 and $40 (£15–£20). **Taxis** are generally waiting to meet most regularly scheduled planes, but if they aren't, you can call **Miguel** (© 8819-9021 or 2640-0261) or **Richard** (© 2640-0003) for a cab.

By Car   Follow the directions above to Montezuma (see "Playa Montezuma," earlier in this chapter). At Cóbano follow the signs to Malpaís and Playa Santa Teresa. It's another 12km (7½ miles) down a rough dirt road that requires four-wheel-drive much of the year, especially during the rainy season.

To drive to Malpaís from Liberia, head out of town on the main road to the Guanacaste beaches, passing through Filadelfia, Santa Cruz, and Nicoya on your way toward the turnoff for the La Amistad Bridge. Continue straight at this turnoff, and follow the directions for this route as listed above.

By Bus & Ferry   Transportes Rodriguez Hermanos (© 2642-0740 or 2642-0219) has three daily buses from San José's Coca-Cola bus station to Malpaís. The buses leave at 7:30 and 11:30am and 3:30pm, and the fare is $11 (£5.50), including the ferry passage. The ride takes a little over 5 hours. The return buses leave Malpaís at 4:20 and 8:20am, and 2:20pm.

Alternately, you can follow the directions above for getting to Montezuma, but get off in Cóbano. From Cóbano, there are buses daily for Malpaís and Santa Teresa at 10:30am and 2:30pm. The fare is $1.50 (75p). Buses return daily to Cóbano at 7am and noon. *Be forewarned:* These bus schedules are subject to change according to demand, road conditions, and the whim of the bus company.

If you miss the bus connection in Cóbano, you can hire a cab to Malpaís for around $15 (£7.50).

ORIENTATION   Malpaís and Santa Teresa are two tiny beach villages. As you reach the ocean, the road forks; Playa Carmen is straight ahead, Malpaís is to your left, and Santa Teresa is to your right. If you continue beyond Santa Teresa, you'll come to the even-more-deserted beaches of playas Hermosa and Manzanillo (not to be confused with beaches of the same names to be found elsewhere in the country). To get to playas

Hermosa and Manzanillo you have to ford a couple of rivers, which can be tricky during parts of the rainy season.

FAST FACTS There are currently no banks or medical clinics in Malpaís or Santa Teresa. All of that is in Cóbano. There is an ATM (by Frank's Place, see below), along with several general stores, public phones, and a few Internet cafes, however, and with the rapid growth, I don't think a bank will be that long in coming. In the case of any medical emergency, you can call Doctor Mel (© **2640-0521**).

If you need a taxi, call **Miguel** (© **8819-9021** or 2640-0261) or **Richard** (© **2640-0003**). If you want to do the driving yourself, you can contact the local offices of **Alamo** (© **2640-0526**) or **Budget Rent A Car** (© **2640-0418**). Or you can head to **Malpaís ATV Rentals** (© **2640-0195**), which has a large stock of ATVs.

FUN ON & OFF THE BEACH

If you decide to do anything here besides sunbathe on the beach and play in the waves, your options include nature hikes, horseback riding, ATV tours, scuba diving, and snorkeling, which most hotels can help arrange. Surfing is a major draw here. There are miles of beach breaks to choose from and a few points to boot. If you want to rent a board or take a lesson, check out the **Malpaís Surf Shop** (© **2640-0173**).

For canopy adventures, head to **Canopy del Pacífico** (© **2640-0091**), which is toward the southern end of Malpaís and just slightly inland. A 2-hour tour over the nearly 1km (½ mile) of cables touches down on eight platforms, features two rappels, and offers good views of both the forest and the ocean below. The cost is $40 (£20).

Finally, any hotel in the area can arrange a horseback-riding or ATV trip into the hills and along the beaches of this region, a guided hike through **Cabo Blanco Nature Reserve,** a sportfishing excursion out onto the high seas, or a trip over to Montezuma.

WHERE TO STAY
VERY EXPENSIVE

Flor Blanca Resort 🌟🌟🌟 *(Finds* This lush and plush hotel is, hands down, the most luxurious option in this neck of the woods and one of the top boutique hotels in the country. The individual villas are huge, with a vast central living area opening onto a spacious veranda. The furnishings, decorations, and architecture boast a mix of Latin American and Asian influences. Most overlook lush gardens, and about half have views through to the sea. Every unit features a large open-air bathroom with a garden shower and teardrop-shape tub set amid flowering tropical foliage. You can opt for either the one-bedroom villas with a four-poster king-size bed in the main bedroom, or a two-bedroom, two-bathroom villa, with two twin beds in a separate upstairs bedroom. There's a modern, full-service spa, as well as a full-size and active dojo on the grounds, where complimentary classes like yoga are regularly offered. The beautiful free-form pool is on two levels, with a sculpted waterfall connecting them and a shady Indonesian-style gazebo off to one side.

Playa Santa Teresa, Cóbano, Puntarenas. © **2640-0232.** Fax 2640-0226. www.florblanca.com. 16 units. $675–$850 (£338–£425) double; $975–$1,250 (£477–£625) 2-bedroom villa for 4; $950 (£475) "honeymoon house." Rates lower during off season; higher during peak weeks. Transfer to and from Tambor airstrip is included. AE, DC, MC, V. No children 13 and under. **Amenities:** Restaurant; bar; pool; small open-air gym; spa; watersports equipment rental; bike rental; limited room service; laundry service. *In room:* A/C, free Wi-Fi, kitchenette, coffeemaker, safe.

EXPENSIVE

Milarepa 🌟 Named after a Buddhist sage, this small collection of individual bungalows is spread around shady grounds fronting the beach, just next door to Flor

Blanca. The bungalows are simple, roomy, and understated. All have wooden floors, a mix of teak and bamboo furniture, beds with mosquito netting, and a private porch. An overhead fan keeps things cool, and there are plenty of windows for cross ventilation. The more expensive units are closest to the beach and have ocean views. There's a midsize pool for when the surf is too rough. The restaurant here, Soma, is excellent.

Playa Santa Teresa, Cóbano, Puntarenas. © 2640-0023. Fax 2640-0168. www.milarepahotel.com. 10 units. $198–$232 (£99–£116) double. Rates include full breakfast and taxes. Rates lower during off season. AE, MC, V. **Amenities:** Restaurant; bar; pool; tour desk; laundry service. *In room:* Wi-Fi, no phone.

MODERATE

In addition to the hotels listed below, the mix of rooms and bungalows at the **Place** (©/fax **2640-0001;** www.theplacemalpais.com) are stylish and reasonably priced.

Moana Lodge   Set on a steep hillside, the rooms here are all decorated in some variation of an African theme. A couple of the higher-situated units have a bit of an ocean view. In addition to being larger, the deluxe rooms come with a stocked minibar, four-poster queen-size bed, and ceiling fan. There's a pretty free-form pool here, with a shady gazebo beside it, as well as some mattresses hung like swings under another shade structure. Though the lodge doesn't have a restaurant, breakfasts are served and guests can use the communal kitchen and barbecue areas.

Malpaís, Cóbano de Puntarenas. © 2640-0230. Fax 2640-0632. www.moanalodge.com. 7 units. $95–$135 (£48–£68) double. Rates include breakfast and taxes. MC, V. **Amenities:** Bar; outdoor pool; Jacuzzi. *In room:* A/C, free Wi-Fi, hair dryer, safe, no phone.

Trópico Latino Lodge ⍟   One of the first hotels in the area, this beachfront spread is still a good choice. The nicest accommodations are the newer private bungalows, which have artistic tile work and finishings and views of the ocean. The original rooms are housed in four duplex units. These are huge—the king-size bamboo bed barely makes a dent in the floor space. There's also a separate sofa bed, as well as a small desk, a wall unit of shelves, and closet space galore. Although none of the older rooms has any ocean view to speak of, they all have private patios with a hammock. The shady grounds are rich in the native pochote tree, which is known for its spiky trunk. The small restaurant has excellent fresh fish and plenty of pasta dishes.

Playa Santa Teresa, Cóbano, Puntarenas. © 2640-0062. Fax 2640-0117. www.hoteltropicolatino.com. 16 units. $103–$155 (£52–£78) double. Rates lower in off season. MC, V. **Amenities:** Restaurant; bar; small free-form pool; small spa; Jacuzzi; laundry service. *In room:* A/C, free Wi-Fi, coffeemaker, safe, no phone.

INEXPENSIVE

Budget travelers can check out **Tranquilo Backpackers** (© 2640-0589; www.tranquilo backpackers.com), which is an outgrowth of a popular San José hostel. This place is located a bit inland off the road running toward Santa Teresa and has a mix of dorm-style and private rooms.

You can also pitch a tent at several spots and makeshift campsites here. Look for camping signs; you should get bathroom and shower access for a few bucks.

Frank's Place   These folks offer a hodgepodge of rooms in a variety of styles, price ranges, and configurations. Nine rooms are very basic and feature a shared bathroom; four units come with private bathrooms, a minifridge, and a tiny television set. Only four rooms feature double beds, although a few come with complete kitchenettes, and some have air-conditioning. The midrange rooms are a decent value and the hotel is well located, but I don't think the higher-priced rooms here are worth it—you can certainly do better for the money. There's a small pool at the center of the complex, as well as an unheated Jacuzzi. The restaurant is a glorified *soda,* but it does serve good Costa Rican cuisine, fresh fish, and a smattering of international dishes. It's also one of the most popular hangouts in Malpaís.

Malpaís, Cóbano de Puntarenas (at the crossroads of Malpaís and Playa Carmen). ©/fax **2640-0096**. 30 units, 9 with shared bathroom. $30 (£15) double with shared bathroom; $45–$85 (£23–£43) double with private bathroom. AE, MC, V. **Amenities:** Restaurant; bar; small pool; Jacuzzi; watersports equipment rental; bike rental; tour desk; laundry service. *In room:* Free Wi-Fi, no phone.

Malpaís Surf Camp & Resort   There's a wide range of accommodations here, reflected in the equally wide range of prices. The most basic rooms are open-air ranchos with gravel floors, lathe-and-bamboo walls, bead curtains for a door, and shared bathrooms. From here, your options get progressively more comfortable, ranging from shared-bathroom bunk-bed rooms to deluxe poolside villas. They'll even let you set up a tent for around $7 (£3.50) per tent, with bathroom and shower access included. There's a refreshing free-form tile pool in the center of the complex, and the large, open main lodge area serves as a combination restaurant, bar, lounge, and surfboard-storage area. As the name implies, this place is run by and caters to surfers, and the overall vibe here is loose and funky. The restaurant serves filling, fresh, and, at times, quite creative cuisine, depending on how accomplished the itinerant surf-chef-of-the-month is. Surf rentals, lessons, and video sessions are all available.

Malpaís, Cóbano de Puntarenas. © **2640-0031**. ©/fax 2640-0061. www.malpaissurfcamp.com. 16 units, 8 with shared bathroom. $15–$20 (£7.50–£10) per person with shared bathroom; $95–$135 (£48–£68) double with private bathroom. AE, MC, V. **Amenities:** Restaurant; bar; midsize pool; small exercise room; watersports equipment rental; bike rental; game room; tour desk; babysitting; laundry service. *In room:* Safe, no phone.

Point Break Hotel   The simple cabins here feature polished concrete floors, inset with cross sections of tree trunks, two twin beds, and three walls comprised largely of screening. They also come with a refrigerator and a small patio area with a couple of chairs. The shared bathrooms and showers are kept quite clean and there's a large lounge area strung with hammocks and featuring a television. Several newer cabins have their own bathrooms. The greatest attraction is the fact that this hotel sits just steps away from one of the best breaks along this stretch of coast. Hence the name and the steady stream of surfers who choose this simple place.

Playa Santa Teresa, Cóbano de Puntarenas. ©/fax **2640-0190**. 7 units, 2 with shared bathroom. $40 (£20) double with shared bathroom; $50–$60 (£25–£30) double with private bathroom and kitchenette. MC, V. **Amenities:** Bar; lounge. *In room:* No phone.

WHERE TO DINE

In addition to the places listed below, you might try **Mary's** (© **2640-0153**), which is a simple open-air joint that features wood-oven baked pizzas, fresh fish, and seafood, and is located toward the northern end of Malpaís. For another fine dining option, in addition to Nectar, head to **Soma** ✿ at Milarepa (see above).

VERY EXPENSIVE

Nectar ✿✿✿ *Finds* FUSION   The dimly lit open-air setting of this poolside and beachfront restaurant is elegant yet casual. There's a Pacific Rim influence to the fusion cuisine served. You can almost always start with some sushi or sashimi made with the daily catch. In addition to fresh seafood and several vegetarian entrees, you might also find lamb, rabbit, or duck on the regularly changing menu. The chef here has begun a business cultivating delectable oysters locally. The creativity, service, and presentation are some of the best you'll find in Costa Rica.

At Flor Blanca Resort in Santa Teresa. (*C* 2640-0232. Reservations recommended. Main courses $15–$38 (£7.50–£19). AE, MC, V. Daily 7am–9:30pm.

INEXPENSIVE

Soda Piedra Mar *(Finds* COSTA RICAN/SEAFOOD   This simple open-air restaurant is set on a rocky outcropping just steps away from the sea. The place is little more than a zinc-roofed shack that seems as if a stiff breeze would quickly level it. There are only a few tables here under the low roof; weather permitting, more tables are set in the sand under the sun or stars. The fare is simple, but the fish is guaranteed fresh, the portions are hearty, and the setting and sunsets are wonderful.

On the beach in Malpaís. (*C* 2640-0069. Main courses $3–$15 (£1.50–£7.50). No credit cards. Daily 8am–8pm.

MALPAIS & SANTA TERESA AFTER DARK

There's not much in the way of raging nightlife here. Some folks make the long and arduous journey over to Montezuma. The most popular bar in Malpaís is **D&N** *(F*, which stands for Day & Night, and is located about 1 block north of the crossroads into town, off the main road. Nearby, you'll find the roadside **Howlin' Monkey Sportsbar.** Surfers and other travelers also tend to gather in the evenings at **Frank's Place** and the **Malpaís Surf Camp.** If you head out toward Santa Teresa, **La Lora** is the most happening spot. This is the place to come on Saturday night to dance some salsa and merengue with some locals.

5 Playa Sámara *(F*

35km (22 miles) S of Nicoya; 245km (152 miles) W of San José

Playa Sámara is a long, broad beach on a gently curved horseshoe-shape bay. Unlike most of the other beaches along this stretch of the Pacific coast, the water here is usually calm and perfect for swimming because an offshore island and rocky headlands break up most of the surf. Playa Sámara is popular both with Tico families seeking a quick and inexpensive getaway and with young Ticos looking to do some serious beach partying. On weekends, in particular, Sámara can get crowded and rowdy. Still, the calm waters and steep cliffs on the far side of the bay make this a very attractive spot, and the beach is so long that the crowds are usually well dispersed. Moreover, if you drive along the rugged coastal road in either direction, you'll discover some truly spectacular and isolated beaches.

ESSENTIALS

GETTING THERE & DEPARTING   By Plane   Sansa (*C* 877/767-2672 in the U.S. and Canada, or 2290-4100 in Costa Rica; www.flysansa.com) flies to Carrillo (15 min. south of Sámara) daily at 6:30am from San José's Juan Santamaría International Airport. The flight might stop first at either Punta Islita or Nosara and takes approximately 1 hour; the fare is $93 (£47) each way. The Sansa flight leaves Carrillo for San José at 9:30am.

Most hotels will arrange to pick you up in Carrillo. If not, you'll have to hire a cab for between $8 and $10 (£4–£5).

Nature Air (*C* 800/235-9272 in the U.S. and Canada, or 2299-6000; www.natureair.com) also has one flight daily to Punta Islita that leaves at 9:40am from

Tobías Bolaños International Airport in Pavas. The fare is $111 (£56) each way. The return flight for San José leaves at 10:40am. Nature Air also flies between Punta Islita and Liberia, Puerto Jimenez, and Quepos.

By Car   Take the Interamerican Highway from San José. Forty-seven kilometers (29 miles) past the turnoff for Puntarenas, you'll see signs and the turnoff for the new La Amistad bridge. After crossing the bridge, continue north to Nicoya. In Nicoya, head more or less straight through town until you see signs for Playa Sámara. From here, it's a well-marked and paved road all the way to the beach.

To drive to Samara from Liberia, head out of town on the main road to the Guanacaste beaches, passing through Filadelfia, Santa Cruz, and Nicoya. Once you reach Nicoya, follow the directions outlined above.

By Bus   Alfaro-Tracopa express buses (© 2222-2666 or 2685-5032) leave San José daily at noon and 6:30pm from Calle 14 between avenidas 3 and 5. The trip lasts 5 hours; the one-way fare is $6.50 (£3.25). Extra buses are sometimes added on weekends and during peak periods, so it's always wise to check.

Alternatively, you can take a bus from this same station to Nicoya and then catch a second bus from Nicoya to Sámara. **Alfaro-Tracopa** buses leave San José roughly every hour between 5:30am and 5pm. The fare is $4.80 (£2.40). The trip can take between 4 and 5½ hours, depending if the bus goes via Liberia or the La Amistad bridge. The latter route is much faster. **Empresa Rojas** (© 2685-5352) buses leave Nicoya for Sámara and Carrillo regularly throughout the day, between 5am and 9pm. The trip's duration is 1½ hours. The fare to Sámara is $1.50 (75p); the fare to Carrillo is $2.20 (£1.10).

Express buses to San José leave daily at 4 and 8am. Buses for Nicoya leave throughout the day between 5am and 9pm. Buses leave Nicoya for San José roughly every hour between 5am and 5pm.

Interbus (© 2283-5573; www.interbusonline.com) has a daily bus that leaves San José for Playa Sámara at 8:15am. The fare is $35 (£18) and they will pick you up at most San José–area hotels.

ORIENTATION   Sámara is a busy little town at the bottom of a steep hill. The main road heads straight into town, passing the soccer field before coming to an end at the beach. Just before the beach is a road to the left that leads to most of the hotels listed below. This road also leads to Playa Carrillo (see below) and the Hotel Punta Islita (p. 229). If you turn right 3 blocks before hitting the beach, you'll hit the coastal road that goes to playas Buena Vista, Barrigona, and eventually Nosara.

FAST FACTS   In case of an emergency, dial © 911. To reach the local police, dial © 2656-0436. There's a small medical clinic in Samara (© 2656-0166). There is also a branch of the **Banco Nacional** (© 2656-0086), on the road to Playa Buena Vista, just as you head out of town. If you need a ride around Samara, or to one of the nearby beaches, you can hire a taxi by calling **Balto** (© 8361-4167) or **Jorge** (© 8830-3002).

FUN ON & OFF THE BEACH

Aside from sitting on the sand and soaking up the sun, the main activities in Playa Sámara seem to be hanging out in the bars and *sodas* and dancing into the early morning hours. But if you're looking for something more, there's horseback riding either on the beach or through the bordering pastureland and forests. Other options include sea kayaking in the calm waters off Playa Sámara, sportfishing, snorkeling and scuba diving, boat tours, mountain biking, and tours to Playa Ostional to see the mass nesting of olive ridley sea turtles. You can inquire about and book any of these tours at your hotel.

You'll find that the beach is nicer and cleaner down at the south end. Better yet, head about 8km (5 miles) south to **Playa Carrillo** ♠♠, a long crescent of soft, white sand. There's almost no development here, so the beach is almost always deserted and there are loads of palm trees providing shade. If you've got a good four-wheel-drive vehicle, ask for directions at your hotel and set off in search of the hidden gems of **Playa Buena Vista** and **Playa Barrigona** ♠♠, which are north of Sámara, less than a half-hour drive away. In late 2007, actor Mel Gibson bought a large estate overlooking Playa Barrigona, and many locals say he actually bought the entire beach. Although his plans for this patch of paradise are still unclear, all beaches in Costa Rica are public property, and access must be provided.

A taxi to Playa Carrillo should cost about $5 to $8 (£2.50–£4) each way. Because it's a bit farther and the roads are a little rougher, expect to pay a little more to reach Playa Buena Vista, and even more for Playa Barrigona.

The folks at **Wingnuts Canopy Tours** (✆ 2656-0153) offer zip-line and harness "canopy tours." The 2-hour outing costs $55 (£28) per person. You'll find their office by the giant strangler fig tree, or *matapalo*, toward the southern end of the beach.

Almost every hotel in the area can arrange sportfishing trips, or you could contact **Samara Sport Fishing** (✆ 2656-0589) or **Kingfisher** ♠ (✆ 2656-0091; www.costaricabillfishing.com).

To learn how to surf, or to rent a board, check in with **C & C Surf Shop and School** (✆ 2656-0628), or **Jesse's Samara Beach Surf School** (✆ 2656-0055).

If you want to head out and try some scuba diving or a snorkel excursion, call **Pura Vida Dive** (✆ 2656-0273 or 8843-2075).

For a bird's-eye view of the area, head over to the **Flying Crocodile** (✆ 2656-8048 or 8827-8858; www.flying-crocodile.com) in Playa Buena Vista. A 20-minute flight will run you $70 (£35).

All of the hotels here can help you arrange any number of tour options, including horseback rides, boat trips, scuba diving, and snorkeling outings. You might also contact **Tío Tigre Tours** (✆ 2656-0098), a good all-around local tour company.

LEARN THE LANGUAGE

If you want to acquire or polish some language skills while here, check in with the **Intercultura Language School** (✆ 866/978-6668 in the U.S. and Canada, or 2656-0127 in Samara; www.samaralanguageschool.com). The facility here even features classes with ocean views, although that might be a detriment to your language learning. These folks offer a range of programs and private lessons and can arrange for a home stay with a local family.

GOING DOWN UNDER

Cavers will want to head 62km (38 miles) northeast of Playa Sámara on the road to the La Amistad bridge. If you don't have a car, your best bet is to get to Nicoya, which is about a half-hour away by bus, and then take a taxi to the park, which should cost about $15 (£7.50). Here, at **Barra Honda National Park** ♠ (✆ 2685-5267 or 2686-6760), there's an extensive system of caves, some of which reach more than 200m (656 ft.) in depth. Human remains and indigenous relics have been found in other caves, but those are not open to the public. Because this is a national park, you'll have to pay the $10 (£5) entrance fee.

If you plan to descend the one publicly accessible cave, you'll also need to rent (or bring your own) equipment and hire a local guide at the park entrance station. Depending upon your group size and bargaining abilities, expect to pay $10 to $30 (£5–£15) per person for a visit to the **Terciopelo Cave,** including the guide, harness, helmet, and flashlight. Furthermore, the cave is open only during the dry season (mid-Nov to Apr). You begin your tour with a descent of 19m (62 ft.) straight down a wooden ladder with a safety rope attached. Inside you'll see plenty of impressive stalactites and stalagmites while visiting several chambers of varying sizes. Even if you don't descend, the trails around Barra Honda and its prominent limestone plateau are great for hiking and bird-watching. Be sure to make a stop at **La Cascada,** a gentle waterfall that fills and passes through a series of calcium and limestone pools, some of them large enough to bathe in. The entire thing is slightly reminiscent of Ocho Rios in Jamaica.

WHERE TO STAY
MODERATE
Fenix Hotel ☆ Set right on the beach, the rooms here are all really studio apartments, with fully equipped kitchenettes. The rooms are simple, but they are kept clean. For cooling off, the hotel has a postage stamp–size pool and some coconut trees for shade. Hammocks are hung in the shade and the ocean is just steps away. The owners are personable and accommodating, and the full kitchens are a boon for families and those looking for longer stays.

Playa Sámara, Nicoya, Guanacaste. ℂ **2656-0158.** Fax 2656-0162. www.fenixhotel.com. 6 units. $80 (£40) double. Rates lower in off season. No credit cards. **Amenities:** Small pool; laundry service. *In room:* A/C, kitchenette, no phone.

Hotel Giada This neat little Italian-owned hotel is located on the left-hand side of the main road into town, about 150m (492 ft.) before the beach. The rooms are all very clean and comfortable and even have small balconies. Breakfast is served in a cool, shady central gazebo. The management is very helpful and can arrange diving or fishing expeditions and horseback-riding trips.

Playa Sámara, Nicoya, Guanacaste. ℂ **2656-0132.** Fax 2656-0131. www.hotelgiada.net. 24 units. $75 (£38) double. Rates include breakfast. Rates lower in off season; higher during peak periods. AE, DC, MC, V. **Amenities:** Restaurant; bar; small pool; tour desk; laundry service. *In room:* A/C, TV, safe.

Las Brisas del Pacífico Hotel This hotel is set amid shady grounds and backs up on a steep hill on a quiet stretch of sand. Most of the rooms are found in the three-story building, up a long and steep flight of stairs at the top of the hill. These have comfortable balconies and walls of glass that provide an excellent view of the bay. The third-floor rooms are the largest here, but the second-floor rooms actually have the best views. At the base of the hill are rooms in stucco duplexes with steeply pitched tile roofs and red-tile patios. The range in prices reflects the range in room size, location, and amenities. However, all of the rooms are rather plain, with decidedly uninspired decor, and you'll definitely have to pay more for air-conditioning. This lack of inspiration also sometimes bleeds over into the service. The restaurant has consistently served up very good fresh seafood and well-prepared pastas.

Playa Sámara (A.P. 11917-1000, San José), Guanacaste. ℂ **2656-0250.** Fax 2656-0076. www.brisas.net. 34 units. $70–$110 (£35–£55) double. Rates include breakfast. Rates lower in the off season, higher during peak weeks. AE, MC, V. **Amenities:** Restaurant; 2 bars; 2 midsize pools; 2 unheated Jacuzzis; limited watersports equipment rental; tour desk; laundry service. *In room:* A/C (in some), safe, no phone.

Samara Tree House Inn ★★   Set right on the beach in the heart of town, this new hotel is my top choice in Samara. The individual units are really small studio apartments. The four namesake rooms are built on raised stilts, made from varnished tree trunks. Inside, they are awash in varnished wood. There's a small sitting area, with large picture windows and a great view up above. And the open-air area underneath each unit is fitted out with a couple of hammocks, a table and chairs, some chaise longues, and a barbecue. There's also a ground-floor unit, which is handicap accessible and quite beautiful in its own right. There's no air-conditioning, but fans are found in every bedroom. No children 11 and under are allowed in the pool at anytime, although they are not prohibited from staying at the hotel.

Playa Sámara, Guanacaste. ⓒ 2656-0733. www.samaratreehouse.com. 5 units. $95 (£44) pool-front double; $115 (£58) beachfront double. Rates include breakfast. Rates lower in the off season, higher during peak weeks. AE, MC, V. **Amenities:** Bar; small outdoor pool; Jacuzzi; laundry service. *In room:* TV, free Wi-Fi, safe, no phone.

Villas Playa Sámara   Toward the southern extreme of Playa Sámara, right on the beach, this place has the best setting and most extensive grounds around. Built to resemble a small village, the hotel consists of numerous villas varying in size from one to three bedrooms. White-stucco exterior walls and red-tile roofs give the whole thing a Mediterranean look, and the whole complex is set right off a nice, quiet, and calm section of beach. The spacious rooms are outfitted with simple furniture and have tiled bathrooms. All the villas have kitchens and patios, and are finished with colorful bedspreads and artwork, basket lampshades, and vertical blinds on the windows. Not all have air-conditioning. This place has many of the facilities and amenities one would expect at a midsize beach resort. However, the upkeep and maintenance have been spotty over the years, and service can be downright bad.

Playa Sámara, Guanacaste. ⓒ **2296-0010** reservations office in San José or 2656-0104 at the resort. Fax 2231-7692. www.villasplayasamara.com. 57 units. $90 (£45) double; $125–$245 (£63–£123) 2- to 3-room villa. Rates lower in the off season, higher during peak weeks. AE, MC, V. **Amenities:** Restaurant; bar; midsize outdoor pool; exercise room; Jacuzzi; bike rental; tour desk; laundry service. *In room:* A/C (in some), no phone.

INEXPENSIVE

You'll find a slew of very inexpensive places to stay along the road into town and around the soccer field. Many of the rooms at these places are less accommodating than your average jail cell. As an alternative, you can pitch a tent right by the beach for a few dollars at **Camping Coco's** (ⓒ 2656-0496). You'll find Camping Coco's several hundred meters south of the downtown. In addition to the places listed below, I also like the tidy, German-run **Hotel Belvedere** (ⓒ 2656-0213; www.samara-costa rica.com), on the hill overlooking the beach.

Casa del Mar *Value*   On the inland side of the beach-access road, 1 block south of the downtown, Casa del Mar is just 50m (164 ft.) from the beach. The rooms here are kept immaculate, and most of them are quite spacious. The place feels like a cool oasis from the harsh Guanacaste sun, with its open-air restaurant, shady central courtyard, and small pool/Jacuzzi. Although the units with shared bathrooms are the best bargains here, I'd opt for a second-floor room with a private bathroom. The owners and staff members are extremely friendly and helpful.

Playa Sámara, Nicoya, Guanacaste. ⓒ 2656-0264. Fax 2656-0129. www.casadelmarsamara.com. 17 units, 11 with private bathroom. $40 (£20) double with shared bathroom; $75 (£36) double with private bathroom and A/C. Rates include full breakfast and taxes. Rates lower in the off season; higher during peak periods. AE, MC, V. **Amenities:** Bar; unheated pool/Jacuzzi; tour desk; laundry service. *In room:* No phone.

Casa Valeria This is the best beachfront budget option in town. The rooms are quite basic and much more rustic than those at either the Belvedere or Casa del Mar, but they are just steps away from the sand and surf. The best bets here are the four individual bungalows. There's a basic restaurant, as well as some tables, chairs, and plenty of hammocks set in the shade of tall coconut palms. This place is popular with European backpackers, and there's a hostel-like feel to the whole operation.

Playa Sámara, Nicoya, Guanacaste. ℂ 2656-0511. Fax 2656-0317. 9 units. $40–$60 (£20–£30) double. Rates include breakfast. V. **Amenities:** Restaurant. *In room:* A/C, minifridge, no phone.

A NEARBY LUXURY HOTEL

Hotel Punta Islita ✸✸✸ *Finds* Set on a high bluff between two mountain ridges that meet the sea, this is one of the most exclusive and romantic luxury resorts in Costa Rica. The rooms here are done in a Santa Fe style, with red Mexican floor tiles, neo-Navajo-print bedspreads, and adobe-colored walls offset with sky-blue doors and trim. Each room has a king-size bed and a private patio with a hammock; a few of these also have a Jacuzzi. The suites come with a separate sitting room and a private two-person plunge pool or Jacuzzi; the villas have two or three bedrooms, their own private swimming pools, and full kitchens. The beach below the hotel is a small crescent of gray-white sand with a calm, protected section at the northern end. It's about a 10-minute hike, but the hotel will shuttle you up and back if you don't feel like walking. There's a rancho bar and grill down there for when you get hungry or thirsty, and a lap pool for when the waves are too rough.

Punta Islita is very involved with the local community, and has sponsored a wide-ranging art program that brings in prominent Costa Rican artists to teach the local residents art and craft skills, while often creating large public works in the process.

Playa Islita (A.P. 242-1225, Plaza Mayor, San José), Guanacaste. ℂ 866/446-4053 in the U.S. and Canada, or 2231-6122 in Costa Rica, 2661-4044 at the hotel. Fax 2231-0715. www.hotelpuntaislita.com. 20 units, 17 villas. $300 (£150) double; $420–$480 (£210–£240) suite; $625–$720 (£313–£360) villa. Rates include continental breakfast. Rates lower in the off season; higher during peak periods. AE, MC, V. **Amenities:** 3 restaurants; bar; small tile pool and lap pool; 9-hole golf course and driving range; 2 lit tennis courts; small exercise room and spa; Jacuzzi; watersports equipment, bike, horse, and 4WD rentals; game room; tour desk; in-room massage; laundry service. *In room:* A/C, TV, free Wi-Fi, minibar, coffeemaker, hair dryer, safe.

DINING & AFTER-DARK DIVERSIONS

There are numerous inexpensive *sodas* in Sámara, and most of the hotels have their own restaurants. If you want to eat overlooking the water, check out **El Ancla** (ℂ 2656-0716) or **Shake Joe's** (ℂ 2656-0252). Both of these are located right on the beach a bit south of downtown. If you head out along the beach north of town, you'll find **El Lagarto** (ℂ 2656-0750), which serves fresh fish and specializes in barbecue.

After dark the most happening place in town is **La Góndola Bar,** which has a pool table, dartboards, and board games. My favorite spot is **El Lagarto** ✸ on the beach a bit north of downtown. You might also try the lounge scene at **Shake Joe's, La Vela Latina,** or **Wana Wana Acuario,** all right near the center of the action. Or you could head a little farther south to **Sol Azteca,** a Mexican bar and restaurant, with a lively nightlife scene and occasional live music.

Las Brasas SPANISH/SEAFOOD This two-story, open-air affair serves authentic Spanish cuisine and well-prepared fresh seafood. The whole fish *a la catalana* is excellent, as is the paella. For something lighter, try the gazpacho Andaluz, a refreshing lunch choice on a hot afternoon. If you have a big party, and order a day or so in advance, they'll roast a whole pig for you. There's a good selection of Spanish wines, a rarity in Costa Rica. Service is attentive yet informal.

On the main road into Sámara, about 90m (295 ft.) before the beach. (📞 **2656-0546**. Reservations recommended in the high season. Main courses $6–$26 (£3–£13). V. Sat–Thurs noon–10pm.

6 Playa Nosara ★ ★

55km (34 miles) SW of Nicoya; 266km (165 miles) W of San José

As is the case in Malpaís, **Playa Nosara** is a bucket term used to refer to several neighboring beaches, spread along an isolated stretch of coast. In addition to the namesake beach, **Playa Guiones, Playa Pelada, Playa Garza,** and (sometimes) **Playa Ostional** are also lumped into this area. In fact, the village of Nosara itself is several kilometers inland from the beach. Playa Nosara marks the northern limit of the Nicoya Peninsula.

Playa Guiones is one of Costa Rica's most dependable beach breaks, and surfers come here in good numbers throughout the year. There's even a tiny strip mall at the crossroads to Playa Guiones; however, the waves are still much less crowded than you would find in and around Jacó or Tamarindo.

The best way to get to Nosara is to fly, but, with everything so spread out, that makes getting around difficult after you've arrived. The roads to, in, and around Nosara are almost always in very rough shape, and there's little sign that this will improve anytime soon.

ESSENTIALS

GETTING THERE & DEPARTING   By Plane   Sansa (📞 877/767-2672 in the U.S. and Canada, or 2290-4100 in Costa Rica; www.flysansa.com) has a daily flight to Nosara, departing from San José's Juan Santamaría International Airport at 8am. The one-way fare for the 50-minute flight is $93 (£47). **Nature Air** (📞 800/235-9272 in the U.S. and Canada, or 2299-6000; www.natureair.com) has one flight daily that leaves at 10am from Tobías Bolaños International Airport in Pavas. The fare is $108 (£54) each way. The return Sansa flight to San José departs Nosara at 9am, and the Nature Air flight leaves at 4:15pm.

Taxis wait for every arrival; fares range between $4 and $8 (£2–£4) to most hotels in Nosara.

By Car   Follow the directions for getting to Playa Sámara (see "Playa Sámara," earlier in this chapter), but watch for a well-marked fork in the road a few kilometers before you reach that beach. The right-hand fork leads to Nosara over another 22km (14 miles) of rough dirt road.

By Bus   An **Alfaro-Tracopa** express bus (📞 2222-2666 in San José, or 2682-0297 in Nosara) leaves San José daily at 6am from Calle 14 between avenidas 3 and 5. The trip's duration is 5½ hours; the one-way fare is $7.70 (£3.85).

You can also take an Alfaro bus from San José to Nicoya and then catch a second bus from Nicoya to Nosara. **Alfaro-Tracopa** buses leave San José roughly every hour between 5:30am and 5pm. The fare is $4.80 (£2.40). The trip can take between 4 and 5½ hours, depending on whether the bus goes via Liberia or the La Amistad bridge. The latter route is much faster. **Empresa Rojas** buses (📞 2686-9089) leave Nicoya for Nosara daily at 5 and 10am, noon, and 3pm. Trip duration is 2 hours; the one-way fare is $1.80 (90p).

The direct Alfaro bus to San José leaves daily at 12:30pm. Buses to Nicoya leave Nosara daily at 5 and 7am, noon, and 3pm. Buses leave Nicoya for San José roughly every hour between 5am and 5pm.

Interbus (© 2283-5573; www.interbusonline.com) runs a daily bus from San José to Playa Nosara at 8:15am; the fare is $45 (£23).

ORIENTATION   The village of Nosara is about 5km (3 miles) inland from the beach. The small airstrip runs pretty much through the center of town; however, most hotels listed here are on or near the beach itself. You'll find the **post office** and **police station** right at the end of the airstrip. There's a small medical clinic and pharmacy (© 2682-0282) in the village as well.

Both **Banco Popular** and **Banco Nacional** have offices in Nosara, with ATMs. If you want to rent a car out here, both **Alamo** (© 2242-7733) and **National** (© 2242-7878) have offices here. Because demand often outstrips supply, I recommend you reserve a car in advance. Alternatively, you can rent an ATV from several operators around town. If you need a **taxi**, call © 2682-0142 or 2682-0236. There's an **Internet cafe** in the village and others at Café de Paris and Harbor Reef Lodge (p. 233).

This area was originally conceived and zoned as a primarily residential community. The maze of dirt roads and lack of any single defining thoroughfare can be confusing for first-time visitors. Luckily, a host of hotel and restaurant signs have gone up in recent years pointing lost travelers in the general direction of their final destination.

FUN ON & OFF THE BEACH

Among the several beaches at Nosara are the long, curving **Playa Guiones** ⊛⊛, **Playa Nosara** ⊛, and the diminutive **Playa Pelada** ⊛. Because the village of Nosara is several miles inland, these beaches tend to be clean, secluded, and quiet. Surfing and bodysurfing are good here, particularly at Playa Guiones, which is garnering quite a reputation as a consistent and rideable beach break. Pelada is a short white-sand beach with three deep scallops, backed by sea grasses and mangroves. There isn't too much sand at high tide, so you'll want to hit the beach when the tide's out. At either end of the beach, rocky outcroppings reveal tide pools at low tide.

With miles of excellent beach breaks and relatively few crowds, this is a great place to learn how to surf. If you want to try to stand up for your first time, check in with the folks at **Safari Surf School** (© 866/433-3355 in the U.S. and Canada, or 2682-0573; www.safarisurfschool.com) or **Corky Carroll's Surf School** (© 888/454-7873 in the U.S. and Canada, or 2682-0385; www.surfschool.net). Both schools specialize in multiday packages with accommodations and meals included, and they rent boards. You can usually sign up for individual or group classes on a daily basis. A morning group lesson should cost between $25 and $35 (£13–£18) per person, while private lessons average around $30 to $50 (£15–£25) per hour.

BIRD- & SEA TURTLE–WATCHING   Bird-watchers should explore the mangrove swamps around the estuary mouth of the Río Nosara. Just walk north from Playa Pelada and follow the riverbank; explore the paths into the mangroves.

If you time your trip right, you can do a night tour to nearby **Playa Ostional** to watch nesting olive ridley sea turtles. These turtles come ashore by the thousands in a mass egg-laying phenomenon known as an *arribada*. These *arribadas* take place 4 to 10 times between July and December; each occurrence lasts between 3 and 10 days. Consider yourself very lucky if you happen to be around during one of these fascinating natural phenomena. Even if it's not turtle-nesting season, you might want to look into visiting Playa Ostional just to have a long, wide expanse of beach to yourself. However, be careful swimming here because the surf and riptides can be formidable. During the dry season (mid-Nov to Apr), you can usually get here in a regular car, but during the rainy season you'll need four-wheel-drive. This beach is part of Ostional National Wildlife Refuge. At the northwest end of the refuge is **India Point,** which is known for its tide pools and rocky outcrops.

The *arribadas* are so difficult to predict that no one runs regularly scheduled turtle-viewing trips, but when the *arribada* is in full swing, several local tour guides and agencies offer tours. Your best bet is to ask the staff at your hotel or check in with Joe at **Iguana Expeditions** (© 2682-4089; www.iguanaexpeditions.com).

FISHING CHARTERS & OTHER OUTDOOR ACTIVITIES   All the hotels in the area can arrange fishing charters for $200 to $500 (£100–£250) for a half-day, or $400 to $1,200 (£200–£600) for a full day. These rates are for one to four people and vary according to boat size and accouterments. **Sunset Sails** (© 2682-0509) offers full-day, half-day, and—of course—sunset cruises.

HORSEBACK RIDING   The folks at **Casa Río Nosara Excursions** (© 2682-0117) have a large stable of well-cared-for horses and a range of beach, jungle, and waterfall rides to choose from. Rates run between $25 and $60 (£13–£30) per person, depending on the size of your group and the length of the tour.

KAYAK TOURS   Based out of the Gilded Iguana hotel and restaurant, **Iguana Expeditions** ★ (© 2682-4089; www.iguanaexpeditions.com) offers a range of full-and half-day tours around the area. Explore the inland coastal mangroves, or combine some open-water paddling with a snorkel break at San Juanillo. These folks also offer hikes to waterfalls and can arrange inexpensive fishing outings in a *panga* (small craft) with a local fisherman. Half-day tours cost between $25 and $50 (£13–£25); full-day tours run between $50 and $100 (£25–£50).

YOGA & MORE   If you want to spend some time getting mind and body together, check in with the **Nosara Yoga Institute** (© 2682-0360; www.nosarayoga.com), which offers intensive and daily yoga classes, teacher trainings, and a host of custom-designed "retreat" options. This is an internationally recognized retreat and teacher training center. Their daily, open, 90-minute classes cost just $10 (£5), and they even provide a mat.

You might also check in to see if anything is being offered up at the Harmony Hotel & Spa (see below).

WHERE TO STAY

In addition to the places listed below, the **Nosara Beach House** ★ (© 2682-0019; www.thenosarabeachhouse.com) on Playa Guiones, has clean and comfortable rooms and a swimming pool—and it's right on the beach to boot. **Giardino Tropicale** (© 2682-4000; www.giardinotropicale.com) is a similar choice, although a bit farther from the beach. For a more intimate option that's also a very good deal, check out the **Nosara B&B** (© 2682-0209; www.nosarabandb.net).

One final hotel that needs mentioning is the **Nosara Beach Hotel** (© 2682-0121; www.nosarabeachhotel.com). You can't miss the giant Russian-style dome topping this hillside hotel, which is the tallest and most striking structure in town. The location and view here are top-notch. However, the place has been in a constant state of construction for a while, rooms are pretty run-down, and service is gruff at times and spotty at best.

EXPENSIVE

Harmony Hotel & Spa ★★ *Finds*   This is easily the most complete, luxurious, and best located choice in the Nosara area. The room decor is simple but attractive, with white-tile floors, contemporary furnishings, and well-designed bathrooms. All the rooms have patios or wooden decks. In fact, even the most basic rooms here, their "Coco" rooms, feature quite large private wooden decks out back, with an outdoor shower. The hotel is geared toward couples, and all are equipped with just one king-size bed, although roll-in beds are available for families or buddies. The bungalows are two-bedroom affairs, with a king-size bed and fold-out sofa in each room and large shared deck area. The hotel has a well-run and pretty spa, with various treatment options and regular yoga classes. One of the best features here is that the beach is only about 90m (295 ft.) away, reached via a short path through some sea grass and dunes.

Playa Nosara, Guanacaste. ✆ **2682-4113.** Fax 2682-4114. www.harmonynosara.com. 16 units, 10 bungalows. $160 (£80) double; $225 (£112) bungalow; $345 (£173) 2-bedroom bungalow. Rates include breakfast buffet. Rates lower in off season; higher during peak periods. AE, MC, V. **Amenities:** Restaurant; bar; midsize pool; spa; lighted tennis court; watersports equipment rental; tour desk; laundry service. *In room:* A/C, TV, free Wi-Fi, minifridge, coffeemaker, safe.

MODERATE

Café de Paris ★   On the main road into Nosara, where it branches off to Playa Guiones, this popular bakery and bistro (reviewed separately below) has some equally popular rooms out back, set behind the restaurant and pool in a series of duplex buildings. All have high ceilings and plenty of room; about half have kitchenettes. A few shady ranchos are spread around the grounds for afternoon lazing. These folks also rent a couple of luxury villas with fabulous views atop a steep hill across the street. In 2007, the owners began focusing solely on weeklong rentals for all their rooms, bungalows, and villas. During the off season, however, you may be able to negotiate a daily rate.

Playa Nosara, Guanacaste. ✆ **2682-0087.** Fax 2682-0089. www.cafedeparis.net. 14 units. $360–$480 (£180–£240) per week; $600–$1,200 (£300–£600) bungalow or villa per week. AE, MC, V. **Amenities:** Restaurant; bar; small pool; game room; tour desk; laundry service. *In room:* A/C, no phone.

Harbor Reef Lodge ★   This hotel caters to surfers, fishermen and all-around vacationers, with clean, spacious rooms close to the beach (about 182m/597 ft. inland from Playa Guiones). The suites come with separate sitting rooms, and a couple even have kitchenettes. There's a cool, oasis-like feel to the lush grounds. The best rooms are the Surf City rooms and suites, which are set around the hotel's second, and larger pool, which is reserved for hotel guests—the other pool, which is just off the restaurant, is open to diners and walk-ins. The hotel offers surf lessons and sportfishing outings and even has a small general store and Internet cafe on the grounds. They also rent out a variety of private homes and villas.

Playa Nosara, Guanacaste. ✆ **2682-0059.** Fax 2682-0060. www.harborreef.com. 22 units. $97–$140 (£49–£70) double; $120–$200 (£60–£100) suite. AE, MC, V. **Amenities:** Restaurant; bar; 2 small pools; watersports equipment rental; bike rental; tour desk; laundry service. *In room:* A/C, TV, free Wi-Fi, fridge, coffeemaker.

Lagarta Lodge   Located on a hillside high over the Nosara River, this small lodge is an excellent choice for bird-watchers and other travelers who are more interested in flora and fauna than the beach. The rooms are spartan but acceptable. The lodge borders its own private reserve, which has trails along the riverbank and through the mangrove and

---

Tips Yo Quiero Hablar Español

You can brush up on or start up your Spanish at the **Rey de Nosara Language School** (ⓒ/fax **2682-0215**; www.reydenosara.itgo.com). It offers group and private lessons according to demand, and can coordinate week or multiweek packages.

---

tropical humid forests here. There are spectacular views from the restaurant and most rooms over the river and surrounding forest, with the beaches of Nosara and Ostional in the distance. You'll want to have your own vehicle if you stay here: The beach is a good 10- to 15-minute hike away, and it's uphill on the way back.

Playa Nosara (A.P. 18-5233), Guanacaste. ⓒ **2682-0035**. Fax 2682-0135. www.lagarta.com. 6 units. $68 (£34) double. Rates lower in off season; higher during peak periods. AE, MC, V. **Amenities:** Restaurant; bar; midsize pool; tour desk. *In room:* No phone.

INEXPENSIVE

The Gilded Iguana ⭐ This long-standing hotel and restaurant began with a few very basic budget rooms. However, it now has a swimming pool, with a high waterfall emptying into it, and six newer, more luxurious rooms. The new rooms have very high ceilings, lots of space, air-conditioning, and minifridges. They are set back from the pool in a row, and sit among some shade trees. The older rooms are much more rustic, and located close to the road, just off the hotel's popular restaurant. These lack air-conditioning, but are more economical. The restaurant here is deservedly popular (see below), and in addition to feeding its guests, draws a lot of the local expatriate community to watch sporting events and listen to the occasional live band.

Playa Guiones, Guanacaste. ⓒ **2682-0259**. www.gildediguana.com. 12 units. $45–$65 (£23–£33) double. Rates lower in off season; higher during peak periods. AE, MC, V. **Amenities:** Restaurant; bar; midsize pool; tour desk; laundry service. *In room:* Minifridge, coffeemaker, no phone.

WHERE TO DINE

In addition to the places mentioned below, **Marlin Bill's** (ⓒ **2682-0458**) is a popular and massive open-air haunt on the hillside on the main road, just across from Café de Paris (see below). You can expect to get good, fresh seafood and American classics here. For Mexican food, try **Pancho's** (ⓒ **2682-0591**) or **Foony's** (ⓒ **2682-0385**), both in Playa Guiones. For Italian, **La Dolce Vita** ⭐ (ⓒ **2682-0107**), on the outskirts of town on the road to Playa Sámara, serves up excellent Italian fare nightly, while closer to town, **Giardino Tropicale** (ⓒ **2682-4000**) also has good Italian fare and brick-oven pizzas. Finally, for local flavor, head to Doña Olga's (no phone), a simple Costa Rican *soda,* located right on the beach in Playa Pelada.

Café de Paris ⭐ *Finds* BAKERY/BISTRO This popular place has wonderful fresh-baked goods and a wide assortment of light bites and full-on meals. You can get pizza or nachos or filling sandwiches on fresh baguettes. There are also hearty salads, as well as fish, meat, and chicken dishes. I enjoy stopping in for a cup of espresso and a fresh almond croissant, and breakfasts are excellent here. Sporting events or movie videos are shown nightly, and there's even a pool table and Internet cafe.

On the main road into Nosara. ⓒ **2682-0087**. Baked goods 75¢–$4 (35p–£2); main courses $4–$17 (£2–£8.50). AE, MC, V. Daily 7am–11pm.

The Gilded Iguana 🐸 SEAFOOD/GRILL   This simple restaurant serves fish so fresh that it's still wiggling: The owner's husband, Chiqui, is a local fisherman. There are also great burgers, Costa Rican *casados,* and a list of nightly specials. If you're in town fishing, they'll cook your catch. Sporting events are shown on a not-quite-big-enough television. There's a separate bar area, on the other side of their new pool, and you can also dine over there. Overall, the vibe is sociable and lively. Most of the tables and chairs here are low-lying affairs; plus-size travelers might find the chairs a bit challenging to get in and out of.

About 90m (295 ft.) inland from the beach at Playa Guiones. © **2682-0259.** Main courses $4–$15 (£2–£7.50). V. Daily 7–9:30am, 11am–2pm, and 5–10pm.

La Luna 🐸 *Finds* INTERNATIONAL   With an enviable location overlooking the water at Playa Pelada and a casually elegant ambience, this little restaurant is an excellent choice. I especially like grabbing one of the outdoor tables closest to the waves for breakfast or lunch. However, it's also quite beautiful at night, with candles spread around generously. The chalkboard menu changes regularly, but will usually include some Thai or Indian curry, as well as pasta dishes, and hearty steaks. Prices are on the high side, and service and hospitality can be spotty at times, but this is still probably the best beachside dining to be had in Nosara.

Playa Pelada. © **2682-0122.** Main courses $8–$36 (£4–£18). MC, V. Daily 11am–10pm.

NOSARA AFTER DARK

When evening rolls around, don't expect a major party scene. Nightlife near the beach seems to center on the **Café de Paris, Marlin Bill's, Blew Dogs, Casa Tucán,** and the **Gilded Iguana.** The last two spots often have live music. In "downtown" Nosara, you'll probably want to check out either the **Tropicana,** the town's long-standing local disco, or the **Beatle Bar,** a U.S.-style bar that also has a branch in Jacó. Be forewarned, as with the Jacó branch, the Beatle Bar here is a popular prostitute pickup spot.

NORTH OF NOSARA

Just north of Nosara lies Playa Ostional, famous for its massive nestings of olive ridley sea turtles (see above). At the northern edge of Playa Ostional where it meets Playa San Juanillo, a few new hotels have sprung up. The best of these is **Hotel Luna Azul** 🐸 (© **8821-0075;** www.hotellunaazul.com), which features beautiful individual bungalows and a great view of the ocean—although the beach is a good distance away.

9

The Northern Zone: Mountain Lakes, Cloud Forests & a Volcano

Costa Rica's northern zone is home to several prime ecotourist destinations, including the misty and mysterious **Monteverde Cloud Forest Reserve** ✸✸✸ and the astoundingly active **Arenal Volcano** ✸✸. There are rainforests and cloud forests, jungle rivers, mountain lakes, lowland marshes, and an unbelievable wealth of birds and other wildlife. Slight changes in elevation create unique microclimates and ecosystems throughout the region. In addition to these natural wonders, this region also provides an intimate glimpse into the rural heart and soul of Costa Rica. Small, isolated lodges abound, and towns and villages remain predominantly small agricultural communities.

This area is also a must for adventure travelers. The northern zone has one of the best windsurfing spots in the world, on **Lake Arenal** ✸, as well as excellent opportunities for mountain biking, hiking, canyoning, and river rafting. Zip-line canopy tours and suspended forest bridges abound. And if you partake in any number of adventure activities, you'll also find several soothing natural hot springs in the area to soak your tired muscles.

1 Puerto Viejo de Sarapiquí ✸

82km (51 miles) N of San José; 102km (63 miles) E of La Fortuna

The Sarapiquí region, named for the principal river that runs through this area, lies at the foot of the Cordillera Central mountain range. To the west is the rainforest of **Braulio Carrillo National Park,** and to the east are **Tortuguero National Park** ✸✸ and **Barra del Colorado National Wildlife Refuge** ✸. In between these protected areas lay thousands of acres of banana, pineapple, and palm plantations. Here you see the great contradiction of Costa Rica: On the one hand, the country is known for its national parks, which preserve some of the largest tracts of rainforest left in Central America; on the other hand, nearly every acre of land outside of these parks, save a few private reserves, has been clear-cut and converted into plantations—and the cutting continues.

Within the remaining rainforest are several lodges that attract naturalists (both amateur and professional). Two of these lodges, **La Selva** and **Rara Avis,** are famous for the research that's conducted on their surrounding reserves. Bird-watching and rainforest hikes are the primary attractions, but more adventure-oriented travelers will find plenty of activities available here, including canopy tours and boating and rafting trips along the Sarapiquí River.

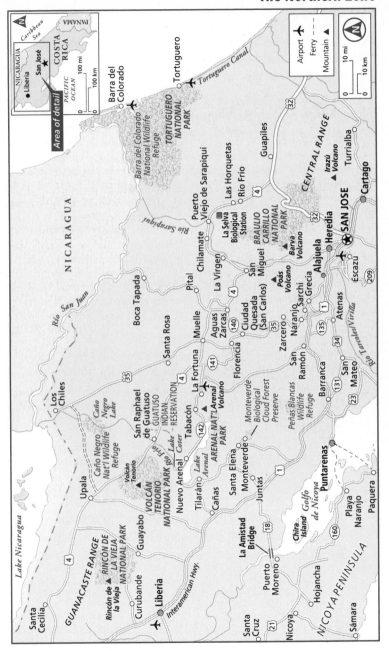

ESSENTIALS

GETTING THERE & DEPARTING   By Car   The Guápiles Highway, which leads to the Caribbean coast, heads north out of downtown San José on Calle 3 before heading east. Turn north before reaching Guápiles on the road to Río Frío, and continue north through Las Horquetas, passing the turnoffs for Rara Avis, La Selva, and El Gavilán lodges before reaching Puerto Viejo.

A more scenic route goes through Heredia, Barva, Varablanca, and San Miguel before reaching Puerto Viejo. This route passes very close to the Poás Volcano and directly in front of the La Paz waterfall. If you want to take this route, head west out of San José, then turn north to Heredia and follow the signs for Varablanca. *Tip:* If you plan to stop on the way to see the **La Paz Waterfall Gardens** (p. 133) or ride the **Rain Forest Aerial Tram** (p. 240), budget *at least* 2 hours to visit either attraction.

By Bus   Empresarios Guapileños buses (© **2222-0610** in San José, or 2710-7780 in Puerto Viejo) leave San José roughly every hour between 6am and 6pm from the **Gran Terminal del Caribe,** on Calle Central, 1 block north of Avenida 11. The buses are marked RIO FRIO, PUERTO VIEJO, or both. There are two routes to Puerto Viejo de Sarapiquí. The faster route heads out on the Guápiles Highway, through Braulio Carrillo National Park and then past Las Horquetas. The slower but more scenic route heads out through Heredia, Varablanca, and La Virgen, passing between the Barva and Poás volcanoes. If you're heading to La Selva, Rara Avis, or El Gavilán lodges, be sure you're on a bus going through Braulio Carrillo and Las Horquetas. The trip takes between 2 and 3 hours, depending on the route taken, the condition of the roads, and the frequency of stops; the fare is around $2.60 (£1.30). Buses for San José leave Puerto Viejo roughly every hour between 6am and 6pm.

ORIENTATION   Puerto Viejo is a very small town, at the center of which is a soccer field. If you continue past the soccer field on the main road and stay on the paved road, and then turn right at the Banco Nacional, you'll come to the Río Sarapiquí and the dock, where you can look into arranging a boat trip.

WHAT TO SEE & DO

BOAT TRIPS   For the adventurous, Puerto Viejo is a jumping-off point for trips down the Río Sarapiquí to Barra del Colorado National Wildlife Refuge and Tortuguero National Park on the Caribbean coast. A boat for up to 10 people will cost you around $200 to $300 (£100–£150) to Barra del Colorado or $250 to $375 (£125–£188) to Tortuguero. If you're interested in this trip, it's worth checking at your hotel or with **Oasis Nature Tours** (© **2766-6108;** www.oasisnaturetours.com). Alternatively, you can head down to the town dock on the bank of the Sarapiquí and see if you can arrange a less expensive boat trip on your own by tagging along with another group or, better yet, with a bunch of locals.

In addition to the longer trips, you can take shorter trips on the river for between $10 and $20 (£5–£10) per person per hour. A trip down the Sarapiquí, even if it's for only an hour or two, provides opportunities to spot crocodiles, caimans, monkeys, sloths, and dozens of bird species.

CANOPY TOUR & MORE   Hacienda Pozo Azul (© **877/810-6903** in the U.S. and Canada, or 2761-1360 in Costa Rica; www.pozoazul.com) is a working cattle farm and one-stop shop for a wide range of adventure activities. These folks have an extensive zip-line canopy tour operation, with 17 platforms connected by 12 different cable runs, in addition to offering white-water rafting and kayaking, horseback riding, guided hikes, and mountain bike tours. They even run a tent-camp and separate rustic lodge, in deep rainforest sites here.

HIKING & GUIDED TOURS   Anyone can take advantage of the 56km (35 miles) of well-maintained **trails at La Selva** ✦ (p. 240). If you're not staying there, however, you'll have to take a guided hike, led by experienced and well-informed naturalists. Half- and full-day hikes ($28/£14 and $36/£18, respectively) are offered daily, but you must reserve in advance (✆ **2766-6565** or 2424-0607; www.threepaths.co.cr). The half-day tours leave at 8am and 1:30pm daily.

My favorite hike starts off with the Cantarrana ("singing frog") trail, which includes a section of low bridges over a rainforest swamp. From here, you can join up with either the near or far circular loop trails—**CCC** and **CCL.** Another good hiking option is the trails and suspended bridges at the **Centro Neotrópico SarapiquíS** (p. 242).

Finally, if you want to visit the Sarapiquí region on a day trip from San José, call either **Costa Rica Fun Adventures** (✆ **2290-6015;** www.crfunadventures.com) or **Ecoscapes Highlights Tour** (✆ **2297-0664;** www.ecoscapetours.com), which run jampacked day trips that combine a bus ride and stop at the Poás Volcano, La Paz waterfall, a visit to a coffee farm, a rainforest hike, and a boat ride on the river for around $83 (£42) per person.

GO BANANAS   The local community of Nogal and Chiquita banana company have combined to offer an interpretive tour of a regional banana plantation. Part theater, part educational presentation, and part site inspection, the tour even features dancing girls. The 2-hour tour is offered every Tuesday at 1:30pm, or by reservation (✆ **8825-0494;** www.chiquitabananashow.com), and costs $15 (£7.50)

A NATURAL-HISTORY THEME PARK   The **Centro Neotrópico SarapiquíS** (p. 242) is a multifaceted natural-history project and tourist attraction. The Alma Ata Archaeological Park is basically an ongoing dig of a modest pre-Columbian gravesite; so far, 12 graves, some petroglyphs, and numerous pieces of ceramic and jewelry have been unearthed. Plans for the park include the reconstruction of a small indigenous village. The hotel also has a small museum that displays examples of the ceramics, tools, clothing, and carvings found here, as well as other natural-history exhibits. Just across the hotel's driveway, you'll find the Chester Field Biological Gardens, which feature well-tended and displayed examples of local medicinal and ornamental plants and herbs, as well as food crops. Admission to the archaeological park, museum, and gardens costs $19 (£10). If you just want to visit the museum, the cost is $12 (£6); it's open daily from 8am to 6pm. A self-guided walk through the botanical gardens is free.

Across the Sarapiquí River from the Centro Neotrópico is the 300-hectare (741-acre) private **Tirimbina Rainforest Center** ✦ (✆ **2761-1579;** www.tirimbina.org), which features a small network of trails and several impressive suspension bridges, both over the river and through the forest canopy. A self-guided walk of the bridges and trails of the reserve costs $15 (£7.50) per person, and a 2-hour guided tour costs $20 (£10) per person—definitely worth the extra few bucks. Night tours and specialized bird-watching tours are also available.

RAFTING & KAYAKING   If you want a fast, wild ride on the river, check in with **Aguas Bravas** (✆ **2292-2072;** www.aguas-bravas.co.cr) or **Aventuras del Sarapiquí** ✦ (✆ **2766-6768;** www.sarapiqui.com). Both companies run trips on a variety of sections of the Sarapiquí River, ranging from Class III to Class V. Trips cost between $45 and $70 (£23–£35) per person. Aventuras del Sarapiquí also runs mountain-biking and horseback riding tours in the area. They rent kayaks, give kayaking classes, and offer kayak trips for more experienced and/or daring river rats, and offer inner-tube floats for those with lesser skill sets still looking to get wet.

Another option is to stay at **Rancho Leona,** in La Virgen de Sarapiquí (© 2761-1019; www.rancholeona.com), a small stained-glass workshop, kayaking center, and rustic guesthouse on the banks of the Río Sarapiquí in the village of La Virgen. Its trips are offered as a package that includes lodging in simple dormitory-style accommodations, all meals, and extensive kayak instruction on the river. They even throw in an hour of Spanish lessons per day. No experience is necessary, and the river here is very calm. Trips for experienced kayakers can also be arranged.

SNAKES UNDER GLASS   Just a few blocks west of the Centro Neotrópico SarapiquíS, you'll find **Jardin de Seprientes (Snake Garden;** © 2761-1059), a collection of over 50 snakes, both venomous and non-venomous, and other reptiles and amphibians. One of the prize attractions here, although not native, is a massive, yellow Burmese python. All are kept in clean, well-lit displays. Admission is $6 (£3) adults, $3 (£1.50) children.

TWO MAJOR ATTRACTIONS EN ROUTE   If you're driving to Puerto Viejo de Sarapiquí via the Guápiles Highway, you might want to stop at the **Rain Forest Aerial Tram** ⚐. You'll see the entrance on your right shortly after passing through the Zurquí tunnel. If you're traveling via Varablanca and La Virgen, you'll want to visit the **La Paz Waterfall Gardens** ⚐⚐, which is right on the winding road to Puerto Viejo de Sarapiquí, about 6km (3¾ miles) beyond Varablanca. For more information, see "What to See & Do" and "Side Trips from San José," in chapter 6.

WHERE TO STAY & DINE

All the lodges listed below arrange excursions throughout the region, including boat trips on the Sarapiquí, guided hikes in the rainforest, and horseback or mountain-bike rides. Also note that rates for the lodges in the "Expensive" category include all meals, taxes, and usually a tour or two, greatly reducing their real cost. In addition to the hotels listed below, **Peace Lodge** (p. 118), located at the La Paz Waterfall Gardens, is almost close enough to be considered lodging in this region.

EXPENSIVE

La Selva Biological Station ⚐   This place caters primarily to students and researchers but also accepts visitors seeking a rustic rainforest adventure. The atmosphere is definitely that of a scientific research center. La Selva, which is operated by the Organization for Tropical Studies (OTS), covers 1,480 hectares (3,656 acres) and is contiguous with Braulio Carrillo National Park. There are miles of well-maintained hiking trails to explore. Researchers estimate that more than 2,000 species of flora exist in this private reserve, and 400-plus species of birds have been identified here. Rooms are basic but large, and the high ceilings help keep them cool. Most have bunk beds and shared bathrooms, although eight have private bathrooms and twin beds, and the two-room family units have a mix of twin and queen-size beds. There's no price difference, so be specific when reserving a room. The dining hall is a big, bright place where students and scientists swap data over fried chicken or fish with rice and beans. Rates are pretty high for what you get, but you can take some solace in the fact that you're helping to support valuable and valiant research and conservation efforts.

Puerto Viejo (A.P. 676-2050, San Pedro, Costa Rica). ☎ 2524-0607 reservations office in San José, or 2766-6565 at the lodge. Fax 2524-0608. www.threepaths.co.cr. 24 units, 16 with shared bathroom. $82 (£41) per person double occupancy. Rates include all meals, half-day tour, and taxes. Rates lower for researchers and student groups. MC, V. **Amenities:** Restaurant; kayak rentals; laundry service. *In room:* No phone.

Selva Verde Lodge 𝄞 *Kids*

This long-standing rainforest lodge is another of the early ecotourist ventures in Costa Rica. Continued expansion and remodeling have kept things comfortable and up-to-date. The all-wood main lodge is a series of buildings connected by covered walkways that keep you dry even though this area receives more than 150 inches of rain each year. The bungalows are across the road and 500m (1,640 ft.) into the forest; they're not as close to the main compound as the lodge rooms, but they offer quite a bit more privacy, as well as air-conditioning and a private screened veranda. Meals are served buffet-style in a beautiful large dining room that overlooks the river. Across the river is a large rainforest preserve. There are several trails on the grounds, a wonderful suspension bridge with a separate zip-line adventure across the river to more trails, and modest butterfly and botanical gardens. The newest addition here is a pretty free-form pool and separate children's pool, and there's also a natural swimming hole right on the river. Selva Verde is located right between the main road (a few kilometers west of Puerto Viejo) and by the Río Sarapiquí.

Chilamate (A.P. 55-3069), Sarapiquí. ☎ 800/451-7111 in the U.S. and Canada, or 2766-6800. Fax 2766-6011. www.selvaverde.com. 45 units, 5 bungalows. $130–$162 (£65–£81) double. Rates include 3 meals daily and taxes. Rates lower in off season. AE, DC, DISC, MC, V. **Amenities:** Restaurant; bar; outdoor pool; tour desk; laundry service. *In room:* Hair dryer, safe.

Sueño Azul Resort 𝄞𝄞 *Kids*

This nature lodge and wellness retreat offers arguably the top accommodations in the area. Set at the juncture of two rivers and backed by rainforest and forested mountains, the setting's pretty darn nice as well. All rooms are spacious, with high ceilings, two double beds, large bathrooms, and a private porch overlooking either one of the rivers or a small lake. Ten of the rooms come with air-conditioning, and one large junior suite has its own outdoor Jacuzzi. Meals are served in an open-air dining room set to take in the view, and a pool, Jacuzzi, bar, and rancho are down by the rivers' edge. The best place to cool off is in the massive outdoor pool, fed and filled by river water from a small waterfall, although there's a more traditional freshwater pool, and you can simply swim in the river at various spots. There's also a good-size spa and yoga facility. A wide range of tours and activities is offered, including rainforest hikes, horseback riding, mountain biking, and fly-fishing, as well as trips to the area's major attractions. The newest attraction here is a trapeze rig, with daily lessons in this high-flying circus art.

Las Horquetas de Sarapiquí (A.P. 3630-1000, San José). ☎ 2253-2020 reservation number in San José, 2764-1048 at the lodge. Fax 2224-3552. www.suenoazulresort.com. 57 units. $144 (£72) double; $163 (£81) suite. Rates lower in off season. Add $20 (£10) for air-conditioning. MC, V. **Amenities:** Restaurant; small pool; activities desk; room service (7am–10pm); laundry service. *In room:* Minibar, hair dryer, safe, no phone.

MODERATE

Although I highly recommend you choose one of the more atmospheric nature lodges listed in this section, if you absolutely must, or for some reason prefer to, stay in Puerto Viejo de Sarapiquí proper, **Hotel El Bambú** (☎ 2766-6005; www.elbambu. com) is a clean, comfortable, and almost modern option.

In addition to the places below, the **Tirimbina Rainforest Center** 𝄞 (☎ 2761-1579; www.tirimbina.org) now has rooms.

Centro Neotrópico SarapiquíS 𝒜 Located on a high bluff fronting the Sarapiquí River, this complex is the most unique project in the Sarapiquí region. The rooms are housed in three large, round buildings, or *palenques*. Based on the traditional pre-Columbian constructions of the area, each of the three *palenques* has a towering thatch roof rising some 18m (59 ft.). All rooms are comfortable and spacious although a little dark, and each has a door leading out to the shared veranda that encircles the building. Smoking is permitted only in the bar and restaurant. The hotel, which has begun calling itself the SarapiquíS Rainforest Lodge, has several interesting attractions, including a small natural-history museum, an on-site excavation of a pre-Columbian graveyard, and a well-marked botanical garden. Just across the river lies the 300-hectare (741-acre) Tirimbina Rainforest Center, with a small network of trails and several impressive suspension bridges, both over the river and through the forest canopy. Tours of the museum and reserve cost extra and are open to guests at other hotels.

A.P. 86-3069, La Virgen de Sarapiquí. ⓒ 2761-1004. Fax 2761-1415. www.sarapiquis.org. 36 units. $104 (£52) double. Rates lower in off season. V. **Amenities:** Restaurant; bar; tour desk; limited room service; babysitting; laundry service; nonsmoking rooms.

Rara Avis *(Finds* Rara Avis is one of the first, most responsible, biologically rich, and isolated ecolodge operations in Costa Rica. There are several options here, but the Waterfall Lodge is by far the most comfortable and popular. It has rustic but comfortable rooms in a two-story building near the main lodge and dining room and just 200m (656 ft.) from its namesake two-tiered waterfall. Each unit here is a corner room with a wraparound porch. For those who want closer communion with nature, Rara Avis has a two-room cabin set deep in the forest beside a river, about a 10-minute hike from the main lodge, as well as three more rustic two-bedroom cabins with shared bathrooms, located in a small clearing about a 5-minute walk from the lodge. Meals are basic Tico-style dishes with lots of beans and rice.

The grounds of Rara Avis are adjacent to Braulio Carrillo National Park, and together the two areas have many miles of trails for you to explore. *Bird-watchers, take note:* More than 362 species of birds have been sighted here, and the lodge consistently has excellent guides and naturalists.

When making reservations, be sure to get directions for how to get to Las Horquetas and information on coordinating your ride on the lodge's tractor. Be forewarned, it's a long, slow, bumpy and muddy ride in a small buggy pulled by a tractor up to the lodge. The tractor leaves just once daily for the very bumpy and plodding 3-hour ride to the lodge.

15km (9⅓ miles) from Las Horquetas (A.P. 8105-1000, San José). ⓒ 2764-1111 for reservations or 2710-8032 at the lodge. Fax 2764-1114. www.rara-avis.com. 16 units, 10 with private bathroom. $50 (£25) per person with shared bathroom; $140–$160 (£70–£80) double with private bathroom. Rates include transportation from Las Horquetas (you can't get there by car), guided hikes, all meals, and taxes. AE, MC, V. **Amenities:** Restaurant. *In room:* No phone.

INEXPENSIVE

In addition to the places listed below, budget travelers might want to check out the **Posada Andrea Cristina** (ⓒ 2766-6265; www.andreacristina.com), which is just on the outskirts of Puerto Viejo and is run by Alex Martínez, an excellent local guide and pioneering conservationist in the region. You may also consider staying at the jungle tent camp or isolated Magsasay Lodge at **Hacienda Pozo Azul** (ⓒ 877/810-6903 in the U.S. and Canada, or 2761-1360; www.pozoazul.com).

Gavilán Sarapiquí River Lodge   On the banks of the Río Sarapiquí just south of Puerto Viejo, Gavilán is surrounded by 100 hectares (247 acres) of forest reserve (secondary forest) and 14 hectares (35 acres) of gardens planted with lots of flowering ginger, heliconia, orchids, and bromeliads. Guest rooms are basic and simply furnished, and the beds are a bit soft for my taste. Still, all have fans and hot water, and there are always fresh-cut flowers. The newest additions here are four "superior" rooms, with much more contemporary appointments and amenities. There's an unheated Jacuzzi in the garden and several open-air ranchos, some of which have hammocks strung up for afternoon siestas. Tico and Continental meals are served buffet-style, and there are always plenty of fresh fruits and juices. Guided hikes through the forest, horseback rides, and river trips are all offered for around $30 (£15) per person.

Puerto Viejo de Sarapiquí (A.P. 445-2010, San José). **©** **2234-9507** or 2766-6743. Fax 2253-6556. www.gavilan lodge.com. 17 units. $55 (£28) double; $75 (£38) superior double. MC, V. **Amenities:** Restaurant; bar; Jacuzzi; laundry service. *In room:* No phone.

La Quinta de Sarapiquí Country Inn   This small, family-run lodge makes a good base for exploring the Sarapiquí region. Located on the banks of the Sardinal River about 15 minutes west of Puerto Viejo, La Quinta caters primarily to nature lovers and bird-watchers. The rooms are located in a half-dozen buildings dispersed around the grounds among richly flowering gardens and connected by covered walkways. They're simple but clean, with good lighting and comfortable bathrooms. Each room has a small patio with a sitting chair or two for gazing out into the garden. The superior rooms have air-conditioning. There are also a small gift shop, a butterfly garden, a frog garden, an extensive insect display, and a vegetable garden and reforestation project on hand. If you don't have a car, call the hotel to see if you can arrange a pickup in Puerto Viejo. Meals are served either buffet- or family-style in the main lodge and will run you an extra $31 (£16) per day.

Chilamate (A.P. 43-3069), Sarapiquí. **©** **2761-1300.** Fax 2761-1395. www.laquintasarapiqui.com. 31 units. $70 (£35) double; $90 (£45) superior double. Children 11 and under stay free in parent's room. AE, MC, V. **Amenities:** Restaurant; bar; small pool; tour desk; laundry service.

2 Arenal Volcano & La Fortuna ★★

140km (87 miles) NW of San José; 61km (38 miles) E of Tilarán

I've visited scores of times, and I never tire of watching red lava rocks tumble down the flanks of **Arenal Volcano,** and listening in awe to its deep rumbling. If you've never experienced them firsthand, the sights and sounds of an active volcano are awe-inspiring. Arenal is one of the world's most regularly active volcanoes. In July 1968, the volcano, which had lain dormant for hundreds of years, surprised everybody by erupting with sudden violence. The nearby village of Tabacón was destroyed, and nearly 80 of its inhabitants were killed. Since that eruption, 1,607m (5,271-ft.) Arenal has been Costa Rica's most active volcano. Frequent powerful explosions send cascades of red-hot lava rocks down the volcano's steep slopes. During the day these lava flows smoke and rumble. However, at night the volcano puts on its most mesmerizing show. If you are lucky enough to be here on a clear and active night—not necessarily a guaranteed occurrence—you'll see the night sky turned red by lava spewing from Arenal's crater. In the past few years, the forests to the south of the volcano have been declared Arenal National Park. Eventually, this park should stretch all the way to Monteverde Biological Cloud Forest Reserve.

Lying at the eastern foot of this natural spectacle is the tiny farming community of **La Fortuna.** This town has become a magnet for volcano watchers, adventure tourists, and assorted travelers from around the world. A host of budget and moderately priced hotels are in and near La Fortuna, and from here you can arrange night tours to the best volcano-viewing spots, which are 17km (11 miles) away on the western slope, on the road to and beyond the Tabacón Grand Spa Thermal Resort.

ESSENTIALS

GETTING THERE & DEPARTING   By Plane   Nature Air (© 800/235-9272 in the U.S. and Canada, or 2299-6000; www.natureair.com) flies to Arenal/La Fortuna daily at 2:50pm from Tobías Bolaños International Airport in Pavas. The flight duration is 30 minutes. Return flights depart for San José at 8:50am. Nature Air also has a daily flight from Tamarindo to Arenal at 7:40am, stopping at Liberia en route, and making the return flight at 3:25pm. One-way fares are $79 (£40) between Arenal and San José, and $140 (£70) between Arenal and Tamarindo.

Sansa (© 877/767-2672 in the U.S. and Canada, or 2290-4100 in Costa Rica; www.flysansa.com) has one daily flight to Arenal La Fortuna from San José's Juan Santamaría International airport at 8am. The flight takes 30 minutes. The fare is $78 (£39) each way. The return flight leaves Arenal at 8:45am. Sansa also has one daily direct flight from Liberia to Arenal at 7:14am, returning at 8:45am.

Taxis are sometimes waiting for all arriving flights. If not, you can call one at © 2479-9605 or 2479-8522. The fare to La Fortuna runs around $20 (£10). Alternately, Nature Air can arrange to have a van waiting for you, for $48 (£24) for up to seven people.

By Car   There are several routes to La Fortuna from San José. The most popular is to head west on the Interamerican Highway and then turn north at Naranjo, continuing north through Zarcero to Ciudad Quesada. From Ciudad Quesada, one route goes through Jabillos, while the other goes through Muelle. The former route is better marked, more popular, slightly shorter, and generally better maintained, but the severe weather and heavy traffic quickly take their toll, and the roads up here can be notoriously bad for long stretches. This route offers wonderful views of the San Carlos valley as you come down from Ciudad Quesada; and Zarcero, with its topiary gardens and quaint church, makes a good place to stop, stretch your legs, and snap a few photos (see "Side Trips from San José," in chapter 6, for more information).

You can also stay on the Interamerican Highway until San Ramón (west of Naranjo) and then head north through La Tigra. This route is also very scenic and passes the Villablanca Cloud Forest & Spa (p. 257). The travel time on any of the above routes is between 2½ and 3½ hours.

Finally, if you combine your visit here with a stop at the Poás Volcano and La Paz Waterfall, or if you stay at a lodge closer to Aguas Zarcas, you can go first to Alajuela or Heredia and then head north to Varablanca before continuing on to San Miguel, where you turn west toward Río Cuarto and Aguas Zarcas. From Aguas Zarcas, continue west through Muelle to the turnoff for La Fortuna. This is the longest route.

By Bus   Buses (© 2255-0567) leave San José for La Fortuna roughly every 2 hours between 6am and 5:30pm from the **Atlántico del Norte** bus station at Avenida 9 and Calle 12. The trip lasts 4 hours; the fare is $3.40 (£1.65). The bus you take might be labeled TILARAN. Make sure it passes through Ciudad Quesada. If so, it passes through

Tips   Boats, Horses & Taxis

You can travel between La Fortuna and Monteverde by boat and taxi, or on a combination boat, horseback, and taxi trip. A 10- to 20-minute boat ride across Lake Arenal cuts out hours of driving around its shores. From La Fortuna to the put-in point is about a 25-minute taxi ride. It's about a 1½-hour four-wheel-drive taxi ride between the Río Chiquito dock on the other side of Lake Arenal and Santa Elena. These trips can be arranged in either direction for between $25 and $45 (£13–£23) per person, all-inclusive.

You can also add on a horseback ride on the Santa Elena/Monteverde side of the lake. There are several routes and rides offered. The steepest heads up the mountains and through the forest to the town of San Gerardo, which is only a 30-minute car ride from Santa Elena. Other routes throw in shorter sections of horseback riding along the lakeside lowlands. With the horseback ride, this trip runs around $50 to $70 (£25–£35) per person.

Warning: The riding is often rainy, muddy, and steep. Many find it much more arduous than awe-inspiring. Moreover, I've received numerous complaints about the condition of the trails and the treatment of the horses, so be very careful and demanding before signing on for this trip. Find out what route you will be taking, as well as the condition of the horses if possible. **Desafío Expeditions** (© 2479-9464; www.desafiocostarica.com) is one of the more reputable operators. They will even drive your car around for you while you take the scenic (and sore) route.

La Fortuna; if not, you'll end up in Tilarán via the Interamerican Highway, passing through the Guanacaste town of Cañas, a long way from La Fortuna.

Alternatively, you can take a bus from the same station to Ciudad Quesada and transfer there to another bus to La Fortuna. These buses depart roughly every 30 minutes between 5am and 7:30pm. The fare for the 2½-hour trip is $2.80 (£1.40). Local buses between Ciudad Quesada and La Fortuna run regularly through the day, although the schedule changes frequently, depending on demand. The trip lasts 1 hour; the fare is $1.50 (75p).

Buses depart **Monteverde/Santa Elena** for Tilarán every day at 7am. This is a journey of only 35km (22 miles), but the trip lasts 2½ hours because the road is in such horrendous condition. People with bad backs should think twice about making the trip, especially by bus. The return bus from Tilarán to Santa Elena leaves at 12:30pm. The fare is $2.20 (£1.10). Buses from Tilarán to La Fortuna depart daily at 8am and 4:30pm, and make the return trip at 8am and 2:30pm. The trip is 3 to 4 hours; the fare is $2.70 (£1.35).

Buses depart La Fortuna for San José roughly every 2 hours between 5am and 5:30pm; in some instances, you might have to transfer in Ciudad Quesada. From there, you can catch one of the frequent buses to San José.

Gray Line (© 2220-2126; www.graylinecostarica.com) has two daily buses from San José to La Fortuna at 9am and 4:45pm. The fare is $33 (£17). **Interbus** (© 2283-5573; www.interbusonline.com) also has two buses daily leaving San José for La

Fortuna at 8:15am and 2:30pm. The fare is $35 (£18). Both companies will pick you up at most San José–area hotels. And both companies also run routes from La Fortuna with connections to most other major destinations in Costa Rica.

ORIENTATION & FAST FACTS   As you enter La Fortuna, you'll see the massive volcano directly in front of you. La Fortuna is only a few streets wide, with almost all the hotels, restaurants, and shops clustered along the main road that leads out of town toward Tabacón and the volcano. There are several information and tour-booking offices and Internet cafes, as well as a couple of pharmacies, general stores, and laundromats on the streets that surround the small central park that fronts the Catholic church. There's a Banco de Costa Rica as you enter La Fortuna, just over the Río Burío bridge, and a Banco Nacional in the center of town, across the park from the church. Both have ATMs.

GETTING AROUND   If you don't have a car, you'll need to either take a cab or go on an organized tour if you want to visit the hot springs or view the volcano eruption. There are tons of taxis in La Fortuna (you can flag one down practically anywhere), and there is always a line of them ready and waiting along the main road beside the central park. A taxi between La Fortuna and Tabacón should cost around $6 (£3). Another alternative is to rent a car when you get here. **Alamo** (© 2479-9090; www.alamocostarica.com) and **Poás** (© 2479-8027; www.carentals.com) both have offices in La Fortuna.

There are also several places to rent scooters and ATVs around town. Provided it's not raining too heavily, this is a good way to get around. Rates run around $35 to $45 (£18–£23) per day for a scooter, and $40 to $70 (£20–£35) for an ATV.

WHAT TO SEE & DO

While in the town of La Fortuna, be sure to spend some time simply people-watching from a bench or grassy spot on the central plaza. It's also worth a quick visit to tour the town's **Catholic church.** This modern church was designed by famous Costa Rican artist Teodorico Quirós, and features an interesting soaring front steeple and clock tower of concrete. In town, you'll find the tiny **Los Abuelos Museum** (© 2479-7306), a very modest collection of old currency, tools, clothing, and household items, collected over several generations by a local family. Admission is $8 (£4), which I think is just a bit ridiculous given the very meager displays. It's open Monday to Saturday from 9am to 4pm.

EXPERIENCING THE VOLCANO 🐾🐾

The first thing you should know is that Arenal Volcano borders a region of cloud forests and rainforests, and the volcano's cone is often socked in by clouds and fog. Many people come to Arenal and never get to see the exposed cone. Moreover, the volcano does go through periods when it is relatively quiet.

The second thing you should know is that you can't climb Arenal Volcano—it's not safe due to the constant activity. Several foolish people who have ignored this warning have lost their lives, and others have been severely injured. The most recent fatalities occurred in August 2000.

Still, waiting for and watching Arenal's regular eruptions is the main activity in La Fortuna and is best done at night when the orange lava glows against the starry sky. Although it's possible simply to look up from the middle of town and see Arenal erupting, the view is best from the north and west sides of the volcano along the road to Tabacón and toward the national park entrance. If you have a car, you can drive along this road, but if you've arrived by bus, you will need to take a taxi or tour.

Arenal National Park constitutes an area of more than 2,880 hectares (7,114 acres), which includes the viewing and parking areas closest to the volcano. The park is open daily from 8am to 10pm and charges $10 (£5) admission per person. The trails through forest and over old lava flows inside the park are gorgeous and fun. (Be careful climbing on those volcanic boulders.) However, at night the view from inside the park is no better than on the roads just outside it.

If you don't have a car and are staying in La Fortuna, every hotel in town and several tour offices offer night tours to the volcano. (They don't actually enter the park; they stop on the road that runs between the park entrance and the Arenal Observatory Lodge.) These tours generally cost between $10 and $25 (£5–£13) per person. Often these volcano-viewing tours include a stop at one of the local hot springs, and the price goes up accordingly (see "Taking a Soothing Soak in Hot Springs," below, for a description of the different options and fees).

Note: Although it's counterintuitive, the rainy season is often a better time to see the exposed cone of Arenal Volcano, especially at night. I don't know why this is, but I've had excellent volcano-viewing sessions at various points during the rainy season; during the dry season the volcano can often be socked in solid for days at a time. The bottom line is that catching a glimpse of the volcano's cone is never a sure thing.

OTHER ADVENTUROUS PURSUITS IN THE AREA

Aside from the impressive volcanic activity, the area around Arenal Volcano is packed with other natural wonders.

ATV   The folks at **Fourtrax Adventures** (© 2479-8444; www.fourtraxadventure. com) offer a 3-hour adventure through the forests and farmlands around La Fortuna. The tour includes a stop at a jungle swimming hole, where you can cool off, as well as a visit to a butterfly farm. You get good views of the volcano, as well as the La Fortuna Waterfall. The cost is $75 (£36) per ATV. A second rider on the same ATV costs $30 (£15).

CANOPY TOURS & CANYONING   There are numerous ways to get up into the forest canopy here. Perhaps the simplest way is to hike the trails and bridges of **Arenal Hanging Bridges** (© 2290-0469; www.hangingbridges.com). Located just over the Lake Arenal dam, this attraction is a complex of gentle trails and suspension bridges through a beautiful tract of primary forest. It's open daily from 7:30am to 4:30pm; admission is $22 (£11). Guided tours, early bird-watching tours, and transportation are also available.

Another option is the **Sky Tram** ✦✦ (© 2479-9944; www.skytrek.com), an open gondola-style ride that begins near the shores of Lake Arenal and rises up, providing excellent views of the lake and volcano. From here you can hike their series of trails and suspended bridges. In the end you can hike down, take the gondola, or strap on a harness and ride their zip-line canopy tour down to the bottom. The zip-line tour here features several very long and very fast sections, with some impressive views of the lake and volcano. The cost is $66 (£33) for the combined tram ride up and zip-line down tour. It's $55 (£27) to ride the tram round-trip.

If you'd like a bigger rush than the canopy tours offer, you could go "canyoning" with **Pure Trek Canyoning** ✦✦ (© 866/569-5723 in the U.S. and Canada, or 2479-1313; www.puretrekcostarica.com) and **Desafío Expeditions** ✦✦ (© 2479-9464;

Taking a Soothing Soak in Hot Springs

Arenal Volcano has bestowed a terrific fringe benefit on the area around it: several naturally heated thermal springs.

Located at the site of the former village that was destroyed by the 1968 eruption, **Tabacón Grand Spa Thermal Resort** ✦✦✦ (© 2519-1900; www. tabacon.com) is the most extensive, luxurious, and expensive spot to soak your tired bones. A series of variously sized pools, fed by natural springs, are spread out among lush gardens. At the center is a large, warm, spring-fed swimming pool with a slide, a swim-up bar, and a perfect view of the volcano. One of the stronger streams flows over a sculpted waterfall, with a rock ledge underneath that provides a perfect place to sit and receive a free hydraulic shoulder massage. The grounds here are extensive and it's worth exploring. The pools and springs closest to the volcano are some of the hottest—makes sense, doesn't it? The resort also has an excellent spa on the grounds offering professional massages, mud masks, and other treatments, as well as yoga classes (appointments required). Most of the treatments are conducted in lovely open-air gazebos surrounded by the rich tropical flora. The spa here even has several permanent sweat lodges, based on a Native American traditional design. A full-service restaurant, garden grill and a couple of bars are available for those seeking sustenance.

Entrance fees are $70 (£35) for adults and $35 (£18) for children 11 and under. This rate includes either a buffet lunch or dinner, and allows admission for a full day. After 6pm, you can enter for $45 (£23) not including any

www.desafiocostarica.com); both offer canyoning adventures. This adventure sport is a mix of hiking through and alongside a jungle river, punctuated with periodic rappels through and alongside the faces of rushing waterfalls. Pure Trek's trip is probably better for first-timers and families with kids, while Desafío's tour is just a bit more rugged and adventurous. Pure Trek charges $90 (£45), while Desafio charges $85 (£42). Both of these companies offer various combination full-day excursions, mixing canyoning with other adventure tours.

There are several other zip-line canopy tours in the area, including the **Arenal Canopy Tour** (© 2479-9769) and **Ecoglide** (© 2479-7120; www.arenalecoglide. com). In fact, the hotel **Montaña de Fuego** (see later in this chapter), even has its own zip-line tour set up.

Finally, while nowhere near as natural, you can also take a bungee jump in La Fortuna at **Arenal Bungee** (© 2479-7440; http://arenalbungee.com). The bungee jump here is a 40m (130 ft.) fall from a steel tower constructed on the outskirts of downtown La Fortuna. You can even try a water landing, as well as a "rocket launch," which is kind of the equivalent of becoming a human sling shot. Jumps, falls, and rocket shots cost $39 (£19). This attraction is open 9:30am to 9:30pm daily, so you can partake in this fun day or night.

FISHING With Lake Arenal just around the corner, fishing is a popular activity here. The big action is *guapote,* a Central American species of rainbow bass. However, meals. The hot springs are open daily from noon to 10pm (spa treatments can actually be scheduled as early as 8am, and hotel guests can enter at 10am). The pools are busiest between 2pm and 6pm. Management enforces a policy of limiting visitors, so reservations (which can be made online or by phone) are recommended. Spa treatments must be purchased separately, and reservations are required.

Baldi Hot Springs (② 2479-9651), next to the Volcano Look Disco, are the first hot springs you'll come to as you drive from La Fortuna toward Tabacón. This place has grown substantially over the years, with many different pools, slides, and bars and restaurants spread around the expansive grounds. However, I find this place far less attractive than either of the other two options mentioned here. There's much more of a party vibe at Baldi, with loud music often blaring at some of the swim-up bars. Admission is $30 (£15).

Just across the street from Baldi Termae is the unmarked entrance of my current favorite local hot spring, **Eco Termales** ★★ (② 2479-8484). Smaller and more intimate than Tabacón, this series of pools set amid lush forest and gardens is almost as picturesque and luxurious, although there are far fewer pools, the spa services are much less extensive, and there is no view of the volcano. Reservations are absolutely necessary here, and total admissions are limited so that it is never crowded. Admission is $24 (£13).

you can also book fishing trips to Caño Negro, where snook, tarpon, and other game fish can be stalked. Most hotels and adventure-tour companies can arrange fishing excursions. Costs run around $100 to $250 (£50–£125) for a half-day, $200 to $500 (£100–£250) for a full day.

HIKING & HORSEBACK RIDING   Horseback riding is a popular activity in this area, and there are scores of good rides on dirt back roads and through open fields and dense rainforest. Volcano and lake views come with the terrain on most rides. Horseback trips to the Río Fortuna waterfall are perhaps the most popular tours sold, but remember, the horse will get you only to the entrance; from there, you'll have to hike a bit. A horseback ride to the falls should cost between $20 and $45 (£10–£22), including the entrance fee.

One popular and strenuous hike is to **Cerro Chato,** a dormant volcanic cone on the flank of Arenal. There's a pretty little lake up here. **Desafío Expeditions** ★ (② 2479-9464; www.desafiocostarica.com) leads a 4- to 5-hour hike for $65 (£33), including lunch.

Aventuras Arenal (② 2479-9133; www.arenaladventures.com), **Desafío Expeditions** ★★ (② 2479-9464; www.desafiocostarica.com), **Jacamar Tours** (② 2479-9767; www.arenaltours.com), and **Sunset Tours** (② 866/417-7352 in the U.S. and Canada, or 2479-9800 in Costa Rica; www.sunsettourcr.com) are the main tour operators. In addition to the above tours, each of these companies offers most of the tours listed in this section, as well as fishing trips and sightseeing excursions on the lake, and transfers to other destinations around Costa Rica.

LA FORTUNA FALLS   Leading the list of side attractions in the area is the impressive **Río Fortuna Waterfall** ☆ (© **2479-8360**), located about 5.5km (3½ miles) outside of town in a lush jungle setting. There's a sign in town to indicate the road that leads out to the falls. You can drive or hike to just within viewing distance. When you get to the entrance to the lookout, you'll have to pay a $6 (£3) entrance fee to actually check out the falls. It's another 15- to 20-minute hike down a steep and often muddy path to the pool formed by the waterfall. The hike back up will take slightly longer. You can swim, but stay away from the turbulent water at the base of the falls—several people have drowned here. Instead, check out and enjoy the calm pool just around the bend, or join the locals at the popular swimming hole under the bridge on the paved road, just after the turnoff for the road up to the falls. The trail to the falls is open daily from 8am to 4pm.

MOUNTAIN BIKING   This region is very well suited for mountain biking. Rides range in difficulty from moderate to extremely challenging. You can combine a day on a mountain bike with a visit to one or more of the more popular attractions here. **Bike Arenal** ☆ (© **866/465-4114** in the U.S. and Canada, or 2479-9454; www.bike arenal.com) is the only dedicated operator in the field, with an excellent collection of top-notch bikes and equipment and a wide range of tour possibilities.

WHITE-WATER RAFTING & CANOEING   For adventurous tours of the area, check out **Desafío Expeditions** ☆☆ (© **2479-9464;** www.desafiocostarica.com) or **Wave Expeditions** ☆☆ (© **2479-7262;** www.waveexpeditions.com). Both companies offer daily raft rides of Class I to II, III, and IV to V on different sections of the Toro, Peñas Blancas, and Sarapiquí rivers. A half-day float trip on a nearby river costs around $45 (£23) per person; a full day of rafting on some rougher water costs $70 to $90 (£35–£45) per person, depending on what section of what river you ride. Both companies also offer mountain biking and most of the standard local guided trips. If you want a wet and personal ride, try Desafío's tour in inflatable kayaks, or "duckies," down the pristine Arenal River.

A more laid-back alternative is to take a canoe tour with **Canoa Aventura** (© **2479-8200;** www.canoa-aventura.com), which offers half-, full-, and multiday excursions on a variety of rivers in the region.

SIDE TRIPS FROM LA FORTUNA

La Fortuna is a great place from which to make a day trip to the **Caño Negro National Wildlife Refuge** ☆. This vast network of marshes and rivers (particularly the Río Frío) is 100km (62 miles) north of La Fortuna near the town of Los Chiles. This refuge is best known for its amazing abundance of bird life, including roseate spoonbills, jabiru storks, herons, and egrets, but you can also see caimans and crocodiles. Bird-watchers should not miss this refuge, although keep in mind that the main lake dries up in the dry season (mid-Apr to Nov), which reduces the number of wading birds. Full-day tours to Caño Negro average between $45 and $60 (£23–£30) per person. However, most of the tours run out of La Fortuna that are billed as Caño Negro never really enter the refuge but instead ply sections of the nearby Río Frio, which features similar wildlife and ecosystems. If you're interested in staying in this area and really visiting the refuge, check out the **Caño Negro Natural Lodge** (see "Where to Stay & Dine Farther Afield," later in this chapter).

You can also visit the **Venado Caverns,** a 45-minute drive away. In addition to plenty of stalactites, stalagmites, and other limestone formations, you'll see bats and cave fish. Tours here cost around $45 (£23). All of the tour agencies and hotel tour desks can arrange or directly offer trips to Caño Negro and Venado Caverns.

SHOPPING

La Fortuna is chock-full of souvenir shops selling standard tourist fare. However, you'll find one of my favorite craft shops here. As you leave the town of La Fortuna toward Tabacón, keep your eye on the right-hand side of the road. When you see a massive collection of wood sculptures and a building reading **Original Grand Gallery** (no phone), slow down and pull over. This local artisan and his family produce works in a variety of styles and sizes. They specialize in faces, many of them larger than a typical home's front door. You can also find a host of animal figures, ranging in style from purely representational to rather abstract. Another good shop for higher-end arts and crafts is **Galería Lunática** (✆ 2479-8255), on the main road in La Fortuna.

WHERE TO STAY IN LA FORTUNA
EXPENSIVE

Magic Mountain Hotel ★★   It was just a matter of time 'til luxury found its way to La Fortuna. Located just on the outskirts of town—as you head toward Tabacón— this new three-story hotel has large and luxurious rooms, with plenty of perks. All come with a private balcony facing the volcano. The junior suites are even bigger, with a separate sitting area, large shower with rainwater shower head, and private volcano-view in-room Jacuzzi. I like no. 506, which is an end unit with spectacular views. There's a spa and large free-form pool, with two separate outdoor Jacuzzis and separate children's pool, as well as the town's only sports bar.

La Fortuna, San Carlos. ✆ **2479-7246.** Fax 2479-7248. www.hotelmagicmountain.com. 46 units. $145 (£73) double; $300 (£150) suite. Rates lower in the off season. Rates include buffet breakfast. AE, MC, V. **Amenities:** Restaurant; bar; outdoor pool; 2 Jacuzzis; spa; tour desk; laundry service. *In room:* A/C, TV, free Wi-Fi, minibar, coffeemaker, hair dryer, safe.

MODERATE

Hotel La Fortuna ★   This long-standing budget stalwart burned down several years ago and was quickly rebuilt near its original state. However, it was recently razed (intentionally) and replaced with a massive and modern five-story building. Centrally located just 1 block south of the gas station, the Hotel La Fortuna now features large, spiffy rooms with a host of modern amenities. The best of these have volcano-view private balconies—ask for a room on the fourth or fifth floor with a volcano view. This hotel has 12 rooms designed for wheelchair accessibility.

La Fortuna, San Carlos. ✆ **2479-9197.** Fax 2479-8563. www.fortunainn.com. 44 units. $75–$95 (£38–£48) double. Rates lower in the off season, higher during peak periods. Rates include buffet breakfast. MC, V. **Amenities:** Restaurant; tour desk. *In room:* A/C, TV, free Wi-Fi, hair dryer.

Hotel San Bosco   Located a block off La Fortuna's main street, the San Bosco offers some of the better rooms to be found right in town. The hotel actually has two styles of rooms. The least expensive rooms are all well maintained and feature tile floors and fans. However, these are standard budget-hotel affairs. The more expensive rooms are much more attractive and have stone walls, tile floors, reading lights, televisions, and benches on the veranda in front. There's an observation deck for volcano viewing on the top floor of the hotel, as well as a helpful front desk staff.

La Fortuna, San Carlos (200m/656 ft. north of the central park). © **2479-9050.** Fax 2479-9109. www.arenal-volcano.com. 34 units. $72–$77 (£36–£39) double. Rates include breakfast. Rates lower in off season. AE, MC, V. **Amenities:** Small pool and separate children's pool; small exercise room; Jacuzzi; tour desk; laundry service. *In room:* A/C, TV, free Wi-Fi, no phone.

INEXPENSIVE

La Fortuna is a tourist boomtown; basic hotels have been popping up here at a phenomenal rate for several years running. Right in La Fortuna you'll find a score of budget options. If you have time, it's worth walking around and checking out a couple. One of the better options is **Arenal Backpackers Resort** (© **2479-7000;** www.arenalbackpackers.com), which bills itself as a five-star hostel. It has both shared-bathroom dorm rooms, and more upscale private rooms, but even backpackers get to enjoy the large pool, Wi-Fi, and volcano views.

There are a couple places both in town and right on the outskirts of La Fortuna that allow camping, with access to basic bathroom facilities, for around $5 to $7 (£2.50–£3.50) per person per night. If you have a car, drive a little bit out of town toward Tabacón and you'll find several more basic cabins and camping sites, some that even offer views of the volcano.

Hotel Las Colinas ★ *(value)*   Like the Hotel La Fortuna (see above), this long-standing downtown hotel was recently torn down and rebuilt. Today, Las Colinas sits as the centerpiece of a new little minimall, which features some shops and a small spa. The rooms range from simple budget accommodations to spiffy junior suites with a private volcano-view balcony and Jacuzzi. The budget rooms come with televisions, but lack the other amenities found in the rest of the rooms. The best feature of the new hotel is its ample rooftop terrace where breakfasts are served. Ecofriendly touches include solar-heated water.

La Fortuna (A.P. 06), San Carlos. © **2479-9305.** Fax 2479-9160. www.lascolinasarenal.com. 19 units. $42 (£21) budget room double; $55–$60 (£27–£30) double; $70 (£35) junior suite. Rates include breakfast and taxes. Rates lower in off season. MC, V (5% surcharge). **Amenities:** Restaurant; tour desk. *In room:* A/C, TV, free Wi-Fi, minifridge, safe.

WHERE TO STAY NEAR THE VOLCANO

While La Fortuna is the major gateway town to Arenal Volcano, for my money, the best places to stay are located on the road between La Fortuna and the National Park.

One other very unique alternative is to stay aboard the **Rain Goddess** (© **866/ 593-3168** in the U.S., or 2231-4299; www.bluwing.com). This luxurious houseboat has four staterooms, ample lounge and dining areas, and cruises around Lake Arenal.

VERY EXPENSIVE

Arenal Kioro ★★   Set on 27 acres of hilly land with two rivers and a small patch of forest, this place is extremely close to Arenal Volcano. The views from the rooms, grounds, pool, and restaurant of this hotel are truly astounding. The rooms themselves are massive and opulent, with soaring high ceilings, large picture windows and glass doors, and a private balcony or patio facing the action. Each has its own four-person modern Jacuzzi tub, with sculpted seats and numerous jets, set below a large picture window with a volcano view. The beds are also set to take in the view. The spa is well designed and offers a wide range of treatment options. There are trails through the grounds, and a host of tours and activities are offered. The restaurant serves excellent international cuisine in a beautiful setting, with a giant wall of windows facing the volcano. These folks recently opened up their own little hot springs spot with a series of sculpted pools and gardens a short drive from the hotel.

On the main road btw. La Fortuna and Lake Arenal, 10km (6 miles) from La Fortuna. © **888/866-5027** in the U.S. and Canada, or 2461-1700. Fax 2461-1710. www.hotelarenalkioro.com. 53 units. $345 (£173) double. Rates include buffet breakfast. Rates lower in off season; higher during peak periods. AE, DC, MC, V. **Amenities:** Restaurant; bar; large outdoor pool; exercise room; spa; Jacuzzi; tour desk; in-room massage; laundry service. *In room:* A/C, TV, minibar, coffeemaker, hair dryer, safe.

Lost Iguana Resort ✦ This place offers large and luxurious rooms with great views of the volcano, although you're a little farther away from the action here than you are at the hotels closer to Tabacón and La Fortuna. The rooms are housed in a series of two-story buildings set on a hillside facing the volcano, and are quite spacious, with either one king-size or two twin beds on bamboo frames, attractive handmade wooden furniture, and interesting decorative touches. All feature a wall of glass letting out on a private balcony or porch, which in itself lets out onto the view. The suites are even larger and feature a Jacuzzi tub on the porch or balcony. You can also reserve one of several villas, which are in effect two-bedroom suites, with a full kitchenette and an extra-long balcony. Just below the open-air restaurant are a pretty two-tiered swimming pool and poolside bar. The hotel has a small network of trails on its own 40 hectares (100 acres) of land, as well as a well-equipped spa set on the lush grounds below the hotel.

On the road to Arenal Hanging Bridges, just over the Lake Arenal dam and to the right. The hotel is about a mile up this road on rough gravel (mailing address: A.P. 63-4417, La Fortuna de San Carlos). © **2267-6148** reservations office in San José, or 2461-0122 at the lodge. Fax 2267-7672. www.lostiguanaresort.com. 41 units. $185 (£92) double; $255 (£128) suite; $395–$460 (£198–£230) villa. Rates include breakfast. AE, MC, V. **Amenities:** Restaurant; bar; midsize pool w/swim-up bar; spa; tour desk; room service (7:30am–9:30pm); in-room massage; laundry service. *In room:* A/C, TV, free Wi-Fi, minifridge, coffeemaker, hair dryer, safe.

Tabacón Grand Spa Thermal Resort ✦✦✦ This is the most-established, extensive, and popular resort in the Arenal area—and for good reason. Many rooms have excellent, direct views of the volcano. Rooms on the upper floors of the 300-block building have the best vistas. However, quite a few of the rooms have obstructed, or no, views. My advice: Book a "Standard Superior," which will come with a view that is definitely worth the $30 (£15) splurge over the straight "Standard."

All rooms are quite spacious, with heavy, dark-stained wooden furniture. Most come with a private terrace or balcony with a table and a couple of chairs. Nine of the rooms are truly accessible to travelers with disabilities. The newer Forest Deluxe rooms are perhaps some of the plusher rooms here, with a private mosaic tile Jacuzzi and plasma-screen television, but, as the name suggests, they come with forest and not volcano views. Guests enjoy privileges at the spectacular hot-springs complex and spa across the street (see "Taking a Soothing Soak in Hot Springs" on p. 248), including slightly extended hours. When you consider the included entrance fee to the hot springs, the rates here are actually rather reasonable.

On the main road btw. La Fortuna and Lake Arenal, Tabacón (P.O. Box 181-1007, Centro Colón, San José). © **877/ 277-8291** in the U.S. and Canada, or 2519-1900 reservations in San José, or 2460-2020 at the resort. Fax 2519-1940. www.tabacon.com. 114 units. $230–$330 (£115–£165) double; $340–$370 (£170–£185) suite. Rates higher during peak periods. AE, DC, MC, V. **Amenities:** 2 restaurants; 2 bars; large pool w/swim-up bar; exercise room; extensive hot springs and spa facilities; Jacuzzi; tour desk; in-room massage; laundry service. *In room:* A/C, TV, Wi-Fi, dataport, coffeemaker, hair dryer, safe.

MODERATE

In addition to the places listed below, there has been ongoing construction along the entire length of the road between La Fortuna and Tabacón over the past years. If you have a car and some time, you might want to stop and check out any new or interesting hotels or cabins that strike your fancy along the way.

Arenal Observatory Lodge ★★   This place is incredibly close to the volcano and is built on a high ridge, with a spectacular view of the cone. Lying in bed at night listening to the eruptions, it's easy to think you're in imminent danger (don't worry—you're not). The best rooms here are the junior suites below the restaurant and main lodge, as well as the four rooms in the Observatory Block, and the White Hawk villa. The "Smithsonian" rooms feature massive picture windows with a direct view of the volcano. The lodge offers a number of guided and unguided hiking options, including a free morning guided hike through their trails and gardens, as well as a wide range of other tours. Meals are served in a dining room with a full wall of glass facing the volcano. This is one of the better nature lodges for travelers with disabilities: Five rooms are truly equipped for wheelchair access, and a paved path extends almost 1km (½ mile) into the rainforest. When you're not hiking or touring the region, you can hang by the volcano-view swimming pool and Jacuzzi.

To get here, head to the national park entrance, stay on the dirt road past the entrance, and follow the signs to the Observatory Lodge. A four-wheel-drive vehicle used to be required for the 9km (5½-mile) dirt road up to the lodge, but two bridges now eliminate the need to ford any major rivers, and a traditional sedan will usually make it even in the rainy season—although you'll always be better off with the clearance afforded by a four-wheel-drive vehicle.

On the flanks of Arenal Volcano (A.P. 13411-1000, San José). ⓒ **2290-7011** reservations number in San José, or 2479-1070 at the lodge. Fax 2290-8427. www.arenalobservatorylodge.com. 42 units. $70 (£35) La Casona double; $93 (£47) standard double; $122 (£61) Smithsonian; $140 (£70) junior suite. Rates include breakfast buffet and are lower in off season. AE, MC, V. **Amenities:** Restaurant; bar; pool; Jacuzzi; tour desk; laundry service. *In room:* No phone.

Montaña de Fuego Inn ★   This modest resort is a collection of individual and duplex cabins spread over hilly grounds. Most have amazing volcano views from their spacious glass-enclosed porches. Some rooms even have back balconies overlooking a forested ravine, in addition to the volcano-facing front porch. The suites and junior suites all have a Jacuzzi tub. I actually prefer the juniors over the full suites, since the Jacuzzis in the juniors are set in front of a volcano-view picture window. Behind the hotel are some rolling hills that lead down to a small river surrounded by patches of gallery forest, where they conduct an adventurous horseback, hiking, and a zip-line canopy tour.

La Palma de la Fortuna (A.P. 82-4417), San Carlos. ⓒ **2460-1220.** Fax 2460-1455. www.montanafuegohotel.com. 69 units. $102–$123 (£51–£61) double; $143–$195 (£72–£83) suite. Rates include buffet breakfast. MC, V. **Amenities:** Restaurant; 2 bars; outdoor pool; spa; 2 Jacuzzis; tour desk; room service (6am-10pm); massage; laundry service. *In room:* A/C, TV, minibar, coffeemaker, hair dryer, safe.

Volcano Lodge ★ *Kids*   This lodge has grown quickly from a small collection of duplex cabins in a single row, to a large and spread-out resort with a wide range of services and amenities. All of the rooms are large and tastefully decorated with heavy wooden furnishings. All come with a small terrace with a couple of wooden rocking chairs, and most of these have great views of the volcano. Several rooms are wheelchair accessible. There are two restaurants here, as well as two outdoor pools, each with a separate heated Jacuzzi and volcano views. One also features a children's pool and playground. A wide range of tours and activities are offered.

La Fortuna de San Carlos. (© **866/208-9819** in the U.S. and Canada, or 2460-6080. Fax 2460-6020. www. volcanolodge.com. 70 units. $110 (£55) double. Rates include continental breakfast. Rates lower in off season. AE, MC, V. **Amenities:** 2 restaurants; 2 bars; 2 pools; small spa; Jacuzzis; tour desk; laundry service. *In room:* A/C, TV, free Wi-Fi, coffeemaker, hair dryer, safe.

INEXPENSIVE

While the hotels located along the road tend to be geared toward higher-end travelers, there are a few options for more budget-conscious travelers. In addition to the inexpensive options in La Fortuna, if you have a car, **Cabinas Los Guayabos** ((©/fax **2460-6644**) and **Cabinas Palo Verde** ((© **2460-9791**) are good, economical options, with views and locations that rival some of the more expensive lodgings listed above.

WHERE TO DINE IN & AROUND LA FORTUNA

Dining in La Fortuna is nowhere near as spectacular as volcano viewing, although, given the area's popularity, there's no lack of options. The favorite meeting places in town are the **El Jardín Restaurant** ((© **2479-9360**) and **Lava Rocks** ((© **2479-8039**); both are on the main road, right in the center of La Fortuna. Other choices include **La Choza de Laurel** ((© **2479-9231**), **Rancho La Cascada** ((© **2479-9145**), and **Restaurante Nene's** ((© **2479-9192**). For Mexican fare, try **Las Brasitas** ((© **2479-9819**). For good pizza and Italian cuisine, try either the new **Anch'io** ((© **8350-4040**) located near the heart of town, or **El Vagabundo** ⭐ ((© **2479-9565**), just on the outskirts.

For some fine and fancy dining, you can try the **Lina's** ⭐ ((© **2479-7246**) at Magic Mountain Hotel, or **Los Tucanes** ⭐⭐ ((© **2460-2020**) restaurant at the Tabacón Grand Spa resort.

Don Rufino ⭐ COSTA RICAN/INTERNATIONAL   Set on a busy corner in the heart of town, this restaurant is easily the best—and the busiest—option right in town. The front wall and bar area open on to the street and are often filled both with local tour guides and tourists. Try the *pollo al estilo de la abuela* (Grandma's chicken), which is baked and served wrapped in banana leaves, or one of the excellent cuts of meat. It's a good choice for breakfast, and the bar stays open most nights until 2am.

Downtown La Fortuna. (© **2479-9997**. Main courses $5–$28 (£2.50–£14). Reservations recommended during the high season. AE, MC, V. Daily 7am–11pm.

El Novillo del Arenal *(Finds)* STEAK/COSTA RICAN   This place is the definition of "nothing fancy." In fact, it's just some lawn furniture (tables and chairs) set on a concrete slab underneath a high, open zinc roof. Still, it has garnered a well-deserved reputation as the best steakhouse in the area. The steaks are big and tender and well prepared. The chicken and fish dishes are huge as well and also nicely done. Meals come with garlic bread, fries, and some slaw. For a real local treat, order some fried yuca as a side. If the night is clear, you can get a good view of any volcanic activity from the parking lot here.

On the road to Tabacón, 10km (6¼ miles) outside of La Fortuna. (© **2479-1910**. Reservations recommended. Main courses $5.50–$12 (£2.75–£6). MC, V. Daily 10am–10pm.

Lava Lounge ⭐ *(Finds)* INTERNATIONAL   This downtown La Fortuna open-air restaurant combines a very simple setting with a sleek and somewhat eclectic menu. Healthy and hearty sandwiches, wraps, and salads are the main offerings here. You can get a traditional burger or one made with fresh grilled tuna. For more substantial fare, there's traditional Costa Rican *arroz con pollo,* and a *casado,* built around a thick pork chop. You can also get several different pasta dishes, and every evening there are dinner specials, which may include some coconut-battered shrimp with a mango salsa, or a prime sirloin steak in a green pepper or red-wine sauce. The decor consists of a series of rustic wooden tables with mostly bench seats.

Downtown La Fortuna, on the main road. ② 2479-7365. Reservations not necessary. Main courses $6–$10 (£3–£5). AE, MC, V. Daily noon–midnight.

LA FORTUNA AFTER DARK

La Fortuna's biggest after-dark attraction is the volcano, but the **Volcano Look Disco** on the road to Tabacón is trying to compete. If you get bored of the eruptions and seismic rumbling, head here for heavy dance beats and mirrored disco balls. In town the folks at Luigi's Hotel have opened a midsize **casino** next door to their hotel and restaurant, while the open-to-the-street bar at **Don Rufino** is a popular spot for a drink. Finally, there's a cozy new sports bar with a pool table and flatscreen televisions on the second floor at the **Hotel Magic Mountain.**

WHERE TO STAY & DINE FARTHER AFIELD

All of the hotels listed in the following three sections are at least a half-hour drive from La Fortuna and the volcano. Most, if not all, offer both night and day tours to Arenal and Tabacón, but they also hope to attract you with their own natural charms.

EAST OF LA FORTUNA

Termales del Bosque *(Finds* The best thing about this hotel is its wonderful **natural hot springs** *(★★.* The series of sculpted pools is set in the midst of rich rainforest, on the banks of a small river. Down by the pools are a natural steam room (scented each day with fresh eucalyptus), a massage room, and a snack-and-juice bar. The trail down here winds through the thick forest, and, if you want to keep on walking, you can take guided or self-guided tours on a network of well-marked trails. Rooms are pretty simple and plain. Still, they are clean and spacious, and most feature a private or shared veranda with views over gardens and rolling hills. There is also a three-bedroom bungalow with a shared bathroom and kitchenette. You can rent horses at the lodge, and a variety of tours are offered. If you aren't staying here, you can use the pools and hike the trails for $10 (£5).

On the road from San Carlos to Aguas Zarcas, just before El Tucano; Ciudad Quesada (A.P. 243-4400), San Carlos. ② 2460-4740. Fax 2460-1356. www.termalesdelbosque.com. 51 units. $61–$71 (£31–£36) double. Rates include full breakfast, unlimited use of the hot springs, and taxes. AE, DC, MC, V. **Amenities:** Restaurant; several hot-spring pools set beside a forest river; tour desk; massage; laundry service. *In room:* A/C, TV, no phone.

Tilajari Resort Hotel *(★ (Kids* This sprawling resort on the banks of the San Carlos River, just outside the farming community of Muelle (28km/17 miles from La Fortuna), makes a good base for exploring this area and offers terrific bird-watching. Most rooms have views of the river; others open onto rich flowering gardens. All have a private balcony or terrace. Large iguanas are frequently sighted on the grounds, and crocodiles live in the river. There's also an orchid garden, a tropical fruit-and-vegetable garden, a medicinal herb garden, and a well-maintained butterfly garden. The large open-air dining room has both formal and informal sections and a bar.

Tilajari is quite popular with Tico families, especially on weekends. This is a great place for your kids to have a chance to interact and play with their Costa Rican counterparts. The lodge arranges tours of the region, including trips to Caño Negro, Arenal Volcano and some hot springs, and Fortuna Falls, for around $60 (£30) per person. Trips into the nearby rainforest (on foot, on horseback, or by tractor), can also be arranged, as can gentle floats on the Peñas Blancas River. The hotel frequently hosts local tennis tournaments, too.

Tilajari is almost directly between La Fortuna, Aguas Zarcas, and Ciudad Quesada, and there are roads leading here from each of these towns.

Muelle (A.P. 81-4400), San Carlos. ⓒ **2469-9091.** Fax 2469-9095. www.tilajari.com. 76 units. $96–$105 (£48–£52) double; $110–$120 (£55–£60) suite. Rates include full breakfast. Rates lower in off season. AE, MC, V. **Amenities:** Restaurant; bar; large pool; 6 lighted tennis courts (2 indoors); exercise room; Jacuzzi; sauna; bike rental; game room; tour desk; laundry service. In room: A/C, TV, hair dryer, safe.

NORTH OF LA FORTUNA

Caño Negro Natural Lodge ⭐   This small nature lodge is the best option in the tiny village of Caño Negro, and it's well located right near the canals and lagoons. If you really want to visit the Caño Negro Wildlife Refuge, either for bird-watching and wildlife viewing or for fishing, this is a good choice. The hotel has spacious grounds full of flowering plants, tropical palms, and fruit trees. The rooms, housed in a series of duplex buildings, are all simple but roomy, clean, and comfortable, with much needed air-conditioning and tasteful decor. To get here, drive toward Los Chiles; several kilometers before Los Chiles, you'll see signs for this hotel and the wildlife refuge. From here, it's 18km (11 miles) on a flat dirt road to the village, refuge, and hotel.

Caño Negro. ⓒ **2265-3302** for reservations in San José, or 2471-1426 direct to the lodge. Fax 2265-4310. www.canonegrolodge.com. 22 units. $95 (£48) double. Rates include continental breakfast. Rates lower in off season. AE, DC, MC, V. **Amenities:** Restaurant; bar; midsize pool; game room; tour desk; laundry service. In room: A/C, safe.

SOUTH OF LA FORTUNA

El Silencio Lodge & Spa ⭐⭐   Built and run by the folks behind Punta Islita (p. 229), this luxurious lodge and spa features a small collection of large and plush individual cabins, set on a hillside in an isolated mountain setting. Each room features a king-size bed with luscious bedding, a modern marble bathroom, and private outdoor Jacuzzi. There are no televisions in the rooms, but the main lodge features a lounge area with a large plasma-screen set and modest DVD library. The spa here offers a range of excellent treatments, and the restaurant specializes in healthy spa cooking—no red meat is served. Hiking around the grounds will take you through their organic gardens, and a relatively easy loop trail passes by three nearby waterfalls. Day tours to Sarchi, Puerto Viejo de Sarapiqui, and Arenal/La Fortuna are all offered.

To reach El Silencio, you must first get to the town of Sarchi. From the Pali supermarket in the center of town, head north and follow the signs. El Silencio is approximately 22km (13 miles) outside of Sarchi.

Bajos del Toro, Alajuela. ⓒ **2291-3044.** Fax 2232-2183. www.elsilenciolodge.com. 16 units. $240 (£120) double. Rates include all meals, non-alcoholic drinks, taxes, and 1 daily hike. Rates lower in off season; higher during peak periods. AE, DC, MC, V. **Amenities:** Restaurant; bar; small spa; tour desk; laundry service. In room: Free Wi-Fi, stocked minibar, coffeemaker, hair dryer, safe.

Villablanca Cloud Forest & Spa ⭐⭐   This plush mountain-retreat hotel consists of a series of Tico-style casitas surrounded by 800 hectares (1,976 acres) of farm and forest. Each casita is built of adobe and has tile floors, open beamed ceilings, and white-washed walls. Inside you'll find a fireplace in one corner, comfortable hardwood chairs, and either one queen-size or two twin beds covered with colorful bedspreads. The deluxe units and suites have a separate sitting area with a fold-out couch and bathrooms with a whirlpool bathtub and a separate shower. In many rooms the bathroom tubs look out through a wall of windows onto lush gardens. Some have private patios. Movies are projected nightly on a screen in their THX theater. Just outside are 11km (6.75 miles) of trails through the **Los Angeles Cloud Forest Reserve.** You can also rent horses or take an adventurous swing through the canopy on a canopy tour here.

Villablanca is off the beaten track, but it is relatively close to San José, and if you're interested in bird-watching or exploring a cloud forest and want to avoid the crowds of Monteverde, this is a good choice. If you're driving, head west out of San José to San Ramón and then head north, following the signs to Villablanca. Or you can take a public bus from San José to San Ramón and then take a taxi for around $15 (£7.50).

San Ramón, Alajuela. ✆ **2461-0300.** Fax 2461-0302. www.villablanca-costarica.com. 34 units. $155 (£78) double; $175 (£88) deluxe; $195 (£98) suite. Rates include buffet breakfast. Rates lower in off season. AE, DC, MC, V. **Amenities:** Restaurant; bar; small spa; tour desk; laundry service. *In room:* Wi-Fi, stocked minifridge, coffeemaker, safe.

A REALLY REMOTE NATURE LODGE
La Laguna del Lagarto Lodge *(Finds)* It's hard to get much more remote than this. Located near the Nicaraguan border, La Laguna del Lagarto Lodge is bordered by more than 480 hectares (1,186 acres) of virgin rainforest that is home to a rich variety of tropical flora and fauna. The accommodations are simple yet comfortable. Most rooms open onto a balcony or veranda with sitting chairs and hammocks. The hotel is named after the two man-made lagoons that sit below the lodge buildings; canoes are available for paddling around these and several other nearby jungle waterways. There are more than 10km (6.25 miles) of well-maintained hiking trails, and the lodge offers trips on the San Carlos River, as well as horseback riding tours. More than 380 species of birds have been spotted here, and the hotel is involved in efforts to preserve the rare green macaw, which is frequently sighted here. In addition to the rainforest, the lodge sits on a small pepper plantation and has lands planted with palmito, pineapple, and other tropical fruits.

To get here, you head first to Pital and then continue on dirt roads to the town of Boca Tapada. It's another 6km (3¾ miles) to the lodge on more bumpy dirt roads. It's also possible to get here on public transportation (call for directions), or you can arrange for the lodge to handle your transportation from San José or La Fortuna (for a cost). Since anyone with four-wheel-drive can make the trip here independently, though, you're best off driving on your own.

Boca Tapada (A.P. 995-1007, San José). ✆ **2289-8163.** Fax 2289-5295. www.lagarto-lodge-costa-rica.com. 20 units. $57 (£29) double. AE, MC, V (5% surcharge). **Amenities:** Restaurant; bar. *In room:* No phone.

3 Along the Shores of Lake Arenal ⊛

200km (124 miles) NW of San José; 20km (12 miles) NW of Monteverde; 70km (43 miles) SE of Liberia

Despite possessing ample charms, this remains one of the least-developed tourism regions in Costa Rica. Lake Arenal, the largest lake in Costa Rica, is the centerpiece here. A long beautiful lake, it is surrounded by rolling hills that are partly pastured and partly forested. There are loads of activities and adventures available both on the lake and in the hills and forests around it. While the towns of Tilarán and Nuevo Arenal remain quiet rural communities, there are several excellent hotels spread out along the shores of the lake.

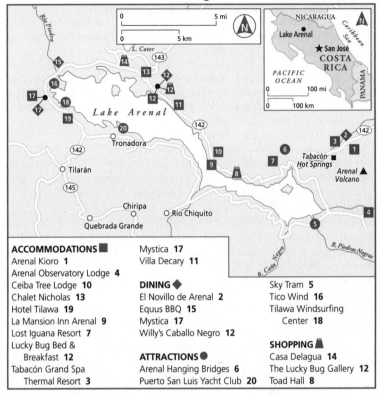

ACCOMMODATIONS ■
Arenal Kioro **1**
Arenal Observatory Lodge **4**
Ceiba Tree Lodge **10**
Chalet Nicholas **13**
Hotel Tilawa **19**
La Mansion Inn Arenal **9**
Lost Iguana Resort **7**
Lucky Bug Bed &
    Breakfast **12**
Tabacón Grand Spa
    Thermal Resort **3**

Mystica **17**
Villa Decary **11**

DINING ◆
El Novillo de Arenal **2**
Equus BBQ **15**
Mystica **17**
Willy's Caballo Negro **12**

ATTRACTIONS ●
Arenal Hanging Bridges **6**
Puerto San Luis Yacht Club **20**

Sky Tram **5**
Tico Wind **16**
Tilawa Windsurfing
    Center **18**

SHOPPING ▲
Casa Delagua **14**
The Lucky Bug Gallery **12**
Toad Hall **8**

Locals here used to curse the winds, which often come blasting across this end of the lake at 60 knots or greater. However, since the first sailboarders caught wind of Lake Arenal's combination of warm, fresh water, steady blows, and spectacular scenery, things have been changing quickly. Even if you aren't a fanatical sailboarder, you might enjoy hanging out by the lake, hiking in the nearby forests, riding a mountain bike on dirt farm roads and one-track trails, and catching glimpses of Arenal Volcano.

The lake's other claim to fame is its rainbow-bass fishing. These fighting fish are known in Central America as *guapote* and are large members of the cichlid family. Their sharp teeth and fighting nature make them a real challenge.

ESSENTIALS

GETTING THERE & DEPARTING   By Car   From San José, take the Interamerican Highway west toward Puntarenas, and then continue north to Cañas. In Cañas, turn east toward Tilarán. The drive takes 4 hours. If you're continuing on to Nuevo Arenal, follow the signs in town, which will put you on the road that skirts the shore of the lake. Nuevo Arenal is about a half-hour drive from Tilarán. You can also drive here from La Fortuna, along a scenic road that winds around the lake. From La Fortuna, it's approximately 1 hour to Nuevo Arenal and 1½ hours to Tilarán.

By Bus   **Transportes Tilaran** buses (© **2258-5792** in San José, 2695-5611 in Tilarán) leave San José for Tilarán daily at 7:30 and 9:30am and 12:45, 3:45, and 6:30pm from Calle 20 and Avenida 3. The trip lasts from 4 to 5½ hours, depending on road conditions; the fare is $3.90 (£1.95).

There are also morning and afternoon buses from **Puntarenas** to Tilarán. The ride takes about 3 hours; the fare is $2.90 (£1.45). (For details on getting to Puntarenas, see "Puntarenas," in chapter 8.) From **Monteverde** (Santa Elena), there is a bus daily at 7am. The fare for the 2-hour trip is $2.20 (£1.10). Buses from **La Fortuna** leave for Tilarán daily at 8am and 4:30pm, returning at 7am and 12:30pm. The trip takes around 2 to 3 hours; the fare is $2.50 (£1.25).

Direct buses to San José leave from Tilarán daily at 5, 7, and 9:30am and 2 and 5pm. Buses to Puntarenas leave at 6am and 1pm daily. The bus to Santa Elena (Monteverde) leaves daily at 12:30pm. Buses also leave regularly for Cañas, and can be caught heading north or south along the Interamerican Highway.

ORIENTATION & FAST FACTS   Tilarán is about 5km (3 miles) from Lake Arenal. All roads into town lead to the central park, which is Tilarán's main point of reference for addresses. If you need to exchange money, check at one of the hotels listed here, or go to the Banco Nacional. If you need a taxi to get to a lodge on Lake Arenal, call **Taxis Unidos Tilarán** (© **2695-5324**). For a taxi in Nuevo Arenal, call **Taxis Nuevo Arenal** (© **2694-4415**).

WHAT TO SEE & DO

ARTS, CRAFTS & DOWN-HOME COOKING   If you're in the area, don't miss **Toad Hall** 👉👉 (© **2692-8020;** www.toadhall-gallery.com). Located 9km (5½ miles) outside of Nuevo Arenal, toward La Fortuna, this roadside gallery and cafe serves up excellent breakfasts, light lunches, and a wide range of coffee drinks and desserts. It also has one of the better-stocked galleries in the country. You'll find the works of Lil Mena, Cecilia Figueres, Patricia Erickson, and Barry Biesanz, among others, as well as a good selection of craftworks.

About halfway between Nuevo Arenal and Tilarán is **Casa Delagua** (© **2692-2101;** www.casadelaguacr.com) the studio, gallery and coffee shop of Costa Rican artist Juan Carlos Ruiz. The **Lucky Bug Gallery** 👉👉 is an excellent roadside arts-and-crafts and souvenir shop, attached to the Lucky Bug Bed & Breakfast (p. 261).

FISHING   Ask at your hotel if you want to try your hand at fishing for *guapote*. A half-day fishing trip should cost around $150 (£75) per boat, and a full day goes for around $250 to $350 (£125–£175). The boats used will usually accommodate up to three people fishing. If you can't arrange this through your hotel, check in with the **Puerto San Luis Yacht Club** (© **2695-5750;** www.puertosanluiscr.com).

HORSEBACK RIDING   Any of the hotels in the area can hook you up with a horseback-riding tour for around $10 to $15 (£5–£7.50) per hour.

MOUNTAIN BIKING   This is a great area to explore on a mountain bike. You can rent bikes from the **Hotel Tilawa** (see "Where to Stay," below).

SWIMMING & HIKING   Up above Lake Arenal on the far side of the lake from Tilarán, you'll find the beautiful little heart-shape **Lake Coter.** This lake is surrounded by forest and has good swimming. (UFO watchers also claim that this is a popular pit stop for extraterrestrials.) A taxi to Lake Coter costs around $10 (£5).

If you feel like strapping on your boots, there are some hiking trails on the far side of Lake Arenal, near the smaller Lake Coter.

WINDSURFING & KITEBOARDING   If you want to try windsurfing, **Tilawa Windsurfing Center** (© 2695-5050; www.windsurfcostarica.com) rents equipment at its facilities on one of the lake's few accessible beaches, about 8km (5 miles) from Tilarán on the road along the west end of the lake. Boards rent for around $55 (£27) per day, and lessons are available. These folks also offer classes and rentals for the new high-octane sport of kiteboarding. Another option that is especially popular with serious sail- and kiteboarders is **Tico Wind** (© 2692-2002; www.ticowind.com), which sets up shop on the shores of the lake each year from December 1 to the end of April, when the winds blow. Rates run around $75 (£38) per day, including lunch, with multiday packages available. If you can't reach them via the phone or website, the folks at **Mystica** (see "Where to Stay," below) can hook you up.

WHERE TO STAY

In addition to the places listed below, the **Ceiba Tree Lodge** (© 2692-8050; www.ceibatree-lodge.com) is a small, simple lodge with a beautiful view and lovely gardens, located on a hill above the lake. **La Mansion Inn Arenal** (© 2692-8018; www.lamansionarenal.com) is an upscale option with a great setting and cozy cabins.

MODERATE

Hotel Tilawa *(Kids*   Built to resemble the Palace of Knossos on the island of Crete, the Hotel Tilawa sits high on the slopes above the lake and has a sweeping vista down to the water. It's primarily a windsurfers' and kiteboarders' hangout, and there's often an untended or sloppy feel to the place, particularly in terms of service and upkeep. Unusual colors and antique paint effects give the hotel a weathered look; inside there are wall murals and other artistic paint treatments throughout. Rooms have dyed cement floors, Guatemalan bedspreads, and big windows. Some have kitchenettes. Tilawa can arrange windsurfing, kiteboarding, mountain-biking, horseback-riding, and fishing trips. There's even a small skate park for radical skateboarders and BMX freestyle bikers, which makes this a good place to bring teenagers. The hotel also features a small spa, an outdoor pool, and one of the few microbrew operations in Costa Rica.

On the road btw. Tilarán and Nuevo Arenal (A.P. 92-5710, Tilarán). © 2695-5050. Fax 2695-5766. www.hotel-tilawa.com. 28 units. $68–$98 (£34–£49) double. Rates lower in off season; higher during peak periods. MC, V. **Amenities:** Restaurant; bar; outdoor pool; Jacuzzi; tennis court; small spa and hot spring Jacuzzi; sailboard, kiteboard, and bike rental nearby; tour desk; laundry service. *In room:* Free Wi-Fi, no phone.

Lucky Bug Bed & Breakfast *(Ꞙ*   An outgrowth of this family's successful restaurant and gift shop, this hotel boasts rooms that are artistic and cheery. Each features an animal motif, from the handmade wood and metal beds, to the hand-painted bathroom tiles, to the individual artworks and wall hangings. The Butterfly and Frog rooms are the best, and each comes with a small balcony. Most have one king-size bed. The largest room is the one ground-floor unit, although I prefer those on the second floor. The rooms are located just above the small lake that's behind the restaurant and gift shop. This lake is stocked with *guapote*, which you can fish for, and, if you're lucky, have cooked up for you at the restaurant.

Nuevo Arenal. © 2694-4515. Fax 2694-4418. www.luckybugcr.com. 5 units. $79–$120 (£40–£60) double. Rates include full breakfast. MC, V. **Amenities:** Restaurant; laundry service. *In room:* Free Wi-Fi, coffeemaker, no phone.

Mystica ⊛ (Value) Set on a high hill above Lake Arenal (about midway btw. Nuevo Arenal and Tilarán), this establishment has simple but spacious and cheery rooms. The painted cement floors are kept immaculate, and the rooms get good ventilation from their large windows. All rooms open onto a long and broad shared veranda with a great view of the lake. There's also one private villa, with a kitchenette, fireplace, and beautiful open deck area. The owners can help you book a wide range of adventures and tours. The hotel has a large open-air yoga platform and sometimes hosts retreats. Perhaps the star attraction here is the hotel's excellent little Italian restaurant and pizzeria by the same name (p. 263).

On the road btw. Tilarán and Nuevo Arenal (A.P. 29-5710, Tilarán). ⓒ **2692-1001.** Fax 2692-2097. www.mystica retreat.com. 7 units. $90 (£45) double; $140 (£70) villa. Rates include continental breakfast. Rates lower in off season. MC, V. **Amenities:** Restaurant; bar; laundry service. *In room:* No phone.

Villa Decary ⊛ (Finds) Named after a French explorer (and a rare palm species that he discovered and named), this small bed-and-breakfast is nestled on a hill above Lake Arenal, midway between the town of Nuevo Arenal and the Arenal Botanical Gardens. Each room comes with one queen-size and one twin bed, large picture windows, and a spacious private balcony with a lake view. The rooms get plenty of light, and the bright Guatemalan bedspreads and white-tile floors create a vibrant look. The separate casitas have full kitchens, more room, and even better views of the lake from their slightly higher perches. Breakfasts are extravagant and memorable, with a steady stream of fresh fruits; fresh juice; strong coffee; homemade pancakes, waffles, or muffins; and usually an excellent omelet or soufflé. There's great bird-watching on the hotel grounds, and howler monkeys are common guests here as well.

Nuevo Arenal (5717 Tilarán, Guanacaste). ⓒ **8383-3012** or ⓒ/fax 2694-4330. www.villadecary.com. 5 units, 3 casitas. $95 (£48) double; $125–$145 (£63–£72) casita for 2. Rates include full breakfast. Extra person $15 (£7.50). MC, V. *In room:* No phone.

INEXPENSIVE

Cabinas Mary Right on Tilarán's large and sunny central park, Cabinas Mary is basic but clean lodging, with a great location and secure parking. The rooms are located on the second floor, upstairs from the restaurant of the same name. All rooms are large, and most have plenty of windows. The restaurant downstairs serves grilled meats and local fare, and is a popular hangout for locals, travelers, and expats alike.

Tilarán (A.P. 89), Guanacaste. ⓒ/fax **2695-5479.** 18 units. $36 (£18) double. Rates include breakfast. V. **Amenities:** Restaurant; bar. *In room:* TV, no phone.

Chalet Nicholas (Value) This friendly American-owned bed-and-breakfast is 2.5km (1½ miles) west of Nuevo Arenal and sits on a hill above the road. This converted home is set on 6 hectares (15 acres) and has pretty flower gardens, an organic vegetable garden, and an orchid garden. Behind the property are acres of forest through which you can hike in search of birds, orchids, butterflies, and other tropical beauties. The upstairs loft room is the largest unit, with its own private deck. All three rooms have a view of Arenal Volcano in the distance. Owners John and Catherine Nicholas go out of their way to make their guests feel at home, although their three Great Danes might intimidate you when you first drive up. All around, it's a really good deal.

Tilarán (A.P. 72-5710), Guanacaste. ⓒ **2694-4041.** www.chaletnicholas.com. 3 units. $58 (£29) double. Rates include full breakfast. No credit cards. 3-hr. horseback-riding tour costs $25 (£12) per person. **Amenities:** Nonsmoking throughout. *In room:* No phone.

Hotel Naralit   This budget hotel is a good bet in Tilarán. The rooms are clean and comfortable, and some even come with air-conditioning. I'd try to land one of the three second-floor rooms that have a nice shared balcony, more natural light, and views of the town's church. The hotel is located across the street from one side of the church, and has its own fenced-in and guarded parking area.

Tilarán, Guanacaste. ⓒ **2695-5393**. Fax 2695-6767. 26 units. $25–$35 (£13–£18) double. MC, V. *In room:* TV, no phone.

WHERE TO DINE

There are numerous inexpensive places to eat in the town of Tilarán, including the restaurant at Cabinas Mary. In Nuevo Arenal, try the pizzas and pastas at **Café del Lago Pizzeria** (ⓒ **2694-4780**). For breakfast, snacks, lunch, and fresh-baked goods, check out **Tom's Pan German Bakery** (ⓒ **2694-4547**). Also worth mentioning is **Equus BBQ** (ⓒ **2692-1101**), a small open-air restaurant in front of the Xiloe Lodge with a view of the lake. It specializes in roast chicken and steaks.

Mystica ⓡ PIZZA/ITALIAN   The restaurant in this Italian-run hotel has a wonderful setting high on a hill overlooking the lake. The large dining room features rustic wooden chairs and tables, varnished wood floors, colorful tablecloths, and abundant flower arrangements. The most striking features, aside from the view, are the large open fireplace on one end and the large brick oven, in the shape of a small cottage, on the other that turns out pizzas. The pastas and delicious main dishes are authentically northern Italian. Whenever possible, Mystica uses fresh ingredients from its own garden.

On the road btw. Tilarán and Nuevo Arenal. ⓒ **2692-1001**. Main courses $5–$14 (£2.50–£7). MC, V. Daily 7:30am–9:30pm.

Willy's Caballo Negro ⓡ *(Finds)* INTERNATIONAL/VEGETARIAN   The German owners of this attractive little roadside cafe serve up two different types of schnitzel, bratwurst, veal *cordon bleu,* and a host of other old-world dishes. However, vegetarians are well served here, and will find several tasty and filling options on the menu, including stuffed potatoes, garden burgers, and eggplant Parmesan. The delicious pesto is made with locally grown organic macadamia nuts and cilantro. Wooden tables are set around the edges of the round dining room, with a high peaked roof. Candles and creative lighting give the place a cozy and warm feel. There's a small, picturesque lake behind the restaurant, a small B&B (see above), and the very interesting Lucky Bug Gallery (see above), run by the owner's triplet daughters.

Nuevo Arenal (about 3km/1¾ miles out of town on the road to Tilarán). ⓒ **2694-4515**. Main courses $5–$11 (£2.50–£5.50). MC, V. Daily 7:30am–8pm.

4 Monteverde ⭐⭐

167km (104 miles) NW of San José; 82km (51 miles) NW of Puntarenas

Monteverde translates as "green mountain," and that's exactly what you'll find at the end of the steep and windy rutted dirt road that leads here. Next to Manuel Antonio, this is Costa Rica's most internationally recognized ecotourism destination. The fame, rapid growth, and accompanying traffic have led some to dub it the Monteverde Crowd Forest. Nevertheless, the reserve itself and the extensive network of private reserves around it are incredibly rich in biodiversity, and a well-organized infrastructure helps guarantee a rewarding experience for both first-time and experienced ecoadventurers.

Tips Today's Forecast . . . Misty & Cool

Make sure you understand that the climatic conditions that make Monteverde such a biological hot spot can leave many tourists feeling chilled to the bone. More than a few visitors are unprepared for a cool, windy, and wet stay in the middle of their tropical vacation, and can find Monteverde a bit inhospitable, especially from August through November.

The village of Monteverde was founded in 1951 by Quakers from the United States who wanted to leave behind a constant fear of war as well as an obligation to support continued militarism through paying U.S. taxes. They chose Costa Rica primarily because it had no standing army. Although Monteverde's founders came here to farm the land, they wisely recognized the need to preserve the rare cloud forest that covered the mountain slopes above their fields, and to that end they dedicated the largest adjacent tract of cloud forest as the Monteverde Biological Cloud Forest Reserve.

Cloud forests are a mountaintop phenomenon. Moist, warm air sweeping in off the ocean is forced upward by mountain slopes, and as this moist air rises, it cools, forming clouds. The mountaintops of Costa Rica are blanketed almost daily in dense clouds, and as the clouds cling to the slopes, moisture condenses on forest trees. This constant level of moisture has given rise to an incredible diversity of innovative life forms and a forest in which nearly every square inch of space has some sort of plant growing. Within the cloud forest, the branches of huge trees are draped with epiphytic plants: orchids, ferns, and bromeliads. This intense botanic competition has created an almost equally diverse population of insects, birds, and other wildlife. Monteverde Biological Cloud Forest Reserve covers 10,400 hectares (25,688 acres) of forest, including several different life zones characterized by different types of plants and animals. Within this small area are more than 2,500 species of plants, including 400 types of orchids, 400 species of birds, and 100 species of mammals. It's no wonder that the reserve has been the site of constant scientific investigations since its founding in 1972.

Tip: For many, the primary goal in visiting Monteverde is to glimpse the rare and elusive **quetzal,** a bird once revered by the pre-Columbian peoples of the Americas. However, if you just care about seeing a quetzal, you should also consider visiting other cloud forest areas. In particular, San Gerardo de Dota and Cerro de la Muerte areas are home to several specialty lodges (see "San Isidro de El General: A Base for Exploring Chirripó National Park" in chapter 10), where you'll find far fewer crowds and often better chances of seeing the famed quetzal.

ESSENTIALS

GETTING THERE & DEPARTING   By Car   From San José, take the Interamerican Highway north. About 20km (12 miles) past the turnoff for Puntarenas, there will be a marked turnoff for Sardinal, Santa Elena, and Monteverde. From this turnoff, the road is paved almost as far as the tiny town of Guacimal. From here it's another 20km (12 miles) to Santa Elena. It should take you a little over 2 hours to reach the turnoff and another 1 hour or so from there.

An alternative route is to continue on the Interamerican Highway until just before the Río Lagarto Bridge. This turnoff isn't always well marked. From the Río Lagarto turnoff, it's 38km (24 miles) to Santa Elena and Monteverde.

Monteverde

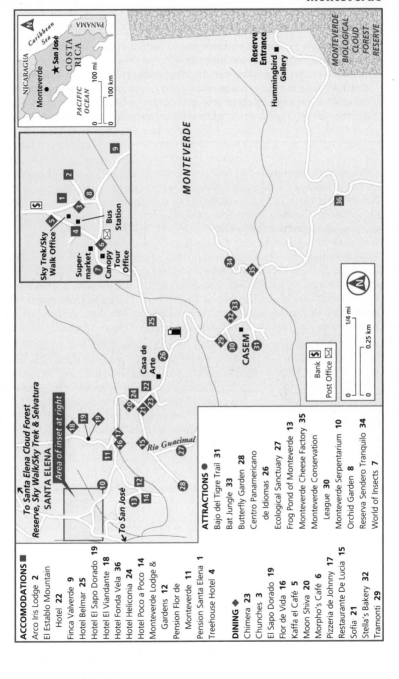

ACCOMODATIONS ■
Arco Iris Lodge **2**
El Establo Mountain
  Hotel **22**
Finca Valverde **9**
Hotel Belmar **25**
Hotel El Sapo Dorado **19**
Hotel El Viandante **18**
Hotel Fonda Vela **36**
Hotel Heliconia **24**
Hotel Poco a Poco **14**
Monteverde Lodge &
  Gardens **12**
Pension Flor de
  Monteverde **11**
Pension Santa Elena **4**
Treehouse Hotel **1**

DINING ◆
Chimera **23**
Chunches **3**
El Sapo Dorado **19**
Flor de Vida **16**
Kaffa el Café **5**
Moon Shiva **20**
Morpho's Café **6**
Pizzeria de Johnny **17**
Restaurante De Lucia **15**
Sofia **21**
Stella's Bakery **32**
Tramonti **29**

ATTRACTIONS ●
Bajo del Tigre Trail **31**
Bat Jungle **33**
Butterfly Garden **28**
Centro Panamericano
  de Idiomas **26**
Ecological Sanctuary **27**
Frog Pond of Monteverde **13**
Monteverde Cheese Factory **35**
Monteverde Conservation
  League **30**
Monteverde Serpentarium **10**
Orchid Garden **8**
Reserva Sendero Tranquilo **34**
World of Insects **7**

Tips Alternative Transport

You can travel between Monteverde and La Fortuna by boat and taxi, or on a combination boat, horseback, and taxi trip. See "Boats, Horses & Taxis" on p. 245 for details. Any of the trips described there can be done in the reverse direction departing from Monteverde. Most hotels and **Desafío Expeditions** (© **2645-5874;** www.monteverdetours.com) can arrange this trip for you. Desafío also offers multiday hikes from Monteverde to Arenal; you spend the night in rustic research facilities inside the Bosque Eterno de los Niños.

Whichever route you take, the final going is slow because the roads into Santa Elena are rough, unpaved dirt-and-gravel affairs. However, once you arrive, the roads in and around Santa Elena are paved, including all the way to Cerro Plano, and about halfway to the Cloud Forest Preserve. Just before you enter the town of Santa Elena, you may be stopped at a little tollbooth collecting 200 colones. The money is ostensibly going to maintain the road, and payment is actually optional.

To drive from Monteverde to La Fortuna, head out of Santa Elena toward Sky Trek and the Santa Elena Cloud Forest Reserve. Follow signs for Tilaran, which are posted at most of the critical intersections. If there's no sign, stick to the most well-worn road. This is a rough dirt road, all the way to Tilaran. From Tilaran, you have mostly well-marked and okay paved roads around the lake, passing first through Nuevo Arenal, and then over the dam and through Tabacón, before reaching La Fortuna.

By Bus **Transmonteverde** express buses (© **2222-3854** in San José, or 2645-5159 in Santa Elena) leave San José daily at 6:30am and 2:30pm from Calle 12 between avenidas 7 and 9. The trip takes around 4 hours; the fare is $4.20 (£2.10). Buses arrive at and depart from Santa Elena. If you're staying at one of the hotels or lodges toward the reserve, you'll want to arrange pickup if possible, or take a taxi or local bus.

A daily Transmonteverde bus departs Puntarenas for Santa Elena at 2:15pm. The bus stop in Puntarenas is across the street from the main bus station. The fare for the 2½-hour trip is $2.70 (£1.35). There's also a daily bus from Tilarán (Lake Arenal) at 12:30pm. Trip duration, believe it or not, is 2 hours (for a 40km/25-mile trip); the fare is $2.20 (£1.10). The express bus departs for San José daily at 6:30am and 2:30pm. The bus from Santa Elena to Puntarenas leaves daily at 6am.

Gray Line (© **2220-2126;** www.graylinecostarica.com) has a daily bus that leaves San José for Monteverde at 8am; the fare is $33 (£17). **Interbus** (© **2283-5573;** www.interbusonline.com) has two daily buses that leave San José for Monteverde at 8:15am and 2:30pm; the fare is $35 (£18). Either of the above companies will pick you up and drop you off at most San José and Monteverde area hotels.

If you're heading to Manuel Antonio, take the Santa Elena/Puntarenas bus and transfer in Puntarenas. To reach Liberia, take any bus down the mountain and get off as soon as you hit the Interamerican Highway. You can then flag down a bus bound for Liberia (almost any bus heading north). The Santa Elena/Tilarán bus leaves daily at 7am. Both **Gray Line** and **Interbus** offer routes with connections to most major destinations in Costa Rica.

GETTING AROUND   There are six buses daily between the town of Santa Elena and the Monteverde Biological Cloud Forest Reserve. The first bus leaves Santa Elena for the reserve at 6am and the last bus from the reserve leaves there at 4pm. The fare is $1.50 (75p). There's also periodic van transportation between the town of Santa Elena and the Santa Elena Cloud Forest Reserve. Ask around town and you should be able to find the current schedule and book a ride for around $2 (£1) per person. A **taxi** (© **2645-6969** or 2645-6666) between Santa Elena and either the Monteverde Reserve or the Santa Elena Cloud Forest Reserve costs around $8 to $10 (£4–£5) for up to four people. Count on paying between $4 and $10 (£2–£5) for the ride from Santa Elena to your lodge in Monteverde. Finally, several places around town rent ATVs, or all-terrain vehicles, for around $45 to $70 (£23–£35) per day. Hourly rates and guided tours are also available. If this is up your alley, try **Aventura** (© **2645-6959**) or **Monteverde Offroader** (© **2645-6463**).

ORIENTATION   As you approach Santa Elena, take the right fork in the road if you're heading directly to Monteverde. If you continue straight, you'll come into the little village of **Santa Elena,** which has a bus stop, a health clinic, a bank, a general store, a laundromat, and a few simple restaurants, budget hotels, souvenir shops, and tour offices. **Monteverde,** on the other hand, is not a village in the traditional sense of the word. There's no center of town—only dirt lanes leading off from the main road to various farms. This main road has signs for all the hotels and restaurants mentioned here, and it dead-ends at the reserve entrance.

For a map of the Cloud Forest Reserve, see the inside front cover of this book.

FAST FACTS   The telephone number for the **local clinic** is © 2645-5076; for the **Red Cross,** © 2645-6128; and for the **local police,** © 911 or 2645-6248. There's a 24-hour gas station about halfway between the town of Santa Elena and the Monteverde Biological Cloud Forest Reserve. The **Farmacia Monteverde** (© **2645-7110**) is right downtown. There's a **Banco Nacional** (© 2645-5610) in downtown Santa Elena and **Coopemex** (© 2645-6948) on the road out to Santa Elena, near Finca Valverde; both have 24-hour ATMs.

EXPLORING THE MONTEVERDE BIOLOGICAL CLOUD FOREST RESERVE ★★★

The **Monteverde Biological Cloud Forest Reserve** (© 2645-5122; www.cct.or.cr) is one of the most developed and well-maintained natural attractions in Costa Rica. The trails are clearly marked, regularly traveled, and generally gentle in terms of ascents and descents. The cloud forest here is lush and largely untouched. Still, keep in mind that most of the birds and mammals are rare, elusive, and nocturnal. Moreover, to all but the most trained of eyes, those thousands of exotic ferns, orchids, and bromeliads tend to blend into one large mass of indistinguishable green. However, with a guide hired through your hotel, or on one of the reserve's official guided 2- to 3-hour hikes,

---

Tips **Seeing the Forest for the Trees, Bromeliads, Monkeys, Hummingbirds . . .**

Because the entrance fee to Monteverde is valid for a full day, I recommend taking an early-morning walk with a guide and then heading off on your own either directly after that hike or after lunch. A guide will certainly point out and explain a lot, but there's also much to be said for walking quietly through the forest on your own or in very small groups. This will also allow you to stray from the well-traveled paths in the park.

you can see and learn far more than you could on your own. At $15 (£7.50) per person, the reserve's tours might seem like a splurge, especially after you pay the entrance fee, but I strongly recommend that you go with a guide.

Perhaps the most famous resident of the cloud forests of Costa Rica is the quetzal, a robin-size bird with iridescent green wings and a ruby-red breast, which has become extremely rare due to habitat destruction. The male quetzal also has two long tail feathers that can reach nearly .6m (2 ft.) in length, making it one of the most spectacular birds on earth. The best time to see quetzals is early morning to midmorning, and the best months are February through April (mating season).

Other animals that have been seen in Monteverde, although sightings are extremely rare, include jaguars, ocelots, and tapirs. After the quetzal, Monteverde's most famous resident used to be the golden toad (*sapo dorado*), a rare native species. However, the golden toad has disappeared from the forest and is feared extinct. Competing theories of the toad's demise include adverse effects of a natural drought cycle, the disappearing ozone layer, pesticides, and acid rain.

ADMISSION, HOURS & TOURS   The reserve is open daily from 7am to 4pm, and the entrance fee is $15 (£7.50) for adults and $7.50 (£3.75) for students and children. Because only 160 people are allowed into the reserve at any one time, you might be forced to wait for a while. Most hotels can reserve a guided walk and entrance to the reserve for the following day for you, or you can get tickets in advance directly at the reserve entrance.

Some of the trails can be very muddy, depending on the season, so ask about current conditions. If the mud is heavy, you can rent rubber boots at the reserve entrance for $2 (£1) per day. They might make your hike much more pleasant. Before venturing into the forest, have a look around the information center. There are several guidebooks available, as well as posters and postcards of some of the reserve's more famous animal inhabitants.

Night tours of the reserve leave every evening at 7:15pm. The cost is $15 (£7.50), including admission to the reserve, a 2-hour hike, and, most important, a guide with a high-powered searchlight. For an extra $2 (£1), they'll throw in round-trip transportation to and from your area hotel.

WHAT TO SEE & DO OUTSIDE THE RESERVE
BIRD-WATCHING & HIKING

You can also find ample bird-watching and hiking opportunities outside the reserve boundaries. Avoid the crowds at Monteverde by heading 5km (3 miles) north from the village of Santa Elena to the **Santa Elena Cloud Forest Reserve** (⚡⚡ (© 2645-5390; www.reservasantaelena.org). This 310-hectare (765-acre) reserve has a maximum elevation of 1,680m (5,510 ft.), making it the highest cloud forest in the Monteverde area. There are 13km (8 miles) of hiking trails, as well as an information center. Because it borders the Monteverde Reserve, a similar richness of flora and fauna is found here, although quetzals are not nearly as common. The $12 (£6) entry fee at this reserve goes directly to support local schools. The reserve is open daily from 7am to 4pm. Three-hour guided tours are available for $15 (£7.50) per person, not including the entrance fee. (Call the number above to make a reservation for the tour.) A night tour ($15/£7.50) is also offered each evening at 7pm.

Sky Walk (⚡⚡ (© 2645-5238; www.skytrek.com) is a network of forest paths and suspension bridges that provides visitors with a view previously reserved for birds, monkeys, and the much more adventurous traveler. The bridges reach 39m (128 ft.)

above the ground at their highest point, so acrophobia could be an issue. The Sky Walk and its sister attraction, **Sky Trek** (see "Canopy & Canyoning Tours," below), are about 3.5km (2¼ miles) outside the town of Santa Elena, on the road to the Santa Elena Cloud Forest Reserve. The Sky Walk is open daily from 7am to 4pm; admission is $17 (£8.50). For an extra $10 (£5), a knowledgeable guide will point out the diverse flora and fauna on the walk. For $50 (£25) per person, you can do the Sky Trek canopy tour and then walk the trails and bridges of the Sky Walk. Reservations are recommended for the Sky Trek; round-trip transportation from Santa Elena is just $2 (£1) per person.

To learn even more about Monteverde, stop in at the **Monteverde Conservation League** (© 2645-5003; www.acmcr.org), which administers the 22,000-hectare (54,000-acre) private reserve **Bosque Eterno de Los Niños (Children's Eternal Forest),** as well as the Bajo del Tigre Trail. The Conservation League has its office on the Cerro Plano road, 50m (164 ft.) before the Butterfly Garden. In addition to being a good source for information, it also sells books, T-shirts, and cards, and all proceeds go to purchase more land for the Bosque Eterno de Los Niños. The **Bajo del Tigre Trail** ⊙ is a 3.5km (2.25-mile) trail that's home to several different bird species not usually found within the reserve. You can take several different loops, lasting anywhere from 1 hour to several hours. The trail starts a little past the CASEM artisans' shop (see "Shopping," below) and is open daily from 8am to 5pm. Admission is $7 (£3.50) for adults and $4 (£2) for students.

You can also go on guided 3-hour hikes at the **Reserva Sendero Tranquilo** ⊙ (© 2645-7711), which is run by the folks at the Sapo Dorado (p. 273) and has 80 hectares (198 acres) of land, two-thirds of which is in virgin forest. This reserve is located up the hill from the cheese factory (p. 272). Both day and night hikes are offered here, and the group size is always small. Prices run $28 (£14) for the 3- to 4-hour day tour, and $20 (£10) for the 2½-hour night tour.

Finally, you can walk the trails and grounds of the **Ecological Sanctuary** ⊙ (© 2645-5869; www.ecologicalsanctuary.com), a family-run wildlife refuge and private reserve located down the Cerro Plano road. This place has four main trails through a variety of ecosystems, and wildlife viewing is often quite good here. There are a couple of pretty waterfalls off the trails. It's open daily from 6:30am to 7pm; admission is $9 (£4.50) for self-guided hiking on the trails; $24 (£12) during the day for a 2-hour guided tour; and $15 (£7.50) for the 1½-hour guided night tour that leaves at 5:30pm.

CANOPY & CANYONING TOURS

Selvatura Park ⊙⊙ (© 2645-5929; www.selvatura.com), located close to the Santa Elena Cloud Forest Reserve, is the best one-stop shop for various adventures and attractions in the area. In addition to an extensive canopy tour, with 15 cables connecting 18 platforms, they also have a network of trails and suspended bridges, a huge butterfly garden, a hummingbird garden, a snake exhibit, and a wonderful insect display and museum. Prices vary depending upon how much you want to see and do. Individually, the canopy tour costs $40 (£20); the walkways and bridges, $20 (£10); the snake and reptile exhibit, $12 (£6); and the butterfly garden and the insect museum, $10 (£5) each. Packages to combine the various exhibits are available, although it's definitely confusing, and somewhat annoying, to pick the perfect package. For $108 (£54), you get the run of the entire joint, all the tours, lunch, and round-trip transportation from your Monteverde hotel.

Another popular option is offered by the folks at **Sky Trek** ★★ (© **2645-5238;** www.skytrek.com), a growing complex of aerial adventures and hiking trails. This is one of the more extensive canopy tours in the country, with two very long cables to cross. The longest of these is some 770m (2,525 ft.) long, high above the forest floor. There are no rappel descents here, and you brake using the pulley system for friction. This tour costs $44 (£22).

One of the oldest canopy tours in the country is run by the **Original Canopy Tour** ★ (© **2645-5243;** www.canopytour.com), which has an office right in the center of Santa Elena. This is one of the more interesting canopy tours in Costa Rica because the initial ascent is made by climbing up the hollowed-out interior of a giant strangler fig. This tour has 11 platforms and two rappels. The 2- to 2½-hour tours run three times daily and cost $45 (£23) for adults, $35 (£18) for students, and $25 (£13) for children 11 and under.

Finally, if you want to add a bit more adventure, and definitely more water, to your adventure, you can try the **Finca Modelo Canyoning Tour** (© **2645-5581;** www. familiabrenestours.com). This tour involves a mix of hiking and then rappelling down the face of a series of forest waterfalls. The tallest of these waterfalls is around 39m (130 ft.). You will get wet on this tour. The cost is $60 (£30).

There's a glut of canopy tours in the Monteverde area, and I can only recommend those mentioned above. Anybody in average physical condition can do any of the adventure tours in Monteverde, but they're not for the fainthearted or acrophobic. Try to book directly with the companies listed above or through your hotel. Beware of touts on the streets of Monteverde, who make a small commission and frequently try to steer tourists to the operator paying the highest percentage.

HORSEBACK RIDING

There's excellent terrain for horseback riding all around Monteverde. **Meg's Riding Stables** (© **2645-5560**), **La Estrella Stables** (© **2645-5075**), **Palomina Horse Tours** (© **2645-5479**), and **Sabine's Smiling Horses** (© **2645-6894;** www.smiling horses.com) are the more established operators, offering guided rides for around $10 to $15 (£5–£7.50) per hour. As I mentioned earlier in "Boats, Horses & Taxis" (p. 245), there are horseback/boat trips linking Monteverde/Santa Elena with La Fortuna. This is certainly an exciting and adventurous means of connecting these two popular destinations, but I've received numerous complaints about the state of the trails and the treatment of the horses, so be very careful before undertaking this trip.

Another option is to set up a day tour and sauna at **El Sol** ★ (© **2645-6672;** www.elsolnuestro.com). Located about a 10-minute car ride down the mountain from Santa Elena, these folks take you on a roughly 3-hour ride either to San Luis or to an isolated little waterfall with an excellent swimming hole. After the ride back, you'll find the wood-burning traditional Swedish sauna all fired up, with a refreshing and beautiful little pool beside it. The tour costs around $60 (£30) per person, including lunch. These folks also have two very rustically luxurious private cabins ($95–$125/£48–£63 double), with excellent views.

OTHER ATTRACTIONS IN MONTEVERDE

It seems as if Monteverde has an exhibit or attraction dedicated to almost every type of tropical fauna. It's a pet peeve of mine, but I really wish these folks would band together and offer some sort of general pass. However, as it stands, you'll have to shell out for each individual attraction.

Butterflies abound here, and the **Butterfly Garden** ✸ (© 2645-5512), located near the Pensión Monteverde Inn, displays many of Costa Rica's most beautiful species. Besides the hundreds of preserved and mounted butterflies, there are a garden and a greenhouse where you can watch live butterflies. The garden is open daily from 9:30am to 4pm, and admission is $9 (£4.50) for adults and $7 (£3.50) for students and children, including a guided tour. The best time to visit is between 9:30am and 1pm, when the butterflies are most active.

If your taste runs toward the slithery, you can check out the informative displays at the **Monteverde Serpentarium** (© 2645-5238; www.snaketour.com), on the road to the reserve. It's open daily from 8am to 8:30pm and charges $8 (£4) for admission. The **Frog Pond of Monteverde** ✸ (© 2645-6320; www.ranario.com), a couple of hundred meters north of the Monteverde Lodge, is probably a better bet. The $10 (£5) entrance gets you a 45-minute guided tour, and your ticket is good for 2 days. A variety of amphibian species populates a series of glass terrariums. In addition, these folks have also added a butterfly garden. This place is open daily from 9am to 8:30pm. I especially recommend that you stop by at least once after dark, when the tree frogs are active.

Fans of invertebrates will want to head to **World of Insects** (© 2645-6859), which features more than 30 terrariums filled with some of the area's more interesting creepy-crawlies. My favorites are the giant horned beetles. This place is 300m (984 ft.) west of the supermarket in Santa Elena. It's open daily from 9am to 7pm; admission is $8 (£4).

Finally, the newest entry in the field is the **Bat Jungle** (© 2645-6566), an in-depth look into the world life and habits of these odd flying mammals. A visit here includes several different types of exhibits, from skeletal remains to a large enclosure where you get to see various live species in action—the enclosure and room are kept dark, and the bats have had their biological clocks tricked into thinking that it's night. It's quite an interesting experience. The Bat Jungle is open daily from 9:30am to 8:30pm. Admission is $10 (£5). In addition to a good gift shop and separate coffee shop, where they make homemade chocolate, these folks also have a small interpretive museum focusing on the history of the Quaker community here. Admission to this museum is $5 (£2.50).

If you've had your fill of birds, snakes, bugs, butterflies, and bats, you might want to stop at the **Orchid Garden** ✸ (© 2645-5308; www.monteverdeorchidgarden. com), in Santa Elena across from the Pension El Tucano. This small botanical garden boasts more than 425 species of orchids. The tour is fascinating, especially the fact that you need (and are given) a magnifying glass to see some of the flowers in bloom. Admission is $7 (£3.50) for adults and $5 (£2.50) for students. It's open daily from 8am to 5pm.

There are several options for those looking for a glimpse into the practices and processes of daily life in this region. My favorite is **El Trapiche Tour** ✸ (© 2645-5834; www.eltrapichetour.com), which gives you a glimpse into the traditional means of harvesting and processing coffee and sugar cane. The 2-hour tour also includes a ride in an ox-drawn cart, and a visit to their coffee farms. Depending upon the season, you may even get to pick a bushel of raw coffee beans. Back at the farmhouse you get to see how the raw materials are then turned into a variety of final products, including cane liquor, raw sugar, and roasted coffee. The tour costs $25 (£13) for adults, and $10 (£5) for children 6 through 12.

Because the vegetation in the cloud forest is so dense, most of the forest's animal residents are rather difficult to spot. If you were dissatisfied with your sightings, even with a naturalist guide leading you, you might want to consider attending a slide show of photographs taken in the reserve. There is a host of daily slide shows around Monteverde. The longest running of these takes place at the **Monteverde Lodge, Hotel El Sapo Dorado,** and **Hotel Belmar** (see "Where to Stay," below), and **Hummingbird Gallery** (see below). Dates, showtimes, and admissions vary, so inquire at your hotel or one of the places mentioned above.

Almost all of the area hotels can arrange a wide variety of other tours and activities, including guided night tours of the cloud forest and night trips to the Arenal Volcano (a tedious 4-hr. ride, each way).

LEARN THE LANGUAGE

The **Centro Panamericano de Idiomas** ✦ (© 2645-5441; www.spanishlanguage school.com) offers immersion language classes in a wonderful setting. A 1-week program with 4 hours of class per day and a home stay with a Costa Rican family costs $465 (£232).

SHOPPING

The best-stocked gift shop in Monteverde is the **Hummingbird Gallery** ✦ (© 2645-5030). You'll find the gallery just outside the reserve entrance. Hanging from trees around it are several hummingbird feeders that attract more than seven species of these tiny birds. At any given moment, there might be several dozen hummingbirds buzzing and chattering around the building and your head. Inside you will find many beautiful color prints of hummingbirds and other local flora and fauna, as well as a wide range of craft items, T-shirts, and other gifts. The Hummingbird Gallery is open daily from 8:30am to 4:30pm.

Another good option is **CASEM** (© 2645-5190), located on the right side of the main road, just across from Stella's Bakery. This crafts cooperative sells embroidered clothing, T-shirts, posters, and postcards with photos of the local flora and fauna, Boruca weavings, locally grown and roasted coffee, and many other items to remind you of your visit to Monteverde. CASEM is open Monday through Saturday from 8am to 5pm and Sunday from 10am to 4pm (closed Sun May–Oct). There is also a well-stocked **gift shop** at the entrance to the Monteverde Biological Cloud Forest Reserve. You'll find plenty of T-shirts, postcards, and assorted crafts here, as well as a selection of science and natural-history books.

Over the years, Monteverde has developed a nice little community of artists. Around town you'll see paintings by local artists such as Paul Smith and Meg Wallace, whose works are displayed at the Fonda Vela Hotel and Stella's Bakery, respectively. You might also check out **Casa de Arte** ✦ (© 2645-5275), which has a mix of arts and crafts in many media and is just off the main road to the reserve, as well as **Flor de Vida** (© 2645-6328), which has some unique custom-made jewelry and clothing.

Finally, it's also worth stopping by the **Monteverde Cheese Factory** to pick up some of the best cheese in Costa Rica. (You can even watch it being processed and get homemade ice cream.) The cheese factory (© 2645-5150) is right on the main road about midway between Santa Elena and the reserve. They offer 1-hour tours at 9am and 2pm, at a cost of $10 (£5).

WHERE TO STAY

When choosing a place to stay in Monteverde, be sure to check whether the rates include a meal plan. In the past almost all the lodges included three meals a day in their prices, but this practice is waning. Check before you assume anything.

EXPENSIVE

El Establo Mountain Hotel From a working stable (*El Establo* translates as "the stable") owned by a local Quaker family, with just a handful of budget rooms, this place has morphed into what is the largest and most extravagant hotel in Monteverde. It is still owned and managed by the same family. However, I think the vision here far exceeds the execution. The design and scale are somewhat out of place with the vibe and aesthetic of Monteverde, and the service can fall short. The rooms are all quite large and have private balconies or patios taking in spectacular views, although the decor appears to have been an afterthought. All rooms come with cable television and are nonsmoking. The honeymoon suites have fabulous views and a private Jacuzzi, but the 400-block of rooms are my favorites. There's one midsize outdoor swimming pool and another slightly smaller pool built under a high open-air roof. El Establo owns 48 hectares (119 acres) of land backing the hotel, and half of that is primary forest. They also have an on-site canopy tour and extensive spa.

Monteverde (A.P. 549-2050, San Pedro). © **2645-5110**. Fax 2645-5041. www.hotelelestablo.com. 115 units. $187 (£94) double; $187–$237 (£94–£119) suite. Rates include breakfast. AE, MC, V. **Amenities:** Restaurant; bar; 2 pools; spa; tour desk; babysitting; laundry service; nonsmoking rooms. *In room:* TV, minifridge, coffeemaker, hair dryer, safe.

Hotel El Sapo Dorado On a steep hill between Santa Elena and the reserve, El Sapo Dorado (named for Monteverde's famous golden toad) offers some of the more charming and comfortable accommodations in Monteverde. The spacious cabins are built of hardwoods both inside and out and are surrounded by a grassy lawn. Big windows let in lots of light, and high ceilings keep the rooms cool during the day. Some of the cabins have fireplaces, a welcome feature on chilly nights and during the rainy season. A remodeling in 2008 has left most cabins updated, with larger, more modern bathrooms, and livelier decor. My favorite rooms are the sunset suites, which have private terraces with views to the Gulf of Nicoya and wonderful sunsets. Not only does El Sapo Dorado own and manage the Reserva Sendero Tranquilo, but it also has a network of well-maintained trails into primary forest on-site.

Monteverde (A.P. 9-5655), Puntarenas. © **2645-5010**. Fax 2645-5180. www.sapodorado.com. 30 units. $122 (£61) double. Rates include breakfast and taxes. Lower rates in the off season. MC, V. **Amenities:** Restaurant; bar; tour desk; massage; laundry service. *In room:* Free Wi-Fi, coffeemaker, hair dryer, safe.

MODERATE

In addition to the hotels listed below, **Hotel Heliconia** (© **2240-7311** reservations office in San José, or 2645-5109 at the hotel; www.hotelheliconia.com) is another good option in this price range, as is **El Sol** (© **2645-6672**; www.elsolnuestro. com), which is about 10 minutes south of Santa Elena, on the road to the Interamerican Highway. Also check out **Hotel Belmar** (© **2645-5201**; www.hotelbelmar.net), a Swiss chalet–style hotel with moderate rates.

Arco Iris Lodge *Value* This is my favorite hotel right in Santa Elena and an excellent value to boot. The rooms are spread out in a variety of separate buildings, including several individual cabins. All have wood or tile floors and plenty of wood accents.

My favorite is the "honeymoon cabin," which has a Jacuzzi tub and its own private balcony with a forest view and good bird-watching, although room nos. 16 and 17 are good choices, also with their own small private balconies. The management here is helpful, speaks five languages, and can arrange a wide variety of tours. Although they don't serve lunch or dinner, breakfast is offered in a spacious and airy dining and lounge building, where refreshments are available throughout the day and evening.

Monteverde (A.P. 003-5655), Puntarenas. © 2645-5067. Fax 2645-5022. www.arcoirislodge.com. 19 units. $75 (£38) double; $180 (£90) honeymoon cabin. AE, MC, V. **Amenities:** Lounge; tour desk; laundry service. *In room:* No phone.

Finca Valverde ⚘ This place is right on the outskirts of Santa Elena, yet once you head uphill to the rooms, you'll feel far from the hustle and bustle of the tiny burg. The standard rooms are set behind the main lodge and restaurant and are reached via a small suspension bridge over a small forest creek. Most have one queen-size and two twin beds. All share a broad common veranda. The junior suites and cabins are larger, more private, and feature bathtubs; these junior suites are the highest up the hill and also have televisions, small refrigerators, and coffeemakers. The grounds are lush and well tended, and meals are served in a large restaurant just off the main lobby.

Monteverde (A.P. 2-5655), Puntarenas. © 2645-5157. Fax 2645-5216. www.monteverde.co.cr. 22 units. $73–$92 (£37–£46) double. Rates include continental breakfast. Rates lower in off season. MC, V. **Amenities:** Restaurant; bar; tour desk; laundry service. *In room:* Free Wi-Fi.

Hotel Fonda Vela ⚘⚘ Although it's one of the older hotels here, Fonda Vela remains one of my top choices in Monteverde. Moreover, this is one of the closer lodges to the Cloud Forest Reserve, a relatively easy 15-minute walk away. Guest rooms are in nine separate buildings scattered among the forests and pastures of this former farm, and most have views of the Nicoya Gulf. The junior suites all come with cable television. The newer block of junior suites, some of which have excellent views, are the best rooms in the house, and I prefer them to the older and larger junior suites. The dining room has great sunset views, and it sometimes even features live music. There's a popular bar here, as well as a small system of private trails. Throughout the hotel, you'll see paintings by co-owner Paul Smith, who also handcrafts violins and cellos and is a musician himself.

Monteverde (A.P. 70060-1000, San José). © 2257-1413 reservations in San José, or 2645-5125 at the lodge. Fax 2257-1416. www.fondavela.com. 40 units. $103 (£51) double; $121 (£61) junior suite. Extra person $9 (£4.50). AE, MC, V. **Amenities:** Restaurant; bar; horse rental; tour desk; laundry service. *In room:* TV, minibar, coffeemaker, hair dryer.

Hotel Poco a Poco ⚘ Located just outside of the town of Santa Elena, this hotel provides many of the perks and comforts of a luxury hotel, at good prices. Some rooms are on the small side, but the beds are firm, and everything is kept neat and contemporary. The best rooms are higher up, away from the road, and have a small private balcony. All rooms come with DVD players, and the hotel maintains a movie-lending library of over 4,000 titles. A heated pool, children's pool, and Jacuzzi are on-site, and the restaurant is excellent.

Monteverde, Puntarenas. © 2645-6000. Fax 2645-6264. www.hotelpocoapoco.com. 30 units. $88 (£44) double. Rates include breakfast. Rates lower in off season; higher during peak periods. MC, V. **Amenities:** Restaurant; bar; small outdoor pool; tour desk; laundry service. *In room:* TV, free Wi-Fi, coffeemaker, hair dryer, safe.

Monteverde Lodge & Gardens ⚘⚘ *Kids* This was one of the first ecolodges in Monteverde, and it remains one of the most popular. Rooms are large and comfortable, and thanks to ongoing upkeep and remodeling are some of the best in town. Most feature angled walls of glass with chairs and a table placed so that avid bird-watchers can do a bit of birding without leaving their rooms. The gardens and secondary forest surrounding the lodge have some gentle groomed trails and are home to quite a few species of birds. Perhaps the lodge's most popular attraction is the large hot tub in a big atrium garden just off the lobby.

The dining room offers great views, good food, and excellent service. The adjacent bar is a popular gathering spot, and there are regular evening slide shows focusing on the cloud forest. Scheduled bus service to and from San José is available, as is a shuttle to the reserve, horseback riding, and a variety of optional tours. The excellent guides here have lots of experience with family groups.

Monteverde (mailing address: SJO 235, P.O. Box 25216, Miami, FL 33102-5216). (℃ **2257-0766** reservations office in San José, or 2645-5057 at the lodge. Fax 2257-1665. www.monteverdelodge.com. 28 units. $95 (£48) double. Rates slightly lower in off season; higher during peak periods. AE, MC, V. **Amenities:** Restaurant; bar; Jacuzzi; tour desk; laundry service. *In room:* Coffeemaker, safe.

INEXPENSIVE

In addition to the hotels listed below, there are quite a few *pensiones* and backpacker specials in Santa Elena and spread out along the road to the reserve. The best of these are **Pensión Santa Elena** (℃ 2645-5051; www.pensionsantaelena.com) and **Pensión Flor de Monteverde** (℃ 2645-5758; www.pensionflordemonteverde.com). A slightly more expensive and modern alternative is the **Hotel El Viandante** (℃ 2645-6475; www.hotelelviandante.com), which is near El Sapo Dorado.

Finally, it's possible to stay in a room right at the **Monteverde Biological Cloud Forest Reserve** (℃ 2645-5122; www.cct.or.cr). A bunk bed, shared bathroom, and three meals per day here run $40 (£20) per person. For an extra $10 (£5) you can get a room with a private bathroom. Admission to the reserve is included in the price.

Treehouse Hotel   Housed in Santa Elena's first, and only, high-rise building, this hotel offers clean and spacious rooms in the center of town. Taking up the third—and highest—floor of this building, the rooms vary in size and the number of beds they feature. The best rooms come with small balconies overlooking the town, although these are also susceptible to street noise, particularly early in the morning and on weekend nights. All rooms feature bright white tile floors, colorful bedspreads, and sparse furnishings. Although the building is modern, it is built around a massive old fig tree, hence the hotel's name.

Santa Elena, Puntarenas. (℃ **2645-7475** or 8389-2573. 7 units. $45 (£23) double. MC, V. **Amenities:** Restaurant; tour desk; laundry service. *In room:* TV, hair dryer, safe, no phone.

WHERE TO DINE

Most lodges in Monteverde have their own dining rooms, and these are the most convenient places to eat, especially if you don't have a car. Because most visitors want to get an early start, they usually grab a quick breakfast at their hotel. It's also common for people to have their lodge pack them a bag lunch to take with them to the reserve, although there's now a decent little *soda* at the reserve entrance. If you're in the mood to eat out, there are several inexpensive restaurants scattered along the road between Santa Elena and Monteverde.

In addition to the places listed below, you can get good pizzas and pastas at **Tramonti** (℃ 2645-6120) and **Pizzeria de Johnny** (℃ 2645-5066), both located out along the road to the reserve. Also, the restaurant at the **Hotel Poco a Poco**

(© 2645-6000) gets good marks with a wide range of international dishes. Finally, **Moon Shiva** (© 2645-6270), located in Cerro Plano, serves a limited menu of Mediterranean and international fare and often features live music or movies.

A popular choice for lunch is **Stella's Bakery** (© 2645-5560), across from the CASEM gift shop. Stella's is open daily from 6am to 9pm. The restaurant is bright and inviting, with lots of varnished woodwork, as well as a few outdoor tables. The selection changes regularly but might include vegetarian quiche, eggplant parmigiana, and different salads. Stella's also features a daily supply of decadent baked goods.

Chimera ★★ FUSION/TAPAS   Building on the success of Sofia (see below), Karen Nielsen has opened this creative, yet casual tapas restaurant. The small menu has a broad scope, with options available in the traditional categories of soups, salads, mains, sides, and dessert, and influences ranging from Asia to Latin America to the Old World. Standout dishes include slow-cooked pork with white beans and caramelized onions and the coconut shrimp "lollipops" with a mango-ginger dipping sauce. And for dessert, don't pass up the chocolate mousse with a sangria syrup. A variety of creative and contemporary cocktails, as well as good wines, are also offered.

Cerro Plano, on the road btw. Santa Elena and the reserve, on your right. © 2645-6081. Reservations recommended during high season. Tapas $3.50–$8.30 (£1.75–£4.15). AE, DC, DISC, MC, V. Daily 11:30am–9:30pm.

El Sapo Dorado ★ INTERNATIONAL   High on a hill above the main road, the original restaurant at El Sapo Dorado continues to offer up great sunsets and food. The menu features such varied options as poached corvina in heart-of-palm sauce, shrimp in a sambuca mushroom sauce, or filet mignon in pepper-cream sauce. The emphasis is on fresh ingredients and healthful preparation, and there are always nightly specials and vegetarian and vegan options as well. If you come in time for a sunset dinner, definitely grab a table in the large, covered dining room, which has full walls of picture windows for taking in the views, or, weather permitting, on their outdoor terrace.

These folks have also opened another restaurant, La Guarida del Sapo, near the main road, in a large building that feels a bit like a church, with high ceilings, a tall central steeple, and plenty of stained glass and ironwork. The menu here is smaller and simpler, with an emphasis on healthy bar food, if such a thing is not too oxymoronic.

On the left as you go from Santa Elena toward the reserve. © 2645-5010. Reservations recommended during high season. Main courses $11–$16 (£5.50–£8). AE, MC, V. Daily 11:30am–9:30pm.

Flor de Vida INTERNATIONAL/VEGETARIAN   With large new digs, this long-standing local favorite continues to serve up some of the best and healthiest fare to be found in Monteverde. Large picture windows line the walls, and there's a small lounge area in one corner, with books, magazines, and board games. When it's cold and windy out, I like to start off with a bowl of their pumpkin-almond soup. For lunch, their veggie burger with roasted potatoes is hard to beat, and for dinner I tend to favor the Thai fish curry. In addition to the regular menu there are always daily specials.

On the road btw. Santa Elena and the reserve, on your right. © 2645-6823. Reservations recommended during high season. Main courses $8–$13 (£4–£6.50). MC, V. Daily 7am–10pm.

Morpho's Café (Value COSTA RICAN/INTERNATIONAL   Probably the best and most popular restaurant in the town of Santa Elena, this simple second-floor affair serves up hearty and economical meals. There are soups, sandwiches, and *casados*

> **Tips** **Take a Break**
>
> If all of the activities in Monteverde have worn you out, stop in at the **Kaffa El Café** (© 2645-6335), a downtown coffee shop, or **Chunches** (© 2645-5147), a bookstore with a small coffee shop and espresso bar that also doubles as a laundromat.

(plates of the day) for lunch and dinner, and delicious fresh-fruit juices, ice-cream shakes, and home-baked desserts throughout the day. The tables and chairs are made from rough-hewn lumber and whole branches and trunks, and the place brims with a light convivial atmosphere. Morpho's is a very popular hangout for backpackers.

In downtown Santa Elena, across from the supermarket. © **2645-5607**. Main courses $5–$12 (£2.50–£6). MC, V. Daily 7am–10pm.

Restaurante De Lucía COSTA RICAN/INTERNATIONAL De Lucía has earned a loyal following for its grilled-to-order meats and fresh fish. All meals come with fresh homemade tortillas and a full accompaniment of side orders and vegetables. They have a good wine selection, too. The sweet *plátanos* prepared on the open grill are delicious. Service is informal and friendly, as is the decor: Heavy wood tables and chairs are spread comfortably around the large dining room.

On the road down to the Butterfly Farm, on your right. © **2645-5337**. Reservations recommended during high season. Lunch $6–$12 (£3–£6); main courses $7–$17 (£3.50–£8.50). AE, MC, V. Daily noon–9pm.

Sofia ★★ *(Finds* COSTA RICAN/FUSION This restaurant serves top-notch eclectic cuisine in a beautiful setting. Start everything off with a mango-ginger mojito and then try one of their colorful and abundant salads. Main courses range from seafood *chimichangas* to chicken breast served in a guava reduction. The tenderloin comes with a chipotle butter sauce, or in a roasted red-pepper and cashew sauce, either way served over a bed of mashed sweet potato. Everything is very well prepared and reasonably priced. There are two good-size dining rooms here; the best seats are close to the large arched picture windows overlooking the neighboring forest and gardens.

Cerro Plano, just past the turnoff to the Butterfly Farm, on your left. © **2645-7017**. Reservations recommended during high season. Main courses $11–$16 (£5.50–£8). AE, DC, DISC, MC, V. Daily 11:30am–9:30pm.

MONTEVERDE AFTER DARK

The most popular after-dark activities in Monteverde are night hikes in one of the reserves and a natural-history slide show (see "Other Attractions in Monteverde," earlier in this chapter). However, if you want a taste of the local party scene, head to **La Taberna** ★, which is just outside of downtown Santa Elena before the Serpentarium. This place attracts a mix of locals and tourists, cranks its music loud, and often gets people dancing. Alternatively, **Flor de Vida, Kaffa El Café,** and **Moon Shiva** sometimes feature live music, theater, or open-mic jam sessions. **El Sapo Dorado** has been hosting live dance bands from San José most Monday evenings.

You'll also want to check to see if there's any live music or other performance at the **Monteverde Amphitheater** (© 2645-6272), a beautiful open-air performance space, up a steep driveway up from Stella's Bakery, next to Bromelia's.

10

The Central Pacific Coast:
Where the Mountains Meet the Sea

After Guanacaste, the beaches of Costa Rica's central Pacific coast are easily the country's most popular. Options here range from the surfer and snowbird hangout of **Jacó,** to the ecotourist mecca of **Manuel Antonio,** to isolated and diminutive **Dominical,** with its jungle-clad hillsides and rainforest waterfalls. The region is also home to some spectacular national parks.

Jacó is the closest major beach destination to San José. It has historically been a top choice for young surfers and citydwelling Costa Ricans. Today, Jacó, and the beaches around it, are booming with a rapidly expanding pool of condominiums, vacation rentals, and retirement homes. Just outside of Jacó sits **Carara National Park** 𝕲𝕲, one of the last places in Costa Rica where you can see the disappearing dry forest join the damp, humid forests that extend south down the coast. If you're lucky, you might even glimpse a scarlet macaw here.

For its part, Manuel Antonio remains one of the country's foremost ecotourist destinations, with a host of hotel and lodging options and an easily accessible national park that combines the exuberant lushness of a lowland tropical rainforest with several gorgeous beaches. **Manuel Antonio National Park** 𝕲𝕲 is home to all four of Costa Rica's monkey species, as well as a wealth of other easily viewed flora and fauna.

If you're looking to get away from it all, **Dominical** and the **beaches south of Dominical** 𝕲 should be your top choice on this coast. Still a small village, the beach town of Dominical is flanked by even more remote and undeveloped beaches, including those found inside **Ballena Marine National Park** 𝕲.

Finally, if you can tear yourself away from the beaches and coastline here, and head slightly inland, you'll find **Chirripó National Park** 𝕲𝕲, a misty cloud forest that becomes a barren *páramo* (a region above 3,000m/9,840 ft.) at the peak of its namesake, Mount Chirripó—the tallest peak in Costa Rica.

The climate here is considerably more humid than that farther north in Guanacaste, but it's not nearly as steamy as along the south Pacific or Caribbean coasts.

1 Playa de Jacó, Playa Hermosa 𝕲 & Playa Herradura

Jacó: 117km (73 miles) W of San José; 75km (47 miles) S of Puntarenas

These beach towns are booming. While Jacó remains the center of the action here, the beaches just north and south of it are also beginning to blossom. **Playa de Jacó** is a long stretch of beach strung with a dense hodgepodge of hotels in all price categories, cheap souvenir shops, seafood restaurants, pizza joints, rowdy bars, and a

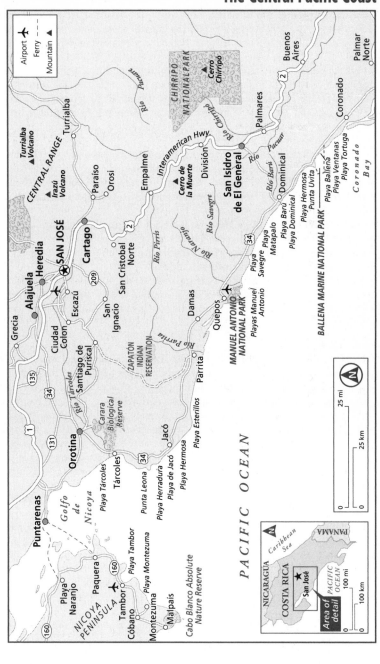

Airport ✈
Ferry - - -
Mountain ▲

Buenos Aires
Palmar Norte
Coronado

CHIRRIPÓ NATIONAL PARK
Cerro Chirripó ▲

Río Pacuar

Turrialba Volcano ▲
Turrialba
CENTRAL RANGE
Turrialba

Interamerican Hwy.
Palmares
Río Pacuar
Río Chirripó

Irazú Volcano ▲
Paraíso
Orosi
Empalme
División
San Isidro de El General
Río General

Cerro de la Muerte ▲

Dominical
Playa Hermosa
Punta Uvita
Playa Ballena
Playa Ventanas
Playa Tortuga

Coronado Bay

SAN JOSÉ ✈
Heredia
Alajuela
Cartago
San Cristobal Norte
Río Pirrís
Río Savegre

Playa Barú
Playa Dominical

BALLENA MARINE NATIONAL PARK

Grecia
Escazú
San Ignacio
Ciudad Colón
Santiago de Puriscal

ZAPATÓN INDIAN RESERVATION

Río Naranjo

Damas
Quepos ✈
Playas Manuel Antonio
Playa Savegre
Playa Matapalo

MANUEL ANTONIO NATIONAL PARK

Río Parrita
Parrita

Carara Biological Reserve
Río Tárcoles

Orotina

Playa Esterillos
Jacó

Playa Tárcoles
Tárcoles
Punta Leona
Playa Herradura
Playa de Jacó
Playa Hermosa

Puntarenas
Golfo de Nicoya

PACIFIC OCEAN

Playa Naranjo
Paquera
Tambor
Cóbano
Montezuma
Malpaís
Playa Tambor
Playa Montezuma

NICOYA PENINSULA

Cabo Blanco Absolute Nature Reserve

25 mi
25 km

N

25 mi
25 km

NICARAGUA
COSTA RICA
San José ★
Caribbean Sea
PANAMÁ
PACIFIC OCEAN
100 mi
100 km

Area of detail

miniature-golf course. The main strip here, which runs parallel to the shoreline, is an overcrowded and congested collection of restaurants, shops, and small strip malls, where pedestrians, bicycles, scooters, cars, and ATVs vie for right of way both day and night.

Still, the number-one attraction here is the surf, and this is definitely a surfer-dominated beach town. Surfers love the consistent beach break here (and at neighboring Playa Hermosa). However, the beach itself is not particularly appealing. It consists of dark-gray sand with lots of little rocks, and it's often very rough. Still, given its proximity to San José, Jacó is almost always packed with a mix of foreign and Tico vacationers.

Just north of Jacó is **Playa Herradura,** a once-forgotten patch of brown sand that is home to the large Los Sueños Marriott Ocean & Golf Resort. North of Herradura, you'll find a few other small beaches and resorts. The high-end St. Regis is taking over one of these beaches, and the elegant boutique hotel Villa Caletas is located on a high hill above another.

To the south of Jacó, **Playa Hermosa** is a black-sand beach with a fast and steep beach break. This is a spot for serious surfers. One of the hotels here has even installed a bank of klieg lights for night surfing. However, be careful; this break can be fierce and is known to humble even experienced riders.

In contrast to the dryness of Guanacaste, these are the first beaches on the Pacific coast to have a tropical feel. The humidity is palpable, and the lushness of the tropical forest is visible on the hillsides surrounding town. In hotel gardens, flowers bloom profusely throughout the year.

ESSENTIALS

GETTING THERE & DEPARTING   By Car   There are several routes to this region. The most popular one is a narrow and winding two-lane road, the "old highway," over and through mountains, known locally as *La Cuesta del Aguacate* (Avocado Hill). This route is equal parts scenic and harrowing—it's not uncommon to encounter buses and trucks passing on blind curves, or to find yourself in a long line of cars stuck behind a slow-moving truck crawling up one of the steep hills. Begin this route by taking the Interamerican Highway west out of San José and exiting just west of Alajuela near the town of Atenas. Follow the numerous signs to any hotel in Jacó or Manuel Antonio. The old highway meets the Costanera Highway a few kilometers west of Orotina. From here it's a straight and flat shot down the coast to Jacó.

Alternatively, you can head out of San José on the highway to Escazú and Santa Ana. Continue to the town of Ciudad Colón; from here, follow signs to Puriscal and then Orotina. This is a similarly scenic and winding route through the mountains, with the same caveats, but it is less traveled and slightly more direct than the more popular route mentioned above. Finally, if you're coming from anywhere in northern Costa Rica, take the Interamerican Highway, get off at the Puntarenas exit, and follow signs to Caldera. From here, head south on the Costanera.

By Bus   **Transportes Jacó** express buses (© **2223-1109** or 2643-3135) leave San José daily every 2 hours between 5am and 7pm from the Coca-Cola bus terminal at Calle 16 between avenidas 1 and 3. The trip takes between 2½ and 3 hours; the fare is $2.50 (£1.25). On weekends and holidays, extra buses are sometimes added, so it's worth calling to check.

Playa Jacó

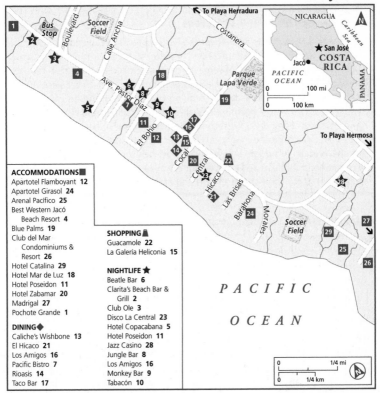

ACCOMMODATIONS ■
Apartotel Flamboyant **12**
Apartotel Girasol **24**
Arenal Pacífico **25**
Best Western Jacó
   Beach Resort **4**
Blue Palms **19**
Club del Mar
   Condominiums &
   Resort **26**
Hotel Catalina **29**
Hotel Mar de Luz **18**
Hotel Poseidon **11**
Hotel Zabamar **20**
Madrigal **27**
Pochote Grande **1**

DINING ◆
Caliche's Wishbone **13**
El Hicaco **21**
Los Amigos **16**
Pacific Bistro **7**
Rioasis **14**
Taco Bar **17**

SHOPPING 🛍
Guacamole **22**
La Galería Heliconia **15**

NIGHTLIFE ★
Beatle Bar **6**
Clarita's Beach Bar &
   Grill **2**
Club Ole **3**
Disco La Central **23**
Hotel Copacabana **5**
Hotel Poseidon **11**
Jazz Casino **28**
Jungle Bar **8**
Los Amigos **16**
Monkey Bar **9**
Tabacón **10**

Gray Line (℃ **2220-2126;** www.graylinecostarica.com) has two buses that leave San José for Jacó daily at 7:30am and 4pm. **Interbus** (℃ **2283-5573;** www.interbus online.com) also has two buses that leave San José for Jacó daily at 8:15am and 2:30pm. Both companies charge $25 (£13) and will pick you up at most San José–area hotels. Both also have outgoing transportation with connections to most major tourist destinations in the country.

Buses from San José to **Quepos** and Manuel Antonio also pass by Jacó. (They let passengers off on the highway about 1km/½ mile from town.) However, during the busy months, some of these buses will refuse passengers getting off in Jacó or will accept them only if they pay the full fare to Quepos or Manuel Antonio. For information and departure times of these buses, see p. 42.

From **Puntarenas,** you can catch daily Quepos-bound buses at 5, 8, and 11am and 12:30, 2:30, and 4:30pm. The buses drop you off on the highway outside of town. The trip's duration is 1 hour; the fare is $2 (£1).

The Jacó bus station is at the north end of town, at a small mall across from the Jacó Fiesta Hotel. Buses for San José leave daily every 2 hours between 5am and 7pm. Buses returning to San José from Quepos pass periodically and pick up passengers on the highway. Because schedules can change, it's best to ask at your hotel about current departure times.

Moments   Don't Feed the Crocs

The Costanera Highway passes over the Tárcoles River just outside the entrance to **Carara National Park,** about 23km (14 miles) south of Orotina. This is a popular spot to pull over and spot some gargantuan crocodiles. Some can reach 3.7 to 4.6m (12–15 ft.) in length. Usually anywhere from 10 to 20 are easily visible, either swimming in the water or sunning on the banks. But be careful. First, you'll be walking on a narrow sidewalk along the side of the bridge with cars and trucks speeding by. And second, there have been numerous car break-ins here, including the seemingly safe restaurant parking lots at the north end of the bridge. Although a new police post has somewhat reduced the risk, I recommend that you don't leave your car or valuables unguarded for long, or better yet, leave someone at the car and take turns watching the crocs.

ORIENTATION   Playa de Jacó is a short distance off the southern highway. One main road runs parallel to the beach, with a host of arteries heading toward the water; you'll find most of the town's hotels and restaurants off these roads.

GETTING AROUND   Almost everything is within walking distance in Jacó, but you can call **Asotaxi** (© 2643-2020 or 2643-1919) for a cab.

You can also rent a bicycle or scooter from a variety of different shops and streetside stands along the main street. A bike rental should run you around $8 to $15 (£4–£7.50) per day, and a scooter should cost between $30 and $50 (£15–£25) per day.

For longer excursions, you can rent a car from **Alamo** (© 2643-2881), **Budget** (© 2643-2265), **Economy** (© 2643-1098), **National** (© 2643-1752), **Payless** (© 2643-3224), or **Zuma** (© 2643-3207). Expect to pay approximately $50 to $70 (£25–£35) for a 1-day rental. You might also consider talking to a local taxi driver, who'd probably take you wherever you want to go for about the same price, saving you some hassle and headache.

FAST FACTS   The **Banco Nacional** (© 2643-3072) and the **Banco de Costa Rica** (© 2643-3695) have branches in town on the main road. Also on the main road, you can find the **Farmacia Jacó** (© 2643-3205) and the well-stocked **Farmacia Fischel** (© 2643-2683), which is in the El Galeone shopping center. A gas station is on the main highway, between Playa Herradura and Jacó, and a 24-hour gas station, **El Arroyo,** is on the highway on the southern edge of Jacó. The **health center** (© 2643-3667) and **post office** (© 2643-2175) are at the Municipal Center at the south end of town. However, the best-equipped medical center is the new **Clinica Santa Catalina** (© 2643-5059), located 4 blocks inland from the Pop's ice-cream shop.

A **public phone office,** where you can make international calls, is in the ICE building on the main road. This office is open Monday through Saturday from 8am to noon and 1 to 5pm. There are half a dozen or more **Internet cafes** in town, as well as several inexpensive full-service laundromats; a **Western Union office** in a small strip mall across from La Hacienda restaurant; a large **Más** × **Menos** supermarket on the main drag in the center of town; and an even larger and more modern **Automercado** supermarket in the strip mall on the main highway near the entrance to Playa Herradura.

FUN ON & OFF THE BEACH

Unfortunately, this beach has a reputation for dangerous riptides (as does most of Costa Rica's Pacific coast). Even strong swimmers have been known to drown in the power rips. At times, storms far offshore cause huge waves to pound on the beach, making it impossible to go into the water much beyond your waist. If this is the case, you'll have to be content with the hotel pool. In general, the far southern end of the beach is the calmest and safest place to swim.

OTHER BEACHES AROUND JACO

As an alternative to Playa de Jacó, you may want to visit other nearby beaches. These beaches are easily reached by car, moped, or bicycle—if you've got a lot of energy. All are signposted, so you'll have no trouble finding them.

Playa Hermosa, 10km (6¼ miles) southeast of Jacó, where sea turtles lay eggs from July to December, is also well known for its great surfing waves. This beach is dark, made of nearly black, yet fine, volcanic sand. If you keep heading south (really southeast) you next come to **Playa Esterillos,** 22km (14 miles) south of Jacó, which is long and wide and almost always nearly deserted. Playa Esterillos is so long, in fact, that there are three separate entrances and sections, Esterillos Oeste, Centro, and Este—West, Center, and East, in order as you head away from Jacó. Just beyond Playa Esterillos is **Playa Bejuco,** another long, wide, nearly deserted stretch of sand.

Heading northwest from Jacó, the first beach you come to is **Playa Herradura,** a hard-packed brown-sand-and-rock beach ringed by lush hillsides. This is home to the Los Sueños Marriott Ocean & Golf Resort. However, the Marriott occupies only one end of the beach here; despite its presence, Playa Herradura still feels a lot more isolated and deserted than Jacó. Finally, **Punta Leona,** just a few kilometers north of Playa Herradura, is a cross between a hotel, a resort, and a private country club, and it has some of the nicer beaches in the area. Although they effectively have restricted access to their beaches for years, this is technically illegal in Costa Rica, and you have the right to enjoy both playas **Manta** and **Blanca,** two very nice white-sand beaches inside the Punta Leona complex. The public access road to these beaches is located south of the main Punta Leona entrance and is not very well marked.

CARARA NATIONAL PARK 🐸🐸

A little more than 15km (9⅓ miles) north of Jacó is **Carara National Park,** a world-renowned nesting ground for **scarlet macaws.** It has a few kilometers of trails open to visitors. There's a loop trail that takes about an hour, and another trail that's open only to tour groups. The macaws migrate daily, spending their days in the park and their nights among the coastal mangroves. It's best to view them in the early morning when they arrive, or around sunset when they head back to the coast for the evening, but a good guide can usually find them for you during the day. Whether or not you see them, you should hear their loud squawks. Among the other wildlife that you might

---

En Route to Jacó: An Isolated Boutique Beauty

If you're planning on heading to the beaches of the central Pacific coast via Ciudad Colón and Puriscal, you might consider a stop at **AmeTierra Hotel & Retreat** 🐸 (© **866/659-3805** in the U.S. and Canada, or 2419-0110 in Costa Rica; www.amatierra.com), a lovely little boutique hotel located about 1½ hours out of San José along this route, and approximately 1 hour from Jacó.

see here are caimans, coatimundis, armadillos, pacas, peccaries, and, of course, hundreds of species of birds.

Be sure to bring along insect repellent or, better yet, wear light cotton long sleeves and pants. (I was once foolish enough to attempt a quick hike while returning from Manuel Antonio, still in beach clothes and flip-flops.) The reserve is open daily from 8am to 4pm. Admission is $10 (£5) per person at the gate.

Several companies offer tours to Carara National Park for around $30 to $45 (£15–£23). Check at your hotel or contact **Gray Line Tours** (© 2643-3231) or **Superior Sightseeing** (© 8393-6626) to set one up. If you're looking for a more personalized tour, contact Lisa Robertson, a knowledgeable and amiable guide who runs **Happy Trails** (© 2643-1894), or you can hike the trails of Carara independently, but my advice is to take a guided tour; you'll learn a lot more about your surroundings.

The muddy banks of the Tárcoles River are home to a healthy population of American crocodiles. Just north of the entrance to the park is a bridge that's a prime spot for viewing both the crocs and the macaw migrations. In Jacó, several operators run daily crocodile tours on the Tárcoles River. These are simple tours in open skiffs or Boston whalers. Most of these companies bring along plenty of freshly killed chicken to attract the reptiles and pump up the adrenaline. Don't expect a highly trained naturalist guide or any semblance of respect for the natural world. Do expect to pay around $20 to $40 (£10–£20) per person for the trip.

Finally, just beyond Carara National Park on the Costanera Sur in the direction of Jacó is a turnoff for some spectacular waterfalls (including a 180m/590-ft. fall) around the town of **Bijagual.** There are several ways to visit these falls, and people run tours from Jacó or from entrances both at the top and bottom of the falls. At the top a local family runs the **Complejo Ecológico La Catarata** (© 2661-8263), which features a basic restaurant and a campground, and also offers horseback tours down to the falls for around $35 (£18). Alternatively, you can hike in from an entrance lower down. The hike takes about 45 minutes each way, and entrance costs $10 (£5) per person. While you're in this area, you can also visit **Pura Vida Botanical Gardens** (© 2200-5040). Admission for the gardens is $15 (£7.50). To get here, turn off at the signs for Hotel Villa Lapas. From there, it's a rough 8km (5 miles) up to the top of the falls.

ACTIVITIES & TOURS

ATV TOURS   Several operations take folks out on ATV tours through the surrounding countryside. Tours range in length from 2 to 6 hours and cost between $50 and $125 (£25–£63) per person. Contact **Paraíso Adventures** (© 2643-2920; www.paraisocostarica.com) or **Jaguar Riders** (© 2643-0180).

BIKING   You can rent a bike for around $8 to $15 (£4–£750) per day or $1 to $2 (50p–£1) per hour. Bikes are available from a slew of shops along the main road. Shop around, and make sure you get a bike that is in good condition and that is comfortable.

CANOPY TOURS   The easiest way to get up into the canopy here is on the **Rain Forest Aerial Tram Pacific** (© 2257-5961; www.rfat.com). A sister project to the original Rain Forest Aerial Tram, this attraction features modified ski-lift type gondolas that take you through and above the transitional forests bordering Carara National Park. The $55 (£28) entrance fee includes the guided 40-minute tram ride, and a guided 45-minute hike on a network of trails. You can also hike the company's trails for as long as you like. These folks also have a zip-line canopy tour on the same grounds, and offer guided tours, including transportation from both San José and any hotel in the area. The Aerial Tram is located a few kilometers inland from an exit just north of the first entrance into Jacó.

There are quite a few zip-line and harness-style canopy tours in this area. **Chiclets Tree Tour** (© 2643-1880) offers up a canopy adventure ($60/£30 per person) in nearby Playa Hermosa. This is an adventurous tour, with 13 platforms set in transitional forest, with some sweeping views of the Pacific. **Villa Lapas** (p. 289) has two different tours through the treetops outside of Jacó. The better and cheaper option is a guided hike on its network of trails and five suspended bridges ($20/£10 per person). The operator also has a relatively low-adrenaline zip-line canopy tour ($35/£18 per person), with seven platforms connected by six cables.

Finally, Jacó is also a good jumping-off point for a trip to **Turu BaRi Tropical Park** (© 2250-0705; www.turubari.com), near Orotina. See chapter 6 for details.

GOLF   The excellent **La Iguana,** an 18-hole golf course at the **Los Sueños Marriott Ocean & Golf Resort** (© 2630-9000; www.golflaiguana.com), is open to nonguests. Greens fees are $155 (£78) for a full round. The price drops to $130 (£65) if you tee off after noon. Club and shoe rentals are available. Marriott guests pay slightly less to play here.

HORSEBACK RIDING   Horseback-riding tours give you a chance to get away from all the development in Jacó and see a bit of nature. Contact **Happy Trails** (© 2643-1894) or **Hermanos Salazar** (© 2643-3203) to make a reservation. Over in Playa Herradura, you can try the **Jacó Equestrian Center** (© 2643-1569). Tours lasting 3 to 4 hours cost anywhere from $35 to $70 (£17–£35).

KAYAKING   Kayak Jacó (© 2643-1233; www.kayakjaco.com) runs a couple of different trips. Tours range from gentle paddles and floats on the Tulin River to combination ocean-kayaking/snorkeling trips on calm Herradura Bay, to full-on kayak surfing at one of the local beach breaks. You can also do some moderate white-water kayaking in easy-to-use inflatable kayaks or try your hand in the ocean on one of the eight-person outrigger canoes. Most options run around 4 hours and include transportation to and from the put-in, as well as fresh fruit and soft drinks during the trip. The tours cost between $50 and $120 (£25–£60) per person, depending on the particular trip and group size.

ORGANIZED TOURS FARTHER AFIELD   If you'll be spending your entire Costa Rican visit in Jacó but would like to see some other parts of the country, you can arrange tours through the local offices of **Gray Line Tours** (© 2643-3231), which operates out of the Best Western Jacó Beach Resort (p. 286). Gray Line offers day tours to Arenal, Poás, and Irazú volcanoes; white-water rafting trips; cruises to Tortuga Island; and trips to Braulio Carrillo National Park and other places. Rates range from $35 to $120 (£18–£60) for day trips. Overnight trips are also available. Thanks to improvements to the road, you can now reach **Manuel Antonio** in about 1 hour from Jacó. In addition to the above-mentioned companies, many local operators offer a variety of tour options in Manuel Antonio, including trips to the national park, the Rainmaker Nature Refuge, and the Damas Island estuary. See the "Manuel Antonio National Park" section (later in this chapter) for more details on the types of tours and activities available there.

SPA   The **Serenity Spa** (© 2643-1624; www.serenityspacr.com) offers massages, as well as mud packs, face and body treatments, and manicures and pedicures. The spa's Jacó branch is on the first floor, among a tiny little cul-de-sac of shops next to Zuma Rent-A-Car. These folks also have operations at Villa Caletas.

SPORTFISHING, SCUBA DIVING & SEABORNE FUN   Since the Los Sueños Marriott resort (p. 289) and its adjacent 250-slip marina opened, most local maritime activity has shifted over here. If you're interested in doing some sportfishing, scuba diving, or any other waterborne activity, I recommend that you check with your hotel or at the marina. Dependable operators that have set up here include **Maverick Sport-fishing Yachts** (© 866/888-6426 in the U.S., or 2637-8824 in Costa Rica; www.maverickyachtscostarica.com), **Costa Rica Dreams** (© 732/901-8625 in the U.S. and Canada or 2637-8942 in Costa Rica; www.costaricadreams.com), and **Cuervo Sport Fishing** (© 800/656-1859 in the U.S. and Canada; www.costarica-fishingcharters.com). A half-day fishing trip for four people costs around $250 to $600 (£125–£300), and a full day costs between $600 and $1,800 (£300–£900).

SURFING   The same waves that often make Playa de Jacó dangerous for swimmers make it one of the most popular beaches in the country with surfers. Nearby **Playa Hermosa, Playa Tulin,** and **Playa Escondida** are also excellent surfing beaches. Those who want to challenge the waves can rent surfboards for around $3 (£1.50) an hour or $10 to $15 (£5–£7.50) per day, and boogie boards for $2 (£1) an hour, from any one of the numerous surf shops along the main road. If you want to learn how to surf, try the **Jacó Surf School** (© 8829-4697; www.jacosurfschool.com) or contact Johnny at **Superior Sightseeing** (© 8393-6626), or ask for him at Club del Mar.

SALSA   If you want to learn a few moves for the late-night dance floors around town, head to **Salsa Star** (© 2643-3886; www.salsastar.com), which offers a "salsa boot camp," that promises to have you dancing like a star after just one 3-hour class. These folks also offer up hip-hop, belly dance, and capoeira lessons.

SHOPPING

If you try to do any shopping in Jacó, you'll be overrun with shops selling T-shirts, cut-rate souvenirs, and handmade jewelry and trinkets. Most of the offerings are of pretty poor quality. Two notable exceptions are **Guacamole** ★ (© 2643-1120), a small clothing store that produces its own line of batik beachwear, and **La Galería Heliconia** ★★ (© 2643-3613), which carries a superb selection of artworks and pottery.

WHERE TO STAY IN PLAYA DE JACO

Because Punta Leona, Playa Herradura, Playa Hermosa de Jacó (not to be confused with either Playa Hermosa in Guanacaste, or Playa Hermosa on the Nicoya Peninsula), Playa Esterillos, and Playa Bejuco are close, many people choose accommodations in these beach towns as well. Selected listings for these towns follow this section.

EXPENSIVE

Best Western Jacó Beach Resort   This remains Jacó's largest and most popular resort hotel. Situated right on the beach, this five-story hotel offers all the amenities and services you could want at a pretty good price. Still, this is a cut-rate resort, and there's little in the way of charm, romance, or true ambience here. The hotel is often packed throughout the high season, and a party atmosphere pervades the place. The open-air lobby is surrounded by lush gardens, and covered walkways connect the hotel's buildings. Rooms are adequate and have tile floors and walls of glass facing balconies; however, not all of the rooms have good views (some face another building), and many of them show the wear and tear of age and heavy occupancy. Ask for a room on a higher floor and with an ocean view. A large percentage of guests opt for an all-inclusive package, but I think you'd do better to sample the many restaurants and dining options around Jacó.

Playa de Jacó (A.P. 962-1000, San José), Puntarenas. ⓒ 800/528-1234 in the U.S. and Canada, or 2643-1000 in Costa Rica. Fax 2643-3833. www.bestwestern.com. 125 units. $131–$162 (£66–£81) double. Rates include breakfast buffet. AE, DC, MC, V. **Amenities:** 2 restaurants; 2 bars; 2 circular pools; tennis court; well-equipped gym; watersports equipment rental; complimentary bike use; tour desk; limited room service; laundry service. *In room:* A/C, TV, free Wi-Fi, coffeemaker, safe.

Club del Mar Condominiums & Resort ⭐⭐ (Kids)   This has long been my top choice in Playa de Jacó, and it remains so. It has a fabulous location, friendly management, and attractively designed rooms. Club del Mar is at the far southern end of the beach, where the rocky hills meet the sand, and where the swimming is probably the safest in town. Most of the rooms are actually one- or two-bedroom condo units, with full kitchens. All are spacious and feature private balconies or porches. There are also eight rooms on the second floor of the large main building, as well as two huge and luxurious penthouse suites up on the third floor. All units come with an ocean view, although some are more open and expansive than others. The grounds are lush and chock-full of flowering heliconia and ginger. There's a midsize multipurpose pool and an excellent open-air restaurant, as well as some modest spa facilities.

Playa de Jacó (A.P. 107-4023), Puntarenas. ⓒ 866/978-5669 in the U.S. and Canada, or 2643-3194 in Costa Rica. Fax 2643-3550. www.clubdelmarcostarica.com. 32 units. $153–$195 (£77–£98) double; $224–$373 (£112–£187) condo; $383 (£186) penthouse. Rates lower in off season; higher during peak weeks. AE, DC, MC, V. **Amenities:** Restaurant; bar; midsize free-form pool; small spa; tour desk; concierge; free Wi-Fi in main building and around pool; room service (8am–9pm); in-room massage; babysitting. *In room:* A/C, TV, fridge, safe.

MODERATE

In addition to the places listed below, the oceanfront **Apartotel Girasol** ⭐ (ⓒ 800/923-2779 or 2643-1591; www.girasol.com), with 16 fully equipped one-bedroom apartments, is a good option, especially for longer stays. **Hotel Poseidon** (ⓒ 888/643-1242 in the U.S. and Canada, or 2643-1642; www.hotel-poseidon.com) is a pretty boutique hotel in the heart of downtown, while **Hotel Catalina** (ⓒ 2643-1237; www.hotelcatalinacr.com) is another good beachfront choice.

Apartotel Flamboyant   Don't let the name fool you: The Flamboyant is actually rather quiet and intimate. The rooms are arranged around a small swimming pool and are only a few steps from the beach. They're all spacious, with simple furnishings, and most have kitchenettes. The more expensive rooms have air-conditioning, televisions, and private balconies. You'll find the hotel on a narrow lane leading toward the ocean, down from Caliche's Wishbone (p. 292).

Playa de Jacó (A.P. 18), Puntarenas. ⓒ 2643-3146. Fax 2643-1068. www.apartotelflamboyant.com. 15 units. $71–$80 (£36–£40) double. AE, MC, V. **Amenities:** Outdoor pool; unheated Jacuzzi. *In room:* Safe, no phone.

Arenal Pacífico ⭐   This is a good midrange option, and it's right on the beach to boot. The rooms are nothing special—and almost none offer an ocean view—but they are clean and cool, and most are pretty spacious. The grounds are lush by Jacó standards—you have to cross a shady bridge over a little stream to get from the parking lot and reception to the rooms and restaurant. I like the second-floor rooms, which have private balconies. The superior rooms are larger, and come with coffeemakers

and minifridges. There are two outdoor pools—one with a little waterfall filling it, another with a round children's pool. The open-air restaurant serves standard Tico and international fare.

Playa de Jacó (A.P. 962-1000, San José), Puntarenas. © **2643-3419**. Fax 2643-3770. www.arenalpacifico.com. 22 units. $98 (£49) double; $121 (£61) superior double. Rates include continental breakfast. Rates lower in off season; higher during peak weeks. AE, MC, V. **Amenities:** Restaurant; bar; 2 outdoor pools; surf- and boogie-board rental; tour desk; laundry service. *In room:* A/C, TV, free Wi-Fi, safe.

Hotel Mar de Luz ★ *Value*   This is one of Playa de Jacó's better deals and a comfortable alternative to the string of cut-rate *cabinas* you'll find crowding this popular beach town. All the rooms are immaculate and comfortable. Some feature stone walls, small sitting areas, and one or two double beds placed on a raised sleeping nook. My only complaint is that in most rooms, the windows are too small and mostly sealed, forcing you to use air-conditioning. In the gardens just off the pools are a couple of grills for guest use. A comfortable common sitting area has a selection of magazines and books. The Dutch owner Victor Keulen seems driven to offer as much comfort, quality, and service as he can for the price. The hotel lies 50m (164 ft.) east of the Hotel Tangeri, right in the center of Jacó.

Playa de Jacó (A.P. 143), Puntarenas. ©/fax **2643-3259**. www.mardeluz.com. 29 units. $100 (£50) double. Rates include breakfast. Rates lower in off season; higher during peak weeks. V. **Amenities:** 2 small-to-midsize adult pools and children's pool; Jacuzzi; game room; tour desk; babysitting; laundry service; nonsmoking rooms. *In room:* A/C, TV, free Wi-Fi, minifridge, coffeemaker, safe, microwave.

Pochote Grande *Value*   Named for a huge old pochote tree on the grounds, this well-kept and attractive hotel is located right on the beach toward the far north end of Jacó. The grounds are shady and lush, and there's a refreshing little pool. All of the rooms are quite large, although sparsely furnished, and have white-tile floors, one queen-size and one single bed, a small fridge, and a balcony or patio. I prefer the second-floor rooms, which are blessed with high ceilings. The modest restaurant and snack bar serve a mixture of Tico, German, and American meals. (The owners are German by way of Africa.)

Playa de Jacó (A.P. 42), Puntarenas. © **2643-3236**. Fax 2220-4979. www.hotelpochotegrande.net. 24 units. $80 (£40) double; $95 (£48) triple. Add $5 (£2.50) for a room with television. Rates lower in off season; higher during peak weeks. AE, MC, V. **Amenities:** Restaurant; bar; pool. *In room:* A/C, free Wi-Fi, fridge, safe, no phone.

INEXPENSIVE

There are quite a few budget hotels around town. Most cater to itinerant surfers, backpackers, and Ticos. If you're looking to stay on the cheap, your best bet is to simply walk the strip and see who's got the best room at the best price. If you walk slightly inland from the center of town, the **Blue Palms** (© **2643-0099**; www.blue-palms. net) offers immaculate rooms and a small swimming pool at budget prices.

There are also several campgrounds in or near Playa de Jacó. **Madrigal** (© **2643-3230**), at the south end of town at the foot of some jungley cliffs, is my favorite. You can also try **El Hicaco** (© **2643-3004**), which is close to the beach but also pretty close to the Disco La Central, so don't expect to get much sleep if you stay here. Also be very careful with your belongings, I've heard several complaints of robberies at the campsites here. Camping runs between $3 and $8 (£1.50–£4) per night.

Hotel Zabamar *Kids*   The Zabamar is set back about 1 block from the beach in a shady compound. The best rooms are in a two-story building closest to the road. These are quite roomy and feature cool tile floors and air-conditioning. The rest of the rooms are also large and have red-tile floors, small refrigerators, ceiling fans, hammocks on their front porches, and *pilas* (laundry sinks) in little gravel-and-palm gardens behind them. Travelers on budgets will appreciate the size of the older, less-expensive rooms. There's a small swimming pool with two separate children's sections that's quite popular with Tico families staying here. Because of the proximity to the town's bars and restaurants, note that it can get noisy in some rooms.

Playa de Jacó, Puntarenas. ℂ 2643-3174. Fax 2643-2645. 20 units. $55–$80 (£28–£40) double. Rates include breakfast. Rates lower in off season; discounts for long-term stays. No credit cards. **Amenities:** Restaurant; small pool. *In room:* No phone.

WHERE TO STAY IN PLAYA HERRADURA & NORTH OF PLAYA DE JACO
VERY EXPENSIVE

In addition to the hotel listed below, there are scores of condominium units for rent at the Los Sueños resort. All come with kitchens, access to swimming pools, and rights to use the golf course here. These are excellent options for families who want to do some cooking, and for longer stays. If you want to rent a condo here, contact **Costa Rica Luxury Rentals** (ℂ 866/525-2188 in the U.S. and Canada, or 2637-7105 in Costa Rica; www.crluxury.com). Rates run between $350 and $440 (£175–£220) nightly for one- and two-bedroom units, to over $1,000 (£500) for some of the more luxurious three-bedroom units.

Los Sueños Marriott Ocean & Golf Resort ★★ *Kids* This resort is a massive, four-story horseshoe facing the beach. The entire thing is done in a Spanish colonial style, with stucco walls, heavy wooden doors, and red-clay roof tiles. The rooms are all spacious and tastefully done. The bathrooms are large and have plenty of counter space. Every room has a balcony, but all are not created equal. Most have only small Juliet-style balconies. Those facing the ocean are clearly superior, and a few of the ocean-facing rooms even have large, comfortable balconies with chaise longues and tables and chairs.

The pool is a vast, intricate maze built to imitate the canals of Venice (in miniature), with private nooks and grottoes; kids love exploring it. Parents will appreciate the excellent children's program. The beach here is calm and good for swimming, although it's one of the least attractive beaches on this coast, with a mix of rocks and hard-packed, dark-brown sand. The Ted Robinson–designed 18-hole golf course winds through some of the neighboring forest and is an excellent, if not particularly challenging, resort course. The Stellaris Casino is the largest and most comfortable I've found at a beach resort in Costa Rica.

Playa Herradura (A.P. 502-4005), San Antonio de Belén. ℂ 888/236-2427 in the U.S., 2298-0844, or 2630-9000 in Costa Rica. Fax 2630-9090. www.marriott.com. 201 units. $219–$309 (£110–£155) double; $439–$650 (£220–£325) suite; $1,250–$1,500 (£625–£750) presidential suite. Rates lower in off season; higher during peak periods. AE, MC, V. **Amenities:** 4 restaurants; coffee shop; 2 bars; lounge; large pool; golf course and pro shop; 9-hole miniature golf course; 4 outdoor lit tennis courts; large health club and spa; children's program; game room; concierge; tour desk; car-rental desk; salon; 24-hr. room service; in-room massage; babysitting; laundry service; nonsmoking rooms; Wi-Fi (for a fee) in most public areas. *In room:* A/C, TV, dataport, minibar, coffeemaker, hair dryer, iron, safe.

Villa Lapas Located on a lush piece of property along the Río Tarcolitos and bordering Carara National Park, Villa Lapas is a good choice if you're looking to combine a bit of ecoadventure and bird-watching with some beach time. The rooms here are spacious, with two double beds, cool red-clay tile floors, air-conditioning, ceiling fans, and a shady veranda with wooden benches for taking in the scenery. The hotel's best feature is its massive, open-air restaurant and deck, which overlooks the river and where buffet-style meals are served. Villa Lapas has 217 hectares (536 acres) of land with excellent trails, a series of suspended bridges crossing the river, and its own canopy tour. The hotel also features a small re-creation of a typical Costa Rican rural village of times gone by. This riverside attraction also has three massive gift shops, an atmospheric old-style Costa Rican bar, and a small chapel. You'll see the signs for Villa Lapas on the left, just after passing Carara National Park. The hotel is about 15 to 25 minutes from the beaches of Jacó, Hermosa, and Herradura.

Tárcoles (A.P. 419-4005, San Antonio de Belén). © 2637-0232. Fax 2637-0227. www.villalapas.com. 55 units. $116 (£58) per person. Rates include 3 meals daily and taxes. Rates lower in off season; higher during peak weeks. AE, MC, V. **Amenities:** 2 restaurants; 2 bars; small pool; 2 Jacuzzis; laundry service. In room: A/C, coffeemaker, safe.

EXPENSIVE

Villa Caletas ★★★ (Finds)   Perched 350m (1,148 ft.) above the sea, Villa Caletas enjoys commanding views of the Pacific over forested hillsides. The rooms are all elegantly appointed and spacious, but you'll definitely want to stay in a villa or suite. Each villa is situated on a patch of hillside facing the sea or forests. They feature white-tile floors, modern bathrooms, and a private terrace for soaking up the views. The larger junior suites come with their own outdoor Jacuzzis. The suites and master suites are larger still—and come with their own private swimming pools. There are only two master suites, and one is a vigorous hike downhill from the main hotel building and restaurants. The same is true of some of the villas and juniors.

The **Zephyr Palace** is a seven-suite addition, located a little bit apart from the main hotel and villas. The rooms here are immense and thematically designed—you can choose from an African suite, an Arabian suite, an Oriental suite, and more. The Imperial suite has its own gym and sauna. All have beautiful ocean views, home theater systems, Jacuzzis, private balconies, and personal concierge service.

A.P. 12358-1000, San José. © 2630-3003. Fax 2637-0404. www.hotelvillacaletas.com. 42 units. $178–$198 (£89–£99) double; $230 (£115) villa; $300–$470 (£150–£235) suite; $450–$600 (£225–£300) Zephyr Palace suites. Rates slightly lower in off season; higher during peak periods. Extra person $35 (£18). AE, MC, V. **Amenities:** 2 restaurants; bar; 2 midsize pools w/spectacular view; spa; concierge; tour desk; beach shuttle; in-room massage; laundry service. In room: A/C, TV, minibar, coffeemaker, hair dryer, safe.

WHERE TO DINE

Playa de Jacó has a wide range of restaurants. Many cater to surfers and budget travelers. In addition to the places listed below, if you're looking for simply prepared fresh seafood, **El Barco de Mariscos** (© 2643-2831) and **El Recreo** (© 2643-3012) are both good bets that serve standard Tico beach fare—fresh seafood, sandwiches, chicken, and steak. For a coffee break and fresh pastries and breads, head to **Café del M@r** (© 2643-1250). **Wahoo Seafood Saloon** (© 2643-1876) offers fresh seafood and Mexican fare. The small restaurant at the **Hotel Poseidon** ★ (© 2643-1642) serves a regularly changing small menu of high-end fusion cuisine. And sushi lovers should head to **Tsunami Sushi** (© 2643-3678), inside the El Galeone strip mall.

On the main road to Jacó, at the first main entrance into town, you'll find the **Lighthouse** (© 2643-3083), a steakhouse, seafood restaurant, and raw bar, which is open 24 hours daily and also has an extensive gift shop.

Over in Playa Herradura are several restaurants, including the Peruvian chain **Inka Grill,** in the new strip mall on the highway near the entrance to the beach. Also, at the Los Sueños marina, you'll find several other options, including **El Galeón** (see below), and **Bambu,** a sushi bar and Pan-Asian restaurant, and **La Linterna,** a fancy Italian restaurant. For lunch or light fare, here, I like the **Hook Up,** an excellent American-style grill and restaurant with a second-floor perch and good views of the boats bobbing at their berths. You can make reservations at any of these latter restaurants by calling ⓒ **2637-8284.**

Finally, **Steve & Lisa's** (ⓒ **2637-0594**), located several miles outside of town, around Tárcoles, is a good place for lunch. The food here is standard Tico fare, but the oceanside setting and views set it apart from other simple *sodas. Note:* There's another restaurant on this road calling itself "Steve & Lisa's," but it's located inland with no view. Definitely head to the one on the water's edge.

VERY EXPENSIVE

El Galeón ⓕⓕ FUSION   This is the top restaurant in a complex of restaurants found at the Los Sueños resort and marina. The setting is elegant, service refined, and the menu wide-ranging, creative, and eclectic. Appetizers range from a Creole gumbo and seafood étoufée, to crisp Asian-spiced soft-shell crabs and sea bass ceviche served with avocado and a local salsa. For a main course, I recommend the pistachio-crusted jumbo shrimp with a Pernod and anis sauce.

At the marina of the Los Sueños Marriott resort (p. 289). ⓒ **2637-8536** or 2637-8331. Reservations recommended. Main courses $16–$38 (£8–£19). AE, MC, V. Daily 6–10pm.

El Nuevo Latino ⓕ LATIN FUSION   The fanciest restaurant inside the Marriott Los Sueños resort offers creative and modern takes on local and regional dishes. The dozen or so tables are set in a narrow room with vaulted ceiling that features a glass wall running its length, fronting a gorgeous pool fed by a series of spouts from a story-high aqueduct. The service and setting are semiformal, but there's no dress code—they realize that you're at the beach and on vacation here. Standout dishes include local shrimp in a rum and sugar-cane glaze served with heart of palms and rice, and tenderloin in a guava–black pepper sauce served with a yucca and bacon tart.

At the Los Sueños Marriott resort (p. 289). ⓒ **2630-9000.** Reservations recommended. Main courses $16–$42 (£8–£21). AE, MC, V. Daily 6–11pm. Closed Mon during the off season.

EXPENSIVE

El Hicaco *Overrated* SEAFOOD/COSTA RICAN   This beachside restaurant has gotten too popular for its own good. There's now a cattle-car feel to the entire operation, and the food is overpriced and quality has declined. But the setting is simply wonderful: right on the edge of the beach, with the majority of the tables outdoors. At night you sit under the stars, surrounded by tall palm trees, with some interesting lighting overhead. If you do come here, stick with the freshly caught grilled seafood or lobster, although there are plenty of meat and chicken selections on the menu as well.

On the beach in downtown Jacó. ⓒ **2643-3226.** www.elhicaco.net. Reservations recommended during high season. Main courses $10–$30 (£5–£15). AE, MC, V. Daily 11am–11pm.

Pacific Bistro ⓕⓕ ASIAN/FUSION   Chef Kent Green changes the menu almost nightly, but fresh seafood and top-quality cuts of meat are always the building blocks for his creative Asian-influenced creations. You'll usually find some fresh tuna, mahimahi, and jumbo shrimp on the menu, but on any given night the sauces will range from a homemade teriyaki to a spicy Thai sauce to coconut curry. Portions are large, but it's worth saving some room for dessert. Set just off the sidewalk on the main drag in town, the restaurant only has six or so tables, so reservations are often essential.

On the main road in Jacó. ℂ 2643-3771. Reservations recommended. Main courses $8–$22 (£4–£11). AE, MC, V. Wed–Mon 6–10pm.

MODERATE

Los Amigos SEAFOOD/INTERNATIONAL   Set on a large corner of a busy intersection in the heart of Jacó, this restaurant serves fresh seafood and adventurous international fare at very reasonable prices. Sturdy wooden tables are spread around the small dining room and open-air patio here. I prefer the patio seating, which looks out over flowering heliconia to the bustle of Jacó's main drag. Fresh tuna can be had Cajun-style or with a spicy mango salsa. There are also several traditional Thai dishes on the menu, as well as some wraps and hearty salads. At night, they play electronic music and have a lively bar scene.

On the main road in Jacó. ℂ 2643-2961. Main courses $7–$30 (£3.50–£15). AE, MC, V. Daily noon–3pm and 6–11pm.

INEXPENSIVE

Caliche's Wishbone ★★ *Finds* SEAFOOD/MEXICAN   This casual spot is popular with surfers and offers Tex-Mex standards and homemade pizzas. However, you can also get excellent fresh fish and perfectly prepared seafood dishes, as well as a variety of sandwiches served in homemade pita bread. The portions are huge. It almost always has fresh tuna lightly seared and served with a soy-wasabi dressing. The nicest tables are streetside on a covered veranda. Inside are more tables, as well as a bar with television sets showing surf videos.

On the main road in Jacó. ℂ 2643-3406. Reservations not accepted. Main courses $4.50–$17 (£2.25–£8.50). V. Thurs–Tues noon–3pm and 6–10pm.

El Pelicano *Finds* SEAFOOD/COSTA RICAN   This simple beachfront restaurant is a lot like El Hicaco was before success went to its head. Heavy wooden tables and chairs are spread around a large, open-air dining room facing the beach and boats bobbing at anchor off Playa Herradura. The menu features a range of ceviches, salads, and main courses, with a heavy—and logical—emphasis on fresh seafood. The *corvina al ajillo* (sea bass in garlic sauce) is excellent, as is the *arroz con mariscos* (rice with seafood). To get here, drive the Playa Herradura road until you hit the beach, and then turn left on the narrow sandy access road.

On the beach in Playa Herradura. ℂ 2637-8910. Reservations recommended during high season. Main courses $6–$23 (£3–£12). MC, V. Daily 11am–10pm.

Rioasis PIZZA/MEXICAN   Rioasis serves hearty burritos, simple pasta dishes, and a wide array of freshly baked wood-oven pizzas. My favorite item is the Greek pizza, with olives, feta cheese, and anchovies, but the barbecue chicken pizza is also delicious. There is both indoor and terrace seating, as well as a bar area, complete with a pool table, dartboards, and a couple of TVs for sports events and surf videos.

On the main road in Jacó. ℂ 2643-3354. Reservations not accepted. Main courses $4–$24 (£2–£12). V. Daily noon–midnight.

Taco Bar ★ *Finds* TACOS   This casual little open-air joint serves up excellent food at great prices. The best option here is to order a one-, two- or three-taco plate with the accompanying salad bar. Choose from fresh fish, chicken, shrimp, calamari, or any combination of them. My favorites are the coconut shrimp and spicy fish fillings. The well-stocked salad bar features a wide range of stand-alone salads, as well as numerous toppings to finish off your tacos. You won't leave here hungry. There are a few wooden tables outdoors under large umbrellas, but most of the seating is around a large "U"-shaped bar. The seats are either high stools or wood planks hung from ropes, like swings. They also serve breakfast, as well as pizzas and a small selection of full entrees, and offer free Wi-Fi for diners.

A half-block inland from Pop's, central Jacó. ⓒ **2643-0222.** Reservations not accepted. Main courses $5–$10 (£2.50–£5). MC, V. Daily 11am–10pm.

PLAYA DE JACO AFTER DARK

Playa de Jacó is the central Pacific's party town, with tons of bars and several discos. **Disco La Central** is packed every night of the high season and every weekend during the off season. La Central is right on the beach near the south end of town. There's a huge open-air hall that features the requisite 1970s flashing lights and suspended mirrored ball, as well as a garden bar in a thatch-roofed building that's a slightly quieter place to have a drink. The disco charges a nominal cover charge. Other popular bars in town are the **Beatle Bar, Club Olé, Jungle Bar** and **Monkey Bar.** All of the aforementioned bars are located along the main strip through town. *Note:* There's a good amount of prostitution in Jacó. It's not uncommon to find working women at any of the above-mentioned places, as well as cruising other bars around town.

For a more casual atmosphere, head to either **Los Amigos** or **Tabacón** ⓕ. Los Amigos has nightly movies projected on a large outdoor wall, while Tabacón has popular pool and foosball tables, and often has live music.

Sports freaks can catch the latest games at **Clarita's Beach Bar & Grill, Hotel Copacabana** (both are right on the beach toward the north end of town), or **Hotel Poseidon** (on a side street near the center of town). The first two serve up good reasonably priced burritos, burgers, and bar food, while the latter offers much the same, as well as some items from their much better restaurant downstairs.

If you're into gaming, head to the **Stellaris Casino** ⓕ at the Los Sueños Marriott resort (ⓒ **2630-9000**), or the **Jazz Casino** (ⓒ **2643-2316**), located at the Hotel Amapola. The latter is a modest casino situated toward the southern end of the main road through Jacó (Av. Pastor Díaz), about a block beyond where it takes a sharp turn inland toward the Costanera Sur.

EN ROUTE SOUTH: PLAYAS HERMOSA, ESTERILLOS & BEJUCO

Playa Hermosa is the first beach you'll hit as you head south from Playa de Jacó. This is primarily a surfers' beach, but it is still a lovely spot to spend some beach time. In fact, even though the surf conditions here can be rather rough and unprotected, and the beach is made of dark volcanic sand, I find Playa Hermosa and the beaches south of it much more attractive than Jacó. After Playa Hermosa you will hit Esterillos, which is actually divided up by rivers into three sections, Esterillos Oeste, Esterillos Centro, Esterillos Este, each with a separate well-marked entrance. Farther south (which because of how the coast turns here, is actually more easterly), lies Playa Bejuco.

At night most folks in Playa Hermosa find their way to the **Backyard,** a raucous surfer bar with a pool table, darts, and hearty food.

Note: While beautiful, isolated, and expansive, the beaches of Hermosa, Esterillos, and Bejuco can be quite rough at times and dangerous for swimming. Caution is highly advised here.

WHERE TO STAY

In addition to the hotels listed below, there are a host of simple hotels and *cabinas* catering to surfers in Playa Hermosa. Prices, conditions, and upkeep can vary greatly. If you've got the time, your best bet is to visit a few until you find the best deal on the cleanest room. **Costa Nera** (✆ 2643-7044) and **Cabinas Las Arenas** (✆ 2643-7013; www.cabinaslasarenas.com) are two good options.

If you're looking for something even more remote and undeveloped, head to Playa Esterillos Este for the **Pelican Hotel** (✆ 2778-8105; www.pelicanbeachfronthotel. com), or head slightly farther south to the nearly deserted Playa Bejuco and the small **Delfin Beach Resort** (✆ 2778-8054; www.delfinbeachfront.com).

Very Expensive

Xandari by the Pacific ★★★ *(Finds*   A sister to the popular, upscale boutique Xandari Resort & Spa (p. 118) in Alajuela, this beachfront boutique resort is very similar in terms of design, style, and aesthetics. All the accommodations here are large, private villas, with high, curved ceilings and loads of artistic touches. I especially like the open, mosaic tile showers that let out on to lush gardens. The Maxima villas here are the top option and come with their own private plunge pool. Most of the villas are beachfront, but those that aren't have large gardens and a wonderful sense of seclusion and romance. *Note:* In order to encourage the enjoyment of the villas, beach, and surrounding nature, the rooms have no televisions. The open-air seafront restaurant serves excellent international fare, with an equal emphasis on healthy fresh ingredients and creative cooking combinations.

Playa Esterillos Centro (mailing address: A.P. 10-6300), Parrita. ✆ 866/363-3212 in the U.S. and Canada, or 2778-7070 in Costa Rica. Fax 2778-7878. www.xandari.com. 20 units. $235–$370 (£118–£185) double. Rates include continental breakfast. Rates lower in off season; higher during peak periods. AE, MC, V. **Amenities:** Restaurant; bar; two lap pools; Jacuzzi; full-service spa; tour desk; room service (7am–9pm); laundry service; all rooms nonsmoking. *In room:* A/C, free Wi-Fi, kitchenette, minibar, coffeemaker, hair dryer, safe.

Expensive

The Backyard   This perennially popular bar and restaurant also has some of the most modern and comfortable accommodations in Playa Hermosa, although they're overpriced for what you get. The two-story building features spacious rooms with dark red terra-cotta tile floors and simple furnishings. The second-floor rooms are definitely nicer than those on the ground floor. The oceanfront end units are classified as suites. They are a bit bigger and do have excellent ocean views. The small pool features a little sculpted-rock waterfall and is quite refreshing on the hot days here. Despite the more elaborate facilities and amenities, this place is still quintessentially a surfer joint, and the main reason to stay here is that this hotel sits directly in front of the principal peaks on Playa Hermosa.

Playa Hermosa de Jacó (A.P. 132), Jacó, Puntarenas. ✆/fax 2643-7011. www.backyardhotel.com. 8 units. $140–$190 (£70–£95) double. Rates lower in off season. AE, MC, V. **Amenities:** Restaurant; bar; small pool; laundry service. *In room:* A/C, TV, safe.

Moderate

Hotel Fuego del Sol ★   This place is right on the beach and offers good value for someone looking for a clean, cool, and comfortable room, as well as easy access to the waves. (It's a much better value than the Backyard, for example.) Most of the rooms are housed in a long, two-story block set perpendicular to the beach. Each comes with a queen-size and twin bed and a private balcony overlooking the free-form pool.

Those closest to the water will also give you a glimpse of the sea. The suites come with king-size beds, a separate sitting room, and fully stocked kitchenette. Everything is well maintained, and the restaurant here boasts a good view of the beach action.

Playa Hermosa, Jacó, Puntarenas. (C) **800/850-4532** in the U.S. and Canada, 2289-6060 reservations office in San José, or 2643-7171 at the hotel. Fax 2288-0123. www.fuegodelsolhotel.com. 22 units. $98 (£49) double; $161–$182 (£81–£91) suite. Rates include breakfast. Lower rates in off season. AE, MC, V. **Amenities:** Restaurant; bar; surf- and boogie-board rental; tour desk; laundry service. *In room:* A/C, TV (in some), safe.

Hotel Playa Bejuco (Kids)

Located just off the beach at Playa Bejuco, this is a younger sister to the popular Mar de Luz hotel in Jacó (p. 288). The two-story hotel is an "L" shape around a central swimming pool and gardens and facing the ocean. The construction features various walls and details made from heavy, smooth river stones. Rooms are spacious, cool, and modern, with red tile floors, simple wooden furnishings, and large bathrooms. The second-floor rooms are the biggest, and feature high ceilings with sleeping lofts, making them good options for families with children. The Belgian chef here serves excellent Continental cuisine.

Playa Bejuco, Puntarenas. (C)/fax **2778-8181.** www.hotelplayabejuco.com. 20 units. $115 (£58) double. Rates include breakfast and taxes. Lower rates in off season. AE, MC, V. **Amenities:** Restaurant; bar; outdoor pool; tour desk; laundry service. *In room:* A/C, TV, minifridge, coffeemaker, safe.

Terraza del Pacífico

Located just over the hill at the start of Playa Hermosa, this hotel has a wonderful setting on a mostly undeveloped section of beach. In the middle of the complex is a circular pool with a swim-up bar and plenty of chaise longues for sunbathing and siestas. Red-tile roofs and faux-stucco walls give the buildings a Mediterranean look, and hardwood balcony railings add a touch of the Tropics. Each guest room has two double beds, a private bathroom, and either a patio or balcony. A couple of suites are considerably larger and even include a kitchenette. The hotel's restaurant and open-air bar are located within a few feet of the high-tide mark. The hotel offers a range of tours, including a nearby canopy tour. Surfing is still the major draw here, and the Terraza hosts several major tournaments each year and has even installed klieg lights on the beach for night surfing.

Playa Hermosa de Jacó (A.P. 168-4023), Jacó, Puntarenas. (C) **2643-3222** or 2440-6862. Fax 2430-7571. www. terrazadelpacifico.com. 62 units. $102 (£51) double; $189–$221 (£95–£111) suite. Rates include full breakfast and taxes. Rates lower in off season; higher during peak weeks. AE, MC, V. **Amenities:** Restaurant; bar; pool w/swim-up bar; laundry service. *In room:* A/C, TV, free Wi-Fi, minibar, safe.

Inexpensive

Cabinas Las Olas   Playa Hermosa is a renowned surfing beach, and this has historically been its most popular surfer hotel. The main building is on a hill by the road. The nicest room here is the "Skybox Suite," located on the top floor, with a great view. Closer to the beach are three A-frame *ranchos*, each of which has a roomy bedroom on the second floor (in the peak of the A) and a single bed, a bunk bed, a kitchenette, and a bathroom on the ground floor. The remaining rooms are found in the main building by the road and parking lot. Between the main building and the *ranchos* is a pool with a small stone waterfall. Out by the ocean there's a restaurant that serves tasty, filling, and economically priced fare, as well as a comfortable, covered two-story palapa for watching the surf action.

Playa Hermosa (A.P. 258-4023), Jacó, Puntarenas. (C)/fax **2643-7021.** www.lasolashotel.com. 8 units. $50–$100 (£25–£50) double. AE, MC, V. **Amenities:** Restaurant; bar; surf- and boogie-board rental; tour desk; laundry service. *In room:* Fridge, safe, no phone.

2 Manuel Antonio National Park ⟨★⟨★

140km (87 miles) SW of San José; 69km (43 miles) S of Playa de Jacó

Manuel Antonio was Costa Rica's first major ecotourist destination and it is still one of its most popular. The views from the hills overlooking Manuel Antonio are spectacular, the beaches (especially those inside the national park) are idyllic, and its jungles are crawling with howler, white-faced, and squirrel monkeys, among other forms of exotic wildlife. The downside is that you'll have to pay more to see it, and you'll have to share it with more fellow travelers than you would at other rainforest destinations around the country. Moreover, development here is threatening to destroy what makes this place so special. What was once a smattering of small hotels tucked into the forested hillside has become a long string of lodgings along the 7km (4⅓ miles) of road between Quepos and the national park entrance. Hotel roofs now regularly break the tree line, and there seems to be no control over zoning and unchecked ongoing construction. A jumble of snack shacks, souvenir stands, and makeshift parking lots line the beach road just outside the park, making the entrance road look more like a shanty than a national park.

Still, this remains a beautiful destination, with a wide range of attractions and activities. Gazing down on the blue Pacific from high on the hillsides of Manuel Antonio, it's almost impossible to hold back a gasp of delight. Offshore, rocky islands dot the vast expanse of blue, and in the foreground, the rich, deep green of the rainforest sweeps down to the water. Even cheap disposable cameras regularly produce postcard-perfect snapshots. It's this superb view that keeps people transfixed on decks, patios, and balconies throughout the area.

One of the most popular national parks in the country, Manuel Antonio is also one of the smallest, covering fewer than 680 hectares (1,680 acres). Its several nearly perfect small beaches are connected by trails that meander through the rainforest. The mountains surrounding the beaches quickly rise as you head inland from the water; however, the park was created to preserve not its beautiful beaches but its forests, home to endangered squirrel monkeys, three-toed sloths, purple-and-orange crabs, and hundreds of other species of birds, mammals, and plants. Once this entire stretch of coast was a rainforest teeming with wildlife, but now only this small rocky outcrop of forest remains.

Those views that are so bewitching also have their own set of drawbacks. If you want a great view, you aren't going to be staying on the beach—in fact, you probably won't be able to walk to the beach. This means that you'll be driving back and forth, taking taxis, or riding the public bus. Also keep in mind that it's hot and humid here, and it rains a lot. However, the rain is what keeps Manuel Antonio lush and green, and this wouldn't be the Tropics if things were otherwise.

If you're traveling on a rock-bottom budget or are mainly interested in sportfishing, you might end up staying in the nearby town of **Quepos,** which was once a quiet banana port; the land to the north was used by Chiquita to grow its bananas. Disease wiped out most of the banana plantations, and now the land is planted primarily with African oil-palm trees. To reach Quepos by road, you pass through miles of these oil-palm plantations. Quepos is coming of age, and currently features a wide variety of restaurants, souvenir and crafts shops, and lively bars. Moreover, it stands to see even more improvement when the new Marina Pez Vela project is completed in early 2009. Located right near the center of town, this complex will feature a modern 270-slip marina, a 100-room hotel, shops, and condominium units.

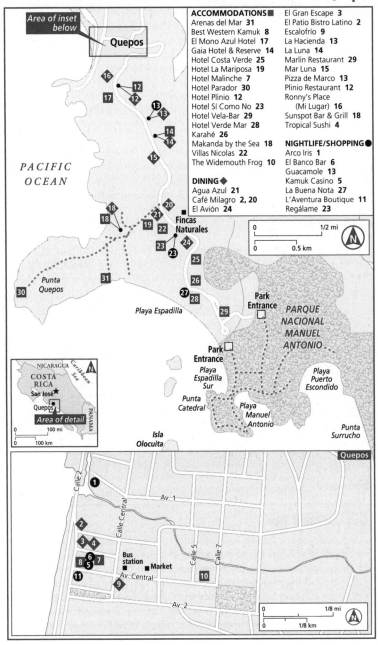

Area of inset below

Quepos

ACCOMMODATIONS ■
Arenas del Mar **31**
Best Western Kamuk **8**
El Mono Azul Hotel **17**
Gaia Hotel & Reserve **14**
Hotel Costa Verde **25**
Hotel La Mariposa **19**
Hotel Malinche **7**
Hotel Parador **30**
Hotel Plinio **12**
Hotel Sí Como No **23**
Hotel Vela-Bar **29**
Hotel Verde Mar **28**
Karahé **26**
Makanda by the Sea **18**
Villas Nicolas **22**
The Widemouth Frog **10**

DINING ◆
Agua Azul **21**
Café Milagro **2, 20**
El Avión **24**

El Gran Escape **3**
El Patio Bistro Latino **2**
Escalofrío **9**
La Hacienda **13**
La Luna **14**
Marlin Restaurant **29**
Mar Luna **15**
Pizza de Marco **13**
Plinio Restaurant **12**
Ronny's Place
  (Mi Lugar) **16**
Sunspot Bar & Grill **18**
Tropical Sushi **4**

NIGHTLIFE/SHOPPING ●
Arco Iris **1**
El Banco Bar **6**
Guacamole **13**
Kamuk Casino **5**
La Buena Nota **27**
L'Aventura Boutique **11**
Regálame **23**

PACIFIC OCEAN

0 ___ 1/2 mi
0 ___ 0.5 km

Fincas Naturales

Punta Quepos

Playa Espadilla

Park Entrance

PARQUE NACIONAL MANUEL ANTONIO

NICARAGUA
Caribbean Sea
COSTA RICA
San José ★
Quepos ■
Area of detail
PANAMA
0 ___ 100 mi
0 ___ 100 km

Park Entrance
Playa Espadilla Sur
Punta Catedral
Playa Manuel Antonio

Playa Puerto Escondido

Punta Surrucho

Isla Olocuita

Quepos

Calle 2
Av. 1
Calle Central
Av. 1
Calle 5
Calle 7
Bus station ■
■ Market
Av. Central
Av. 2

0 ___ 1/8 mi
0 ___ 1/8 km

ESSENTIALS

GETTING THERE & DEPARTING   By Plane   Sansa (☎ **877/767-2672** in the U.S. and Canada, or 2290-4100 in Costa Rica; www.flysansa.com) has nine daily flights to Quepos beginning at 6am, with the final flight departing at 4:20pm from San José's Juan Santamaría International Airport. The flight's duration is 30 minutes; the fare is $64 (£32) each way.

Nature Air (☎ **800/235-9272** in the U.S. and Canada, or 2299-6000; www.natureair.com) flies to Quepos daily at 6 and 9:30am and 1:30 and 4:25pm from Tobías Bolaños International Airport in Pavas. The flight duration is 30 minutes; the fare is $67 (£34) each way.

Both Sansa and Nature Air provide minivan airport-transfer service coordinated with their arriving flights. The service costs around $5 (£2.50) per person each way, depending on where exactly your hotel is located. Speak to your airline's agent when you arrive to confirm your return flight and coordinate a pickup at your hotel for that day if necessary. Taxis also meet incoming flights as well. Expect to be charged between $8 and $12 (£4–£6) per car for up to four people, depending on the distance to your hotel.

When you're ready to depart, **Sansa** (☎ **2777-1912** in Quepos) flights begin departing at 6:44am, with the final flight leaving at 5:04pm. **Nature Air** (☎ **2777-2548** in Quepos) flights leave for San José daily at 7:50 and 11am and 2:10 and 5pm.

By Car   From San José, the most popular route is to take the narrow and winding old highway, which turns off the Interamerican Highway just west of Alajuela near the town of Atenas and joins the Costanera Highway near Orotina. Just follow the many signs to hotels in either Jacó or Manuel Antonio. When you reach Jacó, it's a straight shot and another hour to Manuel Antonio.

Alternatively, you could try the route beginning in Ciudad Colón, a western suburb of San José, and then head out to Puriscal and join the Costanera Highway either near Parrita or Orotina. The route that heads to Parrita is the shortest route, but some sections are not paved and others are in rough shape. Nevertheless, locals often use it, especially during the dry season. Four-wheel-drive vehicles are recommended, but normal two-wheel-drive sedans can usually make it. The route to Orotina is paved the entire way. It is slightly longer than the more popular route mentioned above and not as well marked, but since it passes over a narrow suspension bridge, there are never any trucks or commercial traffic.

Tips Travel Tips

Despite the above caveats, Manuel Antonio is still a fabulous destination with a wealth of activities and attractions for all types and all ages. If you plan carefully, you can avoid many of the problems that detract from its appeal. If you steer clear of the peak months (Dec–Mar), you'll miss most of the crowds. If you must come during the peak months, try to avoid weekends, when the beach is packed with families and young Ticos from San José. If you visit the park early in the morning, you can leave when the crowds begin to show up at midday. In the afternoon you can lounge by your pool or on your patio.

Fun Fact Profitable Palms

On any drive to or from Quepos and Manuel Antonio you will pass through miles and miles of African Palm plantations. Native to West Africa, *Elaeis Guineensis* was planted along this stretch in the 1940s by United Fruit, in response to a blight that was attacking their banana crops. The palms took hold and soon proved quite profitable, being blessed with copious bunches of plum-size nuts that are rich in oil. This oil is extracted and processed in plantations that dot the road between Jacó and Quepos. The smoke and distinct smell of this processing is often easily noticed. The processed oil is then shipped overseas and used in a wide range of products, including soaps, cosmetics, lubricants, and food products.

If you're coming from Guanacaste or any point north, take the Interamerican Highway to the Puntarenas turnoff and head south on the Costanera Highway, the coastal road to Jacó. It's about a 4½-hour drive here from Liberia.

By Bus **Express buses** (© **2223-5567**) to Manuel Antonio leave San José daily at 6am, noon, and 6 and 7:30pm from the Coca-Cola bus terminal at Calle 16 between avenidas 1 and 3. Trip duration is 3½ hours; the fare is $5.50 (£2.25). These buses go all the way to the park entrance and will drop you off at any of the hotels along the way.

Regular buses (© **2223-5567**) to Quepos leave San José daily at 7 and 10am and 2 and 4pm. Trip duration is 4½ hours; the fare is $4.40 (£2.20). These buses stop in Quepos. From here, if you're staying at one of the hotels on the road to Manuel Antonio, you must take a local bus or taxi to your hotel.

Gray Line (© **2220-2126**; www.graylinecostarica.com) has two daily buses that leave San José for Quepos and Manuel Antonio at 7:30am and 4pm; the fare is $33 (£17). The return bus leaves at 10am and 1pm for San José. **Interbus** (© **2283-5573**; www.interbusonline.com) has two daily buses that leave San José for Quepos and Manuel Antonio at 8:15am and 2:30pm; the fare is $35 (£18). Return buses leave at 8:30am and 1:45pm. Both companies will pick you up at most San José—and Manuel Antonio—area hotels and also offer connections to various other popular destinations around Costa Rica.

Buses leave **Puntarenas** for Quepos daily at 5 and 11am and 2:30 and 4:30pm. The ride takes 2½ hours; the fare is $3 (£1.50).

Many of the buses for Quepos stop to unload and pick up passengers in **Playa de Jacó.** If you're in Jacó heading toward Manuel Antonio, you can try your luck at one of the covered bus stops out on the Interamerican Highway (see "Playa de Jacó, Playa Hermosa & Playa Herradura," earlier in this chapter).

From Quepos, buses leave for Manuel Antonio daily, roughly every half-hour, from 6am to 7pm, with one late bus at 10pm. The fare is 30¢ (15p). The ride takes about 15 minutes.

When you're ready to depart, the Quepos bus station (© **2777-0263**) is next to the market, which is 3 blocks east of the water and 2 blocks north of the road to Manuel Antonio. Express buses to San José leave daily at 6 and 9:30am, noon, and 3 and 5pm. Local buses to San José (duration is 4 hr.) leave at 5 and 8am and 2 and 4pm.

In the busy winter months, tickets sell out well in advance, especially on weekends; if you can, purchase your ticket several days in advance. However, you must buy your Quepos-bound tickets in San José and your San José return tickets in Quepos. If you're staying in Manuel Antonio, you can buy your return ticket for a direct bus in advance in Quepos and then wait along the road to be picked up. There is no particular bus stop; just make sure you are out to flag down the bus and give it time to stop—you don't want to be standing in a blind spot when the bus comes flying around a tight corner.

Buses for **Puntarenas** leave daily at 4:30, 7:30, and 10:30am and 3pm. Any bus headed for San José or Puntarenas will let you off in Playa de Jacó.

ORIENTATION Quepos is a little port town at the mouth of the Boca Vieja Estuary. After crossing the bridge into town, take the lower road (to the left of the high road). In 4 blocks, turn left; you'll be on the road to Manuel Antonio. This road winds through town a bit before starting over the hill to all the hotels and the national park. For a map of the national park, see the inside front cover of this book.

GETTING AROUND A taxi between Quepos and Manuel Antonio (or any hotel along the road toward the park) costs between $3 and $6 (£1.50–£3), depending upon the distance. At night or if the taxi must leave the main road (for hotels such as La Mariposa, Parador, Makanda, and Arenas del Mar), the charge is a little higher. If you need to call a taxi, dial © **2777-3080** or 2777-0425. Taxis are supposed to use meters, although this isn't always the case. If your taxi doesn't have a meter, or the driver won't use it, try to negotiate in advance. Ask your hotel desk what a specific ride should cost, and use that as your guide.

The bus between Quepos and Manuel Antonio takes 15 minutes each way and runs roughly every half-hour from 6am to 7pm daily, with one late bus leaving Quepos at 10pm and returning from Manuel Antonio at 10:30pm. The buses, which leave from the main bus terminal in Quepos, near the market, go all the way to the national park entrance before turning around and returning. You can flag down these buses from any point on the side of the road. The fare is 30¢ (15p).

You can also rent a car from **Adobe** (© 2777-4242), **Alamo** (© 2777-3344), **Economy** (© 2777-5260), **Hertz** (© 2777-3365), **National** (© 2777-0368), or **Payless Rent-a-Car** (© 2777-0115) for around $50 (£25) a day. All have offices in downtown Quepos, but with advance notice, someone will meet you at the airport with your car for no extra charge.

If you rent a car, never leave anything of value in it unless you intend to stay within sight of the car at all times. Car break-ins are common here. There are now a couple of parking lots just outside the park entrance that cost around $3 (£1.50) for the entire day. You should definitely keep your car in one of these while exploring the park or soaking up sun on the beach. And although these lots do offer a modicum of protection and safety, you should still not leave anything of value exposed in the car. The trunk is probably safe, though.

If you want to rent a scooter, try **Fast Eddie's Scooter Rental** (© 2777-4127).

FAST FACTS The telephone number of the **Quepos Hospital** is © 2777-0922. In the event of an emergency, you can also call the **Cruz Roja** (Red Cross; © 2777-0116). For the **local police,** call © 2777-1511 or 2777-2117.

The **post office** (© 2777-1471) is in downtown Quepos. There are several pharmacies in Quepos, as well as a pharmacy at the hospital, and another close to the park entrance. There are also a half-dozen or so laundromats and laundry services in town. For film, batteries, and photo developing, try **Todo Foto Quepos** (© 2777-1442).

Several major Costa Rican banks have branches and ATMs in downtown Quepos. An ample array of **Internet cafes** can be found around Quepos and along the road to Manuel Antonio, and many hotels have them as well.

EXPLORING THE NATIONAL PARK

Manuel Antonio is a small park with three major trails. Most visitors come primarily to lie on a beach and check out the white-faced monkeys, which sometimes seem as common as tourists. A guide is not essential here, but unless you're experienced in rainforest hiking, you'll see and learn a lot more with one. A 2- or 3-hour guided hike should cost between $25 and $45 (£13–£23) per person. Almost any of the hotels in town can help you set up a tour of the park. If you decide to explore the park on your own, a basic map is usually available at the park entrance for $1 (50p).

ENTRY POINT, FEES & REGULATIONS   The park (© 2777-5185) is closed on Monday but is open Tuesday through Sunday from 8am to 4pm year-round. You'll find the principal park entrance at **Playa Espadilla,** the beach at the end of the road from Quepos. To reach the park station, you must cross a small, sometimes polluted stream that's little more than ankle-deep at low tide but that can be knee- or even waist-deep at high tide. It's even reputed to be home to a crocodile or two. For years there has been talk of building a bridge over this stream; in the meantime you'll have to either wade it or pay a boatman a small voluntary tip for the very quick crossing. Just over the stream, you'll find the small ranger station where you can pick up the small park map I mentioned above. At the entrance you choose, you will have to pay a fee of $10 (£5) per person to enter. The Parks Service allows only 600 visitors to enter each day, which could mean that you won't get in if you arrive in midafternoon during the high season. Camping is not allowed.

THE BEACHES   **Playa Espadilla Sur** (as opposed to Playa Espadilla, which is just outside the park; see "Hitting the Water," below) is the first beach within the actual park boundaries. It's usually the least crowded and one of the best places to find a quiet shade tree to plant yourself under. However, if there's any surf, this is also the roughest beach in the park. If you want to explore further, you can walk along this soft-sand beach or follow a trail through the forest parallel to the beach. **Playa Manuel Antonio,** which is the most popular beach inside the park, is a short, deep crescent of white sand backed by lush rainforest. The water here is sometimes clear enough to offer good snorkeling along the rocks at either end, and it's usually fairly calm. At low tide Playa Manuel Antonio shows a very interesting relic: a circular stone turtle trap left by its pre-Columbian residents. From Playa Manuel Antonio, there's another slightly longer trail to **Puerto Escondido,** where a blowhole sends up plumes of spray at high tide.

THE HIKING TRAILS   From either Playa Espadilla Sur or Playa Manuel Antonio, you can take a circular hike around a high promontory bluff. The farthest point on this hike, which takes about 25 minutes round-trip, is **Punta Catedral** 🐾🐾, where the view is spectacular. The trail is a little steep in places, but anybody in average shape can do it. I have done it in sturdy sandals, but you might want to wear good hiking shoes. This is a good place to spot monkeys, although you're more likely to see a white-faced monkey than a rare squirrel monkey. Another good place to see monkeys is the

> **_Tips_ Helping Out**
>
> If you want to help efforts in protecting the local environment and the severely endangered squirrel monkey _(mono titi)_, make a donation to **Kids Saving The Rainforest** (© 2777-2592; www.kidssavingtherainforest.org), which was started in 1999 by a couple of local children.

trail inland from Playa Manuel Antonio. This is a linear trail and mostly uphill, but it's not too taxing. It's great to spend hours exploring the steamy jungle and then take a refreshing dip in the ocean.

Finally, there's a trail that leads first to Puerto Escondido (see above) and **Punta Surrucho,** where there are some sea caves. Be careful when hiking beyond Puerto Escondido: What seems like easy beach hiking at low tide becomes treacherous to impassable at high tide. Don't get trapped.

HITTING THE WATER

BEACHES OUTSIDE THE PARK   Playa Espadilla, the gray-sand beach just outside the park boundary, is often perfect for board surfing and bodysurfing. At times it's a bit rough for casual swimming, but with no entrance fee, it's the most popular beach with locals and visiting Ticos. Some shops by the water rent boogie boards and beach chairs and umbrellas. A full-day rental of a beach umbrella and two chaise longues costs around $10 (£5). (These are not available inside the park.) This beach is actually a great spot to learn how to surf, because there are several open-air shops renting surfboards and boogie boards along the road fronting the beach. Rates run between $5 and $10 (£2.50–£5) per hour, and around $30 to $40 (£15–£20) per day. If you want a lesson, check in with the **Manuel Antonio Surf School** (© 2777-4842; www.masurfschool.com), which has a roadside kiosk on the road to Manuel Antonio.

BOATING, KAYAKING, RAFTING & SPORTFISHING TOURS   Adventure Manuel Antonio (© 2777-1084; www.adventuremanuelantonio.com) and **Iguana Tours** (© 2777-2052; www.iguanatours.com) are the most established and dependable tour operators in the area; both offer river rafting, sea kayaking, mangrove tours, and guided hikes.

The two above companies, as well as **Rios Tropicales** (© 2777-4092; www.aventurash2o.com), offer full-day rafting trips for around $85 to $110 (£43–£55). Large multiperson rafts are used during the rainy season, and single-person "duckies" are broken out when the water levels drop. All of the above companies also offer half-day rafting adventures and sea-kayaking trips for around $65 (£33). Depending on rainfall and demand, they will run either the Naranjo or Savegre rivers. I very much prefer the **Savegre River** ✶✶ for its stunning scenery.

Another of my favorite tours in the area is a mangrove tour of the Damas Island estuary. These trips generally include lunch, a stop on Damas Island, and roughly 3 to 4 hours of cruising the waterways. You'll see loads of wildlife. The cost is usually around $60 to $70 (£30–£35).

Among the other boating options around Quepos/Manuel Antonio are excursions in search of dolphins and sunset cruises. **Iguana Tours** (see above) and **Planet Dolphin** (©/fax 2777-1647; www.planetdolphin.com) offer these tours for $40 to $80 (£20–£40) per person, depending upon the size of the group and the length of the cruise. Most tours include a snorkel break and, if lucky, dolphin sightings. **Jungle Coast Jets** (© 2777-1706; www.junglecoastjets.com) offers 2-hour jet-ski tours for $129 (£65) per person. This tour plies the same waters and includes some snorkeling and the possibility of a dolphin encounter.

Quepos is one of Costa Rica's billfish centers, and sailfish, marlin, and tuna are all common in these waters. In the past year or so, fresh and brackish water fishing in the mangroves and estuaries has also become popular. If you're into sportfishing, try hooking up with **Blue Fin Sportfishing** (© 2777-0000; www.bluefinsportfishing.com), **Blue Water** (© 800/807-1585 in the U.S. and Canada or 2777-4841; www.sport fishingincostarica.com), **High Tec Sportfishing** (© 2777-3465; www.hightecsport fishing.com), or **Luna Tours Sportfishing** (© 2777-0725; www.lunatours.net). A full day of fishing should cost between $400 and $1,800 (£200–£900), depending on the size of the boat, distance traveled, tackle provided, and amenities. There's a lot of competition here, so shop around.

SCUBA DIVING & SNORKELING   Manuel Antonio Scuba Divers (© 2777-3483; www.manuelantoniodivers.com) and **Oceans Unlimited** ✪ (© 2777-3171; www.oceansunlimitedcr.com) offer both scuba diving and snorkel outings, as well as certification and resort courses. Because of river run-off and often less-than-stellar visibility close to Quepos, the best trips involve some travel time. However, **Isla del Caño** (p. 333) is only about a 90-minute ride (each way). This is one of the best dive sites in Costa Rica, and I highly recommend it.

OTHER ACTIVITIES IN THE AREA

ATV   If you want to try riding a four-wheel ATV (all-terrain vehicle), check in with the folks at **Fourtrax Adventures** (© 2777-1829; www.fourtraxadventure.com). Their principal tour is a 3-hour adventure through African palm plantations, rural towns, and secondary forest to a jungle waterfall, where you stop for a dip. You cross several rivers and a long suspension bridge. Either breakfast or lunch is served, depending on the timing. Cost is $95 (£48) per ATV. A second rider on the same ATV costs $30 (£15).

BIKING   If you want to do some mountain biking while you're here, check in with **Estrella Tour** (©/fax 2777-1286) in downtown Quepos. Well-maintained bikes rent for around $25 (£13) per day. You can also do a number of different guided tours according to skill level for between $45 and $100 (£23–£50) per day, as well as multiday expeditions.

BUTTERFLY GARDEN   Fincas Naturales/The Nature Farm Reserve ✪ (© 2777-1043; www.butterflygardens.co.cr) is just across from (and run by) Hotel Sí Como No (p. 307). A lovely bi-level **butterfly garden** ✪ is the centerpiece attraction here, but there is also a private reserve and a small network of well-groomed trails through the forest. A 1-hour guided tour of the butterfly garden costs $15 (£7.50) per person, or $35 (£18) when combined with a 1-hour guided hike through the forest. This is also a good place to do a night tour ($30/£15).

CANOPY ADVENTURES   There are several canopy tours in the area. The most adventurous is offered by **Canopy Safari** ✪ (© 2777-0100; www.canopysafari.com), which features 21 treetop platforms connected by a series of cables and suspension bridges. Adventurers use a harness-and-pulley system to "zip" between platforms, using a leather-gloved hand as their only brake. The **Titi Canopy Tour** (© 2777-3130;

www.titicanopytours.com) is a similar but mellower setup. A canopy tour should run you between $50 and $70 (£25–£35) per person.

About 20 minutes outside of Quepos is **Rainmaker Nature Refuge** (© 2777-3565; www.rainmakercostarica.org). The main attraction here is a system of connected suspension bridges strung through the forest canopy, crisscrossing a deep ravine. There are six bridges; the longest is 90m (295 ft.) across. There's also a small network of trails and some great swimming holes. A half-day tour, including a light breakfast, full lunch, round-trip transportation from Quepos, and a guide, costs $70 (£35) per person. Tours leave every morning, and most hotels in the area can book them for you.

HORSEBACK RIDING If your tropical fantasy is to ride a horse down a beach between jungle and ocean, contact **Stable Equus** (© 2777-0001), which charges $35 (£18) for a 2-hour ride in Manuel Antonio. This stable treats its animals more humanely than other stables in the immediate Manuel Antonio area and is also concerned with keeping horse droppings off the beaches. Back in the hills, **Brisas del Nara** (© 2779-1235; www.horsebacktour.com) offers full- and half-day horseback excursions that pass through both primary and secondary forest and feature a swimming stop at a jungle waterfall. A full-day tour with these folks, including breakfast and lunch, costs $65 (£33) per person; and $50 (£25) for a similar half-day tour, with less time on the horse.

SOOTHE YOUR BODY & SOUL There are quite a few massage therapists around Manuel Antonio and a couple of day spas. The best of these are **Raindrop Spa** (© 2777-2880; www.raindropspa.com), **Spa Uno** (© 2777-2607; www.spauno.com), and **Serenity Spa** at the Hotel Sí Como No (p. 307). A wide range of treatments, wraps, and facials are available at all of the above.

Sivana Yoga (© 2777-5268; www.sivanayoga.com) has open classes ($12/£6) Monday through Friday at 8am above the Anaconda restaurant, across from the Hotel Costa Verde. Private classes are also offered.

ULTRALIGHT TOUR If you want a really good view of Manuel Antonio's spectacular scenery, you might sign up with the folks at **Costa Rica Flying Boat** (© 2777-9208; www.flyingboatcostarica.com), who offer ultralight flights out of the Quepos airport. A 20-minute flight runs around $75 (£36).

SHOPPING

If you're looking for souvenirs, you'll find plenty of beach towels, beachwear, and handmade jewelry in a variety of small shops in Quepos and at impromptu stalls down

---

Tips Yo Quiero Hablar Español

Escuela D'Amore (©/fax 2777-1143; www.escueladamore.com) runs language-immersion programs out of a former hotel with a fabulous view on the road to Manuel Antonio. A 2-week conversational Spanish course, including a home stay and two meals daily, costs $995 (£498). Or you can try the **Costa Rica Spanish Institute (COSI)** (© 800/771-5184 in the U.S. and Canada, 2234-1001 or 2777-0021 in Costa Rica; www.cosi.co.cr), which charges $850 (£425) for a similar 2-week program with a home stay.

near the national park. For a good selection, try **La Buena Nota** (*C* **2777-1002**), which is on the road to Manuel Antonio, right near the Karahé hotel (p. 309). The shop is jampacked with all sorts of beachwear, souvenirs, used books, and U.S. magazines and newspapers. It also has a few basic rooms located above the store; if you'd like to find out about renting a house, ask here.

For higher-end gifts, check out **L'Aventura Boutique** (*C* **2777-1019**), on Avenida Central in Quepos. This small shop has a nice collection of woodwork by Barry Biesanz, banana-fabric works by Lil Mena, and pottery by Cecilia "Pefi" Figueres. The Hotel Sí Como No's **Regálame** (www.regalameart.com) gift shop is also pretty well stocked. Finally, one of my favorite shops from Jacó has opened a branch in Manuel Antonio. Look for handmade batik and tie-dye clothing at **Guacamole** (*C* **2777-2071**) in the small Plaza Yara shopping center.

WHERE TO STAY

Take care when choosing your accommodations in Quepos/Manuel Antonio. There are very few true beachfront hotels in Manuel Antonio, so you won't have much luck finding a hotel where you can walk directly out of your room and onto the beach. In fact, most of the nicer hotels here are 1km (½ mile) or so away from the beach, high on the hill overlooking the ocean.

If you're traveling on a rock-bottom budget, you'll get more for your money by staying in Quepos and taking the bus to the beaches at Manuel Antonio every day. The rooms in Quepos might be small, but they're generally cleaner and more appealing than those available in the same price category closer to the park.

VERY EXPENSIVE

In addition to the places listed below, **Bella Vista Villas and Casas** (*C* **866/569-6241** in the U.S. and Canada, or 2777-9081 in Costa Rica; www.buenavistavillas.net) is the latest incarnation of the former Tulemar Resort, and the early indications are that they've finally go this superbly located property running in good shape.

If you're coming for an extended stay with your family or a large group, look into **Escape Villas** ★★ (*C* **877/533-8988** in the U.S., or 2777-5258 in Costa Rica; www.villascostarica.com), which rents a broad selection of very large and luxurious private villas with all the amenities and some of the best views in Manuel Antonio.

Arenas del Mar ★★★ *Finds* Finally, Manuel Antonio has a hotel that combines the best of all worlds—direct beach access, a rainforest setting, fabulous views, and luxurious accommodations. Designed and built by the folks behind Finca Rosa Blanca (p. 117) outside San José, this place is deeply committed to sustainability. Very little was done to disturb the land or surrounding ecosystems during construction. Not all rooms have ocean views, so be sure to specify if you want one. However, all are spacious, with tasteful decor, cool yellow tile floors, and plenty of wood and tile accents. Most have outdoor Jacuzzi tubs on their private balconies. The apartments are immense two-bedroom, three-bathroom affairs with a kitchenette, perfect for families and longer stays. The restaurant, lobby, and main pool are set on the highest point of land here, and several spots have fabulous views of Manuel Antonio's Punta Catedral. *Note:* The beautiful patch of beach right in front of Arenas has for decades been the town's de facto nude beach. Those who might find this offensive can walk farther down the beach or stick to the pools.

Manuel Antonio. *C*/fax **2777-2777**. www.arenasdelmar.com. 38 units. $220 (£110) double; $360 (£180) suite; $580 (£290) 2-bedroom apt. Rates lower in off season; higher during peak periods. Rates include full breakfast. AE, MC, V.

Amenities: Restaurant; bar; snack bar; 2 small outdoor pools; spa; concierge; tour desk; 24-hr. room service; in-room massage; babysitting; laundry service. *In room:* A/C, TV, dataport, free Wi-Fi, minibar, coffeemaker, safe.

Gaia Hotel & Reserve ★★   Making a play for the high-end luxury market, this hotel features chic, postmodern design and decor, with large, well-equipped rooms, tons of amenities, and personalized service. Set on a hilly patch of land, with its own private reserve, the rooms, spa, and restaurant are housed in a series of tall, blocky buildings. The large rooms all have wooden floors, contemporary furnishings, plasma-screen televisions with complete home theater systems, and elaborate bathrooms with massive Jacuzzi tubs. Each guest is assigned a personal concierge. The deluxe suites feature a private rooftop terrace, with a reflecting pool, and shaded lounge chairs. The immense Gaia suite features soaring ceilings, a huge sitting room, and a private pool. The spa is extensive and well-run, with a wide range of treatment options and free daily yoga classes. The restaurant serves excellent fusion cuisine.

Manuel Antonio. © 800/226-2515 in the U.S., or 2777-9797 in Costa Rica. Fax 2777-9126. www.gaiahr.com. 17 units. $260–$330 (£130–£165) double; $350–$495 (£175–£248) suite; $840 (£420) Gaia suite. Rates lower in off season; higher during peak periods. Rates include full breakfast. AE, MC, V. No children under 16 allowed. **Amenities:** Restaurant; bar; multilevel outdoor pool; small gym; extensive spa; concierge; tour desk; 24-hr. room service; in-room massage; laundry service. *In room:* A/C, TV, free Wi-Fi, minibar, coffeemaker, safe.

Hotel La Mariposa ★   Perched on a ridge at the top of the hill between Quepos and Manuel Antonio, La Mariposa (the Butterfly) commands a mountains-to-the-sea vista of more than 270 degrees. The sunsets here are knockouts, and the daytime views are pretty captivating, too. Although this is still one of Manuel Antonio's premier accommodations, expansion and growth have cost this place much of its charm.

The best accommodations are the Premier rooms, housed in two three-story buildings constructed over the foundation of a couple of the original villas. These rooms are large, well equipped, and tastefully decorated, with excellent views. Most of the surviving older villas have been split into separate junior suites and deluxe rooms. Each junior suite has a Jacuzzi out on the small balcony or just inside its sliding glass door. There are also a few standard rooms that are certainly comfortable but without good views. The rooms in the four-story addition to the hotel's main building are quite spacious and have great views, but they don't have much charm or personality.

Manuel Antonio (A.P. 4, Quepos). © 800/549-0157 in the U.S. and Canada, or 2777-0355 in Costa Rica. Fax 2777-0050. www.lamariposa.com. 62 units. $205–$305 (£103–£153) double; $440 (£220) penthouse suite. Rates lower in off season. Extra person $40 (£20). Children 9 and under stay free in parent's room. AE, MC, V. **Amenities:** Restaurant; bar; 4 small pools; concierge; tour desk; complimentary shuttle to and from the national park; in-room massage; babysitting; laundry service. *In room:* A/C, TV, free Wi-Fi, safe.

Makanda by the Sea ★★ *Finds*   A wonderful collection of studio apartments and private villas, Makanda is a great option for anyone looking for an intimate, romantic getaway in Manuel Antonio. Each is individually decorated with flair. If you combine villa no. 1 with the three studios, you get one very large four-bedroom villa, great for a family or a small group (although children 15 and under are not allowed, unless you rent out the entire hotel). Every choice comes with a full kitchenette, cable television, CD player, and either a terrace or a balcony. The grounds are well tended, and intermixed with tropical flowers and Japanese gardens. A full breakfast is delivered to your room each morning. The hotel's pool and Jacuzzi combine intricate and colorful tile work with a view of the jungle-covered hillsides and the Pacific Ocean. Makanda is located halfway down the road to Hotel Parador and Punta Quepos. The hotel is set in thick forest, and, despite the name, is a hefty hike—or short drive—from the beach.

Manuel Antonio (A.P. 29, Quepos). © 888/625-2632 in the U.S., or 2777-0442 in Costa Rica. Fax 2777-1032. www.makanda.com. 11 units. $265 (£133) studio; $400 (£200) villa. Rates include full breakfast. Rates lower in off season; higher during peak periods. AE, MC, V. **Amenities:** Restaurant; bar; midsize pool; Jacuzzi; watersports equipment and bike rental; concierge; tour desk; limited room service; in-room massage and spa services; laundry service. *In room:* TV, free Wi-Fi, kitchenette, stocked minibar, coffeemaker, safe.

EXPENSIVE

Hotel Parador ⭐ This hotel is spread out over more than 4.8 hectares (12 acres) of land on a low peninsula. Its design aims to imitate Spanish Mediterranean grandeur, and the main building is loaded with antiques, including 17th-century Dutch and Flemish oil paintings, a 300-year-old carved wooden horse, and 16th-century church and castle doors. The standard rooms are well appointed but far too small and simple for this price range, and few have any view to speak of. Deluxe rooms offer slightly more space, and those on the second floor have private balconies. The spacious junior suites are located on the top of a hill, giving a good view of the sea and Punta Catedral in the distance. It's a bit of a hike up to these units, although the hotel offers an on-call golf-cart shuttle service. The premium rooms, located in a newer three-story building built on a high spot on the grounds, have the best views and are my first choice here. The hotel runs a shuttle van to the national park, and there's a small, secluded beach about 500m (1,640 ft.) from the hotel.

Manuel Antonio (A.P. 284, Quepos). © 877/506-1414 in the U.S. and Canada, or 2777-1414 in Costa Rica. Fax 2777-1437. www.hotelparador.com. 108 units. $185–$250 (£93–£125) double; $285–$305 (£143–£153) premium; $340 (£170) junior suite; $950 (£475) presidential suite. Rates include breakfast buffet. Rates slightly higher during peak weeks; significantly lower in off season. AE, MC, V. **Amenities:** 2 restaurants; 2 bars; large free-form pool w/swim-up bar and central fountain; tennis court; modern gym and spa; Jacuzzi; concierge; tour desk; room service; free Wi-Fi in main building and around pool; in-room massage; babysitting; laundry service. *In room:* A/C, TV, minibar, coffeemaker, hair dryer, safe.

Hotel Sí Como No ⭐⭐ *Finds* *Kids* This long-standing favorite is a lively, upscale, midsize resort that blends in with and respects the rainforests and natural wonders of Manuel Antonio. This is a place equally suited to families traveling with children and to couples looking for a romantic getaway. All the wood used is farm-grown, and while all the rooms have energy-efficient air-conditioning units, guests are urged to use them only when necessary. The standard rooms are quite acceptable, but it's worth the splurge for a superior or deluxe room or a suite. Most of these are on the top floors of the two- to three-story villas, with spectacular treetop views out over the forest and onto the Pacific. These units all have a bedroom with an adjoining living-room area, a private balcony, and either a kitchenette or a wet bar. There are a series of deluxe suites with lots of space and large garden bathrooms, some of which have private Jacuzzis.

Manuel Antonio (mailing address: Mail Stop SJO 297, P.O. Box 02558216, Miami, FL 33102). © 2777-0777. Fax 2777-1093. www.sicomono.com. 60 units. $190–$240 (£95–£120) double; $275–$310 (£138–£155) suite. Rates include breakfast buffet. Rates lower in off season. Extra person $30 (£15). Children 5 and under stay free in parent's room. AE, MC, V. **Amenities:** 2 restaurants; 2 bars; 2 midsize pools, including 1 w/small water slide; modest spa; 2 Jacuzzis; concierge; tour desk; free beach shuttle; in-room massage; babysitting; laundry service. *In room:* A/C, free Wi-Fi, minibar, coffeemaker, hair dryer, iron, safe.

MODERATE

In addition to the hotels mentioned below, the **Best Western Kamuk Hotel** (© 2777-0811; www.kamuk.co.cr) is a dependable option right in downtown Quepos; it's popular with sportfishing enthusiasts.

El Mono Azul Hotel *(Value)* On the road to Manuel Antonio, just outside of Quepos, the "Blue Monkey" offers clean and comfortable rooms at a good price. The more expensive rooms feature air-conditioning and/or a small television with cable. The newer villas have red-tile floors, separate sitting rooms, and a kitchenette. One room even has a Jacuzzi tub. Though all the rooms feel rather spartan, the place has a lively, hostel-like vibe. The owner is active in a children's arts program aimed at helping preserve the local rainforest and the endangered squirrel monkey. In fact, 10% of your bill goes to this program. The restaurant/pizzeria here is quite popular. Staff members can arrange longer-term rentals of fully equipped apartments and villas.

Manuel Antonio (A.P. 297-6350, Quepos). *©* 800/381-3578 in the U.S., or 2777-2572 in Costa Rica. Fax 2777-1954. www.monoazul.com. 29 units. $60–$80 (£30–£40) double; $80–$150 (£40–£75) villa. Rates lower in off season; higher during peak weeks. AE, DC, MC, V. **Amenities:** Restaurant; bar; lounge; 3 small pools; small gym; game room; tour desk; laundry service. *In room:* A/C, TV, free Wi-Fi, no phone.

Hotel Costa Verde *(★)* This hotel has consistently offered up good values, ocean views, and reasonable proximity to the beaches and national park. Located more than halfway down the hill to Manuel Antonio, about a 10-minute walk from the beach, Costa Verde has rooms in a wide range of sizes and prices. Some of the buildings are quite a hike from the hotel's reception and restaurants, so be sure you know exactly what type of room you'll be staying in and where it's located. The best rooms here have ocean views, kitchenettes, private balconies, and loads of space; some of these don't have air-conditioning, but that's no problem because they feature huge screened walls to encourage cross ventilation. There's also an enormous penthouse suite with a commanding view of the spectacular surroundings. Three small pools are set into the hillside, with views out to the ocean, and the hotel has a couple of miles of private trails through the rainforest.

Manuel Antonio (mailing address: SJO 1313, P.O. Box 025216, Miami, FL 33102). *©* 866/854-7958 in the U.S. and Canada, or 2777-0584 in Costa Rica. Fax 2777-0560. www.costaverde.com. 63 units. $104–$185 (£52–£93) double. Rates lower in off season; higher during peak weeks. AE, MC, V. **Amenities:** 2 restaurants; 3 bars; 3 small pools; tour desk; laundry service. *In room:* A/C and TV (in some units), free Wi-Fi, no phone.

Hotel Plinio The Plinio hotel is built into a steep hillside, so it's a bit of a climb from the parking lot up to the guest rooms and restaurant. That's fitting, considering that rooms have the feel of a treehouse. Floors and walls are polished hardwood, there are rooms with tree-trunk pillars, and the whole complex is set in lush forest. The hotel's suites are the best value. These are built on either two or three levels. Both options have sleeping lofts; the three-story rooms also have rooftop decks. Behind the hotel is a private reserve with 15km (9⅓ miles) of trails and, at the top of the hill, a 15m-tall (49-ft.) observation tower with an incredible view. In addition to the popular **Plinio Restaurant** (p. 311), there's a poolside grill where lunches are served. Plinio is just outside of Quepos on the road toward the national park, so it's a bit far from the park entrance and beaches.

Manuel Antonio (A.P. 71-6350, Quepos). *©* 2777-0055. Fax 2777-0558. www.hotelplinio.com. 12 units. $65–$75 (£33–£38) double; $85–$110 (£42–£55) suite or house. Rates include breakfast buffet in high season. Rates lower in the off season. V. **Amenities:** Restaurant; bar; small pool in lush garden setting; laundry service. *In room:* No phone.

Hotel Verde Mar *(★)* This hotel is a great choice for proximity to the national park and the beach, and I recommend it much more than the similarly priced hotel Karahé. From your room it's just a short walk to the beach (Playa Espadilla) via a raised wooden walkway. All the rooms here have plenty of space, nice wrought-iron queen-size beds, tile floors, a desk and chair, a fan, and a small porch. All but two of the rooms come with a basic kitchenette. Some of the larger rooms even have two queen-size beds. The hotel has no restaurant, but plenty are within walking distance. There's also a small pool here, for when the surf is too rough.

Manuel Antonio (A.P. 348-6350), Quepos. ℂ **877/872-0459** in the U.S. and Canada, or 2777-1805 in Costa Rica. Fax 2777-1311. www.verdemar.com. 24 units. $90–$100 (£45–£50) double; $105–$120 (£53–£60) suite. Rates lower in off season. AE, MC, V. **Amenities:** Small pool. *In room:* A/C, kitchenette, no phone.

Karahé   The Karahé is one of the original and few beachfront hotels in Manuel Antonio. If you stay in one of the more expensive beachfront units, you'll have a plain room with tile floors, two double beds, and a small patio. The least-expensive rooms are just off the reception area and offer neither views nor easy access to the ocean. Be aware that if you opt for one of the villas, you'll have a steep uphill climb from the beach; on the other hand, a couple of these have great views. The gardens here are quite lush and have flowering ginger that often attracts hummingbirds. The hotel can arrange a wide variety of tours and charters, including sportfishing. Karahé is located on both sides of the road about 450m (1,476 ft.) before you reach Playa Espadilla.

Manuel Antonio (A.P. 100-6350, Quepos). ℂ **877/623-3198** in the U.S. and Canada, or 2777-0170 in Costa Rica. Fax 2777-1075. www.karahe.com. 33 units. $100–$150 (£50–£75) double. Rates include continental breakfast. Rates lower in off season. AE, MC, V. **Amenities:** Restaurant; bar; small pool; exercise room; Jacuzzi; tour desk; laundry service. *In room:* A/C, no phone.

Villas Nicolás ★★ ⟨*Value*⟩   These large villas offer a lot of bang for your buck. Built as terraced units up a steep hill in deep forest, they really give you the feeling that you're in the jungle. Most are quite spacious and well appointed, with wood floors, throw rugs, and comfortable bathrooms; some rooms even have separate living rooms and full kitchenettes, which make longer stays comfortable. My favorite features, though, are the balconies, which come with sitting chairs and a hammock. Some of these balconies are massive and have incredible views. In fact, the rooms highest up the hill have views that I'd be willing to pay a lot more for, and a few of them even have air-conditioning. During the high season, the hotel opens an informal restaurant/bar near the pool that serves breakfast and sometimes lunch and dinner, depending on demand.

Manuel Antonio (A.P. 236, Quepos). ℂ **2777-0481**. Fax 2777-0451. www.villasnicolas.com. 20 units. $115–$165 (£58–£83) double. Weekly, monthly, and off season (May–Nov) rates available. AE, MC, V. **Amenities:** Small pool; laundry service. *In room:* A/C (in some units), fridge.

INEXPENSIVE

In addition to the places listed below, the **Widemouth Frog** (ℂ **2777-2798;** www.widemouthfrog.org) is a hostel option in downtown Quepos, which even has its own swimming pool.

Hotel Malinche   A good choice for budget travelers, the Hotel Malinche has consistently been my top choice in this category right in Quepos. The standard rooms are small but have hardwood or tile floors and clean bathrooms. Some of those on the second floor even have small private balconies that open on to a small interior courtyard. The more expensive rooms are larger and have air-conditioning, TVs, and carpets.

Half-block west of downtown bus terminal, Quepos. ℂ **2777-1833**. Fax 2777-0093. hotelmalinche@racsa.co.cr. 24 units. $25–$55 (£13–£28) double. AE, MC, V. *In room:* No phone.

WHERE TO DINE

Scores of dining options are available around Manuel Antonio and Quepos, and almost every hotel has some sort of restaurant. For the cheapest meals around, try a simple *soda* in Quepos, or head to one of the open-air joints on the beach road before the national park entrance. The standard Tico menu prevails, with prices in the $3-to-$8 (£1.45–£3.90) range. Of these, **Marlin Restaurant** (© 2777-1134), right in front of Playa Espadilla, and **Mar Luna** (© 2777-5107), on the main road just beyond Hotel La Colina, are your best bets. For simple pasta, pizzas, and Italian gelato, head to **Escalofrío** (© 2777-0833; downtown Quepos) or **Pizza de Marco** (© 2777-9400; in the Plaza Yara shopping center). In addition to the places listed below, another good option, on the outskirts of Quepos, is **Mi Lugar,** or **"Ronny's Place"** (© 2777-5120; www.ronnysplace.com).

For a taste of the high life, head to the **La Luna** restaurant at Gaia Hotel & Reserve (see above) for their sunset tapas menu. The views are great and the creative tapas are very reasonably priced.

Finally, one of my favorite hangouts has always been **Café Milagro** ★★ (© 2777-1707; www.cafemilagro.com), a homey coffeehouse and gift shop with two locations in the area. The folks here roast their own beans and also have a mail-order service to keep you in Costa Rican coffee year-round. The menu includes a daily selection of freshly baked sweets, simple sandwiches and breakfast items, and a wide range of coffee drinks. You'll find local art for sale on the walls and a good selection of Cuban cigars and international newspapers, too. The original storefront, just over the bridge on your left as you enter Quepos, is now expanded and there's another branch on the main road to Manuel Antonio right across from the turnoff for Hotel La Mariposa.

Agua Azul ★ *Finds* INTERNATIONAL   With a fabulous perch and panoramic view, this open-air restaurant has changed names and owners steadily over the years. It finally seems to have settled down with a menu and management that may just be able to make this place live up to its fantastic setting. Tables by the railing fill up fast, so get here well before sunset if you want to snag one. Start things off with a Tuna Margarita, an inventive version of ceviche with a lime-and-tequila marinade. Main dishes include coconut-crusted mahimahi and Panko-crusted tuna. For lunch there are giant burgers and fresh fish sandwiches. The long wooden bar is a popular hangout, and a good place to order up some appetizers and drinks.

Manuel Antonio, near Villas del Parque. © 2777-5082. Reservations not accepted. Main courses $12–$20 (£6–£10). V. Thurs–Tues 11am–10pm.

El Avión SEAFOOD/INTERNATIONAL   Set on the edge of Manuel Antonio's hillside with a great view of the ocean and surrounding forests, this restaurant is actually housed under some permanent tents and the starboard wing of a retired army transport plane, hence the name El Avión, which means "the Plane." This specific plane was actually shot down by the Sandinista army, leading to a scandal that uncovered illegal CIA supply missions to the Contra rebels in Nicaragua. Today you can enjoy a wide range of seafood and steaks as you take in the unique surroundings and glow of history. However, food quality and service can be inconsistent here—I've had both excellent and roundly disappointing meals—although the setting never falters. Inside the fuselage you'll also find a small bar.

Manuel Antonio. © 2777-3378. Reservations recommended. Main courses $8–$25 (£4–£13). MC, V. Daily noon–11pm.

El Gran Escape ★★ SEAFOOD   This Quepos landmark is consistently one of the most popular restaurants in the area. The fish is fresh and expertly prepared, and the prices are reasonable. If that's not enough of a recommendation, the atmosphere is lively, the locals seem to keep coming back, and the service is darn good for a beach town in Costa Rica. Sturdy wooden tables and chairs fill up the large indoor dining room, and sportfishing photos and an exotic collection of masks fill up the walls. If you venture away from the fish, the menu features hearty steaks, giant burgers, and a wide assortment of delicious appetizers, including fresh tuna sashimi. El Gran Escape's Fish Head Bar is usually crowded and spirited, and if there's a game going on, it will be on the television here. Breakfasts here are also excellent.

On the main road into Quepos, on your left just after the bridge. ⓒ **2777-0395**. Reservations recommended in high season. Main courses $5–$24 (£2.50–£12). V. Daily 7am–11pm.

El Patio Bistro Latino ⭐⭐⭐ NUEVO LATINO/FUSION   This small bistro-style restaurant is an outgrowth of the popular coffeehouse and roasting company Café Milagro. The same attention to detail and focus on quality carries over here. By day you can get a wide range of coffee drinks and specialties, as well as full breakfasts, fresh-baked sweets, and a variety of salads, sandwiches, and light lunch dishes. By night, things get more interesting and this humble little spot serves up some of the best food in Manuel Antonio. Their regularly changing menu features inventive main dishes that take advantage of local ingredients and various regional culinary traditions. So the fresh red snapper may come steamed in a banana leaf with a spicy *mojo,* and the tenderloin could feature a tamarind glaze and be served over some roasted local sweet potatoes *(camote).* Start things off with the calamari sautéed with spicy sausage and fresh corn and served over a spicy flat bread. You may even find some of their home-roasted coffee used as an ingredient in a glaze, sauce, or dessert.

Manuel Antonio. ⓒ **2777-4982**. Reservations recommended. Main courses $6–$19 (£3–£9.50). AE, MC, V. Daily 6am–10pm.

La Hacienda ⭐ INTERNATIONAL   Located on a jungle-facing open-air back patio of the Plaza Yara strip mall, this place is surprisingly intimate and atmospheric, especially at night. Subdued lighting and vines draping down from the high ceiling make you feel as if you are almost in the jungle. The menu is inventive and eclectic. I highly recommend starting things off with the quesadilla of caramelized onions, brie, and fresh mango. For a main dish, the mixed seafood grill for two features shrimp, squid, and fresh fish prepared on a wood-fired grill with a tropical fruit salsa on the side. The dessert menu changes regularly, but almost always features some rich chocolate concoction, as well as a flavored crème brûlée.

In the Plaza Yara, on the road btw. Quepos and Manuel Antonio. ⓒ **2777-3473**. Reservations recommended in high season. Main courses $9–$20 (£4.50–£10). AE, MC, V. Daily 5–10pm.

Plinio Restaurant ⭐⭐ INTERNATIONAL   This is a long-standing, popular restaurant in Manuel Antonio, located at an equally popular hotel. The open-air restaurant is about three stories above the parking lot, so be prepared to climb some steps. It's worth it, though. The broad menu features an enticing mix of international dishes, with a distinct emphasis on Asian fare. The chef uses locally organically grown herbs and veggies. Thai, Indian, and Indonesian dishes are all excellently prepared, and there are always vegetarian options. The shrimp in coconut-milk curry sauce is excellent.

In the Hotel Plinio, 1km (½ mile) out of Quepos toward Manuel Antonio. ⓒ **2777-0055**. Reservations recommended in high season. Main courses $8.50–$20 (£4.25–£10). V. Daily 5–10pm.

Sunspot Bar & Grill ⭐⭐ *Finds* INTERNATIONAL   Dining by candlelight under a purple canvas tent at one of the few poolside tables here is one of the most romantic

dining experiences to be had in Manuel Antonio. The food's some of the best in town as well. The menu changes regularly but features prime meats and poultry and fresh fish, excellently prepared. The rack of lamb might get a light jalapeño-mint or mango chutney, and the chicken breast might be stuffed with feta cheese, kalamata olives, and roasted red peppers and topped with a blackberry sauce. There are nightly specials and a good selection of salads, appetizers, and desserts.

At Makanda by the Sea (p. 306). **(** 2777-0442. Reservations recommended. Main courses $10–$25 (£5–£13). V. Daily 11am–10pm.

Tropical Sushi   SUSHI/JAPANESE   As the name implies, the ambience here is decidedly tropical, with lively pastel colors and Caribbean architectural highlights, but don't let the surroundings fool you: This is still an excellent sushi joint. In addition to fresh tuna and grouper brought in daily by local fishermen, you can get maki, sushi, and sashimi made with Chilean salmon, smoked eel, and deep-fried soft-shell crabs. The sushi bar itself is tiny, and the main dining room is similarly small. The nicest seating here is in the open-air patio. Start things off with some *edamame,* an appetizer of steamed soybeans in their husks, and be sure to try the Crocodile Roll, with its mix of crab, eel, and avocado. The biggest problem here is that, when busy, the service can be excruciatingly slow.

On a side street next to El Gran Escape, Quepos. **(** 2777-1710. Reservations recommended. Maki rolls $4–$12 (£2–£6); main courses $6–$22 (£3–£11). V. Daily 4:30–11pm.

MANUEL ANTONIO AFTER DARK

The bars at the **Barba Roja** restaurant and the **Hotel Sí Como No** (see earlier in this chapter) are good places to hang out and meet people in the evenings. For shooting pool, I head to the **Billfish Sportbar & Grill** at the Byblos Resort (on the main road btw. Quepos and the park entrance). For tapas and local *bocas,* try **Salsipuedes** (roughly midway along the road between Quepos and the National Park entrance), which translates as "get out if you can." If you want live music, **Bambu Jam** ⚡ (along the road btw. Quepos and the park entrance) and **Dos Locos** (in the heart of downtown) are your best bets. In downtown Quepos, **El Banco Bar, Mar y Blues, Sargento Garcia's, Wacky Wanda's,** and the **Fish Head Bar** at El Gran Escape are all popular hangouts.

Night owls and dancing fools have several choices here, although the bulldozing of Mar y Sombra down by the beach has really hurt the scene. The live music at **Bambu Jam** is often salsa and merengue, perfect for dancing. For real late-night action, the local favorite appears to be the **Arco Iris,** which is located just before the bridge heading into town. Admission is usually around $3 (£1.50).

If you enjoy gaming tables, the **Hotel Kamuk** in Quepos and the **Byblos Resort** on the road to Manuel Antonio both have small casinos and will even foot your cab bill if you try your luck and lay down your money.

If you want to see a flick, check what's playing at **Hotel Sí Como No's** (see above) little theater, although you have to eat at the restaurant or spend a minimum at the bar to earn admission.

EN ROUTE TO DOMINICAL: PLAYA MATAPALO

Playa Matapalo is a long expanse of flat beach that's about midway between Quepos and Dominical. It's an easy but bumpy 26km (16 miles) south of Quepos on the Costanera Sur. It's nowhere near as developed as either of those two beaches, but that's part of its charm. The beach here seems to stretch on forever, and it's usually deserted.

The surf and strong riptides frequently make Matapalo too rough for swimming, although surfing and boogie-boarding can be good. Foremost among this beach's charms are peace and quiet.

WHERE TO STAY

Matapalo is a tiny coastal village, although the actual beach is about 1km (½ mile) away. A few very small and intimate lodges are located right on the beach. One of the more interesting is **Bahari Beach Bungalows** (© **2787-5014;** www.baharibeach.com), which offers deluxe tents with private bathrooms, and more standard rooms, right on the beach. If you're looking for a longer stay, check out **Jungle House** (©/fax **2787-5005;** www.junglehouse.com), which has a variety of private houses and bungalows for rent.

El Coquito del Pacifico *(Value)*   Beginning in mid-2008, this place will begin a major transformation into a swank and modern resort-condo-hotel complex. The work, however, should take a year or more to complete, and the current hotel is expected to run as normal in the interim. For now, the rooms at this beachside hotel are all quite large and have white-tile floors and high ceilings and get plenty of natural light. El Coquito also has a small kidney-shaped pool and ample grounds planted with coconut palms and other shade trees. The open-air restaurant is popular with guests and locals alike. When you hit the beach at Matapalo, turn right, and the hotel will be about a block or so north.

Playa Matapalo (Apdo. 6783-1000, San José). © **2787-5028.** Fax 2787-5029. www.elcoquito.com. 6 units. $60–$70 (£30–£35) double. Rates lower in the off season. AE, MC, V. **Amenities:** Restaurant; bar; outdoor pool; laundry service. *In room:* A/C, no phone.

3 Dominical *(★)*

29km (18 miles) SW of San Isidro; 42km (26 miles) S of Quepos; 160km (99 miles) S of San José

With a stunning setting, and miles of nearly deserted beaches backed by rainforest-covered mountains, Dominical and the coastline south of it are excellent places to find uncrowded stretches of sand, spectacular views, remote jungle waterfalls, and abundant budget lodgings. The beach at Dominical itself is one of the prime surf destinations in Costa Rica, with both right and left beach breaks. When the swell is big, the wave here is a powerful and hollow tube, and the town is often packed with surfers. In fact, while the beach at Dominical gets broad, flat, and beautiful at low tide, its primary appeal is to surfers. It is often too rough for casual bathers. However, you will find excellent swimming, sunbathing, and strolling beaches just a little farther south at **Dominicalito, Playa Hermosa,** and inside **Ballena Marine National Park** *(★)*.

Leaving Manuel Antonio, the road south to Dominical runs by mile after mile of oil-palm plantations. However, just before Dominical, the mountains again meet the sea. From Dominical south, the coastline is dotted with tide pools, tiny coves, and cliff-side vistas. Dominical is the largest village in the area and has several small lodges both in town and along the beach to the south. The village enjoys an enviable location on the banks of Río Barú, right where it widens considerably before emptying into the ocean. There's good bird-watching along the banks of the river and throughout the surrounding forests.

ESSENTIALS

GETTING THERE & DEPARTING   **By Plane**   The nearest airport with regular service is in Quepos (see "Essentials" under "Manuel Antonio National Park," earlier in this chapter). From there you can hire a taxi, rent a car, or take the bus.

By Car From San José, head south (toward Cartago) on the Interamerican Highway. Continue on this road all the way to San Isidro de El General, where you turn right and head down toward the coast. The entire drive takes about 4 hours.

You can also drive here from Manuel Antonio/Quepos. Just take the road out of Quepos toward the hospital and airport. Follow the signs for Dominical. It's a straight, albeit bumpy, shot that takes a bit over an hour due to the poor state of the washboard-rutted dirt road. For nearly a decade, this road has been scheduled for paving. If this happens, it should take only a half-hour to cover the 40km (25 miles).

The road from Dominical heading south to Palmar Norte, passing all the beaches mentioned below, is in excellent shape.

By Bus To reach Dominical, you must first go to San Isidro de El General or Quepos. Buses leave San José for San Isidro roughly every hour between 5:30am and 6:30pm. See "Getting There & Departing" in "San Isidro de El General: A Base for Exploring Chirripó National Park," later in this chapter. The trip takes 3 hours; the fare is $3.25 (£1.65). Leave no later than 9am if you want to be sure to catch the 1:30pm bus to Dominical.

From San Isidro de El General, **Transportes Blanco** buses (© **2257-4121** or 2771-4744) leave for Dominical at 7 and 9am and 1:30 and 4pm. The bus station for Dominical is 1 block south of the main bus station and 2 blocks west of the church. Trip duration is 1½ hours; the fare is $1.50 (75p).

From **Quepos,** buses leave daily at 5, 6:30, and 9:30am and 1:30, 5:30, and 7pm. Trip duration is 2 hours; the fare is $3 (£1.50).

When you're ready to leave, buses depart Dominical for San Isidro at 6:45 and 7:15am and 2:30 and 3:30pm. If you want to get to San José the same day, you should catch the morning bus. Buses leave San Isidro for San José roughly every hour between 5am and 6pm. Buses to Quepos leave Dominical at approximately 5:15, 5:45, 8, and 11am and 2:30 and 5:30pm.

ORIENTATION Dominical is a very small village on the banks of Río Barú. The village is to the right after you cross the bridge and stretches out along the main road parallel to the beach. As you first come into town, you'll see the small Pueblo Del Rio shopping center dead ahead of you, where the road hits a "T" intersection. On your left is the soccer field and the heart of the village. To the right, a rough road heads to the river and up along the riverbank. If you stay on the Costanera Highway heading south, just beyond the turnoff into town is a little strip mall, **Plaza Pacífica,** with a couple of restaurants, a pharmacy, bank, and a grocery store.

FAST FACTS If you need any medical care, contact **Dominical Doctor** (© **2787-0129** or 8865-4064), which is inside the Pueblo del Rio minimall. You'll also find a pharmacy in the same little mall.

The closest gas station is about 2km (1¼ miles) north of town on the road to Quepos. Since this road is pretty rough, it's often better to head south along the Costanera to Uvita, where you'll find another gas station. Taxis tend to congregate in front of the soccer field. If you need to call a cab, try **Nelson** (© **8835-9528**) or **Erik** (© **8881-4220**). To rent a car, contact **Alamo** (© **2787-0052**) which has a desk inside the Villas Rio Mar resort.

You can purchase stamps and send mail from the **San Clemente Bar & Grill.** In the little mall built beside the San Clemente Bar & Grill, you'll also find an Internet cafe, and they'll change dollars. There's also a small branch of the **Banco de Costa Rica,** with an ATM, at the Plaza Pacifica.

EXPLORING THE BEACHES & BALLENA MARINE NATIONAL PARK

Because the beach in the village of Dominical itself is unprotected and at the mouth of a river, it's often too rough for swimming. However, you can go for a swim in the calm waters at the mouth of the Río Barú, or head down the beach a few kilometers to the little sheltered cove at **Roca Verde.**

If you have a car, you should continue driving south, exploring beaches as you go. You will first come to **Dominicalito,** a small beach and cove that shelters the local fishing fleet and can be a decent place to swim, but continue on a bit. You'll soon hit **Playa Hermosa,** a long stretch of desolate beach with fine sand. As in Dominical, this is unprotected and can be rough, but it's a nicer place to sunbathe and swim than Dominical.

At the village of Uvita, 16km (10 miles) south of Dominical, you'll reach the northern end of the **Ballena Marine National Park** (⋆, which protects a coral reef that stretches from Uvita south to Playa Piñuela and includes the little Isla Ballena, just offshore. To get to **Playa Uvita** (which is inside the park), turn in at the village of Bahía and continue until you hit the ocean. The beach here is actually well protected and good for swimming. At low tide an exposed sandbar allows you to walk about and explore another tiny island. This park is named for the whales that are sometimes sighted close to shore in the winter months. If you ever fly over this area, you'll also notice that this little island and the spit of land that's formed at low tide compose the perfect outline of a whale's tail. A parks office at the entrance here regulates the park's use and even runs a small turtle-hatching shelter and program. Entrance to the national park is $10 (£5) per person. Camping is allowed here for $2 (£1) per person per day, with access to a public bathroom and shower.

Dominical is a major surf destination. The long and varied beach break here is justifiably popular. In general, the beach boasts powerful waves best suited for experienced surfers. Nevertheless, beginners should check in with the folks at the **Green Iguana Surf Camp** (② 2787-0157; www.greeniguanasurfcamp.com), who offer lessons and comprehensive "surf camps." Rates run around $735 to $795 (£368–£398) per person, based on double occupancy, for a 1-week program including accommodations, lessons, unlimited surfboard use, transportation to various surf breaks, and a T-shirt.

OTHER ACTIVITIES IN THE AREA

Although the beaches stretching south from Dominical should be beautiful enough to keep most people content, there are lots of other things to do. Several local farms offer horseback tours through forests and orchards, and at some of these farms you can even spend the night. **Hacienda Barú** (⋆ (② 2787-0003; fax 2787-0057; www.hacienda baru.com) offers several different hikes and tours, including a walk through mangroves and along the riverbank (for some good bird-watching), a rainforest hike through 80 hectares (198 acres) of virgin jungle, an all-day trek from beach to mangrove to jungle that includes a visit to some Indian petroglyphs, an overnight camping trip, and a combination horseback-and-hiking tour. It even has tree-climbing tours and a small canopy platform 30m (98 ft.) above the ground, as well as one of the more common zip-line canopy tours. Tour prices range from $20 (£10) for the mangrove hike to $60 (£30) for the jungle overnight. If you're traveling with a group, you'll be charged a lower per-person rate, depending on the number of people. Hacienda Barú also has six comfortable cabins with two bedrooms each, full kitchens, and even a living room ($60/£30 double, including breakfast). Hacienda Barú is about 1.5km (1 mile) north of Dominical on the road to Manuel Antonio.

The jungles just outside of Dominical are home to two spectacular waterfalls. The most popular and impressive is the **Santo Cristo** or **Nauyaca Waterfalls** ⚓, a two-tiered beauty with an excellent swimming hole. Most of the hotels in town can arrange for the horseback ride up here, or you can contact **Don Lulo** (© 2787-8013; www.cataratasnauyaca.com) directly. A full-day tour, with both breakfast and lunch, should cost around $45 (£23) per person, including transportation to and from Dominical. The tour is a mix of hiking, horseback riding, and hanging out at the falls. It is also possible to reach these falls by horseback from an entrance near the small village of Tinamaste. (You will see signs on the road.) Similar tours (at similar prices) are offered to the **Diamante Waterfalls,** which are a three-tiered set of falls with a 360m (1,180-ft.) drop, but not quite as spacious and inviting a pool as the one at Santo Cristo.

If you're looking for a bird's-eye view of the area, **Skyline Ultralights** (© 2743-8037; www.flyultralight.com) offers a variety of airborne tours of the area. Near the beach in Uvita, these folks offer options ranging from a 20-minute introductory flight for $65 (£33) to a circuit exploring the Ballena Marine National Park and neighboring mangrove forests lasting a bit over an hour for $150 (£75).

If you want to take a scuba-diving trip out to the rocky sites off of Ballena National Park or all the way out to Isla del Caño, call **Mystic Dive Center** (© 2786-5217; www.mysticdivecenter.com), which has its main office in a small roadside strip mall down toward Playa Tortuga and Ojochal. These folks are only open from December 1 through April 15.

Other adventure activities offered in Dominical include kayak tours of the mangroves, river floats in inner tubes, day tours to Caño Island and Corcovado National Park, and sportfishing. To arrange any of these activities, check in with **Dominical Adventures** (© 2787-0191; at the San Clemente Bar & Grill), **Southern Expeditions** (© 2787-0100; www.southernexpeditionscr.com), or the folks at the **Hotel Roca Verde** (© 2787-0036).

For a fun side trip for anyone interested in snakes and other little critters, head to **Parque Reptilandia** (© 2787-8007; www.crreptiles.com), located a few miles outside of Dominical on the road to San Isidro. This place features over 50 terrariums or enclosed exhibits of snakes, frogs, turtles, and lizards, as well as crocodiles and caimans. It's open daily from 9am to 4:30pm; admission is $10 (£5).

Finally, if you're looking to learn or bone up on your Spanish, **Adventure Education Center** (© 2787-0023; www.adventurespanishschool.com), located right in the heart of town, offers a variety of immersion-style language programs.

WHERE TO STAY

In addition to the places listed below, there are a host of beautiful private homes built on the hillsides above Dominical that are regularly rented out. Most come with several bedrooms and full kitchens, and quite a few have private pools. If you're here for an extended stay and have a four-wheel-drive vehicle (a must for most of these), check in with **Paradise Costa Rica** (© 800/708-4552 in the U.S. and Canada; www.paradisecostarica.com) or with the folks at **Cabinas San Clemente** or **Hotel Roca Verde** (see below for both of these).

Although not yet open at press time, by the start of the 2009 high season, **Kiana Resort** (© 2787-4006; www.kiana-dominical.com) will be a very luxurious all-villa beachfront option just south of the center of the village.

MODERATE

Hotel Diuwak   This little complex offers the best-equipped rooms right near the surf break, although that's not necessarily saying much. The rooms are spartan and bright. About half the rooms come with air-conditioning, and there are a few bigger suites and bungalows for larger groups and families. Most have some sort of private or semiprivate veranda facing lush gardens. At the center of the complex, you'll find a refreshing pool, and in the adjacent shopping center, there's a minimarket. Located about 50m (164 ft.) inland from the beach, this place is a decent option for surfers seeking a little extra comfort just steps away from the waves. However, service and upkeep can be spotty here.

Dominical (mailing address: A.P. 7737-1000, San José). ☏ **2787-0087.** Fax 2787-0089. www.diuwak.com. 18 units. $85–$135 (£43–£68) double. Rates include full breakfast. Rates lower in off season; higher during peak weeks. MC, V. **Amenities:** Restaurant; bar; midsize pool; Jacuzzi; tour desk; laundry service. *In room:* Free Wi-Fi, safe.

Hotel Roca Verde 🏖   This popular hotel offers the best beachfront accommodations in Dominical, although it's a tad south of town. Still, the setting is superb—on a protected little cove with rocks and tide pools. The rooms are located in a two-story building beside the swimming pool. Each room comes with one queen-size and one single bed, and a small patio or balcony. A large open-air restaurant with a popular bar really gets going on Saturday nights. The rooms are a bit close to the bar, so it can sometimes be hard to get an early night's sleep, especially during the high season if the bar is raging.

1km (½ mile) south of Barú River Bridge in Dominical, just off the coastal highway. ☏ **2787-0036.** Fax 2787-0013. www.rocaverde.net. 10 units. $85 (£43) double. Rates lower in off season; higher during peak weeks. MC, V. **Amenities:** Restaurant; bar; small pool; tour desk; laundry service. *In room:* A/C, no phone.

Pacific Edge 🏖 *(Finds*   This place is away from the beach, but the views from each individual bungalow are so stunning that you might not mind. Spread along a lushly planted ridge on the hillside over Dominical, these comfortable cabins have wood floors, solar-heated water, and solar reading lights. Their best feature is surely the private porch with a comfortable hammock in which to laze about and enjoy the view. The restaurant serves breakfast. Dinners are also served upon request, with an emphasis on well-prepared international cuisine. A wide range of tours and activities can be arranged here, and there's a refreshing swimming pool, if you're too tired or lazy to head down to the beach. Pacific Edge is 4km (2½ miles) south of Dominical and then another 1.2km (¾ mile) up a steep and rocky road; four-wheel-drive vehicles are recommended.

Dominical (A.P. 531-8000, Pérez Zeledón). ☏/fax **2787-8010.** www.pacificedge.info. 4 units. $50–$75 (£25–£38) double. AE, MC, V. **Amenities:** Restaurant; midsize pool. *In room:* Minifridge, coffeemaker, no phone.

INEXPENSIVE

As a popular surfer destination, budget lodgings abound in Dominical. I've tried to list the best below, but if you're really counting pennies, it's always a good idea to walk around and check out what's currently available. There are plenty of camping options as well. I recommend **Piramys** (☏ **2787-0196;** piramys@hotmail.com) or **Camping Antorchas** (☏ **2787-0307**), both of which offer basic rooms very close to the beach.

Cabinas San Clemente *(Value*   In addition to running the town's most popular restaurant (see below) and serving as the social hub for the surfers, beach bums, and expatriates passing through, this place offers a variety of accommodations to fit most budgets. Located about 1km (½ mile) from the in-town restaurant, San Clemente has rooms in three separate buildings, right on the beach. Some of the second-floor rooms have wood floors and wraparound verandas and are a good deal in this price range. The grounds are shady, and there are plenty of hammocks. The cheapest rooms are bunk-bed hostel-style affairs in a separate building dubbed the **Dominical Back-packer's Hostel.** Rooms here come with access to a communal kitchen.

Dominical (A.P. 703-8000, Pérez Zeledón). ℂ **2787-0026** or 2787-0055. Fax 2787-0158. 19 units, 16 with private bathroom. $10 (£5) per person with shared bathroom; $30–$70 (£15–£35) double with private bathroom. AE, MC, V. **Amenities:** Restaurant; bar; surf- and boogie-board rental; bike rental; tour desk; laundry service. *In room:* No phone.

Domilocos   Recently expanded and remodeled, this place offers modern and comfortable rooms at a good price. Rooms are simply furnished and on the plain side, but they do have bamboo furnishings, air-conditioning, and large bathrooms. All open onto a common veranda. Since it's about 1 block inland from the beach, this hotel has an isolated location; still, the restaurant and bar are both popular here, so things can get lively.

Dominical. ℂ **2787-0244.** www.domilocos.com. 25 units. $40–$50 (£20–£25) double. MC, V. **Amenities:** Restaurant; bar; laundry service. *In room:* A/C, safe.

Tortilla Flats   This long-standing surfer hotel is another good budget option on the beach. There are several styles of rooms located in a cluster of buildings, including rooms with fans, rooms with air-conditioning, and larger rooms fitted out for groups of surfers. I recommend the second-floor rooms with ocean views. Because the rooms differ so much in size and comfort levels, you should definitely take a look at a few of them before choosing one.

Dominical. ℂ/fax **2787-0168.** www.tortillaflatsdominical.com. 18 units. $35–$60 (£18–£30) double. Rates lower in off season. AE, MC, V. **Amenities:** Restaurant; bar; laundry service. *In room:* No phone.

WHERE TO DINE

On the beach **Tortilla Flats** (ℂ **2787-0033**) is the best and most happening spot, and their menu features some excellent fresh-fish dishes and a touch of fusion cuisine. If you head a little bit south of town, you can check out the restaurant at the **Hotel Roca Verde** (p. 317), which is usually pretty good for freshly grilled fish, steaks, and burgers. For healthy fare, try **Maracatú** (ℂ **2787-0091**), located toward the southern end of town.

　　Soda Nanyoa (ℂ **2787-0164**) is a basic Tico restaurant on the main road, just down a bit from the soccer field, serving local food and fresh seafood at good prices.

Coconut Spice ☙ THAI/INDIAN   Near the mouth of the river, this place continues to serve up dependable and reasonably authentic Thai, Malaysian, Indonesian, and Indian cuisine. The lemon-grass soups and pad Thai are both excellent, and there's a broad selection of different curries and other main dishes. There are several open-air dining spaces, and the best seats actually have a view of the Río Barú.

In the Pueblo del Rio shopping complex, Dominical. ℂ **2787-0073** or 8834-8103. Reservations recommended during the high season. Main courses $8–$15 (£4–£7.50). V. Daily 7:30–9pm.

ConFusione ☙ ITALIAN/INTERNATIONAL   The most refined and romantic restaurant in Dominical proper, this place turns out very good Italian fare, with some other Continental influences. Standout appetizers include a baked gratin of shrimp in brandy sauce and fried fresh mushrooms. There's a long list of pastas and main dishes, and the seafood is always fresh and well prepared. These folks have a modest and fairly priced wine list, and there's a pretty stone bar, which is a pleasant place to hang out, either before or after a meal.

Inside the Domilocos Hotel. (✆ **2787-0244.** Reservations recommended during the high season. Main courses $6.50–$18 (£3.25–£9). MC, V. Daily 7am–11:30pm.

San Clemente Bar & Grill ✯ MEXICAN/AMERICAN   The large wooden tables and bench seats at this convivial place fill up fast most nights. The menu has a large selection of Mexican-American fare ranging from tacos and burritos to sandwiches. You can get any of the former with fresh fish. There are also more substantial plates, as well as nightly specials. Breakfasts here are also excellent. Just off the restaurant is a large indoor space that has a pool and foosball table, and which becomes one of the town's more popular nightspots, particularly on Friday nights. An interesting (and sobering) decorative touch here is the ceiling full of broken surfboards. If you break a board out on the waves, bring it in; they'll hang it and even buy you a bucket of beer.

Next to the soccer field, Dominical. (✆ **2787-0055.** Reservations not accepted. Main courses $4–$16 (£2–£8). MC, V. Daily 7am–10pm.

DOMINICAL AFTER DARK

The big party scenes shift from night to night. **Maracutú** hosts an open jam session every Tuesday and a reggae night every Thursday. The loud and late-night dancing scene usually takes place Fridays at **San Clemente** and Saturdays at **Roca Verde.** In addition, **Thrusters** is a popular surfer bar with pool tables and dartboards, and the bar at **Rio Lindo Resort** has a mellow scene, with occasional live concerts. The bar at **ConFusione** (see above) also frequently has live music.

SOUTH OF DOMINICAL

The beaches south of Dominical are some of the nicest and most unexplored in Costa Rica. With the paving of the Costanera Sur, hotels and *cabinas* have begun popping up all along this route. This is a great area to roam in a rental car—it's a **beautiful drive** ✯✯. One good itinerary is to make a loop from San Isidro to Dominical, down the Costanera Sur, hitting several deserted beaches and then returning along the Interamerican Highway.

Among the beaches you'll find are **Playa Ballena, Playa Uvita, Playa Piñuela, Playa Ventanas,** and **Playa Tortuga.** *Tip:* Most of these beaches are considered part of **Ballena Marine National Park** and are subject to the national park entrance fee of $6 (£3) per person. If you're visiting several of these beaches in 1 day, save your ticket—it's good at all of them.

WHERE TO STAY DOWN SOUTH

In addition to the places listed here, you'll find a campground at Playa Ballena and a couple of basic *cabinas* in Bahía and Uvita. The most popular of these is **El Coco Tico Ecolodge** (✆ **2743-8032;** $40/£20 double), owned and operated by Jorge Díaz, a local legend and enjoyable raconteur who also arranges trips to a nearby waterfall. Coco Tico allows camping as well for around $5 (£2.50) per person. You'll see a sign for Coco Tico on your left as you reach Uvita, traveling south from Dominical. Another similar option is the **Tucan Hotel** (✆ **2743-8140;** www.tucanhotel.com), with a mix of private rooms and dorm accommodations and a friendly hostel-like vibe.

However, if you want to be closer to the beach, check out **Canto de Ballenas** (✆ **2743-8085**), an interesting local cooperative with neat rooms located about .7km (a little less than a half-mile) from the national park entrance at Playa Uvita.

Expensive

Cuna del Angel ✦✦

This hotel has the plushest accommodations along this stretch of coast. The name of this place translates roughly as the Angel's Cradle. All rooms are named after angels, and angel motifs are abundant, as are stained-glass windows and lampshades, carved wood details, tile mosaics, and other artistic touches. The hotel is a bit set in, away from the ocean, but there are pretty good sea views from many rooms and common areas, over the thick forest and gardens here. Rooms come with either an open front patio fronting the pool, or a private balcony. I prefer the second-floor rooms, with the balconies. A wide range of treatments is available at the spa, and they have several well-equipped boats for deep-sea sportfishing.

9km (5½ miles) south of Dominical, just off the coastal highway. © 2787-8436. Fax 2787-8015. www.cunadelangel. com. 16 units. $153 (£77) double. Rates include full breakfast. Rates lower in off season; higher during peak periods. AE, MC, V. **Amenities:** Restaurant; bar; midsize outdoor pool; small spa; Jacuzzi; sauna; steam room; tour desk; laundry service. *In room:* A/C, TV, free Wi-Fi, minifridge, coffeemaker, hair dryer, safe.

La Cusinga Lodge ✦ *(Finds)*

This should be a top choice for bird-watchers and those looking for a comfortable lodge that also feels entirely in touch with the natural surroundings. The individual and duplex cabins feature lots of varnished woodwork and large screened windows on all sides for cross ventilation. Most have interesting stone and tile work in their bathrooms. The small complex is set on a hill overlooking Ballena National Park and Playa Uvita. Heavy stone paths connect the main lodge to the various individual cabins. The "honeymoon cabin" is large, has a private garden sitting area, and a large bathroom with rustic stonemasonry and its own Jacuzzi tub.

Bahía Ballena (A.P. 41-8000). ©/fax 2770-2549. www.lacusingalodge.com. 7 units. $134–$160 (£67–£80) double. Rates include breakfast. MC, V. **Amenities:** Restaurant; bar; tour desk; laundry service. *In room:* No phone.

Moderate

Costa Paraiso Lodge

This hotel offers spacious and functional individual cabins on a rocky point at the north end of Dominicalito beach. All but one of the units come with either a full kitchen or kitchenette, and most have high ceilings and plenty of light and ventilation. Dolphin Lodge and Pelican Roost are the two best rooms here, with spacious living and dining areas. All of the rooms are nonsmoking. There is a small swimming pool, as well as some beautiful tide pools right in front of the hotel; the beach is just a short walk away. For 2009, plans include the construction of two new luxury villas, as well as a bar and restaurant.

2km (1¼ miles) south of Dominical, just off the coastal highway, Dominicalito (A.P. 578-8000, Pérez Zeledón). © 2787-0025. Fax 2787-0338. www.costa-paraiso.com. 5 units. $125–$300 (£63–£150) double. Rates include full breakfast. Rates lower in off season. AE, DC, MC, V. **Amenities:** Small pool; laundry service. *In room:* A/C, free Wi-Fi, fridge, coffeemaker, no phone.

Hotel Villas Gaia ✦

Located off the Costanera Sur just before the town of Ojochal, this small hotel is a collection of separate, spacious wood bungalows. Each bungalow has one single and one double bed, a private bathroom, a ceiling fan, and a small veranda with a jungle view. A few have air-conditioning. I prefer the bungalows farthest from the restaurant, up on the high hill by the swimming pool. The pool and pool area have wonderful views over forest to the sea. A large, open-air dining room down by the parking lot is too close to the highway for my taste but serves tasty, well-prepared international fare. A wide range of tours are available, including trips to Isla del Caño, Corcovado National Park, and Wilson Botanical Gardens.

Playa Tortuga (A.P. 11516-1000, San José). ℭ/fax **2244-0316** reservations in San José, or 2786-5044 at the lodge. www.villasgaia.com. 14 units. $75 (£38) double. Rates include taxes. AE, MC, V. **Amenities:** Restaurant; bar; small pool; tour desk; laundry service. *In room:* A/C ($10/£5 surcharge), no phone.

WHERE TO DINE DOWN SOUTH

In addition to the place mentioned below, you'll also find a similar, French inspired-international restaurant, **Citrus** (ℭ **2786-5175**), in Ojochal. This place is run by the folks who had a wonderful restaurant by the same name, on a converted houseboat docked just off the Costanera.

Exotica ★★ *(Finds* FRENCH/INTERNATIONAL   This place is tucked away deep along the dirt road that runs through Ojochal. With polished concrete floors, roll-up bamboo screens for walls, and only a few tree-trunk slab tables and plastic lawn chairs for furniture, it is nonetheless one of the most popular restaurants in the area. The chalkboard menu changes regularly but might feature such dishes as shrimp in a coconut curry sauce or Chicken Exotica, which is stuffed with bacon, prunes, and cheese and topped with a red-pepper coulis. The lunch menu is much more limited, with a selection of fresh salads and a few more filling mains.

1km (½ mile) inland from the turnoff for Ojochal. ℭ **2786-5050.** Reservations not accepted. Lunch $3–$7 (£1.50–£3.50); main courses $6–$22 (£3–£11). MC, V. Mon–Sat 11am–4:30pm and 6–9pm.

---

4 San Isidro de El General: A Base for Exploring Chirripó National Park

120km (74 miles) SE of San José; 123km (76 miles) NW of Palmar Norte; 29km (18 miles) NE of Dominical

San Isidro de El General is located just off the Interamerican Highway in the foothills of the Talamanca Mountains and is the largest town in this region. Although there isn't much to do right in town, this is the jumping-off point for trips to Chirripó National Park. This is also the principal transfer point if you're coming from or going to Dominical, and most buses traveling the Interamerican Highway stop here.

ESSENTIALS

GETTING THERE & DEPARTING   By Car   The long and winding stretch of the Interamerican Highway between San José and San Isidro is one of the most difficult sections of road in the country. Not only are there the usual car-eating potholes and periodic landslides, but you must also contend with driving over the 3,300m (10,824-ft.) **Cerro de la Muerte (Mountain of Death).** This aptly named mountain pass is legendary for its dense afternoon fogs, blinding torrential downpours, steep drop-offs, severe switchbacks, and unexpectedly breathtaking views. (Well, you wanted adventure travel, so here you go!) Drive with extreme care, and bring a sweater or sweatshirt—it's cold up at the top. It'll take you about 3 hours to get to San Isidro.

Tip: If you want a break from the road, stop for a coffee or meal at **Mirador Vista del Valle** (ℭ **8384-4685** or 8836-3193; at Km 119), a rustic roadside joint with a great view, gift shop, hiking trails, and orchid collection. These folks also have a few rustic cabins, as well as a zip-line canopy tour.

By Bus   Plenty of daily buses will take you to San Isidro. **Musoc** buses (ℭ **2222-2422** in San José, or 2771-3829 in San Isidro) leave from their modern terminal at Calle Central and Avenida 22 roughly hourly between 5:30am and 6:30pm. **Tracopa** (ℭ **2221-4214** or 2771-0468) also runs express buses between San José and San

---

Tips **Little Devils**

If you're visiting the San Isidro area in February, head out to the nearby **Rey Curré** village for the **Fiesta of the Diablitos,** where costumed Boruca Indians perform dances representative of the Spanish conquest of Central America. The 3-day event also includes fireworks and an Indian handicraft market—this is *the* best place in Costa Rica to buy hand-carved Boruca masks. The date varies, so it's best to call the **Costa Rica Tourist Board** (© **800/327-7033** in the U.S. and Canada) for more information.

Isidro that leave roughly every hour between 5am and 6pm from Calle 5, between avenidas 18 and 20. Whichever company you choose, the trip takes a little over 3 hours, and the fare is roughly $3.40 (£1.70). Return buses depart San Isidro for **San José** roughly every hour between 5am and 6pm.

Buses from **Quepos** to San Isidro leave daily at 5am and 1:30pm. Trip duration is 3½ hours; the fare is $3 (£1.50). Buses to or from **Golfito** and **Puerto Jiménez** will also drop you off in San Isidro.

ORIENTATION Downtown San Isidro is just off the Interamerican Highway. A large church fronts the central park, and you'll find several banks, and a host of restaurants, shops, and hotels within a 2-block radius of this park. The main bus station is 2 blocks west of the north end of the central park.

EXPLORING CHIRRIPO NATIONAL PARK 🟊🟊

At 3,759m (12,330 ft.) in elevation, Mount Chirripó is the tallest mountain in Costa Rica. If you're headed up this way, come prepared for chilly weather. Actually, dress in layers and come prepared for all sorts of weather: Because of the great elevations, temperatures frequently dip below freezing, especially at night. However, during the day, temperatures can soar—remember, you're still only 9 degrees from the equator. The elevation and radical temperatures have produced an environment here that's very different from the Costa Rican norm. Above 3,000m (9,840 ft.), only stunted trees and shrubs survive in páramos. If you're driving the Interamerican Highway between San Isidro and San José, you'll pass through a páramo on the Cerro de la Muerte.

Hiking up to the top of Mount Chirripó is one of Costa Rica's best adventures. On a clear day (usually in the morning), an unforgettable **view** 🟊🟊🟊 is your reward: You can see both the Pacific Ocean and the Caribbean Sea from the summit. You can do this trip fairly easily on your own if you've brought gear and are an experienced back-packer. Although it's possible to hike from the park entrance to the summit and back down in 2 days (in fact, some daredevils even do it in 1 day), it's best to allow 3 to 4 days for the trip in order to give yourself time to enjoy your hike fully and spend some time on top because that's where the glacier lakes and páramos are. For much of the way, you'll be hiking through cloud forests that are home to abundant tropical fauna, including the spectacular **quetzal,** Costa Rica's most beautiful bird. However, quetzal sightings on summit climbs are rare. If you really want to see one of these birds, head to one of the specialized lodges listed below.

There are several routes to the top of Mount Chirripó. The most popular, by far, leaves from **San Gerardo de Rivas.** However, it's also possible to start your hike from the nearby towns of **Herradura** or **Canaan.** All these places are within a mile or so of each other, reached by the same major road out of San Isidro. San Gerardo is the most popular because it's the easiest route to the top and has the greatest collections of small hotels and lodges, as well as the National Parks office. Information on all of these routes is available at the parks office.

When you're at the summit lodge, there are a number of hiking options. Just in front of the lodge are Los Crestones (the Crests), an impressive rock formation, with trails leading up and around them. The most popular, however, is to the actual summit (the lodge itself is a bit below), which is about a 2-hour hike that passes through the Valle de los Conejos (Rabbit Valley) and the Valle de los Lagos (Valley of Lakes). Other hikes and trails lead off from the summit lodge, and it's easy to spend a couple of days hiking around here. A few trails will take you to the summits of several neighboring peaks. These hikes should be undertaken only after carefully studying an accurate map and talking to park rangers and other hikers.

ENTRY POINT, FEES & REGULATIONS   Although it's not that difficult to get to Chirripó National Park from nearby San Isidro, it's still rather remote. And to see it fully, you have to be prepared to hike. To get to the trail head, you have three choices: car, taxi, or bus. If you choose to drive, take the road out of San Isidro, heading north toward San Gerardo de Rivas, which is some 20km (12 miles) down the road. Otherwise, you can catch a bus in San Isidro that will take you directly to the trail head in San Gerardo de Rivas. Buses leave daily at 5am from the western side of the central park in San Isidro. It costs 80¢ (40p) one-way and takes 1½ hours. Another bus departs at 2pm from a bus station 200m (656 ft.) south of the park. Buses return to San Isidro daily at 7am and 4pm. A taxi from town should cost around $15 to $20 (£7.50–£10). Because the hike to the summit of Mount Chirripó can take between 6 and 12 hours, depending on your physical condition, I recommend taking a taxi or the early bus so that you can start hiking when the day is still young. Better still, you should arrive the day before and spend the night in San Gerardo de Rivas (there are inexpensive *cabinas* and one nice hotel there) before setting out early the following morning.

Before climbing Mount Chirripó, you must make a reservation and check in with the **National Parks office** (© **2742-5083;** fax 2742-5085) in San Gerardo de Rivas. The office is open from 6:30am to 4:30pm daily. Even if you have a reservation, I highly recommend checking in the day before you plan to climb if possible. If you plan to stay at the lodge near the summit, you must make reservations in advance because accommodations there are limited (see "Staying at the Summit Lodge," below). Note that camping is not allowed in the park. It's possible to have your gear carried up to the summit by horseback during the dry season (Dec–Apr). Guides work outside the park entrance in San Gerardo de Rivas. They charge between $20 and $30 (£10–£15) per pack, depending on size and weight. In the rainy season the same guides work, but they take packs up by themselves, not by horseback. The guides like to take up the packs well before dawn, so arrangements are best made the day before.

The entrance fee to the national park is $15 (£7.50) per day.

STAYING AT THE SUMMIT LODGE   Reservations for lodging on the summit of Mount Chirripó must be made with the National Parks office listed above. This is an increasingly popular destination, and you must reserve well in advance during the dry season. The lodge holds only 25 people and fills up quickly and frequently. *Tip:* Many of the local tour agencies prebook the lodge beds, making it often difficult to impossible to do so on your own. If you can't book a bed by yourself, ask at your hotel, or contact one of the tour agencies listed below in "Other Adventures in & Around San Isidro."

Once you get to the lodge, you'll find various rooms with bunk beds, several bathrooms and showers, and a common kitchen area. There is good drinking water at the lodge. However, blankets, lanterns, and cook stoves are no longer for rent up top, so you have to pack all your own gear, as well as food and water (for the hike up). *Note:* It gets cold up here at night, and the lodge seems to have been designed to be as cold, dark, and cavernous as possible. No consideration was made to take advantage of the ample passive solar potential. The showers are freezing. It costs $10 (£5) per person per night to stay here.

Warning: It can be dangerous for more inexperienced or out-of-shape hikers to climb Chirripó, especially by themselves. It's not very technical climbing, but it is a long, arduous hike. If you're not sure you're up for it, you can just take day hikes out of San Isidro and/or San Gerardo de Rivas, or ask at your hotel about guides.

OTHER ADVENTURES IN & AROUND SAN ISIDRO

If you want to undertake any other adventures while in San Isidro, contact **Costa Rica Trekking Adventures** (② 2771-4582; fax 2771-8841; www.chirripo.com), or **CIPROTUR** (② 2771-6096; www.ecotourism.co.cr). Both offer organized treks through Chirripó National Park, as well as white-water rafting trips and other adventure tours and activities.

Just 7km (4⅓ miles) from San Isidro is **Las Quebradas Biological Center** (②/fax 2771-4131), a community-run private reserve with 2.7km (1¾ miles) of trails through primary rainforest. There's a rustic lodge for visitors and researchers ($25/£13 per person; $15/£7.50 students, including three meals), and camping is also permitted. You can hike the trails here and visit the small information center on-site for $5 (£2.50). From San Isidro, you can take a local bus to Quebradas, but you'll have to walk the last mile to the entrance. You can also take a taxi for around $8 (£4). If you're driving, take the road to Morazán and Quebradas.

WHERE TO STAY & DINE

There are no notable restaurants in San Isidro. The town has its fair share of local joints, but most visitors are content at their hotel restaurant (see below for ideas). If you do venture beyond your hotel, your best options are the **México Lindo** (② 2771-8222) and the **Pizzería El Tenedor** (② 2771-0881), both just off the central park. Although the food is mediocre, the second-floor, open-air balcony seating at **La Cascada** (② 2771-6479) offers some excellent opportunities for people-watching, and is a great place to mingle with locals.

Hotel Diamante Real 🦀 This three-story business-class hotel feels a little out of place in San Isidro. Still, it offers the newest, cleanest, and best-equipped rooms in town, and at a pretty fair price. The rooms themselves lack any sense of style or flair, and could really use a painting or two on the walls. But they are of good size, and boast either a table or desk for working executive types. The deluxe rooms even have Jacuzzi tubs. The restaurant serves respectable, if unimpressive, international and local fare.

San Isidro de El General, 1 block west of the Musoc bus station. ② 2770-6230. Fax 2770-6250. www.hoteldiamante real.com. 21 units. $40–$60 (£20–£30) double. Rates include breakfast. AE, MC, V. **Amenities:** Restaurant; tour desk; room service (7am–10pm); laundry service. *In room:* A/C, TV, free Wi-Fi, hair dryer.

Hotel Iguazú This is a clean, safe, and popular budget choice in San Isidro, although I recommend you splurge and stay at either of the other hotels in this section

> **Tips Rest Your Weary Muscles Here**
>
> If you're tired and sore from so much hiking, be sure to check out the small **Herradura Hot Springs** (📞 8391-8107) located off the road between San Gerardo de Rivas and Herradura. The entrance to the springs is 1km (½ mile) beyond San Gerardo de Rivas. The entrance fee is $3 (£1.50).

if you can afford it. The rooms are basic and come in different sizes with different arrangements of beds, but all have small televisions. The rooms are definitely in better shape than those at the even more popular budget choice, the Hotel Chirripó. The hotel is on the second and third floors of the Gallo Mas Gallo department store, half a block away from the Musoc bus station. Some might find this convenient; others might find it too noisy. In 2007, they opened an annex, El Nuevo Iguazú, which is several blocks away, and very similar, although all rooms here have private bathrooms.

San Isidro de El General (above the Gallo Mas Gallo store). 📞 **2771-2571.** Fax 2771-0076. 22 units, 17 with private bathroom. $12 (£6) double with shared bathroom; $25 (£13) double with private bathroom. V. *In room:* TV.

Hotel Los Crestones This two-story hotel is a few blocks south of downtown, and away from most of the traffic noise of this busy little city, although it is still on the main route that heads out of town toward Dominical. All rooms are relatively large and come with air-conditioning, but it costs an extra $10 (£5) to use it. The televisions are also pretty small. I recommend the units on the second floor, which share a broad tiled veranda. There's a midsize outdoor swimming pool and Jacuzzi.

San Isidro de El General (southwest side of the stadium). 📞 **2770-1200.** Fax 2770-5047. www.hotelloscrestones. com. 27 units. $50–$60 (£25–£30) double. Rates include breakfast. MC, V. **Amenities:** Restaurant; outdoor pool; tour desk; laundry service. *In room:* A/C, TV, free Wi-Fi.

WHERE TO STAY CLOSER TO THE TRAIL HEAD

If you're climbing Mount Chirripó, you'll want to spend the night as close to the trail head as possible. As mentioned above, several basic *cabinas* right in San Gerardo de Rivas charge between $5 and $15 (£2.50–£7.50) per person. The best of these are **El Descanso** (📞 8369-0067 or 2742-5061) and **Roca Dura** (📞 8363-7318; luisrocadura@ hotmail.com). If you're looking for a little more comfort, check out the lodge listed below.

Talari Mountain Lodge ⭐ This small mountain getaway is nothing fancy, but it is one of the nicer options right around San Isidro, and it also makes a good base for exploring or climbing Mount Chirripó. The rooms are in two separate concrete-block buildings. Most come with one double and one single bed, although one room can handle a family of four in one double and two single beds. Each room comes with a small fridge and a small patio. I prefer the four rooms that face the Talamanca Mountains. There are plenty of fruit trees around and good bird-watching right on the grounds. (They've identified more than 222 bird species here.) The hotel borders the Río General and maintains some forest trails. Talari is located 8km (5 miles) outside of San Isidro, and a staff member picks you up in town for free with advance notice. This lodge is also about 11km (6¾ miles) from San Gerardo de Rivas, so you'll probably have to arrange transportation to and from the park entrance.

Rivas, San Isidro (A.P. 517-8000, Pérez Zeledón). 📞/fax **2771-0341.** www.talari.co.cr. 8 units. $59 (£30) double. Rates include full breakfast and taxes. AE, MC, V. Closed Sept 16–Oct 31. **Amenities:** Restaurant; bar; small pool and separate children's pool; tour desk; laundry service. *In room:* Fridge, no phone.

EN ROUTE TO SAN JOSE: THREE PLACES TO SEE QUETZALS IN THE WILD

Between San Isidro de El General and San José, the Interamerican Highway climbs to its highest point in Costa Rica and crosses over the Cerro de la Muerte. This area is one of the best places in Costa Rica to see quetzals. March, April, and May is nesting season for these birds, and this is usually the best time to see them. However, it's often possible to spot them year-round here. On my first visit here, a 2-hour hike without a guide, my small group spotted eight of these amazing birds. I was hooked.

In addition to the places listed below, **Dantica Cloud Forest Lodge** (© 2740-1067; www.dantica.com) is a small collection of private bungalows in a beautiful forested setting in this region, near the town of San Gerardo de Dota.

Albergue Mirador de Quetzales   This family-run lodge is also known as Finca Eddie Serrano. The rooms in the main lodge are quite basic, with wood floors, bunk beds, and shared bathrooms. Eight separate A-frames provide a bit more comfort and a private bathroom. Meals are served family-style in the main lodge. But quetzals, not comfort, are the main draw here, and if you come between December and May, you should have no trouble spotting plenty of them. There are good hiking trails through the cloud forest, and the Serrano family members are genial hosts and good guides. On a clear day you can see the peaks of five volcanoes from the hotel's lookout—but it's not that clear often.

Carretera Interamericana Sur Km 70 (A.P. 985-7050, Cartago), about 1km (½ mile) down a dirt road from the highway. ©/fax 8381-8456. 11 units. $45 (£23) per person. Rate includes breakfast and dinner, a 2-hr. tour, and taxes. AE, MC, V. **Amenities:** Restaurant; bar. *In room:* No phone.

Savegre Mountain Hotel   This working apple-and-pear farm, which also has more than 240 hectares (593 acres) of primary forest, has acquired a reputation for superb bird-watching—it's one of the best places in the country to see quetzals. The rooms are clean and comfortable, but spartan, but if you're serious about birding, this shouldn't matter. In addition to the quetzals, some 170 other species have been spotted here. Hearty Tico meals are served, and if you want to try your hand at trout fishing, you might luck into a fish dinner. You'll find this lodge 9km (5½ miles) down a dirt road off the Interamerican Highway. This road is steep and often muddy, and four-wheel-drive is recommended, although not necessary.

Carretera Interamericana Sur Km 80, San Gerardo de Dota (A.P. 482, Cartago). © 2740-1028. Fax 2740-1027. www.savegre.co.cr. 41 cabins. $179–$254 (£90–£127) double. Rates include all meals, nonalcoholic drinks, entrance to their reserve, and taxes. Rates slightly lower in the off season. AE, MC, V. **Amenities:** Restaurant; bar; tour desk; laundry service.

Trogon Lodge 🌟 *Finds*   This is the most attractive and comfortable of the lodges in the area. The rooms are rather basic, but the grounds, setting, and amenities are much nicer than at the lodges listed above. The rooms are all of good size, with wood floors, wood walls, a shared veranda, and one double and one twin bed. Room nos. 15 and 16 are my favorites; they are the farthest from the main lodge and have great views of the river. The family-style meals often feature fresh trout from their well-stocked trout ponds; as at Savegre Mountain Hotel, more than half the fun is catching it yourself. These folks also have their own little zip-line canopy tour.

Carretera Interamericana Sur Km 80, San Gerardo de Dota (A.P. 10980-1000, San José). © 2293-8181 in San José, or 2740-1051 at the lodge. Fax 2239-7657. www.grupomawamba.com. 23 units. $78 (£39) double; $138 (£69) junior suite with Jacuzzi. A full meal package runs $35 (£18) per person. AE, MC, V. **Amenities:** Restaurant; bar; tour desk; laundry service; pool table; TV room in lodge. *In room:* No phone.

11

The Southern Zone

Costa Rica's southern zone is an area of rugged beauty, with vast expanses of virgin lowland rainforest and few cities, towns, or settlements. Lushly forested mountains tumble into the sea, streams still run clear and clean, scarlet macaws squawk raucously in the treetops, and dolphins frolic in the **Golfo Dulce.** The **Osa Peninsula** is the most popular attraction in this region and one of the premier ecotourism destinations in the world. It's home to **Corcovado National Park** ★★★, the largest single expanse of lowland tropical rainforest in Central America, and its sister, **Piedras Blancas National Park** ★★. Scattered around the edges of these national parks and along the shores of the Golfo Dulce are some of the country's finest nature lodges. These lodges, in general, offer comfortable to nearly luxurious accommodations, attentive service, knowledgeable guides, and a wide range of activities and tours, all close to the area's many natural wonders.

But this beauty doesn't come easy. You must have plenty of time (or plenty of money—or, preferably, both) and a desire for adventure. It's a long way from San José, and many of the most fascinating spots can be reached only by small plane or boat—although hiking and four-wheeling will get you into some memorable surroundings as well. In many ways, this is Costa Rica's final frontier, and the cities of Golfito and Puerto Jiménez are nearly as wild as the jungles that surround them. Tourism is still underdeveloped here; there are no large resorts in this neck of the woods. Moreover, the heat and humidity are more than many people can stand. So it's best to put some forethought into planning a vacation down here, and it's usually wise to book your rooms and transportation in advance.

1 Drake Bay ★★

145km (90 miles) S of San José; 32km (20 miles) SW of Palmar

While Drake Bay remains one of the most isolated places in Costa Rica, the small town located at the mouth of the **Río Agujitas** has boomed somewhat in recent years. Most of that is due to the year-round operation of the small airstrip here, and the sometimes passable condition of the rough dirt road connecting Drake Bay to the coastal highway—just a few years ago there was no road, and the nearest regularly functioning airstrip was in Palmar Sur. That said, the lodges listed here remain quiet and remote getaways catering to naturalists, anglers, scuba divers, and assorted vacationers. Tucked away on the northern edge of the Osa Peninsula, Drake Bay is a great place to get away from it all.

The bay is named after Sir Francis Drake, who is believed to have anchored here in 1579. Emptying into a broad bay, the tiny Río Agujitas acts as a protected harbor for small boats and is a great place to do a bit of canoeing or swimming. It's here that many of the local lodges dock their boats. Stretching south from Drake Bay are miles

---

Tips Helping Out

If you want to help local efforts in protecting the fragile rainforests and wild areas of the Osa Peninsula, contact the **Corcovado Foundation** (© 2297-3013; www.corcovadofoundation.org) or the **Friends of the Osa** (© 2735-5756; www. osaconservation.org).

Moreover, if you're looking to really lend a hand, both of the aforementioned groups have volunteer programs ranging from trail maintenance to environmental and English-language education to sea-turtle-nesting protection programs.

---

of deserted beaches and dense primary tropical rainforest. Adventurous explorers will find tide pools, spring-fed rivers, waterfalls, forest trails, and some of the best bird-watching in all of Costa Rica. If a paradise such as this appeals to you, Drake Bay makes a good base for exploring the peninsula.

South of Drake Bay lay the wilds of the **Osa Peninsula,** including **Corcovado National Park.** This is one of Costa Rica's most beautiful regions, yet it's also one of its least accessible. Corcovado National Park covers about half of the peninsula and contains the largest single expanse of virgin lowland rainforest in Central America. For this reason, Corcovado is well known among naturalists and researchers studying rainforest ecology. If you come here, you'll learn firsthand why they call them rainforests: Some parts of the peninsula receive more than 250 inches of rain per year.

Puerto Jiménez (see later in this chapter) is the best base to choose if you want to spend a lot of time hiking in and camping inside Corcovado National Park. Drake Bay is primarily a collection of mostly high-end hotels, very isolated and mostly accessible only by boat. Travelers using these hotels can have great day hikes and guided tours into Corcovado Park, but Puerto Jiménez is the place if you want to have more time in the park or to explore independently. (It has a range of budget hotels, the parks office, and "taxi/bus" service to Carate and Los Patos, from which visitors can hike into the various stations.) From the Drake Bay side, you're much more dependent on a boat ride/organized tour from one of the lodges to explore the park; these lodges offer many other guided outings in addition to visits to the park.

ESSENTIALS

Because Drake Bay is so remote, I recommend that you have a room reservation and transportation arrangements (usually arranged with your hotel) before you arrive. Most of the lodges listed here are scattered along several kilometers of coastline, and it is not easy to go from one to another looking for a room.

Tip: A flashlight and rain gear are always useful to have on hand in Costa Rica; they're absolutely essential in Drake Bay.

GETTING THERE   By Plane   Most people fly directly into the little airstrip at Drake Bay, although some tourists still fly to Palmar Sur: All lodges will either arrange transportation for you, or include it in their packages. **Sansa** (© 877/767-2672 in the U.S. and Canada, or 2290-4100 in Costa Rica; www.flysansa.com) flies directly to Drake Bay daily at 6 and 10:53am and 12:18, 1:10, and 2:31pm from San José's Juan Santamaría International Airport. The return flights leave Drake Bay at 7 and

Tapantí National Park

To San José

Cerro de la Muerte

CHIRRIPÓ INDIAN RESERVATION

TALAMANCA INDIAN RESERVATION

BRIBRI INDIAN RESERVATION

Cerro Chirripó

TALAMANCA RANGE (CORDILLERA DE TALAMANCA)

LA AMISTAD INTERNATIONAL PARK

San Isidro de El General

PANAMA

Peñas Blancas

Interamerican Hwy.

SALITRE INDIAN RESERVATION

Cerro Kámuk

Dominical

To Quepos & Manuel Antonio

Río Pacuare

Buenos Aires

El Brujo

Punta Uvita

Playa Ballena

BALLENA MARINE NATIONAL PARK

Playa Piñuela

Ojochal

Ciudad Cortes

Palmar Norte

Boca Brava

Palmar Sur Airport

CURRÉ INDIAN RESERVATION

Coronado Bay

Río Sierpe Sierpe

Sierpe

Sabanilla

Sabalito

Piedras Blancas

San Vito

Wilson Botanical Garden

Caño Island

Drake Bay

Río Chocuaco

PIEDRAS BLANCAS NATIONAL PARK

Golfito Airport

Río Claro

Caño Island Biological Reserve

Chocuaco Lake

Rincón

La Palma

Playa Cativa

Golfito

To Panama

Ciudad Neily

San Pedrillo

Corcovado Lake

OSA INDIAN RESERVATION

Los Patos Ranger Station

OSA PENINSULA

El Tigre

Playa Zancudo

Zancudo

Río Colorado

Lake Colorado

CORCOVADO NATIONAL PARK

Puerto Jiménez

Playa Tamale

Playa Pavones

Pavones

Playa Sirena

La Leona Ranger Station

Carate

Cabo Matapalo

Punta Banco

PANAMA

PACIFIC OCEAN

NICARAGUA

Caribbean Sea

COSTA RICA

San José

N

PACIFIC OCEAN

PANAMA

Area of detail

0   100 mi

0   100 km

Airport ✈

Ferry

Mountain ▲

Ranger Station

0   50 mi

0   50 km

Punta Burica

N

11:30am and 2 and 2:30pm. The flight takes 50 minutes; the fare is $104 (£52) each way. Flights also departs San José daily at 9 and 9:30am for Palmar Sur; the fare is $94 (£47) each way.

Sansa also now has twice-daily flights between Drake Bay and Puerto Jiménez. This 25-minute flight leaves Drake Bay at 7 and 11:55am. The return flights leave Puerto Jiménez at 1:28 and 3:42pm. The one-way fare is $40 (£20).

Nature Air (© **800/235-9272** in the U.S. and Canada, or 2299-6000; www. natureair.com) has one direct flight to Drake Bay departing daily from Tobías Bolaños International Airport in Pavas at 8:15am. Flight duration is 40 minutes; the fare is $111 (£56) each way. Return flights leave Drake Bay at 9:05am and 3:50pm. The latter return flight is actually to Golfito, but it makes an onward connection to San José. It also has a daily flight to Palmar Sur that departs at 9am and sometimes stops at Quepos en route. The flight takes a little over an hour, and the fare is $99 (£50) each way.

If your travels take you to Drake Bay via Palmar Sur, you must then take a 15-minute bus or taxi ride over dirt roads to the small town of **Sierpe.** This bumpy route runs through several banana plantations and quickly past some important archaeological sites. In Sierpe you board a small boat for a 40km (25-mile) ride to Drake Bay; see "By Taxi & Boat from Sierpe," below. The first half of this trip snakes through a maze of mangrove canals and rivers before heading out to sea for the final leg to the bay. *Warning:* Entering and exiting the Sierpe River mouth is often treacherous; I've had several very white-knuckle moments here.

By Bus   Tracopa-Alfaro express buses (© **2221-4214** or 2223-7685) leave San José daily for Palmar Norte at 5, 7, 8:30, and 10am, and 1, 2:30, and 6pm from Calle 5 between avenidas 18 and 20. Bus trips take 6 hours; the fare is $8 (£4).

You can also catch any Golfito-bound bus from this same station and get off in Palmar Norte. Once in Palmar Norte, ask when the next bus goes out to Sierpe. If it doesn't leave for a while (buses aren't frequent), consider taking a taxi (see below).

By Taxi & Boat from Sierpe   When you arrive at either the Palmar Norte bus station or the Palmar Sur airstrip, you'll most likely first need to take a taxi to the village of Sierpe. The fare should be around $15 (£7.50). If you're booked into one of the main lodges, chances are your transportation is already included. Even if you're not booked into one of the lodges, a host of taxi and minibus drivers offer the trip. When you get to Sierpe, head to the dock and try to find space on a boat. This should run you another $15 to $30 (£7.50–£15). If you don't arrive early enough, you might have to hire an entire boat, which usually runs around $80 to $140 (£40–£70) for a boat that can carry up to six passengers. Make sure that you feel confident about the boat and skipper, and, if possible, try to find a spot on a boat from one of the established lodges in Drake Bay.

By Car   I don't recommend driving to Drake Bay. But if you insist, take the Interamerican Highway east out of San José (through San Pedro and Cartago) and continue south on this road. In about 3 hours you'll reach San Isidro de El General. Although you can continue on the Interamerican Highway all the way south, it is faster, smoother, and safer to turn off in San Isidro and head to Dominical, picking up the Southern Highway or Costanera Sur in Dominical. From here it's a fast and smooth shot down Palmar Norte, where you'll meet up again with the Interamerican Highway. South of Palmar take the turnoff for La Palma and Puerto Jiménez (at the town of Chacarita; it's clearly marked). Then at Rincón, turn onto the rough road

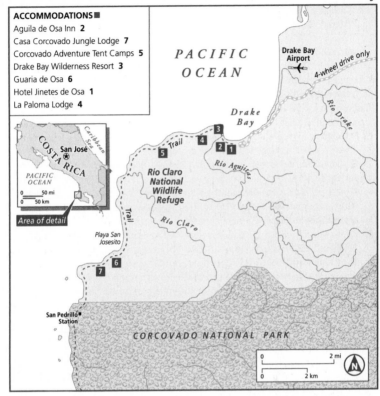

ACCOMMODATIONS ■
Aguila de Osa Inn **2**
Casa Corcovado Jungle Lodge **7**
Corcovado Adventure Tent Camps **5**
Drake Bay Wilderness Resort **3**
Guaria de Osa **6**
Hotel Jinetes de Osa **1**
La Paloma Lodge **4**

leading into Drake Bay. This road fords some 10 rivers and is often not passable during the rainy season. Moreover, it only reaches into the small heart of the village of Drake Bay, though almost all of the hotels I've listed below are farther out along the peninsula, where only boats reach. In fact, the only hotels that you can actually drive up to are very basic cabins in town. For the rest, you'd have to find someplace secure to leave your car and either haul your bags quite a way or get picked up in a boat.

DEPARTING   If you're not flying directly out of Drake Bay, have your lodge arrange a boat trip back to Sierpe for you. Be sure that the lodge also arranges for a taxi to meet you in Sierpe for the trip to Palmar Sur or Palmar Norte. (If you're on a budget, you can ask around to see whether a late-morning public bus is still running from Sierpe to Palmar Norte.) In the two Palmars you can make onward plane and bus connections. At the Palmar Norte bus terminal, almost any bus heading north will take you to San José, and almost any bus heading south will take you to Golfito.

WHAT TO SEE & DO
Beaches, forests, wildlife, and solitude are the main attractions of Drake Bay. Although Corcovado National Park (see "Puerto Jiménez: Gateway to Corcovado National Park," below) is the area's star attraction, there's plenty to soak up in and around Drake Bay. The Osa Peninsula is home to an unbelievable variety of plants and animals: more

Those Mysterious Stone Spheres

Although Costa Rica lacks the great cities, giant temples, and bas-relief carvings of the Maya, Aztec, and Olmec civilizations of northern Mesoamerica, its pre-Columbian residents did leave a unique legacy that continues to cause archaeologists and anthropologists to scratch their heads and wonder. Over a period of several centuries, hundreds of painstakingly carved and carefully positioned granite spheres were left by the peoples who lived throughout the Diquis Delta, which flanks the Terraba River in southern Costa Rica. The orbs, which range from grapefruit size to more than 2m (6½ ft.) in diameter, can weigh up to 15 tons, and many reach near-spherical perfection.

Archaeologists believe that the spheres were created during two defined cultural periods. The first, called the Aguas Buenas period, dates from around A.D. 100 to 500. Few spheres survive from this time. The second phase, during which spheres were created in apparently greater numbers, is called the Chiriquí period and lasted from approximately A.D. 800 to 1500. The "balls" believed to have been carved during this time frame are widely dispersed along the entire length of the lower section of the Terraba River. To date, only one known quarry for the spheres has been discovered, in the mountains above the Diquis Delta, which points to a difficult and lengthy transportation process.

Some archaeologists believe that the spheres were hand-carved in a very time-consuming process, using stone tools, perhaps aided by some sort of firing process. However, another theory holds that granite blocks were placed at the bases of powerful waterfalls, and the hydraulic beating of the water eventually turned and carved the rock into these near-perfect spheres. And more than a few proponents have credited extraterrestrial intervention for the creation of the stone balls.

Most of the stone balls have been found at the archaeological remains of defined settlements and are associated with either central plazas or known burial sites. Their size and placement have been interpreted to have both social and celestial importance, although their exact significance remains a mystery. Unfortunately, many of the stone balls have been plundered and are currently used as lawn ornaments in the fancier neighborhoods of San José. Some have even been shipped out of the country. The **Museo Nacional de Costa Rica** (p. 130) has a nice collection, including one massive sphere in its center courtyard. It's a never-fail photo op. You can also see the stone balls near the small **airports in Palmar Sur** and **Drake Bay,** and on **Isla del Caño** (which is 19km/12 miles off the Pacific coast near Drake Bay).

than 140 species of mammals, 385 species of birds, and 130 species of amphibians and reptiles. You aren't likely to see anywhere near all of these animals, but you can expect to see quite a few, including several types of monkeys, coatimundis, scarlet macaws, parrots, and hummingbirds. Other park inhabitants include jaguars, tapirs, sloths, and crocodiles. If you're lucky, you might even see one of the region's namesake *osas,* or giant anteaters.

Around Drake Bay and within the national park are many miles of trails through rainforests and swamps, down beaches, and around rock headlands. All of the lodges listed below offer guided excursions into the park. It's also possible to begin a hike around the peninsula from Drake Bay.

One of the most popular excursions from Drake Bay is a trip out to **Isla del Caño** and the **Caño Island Biological Reserve** for a bit of exploring and snorkeling or scuba diving. The island is about 19km (12 miles) offshore from Drake Bay and was once home to a pre-Columbian culture about which little is known. A trip to the island will include a visit to an ancient cemetery, and you'll also be able to see some of the stone spheres believed to have been carved by this area's ancient inhabitants (see the above box, "Those Mysterious Stone Spheres"). Few animals or birds live on the island, but the coral reefs just offshore teem with life and are the main reason most people come here. This is one of Costa Rica's prime **scuba spots**. Visibility is often quite good, and there's even easily accessible snorkeling from the beach. All of the lodges listed below offer trips to Isla del Caño.

All lodges in the area also offer a host of half- and full-day tours and activities, including hikes in Corcovado National Park, horseback rides, and sportfishing. In some cases, tours are included in your room rate or package; in others, they must be bought a la carte. Other options include mountain biking and sea kayaking. Most of these tours run between $60 and $120 (£30–£60), depending on the activity, with scuba diving ($90–$135/£45–£68 for a two-tank dive) and sportfishing ($450–$1,400/ £225–£700, depending on the size of the boat and other amenities) costing a bit more.

One of the most interesting tour options in Drake Bay is a 2-hour **night tour** (© **8382-1619;** www.thenighttour.com; $35/£18 per person) offered by Tracie Stice, who is affectionately known as the "Bug Lady." Equipped with flashlights, participants get a bug's-eye view of the forest at night. You might see reflections of some larger forest dwellers, but most of the tour is a fascinating exploration of the nocturnal insect and arachnid world. Consider yourself lucky if she finds the burrow of a trap-door spider or large tarantula. Avoid this tour if you are helplessly arachnophobic. Also, the folks from the **Original Canopy Tour** (© **2291-4465;** www.canopy tour.com) have set up an operation in Drake Bay in the forest behind the Hotel Jinetes de Osa. The 2½-hour tour costs $55 (£28) per person. Any hotel in the area can book either of the above tours for you.

WHERE TO STAY & DINE

Given the remote location and logistics of reaching Drake Bay, as well as the individual isolation of each hotel, nearly all of the hotels listed below deal almost exclusively

---

Tips **Combing for Beaches**

While the beach at Drake Bay itself is acceptable and calm for swimming, it's far from spectacular. The most popular swimming beach is a pretty small patch of sand, known locally as Cocalito beach, about a 7-minute hike down from La Paloma Lodge. The nicest beaches around involve taking a day trip to either Isla del Caño or San Josesito. The latter is a stunning beach farther south on the peninsula with excellent snorkeling possibilities.

in package trips that include transportation, meals, tours, and taxes. I've listed the most common packages, although all the lodges will work with you to accommodate longer or shorter stays. Nightly room rates are listed only where they're available and practical, generally at the more moderately priced hotels.

In addition to the places listed below, **Guaria de Osa** ✆ (© **510/235-4313** in the U.S., or 8358-9788 in Costa Rica; www.guariadeosa.com) is a beautiful lodge near the Río Claro that specializes in yoga, spiritual, and educational retreats.

In addition to the hotels listed below, you could try **Corcovado Adventure Tent Camps** (© **831/345-8484** in the U.S., or 8384-1679 in Costa Rica; www.corcovado. com). A semi-permanent tent, with three-squares per day and use of the facilities and watersports equipment, will run you around $70 (£35) per person, per day. Shared bathrooms are clean and the setting is beautiful, but meals and accommodations are a bit basic for the price.

VERY EXPENSIVE

Aguila de Osa Inn ✆   This luxurious hillside lodge is a great choice for serious sportfishers and scuba divers. Situated high on a hill overlooking Drake Bay and the Pacific Ocean, the Aguila de Osa Inn offers large, attractively decorated rooms, with hardwood or tile floors, ceiling fans, large bathrooms, and excellent views. Varnished wood and bamboo abound. A bar is built atop some rocks on the bank of the Río Agujitas, and the open-air dining room is set amid lush foliage with a partial view of the bay through the leaves, close to river level. Meals are excellent and filling, and the kitchen leaves a fresh Thermos of coffee outside each room every morning. Service, upkeep, and attention are top-notch here. The biggest drawback, however, is the lack of a swimming pool, which most of the other high-end places here have.

Drake Bay (mailing address: Interlink 898, P.O. Box 025635, Miami, FL 33102). © **866/924-8452** in the U.S., or 2296-2190 in Costa Rica. Fax 2232-7722. www.aguiladeosainn.com. 13 units. $541–$581 (£271–£291) for 3 days/2 nights; $769–$870 (£385–£435) for 4 days/3 nights. Rates are per person based on double occupancy and include round-trip transportation from Palmar Sur, all meals, and taxes. Lower rates in off season. AE, MC, V. **Amenities:** Restaurant; bar; fleet of sportfishing and dive vessels; laundry service. *In room:* No phone.

Casa Corcovado Jungle Lodge ✆   This very isolated jungle resort is the closest lodge to Corcovado National Park on this end of the Osa Peninsula. The rooms are all private bungalows built on the grounds of an old cacao plantation on the jungle's edge. The bungalows are very spacious, with one or two double beds (each with mosquito netting) and a large tiled bathroom. Family-style meals are served in the main lodge, although most guests take lunch with them to the beach or on one of the various tours available. Late afternoons are usually enjoyed from a high point overlooking the sea and sunset, with your beverage of choice in hand. Access is strictly by small boat, and sometimes the beach landing can be a bit rough and wet. When the sea is calm, the beach is great for swimming; when it is rough, it's a great place to grab a hammock in the shade and read a book. The lodge has two pretty swimming pools, both surrounded by thick rainforest, and a wide range of tours and activities is available.

Osa Peninsula (mailing address: Interlink 253, P.O. Box 526770, Miami, FL 33152). © **888/896-6097** in the U.S., or 2256-3181 in Costa Rica. Fax 2256-7409. www.casacorcovado.com. 14 units. $810–$840 (£405–£420) per person for 3 days/2 nights with 1 tour; $970–$1,000 (£485–£500) for 4 days/3 nights with 2 tours. Rates are based on double occupancy and include round-trip transportation from San José, all meals, park fees, and taxes. Rates higher during peak weeks; lower in off season. AE, MC, V. **Amenities:** Restaurant; 2 bars; 2 outdoor pools; laundry service. *In room:* Stocked minibar, safe, no phone.

La Paloma Lodge ★★★ *(Finds)* On a steep hill overlooking the Pacific, with Isla del Caño in the distance, the luxurious individual bungalows at La Paloma offer expansive ocean views that, combined with the attentive service, make this my top choice in Drake Bay. All of the bungalows feature private verandas, and are set among lush foliage facing the Pacific. The large two-story Sunset Ranchos are the choice rooms here, with fabulous panoramic views. The other cabins are a tad smaller, but all are plenty spacious and beautifully appointed, and feature luxurious bathrooms and pretty good ocean views as well. Standard rooms, located in one long building, are smaller and less private than the cabins, but they're still attractive and have good views from their hammock-equipped balcony. The beach is about a 7-minute hike down a winding jungle path, and the lodge also offers scuba certification courses along with free water equipment like surfboards. Hearty and delicious meals are served family-style in the restaurant.

Drake Bay (mailing address: A.P. 97-4005, San Antonio de Belén). © **2293-7502** or ©/fax 2239-0954. www.lapaloma lodge.com. 11 units. $1,100–$1,400 (£550–£700) per person for 4 days/3 nights with 2 tours; $1,245–$1,620 (£623–£810) per person for 5 days/4 nights with 2 tours. Rates are based on double occupancy and include round-trip transportation from San José, all meals, park fees, indicated tours, and taxes. Rates slightly lower in off season. AE, MC, V. **Amenities:** Restaurant; bar; small tile pool w/spectacular view; free Wi-Fi around the main lodge; laundry service. *In room:* Minibar, safe, no phone.

EXPENSIVE
Drake Bay Wilderness Resort ★ This is one of the best-located lodges at Drake Bay. It backs onto the Río Agujitas and fronts the Pacific. The rooms here are less fancy than those at the resort lodges listed above, but they are clean and comfortable, with ceiling fans, small verandas, good mattresses on the beds, and private bathrooms. The best room is a pretty, deluxe honeymoon suite on a little hill toward the rear of the property, with a great view of the bay. There are also five budget cabins that share bathroom and shower facilities.

Because it's on a rocky spit, there isn't a good swimming beach on-site, but there's a saltwater pool in front of the bay, and, depending on the tide, you can bathe in a beautiful small tide pool formed by the rocks. The resort offers a wide range of tour options, and runs a small butterfly farm and iguana-breeding project on some land inland from Drake Bay, where you can even spend the night. The restaurant's family-style meals are filling, with an emphasis on fresh seafood and fresh fruits.

Drake Bay (A.P. 13710-1000, San José). © **561/762-1763** in the U.S., or ©/fax 2770-8012 in Costa Rica. www.drakebay.com. 25 units. $90 (£45) per person per day with shared bathroom; $130–$160 (£65–£80) per person per day standard and deluxe. Rates include all meals and taxes. $695 (£348) per person for 4 days/3 nights with 2 tours, including all meals and taxes. Rates lower in off season. AE, MC, V. **Amenities:** Restaurant; bar; small saltwater pool; free use of canoes and kayaks; free same-day laundry service. *In room:* Free Wi-Fi, hair dryer, no phone.

MODERATE
Hotel Jinetes de Osa *(Value)* This is a good option right in the village of Drake Bay, and a popular choice for serious divers and adventure tourists. Although no longer a budget lodging, it does offer a reasonable alternative to the more upscale options in the area. The best rooms here are spacious and well-appointed, and even have a view of the bay. The hotel is pretty close to the docks on the Río Agujitas, which is a plus for those traveling independently or with heavy bags. A wide range of tours and activities are available, as are dive packages, weekly packages, and PADI certification courses. For true budget travelers, camping is allowed just behind the main lodge.

Drake Bay (mailing address: 831 S. Newcombe Way, Lakewood, CO 80226). (©) **866/553-7073** in the U.S. and Canada, or (©)/fax 2231-5806 in Costa Rica. www.drakebayhotel.com. 9 units, 7 with private bathroom. $120–$160 (£60–£80) double. Rates include 3 meals daily. MC, V. **Amenities:** Restaurant; bar. *In room:* Free Wi-Fi, no phone.

2 Puerto Jiménez ⟨★⟩: Gateway to Corcovado National Park

35km (22 miles) W of Golfito by water (90km/56 miles by road); 85km (53 miles) S of Palmar Norte

Don't let its small size and languid pace fool you. Puerto Jiménez is actually a bustling little burg, where rough jungle gold-panners mix with wealthy ecotourists, budget backpackers, serious surfers, and a smattering of celebrities seeking a small dose of anonymity and escape. Located on the southeastern tip of the Osa Peninsula, the town itself is just a couple of streets wide in any direction, with a ubiquitous soccer field, a handful of general stores, some inexpensive *sodas* (diners), and several bars. Scarlet macaws fly overhead, and mealy parrots provide wake-up calls.

Corcovado National Park has its headquarters here, and this town makes an excellent base for exploring this vast wilderness area. Signs in English on walls around town advertise a variety of tours, including a host of activities outside of the park. If the in-town accommodations are too budget-oriented, you'll find several far more luxurious places farther south on the Osa Peninsula. This is also a prime surf spot. **Cabo Matapalo** (the southern tip of the Osa Peninsula) is home to several very dependable right point breaks. When it's working, the waves at Pan Dulce and Backwash actually connect, and can provide rides almost as long and tiring as those to be had in more famous Pavones (see "Playa Pavones: A Surfer's Mecca," later in this chapter).

ESSENTIALS

GETTING THERE & DEPARTING By Plane Sansa ((©) **877/767-2672** in the U.S. and Canada, or 2290-4100 in Costa Rica; www.flysansa.com) has flights to Puerto Jiménez daily at 6 and 10:53am and 12:18, 1:10, and 2:31pm from San José's Juan Santamaría International Airport. The flight takes 55 minutes; the cost is $102 (£51) each way. Sansa flights depart Puerto Jiménez for San José daily at 7:34am and 12:27, 1:28, and 3:41pm.

Sansa also now has twice-daily flights between Puerto Jiménez and Drake Bay. This 25-minute flight leaves Puerto Jiménez at 1:28 and 3:42pm. Flights to Puerto Jiménez leave Drake Bay at 7 and 11:55am. The one-way fare is $40 (£20).

Nature Air ((©) **800/235-9272** in the U.S. and Canada, or 2299-6000; www.natureair.com) has flights to Puerto Jiménez departing from Tobías Bolaños International Airport in Pavas at 6:10, 8:30, and 10:50am and 3:40pm daily. The flight takes 50 minutes; the fare is $111 (£56) each way. Nature Air flights to San José depart daily at 7:15, 9:30, and 11:50am and 4:40pm.

Note that due to the remoteness of this area and the unpredictable flux of traffic, both Sansa and Nature Air frequently improvise on scheduling. Sometimes this means an unscheduled stop in Quepos or Golfito either on the way to or from San José, which can add some time to your flight. Less frequently it might mean a change in departure time, so it's always best to confirm. Also, lodges down here sometimes run charters, so it pays to ask them as well.

Taxis are generally waiting to meet all incoming flights. A ride into downtown Puerto Jimenez should cost around $3 (£1.50). If you're staying at a hotel outside of downtown, it's best to have them arrange for a taxi to meet you. Otherwise you can hire one at the airstrip. Depending upon how far out on the peninsula you are staying, it

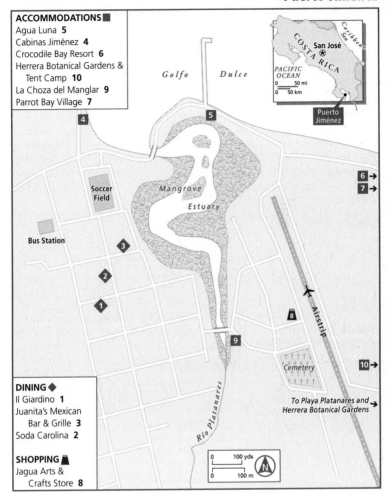

Puerto Jimenez

ACCOMMODATIONS ■
Agua Luna **5**
Cabinas Jiménez **4**
Crocodile Bay Resort **6**
Herrera Botanical Gardens &
 Tent Camp **10**
La Choza del Manglar **9**
Parrot Bay Village **7**

Golfo   Dulce

COSTA RICA

San José ✸

PACIFIC
OCEAN

Caribbean Sea

0   50 mi
0   50 km

Puerto
Jiménez

Soccer
Field

Mangrove
Estuary

Bus Station

Airstrip

Cemetery

Rio Platanares

To Playa Platanares and →
Herrera Botanical Gardens

0   100 yds
0   100 m

N

DINING ◆
Il Giardino **1**
Juanita's Mexican
 Bar & Grille **3**
Soda Carolina **2**

SHOPPING 🛍
Jagua Arts &
 Crafts Store **8**

could cost up to $80 (£40) for a rugged four-wheel-drive vehicle that can carry up to four people.

By Car Take the Interamerican Highway east out of San José (through San Pedro and Cartago) and continue south on this road. In about 3 hours, you'll reach San Isidro de El General. Although you can continue on the Interamerican Highway all the way south, it is currently faster, smoother, and safer to turn off in San Isidro and head to Dominical, picking up the Southern Highway or Costanera Sur in Dominical. From here it's a fast and smooth shot down Palmar Norte, where you'll meet up again with the Interamerican Highway. Take the turnoff for La Palma, Rincón, and Puerto Jiménez. This road is paved at first, but at Rincón it turns to gravel. The last 35km (22 miles) are slow and rough, and, if it's the rainy season (mid-Apr to Nov), it'll be too muddy for anything but a four-wheel-drive vehicle.

By Bus   A **Transportes Blanco-Lobo** express bus ((C) **2257-4121** in San José or 2771-4744 in Puerto Jiménez) leaves San José daily at noon from Calle 12 between avenidas 7 and 9. The trip takes 8 hours; the fare is $7 (£3.50). Buses depart Puerto Jiménez for San José daily at 5am.

By Boat   There are now fast speedboats working as boat taxis between Puerto Jiménez and Golfito. The fare is $5 (£2.50), and the ride takes a little under 30 minutes. These boats leave five or six times throughout the day, beginning at around 5am and finishing up at around 5pm. Ask around town, or at the docks for current schedules.

There is also a daily passenger launch. This slower boat takes 1½ hours; and the fare is $3 (£1.50). The ferry leaves the public dock in Golfito at 6am for Puerto Jiménez. The return trip to Golfito leaves Puerto Jiménez's municipal dock at 11:30am. It's possible to charter a water taxi in Golfito for the trip across to Puerto Jiménez, as well. You'll have to pay between $40 and $80 (£20–£40) for an entire launch, some of which can carry up to 12 people.

ORIENTATION   Puerto Jiménez is a dirt-lane town on the southern coast of the Osa Peninsula. The public dock is over a bridge past the north end of the soccer field; the bus stop is 2 blocks east of the center of town. You'll find a couple of Internet cafes in town; the best of these is **Cafe Net El Sol** ((C) **2735-5719;** www.soldeosa.com), which is a great place to book tours and get information, and is also a Wi-Fi hotspot.

Four-wheel-drive taxis are actually fairly plentiful in Puerto Jiménez. You can usually find them cruising or parked along the main street in town. Alternatively, you can call **Andy** ((C) **8819-8210**), **Luis** ((C) **8837-3120**), **Marvin** ((C) **8345-3123**), or **Orlando** ((C) **8836-8241**). You can even rent a car down here from **Solid Car Rental** ((C) **2735-5777;** www.solidcarrental.com).

EXPLORING CORCOVADO NATIONAL PARK ★★★

Exploring Corcovado National Park is not something to be undertaken lightly, but neither is it the expedition that some people make it out to be. The weather is the biggest obstacle to overnight backpacking trips through the park. Within a couple of hours of Puerto Jiménez (by 4WD vehicle) are several entrances to the park; however, there are no roads in the park, so once you reach any of the entrances, you'll have to start hiking. The heat and humidity are often quite extreme, and frequent rainstorms can make trails fairly muddy. If you choose the alternative—hiking on the beach— you'll have to plan your hiking around the tides when often there is no beach at all and some rivers are impassable.

Because of its size and remoteness, Corcovado National Park is best explored over several days; however, it is possible to enter and hike a bit of it for day trips. The best way to do this is to book a tour with your lodge on the Osa Peninsula, from a tour company in Puerto Jiménez, or through a lodge in Drake Bay (see "Where to Stay & Dine," above).

GETTING THERE & ENTRY POINTS   The park has four primary entrances, which are really just ranger stations reached by rough dirt roads. When you've reached them, you'll have to strap on a backpack and hike. Perhaps the easiest one to reach from Puerto Jiménez is **La Leona ranger station,** accessible by car, bus, or taxi.

If you choose to drive, take the dirt road from Puerto Jiménez to Carate (Carate is at the end of the road). From Carate, it's a 3km (1¾-mile) hike to La Leona. To travel there by "public transportation," pick up one of the collective buses (actually, a 4WD pickup truck with a tarpaulin cover and slat seats in the back) that leave Puerto

---

Tips **Trail Distances in Corcovado National Park**

It's 14km (8.5 miles) from La Leona to Sirena. From Sirena to San Pedrillo, it's 23km (14 miles) along the beach. From San Pedrillo, it's 20km (13 miles) to Drake Bay. It's 19km (12 miles) between Sirena and Los Patos.

Jiménez for Carate daily at 6am and 1:30pm, returning at 9am and 4pm. Remember, these "buses" are very informal and change their schedules regularly to meet demand or avoid bad weather, so always ask in town. The one-way fare is around $8 (£4). A small fleet of these pickups leaves just south of the new bus terminal, and will stop to pick up anyone who flags them down along the way. Your other option is to hire a taxi to suit your schedule, which will charge approximately $70 to $80 (£35–£40) each way to or from Carate.

En route to Carate, you will pass several campgrounds and small lodges as you approach the park. If you are unable to get a spot at one of the campsites in the park, you can stay at one of these and hike the park during the day.

You can also travel to **El Tigre,** about 14km (8¾ miles) by dirt road from Puerto Jiménez, where there's another ranger station. But note that trails from El Tigre go only a short distance into the park.

The third entrance is in **Los Patos,** which is reached from the town of La Palma, northwest of Puerto Jiménez. From here, there's a 19km (12-mile) trail through the center of the park to **Sirena,** a ranger station and research facility (see "Beach Treks & Rainforest Hikes," below). Sirena has a landing strip that is used by charter flights.

The northern entrance to the park is **San Pedrillo,** which you can reach by hiking from Sirena or by taking a boat from Drake Bay or Sierpe (see "Beach Treks & Rainforest Hikes," below). It's 14km (8¾ miles) from Drake Bay.

If you're not into hiking in the heat, you can charter a plane in Puerto Jiménez to take you to Carate or Sirena. A five-passenger plane should cost around $200 to $400 (£100–£200) one-way, depending on your destination. Contact **Alfa Romeo Air Charters** (© 2735-5353 or 2735-5112; www.alfaromeoair.com) for details.

FEES & REGULATIONS   Park admission is $10 (£5) per person per day. Only the Sirena station is equipped with dormitory-style lodgings and a simple *soda,* but the others have basic campsites and toilet facilities. All must be reserved in advance by contacting the **ACOSA** (Area de Conservacion de Osa) in Puerto Jiménez (© 2735-5036; fax 2735-5276; pncorcovado@hotmail.com) For a good overview of the park and logistics, check out **www.corcovado.org**. Its offices are adjacent to the airstrip. Only a limited number of people are allowed to camp at each ranger station, so make your reservations well in advance.

BEACH TREKS & RAINFOREST HIKES   The park has quite a few good hiking trails. Two of the better-known ones are the beach routes, starting at either the La Leona or San Pedrillo ranger stations. None of the hikes is easy, but the forest route from the Los Patos ranger station to Sirena, although long, is less taxing than either of the beach treks, which can be completed only when the tide is low. The route between the Los Patos/Sirena hike is 19km (12 miles) through beautiful rainforest.

Sirena is a fascinating destination. As a research facility and ranger station, it's frequented primarily by scientists studying the rainforest. One of the longest hikes, from San Pedrillo to Sirena, can be done only during the dry season. Between any two

---

Tips **Important Corcovado Tips**

If you plan to hike the beach trails from La Leona or San Pedrillo, be sure to pick up a tide table at the park headquarters' office in Puerto Jiménez. The tide changes rapidly; when it's high, the trails and river crossings can be dangerous or impassable.

If you plan to spend a night or more in the park, you'll want to stock up on food, water, and other essentials while you're in Puerto Jiménez. There's a minimarket in Carate, but the selection is limited. Although most of the stations have simple *sodas,* you need to reserve in advance if you plan to take your meals at any of these.

---

stations, the hiking is arduous and takes all day, so it's best to rest for a day or so between hikes if possible.

Remember, this is quite a wild area. Never hike alone, and take all the standard precautions for hiking in the rainforest. In addition, be especially careful about swimming in any isolated rivers or river mouths because most rivers in Corcovado are home to crocodiles.

WHERE TO STAY & DINE IN THE PARK: CAMPSITES, CABINS & CANTINAS Reservations are essential at the various ranger stations if you plan to eat or sleep inside the park (see "Fees & Regulations," above). **Sirena** has a modern research facility with dormitory-style accommodations for 28 persons, as well as a campground, *soda,* and landing strip for charter flights. There is also camping at the **La Leona, Los Patos,** and **San Pedrillo** ranger stations. Every ranger station has potable water, but it's advisable to pack in your own; whatever you do, don't drink stream water. Campsites in the park are $4 (£2) per person per night. A dorm bed at the Sirena station will run you $12 (£6)—you must bring your own sheets, and a mosquito net is highly recommended—and meals here are another $35 (£18) per day. Everything must be reserved in advance.

ACTIVITIES OUTSIDE THE PARK

While Puerto Jiménez has typically been a staging ground for adventures much farther out toward Carate and the park, quite a few activities and tours can be undertaken closer to town.

If you're looking to spend some time on the beach, head just east of town for a long pretty stretch of sand called **Playa Plantanares.** The waves are generally fairly gentle, and quite a few hotels have begun to pop up here. If you head farther out the peninsula, you'll come to the beaches of **Pan Dulce, Backwash,** and **Matapalo,** all major surf spots with consistently well-formed right point breaks. When the waves aren't too big, these are excellent places to learn how to surf.

Kayaking trips around the estuary and up into the mangroves and out into the gulf are popular. Contact **Escondido Trex** ⊕ (© **2735-5210;** www.escondidotrex.com), which has an office in the Soda Carolina (see "Where to Dine in Puerto Jiménez," below). There are daily paddles through the mangroves, as well as sunset trips where you can sometimes see dolphins. These folks also do guided rainforest hikes and can have you rappelling down the face of a jungle waterfall. More adventurous multiday kayak and camping trips are also available, in price and comfort ranges from budget to luxury (staying at various lodges around the Golfo Dulce and Matapalo). They'll even take you gold-panning (although there are no guarantees that your panning will pay for the trip).

If you're in Puerto Jiménez, be sure to check out the **Herrera Botanical Gardens** (© 2735-5210). These gardens are just outside of town, and the entrance is across from Crocodile Bay. The whole project encompasses over 260 acres of botanical gardens, working permaculture gardens, and secondary forest. There are even a few platforms built high in the trees here and reached by climbing a ladder. A 2½-hour guided tour of the gardens costs $15 (£7.50), although you can wander the gardens yourself, with a self-guiding map, for just $4 (£2).

For a real adventure, check in with **Psycho Tours** (© 8353-8619; www.psychotours.com). These folks, who also call themselves Everyday Adventures, run a variety of adventure tours, but their signature combo trip features a free climb up (with a safety rope attached) the roots and trunks of a 200-foot-tall strangler fig. You can climb as high as your ability allows, but most try to reach a natural platform at around 18m (60 ft.), where you take a leap of faith into space and be belayed down by your guide. This is preceded by an informative hike through primary rainforest, often wading through a small river, and followed by a couple of rappels down jungle waterfalls, the highest of which is around 30m (100 ft.). You can do either one of the above adventures separately, but I recommend the 5- to 6-hour combo tour, which costs $110 (£55).

If you're interested in doing some **bill-fishing** or **deep-sea fishing,** you'll probably want to stay at or fish with **Crocodile Bay Lodge** (© 800/733-1115 in the U.S. and Canada, or 2735-5631 in Costa Rica; www.crocodilebay.com). This upscale fishing lodge is close to the Puerto Jiménez airstrip. Alternatively, call Mike Hennessy at **Cabo Matapalo Sportfishing** (© 8382-7796; www.cabo-matapalo.com). Mike is a long-time resident and one of the best captains around. You can also check around the public dock for notices put up by people with charter boats. Rates can run between $400 and $2,400 (£200–£1,200) for a full day, or between $100 and $900 (£50–£450) for a half-day, depending on the boat, tackle, number of anglers, and fishing grounds.

If you want to learn to surf, contact **Mike's Surf School** (© 8382-7796), which is also run by Mike Hennessy, and located near some excellent learning waves on Pan Dulce beach.

To explore the rugged roads, trails, and beaches of this area by ATV or mountain bike, contact **Osa Discoveries** (© 2735-5260; www.osadiscoveries.com). **Osa Aventura** (©/fax 2735-5758 or 8830-9832; www.osaaventura.com), **Sol de Osa** (© 2735-5702; www.soldeosa.com), and **Tom Kayak's Osa Info** (© 8838-2314) are other local tour companies that offer a host of guided tours around the Osa Peninsula and into Corcovado National Park. Rates run between $35 and $120 (£18–£60) depending upon group size and the tour or activity chosen.

SHOPPING

Jagua Arts & Craft Store (© 2735-5267) is near the airstrip, and is definitely worth a visit. Owner Karen Herrera has found excellent local and regional art and craft works, including some excellent jewelry and blown glass. *Tip:* Many folks head to this store while waiting for their departing flight out of Puerto Jiménez. Be sure to give yourself enough time, as the store has a somewhat extensive collection.

WHERE TO STAY IN PUERTO JIMENEZ
VERY EXPENSIVE
Crocodile Bay Resort ⚓ Originally, and still primarily a sportfishing resort, this place also caters to other sorts of adventure travelers. The rooms are the best you'll find right in Puerto Jiménez, with tons of space and private balconies or verandas—try for a garden-facing second-floor unit. The hotel has excellent facilities and expansive grounds. In addition to a large modern fleet of fishing boats, with top-notch crew and equipment, they have a well-staffed activities and tour desk, and a large spa. The food and service here are also excellent.

Puerto Jiménez. ℂ **800/733-1115** in the U.S. and Canada, or 2735-5631 in Costa Rica. www.crocodilebay.com. 40 units. $300 (£150) double. Rates include breakfast. Rates lower in off season; higher during peak weeks. A wide range of fishing and adventure-tour packages are available. AE, MC, V. **Amenities:** Restaurant; bar; outdoor swimming pool; Jacuzzi; large modern spa; game room; watersports equipment rental; tour desk; laundry service. *In room:* A/C.

EXPENSIVE
Parrot Bay Village There's a small-resort feel to this collection of individual cabins—despite being just a short walk from town, it feels miles away. The smaller cabins are octagonal and have just one double bed, while the larger ones each feature a sleeping loft with a double and single bed above and a double bed below. Amenities include a small restaurant and bar, along with a large central deck with a view of the gulf and a pretty good sportfishing operation. The grounds also include a pretty patch of beach and a semi-groomed trail through the mangroves.

A.P. 91, Puerto Jiménez. ℂ **866/551-2003** in U.S., or 2735-5180 in Costa Rica. Fax 2735-5568. www.parrotbay village.com. 9 units. $145 (£73) double. Rates include breakfast and local airport transfers. Rates lower in off season; higher during peak weeks. MC, V. **Amenities:** Restaurant; bar; watersports equipment rental and free kayak use; tour desk; laundry service. *In room:* A/C, hair dryer, no phone.

MODERATE
Agua Luna Agua Luna is located right at the foot of the town's public dock and backs up to a mangrove forest. The older rooms directly face the gulf across a fenced-in gravel parking area. The most surprising feature in each of these rooms is the bathroom, which includes both a shower and a tub facing a huge picture window that looks into the mangroves. There are two double beds in each room, and on the tiled veranda out front, you'll find hammocks for lounging. The newer rooms are a half-block away and are smaller and less attractive than those in the original building, although room nos. 4 and 5 in this building do overlook the mangroves.

In front of the public dock, Puerto Jiménez. ℂ/fax **2735-5393**. 20 units. $60–$75 (£30–£38) double. V. **Amenities:** Restaurant; laundry service. *In room:* A/C, TV, minifridge.

La Choza del Manglar A short distance from the airstrip, this long-standing hotel is one of the better in-town options. The rooms are clean and comfortable, probably the most modern and tastefully decorated rooms you'll find in Puerto Jiménez proper. All rooms have air-conditioning, and about half have televisions. However, the private cabins have fans only. The hotel has several acres of mangroves and gardens, and the bird-watching and wildlife viewing are pretty good. The restaurant serves Costa Rican and international fare in a large, open-air space with colorful murals covering all of the walls. While this is a good in-town option, you're still several hundred meters or more from the water and from downtown Puerto Jiménez.

125m (410 ft.) west of the airstrip, Puerto Jiménez. ℂ **888/467-3181** in the U.S. and Canada, or ℂ/fax 2735-5605 in Costa Rica. www.manglares.com. 10 units. $59–$99 (£29–£49) double. Rates include taxes. Rates higher during peak weeks; lower in off season. MC, V. **Amenities:** Restaurant; bar; tour desk; laundry service. *In room:* Free Wi-Fi, no phone.

INEXPENSIVE

In addition to the places listed below, you can camp or take advantage of some simple screened-in rooms at the beautiful **Herrera Botanical Gardens and Tent Camp** (*©* **2735-5210**). Rates run around $12 to $15 (£6–£7.50) per person to camp; it's $20 (£10) per person in a screened-in room, with access to a communal kitchen, bathroom, and shower facilities, and unlimited access to the trails and gardens. If you don't have your own tent, they can rent you one.

Cabinas Jiménez *(Value* Located right on the waterfront at the north end of the soccer field, this perennial budget favorite has improved with age. All of the rooms have air-conditioning, tile floors, hot-water showers, and hand-carved headboards and Guatemalan bedspreads on the beds. Some have little fridges and coffeemakers. Three units even have views of the water, with a broad shared veranda in front, and there's one private bungalow that's the choice room in the house. The wide range in prices, in fact, reflects the range in size and location of the rooms. But even the most basic standard room here is a good option.

Downtown, 50m (164 ft.) north of the soccer field, Puerto Jiménez, Puntarenas. *©* **2735-5090**. www.cabinas jimenez.com. 10 units. $45–$80 (£23–£40) double. MC, V. *In room:* A/C, no phone.

WHERE TO STAY IN PLAYA PLANTANARES
VERY EXPENSIVE

Iguana Lodge *©* This place has a variety of rooms and bungalows. The two-story casitas are their top option: These are set amid lush gardens just steps from the sand. Hardwood floors, bamboo furniture, and mosquito netting over orthopedic mattresses all add up to rustic tropical elegance. The lower units have delightful semi-outdoor garden showers, and all come with either a large covered balcony or veranda. Still, I prefer the second-floor rooms for their views and elevation. By November 2008, they expect to have completed a pool and small spa. These folks also rent out a separate, private three-bedroom villa.

Playa Plantanares. *©* **8829-5865** or 8848-0752. Fax 2735-5436. www.iguanalodge.com. 19 units. $135 (£68) double club room; $310 (£155) casita double. Rates include breakfast. Rates lower in off season; higher during peak weeks. Rates of the casita include dinner as well. MC, V. **Amenities:** Restaurant; bar; watersports equipment rental; laundry service. *In room:* No phone.

WHERE TO DINE IN PUERTO JIMENEZ

In addition to the places listed below, locals also seem to enjoy the pizzas and occasional sushi at the open-air downtown Italian joint, **Il Giardino** (*©* **2735-5129**).

Juanita's Mexican Bar & Grille *© (Value* MEXICAN This place offers good, hearty California-style Mexican food and seafood served up in a lively, convivial atmosphere. You can get fajitas with chicken, beef, fish, or even grilled vegetables. Juanita's also has pizza by the slice or pie, and will deliver, although I'm not sure how far out the peninsula their drivers will go. There are nightly specials and a popular happy hour. You can also order breakfast a la carte, or you can load up on an abundant breakfast buffet.

Downtown, Puerto Jiménez. *©* **2735-5056**. Reservations not accepted. Main courses $4–$15 (£2–£7.50). V. Daily 7am–midnight.

Soda Carolina COSTA RICAN   Set in the center of the town's main street, and otherwise known as the "Bar, Restaurante y Cabinas Carolina," this is the town's budget travelers' hangout and also serves as an unofficial information center. The walls are painted with colorful jungle and wildlife scenes. As for the fare, seafood is the way to go. There's good fried fish as well as a variety of ceviches. The black-bean soup is usually tasty, and the *casados* (plates of the day) are filling and cost around $3.50 (£1.70).

On the main street. © 2735-5185. Reservations not accepted. Main courses $3.50–$9 (£1.75–£4.50). V. Daily 7am–10pm.

WHERE TO STAY & DINE AROUND THE OSA PENINSULA

As with most of the lodges in Drake Bay, the accommodations listed in this section include three meals a day in their rates and do a large share of their bookings in package trips. Per-night rates are listed, but the price categories have been adjusted to take into account the fact that all meals are included. Ask about package rates if you plan to take several tours and stay awhile: They could save you money.

In addition to the lodges listed below, there are several other options, ranging from small bed-and-breakfasts to fully equipped home rentals. Surfers, in particular, might want to inquire into one of the several rental houses located close to the beach at Matapalo. Your best bet for alternative accommodations is to contact Isabel at **Osa Tropical** (© 2735-5062; www.osatropical.com).

Finally, there's been a small boom of lodges out in Carate. In addition to the tent lodge listed below you can look into **La Leona Eco-Lodge** (© 2735-5705; www. laleonalodge.com), another tent camp option on the outskirts of the national park, and **Lookout Inn** (© 815/955-1520 in the U.S., or 2735-5431 in Costa Rica; www.lookout-inn.com), a more traditional lodge option right in Carate. Often used for yoga retreats, **Luna Lodge** ◈ (© 888/409-8448 in the U.S., or 8380-5036; www.lunalodge.com) has luxurious rooms and private cabins with great views over the jungle, and they even have some permanent, large tents for the more budget-conscious travelers.

VERY EXPENSIVE

The following lodges are some of the best ecolodges Costa Rica has to offer, and most are pretty pricey. However, keep in mind that despite paying top dollar, there are no TVs, no in-room telephones, no air-conditioning, no discos, very limited shopping, and no paved roads. There are also no crowds and very few modern distractions.

Bosque del Cabo Rainforest Lodge ◈◈◈ *(Finds)*   This secluded jungle lodge is my favorite spot in this neck of the woods. The individual cabins are all spacious and attractively furnished, have wooden decks or verandas to catch the ocean views, and are set amid beautiful gardens. The deluxe cabins come with king-size beds and slightly larger deck space. The Congo cabin is my choice for its spectacular view of the sunrise from your bed. All cabins have indoor bathrooms; while tiled showers are set outdoors amid flowering heliconia and ginger. About half of the units also have outdoor bathtubs.

There's a trail down to a secluded beach that has some tide pools and ocean-carved caves. Another trail leads to a jungle waterfall, and several others wind through the rainforests of the lodge's 260-hectare (650-acre) private reserve. The wildlife viewing here is excellent. If you're too lazy to hike down to the beach, there's a beautiful pool by the main lodge. Other attractions include a canopy platform 36m (118 ft.) up a

Manu tree, reached along a 90m (295-ft.) zip line, as well as a bird- and wildlife-watching rancho set beside a little lake on the edge of their tropical gardens and surrounded by forest. Trips to the national park or fishing excursions can be arranged, as can guided hikes, sea kayaking, and a host of other activities and tours. These folks also rent out two separate, fully equipped houses that are quite popular, along with a couple of cabins set inland by their gardens.

Osa Peninsula (mailing address: Interlink 528, P.O. Box 02-5635, Miami, FL 33102). ℂ/fax **2735-5206** or 8389-2846. www.bosquedelcabo.com. 10 units. $350–$390 (£175–£195) double. Rates include 3 meals daily and taxes. $25 (£13) round-trip transportation from Puerto Jiménez. MC, V. **Amenities:** Restaurant; bar; midsize pool; surfboard rental; in-room or rainforest massage; laundry service. *In room:* No phone.

El Remanso ☀☀   This collection of individual cabins and two-story units is set in a deep patch of primary forest bordering Bosque del Cabo. The best view of the ocean, over and through thick forest, can be had from the two-story deluxe La Vanilla unit, which can be rented whole or split into two separate one-bedroom affairs. The upstairs room here is the best in the house, with plenty of space, varnished wood floors, and a spacious balcony. All of the private cabins feature polished cement floors, a queen-size bed, and separate fold-down futon. If you want an individual cabin, Azul de Mar has the best view. A host of adventure activities are available, including tree climbing, waterfall rappelling, and a zip-line canopy tour. They also have a large, open-air yoga platform, and frequently host yoga groups. For chilling out, there's a small oval pool set in a stone deck area with great views to the ocean. The meals here are fresh, filling, and expertly prepared. Breakfasts can even be taken on a platform high atop a rainforest tree. The owners are committed to environmental protection. In fact, Joel and Belen Stewart met aboard the Greenpeace vessel *Rainbow Warrior*, which Joel captained for a number of years.

Osa Peninsula. ℂ **2735-5569.** Fax 2735-5126. www.elremanso.com. 14 units. $300–$380 (£150–£190) double. Rates include 3 meals daily and all taxes. Rates lower in off season; slightly higher during peak periods. MC, V. **Amenities:** Restaurant; bar; small pool; tour desk; laundry service. *In room:* No phone.

Lapa Ríos ☀☀   This is one of Costa Rica's pioneering and most famous ecolodges. The hotel consists of eight duplex buildings perched along a steep ridge. Each spacious room is totally private and oriented toward the view. Walls have open screenings, and the ceiling is a high-peaked thatched roof. Mosquito nets drape languidly over the rooms' two queen-size beds. A large deck and small tropical garden, complete with a hammock and outdoor shower, more than double the living space. There's an indoor shower in each room, which features open screen walls letting out on the view, so it's not all that different from being outdoors. *Note:* It's a bit of a hike back and forth from the main lodge to the farthest rooms.

The centerpiece of the lodge's large open-air dining room is a 15m (49-ft.) spiral staircase that leads to an observation deck tucked beneath the peak of the building's thatched roof. Just off the main lodge is a pretty little pool with great views. The beach, however, is a good 15-minute hike away. There's also another open-air yoga platform, where classes are sometimes offered. Lapa Ríos is surrounded by its own 400-hectare (988-acre) private rainforest reserve, which is home to scarlet macaws, toucans, parrots, hummingbirds, monkeys, and myriad other wildlife.

Osa Peninsula (mailing address: SJO-706, Box 025216, Miami, FL 33102). ℂ **2735-5130.** Fax 2735-5179. www. laparios.com. 16 units. $590 (£295) double. Rates include 3 meals daily, round-trip transportation btw. the lodge and

Puerto Jiménez, and taxes. Discounts for children 10 and under. AE, MC, V. **Amenities:** Restaurant; bar; small pool; tour desk; massage; laundry service; nonsmoking rooms. *In room:* Safe, no phone.

MODERATE

Corcovado Lodge Tent Camp ⭐ If you're looking for a balanced blend of comfort and adventure, check out Corcovado Lodge Tent Camp, which is built on a low bluff right above the beach. Forested mountains rise up behind the camp, and just a few minutes' walk away is the entrance to the national park. Accommodations are in large tents pitched on wooden decks. Each tent has two twin beds, a table, a couple of plastic garden chairs on the front deck, and an ocean view. Shared toilets and showers are a short walk away, but there are enough that there's usually no waiting.

Meals are served family-style in a large open-air dining room furnished with picnic tables. A separate screen-walled building is furnished with hammocks, a small bar, a Ping-Pong table, and a few board games. Services at the lodge include guided walks and excursions, such as hikes through the national park and horseback rides on the beach. The lodge features a canopy platform located 36m (118 ft.) up an ancient guapinol tree. If you're truly adventurous, you can spend the night in a tent atop the platform. (Just don't wake up on the wrong side of the tent.)

Simply reaching this lodge is an adventure in itself. Most guests take a five-seat chartered plane to the gravel landing strip at Carate and then walk for around 30 minutes along the beach to the lodge. Don't worry: Your bags are hauled in on a mule-drawn cart. If you have a four-wheel-drive vehicle, you can get as far as Carate, arrange for safe parking, and then walk the remaining 1.6km (1 mile).

Osa Peninsula (mailing address: SJO 235, P.O. Box 025216, Miami, FL 33102-5216). © **800/886-2609** in the U.S. and Canada, or 2257-0766 in Costa Rica. Fax 2257-1665. www.corcovadolodge.com. 20 tents, all with shared bathrooms. $128 (£64) double. Rates include 3 meals daily. Rates lower in off season; slightly higher during peak periods. Multiday packages, including transportation and tours, are available. AE, MC, V. **Amenities:** Restaurant; bar; laundry service. *In room:* No phone.

PUERTO JIMENEZ AFTER DARK

If you're looking for any after-tours action in Puerto Jiménez, I recommend you start off at either **Juanita's Mexican Bar & Grille** or the **Soda Carolina.** If you want to dance, there's basically just one option, the **Delfines Discoteque,** which is near the bus station.

3 Golfito: Gateway to the Golfo Dulce

87km (54 miles) S of Palmar Norte; 337km (209 miles) S of San José

Despite being the largest and most important city in Costa Rica's southern zone, Golfito, in and of itself, is neither a popular nor a particularly inviting tourist destination. In its prime, this was a major banana port, but following years of rising taxes, falling prices, and labor disputes, United Fruit pulled out in 1985. Things may change in the future, as rumors perennially abound about the potential construction of an international airport nearby, major marina right on the bay, or large-scale tuna farm just offshore. But for the moment, none of these megaprojects have gotten off the drawing board.

That said, Golfito is still a major sportfishing center and a popular gateway to a slew of nature lodges spread along the quiet waters, isolated bays, and lush rainforests of the Golfo Dulce, or "Sweet Gulf." In 1998, much of the rainforest bordering the

Golfo Dulce was officially declared the **Piedras Blancas National Park** 🐾🐾, which includes 12,000 hectares (29,640 acres) of primary forests, as well as newly protected secondary forests and pasturelands.

Golfito is set on the north side of the Golfo Dulce, at the foot of lush green mountains. The setting alone gives Golfito the potential to be one of the most attractive cities in the country. However, the areas around the municipal park and public dock are somewhat seedy and the "downtown" section is quite run-down. Still, if you go a little bit farther along the bay, you come to the old United Fruit Company housing. Here you'll find well-maintained wooden houses painted bright colors and surrounded by neatly manicured gardens. Toucans are commonly sighted. It's all very lush and green and clean—an altogether different picture from that painted by most port towns in this country. When a duty-free zone was opened here, these old homes experienced a minor renaissance and several were converted into small hotels. Ticos come here in droves on weekends and throughout December to take advantage of cheap prices on name-brand goods and clothing at the duty-free zone; sometimes all these shoppers make finding a room difficult.

ESSENTIALS

GETTING THERE & DEPARTING   By Plane   Sansa (© 877/767-2672 in the U.S. and Canada, or 2290-4100 in Costa Rica; www.flysansa.com) has five daily flights to Golfito, with the first one departing San José's Juan Santamaría International Airport at 5:30am. The latest flight leaves at 2:19pm during the high season, and 1:50pm during the off season. Trip duration is 1 hour; the fare is $102 (£51) each way. Sansa flights return to San José daily beginning at 6:43am, with the last flight departing at 1:03pm in the low season, and 4:44pm in the high season.

Nature Air (© 800/235-9272 in the U.S. and Canada, or 2299-6000; www. natureair.com) has flights to Drake Bay departing daily from Tobías Bolaños International Airport in Pavas at 6:05am and 3pm. Flight duration is 50 minutes on the direct morning flight, and 70 minutes on the later flight, which stops first in Drake Bay; the fare is $108 (£54) each way.

By Car   Take the Interamerican Highway east out of San José (through San Pedro and Cartago) and continue south on this road. In about 3 hours, you'll reach San Isidro de El General. Although you can continue on the Interamerican Highway all the way south, it is currently faster, smoother, and safer to turn off in San Isidro and head to Dominical, picking up the Southern Highway or Costanera Sur in Dominical. From here it's a fast and smooth shot down to Palmar Norte, where you meet up again with the Interamerican Highway. When you get to Río Claro, you'll notice a couple of gas stations and quite a bit of activity. Turn right here and follow the signs to Golfito. If you end up at the Panama border, you've missed the turnoff by about 32km (20 miles). The complete drive takes about 6 hours. On most of the Interamerican Highway, you'll have to contend with potholes of sometimes gargantuan proportions. Just remember, if the road is suddenly smooth and in great shape, you can bet that around the next bend there will be a bottomless pothole that you can't swerve around. Take it easy.

By Bus   Express buses leave San José daily at 7am and 3pm from the **Tracopa** station on the Plaza Viquez at Calle 5 between avenidas 18 and 20 (© 2221-4214). The trip takes 7½ hours; the fare is $6 (£3). Buses depart Golfito for San José daily at 5am and 1:30pm from the bus station near the municipal dock.

By Boat   There are now fast speedboats working as boat taxis between Golfito and Puerto Jiménez. The fare is $5 (£2.50), and the ride takes a little under 30 minutes. These boats leave five or six times throughout the day, beginning at around 5am and finishing up at around 5pm. Ask at the *muellecito* (public dock) for current schedules.

There is also a daily passenger launch. This slower boat takes 1½ hours; and the fare is $3 (£1.50). The ferry leaves the public dock in Golfito at 6am for Puerto Jiménez. The return trip to Golfito leaves Puerto Jiménez's municipal dock at 11:30am.

It's also possible to charter a water taxi in Golfito for the trip across to Puerto Jiménez. You'll have to pay between $40 and $80 (£20–£40) for an entire launch, some of which can carry up to 12 people.

GETTING AROUND   Taxis are plentiful in Golfito, and are constantly cruising the main road, all the way from the entrance of town to the duty-free port. A taxi ride anywhere in town should cost around $1 (50p). Local buses also ply this loop. The fare for the bus is 15¢ (10p).

If you drive down here and head out to one of the remote lodges on the gulf, you can leave your car at Samoa del Sur (see "Where to Stay" below) for around $10 (£5) per day.

If you can't get to your next destination by boat, bus, commuter airline, or car, **Alfa Romeo Air Charters** (© 2735-5353 or 2735-5112; www.alfaromeoair.com) runs charters to most of the nearby destinations, including Carate, Drake Bay, Sirena, and Puerto Jiménez. A five-passenger plane should cost around $200 to $400 (£100–£200) one-way, depending on your destination.

FAST FACTS   To avoid the bureaucracy and frequently long lines at the banks, you can **exchange money** at the gas station, or "La Bomba," in the middle of town. A **laundromat** on the upper street of the small downtown charges around $3 (£1.50) for an average-size load.

EXPLORING THE AREA

You won't find any really good swimming beaches right in Golfito. The closest spot is **Playa Cacao,** a short boat ride away, although this is not one of my favorite beaches in Costa Rica. You should be able to get a ride here for around $5 (£2.50) per person from one of the boat taxis down at the public docks. However, you might have to negotiate hard because these boatmen like to gouge tourists whenever possible. If you really want some beach time, I recommend staying at one of the hotels in the Golfo Dulce (see "Where to Stay," below) or heading over to **Playa Zancudo** (see "Playa Zancudo," later in this chapter).

About a 20-minute drive over a rough dirt road from Golfito will bring you to the **Avellana Waterfall & Trails** (© 8877-4004). Admission to the site costs $5 (£2.50) and includes a 2-hour guided hike through the forests and a visit to a beautiful forest waterfall, with several refreshing pools perfect for swimming. A taxi should charge around $10 (£5) for the ride, one-way. Horseback riding is available, and they even have a zip-line canopy tour. Camping is also allowed, and meals are served by the friendly owners of the land, the local Gamba family. However, for most folks, the best way to visit this site is to go as part of an organized trip with **Land Sea Tours** (© 2775-1614).

The waters off Golfito also offer some of the best **sportfishing** in Costa Rica. If you'd like to try hooking into a possible world-record marlin or sailfish, contact

Banana Bay Marina (© **800/245-1635** in the U.S. and Canada, or 2775-0838 in Costa Rica; www.bananabaymarina.com). These folks have a full-service marina, a few waterside rooms for guests, and a fleet of sportfishing boats and captains. A full-day fishing trip costs between $800 and $2,200 (£400–£1100). You can also try the **Zancudo Lodge** (© **800/854-8791** in the U.S. and Canada, or 2776-0008 in Costa Rica; www.thezancudolodge.com), which is based in nearby Playa Zancudo. The lodge can arrange pickup in Golfito, and I prefer the lodgings and scenery out in Zancudo to what you'll find in Golfito.

There's no steady charter fleet here, but itinerant sailors often set up shop for a season or so. If you're looking to charter a sailboat, you should check with **Banana Bay Marina** or **Las Gaviotas Hotel** (p. 350).

About 30 minutes by boat out of Golfito, you'll find **Casa Orquídeas** ⊕⊕, a private botanical garden lovingly built and maintained by Ron and Trudy MacAllister. Most hotels in the area offer trips here, including transportation and a 2-hour tour of the gardens. During the tour, you'll sample a load of fresh fruits picked right off the trees. If your hotel can't, you can book a trip out of Golfito with **Land Sea Tours** (© **2775-1614**). The entrance and guided tour is only $5 (£2.50) per person, but it will cost you between $50 and $60 (£25–£30) to hire a boat for the round-trip ride.

If you have a serious interest in botanical gardens or bird-watching, consider an excursion to **Wilson Botanical Gardens** ⊕⊕⊕ at the Las Cruces Biological Station (© **2524-0607** in San José, or 2773-4004 at the gardens; www.threepaths.co.cr), just outside the town of San Vito, about 65km (40 miles) to the northeast. The gardens are owned and maintained by the Organization for Tropical Studies and include more than 7,000 species of tropical plants from around the world. Among the plants grown here are many endangered species, which make the gardens of interest to botanical researchers. Despite the scientific aspects of the gardens, there are so many beautiful and unusual flowers amid the manicured grounds that even a neophyte can't help but be astounded. All this luscious flora has attracted at least 360 species of birds. A full-day guided walk, including lunch, costs $36 (£18); a half-day guided walk costs $18 (£9). If you'd like to stay the night here, there are 12 well-appointed rooms. Rates, which include one guided walk, three meals, and taxes, run around $82 (£41) per person; you definitely need to make reservations if you want to spend the night, and it's usually a good idea to make a reservation for a simple day visit and hike. The gardens are about 6km (3¾ miles) before San Vito. To get here from Golfito, drive out to the Interamerican Highway and continue south toward Panama. In Ciudad Neily, turn north. A taxi from Golfito should cost around $40 (£20) each way.

WHERE TO STAY
IN GOLFITO
Moderate
Centro Turístico Samoa del Sur   This is the best-located hotel on the waterfront, and it features a popular restaurant and bar. The rooms are spacious and clean. Varnished wood headboards complement two firm and comfortable queen-size beds. With red-tile floors, modern bathrooms, and carved-wood doors, the rooms all share a long, covered veranda that's set perpendicular to the gulf, so the views aren't great. If you want to watch the water, you're better off grabbing a table at the restaurant, or walking out to the docks at their small marina. The hotel also has a swimming pool,

a volleyball court, and a large gift shop with an extensive shell-and-coral collection that they bill as a museum.

100m (328 ft.) north of the public dock, Golfito. © 2775-0233. Fax 2775-0573. www.samoadelsur.com. 14 units. $60–$90 (£30–£45) double. AE, MC, V. **Amenities:** Restaurant; bar; midsize outdoor pool; tour desk; kayak rental; room service (7am–midnight); laundry service. *In room:* A/C, TV.

Hotel Sierra ⟨𝒦⟩   This resort-style hotel is the most luxurious option in Golfito, although that isn't saying much. Right beside the airstrip and walking distance to the duty-free zone, the Hotel Sierra was originally built as a business-class option geared toward middle-class Ticos in town to shop. It's currently trying to sell itself as a sport-fishing and ecotourism lodge, but it's not particularly well located for either. The Sierra is constructed to be as open and breezy as possible, and covered walkways connect the hotel's various buildings. The rooms are spacious and have windows on two sides to let in plenty of light. The swimming pool is the largest and most appealing in town, and the restaurant serves good, affordable international fare. One of the biggest draws here is the small casino, which is popular with guests and locals alike.

Beside the airstrip (A.P. 37), Golfito. © 2775-0666. Fax 2775-0506. www.hotelsierra.com. 72 units. $80 (£40) double. AE, MC, V. **Amenities:** Restaurant; bar; casino; midsize outdoor pool; tour desk; car rental; room service (7am–10pm); laundry service. *In room:* A/C, TV, safe.

Inexpensive

El Gran Ceibo ⟨Value⟩   This little motel-like option at the entrance to Golfito is a good choice. It's named after the giant ceibo tree you'll see standing over it near the entrance. The rooms are clean, bright, comfortable, and relatively spacious. All feature small verandas with some sitting chairs. About half of them come with air-conditioning and cable TV; although you pay more for these, they're still quite affordable. The others have just fans and cold-water showers. There are nice views over the gulf from the grounds and some of the rooms.

On the left, just as you enter Golfito. © 2775-0403. Fax 2775-2303. www.hotel-elgranceibo.com. 27 units. $25–$50 (£13–£25) double. AE, MC, V. **Amenities:** Restaurant; bar; pool; laundry service. *In room:* A/C and TV in some units, no phone.

Golfo Azul   Azul offers clean rooms and a quiet location in an attractive section of the old banana company compound near the Depósito Libre (free port). Most of the guests here are Ticos in town to shop at the duty-free shops. The smallest rooms are cramped, but there are larger rooms, some with high ceilings, making them feel even more spacious. Some rooms come with televisions. Bathrooms are tiled and have hot water. The hotel's restaurant serves breakfast only.

Barrio Alameda, 300m (984 ft.) south of the Depósito Libre, Golfito. © 2775-0871. Fax 2775-0004. 18 units. $15–$30 (£7.50–£15) double. V. **Amenities:** Restaurant. *In room:* A/C, no phone.

Las Gaviotas Hotel   Situated just at the start of Golfito proper—a short taxi or bus ride from the "downtown"—Las Gaviotas has long been a popular choice. The waterfront location is the hotel's greatest asset. There is a long pier that attracts the sailboat and sportfishing crowd. For landlubbers, there's a small pool built out near the gulf. Guest rooms, which are set amid attractive gardens, all face the ocean, and although they're quite large, they're spartan and show their age. There are small, tiled patios in front of all the rooms, and the cabanas have little kitchens. A large, open-air restaurant looks over the pool to the gulf; it's a great view, but the food leaves much to be desired. Just around the corner is a large, open-air bar.

A.P. 12-8201, Golfito. © **2775-0062**. Fax 2775-0544. 18 units, 3 cabanas. $42–$56 (£21–£28) double; $85 (£43) cabana. AE, DC, MC, V. **Amenities:** Restaurant; bar; small pool; tour desk; room service 7am–10pm; laundry service. *In room:* A/C, TV.

WHERE TO DINE
MODERATE
Bilge Bar, Restaurant & Grill ⚑ INTERNATIONAL/SEAFOOD   The open-air restaurant attached to the Banana Bay Marina is the best restaurant in Golfito. The seafood is fresh and excellently prepared, but you can also get hearty steaks and great burgers. I personally recommend the fresh-fish burger. Grab a table toward the water and watch the boats bob up and down while you enjoy your meal.

At the Banana Bay Marina, on the waterfront in downtown Golfito. © **2775-0838**. Reservations not necessary. Main courses $6–$17 (£3–£8.50). AE, MC, V. Daily 7am–9pm.

Samoa del Sur INTERNATIONAL   This large, open-air place features an extensive menu of Continental and French dishes (the owners are French), including such specialties as onion soup, salade niçoise, filet of fish meunière, and, in a nod to their southern neighbor, paella. There are also pizzas and spaghetti. In addition to the food, the giant rancho houses a pool table, several high-quality dartboards, and two big-screen TVs. The bar sometimes stays open all night.

100m (328 ft.) north of the public dock. © **2775-0233**. Reservations not accepted. Main courses $6.50–$30 (£3.25–£15). AE, MC, V. Daily 7am–midnight.

INEXPENSIVE
Bar & Restaurant La Cubana COSTA RICAN   This small, open-air restaurant with a basic menu commands a good view of the gulf from its location on the bluff of a small hill. It serves hearty meals at rock-bottom prices: A fresh, whole fish in garlic sauce costs around $5 (£2.50). The bar is a quiet spot to have a drink in the evening.

150m (492 ft.) east of the gas station, on the upper road through downtown Golfito. No phone. Main courses $4–$12 (£2–£6). No credit cards. Tues–Sun 6am–10pm.

GOLFITO AFTER DARK
Golfito is a rough-and-tumble port town, and it pays to be careful here after dark. Right in town, about 1½ blocks inland and uphill from the *muellecito,* **Latitude 8** is the most popular spot. Most folks stick pretty close to their hotel bar and restaurant. Of these, the bar/restaurants at **Las Gaviotas** and **Samoa del Sur** are, by far, the liveliest. If you're feeling lucky, you can head to the **casino** at the **Hotel Sierra.**

FARTHER AFIELD ON THE GOLFO DULCE
The lodges listed here are located on the shores of the Golfo Dulce. There are no roads into this area, so you must get to the lodges by boat. I recommend that you have firm reservations when visiting this area, so your transportation should be arranged. If worse comes to worst, you can hire a boat taxi at the *muellecito* (little dock), which is located on the water just beyond the gas station, or "La Bomba," in Golfito, for between $20 and $40 (£10–£20), depending on which lodge you are staying at.

In addition to the lodges listed below, **Villas Corcovado** ⚑ (© **2296-8597;** www. villacorcovado.com) is another excellent option.

Very Expensive

Playa Nicuesa Rainforest Lodge ★★★ *(Finds)*   Set on its own private bay, with a large stretch of black-sand beach, this is the most impressive lodge along the shores of the Golfo Dulce. While the four Mango Manor rooms are certainly very comfortable, you'll definitely want to snag one of the individual cabins. These are all set amid dense forest and are made almost entirely of wood, with large open-air showers, private verandas, and a true sense of being in touch with nature. The main lodge building is a huge, open-air affair with an abundance of varnished wood and a relaxed inviting vibe that induces one to grab a book, board game, or chat with other guests. There's an excellent network of trails on the lodge's 66 hectares (165 acres), and a whole host of tours and activities are offered. Meals are served family-style, and are inventive and tasty.

Golfo Dulce (A.P. 56, Golfito). (© 866/504-8116 in the U.S., or 2258-8250 in Costa Rica. Fax 2735-5043. www.nicuesa lodge.com. 8 units. $340–$380 (£170–£190) double. Rates include all meals, taxes, and transfers to and from either Golfito or Puerto Jiménez. A 2-night minimum stay is required. Closed Oct 1–Nov 15. AE, MC, V. **Amenities:** Restaurant; bar; watersports equipment; laundry service. *In room:* Safe, no phone.

Expensive

Golfo Dulce Lodge ★   This small, Swiss-run lodge is just down the beach from Casa Orquídeas, about a 30-minute boat ride from Golfito. The five separate cabins and main lodge buildings are all set back away from the beach about 500m (1,640 ft.) into the forest. The cabins are spacious and airy, and feature either a twin and a double bed or three single beds. In addition, there are large bathrooms, solar hot-water showers, a small sitting area, and a porch with a hammock. The rooms are all comfortable and well appointed, and even feature private verandas, but they are not nearly as nice as the cabins. Meals are served in a two-story open rancho with an observation deck, located beside the small swimming pool. The lodge offers jungle hikes, river trips, and other guided tours.

Golfo Dulce (A.P. 137-8201, Golfito). ((© 8821-5398. Fax 2775-0573. www.golfodulcelodge.com. 8 units. $285–$345 (£143–£173) per person double occupancy for 4-day/3-night stay. Rates include 3 meals daily and taxes. Add $25 (£13) per person for transportation to and from Golfito. Rates lower in off season; higher during peak weeks. No credit cards. **Amenities:** Restaurant; bar; small outdoor pool; nature trails; laundry service. *In room:* No phone.

4 Playa Zancudo ★

19km (12 miles) S of Golfito by boat; 35km (22 miles) S of Golfito by road

Playa Zancudo is one of Costa Rica's most isolated and undeveloped beach destinations. If you're looking for a remote and low-key beach getaway, it's hard to beat Zancudo. It's pretty far from just about everything, and there are relatively few places to stay, so it's virtually never crowded. However, the small number of hotel rooms to be had means that the better ones, such as those listed here, can fill up fast in the high season. The beach itself is long and flat, and because it's protected from the full force of Pacific waves, it's one of the calmest beaches on this coast and relatively good for swimming, especially toward the northern end. There's a splendid view across the Golfo Dulce, and the sunsets are hard to beat.

ESSENTIALS

GETTING THERE   By Plane   The nearest airport is in Golfito. See "Golfito: Gateway to the Golfo Dulce," earlier in this chapter, for details. To get from the airport to Playa Zancudo, your best bets are by boat or taxi.

Tips Park It

If you drive down to Golfito, you can leave your car at Samoa del Sur (see "Where to Stay," above) and take one of the waterborne routes mentioned above. They charge around $10 (£5) per day, and the lot is very secure.

By Boat Water taxis can be hired in Golfito to make the trip out to Playa Zancudo; however, trips depend on the tides and weather conditions. When the tide is high, the boats take a route through the mangroves. This is by far the calmest and most scenic way to get to Zancudo. When the tide is low, they must stay out in the gulf, which can get choppy at times. It costs around $15 (£7.50) per person for a water taxi, with a minimum charge of $35 (£18). If you can round up any sort of group, be sure to negotiate. The ride takes about 30 minutes.

Also, there's a passenger launch from the *muellecito* (little dock) in Golfito, which normally leaves daily at around noon. Because the schedule sometimes changes, be sure to ask in town about current departure times. The trip lasts 40 minutes; the fare is $5 (£2.50). The *muellecito* is next to the town's principal gas station, "La Bomba."

If you plan ahead, you can call **Zancudo Boat Tours** (© 2776-0012; www.loscocos.com) and arrange for pickup in Golfito or Puerto Jiménez. The trip costs $15 (£7.50) per person each way from Golfito or Puerto Jiménez, with a $40 (£19) minimum from Golfito and $60 (£30) minimum from Puerto Jiménez. Zancudo Boat Tours also includes land transportation to your hotel in Playa Zancudo—a very nice perk because there are so few taxis in town.

By Car If you've got a four-wheel-drive vehicle, you can make it out to Zancudo even in the rainy season. To get here, follow the directions for driving to Golfito, but don't go all the way into town. The turnoff for playas Zancudo and Pavones is at El Rodeo, about 4km (2½ miles) outside of Golfito, on the road in from the Interamerican Highway. About 20 minutes past the turnoff, you'll have to wait and take a small diesel-operated crank ferry. The fare is $1 (50p) per vehicle. The ferry generally operates from around 5am until 8pm; however, the hours can be erratic. Moreover, at very low tides the ferry can't run, so sometimes you must wait a couple of hours. After the ferry, you should follow the few signs and the flow of traffic (if there is any) or stick to the most worn route when in doubt.

When the ferry's not running, or waiting for the tide to come in, there's an alternative route from Paso Canoas (at the border), via the towns of La Cuesta and Laurel. This route meets the route mentioned above at the small village of Conte.

A four-wheel-drive **taxi** costs around $40 (£20) from Golfito. It takes about 1 hour when the road is in good condition, and about 2 hours when it's not. For info on getting here from San José, see p. 42.

By Bus It's possible to get to Zancudo by bus, but I highly recommend coming by boat from Golfito, or your own car. If you insist, you can catch one of the Pavones buses in front of the gas station "La Bomba" in downtown Golfito and get off in the village of Conte (at around 4pm). In theory, a Zancudo-bound bus should be waiting. However, this is not always the case, and you may have to wait, hitchhike, or spring for a cab, if any can be found. The entire trip takes about 3 hours; the fare is $3 (£1.50).

DEPARTING The public launch to Golfito leaves daily at 7am from the dock near the school, in the center of Zancudo. You can also arrange a water taxi back to Golfito, but it's best to work with your hotel owner and make a reservation at least 1 day in advance. **Zancudo Boat Tours** will take you for $15 (£7.50) per person, with a $40 (£19) minimum. Zancudo will also take you to **Pavones** or the **Osa Peninsula.** It costs the same $15 (£7.50) per person, but there's a minimum charge of $60 (£30). The bus to Golfito leaves Zancudo each morning at 5:30am. You can catch the bus anywhere along the main road.

ORIENTATION Zancudo is a long, narrow peninsula (sometimes only 90m/295 ft. or so wide) at the mouth of the Río Colorado. On one side is the beach; on the other is a mangrove swamp. There is only one road that runs the length of the beach, and along this road, spread out over several kilometers of long, flat beach, you'll find the hotels I mention here. It's about a 20-minute walk from the public dock near the school to the popular Cabinas Sol y Mar.

WHAT TO SEE & DO (OR HOW NOT TO DO ANYTHING)

The main activity at Zancudo is relaxing, and people take it seriously. There are hammocks at almost every lodge, and if you bring a few good books, you can spend quite a number of hours swinging slowly in the tropical breezes. The beach along Zancudo is great for swimming. It's generally a little calmer on the northern end and gets rougher (good for bodysurfing) as you head south. There are a couple of bars and even a disco, but visitors are most likely to spend their time just hanging out at their hotel or in restaurants meeting like-minded folks, reading a good book, or playing board games. If you want to take a horseback ride on the beach, ask at your hotel; they should be able to arrange it for you.

Susan and Andrew Robertson, who run Cabinas Los Cocos, also operate **Zancudo Boat Tours** (© 2776-0012; www.loscocos.com), which offers snorkeling trips, kayaking tours, trips to the Casa Orquídeas Botanical Garden, hikes on the Osa peninsula, a trip up the Río Coto to watch birds and wildlife, and more. Tour prices are $45 to $80 (£23–£40) per person per tour, with discounts available for larger groups.

For fishing, contact the **Zancudo Lodge** (see below). A full day of fishing with lunch and beer should cost between $600 and $1,600 (£300–£800) per boat.

Because there's a mangrove swamp directly behind the beach, mosquitoes and sand flies can be a problem when the winds die down, so be sure to bring insect repellent.

WHERE TO STAY

If you're planning on an extended stay, there are quite a few fully equipped beach houses for rent. Once again, Susan and Andrew at **Los Cocos** (© 2776-0012; www.loscocos.com) are your best bet for lining up one of these houses.

VERY EXPENSIVE

The Zancudo Lodge Primarily a fishing lodge, this hotel is located at the north end of Zancudo, and is, by far, the most luxurious option around. All of the rooms look out onto a bright green lawn of soft grass and the small swimming pool and Jacuzzi; the beach is just a few steps beyond. Most of the rooms are in a long two-story building and feature tile floors, clean, modern bathrooms, and small verandas. There are four suites that have separate sitting rooms, hardwood floors, and more space. The lodge offers many different types of fishing excursions and packages, and boasts more than 50 world-record catches. This place is still sometimes called Roy's Zancudo Lodge, although Roy sold the place back in 2006.

Playa Zancudo (A.P. 41, Golfito). © **800/854-8791** in the U.S., or 2776-0008 in Costa Rica. Fax 2776-0011. www.thezancudolodge.com. 26 units. $185 (£90) per person nonfishing; $400–$500 (£200–£250) including full-day fishing. Rates are per person double occupancy and include all meals, drinks (alcoholic and carbonated), and taxes. Multiday packages available. V. **Amenities:** Restaurant; bar; pool; Jacuzzi; laundry service. *In room:* A/C, TV, dataport, stocked minibar, coffeemaker, hair dryer.

MODERATE

Cabinas Los Cocos ★ *Finds*   If you've ever pondered throwing it all away and setting up shop in a simple house by the beach, these kitchen-equipped cabins might be a good place for a trial run. Set under the trees and only a few meters from the beach, the four cabins are quiet and semi-isolated from one another. Two of them served as banana-plantation housing in a former life, until they were salvaged and moved here. These wood houses have big verandas and bedrooms, and large eat-in kitchens. Bathrooms are down a few steps in back and have hot water. The two newer cabins also offer plenty of space, small kitchenettes, and a private veranda, as well as comfortable sleeping lofts. If you plan to stay in Zancudo for a while, this is a perennially good choice. The owners, Susan and Andrew Robertson, run Zancudo Boat Tours, so if you want to do some exploring or need a ride into Golfito or Puerto Jiménez, they're the folks to see. Finally, these folks also rent out several wonderful beach houses around Zancudo.

Playa Zancudo (A.P. 88, Golfito). ©/fax **2776-0012.** www.loscocos.com. 4 units. $60 (£30) double. Rates lower in off season. Weekly discounts available. No credit cards. *In room:* Kitchenette, no phone.

Oasis on the Beach ★   Located toward the southern end of Zancudo, the Oasis is an intimate and isolated option. My favorite rooms here are the three individual bungalows. Although they are simple and lack the air-conditioning of the villa rooms, they are plenty spacious and I like their wood floors, private front porches, large bathrooms, and rustic yet comfortable feel. The villa is a two-story building with rooms upstairs and down that feature tile floors and air-conditioning. The upstairs unit has a high peaked ceiling and a great view over the Golfo Dulce to Cabo Matapalo from its private balcony. The restaurant here is quite good, with weekly pizza nights featuring homemade pizzas made in a wood-fired brick oven.

Playa Zancudo (A.P. 17, Golfito). ©/fax **2776-0087.** www.oasisonthebeach.com. 5 units. $65–$75 (£33–£38) double. Rates lower in off season. Weekly discounts available. V. **Amenities:** Restaurant; bar; laundry service. *In room:* Minifridge, coffeemaker, no phone.

INEXPENSIVE

Cabinas Sol y Mar ★ *Value*   This friendly owner-run establishment is one of the most popular lodgings in Zancudo. There are two individual bungalows and two rooms in a duplex building with a shared veranda. I prefer the individual rooms for their privacy. The bathrooms in these have unusual showers that feature a tiled platform set amid smooth river rocks. There's also a small budget cabin that is quite a good deal, as well as a fully equipped house for longer stays. You can even camp here for a few bucks per night. All of the options are just steps away from the sand. The hotel's open-air restaurant is one of the best and most popular places to eat in Zancudo.

Playa Zancudo (A.P. 87-8201, Golfito). © **2776-0014.** www.zancudo.com. 6 units. $22–$42 (£11–£21) double. Rates lower in off season. No credit cards. **Amenities:** Restaurant; bar. *In room:* Free Wi-Fi, no phone.

WHERE TO DINE

In addition to the place listed below, you'll do well to try the wood-oven pizza and nightly specials at the **Oasis on the Beach** ★ (© **2776-0087**). You might also try the tasty Italian meals at **Restaurante Macondo** (© **2776-0157**) or **Alberto's Puerta**

Negra (© 2776-0181). And if you want basic Tico fare and some local company, head to **Soda Sussy** (© 2776-0107) or **Soda Katherine** (© 2776-0124).

Finally, for a good breakfast, lunch, or dinner, or perhaps just a midday ice-cream treat, check out the little open-air cafe at **Oceanos Cabinas** ⭐ (© 2776-0921; www.oceanocabinas.com).

Sol y Mar ⭐⭐ *Value* INTERNATIONAL/SEAFOOD   This is the best and most popular restaurant in Playa Zancudo. The reasonably priced menu is heavy on seafood, but features some items you won't find at most places in town, including thick-cut pork chops in a teriyaki sauce. The fresh seared tuna is always excellent, as are the twice-weekly barbecues on Monday and Friday. This is also my top choice for breakfast—the breakfast burrito should get you through most of the day. A regular horseshoe tournament takes place on Sundays throughout the high season, and there's free Wi-Fi available at the bar and restaurant.

At Cabinas Sol y Mar. © 2776-0014. Reservations not necessary. Main courses $3–$14 (£1.50–£7). No credit cards. Daily 7am–9pm.

5 Playa Pavones: A Surfer's Mecca ⭐

40km (25 miles) S of Golfito

Hailed as the world's longest rideable left point break, Pavones is a legendary destination for surfing. It takes around 1.8m (6 ft.) of swell to get this wave cranking, but when the surf's up, you're in for a long, long ride—so long, in fact, that it's much easier to walk back through town to where the wave is breaking than to paddle back. The swells are most consistent during the rainy season, but you're likely to find surfers here year-round. Locals tend to be pretty possessive around here (both the wave and local properties have engendered bitter disputes), so don't be surprised if you receive a cool welcome.

Other than surfing, nothing much goes on here; however, the surrounding rainforests are quite nice, and the beaches feature some rocky coves and points that give Pavones a bit more visual appeal than Zancudo. If you're feeling energetic, you can go for a horseback ride or hike into the rainforests that back up this beach town, or stroll south on the beaches that stretch toward Punta Banco and beyond, all the way to the Panamanian border. This is a forgotten and isolated destination catering almost exclusively to backpackers. So be prepared, Pavones is a tiny village with few amenities, and most of the accommodations are quite basic.

ESSENTIALS

GETTING THERE & DEPARTING   By Plane   The nearest airport with regularly scheduled flights is in Golfito (p. 346). See "By Car" and "By Bus," below, for how to get to Pavones from the Golfito airport. There is a private strip at Tiskita Jungle Lodge (see below). Depending on space, you might be able to arrange transportation to Pavones on one of its charter flights even if you are not staying there.

By Car   If you've got a four-wheel-drive vehicle, you can make it out to Pavones even in the rainy season. To get here, follow the directions for driving to Golfito, but don't go all the way into town. The turnoff for playas Zancudo and Pavones is at El Rodeo, about 4km (2½ miles) outside of Golfito, on the road in from the Interamerican Highway. About 20 minutes past the turnoff, you'll have to wait and take a small diesel-operated crank ferry. Fare is $1 (50p) per vehicle. The ferry generally operates from around 5am until 8pm; however, the hours can be erratic. Moreover, at very low tides the ferry can't run, so sometimes you must wait a couple of hours. A four-wheel-drive taxi from Golfito to Pavones will cost between $50 and $60 (£25–£30). It takes around 2 hours.

When the ferry's not running, or waiting for the tide to come in, there's an alternative route from Paso Canoas (at the border), via the towns of La Cuesta and Laurel. This route meets the route mentioned above at the small village of Conte.

By Bus   There are two daily buses (© **2775-0365**) to Pavones from Golfito at 10am and 3pm. Trip duration is 2½ hours; the fare is $3 (£1.50). Buses to Golfito depart Pavones daily at 5:30am and 12:30pm. This is a very remote destination, and the bus schedule is subject to change, so it always pays to check in advance.

ORIENTATION   You can now find an Internet connection at **Esquina del Mar** in the heart of the village. If there are no waves, or you want some other form of exercise, check in with the folks at **Shooting Star Yoga** (© **8393-6982**; www.yoga pavones.com).

WHERE TO STAY & DINE

Right in Pavones, several very basic lodges cater to itinerant surfers by renting rooms for between $10 and $20 (£5–£10) per night for a double room; most take walk-in reservations since they don't have phones. There are also a couple of *sodas* where you can get Tico meals. The most popular spot for both cheap meals and cheap rooms is **Esquina del Mar** (no phone), which is right on the beach's edge, in front of the fattest part of the surf break. However, for in-town lodgings, I prefer **Mira Olas** (© **8393-7742**; www.miraolas.com), about 2 blocks uphill from the soccer field.

For light meals, I recommend **Café de la Suerte** (© **8879-0302**), a lively little joint located across from Esquina del Mar that serves breakfasts and lunches and specializes in vegetarian items, freshly baked goods, and fresh-fruit smoothies. For dinner, check out either the pizzas and Italian cuisine at **Pizzeria Valeri** (no phone) or the falafel and Mediterranean cuisine at **La Manta Club** (www.la-manta.com), where the day's surf action or a first-run movie is usually broadcast on a large screen.

EXPENSIVE

Tiskita Jungle Lodge ★★ *Finds*   This small ecolodge is nearly on the Panamanian border, with the beach on one side and rainforest-clad hills behind. The lodge itself is set on a hill a few hundred meters from the beach and commands a superb view of the ocean. There's a dark-sand swimming beach, tide pools, jungle waterfalls, a farm and forest to explore, and great bird-watching. Most of the land here is primary rainforest; the rest is a mix of secondary forest, reforestation projects, orchards, and pastures. Accommodations are in cozy rustic cabins with screen walls and verandas. Constructed of local hardwoods, the cabins have a very tropical feel. My favorite cabin is no. 6, which has a great view and ample deck space. Some cabins have two or three rooms, making them great for families but less private for couples. Most of the bathrooms are actually outdoors, although they are private and protected, allowing you to take in the sights and sounds as you shower and shave. Meals are served family-style in the open-air main lodge. Although they're not fancy, they're certainly tasty and filling, and you'll be eating plenty of ingredients straight from the gardens.

The lodge is more than 8 hours from San José by car, so most guests take advantage of the package tours, which can include air transportation to a private landing strip.

Pavones (A.P. 13411-1000, San José), 6km (3¾ miles) down the road from Pavones. ✆ **2296-8125**. Fax 2296-8133. www.tiskita-lodge.co.cr. 17 units. $260 (£130) double. Rates include 3 meals and 1 guided walk daily, and all taxes. Packages with transportation to and from Golfito or Puerto Jiménez are available. AE, MC, V. **Amenities:** Restaurant; bar; small pool; limited watersports equipment; laundry service. *In room:* No phone.

MODERATE

In addition to the place below, the new **Riviera Riverside Villas** (✆ **2776-2396;** www.pavonesriviera.com) offers modern, plush individual cabins, as well as several fully equipped house rentals, located a block or so inland from the water, right alongside the Río Claro (Clear River). **Cabinas La Ponderosa** (✆ **8824-4145;** www.cabinas laponderosa.com), is a small, beachfront collection of cabins and private, rustic villas, a little bit out of town, on the way to Punta Banco.

Casa Siempre Domingo   This small hillside inn offers up the best accommodations right in Pavones. The rooms all feature high ceilings, tile floors, and two double beds (one room has two doubles and a twin). The high beds are custom-made constructions, and they're uncommonly high off the ground. The owner says the design helps capture breeze from the picture windows, but if there's not enough, you can always crank up the air-conditioning. Meals are served on picnic tables in the large interior common space, and there is also a separate sitting room with satellite TV. The nicest feature is the huge deck, with its ocean view.

Pavones (A.P. 91, Golfito), several hundred meters south of downtown Pavones. ✆ **8820-4709**. www.casa-domingo.com. 4 units. $80 (£40) double. Rate includes breakfast and taxes. No credit cards. *In room:* A/C, no phone.

12

The Caribbean Coast

Costa Rica's Caribbean coast is a world apart from the rest of the country. The pace is slower, the food is spicier, the tropical heat is more palpable, and the rhythmic lilt of patois and reggae music fills the air.

This remains one of Costa Rica's least discovered and explored regions. More than half of the coastline here is still inaccessible except by boat or small plane. This inaccessibility has helped preserve large tracts of virgin lowland rainforest, which are now set aside as **Tortuguero National Park** ✿✿ and **Barra del Colorado National Wildlife Refuge** ✿. These two parks, on the northern reaches of this coast, are among Costa Rica's most popular destinations for adventurers and ecotravelers. Of particular interest are the sea turtles that nest here. Farther south, **Cahuita National Park** ✿ is another popular national park in this area, located just off its namesake beach village. It was set up to preserve 200 hectares (494 acres) of coral reef, but its palm tree–lined beaches and gentle trails are stunning.

So remote was the Caribbean coast from Costa Rica's population centers in the Central Valley that it developed a culture all its own. The original inhabitants of the area included people of the Bribri, Cabécar, and Kéköldi tribes, and these groups maintain their cultures on indigenous reserves in the Talamanca Mountains. In fact, until the 1870s, there were few non-Indians in this area. However, when Minor Keith built the railroad to San José and began planting bananas, he brought in black laborers from Jamaica and other Caribbean islands to lay the track and work the plantations. These workers and their descendants established fishing and farming communities up and down the coast. Today dreadlocked Rastafarians, reggae music, Creole cooking, and the English-based patois of this Afro-Caribbean culture give this region a quasi-Jamaican flavor. Many visitors find this striking contrast with the Spanish-derived Costa Rican culture fascinating.

Today, the Caribbean coast's main city of **Limón** is a major commercial port and budding cruise ship port of call.

Over the years, the Caribbean coast has garnered a reputation as being a dangerous, drug-infested zone, rife with crime and danger. Although there have been several high-profile crimes in the area, overall this reputation is exaggerated. The same crime and drug problems found here exist in San José and most of the more popular beach destinations on the Pacific coast. Use common sense and take normal precautions and you should have no problems on the Caribbean coast.

1 Barra del Colorado (★

115km (71 miles) NE of San José

Most visitors to Barra del Colorado come for the fishing. Tarpon and snook fishing are world-class, or you can head farther offshore for some deep-sea action. Barra del Colorado is part of the same ecosystem as Tortuguero National Park (see below); as in Tortuguero, there's an abundance of wildlife and rainforest fauna in the rivers and canals, which are accessible only by boat.

Named for its location at the mouth of the Río Colorado up near the Costa Rica–Nicaragua border, Barra del Colorado can be reached only by boat or small plane. There are no roads in or out of Barra del Colorado. The town itself is a small, ramshackle collection of raised stilt houses, and it supports a diverse population of Afro-Caribbean and Miskito Indian residents, Nicaraguan emigrants, and transient commercial fishermen.

It's hot and humid here most of the year, and it rains a lot, so although some of the lodges have at times risked offering a "tarpon guarantee," they're generally hesitant to promise anything in terms of the weather.

ESSENTIALS

GETTING THERE & DEPARTING   By Plane   Most folks come here on multi-day fishing packages, and most of the lodges in this area either operate charter flights as part of their package trips or will book you a flight.

Sansa (ⓒ 877/767-2672 in the U.S. and Canada, or 2290-4100 in Costa Rica; www.flysansa.com) has a flight that departs at 5:45am Monday, Friday, and Saturday for Barra del Colorado from San José's Juan Santamaría International Airport. The return flight to San José leaves Barra del Colorado daily at 6:55am. Flight duration is 45 minutes; the fare is $95 (£48) each way.

Nature Air (ⓒ 800/235-9272 in the U.S. and Canada, or 2299-6000; www. natureair.com) has a daily flight that departs the Tobías Bolaños International Airport in Pavas at 6:25am. Flight duration is 1 hour and 35 minutes, with stops in Limón and Tortuguero en route. The fare is $96 (£48) each way. The return flight leaves Barra del Colorado at approximately 7:10am.

By Boat   It is also possible to travel to Barra del Colorado by boat from **Puerto Viejo de Sarapiquí** (see chapter 9). Expect to pay $200 to $300 (£100–£150) each way for a boat that holds up to 10 people. Check at the public dock in Puerto Viejo de Sarapiquí. **Río Colorado Lodge** (ⓒ 800/243-9777 in the U.S. and Canada, or 2232-4063) runs its own launch between Barra del Colorado and Puerto Viejo de Sarapiquí (and sometimes btw. Barra and Limón), including land transportation between Puerto Viejo de Sarapiquí and San José. If you're staying at the Río Colorado Lodge, be sure to ask about this option (for at least one leg of your trip) when booking; the hotel doesn't discriminate—you can arrange transportation even if you aren't staying there. For $198 (£99) per person, you can arrange a pickup in San José, a minibus to the boat, a trip down the river to Barra, overnight accommodations at Río Colorado Lodge, and a return trip the next day, with all meals and taxes included.

ORIENTATION   The Río Colorado neatly divides the town of Barra del Colorado. The airstrip is in the southern half of town, as are most of the lodgings. The lodges that are farther up the canals will meet you at the airstrip with a small boat.

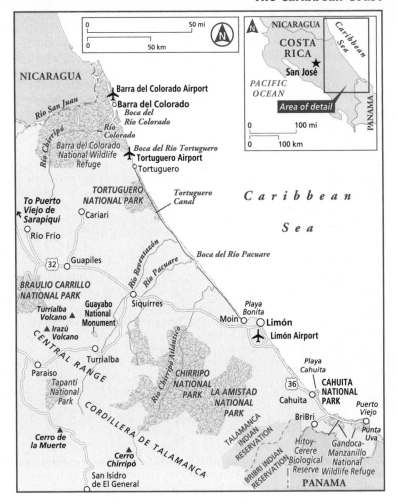

The Caribbean Coast

FISHING, FISHING & MORE FISHING

Almost all the lodges here specialize in fishing packages. If you don't fish, you may wonder just what in the world you're doing here. Even though there are excellent opportunities for bird-watching and touring jungle waterways, most lodges still merely pay lip service to ecotourists and would rather see you with a rod and reel.

Fishing takes place year-round. You can do it in the rivers and canals, in the very active river mouth, or offshore. Most anglers come in search of the tarpon, or silver king. **Tarpon** can be caught year-round, both in the river mouth and, to a lesser extent, in the canals; however, they are much harder to land in July and August—the two rainiest months—probably because the river runs so high and is so full of runoff and debris. **Snook,** an aggressive river fish, peak in April, May, October, and November; fat snook, or *calba,* run heavy November through January. Depending on how far out to sea you venture, you might hook up with **barracuda, jack, mackerel** (Spanish and king), **wahoo, tuna, dorado, marlin,** or **sailfish.** In the rivers and canals, fishermen regularly bring in *mojarra, machaca,* and *guapote* (rainbow bass).

Following current trends in sportfishing, more and more anglers have been using fly rods, in addition to traditional rod-and-reel setups, to land just about all the fish mentioned above. To fish here, you'll need both salt- ($24/£12) and freshwater ($30/£15) fishing licenses. The lodges here either include these in your packages or can readily provide the licenses for you.

Nonfishers should see whether their lodge has a good naturalist guide or canoes or kayaks for rent or use.

WHERE TO STAY & DINE

Almost all of the hotels here specialize in package tours, including all your meals, fishing and tackle, taxes, and usually your transportation and liquor too, so rates are high. There are no dependable budget hotels, and Barra remains a remote and difficult destination for independent and budget travelers. In addition to the places listed below, **Casa Mar Lodge** (© **800/543-0282** in the U.S. and Canada, or 2710-8093 in Costa Rica; www.casamarlodge.com) is a long-standing fishing lodge that is popular with hard-core anglers.

Río Colorado Lodge ⋆   This rustic lodge is one of the country's oldest and best-known fishing lodges. It was founded and built more than 30 years ago by local legend Archie Fields. The rooms are comfortable but decidedly rustic, with many showing the wear and tear of the years. The "honeymoon suite" is basically a standard room with a small mirror hung by ropes over the bed. As at Silver King Lodge, the whole complex is tied together by covered walkways.

The nicest feature here is the large covered deck out by the river, where breakfast is served. Dinner is dished out family-style in the second-floor dining room. There's also a large bar (where lunch is served) with satellite TV, pool table, and dartboard. The lodge runs a small "zoo" and participates in a macaw breeding project, as well as local education efforts. While their hearts may be in the right place, I find the zoo and cage conditions here rather desultory.

This lodge runs riverboat tours (see "Essentials," above) for those interested in cruising to either Puerto Viejo de Sarapiquí or Limón, as well as several other smaller launches for a variety of tours and outings.

Barra del Colorado (A.P. 5094-1000, San José). © **800/243-9777** in the U.S. and Canada, or 2232-4063 in Costa Rica. Fax 2231-5987. www.riocoloradolodge.com. 18 units. $2,239–$2,587 (£1,120-£1,294) per person double occupancy for 7 days/6 nights with 4 full days of fishing, including 2 nights lodging in San José, all meals and drinks at the lodge, boat, guide, fuel, licenses, and taxes. Nonfishing guests $120–$170 (£60–£85) per person per day. AE, MC, V. Amenities: Restaurant; bar; Jacuzzi; laundry service; tackle shop; 2 wheelchair-accessible rooms. In room: A/C, TV (in some), no phone.

Silver King Lodge ⋆⋆ (Finds)   This is the most upscale lodge in Barra del Colorado. They take their fishing seriously here—there's a large selection of modern boats and equipment, as well as a full tackle shop—but Silver King also emphasizes comfort. The rooms are immense, with two double beds, a desk and chair, luggage racks, fishing racks, air-conditioning, an overhead fan, and a roomy closet. The floors and walls are all varnished hardwood, and the ceilings are finished in bamboo. The entire complex is built on raised stilts and connected by covered walkways (useful during the frequent downpours).

The meals here are truly exceptional, with some of the best buffet-style lodge cooking I've ever had. Each all-you-can-eat meal is anchored with at least two main dishes and a wide variety of appetizers, salads, side dishes, and desserts. You should be eating plenty of fish during your stay—coconut-battered snook nuggets with a pineapple-wasabi dip were just one of the highlights of my culinary indulgences here. These folks also have a photographer snapping away digital shots of all the offshore action and give you a personalized CD of photos from your stay at no extra cost.

Barra del Colorado (mailing address: Interlink 399, P.O. Box 02-5635, Miami, FL 33102). © 800/847-3474 in the U.S., or ©/fax 2711-0708 in Costa Rica. www.silverkinglodge.net. 10 units. $1,875–$2,150 (£938–£1,075) per person double occupancy for 3 full days of fishing, air transportation to and from Barra del Colorado from San José, all meals at the lodge, liquor, and taxes; $350 (£175) per person per extra day, including all fishing, meals, liquor, and taxes; $175 (£88) per person for nonfishers, with no ground transportation. AE, MC, V. Closed throughout the months of July, Aug, and Dec. **Amenities:** Restaurant; bar w/satellite TV; small pool; enclosed Jacuzzi; massage; free daily laundry service; Internet for free in lobby. *In room:* A/C, free Wi-Fi, coffeemaker, no phone.

2 Tortuguero National Park ★★

250km (155 miles) NE of San José; 79km (49 miles) N of Limón

Sometimes dubbed "the Venice of Costa Rica," Tortuguero is connected to Limón, and the rest of mainland Costa Rica, by a series of rivers and canals. This aquatic highway is lined almost entirely with a dense tropical rainforest that is home to howler and spider monkeys, three-toed sloths, toucans, and great green macaws. A trip through the canals is nothing like touring around Venice in a gondola, but it is a lot like cruising the Amazon basin—on a much smaller scale.

"Tortuguero" comes from the Spanish name for the giant sea turtles *(tortugas)* that nest on the beaches of this region every year from early March to mid-October (prime season is July–Oct, and peak months are Aug and Sept). The chance to see this nesting attracts many people to this remote region, but just as many come to explore the intricate network of jungle canals that serve as the region's main transportation arteries.

Very important: More than 200 inches of rain fall here annually, so you can expect a downpour at any time of the year. Most of the lodges will provide you with rain gear (including ponchos and rubber boots), but it can't hurt to carry your own.

Independent travel is not the norm here, although it's possible. Most travelers rely on their lodge for boat transportation through the canals and into town. At most of the lodges around Tortuguero, almost everything (bus rides to and from, boat trips through the canals, and even family-style meals) is done in groups. This group feeling can be intimate and rewarding, or overwhelming and impersonal.

ESSENTIALS

GETTING THERE & DEPARTING   By Plane   Nature Air (© 800/235-9272 in the U.S. and Canada, or 2299-6000; www.natureair.com) has one flight that departs daily at 6:15am for Tortuguero from Tobías Bolaños International Airport in Pavas. The flight takes approximately 55 minutes; the fare is $91 (£46) each way. The return flight leaves Tortuguero daily at around 7:30am for San José.

Sansa (© 877/767-2672 in the U.S. and Canada, or 2290-4100 in Costa Rica; www.flysansa.com) has a daily flight for Tortuguero from San José's Juan Santamaría International Airport. The flight departs at 5:45am on Monday, Friday, and Saturday, and at 6:12am the rest of the week. The flight is direct and 45 minutes long when leaving at 6:12am. It takes about 30 minutes longer the other days, with a preliminary stop in Barra de Colorado. The fare is $95 (£50) each way. The return flight leaves Tortuguero daily at 6:50am for San José, stopping in Barra del Colorado en route.

It always pays to check with both Sansa and Nature Air. Additional flights are often added during the high season, and departure times can vary according to weather or the whim of the airline. In addition, many lodges in this area operate charter flights as part of their package trips.

Be sure to arrange with your hotel to pick you up at the airstrip. Otherwise you'll have to plead with one of the other hotel's boat captains to give you a lift, which they will usually do, either for free or for a few dollars.

By Car It's not possible to drive to Tortuguero. If you have a car, your best bet is either to leave it in San José and take an organized tour; or drive it to Limón or Moín, find a secure hotel or public parking lot, and then follow the directions for arriving by boat below. You can also leave your car at the lot at Caño Blanco Marina (p. 367), but you should try to arrange your boat transportation and lodging in advance. There is a road sign declaring TORTUGUERO at the turnoff for Caño Blanco Marina. There is also secure parking in La Pavona, which is useful for those meeting the boats plying the Cariari and La Pavona route outlined below.

By Boat Flying to Tortuguero is convenient if you don't have much time, but a boat trip through the canals and rivers of this region is often the highlight of any visit to Tortuguero. However, be forewarned: Although this trip can be stunning and exciting, it can also be long, tiring, and uncomfortable. You'll first have to ride by bus or minivan from San José to Moín, Caño Blanco, or one of the other embarkation points; then it's 2 to 3 hours on a boat, usually with hard wooden benches or plastic seats. All of the more expensive lodges listed offer their own bus and boat transportation packages, which include the boat ride through the canals. However, if you're coming here on the cheap and plan to stay at one of the less expensive lodges or at a budget *cabina* in Tortuguero, you will have to arrange your own transportation. In this case, you have a few options.

The most traditional option is to get yourself first to Limón and then to the public docks in **Moín,** just north of Limón, and try to find a boat on your own. You can reach Limón easily by public bus from San José (see "Getting There & Departing" under "Limón: Gateway to Tortuguero National Park & Southern Coastal Beaches," later in this chapter). If you're coming by car, make sure you drive all the way to Limón or Moín, unless you have arrangements out of Cariari or Caño Blanco Marina.

If you arrive in Limón by bus, you might be able to catch one of the periodic local buses to Moín right there at the main bus terminal; it costs around 50¢ (25p). Otherwise, you can take a taxi for around $6 (£3), for up to four people. At the docks, you should be able to negotiate a fare of between $40 and $70 (£20–£35) per person round-trip. These boats tend to depart between 8 and 10am every morning. You can stay as many days as you like in Tortuguero, but be sure to arrange with the captain to be there to pick you up when you're ready to leave. The trip from Moín to Tortuguero takes between 3 and 4 hours.

As I mentioned above, it is possible to get to Tortuguero by bus and boat from Cariari. For backpackers and budget travelers, this is the cheapest and most reliable means of reaching Tortuguero from San José. To take this route, begin by catching the 9 or 10:30am direct bus to Cariari from the **Gran Terminal del Caribe,** on Calle Central, 1 block north of Avenida 11 (✆ **2222-0610**). The fare is $2.30 (£1.15). This bus will actually drop you off at the main bus terminal in Cariari, from which you'll have to walk 5 blocks north to a separate small bus station. Look for a booth marked COOPETRACA or Clic Clic. At these booths you can buy your bus ticket for La Pavona. The bus fare is around $2 (£1). Buy a ticket for the noon bus (a later bus leaves at 3pm). A boat will be waiting to meet the bus at the dock at the edge of the river at around 1:30pm (and again at 4:30pm). Check with each of the two boat services you will find at the dock in La Pavona and pay on board. The boat fare to Tortuguero is not regulated, and the price sometimes varies for foreigners. It can be as low as $3 (£1.50) each way, which is what locals pay. However, the boat captains often try to gouge tourists. Stand firm; you should not have to pay more than $6 (£3). Return boats leave Tortuguero for La Pavona every morning at 6 and 11:30am, and 3pm, making return bus connections to Cariari.

Warning: Be careful if you decide to take this route. I've received reports of unscrupulous operators providing misinformation to tourists. *Note:* Folks from a company called **Bananera** have set up shop at the Gran Terminal del Caribe and in Cariari, offering to sell you "packaged transportation" to Tortuguero. However, all they are doing is charging you extra to buy the individual tickets described above. Be especially careful if the folks selling you boat transportation aggressively steer you to a specific hotel option, claim that your first choice is full, or insist that you must buy a package with them that includes the transportation, lodging, and guide services. If you have doubts or want to check on the current state of this route, contact the naturalist guide Daryl Loth in Tortuguero (© **8833-0827**; safari@racsa.co.cr). Or you can check out the site www.tortugerovillage.com, which has detailed directions about how to get to Tortuguero by a variety of routes.

Finally, it's also possible, albeit expensive, to travel to Tortuguero by boat from **Puerto Viejo de Sarapiquí** (see chapter 9). Expect to pay $250 to $375 (£125–£188) each way for a boat that holds up to 10 people. Check at the public dock in Puerto Viejo de Sarapiquí if you're interested. The ride usually takes about 3 to 4 hours, and the boats tend to leave in the morning.

ORIENTATION   Tortuguero is one of the most remote locations in Costa Rica. There are no roads into this area and no cars in the village, so all transportation is by boat or foot. Most of the lodges are spread out over several kilometers to the north of the village of Tortuguero on either side of the main canal; the small airstrip is at the north end of the beachside spit of land. At the far northern end of the main canal, you'll see the **Cerro de Tortuguero (Turtle Hill),** which, at some 119m (390 ft.), towers over the area. The hike to the top of this hill is a popular half-day tour and offers some good views of the Tortuguero canals and village, as well as the Caribbean Sea.

Tortuguero Village is a tiny collection of houses connected by footpaths. The village is spread out on a thin spit of land, bordered on one side by the Caribbean Sea and on the other by the main canal. At most points, it's less than 300m (984 ft.) wide. In the center of the village, you'll find a small children's playground and a soccer field, as well as a kiosk that has information on the cultural and natural history of this area.

If you stay at a hotel on the ocean side of the canal, you'll be able to walk into and explore the village at your leisure; if you're across the canal, you'll be dependent on the lodge's boat transportation. However, some of the lodges across the canal have their own network of jungle trails that might appeal to naturalists.

FAST FACTS   There are no banks, ATMs, or currency-exchange houses in Tortuguero, so be sure to bring sufficient cash in colones to cover any expenses and incidental charges. The local hotels and shops generally charge a hefty commission to exchange dollars. There is an **information center** (© 8833-0827) in town in front of the Catholic church. This is a good place for independent travelers looking to arrange local tours and onward travel. You'll find a dependable Internet cafe at **La Casona** (© 2709-8092), a small restaurant and budget hotel in the heart of the village.

EXPLORING THE NATIONAL PARK

According to existing records, sea turtles have frequented Tortuguero National Park since at least 1592, largely due to its extreme isolation. Over the years, turtles were captured and their eggs were harvested by local settlers; by the 1950s this practice became so widespread that turtles faced extinction. Regulations controlling this mini-industry were passed in 1963, and in 1970 Tortuguero National Park was established.

Today four different species of sea turtles nest here: the green turtle, the hawksbill, the loggerhead, and the giant leatherback. The prime nesting period is from **July to mid-October** (Aug–Sept are peak months). The park's beaches are excellent places to watch sea turtles nest, especially at night. As appealingly long and deserted as they are, however, the beaches are not appropriate for swimming. The surf is usually very rough, and the river mouths have a nasty habit of attracting sharks that feed on the turtle hatchlings and many fish that live here.

Green turtles are perhaps the most common turtle found in Tortuguero, so you're more likely to see one of them than any other species if you visit during the prime nesting season. **Loggerheads** are very rare, so don't be disappointed if you don't see one. The **giant leatherback** is perhaps the most spectacular sea turtle to watch laying eggs. The largest of all turtle species, the leatherback can grow to 2m (6½ ft.) long and weigh well over 1,000 pounds. It nests from early March to mid-April, predominantly in the southern part of the park.

You can explore the park's rainforest, either by foot or by boat, and look for some of the incredible varieties of wildlife that live here: jaguars, anteaters, howler monkeys, collared and white-lipped peccaries, some 350 species of birds, and countless butterflies, among others. Boat tours are far and away the most popular way to visit this park, although one frequently very muddy trail starts at the park entrance and runs for about 2km (1¼ miles) through the coastal rainforest and along the beach.

ENTRY POINT, FEES & REGULATIONS   The Tortuguero National Park entrance and ranger station are at the south end of Tortuguero Village. Admission to the park is $10 (£5). However, most people visit Tortuguero as part of a package tour. Be sure to confirm whether the park entrance is included in the price. Moreover, only

---

Turtle Tips

- Visitors to the beach at night must be accompanied by a licensed guide. Tours generally last between 2 and 4 hours.
- Sometimes you must walk quite a bit to encounter a nesting turtle. Wear sneakers or walking shoes rather than sandals. The beach is very dark at night, and it's easy to trip or step on driftwood or other detritus.
- Wear dark clothes. White T-shirts are not permitted.
- Flashlights, flash cameras, and lighted video cameras are prohibited on turtle tours.
- Smoking is prohibited on the beach at night.

certain canals and trails leaving from the park station are actually within the park. Many hotels and private guides take their tours to a series of canals that border the park and are very similar in terms of flora and fauna but don't require a park entrance. When the turtles are nesting, you will have to arrange a night tour in advance with either your hotel or one of the private guides working in town. These guided tours generally run between $10 and $15 (£5–£7.50). Flashlights and flash cameras are not permitted on the beach at night because the lights discourage the turtles from nesting.

ORGANIZED TOURS   Most visitors come to Tortuguero on an organized tour. All of the lodges listed below, with the exception of the most inexpensive accommodations in Tortuguero Village, offer package tours that include various hikes and river tours; this is generally the best way to visit the area.

In addition, several San José–based tour companies offer budget 2-day/1-night excursions to Tortuguero, including transportation, all meals, and limited tours around the region. Prices for these trips range between $90 and $200 (£45–£100) per person, and—depending on price—guests are lodged either in one of the basic hotels in Tortuguero Village or one of the nicer lodges listed below. Reputable companies offering these excursions include the **Learning Trips** (© 800/723-2674 in the U.S. and Canada, or 2258-2293 in Costa Rica; www.costa-rica.us) and **Caño Blanco Marina** (© 2256-9444). There are even 1-day trips that spend almost all their time coming and going but that do allow for a quick tour of the canals and lunch in Tortuguero. These trips are good for travelers who like to be able to say, "Been there, done that," and they generally run between $80 and $100 (£40–£50) per person. However, these trips spend most of their time traveling to and from Tortuguero. If you really want to experience Tortuguero, I recommend staying for at least 2 nights.

Alternately, you could go with **Fran and Modesto Watson** ✦ (© 2226-0986; www.tortugerocanals.com), who are pioneering guides in this region and operate their own boat. The couple offers a range of overnight and multiday packages to Tortuguero, with lodging options at most of the major lodges here.

BOAT CANAL TOURS   Aside from watching the turtles nest, the unique thing to do in Tortuguero is tour the canals by boat, keeping your eye out for tropical birds and native wildlife. Most lodges can arrange a canal tour for you, but you can also arrange a tour through one of the operators in Tortuguero Village. I recommend **Daryl Loth** (© 8833-0827; safari@racsa.co.cr), who runs the Casa Marbella (see below) in the center of the village. I also recommend **Ernesto Castillo,** who can be reached through Cabinas Sabina or by asking around the village. If neither of these guides is available, ask for a recommendation at the **Jungle Shop** (© 2709-8072) or at the **Caribbean Conservation Corporation's Museum** (© 2709-8091). Most guides charge between $10 and $15 (£5–£7.50) per person for a tour of the canals. If you travel through the park, you'll also have to pay the park entrance fee ($10/£5 per person).

EXPLORING THE VILLAGE

The most popular attraction in town is the small **Caribbean Conservation Corporation's Visitors' Center and Museum** ✦ (© 2709-8091; www.cccturtle.org). The museum has information and exhibits on a whole range of native flora and fauna, but its primary focus is on the life and natural history of the sea turtles. Most visits to the museum include a short, informative video on the turtles. There's a small gift shop here, and all the proceeds go toward conservation and turtle protection. The museum is open Monday through Saturday from 10am to noon and 2 to 5:30pm, and Sunday from 2 to 5pm. There's a $1 (50p) admission charge, but more generous donations are encouraged.

In the village you can also rent dugout canoes, known in Costa Rica as *cayucos* or *pangas*. Be careful before renting and taking off in one of these; they tend to be heavy, slow, and hard to maneuver, and you might be getting more than you bargained for. **Miss Junie** (© 2709-8102) rents lighter and more modern fiberglass canoes for around $10 (£5) for a half-day.

You'll find a couple of souvenir shops on the main footpath near the center of the village. About 182m (597 ft.) of this path was recently paved with concrete. The **Paraíso Tropical Gift Shop** has the largest selection of gifts and souvenirs, by far. But I prefer the **Jungle Shop,** which has a higher-end selection of wares and donates 10% of its profits to local schools.

PLAYING TARZAN IN TORTUGUERO

It was only a matter of time 'til Tortuguero caught up with the rest of the country, and you can now experience the thrill of a zip-line canopy tour here. **Secrets of the Jungle** (© 2709-8209; www.secretsofthegreenjungle.com) charges $35 (£18) for a chance to glide from treetop platform to treetop platform through the dense forests of this area. The tour, which includes local guides, also features some hiking and suspended pedestrian bridges.

WHERE TO STAY & DINE

Although the room rates below may appear high, keep in mind that they usually include round-trip transportation from San José (which amounts to approx. $100–$140/£50–£70 per person), plus all meals, taxes, and usually some tours. When broken down into nightly room rates, most of the lodges are really charging only between $60 and $120 (£30–£60) for a double room. Note: When I list package rates below, I have always listed the least expensive travel option, which is a bus and boat combination both in and out. All of the lodges also offer packages with the option of a plane flight either one or both ways.

Most visitors take all their meals, as part of a package, at their hotel. There are a couple of simple *sodas* (diners) and local restaurants in town. The best of these are **La Casona** (© 2709-8092) and the **Buddha Café** (© 2709-8084).

VERY EXPENSIVE

Manatus Hotel ★★   This intimate new hotel offers the only true luxury accommodations in Tortuguero. The large rooms are plush and well-equipped, with two queen-size beds, high ceilings, wood floors, tasteful local furnishings, and a host of amenities you won't find anywhere else in the area. I prefer the second-floor rooms, with high peaked ceilings and exposed wood beams. Meals and service are top-notch here, and they even have the only spa (albeit small) of any local hotel, as well as an on-site art gallery. The amoeba-shaped pool is set just off the dark waters of the Tortuguero canal, with a broad deck and plenty of inviting chaise longues surrounding it.

Tortuguero. © **2239-4854** reservations in San José, or 2709-8197 at the hotel. Fax 2239-4854. www.manatushotel. com. 12 units. $640 (£320) double for 2 days/1 night; $830 (£415) double for 3 days/2 nights. Rates include round-trip transportation from San José, 3 meals daily, taxes, and daily tours. Rates lower in off season. AE, MC, V. **Amenities:** Restaurant; bar; free-form pool; small spa and exercise room; game room; tour desk; room service; laundry service. *In room:* A/C, TV, minibar, safe.

EXPENSIVE

Laguna Lodge ⚡ This popular lodge is 2km (1¼ miles) north of Tortuguero Village, on the ocean side of the main canal (which allows you to walk along the beach and into town at your leisure). All rooms are spacious and attractive. Most have wood walls, waxed hardwood floors, and tiled bathrooms with screened upper walls to let in air and light. Each room also has a little shared veranda overlooking flowering gardens. The large dining area is on a free-form deck that extends out over the Tortuguero Canal. Another covered deck, also over the water, is strung with hammocks for lazing away the afternoons. Several covered palapa huts, also strung with hammocks, have been built among the flowering ginger and hibiscus. There's a large landscaped pool, with a poolside bar and grill, as well as a butterfly garden and botanical garden. All the standard Tortuguero tours are available.

Tortuguero (A.P. 173-2015, San José). ℂ **2272-4943** for reservations, or 2709-8082 at the lodge. Fax 2272-4927. www.lagunatortuguero.com. 80 units. $510 (£255) double for 2 days/1 night; $568 (£284) double for 3 days/2 nights. Rates include round-trip transportation from San José, tours, taxes, and 3 meals daily. Rates lower in the off season. AE, DC, MC, V. **Amenities:** Restaurant; 2 bars; large free-form pool; laundry service. *In room:* No phone.

Mawamba Lodge ⚡ Located just north of Tortuguero Village on the ocean side of the canal, Mawamba is quite similar to Laguna Lodge—perhaps because the two lodges are owned by brothers. Rooms have varnished wood floors, twin beds, hot-water showers, ceiling fans, and verandas with rocking chairs. All rooms are painted in bright Caribbean colors. In 2008, a few "superior rooms" were added, with king-size beds and a few extra amenities, like hair dryers and a bathtub. The gardens are lush and overgrown with flowering ginger, heliconia, and hibiscus. There are plenty of hammocks around for anyone who wants to kick back and a beach volleyball court for those who don't. These folks also offer an extensive menu of kayaking tours and excursions, including one package in which you actually kayak part of the way into Tortuguero. On the premises are a small gift shop, a small butterfly garden, a game room, and nightly lectures and slide shows that focus on the natural history of this area.

Tortuguero (A.P. 10980-1000, San José). ℂ **2293-8181** or 2709-8100. Fax 2239-7657. www.grupomawamba.com. 54 units. $446 (£223) double for 2 days/1 night; $560 (£280) double for 3 days/2 nights. Rates include round-trip transportation from San José, 3 meals daily, taxes, and some tours. Rates lower in off season. AE, MC, V. **Amenities:** Restaurant; bar; free-form pool; laundry service. *In room:* No phone.

Pachira Lodge ⚡ The rooms in this lodge are in a series of four-plex buildings perched on stilts and connected by covered walkways in a dense section of secondary forest set in a little bit from the main canal. Each room is spacious and clean, with varnished wood floors, painted wood walls, two double beds, ceiling fans, and plenty of cross ventilation. The covered walkways come in handy when it rains. Standard buffet meals are served in a large, screened-in dining room. There's a large, cool pool in the shape of a turtle, with children's wading pools built into the flippers. Bilingual guides and all the major tour options are available.

Tortuguero (A.P. 1818-1002, San José). ℂ **2223-1682** or 2256-7080. Fax 2223-1119. www.pachiralodge.com. 34 units. $376 (£188) double for 2 days/1 night; $538 (£269) double for 3 days/2 nights. Rates include round-trip transportation from San José, 3 meals daily, taxes, and tours. AE, MC, V. **Amenities:** Restaurant; bar; pool; laundry service. *In room:* No phone.

Turtle Beach Lodge This isolated ecolodge is located 8km (5 miles) north of the village of Tortuguero, about 20 minutes away by boat. The grounds are set on a narrow strip of land between the Caribbean Sea and the Caño Palma canal. The accommodations are somewhat more spartan than those at the lodges listed above, but they are still clean and comfortable. The rooms are housed in a series of long buildings. Most feature exterior walls that are solid on the bottom half and pure screening above. The best rooms are the corner units, which get the most airflow and circulation. All have some form of shared or private verandas. Given its location, this is one of the more convenient lodges for viewing the turtle nestings. There's a small, turtle-shaped pool in the center of the grounds, and they have a stable of horses available for riding tours.

Caño Palma, Tortuguero. ⓒ 2248-0707 in San José, or 8837-6969 at the lodge. Fax 2257-4409. www.turtlebeach lodge.com. 47 units. $380 (£190) double for 2 days/1 night; $510 (£255) double for 3 days/2 nights. Rates include round-trip transportation from San José, 3 meals daily, and tours. AE, MC, V. **Amenities:** Restaurant; bar; lounge w/satellite TV; Internet cafe; pool; laundry service. *In room:* No phone.

MODERATE

Tortuga Lodge ⭐⭐ (Kids)   This one of the oldest lodges in Tortuguero, and still one of the best. My favorite feature here is the long multilevel deck off the main dining room, where you can sit and dine, sip a cool tropical drink, or just take in the view as the water laps against the docks at your feet. There's also a lovely little pool built by the water's edge that's designed to look like it blends into Tortuguero's main canal. All the rooms feature contemporary furniture, Caribbean-influenced decor, and loads of freshly varnished hardwood. If possible, I'd opt for the second-floor rooms, which feature varnished wood walls and floors and come with a small, covered veranda. There's also a new two-bedroom, two-bathroom second-floor penthouse suite for families or those wanting more space. There are several acres of forest behind the lodge, and a few kilometers of trails wind their way through the trees. This is a great place to look for howler monkeys and colorful poison-arrow frogs.

Tortuguero (mailing address: SJO 235, P.O. Box 025216, Miami, FL 33102-5216). ⓒ 800/886-2609 in the U.S. and Canada, or 2257-0766 reservations in San José or 2710-8016 at the lodge. Fax 2257-1665. www.tortugalodge.com. 27 units. $102 (£51) double; $160 (£80) penthouse. A full-meal plan costs $50 (£25) per person Rates lower in off season; slightly higher during peak periods. Package rates with transportation, meals, and tours are available. AE, MC, V. **Amenities:** Restaurant; bar; small pool; game room; laundry service. *In room:* No phone.

INEXPENSIVE

Several basic *cabinas* in the village of Tortuguero offer budget lodgings for between $8 and $15 (£4–£7.50) per person. **Cabinas Miss Junie** (ⓒ 2709-8102) and **Cabinas Miss Miriam** (ⓒ 2709-8107) are the traditional favorites, although in my opinion, the best of the batch are the **Cabinas Icaco** (ⓒ 2709-8044), **Cabinas La Casona** (ⓒ 2709-8092), and **Cabinas Tortuguero** (ⓒ 2709-8114).

Casa Marbella ⭐ (Value)   Right in the village of Tortuguero, this converted house is an excellent option for budget travelers looking for a bit more comfort and care than that offered at most of the other inexpensive in-town options. It's also a good alternative for those wishing to avoid the large groups and cattle-car-like operations of most big lodges here. The rooms all have high ceilings, tile floors, firm mattresses, and white walls with varnished wood trim. Owner Daryl Loth is a longtime resident and well-respected naturalist guide. Breakfast is served on a little patio facing the main Tortuguero canal in back of the house. A library and lounge area complement the facilities, and a wide range of tours can be arranged. The newest addition here is two "superior" rooms, with direct views of the canal.

Tortuguero, Limón. ⓒ/fax 2709-8011 or ⓒ 8833-0827. http://casamarbella.tripod.com. 8 units. $35–$40 (£18–£20) double; $50–$60 (£25–£30) superior. Rates include breakfast. No credit cards. *In room:* No phone.

3 Limón: Gateway to Tortuguero National Park & Southern Coastal Beaches

160km (99 miles) E of San José; 55km (34 miles) N of Puerto Viejo

It was just offshore from present-day Limón, in the lee of Isla Uvita, that Christopher Columbus is said to have anchored in 1502, on his fourth and final voyage to the New World. Believing that this was potentially a very rich land, he christened it Costa Rica ("Rich Coast"). While never supplying the Spanish crown with much in the way of gold or jewels, the spot where he anchored has proved over the centuries to be the best port on Costa Rica's Caribbean coast—so his judgment wasn't all bad. From here the first bananas were shipped to North America in the late 19th century. Today Limón is primarily a rough-and-tumble port city that ships millions of pounds of bananas northward every year. It also receives a fair share of the country's ocean-borne imports and a modest number of cruise ship callings. On days when a cruise ship is in port, you'll find the city bustling far beyond the norm.

Limón is not generally considered a tourist destination, and few tourists take the time to tour the city, except those stopping here on cruise ships. Very few choose to stay here, and I don't recommend it except during Carnaval—and even then you're better off in Cahuita or Puerto Viejo. Most travelers use it primarily as a gateway to Tortuguero to the north or the beaches of Cahuita and Puerto Viejo to the south. However, if you do spend some time in Limón, take a seat in Parque Vargas along the seawall and watch the city's citizens go about their business. You may even spot some sloths living in the trees here. Take a walk around town if you're interested in architecture. When banana shipments built this port, many local merchants erected elaborately decorated buildings, several of which have survived the city's many earthquakes, humid weather, and salty sea air. There's a certain charm in the town's fallen grace, drooping balconies, rotting woodwork, and chipped paint. Just be careful, particularly after dark and outside of the city center—Limón has earned a reputation for frequent muggings and robberies.

If you want to get in some beach time while you're in Limón, hop in a taxi or a local bus and head north a few kilometers to **Playa Bonita,** a small public beach. Although the water isn't very clean and is usually too rough for swimming, the setting is much more attractive than downtown. This beach is popular with surfers.

ESSENTIALS

GETTING THERE & DEPARTING   By Plane   Nature Air (© 800/235-9272 in the U.S. and Canada, or 2299-6000; www.natureair.com) has one flight that departs daily at 1pm for Limón from the Tobías Bolaños International Airport in

---

Tips A Fall Festival

The biggest event of the year in Limón, and one of the liveliest festivals in Costa Rica, is the annual **Carnaval,** which is held around Columbus Day (Oct 12). For a week, languid Limón shifts into high gear for a nonstop bacchanal orchestrated to the beat of reggae, soca, and calypso music. During the revelries, residents don costumes and take to the streets in a dazzling parade of color. If you want to experience Carnaval, make your reservations early because hotels fill up fast. (This advice goes for the entire coast.)

Pavas. The flight takes 45 minutes. This flight continues on to Bocas del Toro, Panama. The return flight leaves Limón for San José at 3:30pm. The fare is $87 (£44) one-way.

By Car   The Guápiles Highway heads north out of San José on Calle 3 before turning east and passing close to Barva Volcano and through the rainforests of Braulio Carrillo National Park en route to Limón. The drive takes about 2½ hours and is spectacularly beautiful, especially when it's not raining or misty. Alternately, you can take the old highway, which is also scenic but much slower. This highway heads east out of San José on Avenida Central and passes through San Pedro before reaching Cartago. From Cartago on, the road is narrow and winding and passes through Paraíso and Turrialba before descending out of the mountains to Siquirres, where the old highway meets the new. This route takes around 4 hours, more or less, to get to Limón.

By Bus   **Transportes Caribeños** buses (© **2222-0610** in San José, or 2758-2575 in Limón) leave San José every half-hour daily between 5am and 7pm from the Caribbean bus terminal (Gran Terminal del Caribe) on Calle Central, 1 block north of Avenida 11. Friday through Sunday, the last bus leaves an hour later at 8pm. Trip duration is 2½ to 3 hours. The buses are either direct or local *(corriente),* and they don't alternate in any particularly predictable fashion. The local buses are generally older and less comfortable and stop en route to pick up passengers from the roadside. I highly recommend taking a direct bus, if possible. The fare is $4.50 (£2.25) one-way.

Buses leave Limón for San José every half-hour between 6am and 7:30pm, and similarly alternate between local and direct, with the last bus leaving 1 hour later Friday through Sunday. The Limón bus terminal is on the main road into town, several blocks west of the downtown area and Parque Vargas. Buses (© **2758-1572** for the terminal) to **Cahuita** and **Puerto Viejo** leave from here roughly every hour from 5am to 6pm daily. Buses to **Punta Uva** and **Manzanillo,** both of which are south of Puerto Viejo, leave Limón daily at 6 and 10:30am and 3 and 6pm, from the same station.

ORIENTATION   Nearly all addresses in Limón are measured from the central market, which is aptly located smack-dab in the center of town, or from Parque Vargas, which is at the east end of town fronting the sea. The cruise ship dock is just south of Parque Vargas. A pedestrian mall runs from Parque Vargas to the west for several blocks.

FAST FACTS   A host of private and national banks are located in the small downtown area. You can reach the **local police** at © **2758-1148** and the **Red Cross** at © **2758-0125.** The **Tony Facio Hospital** (© **2758-0580**) is just outside of the downtown area on the road to Playa Bonita.

WHERE TO STAY & DINE

In addition to the hotels listed below, if you want to be right on the beach at Playa Bonita, check out the **Beach Hotel Cocori** (© **2795-1670;** fax 2795-2930), a simple hotel with a great location; the neighboring beach bar and disco can be loud, though.

Park Hotel ⓐ   This is easily, and perennially, the best option in Limón proper—although there really isn't much competition. The hotel has an excellent location fronting the ocean, across the street from the fire station. Unlike much of Limón, which seems to be in a state of prolonged and steady decay, the Park Hotel receives regular and fairly competent upkeep year in and year out. Ask for a room on the ocean side of the hotel because these are brighter, quieter, and cooler than those that face the fire station, although they're also slightly more expensive. The suites have private oceanview balconies and larger bathrooms with tubs. The large, sunny dining room off the lobby serves standard Tico fare at very reasonable prices.

Av. 3, btw. calles 1 and 3 (A.P. 35-7300), Limón. ✆ 2758-3476 or 2798-0555. Fax 2758-4364. 32 units. $52–$65 double (£26–£33). AE, MC, V. **Amenities:** Restaurant. *In room:* A/C, TV, safe.

EN ROUTE SOUTH

Staying at the place listed below is a great way to combine some quiet beach time on the Caribbean coast with a more active ecolodge and bird-watching experience into one compact itinerary.

Selva Bananito Lodge ★★ *(Finds)*   The individual raised-stilt cabins here are spacious and comfortable, with an abundance of varnished woodwork. Inside are two double beds, a desk and chair, and some fresh flowers, as well as a large private bathroom. Outside is a wraparound veranda with a hammock and some chairs. It all adds up to what I call rustic luxury. Half the cabins have views of the Bananito River and a small valley; the other half have views of the Matama Mountains (part of the Talamanca mountain range). There are no electric lights at Selva Bananito, but each evening as you dine by candlelight, your cabin's oil lamps are lit for you. Hot water is provided by solar panels. There's a wide range of tours and activities, including rainforest hikes and horseback rides in the jungle, tree climbing, self-guided trail hikes, and even the opportunity to rappel down the face of a jungle waterfall.

The owners are very involved in conservation efforts in this area, and approximately two-thirds of the 840 hectares (2,100 acres) here are primary forest managed as a private reserve. You'll need a four-wheel-drive vehicle to reach the lodge itself, although most folks leave their rental cars in Bananito and let the lodge drive them the final bit. You can also arrange to be picked up in San José.

Bananito (A.P. 2333-2050, San Pedro). ✆ 2253-8118. Fax 2280-0820. www.selvabananito.com. 11 units. $260–$280 double (£130–£140). Rates include 3 meals daily and all taxes. Rates lower in off season. No credit cards. **Amenities:** Restaurant; activity desk. *In room:* No phone.

4 Cahuita ★

200km (124 miles) E of San José; 42km (26 miles) S of Limón; 13km (8 miles) N of Puerto Viejo

Cahuita is a tiny Caribbean beach village and the first "major" tourist destination heading south out of Limón. Nevertheless, the boom going on in Puerto Viejo and the beaches south of Puerto Viejo have in many ways passed Cahuita by. Depending on your point of view, that can be a reason to stay here or to decide to head farther south. Any way you slice it, Cahuita is one of the most laid-back villages in Costa Rica. The few dirt and gravel streets here are host to a languid parade of pedestrian traffic, parted occasionally by a bicycle, car, or bus. After a short time, you'll find yourself slipping into the heat-induced torpor that affects anyone who ends up here.

The village traces its roots to Afro-Caribbean fishermen and laborers who settled in this region in the mid-1800s, and today the population is still primarily English-speaking blacks whose culture and language set them apart from other Costa Ricans.

People come to Cahuita for its miles of pristine beaches, which stretch both north and south from town. The southern beaches, the forest behind them, and the coral reef offshore (one of just a handful in Costa Rica) are all part of **Cahuita National Park.**

Silt and pesticides washing down from nearby banana plantations have taken a heavy toll on the coral reefs, so don't expect the snorkeling to be world-class. But on a calm day, it can be pretty good, and the beaches are idyllic every day. It can rain almost any time of year here, but the most dependably dry months are September and October.

ESSENTIALS

GETTING THERE & DEPARTING   By Plane   The closest airport to Cahuita is found in Limón (see above). A taxi from the airport to Cahuita should cost around $15 (£7.50). You can also just walk the long block from the airport terminal to the main road south and flag down any of the frequent buses that pass by.

By Car   Follow the directions above for getting to Limón. As you enter Limón, about 5 blocks before the busiest section of downtown, watch for a paved road to the right, just before the railroad tracks. Take this road south to Cahuita, passing the airstrip and the beach on your left as you leave Limón. Alternatively, there's a turnoff with signs for Sixaola and La Bomba several miles before Limón. This winding short-cut skirts the city and puts you on the coastal road several miles south of town.

By Bus   Mepe express buses (© 2257-8129) leave San José daily at 6 and 10am, noon, and 2 and 4pm from the new Caribbean bus terminal (Gran Terminal del Caribe) on Calle Central, 1 block north of Avenida 11. The trip's duration is 4 hours; the fare is $6.50 (£3.25). During peak periods, extra buses are often added. However, it's wise to check because this bus line **(Mepe)** is one of the most fickle.

Alternatively, you can catch a bus to **Limón** (see above) and then transfer to a Cahuita- or Puerto Viejo–bound bus (© 2758-1572) in Limón. These latter buses leave roughly every hour between 5am and 6pm from in front of Radio Casino, which is 1 block north of the municipal market. Buses from Limón to Manzanillo also stop in Cahuita and leave from the same spot daily at 6 and 10am and 3 and 6pm. The trip takes 1 hour; the fare is $1.50 (75p).

Gray Line (© 2220-2126; www.graylinecostarica.com) has a daily bus that leaves San José for Cahuita at 9:30am. The fare is $33 (£17). The return bus leaves Cahuita at 7:20am. **Interbus** (© 2283-5573; www.interbusonline.com) has a daily bus that leaves San José for Cahuita at 7:50am. The fare is $35 (£18). Interbus buses leave Cahuita daily at both 7:20am and 3:15pm. Both companies will pick you up at most area hotels in both San José and Cahuita, and both offer connections to various other destinations around Costa Rica.

Buses departing **Puerto Viejo** and Sixaola (on the Panama border) stop in Cahuita at approximately 7, 8, 9:30, and 11:30am, and 4:30pm en route to San José. How-ever, this schedule is far from precise, so it's always best to check with your hotel. Moreover, these buses are often full, particularly on weekends and throughout the high season. To avoid standing in the aisle all the way to San José, it is sometimes bet-ter to take a bus first to Limón and then catch one of the frequent Limón–San José buses. Buses to Limón pass through Cahuita regularly throughout the day. Another tactic I've used is to take a morning bus to Puerto Viejo, spend the day down there, and board a direct bus to San José at its point of origin, thereby snagging a seat.

ORIENTATION   There are only about eight dirt streets in Cahuita. The highway runs parallel to the coast, with three main roads running perpendicular. The north-ernmost of these roads bypasses town and brings you to the northern end of Playa Negra. It's marked with signs for the Magellan Inn and other hotels up on this end. The second road in brings you to the southern end of Playa Negra, a half-mile closer to town. The third road is the principal entrance into town. The village's main street in town, which runs parallel to the highway, dead-ends at the entrance to the national park (a footbridge over a small stream).

Buses drop their passengers by a small public park in front of Coco's Bar (see below). Across from the park you'll find a helpful large-scale map of the town. If you come in on the bus and are staying at a lodge on Playa Negra, ask around town for a cab or head out walking north on the street that runs between Coco's Bar and the small park. This road curves to the left and continues a mile or so out to Playa Negra.

FAST FACTS   You can wash your clothes at the self-service **laundromat** in front of Cabinas Vaz. One load in the washer or dryer costs $1.50 (75p). The **police station** (© 2755-0217) is located where the road from Playa Negra turns into town. The **post office** is next door to the police station.

If you can't find a **cab** in town, try calling **René** (© 2755-0243), **Wayne** (© 2755-0078), or **Dino** (© 2755-0012). You can also rent a scooter from **Sucurucú** (© 2755-0218), which is located in the village, at Cabinas Vaz.

EXPLORING CAHUITA NATIONAL PARK ☙

On arrival, you'll immediately feel the call of the long scimitar of beach that stretches south from the edge of town. This beach can be glimpsed through the trees from Cahuita's sun-baked main street and extends a promise of relief from the heat. Although the lush coastal forest and picture-perfect palm lines are a tremendous draw, the park was actually created to preserve the 240-hectare (787-acre) **coral reef** that surrounds it. The reef contains 35 species of coral and provides a haven for hundreds of brightly colored tropical fish. You can walk on the beach itself or follow the trail that runs through the forest just behind the beach to check out the reef.

The best place to swim is just before or beyond the **Río Perezoso (Lazy River)**, several hundred meters inside Cahuita National Park. The trail behind the beach is great for bird-watching, and if you're lucky, you might see some monkeys or a sloth. The loud grunting sounds you'll hear off in the distance are the calls of howler monkeys, which can be heard from more than a kilometer away. Nearer at hand, you're likely to hear crabs scuttling amid the dry leaves on the forest floor—a half-dozen or so species of land crabs live in this region—my favorites are the bright orange-and-purple ones.

The trail behind the beach stretches a little more than 6.4km (4 miles) to the southern end of the park at **Puerto Vargas,** where you'll find a beautiful white-sand beach, the park headquarters, and a primitive campground with showers and outhouses. It's a nice, flat walk, but a rewarding one because there's good wildlife viewing and access to the beach. The reef is off the point just north of Puerto Vargas, and you can snorkel here. If you don't dawdle, the hike to Puerto Vargas should take no more than 2 hours each way. Bring plenty of mosquito repellent because this area can be buggy.

Although there's snorkeling at Puerto Vargas, the nicest coral heads are several hundred meters offshore, and it's best to have a boat take you out. A 3-hour **snorkel trip** costs between $15 and $30 (£7.50–£15) per person with equipment. You can arrange one with any of the local tour companies listed below. *Note:* These trips are best taken when the seas are calm—for safety's sake, visibility, and comfort.

ENTRY POINTS, FEES & REGULATIONS   The **in-town park entrance** is just over a footbridge at the end of the village's main street. It has bathroom facilities, changing rooms, and storage lockers. This is the best place to enter if you just want to spend the day on the beach and maybe take a little hike in the bordering forest.

The alternate park entrance is at the southern end of the park in **Puerto Vargas.** This is where you should come if you plan to camp at the park or if you don't feel up to hiking a couple of hours to reach the good snorkeling spots. The road to Puerto Vargas is approximately 5km (3 miles) south of Cahuita on the left.

Officially, **admission** is $10 (£5) per person per day, but this is collected only at the Puerto Vargas entrance. You can enter the park from the town of Cahuita for free or with a voluntary contribution. The park is open from dawn to dusk for day visitors.

Camping is an extra $2 (£1) per person. Fifty campsites at Puerto Vargas stretch along for several kilometers and are either right on or just a few steps from the beach. My favorite are those farthest from the entrance. A small ranger station has basic shower and bathroom facilities, but they're a bit far from some of the better campsites.

GETTING THERE **By Car** The turnoff for the Puerto Vargas entrance is clearly marked 7km (4⅓ miles) south of Cahuita.

By Bus Your best bet is to get off a Puerto Viejo- or Sixaola-bound bus at the turnoff for the Puerto Vargas entrance (well marked, but tell the bus driver in advance). The guard station/entrance is only about 500m (1,640 ft.) down this road. However, the campsites are several kilometers farther, so it's a long hike with a heavy pack.

BEACHES & ACTIVITIES OUTSIDE THE PARK

Outside the park the best place for swimming is **Playa Negra.** The stretch right in front of the Atlantida Lodge is my favorite spot here.

There are plenty of options for organized adventure trips or tours while in Cahuita. I recommend **Cahuita Tours and Adventure Center** (© 2755-0000; www.cahuita tours.com), on the village's main street heading out toward Playa Negra. They offer a wide range of tour and activity options, including glass-bottom-boat and snorkeling trips ($25/£13 per person), jungle tours ($35–$45/£18–£23), white-water rafting trips ($100/£50), and jeep tours to a nearby Bribri Reservation ($80/£40).

Turística Cahuita Information Center (©/fax 2755-0071), also on the main road heading toward Playa Negra, and **Roberto Tours** (© 2755-0117), 50m (164 ft.) south of the bus stop, offer similar tours at similar prices. Most of the companies offer multiday trips to Tortuguero, as well as to Bocas del Toro, Panama.

Brigitte (© 2755-0053; www.brigittecahuita.com) rents horses for $12 (£6) per hour (you must have experience riding) and offers guided horseback tours for $35 to $40 (£18–£20). She also rents mountain bikes for $8 (£4) per day, and even has a few rooms available.

On the main highway, just north of the main entrance to Cahuita, is the **Mariposario Cahuita** (© 2755-0361), a large, informative butterfly-farm attraction that charges $8 (£4) and is open daily from 8:30am to 3:30pm. It's best to come in the early morning on a sunny day, when the butterflies are most active.

Bird-watchers and sloth lovers should head north 9km (5½ miles) to **Aviarios del Caribe and the Buttercup Sloth Rescue Center** ★★ (©/fax 2750-0775; www.sloth rescue.org). The folks here run a sloth rehabilitation project and also offer guided canoe tours through the surrounding estuary and river system. More than 330 species of birds have been spotted here. The 3½-hour canoe tour costs $30 (£15) per person and leaves at 6am and 3pm. There's also a 1¼-hour canoe tour combination that includes a visit to the sloth rehabilitation center and a self-guided hike on its trails for $20 (£10) per person. This option is available between 8am and 2:30pm. It's best to make reservations in advance.

SHOPPING

For a wide selection of beachwear, local crafts, cheesy souvenirs, and batik clothing, try **Boutique Coco Miko** or **Boutique Bambata,** which are both on the main road near the entrance to the park. The latter is also a good place to have your hair wrapped in colorful threads and strung with beads. Out toward Playa Negra, similar wares are offered at the **Cahuita Tours** gift shop. Handmade jewelry and crafts are sold by local and itinerant artisans in makeshift stands near the park entrance.

Ask around town for a copy of Paula Palmer's *What Happen: A Folk-History of Costa Rica's Talamanca Coast* (Zona Tropical; 2005). The book is a history of the region based on interviews with many of the area's oldest residents. Much of it is in the traditional Creole language, from which the title is taken. It makes fun and interesting reading, and you just might bump into someone mentioned in the book.

If you are interested in the local music scene, pick up a disc by Walter "Gavitt" Ferguson. The local 87-year-old calypso singer and songwriter is a living legend and has two CDs of original songs, *Babylon* and *Dr. Bombodee.* Ask around town and you should be able to find a copy. If you're lucky, you might even bump into Gavitt.

WHERE TO STAY

MODERATE

El Encanto Bed and Breakfast 🗚🗚 *Value*   The individual bungalows at this little bed-and-breakfast are set in from the road on spacious and well-kept grounds. The bungalows themselves are also spacious and have attractive touches such as wooden bed frames, arched windows, Mexican-tile floors, Guatemalan bedspreads, and framed Panamanian *molas* hanging on the walls. There is a separate two-story, three-bedroom, two-bathroom house with a full kitchen at the rear of the grounds, as well as a deluxe room. Hearty breakfasts are served in the small open dining room surrounded by lush gardens. Nice extra touches here include a small kidney-shaped pool, a wood-floored meditation hall, a covered garden gazebo, and an open-air massage room.

Cahuita (A.P. 7302-7), Limón (just outside of town on the road to Playa Negra). ✆ **2755-0113.** Fax 2755-0432. www.elencantobedandbreakfast.com. 7 units. $65–$85 (£33–£43) double. Rates include full breakfast. Rates slightly lower in off season; higher during peak weeks. MC, V. **Amenities:** Small pool. *In room:* No phone.

Hotel La Diosa 🗚   Close to the sea north of Playa Negra, this hotel has some of the coziest and most inviting rooms around, with excellent facilities and friendly hosts. The best rooms here have air-conditioning and private Jacuzzis. All have cool tile floors, rattan furnishings, and plenty of ventilation. There's a midsize pool, as well as a yoga and meditation room. While breakfast is served daily, there's no restaurant. The hotel is just steps from the sea, but the coast here is rugged and made up mostly of sharp coral, and not very suitable for swimming. Still, the gardens are lush and beautiful, and a relaxed and welcoming vibe pervades this place.

Cahuita, Limón (north of town, inland from the Playa Negra road). ✆ **877/632-3198** in the U.S. and Canada, or 2755-0055 in Costa Rica. Fax 2755-0321. www.hotelladiosa.net. 18 units. $55–$85 (£28–£43) double. Rates include full breakfast. Rates slightly lower in off season; higher during peak weeks. MC, V. **Amenities:** Midsize pool. *In room:* No phone.

Magellan Inn 🗚   With an understated sense of tropical sophistication, this small inn has thrived over the years. The carpeted rooms have French doors, vertical blinds, tiled bathrooms with hardwood counters, and two joined single beds. Each room has its own tiled veranda with a Persian rug and bamboo sitting chairs. About half of the rooms have air-conditioning. Although there's a ceiling fan over each bed, the non-air-conditioned

rooms could use a bit more ventilation. The combination bar/lounge and dining room features even more Persian-style rugs and wicker furniture. Most memorable of all are the hotel's sunken pool and lush gardens, both of which are built into a crevice in the ancient coral reef that underlies this entire region—which leads to good bird-watching.

At the far end of Playa Negra (about 2km/1¼ miles north of Cahuita), Cahuita (A.P. 1132), Limón. ©/fax **2755-0035.** www.magellaninn.com. 6 units. $69 (£35) double; $99 (£49) double with A/C. Rates include continental breakfast. Rates slightly lower in off season; higher during peak weeks. AE, MC, V. **Amenities:** Bar; lounge; small pool; tour desk; laundry service. In room: Free Wi-Fi, no phone.

INEXPENSIVE

In addition to the places listed below, **Spencer's Seaside Cabinas** (© **2755-0027**) and its somewhat funky collection of budget rooms is worth considering; its rooms are set just a few feet from the water in the heart of town. Another option is **Hotel Belle Fleur** (© **2755-0283;** hotelbellefleur@hotmail.com), which has neat and cheery rooms set just a few feet back from the main road, close to the national park entrance.

Alby Lodge ★ (Value) With the feel of a small village, Alby Lodge is a fascinating little place hand-built by its German owners. Although the four small cabins are close to the center of the village, they're surrounded by a large lawn and feel secluded. The cabins are quintessentially tropical, with thatched roofs, mosquito nets, hardwood floors and beams, big shuttered windows, tile bathrooms, and a hammock slung on the front porch. There's no restaurant here, but you may cook your own meals in a communal kitchen area if you wish. The turnoff for the lodge is on your right just before you reach the national park entrance; the hotel is about 136m (446 ft.) down a narrow, winding lane from here.

Cahuita (A.P. 840), Limón. ©/fax **2755-0031.** www.albylodge.com. 4 units. $40 (£20) double; $45 (£23) triple; $50 (£25) quad. Children 11 and under stay free in parent's room. No credit cards. In room: Free Wi-Fi, safe, no phone.

Cabinas Arrecife Located near the water, next to Restaurant Edith (p. 379), this row of basic rooms is an excellent budget choice in Cahuita. Each room comes with a double and a single bed, a table fan, and tile floors. There's not a lot of room to move around, but things are pretty clean and well kept for this price range. A shared veranda boasts some chairs for sitting, where you can catch a glimpse of the sea through a dense stand of coconut palms. If you want to be closer to the sea, grab one of the hammocks strung on the palms or sit in the small, open restaurant, which serves breakfast every day and dinners according to demand.

Cahuita (about 100m/328 ft. east of the post office), Limón. ©/fax **2755-0081.** 12 units. $25–$30 (£13–£15) double. AE, MC, V. **Amenities:** Restaurant. In room: No phone.

WHERE TO DINE

Coconut meat and milk figure in a lot of the regional cuisine here. Most nights, local women cook up pots of various local specialties and sell them from the front porches of the two discos or from streetside stands around town; a full meal will cost you around $2 to $5 (£1–£2.50).

In addition to the places listed below, **Restaurante Cactus** (© **2755-0276**) serves good thin-crust pizzas, and **Caribbean Roots & Culture** (© **8811-9351**) cooks up excellent Pan-Caribbean and vegetarian fare. Another local favorite is **Relax** (© **2755-0322**), which serves a mix of local, Italian, and Mexican food in a new, expanded space on the road between Cahuita and Puerto Viejo.

Cha Cha Cha &&& SEAFOOD/INTERNATIONAL Fresh seafood and grilled meats, simply and expertly prepared—What more could you ask from a casual, open-air restaurant in a funky beach town? In addition to the fresh catch of the day and filet mignon, the eclectic menu here includes everything from jerk chicken and Thai shrimp salad to pasta primavera and fajitas. The grilled squid salad with a citrus dressing is one of the house specialties and a great light bite. The restaurant occupies the ground floor of an old wooden building. Everything is painted pure white, with some blue trim and accents. The restaurant has only a half-dozen or so tables that fill up fast.

On the main road in town, 3 blocks north of Coco's Bar. ✆ **8394-4153** or 2755-0476. Reservations recommended during the high season. Main courses $6–$21 (£3–£11). MC, V. Tues–Sun 2–10pm.

Restaurant Edith & *Finds* CREOLE/SEAFOOD This place is a local institution, and deservedly so. If you want a taste of the local cuisine in a homey, sit-down environment, this is the place. Miss Edith's daughters do most of the cooking and serving today, but you might just find her on hand. The menu is long, with lots of local seafood dishes and Creole combinations such as yuca in coconut milk with meat or vegetables. The sauces have spice and zest and are a welcome change from the typically bland fare served up elsewhere in Costa Rica. After you've ordered, it's usually no more than 45 minutes until your meal arrives. It's often crowded, so don't be bashful about sitting down with total strangers at any of the big tables. Hours can be erratic; it sometimes closes without warning. However, with advance notice, and some cajoling, Miss Edith can even be tempted into giving classes in local cooking.

By the police station, Cahuita. ✆ **2755-0248**. Reservations not accepted. Main courses $5–$20 (£2.50–£10). No credit cards. Mon–Sat 11am–10pm; Sun 4–9pm.

Sobre Las Olas & SEAFOOD/ITALIAN Set on a slight rise of rocks above a coral cove and breaking waves, this place has by far the best location in Cahuita. The Italian owners serve a mix of local and Italian fare. They serve excellent fresh squid or shrimp in a tangy local coconut milk sauce, as well as a host of pasta dishes. The fresh grilled snapper is also always a good way to go. I especially like this place for lunch, since you can really enjoy the view of the clear blue Caribbean Sea then. If weather permits, grab one of the outdoor tables set in the shade of coconut palms. After you finish eating, slide over and into one of the hammocks strung between those palms.

Just north of town on the road to Playa Negra. ✆ **2755-0109**. Reservations not necessary. Main courses $8–$20 (£4–£10). MC, V. Wed–Mon noon–10pm.

CAHUITA AFTER DARK

Coco's Bar &, a classic Caribbean watering hole at the main crossroads in town, has traditionally been the place to spend your nights (or days, for that matter) if you like cold beer and very loud reggae and soca music. Toward the park entrance, the **National Park Restaurant** has a popular bar and disco on most nights during the high season and on weekends during the off season.

5 Puerto Viejo &&

200km (124 miles) E of San José; 55km (34 miles) S of Limón

Puerto Viejo is the hottest spot on Costa Rica's Caribbean coast. And I'm not just talking about the sometimes stifling heat. Even though Puerto Viejo is farther down the road from Cahuita, it's much more popular, with a livelier vibe and more ongoing development. Much of this is due to the many surfers who come here to ride the town's famous and fearsome Salsa Brava wave, and only slightly mellower Playa Cocles beach break. Nonsurfers will appreciate the abundance of excellent swimming beaches, plenty of active adventure options, nearby rainforest trails, and some great local and international restaurants.

As you head still farther south, you will come to the most beautiful beaches on this coast, with white sand and turquoise seas. When it's calm (Aug–Oct), the waters down here are some of the clearest anywhere in the country, with good snorkeling among the nearby coral reefs.

This is the end of the line along Costa Rica's Caribbean coast. After the tiny town of Manzanillo, some 15km (9⅓ miles) south of Puerto Viejo, a national wildlife reserve stretches a few final kilometers to the Panamanian border.

This area gets plenty of rain, just like the rest of the coast (Sept–Oct are your best bets for sun, although it's not guaranteed even in those months).

ESSENTIALS
GETTING THERE & DEPARTING   By Plane   The closest airport to Puerto Viejo is in Limón (see "Limón: Gateway to Tortuguero National Park & Southern Coastal Beaches," earlier in this chapter). A taxi from the airport to Cahuita should cost around $20 (£10). Alternately, you can just walk the long block from the airport terminal to the main road south and flag down any of the frequent buses that pass by.

By Car   To reach Puerto Viejo, continue south from Cahuita for another 16km (10 miles). Watch for a prominent fork in the highway. The right-hand fork continues on to Bribri and Sixaola. The left-hand fork (it actually appears to be a straight shot) takes you into Puerto Viejo on 5km (3 miles) of paved road.

By Bus   Mepe express buses (© **2257-8129** in San José, or 2750-0023 in Puerto Viejo) to Puerto Viejo leave San José daily at 6 and 10am, noon, and 2 and 4pm from the new Caribbean terminal (Gran Terminal del Caribe) on Calle Central, 1 block north of Avenida 11. The trip's duration is 4½ to 5 hours; the fare is $7 (£3.50). During peak periods extra buses are sometimes added. Always ask if the bus is going into Puerto Viejo (you do not want to get dropped off at the turnoff for Sixaola) and if it's continuing on to **Manzanillo** (especially helpful if you're staying in a hotel south of town). Regardless, don't be surprised if it doesn't do exactly what you were told.

Gray Line (© **2220-2126;** www.graylinecostarica.com) has a daily bus that leaves San José for Puerto Viejo at 9:30am. The fare is $33 (£17). The return bus leaves Puerto Viejo at 7am. **Interbus** (© **2283-5573;** www.interbusonline.com) has a daily bus that leaves San José for Puerto Viejo at 7:50am. The fare is $35 (£18). Interbus buses leave Puerto Viejo daily at both 7am and 2:50pm. Both companies will pick you up at most area hotels in both San José and Puerto Viejo, and both offer connections to various other destinations around Costa Rica.

Alternatively, you can catch a bus to **Limón** (see earlier in this chapter for details) and then transfer to a Puerto Viejo–bound bus in Limón. These latter buses (© **2758-1572**) leave roughly every hour between 5am and 6pm from in front of Radio Casino, which is 1 block north of the municipal market. Buses from Limón to Manzanillo also stop in Puerto Viejo and leave daily at 6 and 10:30am and 3 and 6pm. The trip takes 1½ hours; the fare is $2 (£1).

If you arrive in Puerto Viejo by bus, be leery of hucksters and touts offering you hotel rooms. In most cases, they just work on a small commission from whatever hotel

Puerto Viejo

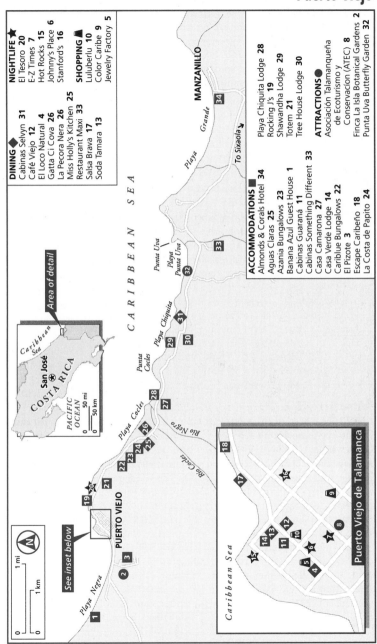

DINING ◆
Cabinas Selvyn **31**
Café Viejo **12**
El Loco Natural **4**
Gatta Ci Cova **26**
La Pecora Nera **26**
Miss Holly's Kitchen **25**
Restaurant Maxi **33**
Salsa Brava **17**
Soda Tamara **13**

NIGHTLIFE ★
El Tesoro **20**
E-Z Times **7**
Hot Rocks **15**
Johnny's Place **6**
Stanford's **16**

SHOPPING 🛍
Luluberlu **10**
Color Caribe **9**
Jewelry Factory **5**

ACCOMMODATIONS ■
Almonds & Corals Hotel **34**
Aguas Claras **25**
Azania Bungalows **23**
Banana Azul Guest House **1**
Cabinas Guaraná **11**
Cabinas Something Different **33**
Casa Camarona **27**
Casa Verde Lodge **14**
Cariblue Bungalows **22**
El Pizote **3**
Escape Caribeño **18**
La Costa de Papito **24**
Playa Chiquita Lodge **28**
Rocking J's **19**
Shawandha Lodge **29**
Totem **21**
Tree House Lodge **30**

ATTRACTIONS ●
Asociación Talamanqueña
de Ecoturismo y
Conservación (ATEC) **8**
Finca La Isla Botanical Gardens **2**
Punta Uva Butterfly Garden **32**

or *cabina* is hiring, and, in some cases, they'll steer you away from one of my recommended hotels or falsely claim that it is full.

Express buses leave Puerto Viejo for San José daily at 7:30, 9, and 11am, and 4pm. Buses for Limón leave daily at 6 and 9am, and 1, 4, and 5pm. Buses to **Punta Uva** and **Manzanillo** leave Puerto Viejo daily around 7:30am, noon, and 4:30 and 7:30pm. These buses return from Manzanillo at 5 and 8:15am and 12:45 and 5pm.

ORIENTATION The road in from the highway runs parallel to Playa Negra, or Black Sand Beach (this is not the same one I talked about in Cahuita), for a couple hundred meters before entering the village of Puerto Viejo, which has all of about 10 dirt streets. The sea is on your left and forested hills on your right as you come into town. It's another 15km (9⅓ miles) south to Manzanillo. This road is paved all the way to Manzanillo, although some sections are nonetheless in fairly rough shape.

FAST FACTS **Public phones** are located around town and at several hotels. Those looking to change money should head to the **Banco de Costa Rica** branch on the main road in town. There's also a **Banco Nacional** branch in **Bribri,** about 10km (6 miles) away. Both of these banks have ATMs. You'll find the **post office** in the tiny strip mall behind Café Viejo. There is a **Guardia Rural police office** (© 2750-0230) on the beach, near Johnny's Place (see later in this chapter).

There are several little Internet cafes around town. There are also a couple of full-service laundromats—the one at **Café Rico** (© 2750-0325) will give you a free cup of coffee, cappuccino, or espresso while you wait.

There are a handful of taxi drivers in town. You'll either find them hanging around the *parquecito* (little park), or you can try calling **Bull** (© 2750-0112 or 8836-8219) or **Delroy** (© 2750-0132). You can rent scooters and bicycles from several operators in town. I like **Sucurucú** (© 2750-0700), which is just south of the bus stop, and **Dragon Scooter Rentals** (© 2750-0728), which is across from the restaurant Salsa Brava, at the stand for **Aventuras Bravas.**

WHAT TO SEE & DO

CULTURAL & ADVENTURE TOURS The **Asociación Talamanqueña de Eco-turismo y Conservación** (ATEC; Talamancan Association of Ecotourism and Conservation; © 2750-0398 or ©/fax 2750-0191; www.ateccr.org), across the street from the Soda Tamara, is concerned with preserving the environment and cultural heritage of this area and promoting ecologically sound development. (If you plan to stay in Puerto Viejo for an extended period of time and would like to contribute to the community, ask about volunteering.) In addition to functioning as the local information center, Internet cafe, and traveler's hub, ATEC runs a little shop that sells T-shirts, maps, posters, and books.

ATEC also offers quite a few tours, including **half-day walks** that focus on nature and either the local Afro-Caribbean culture or the indigenous Bribri culture. These walks pass through farms and forests, and along the way you'll learn about local history, customs, medicinal plants, and Indian mythology, and have an opportunity to see sloths, monkeys, iguanas, keel-billed toucans, and other wildlife. There is a range of different walks through the nearby Bribri Indians' Kéköldi Reserve, as well as more strenuous hikes through the primary rainforest. **Bird walks** and **night walks** will help you spot more of the area wildlife; there are even overnight treks. The local guides have a wealth of information and make a hike through the forest a truly educational experience. Half-day walks (and night walks) are $20 to $35 (£10–£18), and a full-day

---

Tips **South Caribbean Music Festival**

Each year, the folks at Playa Chiquita Lodge (p. 390) organize a month-long festival of concerts and workshops featuring local and national musical groups
and solo artists. The dates vary, but the festival tends to fall somewhere during
the months of March and April and always ends the week before Easter. Concerts are usually held on Friday and weekends at Playa Chiquita Lodge and
other venues around the area.

---

tour costs between $33 and $80 (£17–£40). ATEC can arrange snorkeling trips to the
nearby coral reefs, as well as snorkeling and fishing trips in dugout canoes. A half-day
of snorkeling or fishing costs around $20 to $45 (£10–£23) per person.

ATEC can also help you arrange overnight and multiday **camping trips** into the
Talamanca Mountains and through neighboring indigenous reserves, as well as trips
to Tortuguero and even a 7- to 10-day transcontinental trek to the Pacific coast. Some
tours require minimum groups of 5 or 10 people and several days' advance notice. The
ATEC office is open daily from 8am to 9pm.

Local tour operators **Exploradores Outdoors** *ℱ* (ℂ **2750-0641;** www.exploradores
outdoors.com), **Puerto Viejo Tours & Rentals** (ℂ **2750-0411**), and **Terraventuras** *ℱ*
(ℂ **2750-0750;** www.terraventuras.com) all offer a whole host of half- and full-day
adventure tours into the jungle or sea for between $25 and $100 (£13–£50) per person. One popular tour is Terraventuras' zip-line canopy tour, which features 23 treetop platforms, a large harnessed swing, and a rappel.

One of the more educational tours is the 2-hour **Chocolate Tour** (ℂ **2750-0075**)
through a working organic cacao plantation and chocolate production facility. The
tour shows you the whole process of growing, harvesting, and processing cacao, and
of course there's a tasting at the end. The tour is run by reservation only, and costs $15
(£7.50) per person, with a four-person minimum.

Scuba divers can check in with **Aquamor** *ℱ* (ℂ **2759-9012**) or **Reef Runners
Dive Shop** (ℂ **2750-0480**). Both operations frequent a variety of dive sites between
Punta Uva and Manzanillo, and if you're lucky the seas will be calm and visibility
good—although throughout most of the year it can be a bit rough and murky here.
Aquamor is based down in Manzanillo (where you'll find the best reefs), while Reef
Runners has an office in downtown Puerto Viejo.

A LITTLE MIND & BODY REVITALIZATION   If you're looking for some day-
spa pampering, check out **Pure Jungle Spa** *ℱℱ* (ℂ **2750-0536;** www.purejungle
spa.com). Located at La Costa de Papito (see below), these folks have a wide range of
massage and treatment options at reasonable rates. They make many of their own oils,
masks, wraps, and exfoliants.

Better suited to a longer stay, **Samasati** *ℱ* (ℂ **800/563-9643** in the U.S., or 2756-
8015 in Costa Rica; www.samasati.com) is a lovely jungle yoga retreat and spa, with
spectacular hillside views of the Caribbean Sea and surrounding forests. Rates here run
between $75 and $162 (£38–£81) per person per day, depending on occupancy and
room type, and include three vegetarian meals per day and taxes. A wide range of tour,
massage, and yoga packages are available. If you're staying elsewhere in Puerto Viejo
or Cahuita, you can come up for yoga classes ($12/£6), meditations ($5/£2.50), or

private massages ($75–$85/£38–£43) with advance notice. Samasati is located a couple of kilometers before Puerto Viejo (near the turnoff for Bribri) and roughly 1.6km (1 mile) up into the jungle.

NOT YOUR EVERYDAY GARDENS   One of the nicest ways to spend a day in Puerto Viejo is to visit the **Finca La Isla Botanical Gardens** 🌟🌟 (✆ **2750-0046** or 8886-8530; crgarden@mac.com), a couple hundred meters inland from the Black Sand Beach on a side road just north of El Pizote lodge. Peter Kring and his late wife Lindy have poured time and love into the creation of this meandering collection of native and imported tropical flora. You'll see medicinal, commercial, and just plain wild flowering plants, fruits, herbs, trees, and bushes. Visitors get to gorge on whatever is ripe at the moment. There's also a rigorous rainforest loop trail leaving from the grounds. The gardens are generally open Friday through Monday from 10am to 4pm, but visits at other times can sometimes be arranged in advance. Entrance to the garden or loop trail is $5 (£2.50) per person, or $10 (£5) with the guided tour.

Cacao Trails 🌟 (✆ **2756-8186;** www.cacaotrails.com) is a one-stop attraction featuring botanical gardens, a small serpentarium, an open-air museum demonstrating the tools and techniques of cacao cultivation and processing, and a series of trails. There's also a large open-air restaurant, and a swimming pool for cooling off. You can also take canoe rides on the bordering Carbon River, and even watch sea turtles lay their eggs during the nesting season. Admission to the attraction is $25 (£13), including a guided tour. A full-day tour, including lunch and a canoe trip, as well as the guided tour, costs $47 (£24). During turtle nesting season, they do night tours to watch sea turtles lay their eggs.

Near Punta Uva, you'll find the **Punta Uva Butterfly Garden** 🌟 (✆ **2750-0086**). This small yet well-run facility is the only butterfly-breeding and production facility along the coast, and it's open daily from 8am to 4pm. Admission is $5 (£2.50) for adults; children enter free.

Finally, down around Playa Chiquita, at the Tree House Lodge (see below), there's the **Green Iguana Conservation Tour** (✆ **2750-0706;** www.greeniguana.com). This educational tour focuses on the life cycle, habits, and current situation of this endangered reptile. The tour features a walk around a massive natural enclosure, as well as a video presentation. The cost is $15 (£7.50).

SUNNING & SURFING   **Surfing** has historically been the main draw here, but increasing numbers of folks are coming for the miles of beautiful and uncrowded **beaches** 🌟🌟, acres of lush rainforests, and laid-back atmosphere. If you aren't a surfer, the same activities that prevail in any quiet beach town are the norm here—sunbathe, go for a walk on the beach, read a book, or take a nap. If you have more energy, there's a host of tours and hiking options, or you can rent a bicycle or a horse. For swimming and sunbathing, locals like to hang out on the small patches of sand in front of Stanford's Disco and Johnny's Place. There are small, protected tide pools in front of each of these bars for cooling off.

If you want a more open patch of sand and sea, head north out to **Playa Negra,** along the road into town, or, better yet, to the beaches south of town around Punta Uva and all the way down to Manzanillo, where the coral reefs keep the surf much more manageable (see "Manzanillo & the Manzanillo-Gandoca Wildlife Refuge," below).

Just offshore from the tiny village park is a shallow reef where powerful storm-generated waves sometimes reach 6m (20 ft.). **Salsa Brava,** as it's known, is the prime surf break on the Caribbean coast. Even when the waves are small, this spot is recommended only for very experienced surfers because of the danger of the reef. Other popular beach breaks are south of town on Playa Cocles. If you're interested in surf lessons or want to rent a board, check in with **Aventuras Bravas** (© 8849-7600). They charge $10 (£5) for a half-day board rental, and $15 (£7.50) for a full-day rental.

Several operators and makeshift roadside stands offer bicycles, scooters, boogie boards, surfboards, and snorkel gear for rent. Shop around to compare prices and the quality of the equipment before settling on any one.

ANOTHER WAY TO GET WET & WILD **Exploradores Outdoors** ✦ (© 2222-6262 in San José, or 2750-2020 in Puerto Viejo; www.exploradoresoutdoors.com) runs daily white-water rafting trips on the Pacuare and Reventazón rivers. The full-day trip, including transportation, breakfast, and lunch, is $95 (£48). If you want to combine white-water rafting with your transportation to or from the Caribbean coast, they can pick you up at your hotel in San José with all your luggage, take you for a day of white-water rafting, and drop you off at day's end at your hotel anywhere on the Caribbean coast from Cahuita to Manzanillo. You can also choose to use the option in the other direction.

MANZANILLO & THE MANZANILLO-GANDOCA WILDLIFE REFUGE ✦✦

If you continue south on the coast road from Puerto Viejo, you'll come to a couple of even smaller villages. **Punta Uva** ✦✦ is 8km (5 miles) away, and **Manzanillo** ✦✦ is about 15km (9⅓ miles) away. For a good day trip, you can catch the 7:15am bus from Puerto Viejo down to Manzanillo and then catch the 5:15pm bus back. There are several other buses running this route throughout the day, although it's always wise to check with ATEC about current local bus schedules. You could also hire a cab for around $6 (£3) to Punta Uva or $10 (£5) to Manzanillo. Alternatively, it's about 1½ hours each way by bicycle, with only two relatively small hills to contend with. Although the road is ostensibly paved all the way to Manzanillo, between the near-constant potholes and washed-out sections, it's almost like riding an off-road trail. It's also possible to walk along the beach all the way from Puerto Viejo to Manzanillo, with just a couple of short and well-worn detours inland around rocky points. However, I recommend you catch a ride down to Manzanillo and save your walking energies for the trails and beaches inside the refuge.

Manzanillo is a tiny village with only a few basic *cabinas* and funky *sodas,* although this has been changing in recent years. The most popular place to eat and hang out is **Restaurant Maxi** ✦ (© 2759-9086), an open-air joint located on the second floor of an old wooden building facing the sea. This place gets packed on weekends, especially for lunch.

The **Manzanillo-Gandoca Wildlife Refuge** ✦✦ encompasses the small village and extends all the way to the Panamanian border. Manatees, crocodiles, and more than 350 species of birds live within the boundaries of the reserve. The reserve also includes the coral reef offshore—when the seas are calm, this is the best **snorkeling** and **diving** spot on this entire coast. Four species of **sea turtles** nest on one 8.9km (5½-mile) stretch of beach within the reserve between March and July. Three species of dolphins also inhabit and frolic in the waters just off Manzanillo. Many local tour guides and operators offer boat trips out to spot them.

If you want to explore the refuge, you can easily find the single, well-maintained trail by walking along the beach just south of town until you have to wade across a small river. On the other side, you'll pick up the trail head. Otherwise, you can ask around the village for local guides or check out **Aquamor** ✋ (☎ 2759-9012), a kayak and dive operation located on the one main road in town. These folks rent kayaks for $6 (£3) per hour and offer a variety of guided excursions for between $15 and $65 (£7.50–£33) per person. Depending on tides and sea conditions, this is a great way to explore the mangroves and estuaries, visit several nearby beaches, and even snorkel or dive the nearby coral reef. A one-tank beach dive, with equipment and guide, costs $30 (£15) per person. They have a variety of tour and diving options, including PADI dive-certification courses, hikes into the Talamanca Mountains, dolphin-watching excursions, and trips to Bocas del Toro, Panama.

Sportfishers should check in with **Bacalao Tours** (☎ 2759-9116).

(ORGANIC) PEAS & LOVE ✋ Inside the Manzanillo-Gandoca refuge is the **Punta Mona Center For Sustainable Living & Education** (☎ 2222-4568; www. puntamona.org). With organic permaculture gardens and a distinctly alternative vibe, this place is open for day visits, overnight stays, and work-exchange and educational programs. A day trip to visit the center, its garden, and facilities, including a vegetarian organic lunch, costs $40 (£20); overnight stays cost $35 (£18), including three meals.

SHOPPING

Puerto Viejo attracts a lot of local and international bohemians, who seem to survive solely on the sale of handmade jewelry, painted ceramic trinkets (mainly pipes and cigarette-lighter holders), and imported Indonesian textiles. You'll find them at makeshift stands set up by the town's *parquecito* (little park), a few wooden benches in front of the sea between Soda Tamara and Stanford's.

In addition to the makeshift outdoor stands is a host of well-stocked gift and crafts shops in town. The **Jewelry Factory** and **Color Caribe,** both on the main road into town, sell a wide range of jewelry, crafts, and gift items, as well as Costa Rican hammocks. **Luluberlu** ✋, located inland across from Cabinas Guaraná, features locally produced craftwork, including shell mobiles and mirrors with mosaic-inlaid frames, as well as imports from Thailand and India. For ceramics, head south to Playa Chiquita and check out the traditional Japanese-style works at **Raku Art.**

Tip: My favorite local purchase is locally produced chocolate, which comes wrapped in wax paper the size and shape of a roll of quarters. They come plain or flavored with coconut, peanuts, mint, ginger, or raisins, and can be found for sale at many gift shops and restaurants around town.

Finally, if you need a book to read on the beach, head just south of town to **Echo Books,** which has a good supply of new and used books, as well as a small cafe and gift shop. The owner also specializes in making homemade truffles and other chocolate treats from local cacao.

WHERE TO STAY IN PUERTO VIEJO

For a longer stay, close to town, you might want to check out **Cashew Hill Jungle Cottages** (☎ 2750-0256; www.cashewhilllodge.co.cr). On a hill just on the outskirts of town, these are simple but immaculate individual one- and two-bedroom bungalows, with kitchenettes.

MODERATE

In addition to the hotel listed below, **Escape Caribeño** (© 2750-0103; www.escape caribeno.com), is another good option in this price range, located on the outskirts of town, just south of Salsa Brava.

El Pizote   This hotel is 100m (328 ft.) or so inland from a long, quiet stretch of Playa Negra, about 400m (1,312 ft.) before you reach downtown proper. The four deluxe bungalows are modern concrete-block affairs, with a small kitchenette, two separate bedrooms, one small bathroom, air-conditioning, and a private porch. Although older and funkier, the standard bungalows have much more character. These raised wooden buildings have dark, stained wood walls; steeply pitched roofs; ceiling fans; private porches; and larger step-down bathrooms. The standard rooms are housed in a U-shaped wooden building near the large, free-form pool. These rooms are cool, and come with two double beds, a ceiling fan, and a shared wraparound veranda. Everything is set amid extensive, lush gardens, assorted tropical fruit trees, and a few towering rainforest trees. There are hiking trails in the adjacent forest, and there's good bird-watching here, too. My biggest complaint about the place is that upkeep and service are erratic.

Just off the main road, about 275m (902 ft.) before you enter downtown, Puerto Viejo, Limón. © 2750-0088. Fax 2750-0226. www.pizotelodge.com. 22 units. $63 (£32) double; $79 (£40) double bungalow; $109 (£55) double deluxe. Rates lower in off season. AE, MC, V. **Amenities:** Restaurant; bar; pool and adjacent kids' pool; laundry service. *In room:* No phone.

INEXPENSIVE

True budget hounds will find an abundance of basic hotels and *cabinas* in downtown Puerto Viejo in addition to those listed below. Of these, **Hotel Pura Vida** (©/fax 2750-0002; www.hotel-puravida.com) and **Kaya's Place** (© 2750-0690; www.kayas place.com) are both good bets; however, the most popular spot for backpackers, surfers, and students is **Rocking J's** (© 2750-0657; www.rockingjs.com), a sprawling compound offering simple rooms, camping spaces, and a "hammock hotel."

Banana Azul Guest House 🐾 *Finds*   Located at the northern end of Playa Negra, on the north end of town, this newer hotel is earning fast friends and hearty praise. Rooms abound in varnished hardwoods. Inside they are quite simple, with minimal furnishings and amenities, and an overhead or floor fan. Most are on the second floor of the main lodge building, and open onto a broad veranda with ocean views. The end-unit Howler Monkey suite is the best room here. The garden bath suites are larger units, with satellite TVs and a large open-air bathtub in their private gardens—hence, the name. Filling breakfasts are served in the common lounge area, and drinks are available throughout the day. An almost private section of beach sits just in front of the hotel, and stretches on for miles north, all the way to Cahuita National Park. No children 15 and under are permitted.

Playa Negra Puerto Viejo, Limón. © 2750-2035 or 8351-4582. www.bananaazul.com. 12 units. $48–$59 (£24–£29) double; $105 (£53) suite. Rates include full breakfast. Weekly and monthly rates available. Discounts offered for cash payments. MC, V. **Amenities:** Bike rental; watersports equipment rental; tour desk; laundry service. *In room:* Free Wi-Fi, safe, no phone.

Cabinas Guaraná   This is another of the better options right in town, although it is several blocks from the water. The spacious rooms are painted in bright primary colors, with equally bright and contrasting trim. Rooms come with either two or three full-size beds, or a queen-size with one or two full beds. All come with tile floors, a ceiling fan, and mosquito netting. Guests can use the hotel's fully equipped kitchen to whip up meals, and there's an interesting little sitting area on a platform high up a tree on the property.

1½ blocks inland from Café Viejo, Puerto Viejo, Limón. ©/fax **2750-0244**. www.hotelguarana.com. 12 units. $35–$45 (£18–£24) double. Rates slightly lower in off season; higher during peak weeks. AE, DC, MC, V. **Amenities:** Lounge; bike rental. *In room:* Free Wi-Fi, safe, no phone.

Cabinas Jacarandá *(Value* This small hotel has a few nice touches that set it apart from the others in the area. Guatemalan bedspreads add a dash of color and tropical flavor, as do tables made from sliced tree trunks. Most rooms and walkways feature intricate and colorful tile work; in addition, Japanese paper lanterns cover the lights, mosquito nets hang over the beds, and covered walkways connect the various buildings in this budding compound. Massage and yoga classes are offered on-site. If you're traveling in a group, you'll enjoy the space and atmosphere of the biggest room here. If the hotel is full, the owners also rent a few nearby bungalows.

1½ blocks inland from Café Viejo, Puerto Viejo, Limón. ©/fax **2750-0069**. www.cabinasjacaranda.net. 14 units, 13 with private bathroom. $35–$45 (£18–£23) double. MC, V. *In room:* No phone.

Casa Verde Lodge ★★ *(Value* This is my favorite hotel right in Puerto Viejo town, regardless of the price. A quiet sense of tropical tranquillity pervades this place. The rooms are spread around a small but growing complex. Most are large, with high ceilings, tile floors, private bathrooms, and a private veranda. The rooms with shared bathrooms are housed in a raised building with a wide, covered breezeway between the rooms. The front and back porches of this building are hung with hammocks and surrounded by lush gardens, where you'll find the showers and toilets. There are also two fully equipped apartments available in a neighboring duplex. Everything is very well maintained, and even the shared bathrooms are kept immaculate. The hotel also features a small but well-stocked gift shop, a poison-dart-frog garden, a good-size outdoor pool with a waterfall, and a separate outdoor massage hut. Even though it's an in-town choice, there's great bird-watching all around the grounds.

A.P. 37-7304, Puerto Viejo, Limón. © **2750-0015**. Fax 2750-0047. www.cabinascasaverde.com. 17 units, 9 with private bathroom. $40–$50 (£20–£25) double with shared bathroom; $70 (£35) double with private bathroom. Rates include taxes. Rates slightly lower in off season; higher during peak weeks. Discounts offered for cash payments. AE, MC, V. **Amenities:** Pool; bike rental; tour desk. *In room:* No phone.

WHERE TO STAY BETWEEN PUERTO VIEJO & MANZANILLO

All the hotels listed below are located along the road south of Puerto Viejo heading toward Manzanillo. This is one of the most beautiful and isolated stretches of beach in Costa Rica. The single coastal road here has been paved all the way to Manzanillo, greatly improving access to this area. I recommend that you rent a car if you plan to stay at one of these hotels because public transportation is sporadic and taxis aren't always available. If you arrive by bus, however, a rented bicycle or scooter might be all you need to get around once you are settled.

VERY EXPENSIVE

In addition to the place listed below, the former tent camp **Almonds & Corals Hotel** (© **2272-2024** reservations in San José, or 2759-9057 at the hotel; www.almonds andcorals.com) now offers rustically luxurious bungalows and suites in a lush forest setting near Manzanillo.

Tree House Lodge ☆☆☆ *Finds*   The four individual houses here are the most unique and stylish options on this coast. All are distinct and quite large, with fluid and fanciful architectural details and tons of brightly varnished woodwork. As the name implies, the Tree House is built into and around a large *sangrillo* tree. The Beach House is closest to the sea and actually features an ocean view from its kitchen and broad deck. However, the crowning achievement is the three-bedroom, two-bathroom Beach House Suite, with its spectacular domed bathroom, which during the day is lit by sunlight streaming through scores of colored glass skylights. All of the houses are beautiful, and you'll spend much of your time here marveling at the creative touches and one-off furniture. This property is set right off Punta Uva, one of the nicest swimming beaches on this coast.

Punta Uva, Puerto Viejo, Limón. © **2750-0706**. www.costaricatreehouse.com. 4 units. $200–$350 (£100–£175) double. Rates lower in off season, higher during peak weeks. No credit cards. *In room:* Full kitchen, safe.

MODERATE

Although I find all of the options listed in this section far more charming, surfers might look into **Totem** (© **2750-0758**; www.totemsite.com), which offers very comfortable rooms, set just off the road, right in front of the beach break in Playa Cocles.

Aguas Claras ☆ *Finds*   These brightly painted individual bungalows are built on raised stilts and feature fancy gingerbread trim. They are all of wood construction, and all come with private verandas and fully equipped kitchens—although some have just a two-burner cook-top, while others come with a full stove and oven. Inside, they are bright and airy, with either wood or tile floors. There are two 1-bedroom cottages, two 2-bedroom affairs, and one 3-bedroom house. The compound is just a few steps away from a lovely section of Playa Chiquita, and the restaurant here, Miss Holly's Kitchen (see below), is excellent. Maid service is provided every other day. If you book 5 nights, the sixth night is free.

Playa Chiquita, Puerto Viejo, Limón. © **2750-0131**. Fax 2750-0368. www.aguasclaras-cr.com. 5 bungalows. $70–$220 (£35–£110) bungalow. Rates lower in off season; higher during peak weeks. AE, DC, MC, V. **Amenities:** Restaurant; laundry service. *In room:* Kitchenette, no phone.

Azania Bungalows ☆ *Finds*   This collection of individual bungalows is an excellent option for those seeking a quiet, romantic tropical getaway. The spacious bungalows are set apart from each other amid the hotel's high flowering gardens, giving each a sense of seclusion. All come with one queen-size bed and one double bed downstairs and another double bed in the small loft. The thatch roofs are high-pitched and, combined with large screened windows, allow for good cross ventilation. The lounge area features a television with satellite TV, a small lending library, and a collection of board games. Some of the best features here include the refreshing free-form swimming pool and the open-air thatch-roofed poolside restaurant.

Playa Cocles, Puerto Viejo, Limón. © **2750-0540**. Fax 2750-0371. www.azania-costarica.com. 10 bungalows. $85 (£43) double. Rates include full breakfast. Rates lower in off season; higher during peak weeks. AE, DC, MC, V. **Amenities:** Restaurant; lounge; pool; bike rental; tour desk; laundry service. *In room:* Free Wi-Fi, fridge, safe, no phone.

Cariblue Bungalows ☆☆   This boutique resort is a wonderful choice in this neck of the woods. The rooms are spread around the well-tended and lush grounds. My favorites are the raised-stilt wood bungalows, with spacious bedrooms featuring either one king-size bed and one single bed or two queen-size beds. The beds are covered with mosquito nets, and there's a small veranda with a hammock. The nicest features here are the bathrooms, with their intricate mosaic tile designs. Deluxe bungalows come with televisions and air-conditioning. The standard rooms are in a couple of concrete-block buildings with high-pitched thatch roofs. They are also spacious and comfortable, but not quite as private or charming as the bungalows. Another option is a two-bedroom house with a full kitchen, for families or for longer stays. A very inviting free-form swimming pool has a swim-up bar, and the restaurant here tends to serve excellent Italian and local cuisine. Cariblue is located about 90m (295 ft.) or so inland from the southern end of Playa Cocles.

Playa Cocles, Puerto Viejo (A.P. 51-7304), Limón. ℂ **2750-0035** or ℂ/fax 2750-0057. www.cariblue.com. 16 units, 1 house. $90–$110 (£45–£55) double; $220 (£110) house. Rates include breakfast buffet. Rates slightly lower in off season. AE, MC, V. **Amenities:** Restaurant; bar/lounge; pool; Jacuzzi; bike rental; tour desk; laundry service. *In room:* Free Wi-Fi, hair dryer, safe, no phone.

Casa Camarona Casa Camarona has the enviable distinction of being one of the very few hotels in this area right on the beach. There's no road to cross and no path through the jungle—just a small section of shady gardens separates you from a quiet section of Playa Cocles and the Caribbean Sea. The rooms are in two separate two-story buildings. Definitely get a room on the second floor: Up there you'll find spacious rooms painted in pleasant pastels, with plenty of cross ventilation and a wide shared veranda. I don't know who designed the first-floor rooms, but several of them have such low ceilings that I felt as tall as Yao Ming—and believe me, I'm not. The hotel keeps some chaise longues on the beach under the shade of palm trees, and a beach bar is open during the day, so you barely have to move to quench your thirst.

Playa Cocles, Puerto Viejo, Limón (mailing address: A.P. 2270-1002, Paseo de los Estudiantes, San José). ℂ **2283-6711** or 2750-0151. Fax 2222-6184. www.casacamarona.co.cr. 17 units. $66 (£33) double. Rates include continental breakfast and taxes. AE, MC, V. **Amenities:** Restaurant; bar. *In room:* A/C (in some—extra $13/£6.50), no phone.

Playa Chiquita Lodge *(Kids* Set amid the shade of large old trees a few kilometers south of Puerto Viejo toward Punta Uva (watch for the sign), this lodge has several wooden buildings set on stilts and connected by a garden walkway. Wide verandas offer built-in seating and rocking chairs. The spacious rooms have received steady upkeep and upgrading and are painted in bright colors. Throughout the day, free bananas and coffee are available. The owners have three children, ranging from a young child to a couple of teenagers. Guests are invited to join in the nightly family-style dinners, and travelers, especially those with kids, often feel like part of the family. A short trail leads down to a semiprivate little swimming beach with tide pools and beautiful turquoise water. This stretch of beach is the site of a daily 4pm volleyball game. These folks also rent out fully equipped houses for those interested in longer stays or more privacy and independence.

Puerto Viejo, Limón. ℂ **2750-0062** or ℂ/fax 2750-0408. www.playachiquitalodge.com. 12 units. $60 (£30) double. Rates lower in off season; slightly higher during peak weeks. Rates include breakfast. AE, MC, V. **Amenities:** Restaurant. *In room:* Free Wi-Fi, no phone.

Shawandha Lodge *(Finds* Isolated and romantic, the individual bungalows here are rustically luxurious. Creative flourishes abound. The thatch-roofed, raised bungalows feature high-pitched ceilings, varnished wood floors, and either one king-size bed or a mix of queen-size and single beds. The bathrooms are practically works of art, each with original, intricate mosaics of hand-cut tile highlighting a large, open shower. Every bungalow has its own spacious balcony, with both a hammock and a couch, where you can lie and look out on the lush, flowering gardens. The beach is easily accessed by a private path, and a host of activities and tours can be arranged.

There's a large open-air restaurant and lounge where meals and drinks are served. The menu is an eclectic mix, featuring fresh fish and meats in a variety of French, Caribbean, and Polynesian sauces.

Puerto Viejo, Limón. ℭ **2750-0018.** Fax 2750-0037. www.shawandhalodge.com. 13 units. $105 (£53) double. Rates lower in off season; higher during peak weeks. Rates include full breakfast. AE, MC, V. **Amenities:** Restaurant; laundry service. *In room:* No phone.

INEXPENSIVE

Down in Manzanillo, the simple **Cabinas Something Different** (ℭ 2759-9014) is a good option, while **Congo Bongo** (ℭ **2759-9016;** www.congo-bongo.com) offers fully equipped houses in a lush forest setting.

La Costa de Papito 🏆 *Value*   This small collection of individual and duplex cabins offers some of the same feel and character as Shawandha and Cariblue, with fewer amenities and less luxury—but at lower rates. La Costa de Papito is just across from Playa Cocles, about 1.6km (1 mile) south of Puerto Viejo. The wooden bungalows come with one or two double beds, artfully tiled bathrooms, and an inviting private porch with a table and chairs and either a hammock or a swing chair. There's also a larger, two-bedroom unit. In 2007, they added a restaurant, as well as a small gym. The Pure Jungle Spa (see above) here is an excellent little day spa.

Playa Cocles, Puerto Viejo, Limón. ℭ/fax **2750-0080** or ℭ 2750-0704. www.lacostadepapito.com. 13 units. $54–$74 (£27–£37) double. Rates lower in off season. AE, DISC, MC, V. **Amenities:** Restaurant; bar; small spa; bike rental; laundry service. *In room:* No phone.

WHERE TO DINE IN PUERTO VIEJO

To really sample the local cuisine, you need to look up a few local women. Ask around for **Miss Dolly, Miss Sam, Miss Isma,** and **Miss Irma,** who all serve up sit-down meals in their modest little *sodas.* In addition to locally seasoned fish and chicken served with rice and beans, these joints are usually a great place to find some *pan bon* (a local sweet, dark bread), ginger cakes, *paty* (meat-filled turnovers), and *rondon* (see below). Just ask around for these women, and someone will direct you to them. In a similar vein, but with a fancier, large restaurant space, is **Miss Elena Brown,** who has set up shop on the outskirts of downtown, on the road heading south.

If you're looking for a light bite for breakfast, lunch, or a snack, check out **Pan Pay** (ℭ 2750-0081), a French-run bakery and sandwich shop located next to Johnny's Place (see "Puerto Viejo After Dark," below). Also, **Jammin' Juice and Jerk Center** (ℭ 8826-4332), in the same building, specializes in jerk chicken, salads, and fresh juices. For casual fare, try **E-Z Times** (ℭ 2750-0663), which is right in front of the water near the heart of town, and for Thai and Middle Eastern fare, head to **Chile Rojo** (ℭ 2750-0025).

Puerto Viejo has a glut of excellent Italian restaurants; in addition to the places listed below, **Amimodo** (ℭ 2750-0257) and **Trattoria da Cesare** (ℭ 2750-0161) are both fine restaurants.

For breakfasts, desserts and hearty, healthy lunches, there's **Bread & Chocolate** (ℭ 2750-0723). And if you're just looking for something to cool you off, try the new **Mighty River's Ice Cream & Coffee Shop** (ℭ 2750-2016), which has delicious homemade ice cream.

Café Viejo 🏆 ITALIAN   This place is set right on the busiest corner of "downtown" Puerto Viejo. White gauze curtains help to slightly shield this open-air spot from the hustle and bustle just outside. Still, it's often loud and crowded inside as well, and

---

Tips **That Rundown Feeling**

Rundown (or *rondon*) soup is a spicy coconut milk–based soup or stew made with anything the cook can run down—it usually includes a mix of local tubers (potato, sweet potato, or yuca), other vegetables (carrots or corn), and often some fish and/or seafood. Be sure to try this authentic taste of the Caribbean.

---

that's part of the charm of this popular place. You can get a wide range of pastas and thin-crust wood-oven pizzas here, as well as more substantial fish, chicken, and meat entrees. The grilled whole fresh fish is an especially good option. On weekends, a late-night lounge often develops here, with electronic music and dancing.

On the main road. ℂ 2750-0817. Main courses $9–$30 (£4.50–£15). MC, V. Wed–Mon noon–1am.

El Loco Natural ★★ *(Finds* INTERNATIONAL   A friendly, hippie vibe pervades this second-floor open-air restaurant. Seating is at heavy wooden tables, and if the few smaller, more private tables are taken, you can take any empty seat at one of the larger communal tables. The short menu features several vegetarian items, as well as fresh fish and some chicken and meat dishes, prepared in curry, Thai, and Mexican sauces. There's often live music here, ranging from reggae to jazz to Latin American folk.

On the main road just south of downtown. ℂ 2750-0263. Main courses $4–$14 (£2–£7). No credit cards. Thurs–Mon 6–10pm.

Salsa Brava ★★ SPANISH/MEDITERRANEAN   Fresh grilled seafood and meats are the specialty here, and everything is simply yet expertly prepared. There's usually a wide range of fresh-caught fish available, grilled either whole or in filets, plus grilled calamari, shrimp, or filet mignon, as well as several hearty vegetarian options. Wash down whatever you choose with the homemade sangria. The dozen or so wooden tables are painted bright primary colors and are set on a gravel floor under an open-air thatched roof. Service is attentive and informal, and there's occasional live jazz to accompany your dinner.

On the left-hand side of the main road heading south of Puerto Viejo, just after El Bambú. ℂ 2750-0241. Main courses $8–$17 (£4–£8.50). MC, V. Tues–Sun noon–10pm.

Soda Tamara *(Value* COSTA RICAN   This little restaurant has long been popular with budget-conscious travelers and has an attractive setting for such an economical place. The painted picket fence in front gives the restaurant a homey feel, and the best seats can be found on the front veranda facing the street, or in the large open-air dining area. The menu features standard fish, chicken, and meat entrees, served with a hefty helping of Caribbean-style rice and beans. You can also get *patacones* (fried chips made out of plantains) and a wide selection of fresh-fruit juices. At the counter inside, you'll find homemade cocoa candies and unsweetened cocoa biscuits made by several women in town. They're definitely worth a try. Soda Tamara also has a second-floor open-air bar that's open nightly from 6pm until the last straggler calls it quits.

On the main road. ℂ 2750-0148. Main courses $4–$15 (£2–£7.50). AE, MC, V. Daily 11am–11pm.

WHERE TO DINE BETWEEN PUERTO VIEJO & MANZANILLO

As the beaches stretching south of Puerto Viejo keep getting more popular, there has been a corresponding increase in the number of places to grab a meal. In addition to the restaurants listed above and below, **Johanna Restaurante** (© 8887-6203) in Playa Cocles, and **Cabinas Selvyn** (no phone) at Punta Uva, are both excellent options for local cuisine and fresh seafood.

Finally, if you make it as far south as Manzanillo, **Restaurant Maxi** ⍟ (© 2759-9086) is your best bet. This open-air spot is always packed, especially for lunch. A fresh-fish plate will cost you between $5 and $8 (£2.50–£4); lobster, in season, will cost around $14 (£7). Whatever you order comes with rice and beans, *patacones* (fried plantain chips), and a small side of cabbage salad.

Gatta Ci Cova ⍟ *(Value* ITALIAN   An extension and variation on their nearby and extremely popular restaurant, La Pecora Nera (see below), this simple place serves a range of panini sandwiches and thin-crust pizzas. Located in an open, two-story building, the main dining room is on the second floor, watched over by a giant stuffed black jaguar on the stairway railing. Downstairs is a more informal bar area. Try the four-cheese pizza with fresh pear slices and pine nuts, or the fresh fish panino with grilled zucchini and olive paste. There's always a two-course daily plate of an antipasto and pasta dish, with a glass of wine or beer for around $10 (£5). This is a great place for lunch or a light dinner.

Just beyond the soccer field on the main road through Cocles. © 2750-0490. Reservations not necessary. Pizzas and panini $3–$10 (£1.50–£5). AE, MC, V. Tues–Sun noon–10:30pm.

La Pecora Nera ⍟⍟⍟ *(Finds* ITALIAN   This open-air joint on the jungle's edge has a deserved reputation as the finest Italian restaurant in the region, if not the country. Owner Ilario Giannoni is a whirlwind of enthusiasm and activity, switching hats all night long from maitre d' to chef to waiter to busboy in an entertaining blur. Sure, he's got some help, including his grandmother, who makes gnocchi, but it seems like he's doing it single-handedly. The menu has a broad selection of pizzas and pastas, but your best bet is to just ask Ilario what's fresh and special for that day, and to trust his instincts and inventions. I've had fabulous fresh pasta dishes and top-notch appetizers every time I've visited. The gnocchi here is light and mouthwatering. The main dishes come with a variety of side dishes.

50m (164 ft.) inland from a well-marked turnoff on the main road south just beyond the soccer field in Cocles. © 2750-0490. Reservations recommended. Main courses $7–$28 (£3.50–£14). AE, MC, V. Tues–Sun 5:30–11pm.

Miss Holly's Kitchen ⍟ *(Finds* INTERNATIONAL   Although they only serve breakfast and lunch, this little cafe is a favorite spot for locals and visitors alike. Breakfasts feature fresh baked goods, omelets, and local favorites such as rice and beans with eggs. For lunch the menu shifts to a range of green and hearty salads, and various sandwiches. I like grabbing one of the tables on the small wooden cottage's wraparound veranda. But you can also just order at the deli counter inside and have a picnic on the beach. If you're traveling with a laptop, this is a great place to take advantage of some free Wi-Fi.

At Aguas Clara, Playa Chiquita. © 2750-0131. Breakfast $4–$6 (£2–£3); sandwiches and salads $3–$6 (£1.50–£3). MC, V. Wed–Mon 8am–4pm.

PUERTO VIEJO AFTER DARK

There are two main disco/bars in town. **Johnny's Place** ⍟⍟ is near the Rural Guard station, about 100m (328 ft.) or so north of the ATEC office. You'll find **Stanford's** overlooking the water out near Salsa Brava just as the main road heads south of town. Both have small dance floors with ground-shaking reggae, dub, and rap rhythms blaring. The

On to Panama

Costa Rica's southern zone, particularly Puerto Viejo, is a popular jumping-off point for trips into Panama. The nearest and most popular destination is the island retreat of Bocas del Toro. Most tour agencies and hotel desks in the area can arrange tours to Panama. If you're doing it yourself, it's easiest to fly directly from Limón on **Nature Air** (ℂ **800/235-9272** in the U.S. and Canada, or **2299-6000**; www.natureair.com), which has a daily flight that departs the Tobías Bolaños International Airport in Pavas at 1pm, stopping in Limón en route to pick up and discharge passengers. The one-way fare from Limón is $87 (£44). You can also take the local buses to the border at Sixaola. All the border formalities can be handled easily at the border, and onward bus connections wait on the Panamanian side to take you to Bocas del Toro.

If you're planning on spending any time touring around Panama, be sure to pick up a copy of *Frommer's Panama.*

action usually spills out from the dance floor at both joints on most nights. I like the atmosphere better at Johnny's, although both have tables, chairs, and candles set out on the sand, near the water's edge.

One of the more popular places in town is **Hot Rocks,** a large dirt lot with some canvas catering tents over its bar and some of its table area. This place, which is located right where the main road hits the water, has a huge screen upon which several late-run movies are projected each night. Another option is the **Sunset Bar,** which is near the water, beside the bus station, and sometimes features live music. For a more sophisticated ambience try the downtown **Baba Yaga,** or the ocean-side **E-Z Times.** An open-air bar on the second floor of **Soda Tamara** (p. 392) is a casual and quiet place to gather after dark. Finally, for a more local scene, check out **Bar Maritza's,** which really seems to go off on Sunday nights.

You can also take advantage of the pool table, board games, and DirecTV (usually showing sporting events) at **El Dorado,** in front of the ATEC office, as an alternative to the loud music and dance scenes of the other joints mentioned above.

Heading just south out of town, the **Cut Back** is a popular spot with backpackers and bohemians, with a solid after-hours scene. Farther south of town, at the start of Playa Cocless, **El Tesoro** shows large-screen movies every night.

Appendix A:
Fast Facts, Toll-Free
Numbers & Websites

1 Fast Facts: Costa Rica

AMERICAN EXPRESS American Express Travel Services is represented in Costa Rica by **ASV Olympia,** Oficentro La Sabana, Sabana Sur, in San José (© **2242-8585**), which can issue traveler's checks and replacement cards and provide other standard services. To report lost or stolen Amex traveler's checks within Costa Rica, call the number above or © **2257-0155,** or call collect to 313/271-7887 in the United States.

AREA CODES There are no area codes in Costa Rica. All local phone numbers are eight-digit numbers. However, toll-free numbers are inconsistent. Some begin with 800, others with 0800. Moreover, some actually have eight digits following the 800 or 0800.

ATM NETWORKS & CASHPOINTS See "Money & Costs," p. 46.

BUSINESS HOURS Banks are usually open Monday through Friday from 9am to 4pm, although many have begun to offer extended hours. Post offices are generally open Monday through Friday from 8am to 5:30pm, and Saturday from 7:30am to noon. (In small towns, post offices often close on Sat.) Stores are generally open Monday through Saturday from 9am to 6pm (many close for 1 hr. at lunch) but stores in modern malls generally stay open until 8 or 9pm and don't close for lunch. Most bars are open until 1 or 2am, although some go later.

CAR RENTALS See "Toll-Free Numbers & Websites," below, and "Getting There & Getting Around," in "Planning Your Trip to Costa Rica," on p. 37.

CUSTOMS **What You Can Bring Into Costa Rica** Visitors entering Costa Rica are officially entitled to bring in 500 grams of tobacco, 5 liters of liquor, and US$500 in merchandise. Cameras, computers, and electronic equipment for personal use are permitted duty-free. Customs officials in Costa Rica seldom check tourists' luggage.

What You Can Take Home from Costa Rica Every country has rules stating what its citizens are allowed to bring back. Be sure to understand your country's rules before beginning your trip to Costa Rica.

U.S. Citizens: For specifics on what you can bring back and the corresponding fees, download the invaluable free pamphlet *Know Before You Go* at **www. cbp.gov** (click on "Travel," and then click on "Know Before You Go! Online Brochure"). Or contact the **U.S. Customs & Border Protection (CBP),** 1300 Pennsylvania Ave., NW, Washington, DC 20229 (© **877/287-8667**) and request the pamphlet.

Canadian Citizens: For a clear summary of Canadian rules, write for the booklet *I Declare,* issued by the Canada Border Services Agency (© 800/461-9999 in Canada, or 204/983-3500; www.cbsa-asfc.gc.ca).

U.K. Citizens: For information, contact **HM Customs & Excise** at ✆ **0845/010-9000** (from outside the U.K., 020/8929-0152), or consult their website at **www.hmce.gov.uk**.

Australian Citizens: A helpful brochure available from Australian consulates or Customs offices is *Know Before You Go*. For more information, call the **Australian Customs Service** at ✆ **1300/363-263**, or log on to **www.customs.gov.au**.

New Zealand Citizens: Most questions are answered in a free pamphlet available at New Zealand consulates and Customs offices: *New Zealand Customs Guide for Travellers, Notice no. 4*. For more information, contact **New Zealand Customs**, The Customhouse, 17–21 Whitmore St., Box 2218, Wellington (✆ **04/473-6099** or 0800/428-786; **www.customs.govt.nz**).

DRINKING & DRUG LAWS   Alcoholic beverages are sold every day of the week throughout the year, with the exception of the 2 days before Easter and the 2 days before and after a presidential election. The legal drinking age is 18, although it's only sporadically enforced. Liquor—everything from beer to hard spirits—is sold in specific liquor stores, as well as at most supermarkets and even convenience stores.

Drug laws in Costa Rica are strict, and you don't want your vacation ruined by a protracted interaction with the local police and judicial systems. Many prescription drugs are sold over-the-counter here, but often the names are different from those in the United States and Europe. It's always best to have a prescription from a doctor.

DRIVING RULES   See "Getting There & Getting Around," p. 42.

DRUGSTORES   Called *farmacias* in Spanish, drugstores are quite common throughout the country. Those at hospitals and major clinics are often open 24 hours a day.

ELECTRICITY   The standard in Costa Rica is the same as in the United States: 110 volts AC (60 cycles). However, three-pronged outlets can be scarce, so it's helpful to bring along an adapter.

Wherever you go, bring a **connection kit** of the right power and phone adapters, a spare phone cord, and a spare Ethernet network cable—or find out whether your hotel supplies them to guests.

EMBASSIES & CONSULATES   The following are located in San José: **United States Embassy,** in front of Centro Comercial, on the road to Pavas (✆ **2519-2000,** or 2220-3127 after-hours in case of emergency); **Canadian Consulate,** Oficentro Ejecutivo La Sabana, Edificio 5 (✆ **2242-4400**); and **British Embassy,** Paseo Colón between calles 38 and 40 (✆ **2258-2025**). There are no Australian or New Zealand embassies in San José.

EMERGENCIES   In case of any emergency, dial ✆ **911** (which should have an English-speaking operator); for an ambulance, call ✆ **128;** and to report a fire, call ✆ **118.** If 911 doesn't work, you can contact the police at ✆ **2222-1365** or 2221-5337, and hopefully they can find someone who speaks English.

GASOLINE (PETROL)   Gasoline is sold as "regular" and "super." Both are unleaded; super is just higher octane. Diesel is available at almost every gas station as well. When going off to remote places, try to leave with a full tank of gas because gas stations can be hard to find. If you need to gas up in a small town, you can sometimes get gasoline from enterprising families who sell it by the liter from their houses. Look for hand-lettered signs that say GASOLINA. At press time a liter of super cost 573 colones, or roughly $4.35 (£2.20) per gallon.

HOLIDAYS   For more information on holidays see "Calendar of Events," on p. 40.

HOSPITALS In San José try Clínica Bíblica (Avenida 14 btw. calles Central and 1), which offers emergency services to foreign visitors at reasonable prices (© **2522-1000;** www.clinicabiblica. com), or the **Hospital CIMA** (© **2208-1000;** www.hospitalsanjose.net), located in Escazú on the Próspero Fernández Highway, which connects San José and the western suburb of Santa Ana and has the most modern facilities in the country.

INSURANCE Medical Insurance For travel overseas, most U.S. health plans (including Medicare and Medicaid) do not provide coverage, and the ones that do often require you to pay for services upfront and reimburse you only after you return home.

As a safety net, you may want to buy travel medical insurance, particularly if you're traveling to a remote or high-risk area where emergency evacuation might be necessary. If you require additional medical insurance, try **MEDEX Assistance** (© 410/453-6300; www.medex assist.com) or **Travel Assistance International** (© **800/821-2828;** www.travel assistance.com; for general information on services, call the company's **Worldwide Assistance Services, Inc.,** at © 800/777-8710).

Canadians should check with their provincial health plan offices or call **Health Canada** (© 866/225-0709; www. hc-sc.gc.ca) to find out the extent of their coverage and what documentation and receipts they must take home in case they are treated overseas.

Travelers from the U.K. should carry their European Health Insurance Card (EHIC), which replaced the E111 form as proof of entitlement to free/reduced cost medical treatment abroad (© 0845/606-2030; www.ehic.org.uk). Note, however, that the EHIC only covers "necessary medical treatment," and for repatriation costs, lost money, baggage, or cancellation, travel insurance from a reputable company should always be sought (www.travelinsuranceweb.com).

Travel Insurance The cost of travel insurance varies widely, depending on the destination, the cost and length of your trip, your age and health, and the type of trip you're taking, but expect to pay between 5% and 8% of the vacation itself. You can get estimates from various providers through **InsureMyTrip.com**. Enter your trip cost and dates, your age, and other information, for prices from more than a dozen companies.

U.K. citizens and their families who make more than one trip abroad per year may find an annual travel insurance policy works out cheaper. Check **www.money supermarket.com**, which compares prices across a wide range of providers for single- and multitrip policies.

Most big travel agents offer their own insurance and will probably try to sell you their package when you book a holiday. Think before you sign. **Britain's Consumers' Association** recommends that you insist on seeing the policy and reading the fine print before buying travel insurance. The **Association of British Insurers** (© **020/7600-3333;** www.abi. org.uk) gives advice by phone and publishes *Holiday Insurance,* a free guide to policy provisions and prices. You might also shop around for better deals: Try **Columbus Direct** (© **0870/033-9988;** www.columbusdirect.net).

Trip-Cancellation Insurance Trip-cancellation insurance will help retrieve your money if you have to back out of a trip or depart early, or if your travel supplier goes bankrupt. Trip cancellation traditionally covers such events as sickness, natural disasters, and State Department advisories. The latest news in trip-cancellation insurance is the availability of **expanded hurricane coverage** and the

"any-reason" cancellation coverage—which costs more but covers cancellations made for any reason. You won't get back 100% of your prepaid trip cost, but you'll be refunded a substantial portion. **Travel-Safe** (© **888/885-7233;** www.travelsafe.com) offers both types of coverage. Expedia also offers any-reason cancellation coverage for its air-hotel packages. For details, contact one of the following recommended insurers: **Access America** (© 866/807-3982; www.accessamerica.com); **Travel Guard International** (© 800/826-4919; www.travelguard.com); **Travel Insured International** (© 800/243-3174; www.travelinsured.com); and **Travelex Insurance Services** (© 888/457-4602; www.travelex-insurance.com).

LANGUAGE   Spanish is the official language of Costa Rica. However, in most tourist areas, you'll be surprised by how well Costa Ricans speak English. *Frommer's Spanish PhraseFinder & Dictionary* (Wiley Publishing, 2006) is probably the best phrase book to bring with you.

LAUNDROMATS   Dry cleaners and laundromats—be they full-service or self-serve—are few and far between in Costa Rica. Hotel laundry services, which can sometimes be expensive, are far more common. For listings of laundromats, see individual city and town sections.

LEGAL AID   If you need legal help, your best bet is to first contact your local embassy or consulate. See "Embassies & Consulates" above for contact details. Alternatively, you can pick up a copy of the *Tico Times,* which usually carries advertisements from local English-speaking lawyers.

LOST & FOUND   Be sure to tell all of your credit card companies the minute you discover your wallet has been lost or stolen and file a report at the nearest police precinct. Your credit card company or insurer may require a police report number or record of the loss. Most credit card companies have an emergency toll-free number to call if your card is lost or stolen; they may be able to wire you a cash advance immediately or deliver an emergency credit card in a day or two. In Costa Rica, Visa's emergency number is © **0800/011-0030.** American Express cardholders and traveler's check holders should call © **0800/012-3211.** MasterCard holders should call © **0800/011-0184.** For other credit cards, or for a local representative of the above companies, call **Credomatic** © **2295-9898.**

If you need emergency cash over the weekend when all banks and American Express offices are closed, you can have money wired to you via **Western Union** (© **800/777-7777** in Costa Rica; www.westernunion.com).

MAIL   At press time, it cost 155 colones (31¢/15p) to mail a letter to the United States, and 180 colones (36¢/17p) to Europe. You can get stamps at a post office and at some gift shops in large hotels. Given the Costa Rican postal service's track record, I recommend paying an extra 600 colones ($1.20/60p) to have anything of any value certified. Better yet, use an international courier service or wait until you get home to post it. **DHL,** on Paseo Colón between calles 30 and 32 (© **2209-0000;** www.dhl.com); **EMS Courier,** with desks at the principal metropolitan post offices (© **800/900-2000** or 2202-2900); **FedEx,** which is based in Heredia but will arrange pickup anywhere in the San José metropolitan area (© **800/463-3339;** www.fedex.com); and **United Parcel Service,** in Pavas (© **2290-2828;** www.ups.com), all operate in Costa Rica. *Note:* Despite what you may be told, packages sent overnight to U.S. addresses tend to take 3 to 4 days.

If you're sending mail *to* Costa Rica, it generally takes between 10 and 14 days to reach San José, although it can take as much as a month to get to the more remote corners of the country. Plan ahead. Also note that many hotels and ecolodges have mailing addresses in the United States. Always use these addresses when writing from North America or Europe. Never send cash, checks, or valuables through the Costa Rican mail system.

MEASUREMENTS   Costa Rica uses the metric system. See the chart on the inside front cover of this book for details on converting metric measurements to non-metric equivalents.

NEWSPAPERS & MAGAZINES   There are six Spanish-language dailies in Costa Rica and one English-language weekly, the *Tico Times.* In addition, you can get *Time, Newsweek,* and several U.S. newspapers at some hotel gift shops and a few of the bookstores in San José. If you understand Spanish, *La Nación* is the paper you'll want. Its "Viva" and "Tiempo Libre" sections list what's going on in the world of music, theater, dance, and more.

PASSPORTS   The websites listed provide downloadable passport applications as well as the current fees for processing applications. For an up-to-date, country-by-country listing of passport requirements around the world, go to the "International Travel" tab of the U.S. State Department at **http://travel.state. gov.** Allow plenty of time before your trip to apply for a passport; processing normally takes 4 to 6 weeks (3 weeks for expedited service) but can take longer during busy periods (especially spring). And keep in mind that if you need a passport in a hurry, you'll pay a higher processing fee.

For Residents of Australia   You can pick up an application from your local post office or any branch of Passports Australia, but you must schedule an interview at the passport office to present your application materials. Call the **Australian Passport Information Service** at © **131-232,**

or visit the government website at www.passports.gov.au.

For Residents of Canada   Passport applications are available at travel agencies throughout Canada or from the central **Passport Office,** Department of Foreign Affairs and International Trade, Ottawa, ON K1A 0G3 (© **800/567-6868;** www.ppt.gc.ca). *Note:* Canadian children who travel must have their own passport. However, if you hold a valid Canadian passport issued before December 11, 2001, that bears the name of your child, the passport remains valid for you and your child until it expires.

For Residents of Ireland   You can apply for a 10-year passport at the **Passport Office,** Setanta Centre, Molesworth Street, Dublin 2 (© **01/671-1633;** www. irlgov.ie/iveagh). Those 17 and under and 65 and over must apply for a 3-year passport. You can also apply at 1A South Mall, Cork (© **21/494-4700**) or at most main post offices.

For Residents of New Zealand   You can pick up a passport application at any New Zealand Passports Office or download it from their website. Contact the **Passports Office** at © **0800/225-050** in New Zealand or 04/474-8100, or log on to www.passports.govt.nz.

For Residents of the United Kingdom   To pick up an application for a standard 10-year passport (5-year passport for children 15 and under), visit your nearest passport office, major post office, or travel agency or contact the **United Kingdom Passport Service** at © **0870/ 521-0410** or search its website at www. ukpa.gov.uk.

For Residents of the United States: Whether you're applying in person or by mail, you can download passport applications from the U.S. State Department website at **http://travel.state.gov.** To find your regional passport office, either check the U.S. State Department website or call the **National Passport Information Center** toll-free number (© 877/487-2778) for automated information.

POLICE   In most cases, dial © **911** for the police, and you should be able to get someone who speaks English on the line. Other numbers for the **Judicial Police** are © **2222-1365** and 2221-5337. The numbers for the **Traffic Police (Policía de Tránsito)** are © **2222-9330** and 2222-9245.

SMOKING   While not as bad as most of Europe, a large number of Costa Ricans smoke, and public smoking regulations and smoke-free zones have yet to take hold. Restaurants are required by law to have nonsmoking areas, but enforcement is often lax, air-circulation poor, and the separating almost nonexistent. Bars, as a whole, are often very smoke-filled in Costa Rica.

Most higher-end hotels have at least some nonsmoking rooms. However, many midrange hotels and most budget options are pretty laissez-faire when it comes to smoking. Whenever possible, the presence of nonsmoking rooms is noted in the listing description information.

TAXES   All hotels charge 16.3% tax. Restaurants charge 13% tax and also add on a 10% service charge, for a total of 23% more on your bill.

There is a $26 (£13) departure tax for all visitors leaving by air. This tax must be purchased prior to check-in. There are desks at the main terminal of all international airports where you can pay this tax. Some local travel agencies and hotels offer to purchase the departure tax in advance, as a convenience for tourists. You must give them authorization, as well as your passport number, and pay a small service fee.

Although you can pay the airport exit tax with a credit card, it is charged as a cash advance. Most credit card companies hit this kind of transaction with a fee and begin charging interest on it immediately. It is best to pay the airport tax in cash, either dollars or colones.

TIME   Costa Rica is on Central Standard Time (same as Chicago and St. Louis), 6 hours behind Greenwich Mean Time. Costa Rica does not use daylight saving time, so the time difference is an additional hour April through October.

TIPPING   Tipping is not necessary in restaurants, where a 10% service charge is always added to your bill (along with a 13% tax). If service was particularly good, you can leave a little at your own discretion, but it's not mandatory. Porters and bellhops get around 75¢ (40p) per bag. You don't need to tip a taxi driver unless the service has been superior; a tip is not usually expected. (Note that it's also not uncommon for passengers to sit in the front seat with the driver.)

TOILETS   These are known as *sanitarios, servicios sanitarios,* or *baños.* They are marked *damas* (women) and *hombres* or *caballeros* (men). Public restrooms are hard to come by. You will almost never find a public restroom in a city park or downtown area. There are usually public restrooms at most national-park entrances, and much less frequently inside the national park. (There are usually plenty of trees and bushes.) In the towns and cities, it gets much trickier. One must count on the generosity of some hotel or restaurant. Same goes for most beaches. However, most restaurants, and, to a lesser degree, hotels, will let you use their facilities, especially if you buy a soft drink or something. Bus and gas stations often have restrooms, but many of these are pretty grim.

USEFUL PHONE NUMBERS   For directory assistance, call © **113;** for international directory assistance, call © **124;** and for the exact time (in Spanish), call © **112.**

U.S. Dept. of State Travel Advisory ℂ 202/647-5225 (staffed 24 hr.)

U.S. Passport Agency ℂ 202/647-0518

U.S. Centers for Disease Control International Traveler's Hotline: ℂ 404/332-4559

Throughout the book, I haven't listed phone numbers for bars or clubs in small towns and villages. Reservations are never necessary, and in most cases you're never more than a few blocks away if you need to find out if it's open. The same is true for most shops and souvenir stands in these smaller destinations, towns, and villages. If for any reason you need to contact one of these places, ask at your hotel desk, and they'll certainly have the number.

WATER   Although the water in San José is generally safe to drink, water quality varies outside the city. Because many travelers have tender digestive tracts, I recommend playing it safe and sticking to bottled drinks as much as possible. Also avoid ice. See p. 49 in "Planning Your Trip to Costa Rica" for more advice.

2 Toll-Free Numbers & Websites

MAJOR U.S. AIRLINES

American Airlines
ℂ 800/433-7300 (in U.S. or Canada)
ℂ 020/7365-0777 (in U.K.)
www.aa.com

Continental Airlines
ℂ 800/523-3273 (in U.S. or Canada)
ℂ 084/5607-6760 (in U.K.)
www.continental.com

Delta Air Lines
ℂ 800/221-1212 (in U.S. or Canada)
ℂ 084/5600-0950 (in U.K.)
www.delta.com

Frontier Airlines
ℂ 800/432-1359
www.frontierairlines.com

Spirit Airlines
ℂ 800/772-7117
www.spiritair.com

United Airlines
ℂ 800/864-8331 (in U.S. and Canada)
ℂ 084/5844-4777 (in U.K.)
www.united.com

US Airways
ℂ 800/428-4322 (in U.S. and Canada)
ℂ 084/5600-3300 (in U.K.)
www.usairways.com

BUDGET & DOMESTIC AIRLINES

Nature Air
ℂ 800/235-9272 (in U.S. and Canada)
www.natureair.com

Sansa
ℂ 877/767-2672 (in U.S. and Canada)
www.flysansa.com

CAR-RENTAL AGENCIES

Alamo
ℂ 800/GO-ALAMO (800/462-5266)
www.alamo.com

Avis
ℂ 800/331-1212 (in U.S. and Canada)
ℂ 084/4581-8181 (in U.K.)
www.avis.com

Budget
ℂ 800/527-0700 (in U.S.)
ℂ 087/0156-5656 (in U.K.)
ℂ 800/268-8900 (in Canada)
www.budget.com

Dollar
ℂ 800/800-4000 (in U.S.)
ℂ 800/848-8268 (in Canada)
ℂ 080/8234-7524 (in U.K.)
www.dollar.com

Hertz
© 800/645-3131
© 800/654-3001 (for international
   reservations)
www.hertz.com

National
© 800/CAR-RENT (800/227-7368)
www.nationalcar.com

MAJOR HOTEL & MOTEL CHAINS

Best Western International
© 800/780-7234 (in U.S. and Canada)
© 0800/393-130 (in U.K.)
www.bestwestern.com

Clarion Hotels
© 800/CLARION [252-7466] or
   877/424-6423 (in U.S. and Canada)
© 0800/444-444 (in U.K.)
www.choicehotels.com

Crowne Plaza Hotels
© 888/303-1746
www.ichotelsgroup.com/crowneplaza

Doubletree Hotels
© 800/222-TREE (800/222-8733)
   (in U.S. and Canada)
© 087/0590-9090 (in U.K.)
www.doubletree.com

Four Seasons
© 800/819-5053 (in U.S. and Canada)
© 0800/6488-6488 (in U.K.)
www.fourseasons.com

Hampton Inn
© 800/HAMPTON (800/426-4766)
www.hamptoninn.hilton.com

Payless
© 800/PAYLESS (800/729-5377)
www.paylesscarrental.com

Thrifty
© 800/367-2277
© 918/669-2168 (international)
www.thrifty.com

Hilton Hotels
© 800/HILTONS (800/445-8667)
   (in U.S. and Canada)
© 087/0590-9090 (in U.K.)
www.hilton.com

Hyatt
© 888/591-1234 (in U.S. and Canada)
© 084/5888-1234 (in U.K.)
www.hyatt.com

InterContinental Hotels & Resorts
© 800/424-6835 (in U.S. and Canada)
© 0800/1800-1800 (in U.K.)
www.ichotelsgroup.com

Marriott
© 877/236-2427 (in U.S. and Canada)
© 0800/221-222 (in U.K.)
www.marriott.com

Quality
© 877/424-6423 (in U.S. and Canada)
© 0800/444-444 (in U.K.)
www.QualityInn.ChoiceHotels.com

Radisson Hotels & Resorts
© 888/201-1718 (in U.S. and Canada)
© 0800/374-411 (in U.K.)
www.radisson.com

Appendix B: Glossary of Spanish Terms & Phrases

Costa Rican Spanish is neither the easiest nor the most difficult dialect to understand. Ticos speak at a relatively relaxed speed and enunciate clearly, without dropping too many final consonants. The *y* and *ll* sounds are subtly, almost inaudibly, pronounced. Perhaps the most defining idiosyncrasy of Costa Rican Spanish is the way Ticos overemphasize, and almost chew, their *r*'s.

If you're looking for a more comprehensive dictionary and language resource, pick up a copy of *Frommer's Spanish PhraseFinder& Dictionary,* or *Frommer's Spanish Phrasebook and Culture Guide.* Both are excellent pocket books with a wealth of information to make your travel interactions more rewarding.

1 Basic Words & Phrases

English	Spanish	Pronunciation
Hello	**Buenos días**	*bweh*-nohss *dee*-ahss
How are you?	**¿Cómo está usted?**	*koh*-moh ehss-*tah* oo-*stehd*
Very well	**Muy bien**	mwee byehn
Thank you	**Gracias**	*grah*-syahss
Goodbye	**Adiós**	ad-*dyohss*
Please	**Por favor**	pohr fah-*vohr*
Yes	**Sí**	see
No	**No**	noh
Excuse me (to get by someone)	**Perdóneme**	pehr-*doh*-neh-meh
Excuse me (to begin a question)	**Disculpe**	dees-*kool*-peh
Give me	**Deme**	*deh*-meh
Where is . . . ?	**¿Dónde está . . . ?**	*dohn*-deh ehss-*tah*
the station	**la estación**	la ehss-*tah*-syohn
the bus stop	**la parada**	la pah-*rah*-dah
a hotel	**un hotel**	oon oh-*tehl*
a restaurant	**un restaurante**	oon res-tow-*rahn*-teh
the toilet	**el servicio**	el ser-*vee*-syoh
To the right	**A la derecha**	ah lah deh-*reh*-chah
To the left	**A la izquierda**	ah lah ees-*kyehr*-dah
Straight ahead	**Adelante**	ah-deh-*lahn*-teh

English	Spanish	Pronunciation
I would like . . .	**Quiero . . .**	*kyeh*-roh
to eat	**comer**	ko-*mehr*
a room	**una habitación**	oo-nah ah-bee-tah-*syohn*
How much is it?	**¿Cuánto?**	*kwahn*-toh
The check	**La cuenta**	la *kwen*-tah
When?	**¿Cuándo?**	*kwan*-doh
What?	**¿Qué?**	keh
Yesterday	**Ayer**	ah-*yehr*
Today	**Hoy**	oy
Tomorrow	**Mañana**	mah-*nyah*-nah
Breakfast	**Desayuno**	deh-sah-*yoo*-noh
Lunch	**Almuerzo**	ahl-*mwehr*-soh
Dinner	**Cena**	*seh*-nah
Do you speak	**¿Habla usted**	*ah*-blah oo-*stehd*
English?	**inglés?**	een-*glehss*
I don't understand	**No entiendo muy**	noh ehn-*tyehn*-do mwee
Spanish very well.	**bien el español.**	byehn el ehss-pah-*nyohl*

NUMBERS

1	**uno** (*oo*-noh)		16	**dieciséis** (dyeh-see-*sayss*)
2	**dos** (dohss)		17	**diecisiete** (dyeh-see-*syeh*-teh)
3	**tres** (trehss)		18	**dieciocho** (dyeh-see-*oh*-choh)
4	**cuatro** (*kwah*-troh)		19	**diecinueve** (dyeh-see-*nweh*-beh)
5	**cinco** (*seen*-koh)		20	**veinte** (*bayn*-teh)
6	**seis** (sayss)		30	**treinta** (*trayn*-tah)
7	**siete** (*syeh*-teh)		40	**cuarenta** (kwah-*rehn*-tah)
8	**ocho** (*oh*-choh)		50	**cincuenta** (seen-*kwehn*-tah)
9	**nueve** (*nweh*-beh)		60	**sesenta** (seh-*sehn*-tah)
10	**diez** (dyehss)		70	**setenta** (seh-*tehn*-tah)
11	**once** (*ohn*-seh)		80	**ochenta** (oh-*chehn*-tah)
12	**doce** (*doh*-seh)		90	**noventa** (noh-*behn*-tah)
13	**trece** (*treh*-seh)		100	**cien** (syehn)
14	**catorce** (kah-*tohr*-seh)		1,000	**mil** (meel)
15	**quince** (*keen*-seh)			

DAYS OF THE WEEK

English	Spanish	Pronunciation
Monday	**lunes**	(*loo*-nehss)
Tuesday	**martes**	(*mahr*-tehss)
Wednesday	**miércoles**	(*myehr*-koh-lehs)
Thursday	**jueves**	(*wheh*-behss)
Friday	**viernes**	(*byehr*-nehss)
Saturday	**sábado**	(*sah*-bah-doh)
Sunday	**domingo**	(doh-*meen*-goh)

2 Some Typical Tico Words & Phrases

Birra   Slang for beer.

Boca   Literally means "mouth," but also a term to describe a small appetizer served alongside a drink at many bars.

Bomba   Translates literally as "pump" but is used in Costa Rica for "gas station."

Brete   Work, or job.

Casado   Literally means "married," but is the local term for a popular restaurant offering that features a main dish and various side dishes.

Chapa   Derogatory way to call someone stupid or clumsy.

Chepe   Slang term for the capital city, San José.

Choza   Slang for house or home.

Chunche   Knickknack; thing, as in "whatchamacallit."

Con mucho gusto   With pleasure.

De hoy en ocho   In 1 week's time.

Diay   An untranslatable but common linguistic punctuation, often used to begin a sentence.

Estar de chicha   To be angry

Goma   Hangover.

Harina   Literally "flour," but used to mean money.

La sele   Short for *la selección,* the Costa Rican national soccer team.

Limpio   Literally means "clean," but is the local term for being broke, or having no money

Macha or **machita**   A blond woman.

Mae   Translates like "man"; used by many Costa Ricans, particularly teenagers, as frequent verbal punctuation.

Maje   A lot like *mae,* above, but with a slightly derogatory connotation.

Mala nota   Bad vibe, or bad situation.

Mala pata   Bad luck.

Mejenga   An informal, or pickup, soccer game.

Pachanga or **pelón**   Both terms are used to signify a big party or gathering.

Ponga la maría, por favor   This is how you ask taxi drivers to turn on the meter.

Pulpería   The Costa Rican version of the "corner store" or small market.

Pura paja   Pure nonsense or BS.

Pura vida   Literally, "pure life"; translates as "everything's great."

Qué torta   What a mess; what a screw-up.

Si Dios quiere   God willing; you'll hear Ticos say this all the time.

Soda   A casual diner-style restaurant serving cheap Tico meals.

Tico   Costa Rican.

Tiquicia   Costa Rica.

Tuanis   Means the same as *pura vida,* above, but is used by a younger crowd.

Una teja   100 colones.

Un rojo   1,000 colones.

Un tucán   5,000 colones.

Upe!   Common shout to find out if anyone is home; used frequently since doorbells are so scarce.

Zarpe   Last drink of the night, or "one more for the road."

3 Menu Terms

FISH

Almejas   Clams
Atún   Tuna
Bacalao   Cod
Calamares   Squid
Camarones   Shrimp
Cangrejo   Crab
Ceviche   Marinated seafood salad
Dorado   Dolphin or mahimahi

Langosta   Lobster
Lenguado   Sole
Mejillones   Mussels
Ostras   Oysters
Pargo   Snapper
Pulpo   Octopus
Trucha   Trout

MEATS

Albóndigas   Meatballs
Bistec   Beefsteak
Cerdo   Pork
Chicharrones   Fried pork rinds
Cordero   Lamb
Costillas   Ribs

Jamón   Ham
Lengua   Tongue
Pato   Duck
Pavo   Turkey
Pollo   Chicken
Salchichas   Sausages

VEGETABLES

Aceitunas   Olives
Alcachofa   Artichoke
Berenjena   Eggplant
Cebolla   Onion
Elote   Corn on the cob
Ensalada   Salad
Espinacas   Spinach
Frijoles   Beans

Lechuga   Lettuce
Maíz   Corn
Palmito   Heart of palm
Papa   Potato
Pepino   Cucumber
Tomate   Tomato
Yuca   Yucca, cassava, or manioc
Zanahoria   Carrot

FRUITS

Aguacate   Avocado
Banano   Banana
Carambola   Star fruit
Cereza   Cherry
Ciruela   Plum
Durazno   Peach
Frambuesa   Raspberry
Fresa   Strawberry
Granadilla   Sweet passion fruit
Limón   Lemon or lime
Mango   Mango

Manzana   Apple
Mango   Mango
Maracuya   Tart passion fruit
Melón   Melon
Mora   Blackberry
Naranja   Orange
Papaya   Papaya
Piña   Pineapple
Plátano   Plantain
Sandía   Watermelon
Toronja   Grapefruit

BASICS

Aceite   Oil
Ajo   Garlic
Arreglado   Small meat sandwich
Azúcar   Sugar
Casado   Plate of the day
Gallo   Corn tortilla topped with meat or chicken
Gallo pinto   Rice and beans
Hielo   Ice
Mantequilla   Butter
Miel   Honey

Mostaza   Mustard
Natilla   Sour cream
Olla de carne   Meat and vegetable soup
Pan   Bread
Patacones   Fried plantain chips
Picadillo   Chopped vegetable side dish
Pimienta   Pepper
Queso   Cheese
Sal   Salt
Tamal   Filled cornmeal pastry
Tortilla   Flat corn pancake

DRINKS

Agua purificada   Purified water
Agua con gas   Sparkling water
Agua sin gas   Plain water
Bebida   Drink
Café   Coffee
Café con leche   Coffee with milk
Cerveza   Beer
Chocolate caliente   Hot chocolate

Jugo   Juice
Leche   Milk
Natural   Fruit juice
Natural con leche   Milkshake
Refresco   Soft drink
Ron   Rum
Té   Tea
Trago   Alcoholic drink

OTHER RESTAURANT TERMS

Al grill   Grilled
Al horno   Oven-baked
Al vapor   Steamed
Asado   Roasted
Caliente   Hot
Cambio or **vuelto**   Change
Cocido   Cooked
Comida   Food
Congelado   Frozen
Crudo   Raw
El baño   Toilet

Frío   Cold
Frito   Fried
Grande   Big
La cuenta   The check
Medio   Medium
Medio rojo   Medium rare.
Muy cocido   Well-done
Pequeño   Small
Poco cocido or **rojo**   Rare
Tres cuartos   Medium-well-done

4 Other Useful Terms

HOTEL TERMS

Aire acondicionado   Air-conditioning
Almohada   Pillow
Baño   Bathroom
Baño privado   Private bathroom
Calefacción   Heating
Cama   Bed
Cobija   Blanket
Colchón   Mattress
Cuarto or **Habitación**   Room
Escritorio   Desk

Habitación simple/sencilla   Single room
Habitación doble   Double room
Habitación triple   Triple room
Llave   Key
Mosquitero   Mosquito net
Sábanas   Sheets
Seguro de puerta   Door lock
Telecable   Cable TV
Ventilador   Fan

TRAVEL TERMS

Aduana   Customs
Aeropuerto   Airport
Avenida   Avenue
Avión   Airplane
Aviso   Warning
Bus   Bus
Calle   Street
Cheques viajeros   Traveler's checks
Correo   Mail, or post office
Cuadra   City block
Dinero or **plata**   Money
Embajada   Embassy
Embarque   Boarding
Entrada   Entrance

Equipaje   Luggage
Este   East
Frontera   Border
Lancha or **bote**   Boat
Norte   North
Oeste   West
Occidente   West
Oriente   East
Pasaporte   Passport
Puerta de salida or **puerta de embarque**   Boarding gate
Salida   Exit
Tarjeta de embarque   Boarding pass
Vuelo   Flight

EMERGENCY TERMS

¡Auxilio!   Help!
Ambulancia   Ambulance
Bomberos   Fire brigade
Clínica   Clinic or hospital
Doctor or **médico**   Doctor
Emergencia   Emergency
Enfermo/enferma   Sick
Enfermera   Nurse

Farmacia   Pharmacy
Fuego or **incendio**   Fire
Hospital   Hospital
Ladrón   Thief
Peligroso   Dangerous
Policía   Police
¡Váyase!   Go away!

Appendix C:
Costa Rican Wildlife

For such a small country, Costa Rica is incredibly rich in biodiversity. With just .01% of the earth's landmass, Costa Rica is home to some 5% of its biodiversity. Whether you come to Costa Rica to check 100 or so species off your lifetime list, or just to check out of the rat race for a week or so, you'll be surrounded by a rich and varied collection of flora and fauna. The information below is meant to be a selective introduction to some of what you might see.

In many instances, the prime viewing recommendations should be taken with a firm dose of reality. Most casual visitors and even many dedicated naturalists will never see a wildcat or kinkajou. However, anyone working with a good guide should be able to see a broad selection of Costa Rica's impressive flora and fauna.

There are scores of good field guides out there; two of the best general guides are *The Field Guide to the Wildlife of Costa Rica,* by Carrol Henderson (University of Texas Press, 2002), and *Costa Rica: Traveller's Wildlife Guides,* by Les Beletsky (Interlink Books, 2004). Bird-watchers will want to pick up one or both of the following two books: *A Guide to the Birds of Costa Rica,* by F. Gary Stiles and Alexander Skutch (Cornell University Press, 1989) and *Birds of Costa Rica,* by Richard Garrigues and Robert Dean (Cornell University Press, 2007). Other specialized guides to mammals, reptiles, insects, flora, and more are also available. In Costa Rica, **Seventh Street Books,** on Calle 7 between avenidas 1 and Central in San José (© **2256-8251**) always has a great selection.

See "The Lay of the Land" in chapter 2 for more information, as well as "Tips on Health, Safety & Etiquette in the Wilderness" in chapter 5.

1 Fauna

MAMMALS

Costa Rica has more than 230 species of mammals. Roughly half of these are bats. While it is very unlikely that you will spot a wildcat, you have good odds of catching a glimpse of a monkey, coatimundi, peccary, or sloth, or more likely any number of bats.

SCIENTIFIC NAME   *Panthera onca*

WORTH NOTING   This cat measures from 1 to 1.8m (3½–6 ft.) plus tail and is distinguished by its tan/yellowish fur with black spots. Often called simply *tigre* (tiger) in Costa Rica.

PRIME VIEWING   Jaguars exist in all major tracts of primary and secondary forest in Costa Rica, as well as some open savannas. However, jaguars are endangered and extremely hard to see in the wild. The largest concentrations of jaguars can be found in Corcovado National Park on the Osa Peninsula.

Jaguar

Ocelot

SCIENTIFIC NAME   *Leopardus pardalis*

WORTH NOTING   Known as *manigordo,* or "fat paws," in Costa Rica, the tail of this small cat is longer than its rear leg, which makes for easy identification. **Ocelots** are mostly nocturnal, and they sleep in trees.

PRIME VIEWING   Forests in all regions of Costa Rica, with the greatest concentration found on the Osa Peninsula.

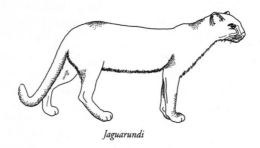

Jaguarundi

SCIENTIFIC NAME   *Herpailurus yaguarondi*

WORTH NOTING   This smallish to midsize cat, with a solid black, brown, or reddish coat, can occasionally be spotted in a clearing or climbing trees. The **jaguarundi** has a unique look for a wild cat, with a face often compared to that of a weasel or otter. Jaguarundi are diurnal hunters.

PRIME VIEWING   Most frequently spotted in middle elevation moist forests. Sometimes mistaken for a *tayra.*

SCIENTIFIC NAME   *Agouti paca*

WORTH NOTING   The **paca,** a nocturnal rodent, inhabits the forest floor, feeding on fallen fruit, leaves, and some tubers dug from the ground.

PRIME VIEWING   Known as *tepezquintle* in Costa Rica, these are most often found near water throughout many habitats of Costa Rica, from river valleys to

Paca

Tayra

swamps to dense tropical forest. However, since they're nocturnal, you're much more likely to see their smaller cousin, the diurnal agouti or *guatusa*.

SCIENTIFIC NAME *Eira barbara*

WORTH NOTING This midsize rodent is in the weasel family. **Tayras** run from dark brown to black, with a brown to tan head and neck. Long and low to the ground, they have a long bushy tail.

PRIME VIEWING Known as *tolumuco* or *gato de monte* in Costa Rica, tayras are found across the country, in forests as well as plain areas, and in trees, as well as on the ground.

SCIENTIFIC NAME *Tapirus bairdii*

WORTH NOTING Known as the *danta* or *macho de monte*, **Baird's tapir** is the largest land mammal in Costa Rica. Tapirs are active both day and night, foraging along riverbanks, streams, and forest clearings.

PRIME VIEWING An endangered species, tapirs can be found in wet forested areas, particularly on the Caribbean and south Pacific slopes.

SCIENTIFIC NAME *Nasua narica*

WORTH NOTING Known as *pizote* in Costa Rica, the raccoonlike **coatimundi** can adapt to habitat disturbances and is often spotted near hotels and nature lodges. Active both day and night, it is equally comfortable on the ground and in trees.

PRIME VIEWING Found in a variety of habitats across Costa Rica, from dry scrub to dense forests, on the mainland as well as the coastal islands. Social animals, they are often found in groups of 10 to 20.

Coatimundi

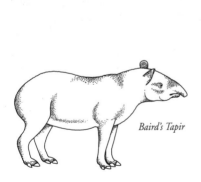
Baird's Tapir

SCIENTIFIC NAME *Tayassu tajacu*

WORTH NOTING Called *saino* or *chancho de monte* in Costa Rica, the **collared peccary** is a black or brown piglike animal that travels in small groups (larger where populations are still numerous) and has a strong musk odor.

PRIME VIEWING Low- and middle-elevation forests in most of Costa Rica.

SCIENTIFIC NAME *Tamandua mexicana*

Collared Peccary

*Northern
Tamandua*

WORTH NOTING   Also known as the collared anteater (*oso hormiguero* in Spanish), the **northern Tamandua** grows up to 77 centimeters (30 in.) long, not counting its thick tail, which can be as long its body. It is active diurnally and nocturnally.

PRIME VIEWING   Low- and middle-elevation forests in most of Costa Rica.

SCIENTIFIC NAME   *Bradypus variegatus*

WORTH NOTING   The larger and more commonly sighted of Costa Rica's two sloth species, the **three-toed sloth** has long, coarse brown-to-gray fur and a distinctive eye band. They have three long and sharp claws on each foreleg. Except for brief periods used for defecation, these slow-moving creatures are entirely arboreal.

PRIME VIEWING   Low- and middle-elevation forests in most of Costa Rica. While sloths can be found in a wide variety of trees, they are most commonly spotted in the relatively sparsely leaved Cecropia (see later in this appendix).

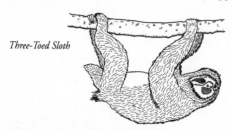

Three-Toed Sloth

SCIENTIFIC NAME   *Alouatta palliata*

WORTH NOTING   Known locally as *mono congo,* the highly social **mantled howler monkey** grows to 56 centimeters (22 in.) in size and often travels in groups of 10 to 30. The loud roar of the male can be heard as far as 1.6km (1 mile) away.

PRIME VIEWING   Wet and dry forests across Costa Rica. Almost entirely arboreal, they tend to favor the higher reaches of the canopy.

SCIENTIFIC NAME   *Cibus capucinus*

WORTH NOTING   Known as both *mono carablanca and mono capuchin* in Costa Rica, the white-faced or capuchin monkey is a midsize species (46cm/18 in.) with

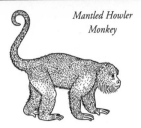

Mantled Howler Monkey

White Faced Monkey

distinct white fur around its face, head, and forearms. It can be found in forests all around the country and often travels in large troops or family groups.

PRIME VIEWING   Wet and dry forests across Costa Rica.

SCIENTIFIC NAME   *Saimiri oerstedii*

WORTH NOTING   The smallest and friskiest of Costa Rica's monkeys, the **red-backed squirrel monkey,** or *mono titi,* is also its most endangered. Active in the daytime, these monkeys travel in small to midsize groups. Squirrel monkeys do not have a prehensile tail.

PRIME VIEWING   Manuel Antonio National Park and Corcovado National Park.

SCIENTIFIC NAME   *Ateles geoffroyi*

WORTH NOTING   Known as both *mono araña and mono colorado* in Costa Rica, the **spider monkey** is one of the more acrobatic monkey species. A large monkey (64cm/25 in.) with brown or silvery fur, it has long thin limbs and a long prehensile tail. It is active both day and night, and travels in small to midsize bands or family groups.

PRIME VIEWING   Wet and dry forests across Costa Rica.

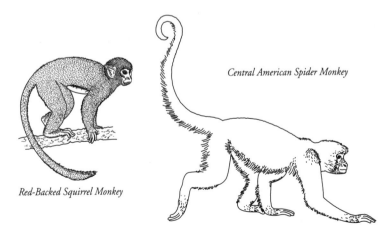

Central American Spider Monkey

Red-Backed Squirrel Monkey

SCIENTIFIC NAME   *Dasypus novemcinctus*

WORTH NOTING   This is the most common armadillo species. **Armadillo** is Spanish for "little armored one," and that's an accurate description of this hard-carapace

Nine-banded Armadillo

carrying mammal. The **nine-banded armadillo** can reach 65cm (26 in.) in length and weigh up to 4.5kg (9.9 lb.). The female gives birth to identical quadruplets from one single egg.

PRIME VIEWING   Low- and middle-elevation forests, as well as farm lands, in most of Costa Rica. These prehistoric-looking animals are nocturnal and terrestrial.

BIRDS

Costa Rica has more than 880 identified species of resident and migrant birds. The variety of habitats and compact nature of the country make it a major bird-watching destination.

SCIENTIFIC NAME   *Jabiru mycteria*

WORTH NOTING   One of the largest birds in the world, the **jabiru stork** stands 1.5m (5 ft.) tall, with a wingspan of 2.4m (8 ft.) and a .3m (1 ft.) bill. An endangered species, the jabiru is very rare, with only a dozen or so nesting pairs in Costa Rica.

PRIME VIEWING   The wetlands of Palo Verde National Park and Caño Negro Wildlife Reserve are the best places to try to spot the jabiru stork. The birds arrive in Costa Rica from Mexico in November and fly north with the rains in May or June.

SCIENTIFIC NAME   *Ramphastos sulfuratus*

WORTH NOTING   The rainbow-colored canoe-shape bill and brightly colored feathers make the **keel-billed toucan** a favorite of bird-watching tours. The toucan can grow to about 51 centimeters (20 in.) in length. It's similar in size and shape to the chestnut mandibled toucan. Costa Rica also is home to several smaller toucanet and aracari species.

PRIME VIEWING   Lowland forests on the Caribbean and north Pacific slopes.

Jabiru Stork

Keel-Billed Toucan

SCIENTIFIC NAME   *Ara macao*

WORTH NOTING   Known as *guacamaya* or *lapa* in Costa Rica, the **scarlet macaw** is a long-tailed member of the parrot family. It can reach 89 centimeters (35 in.) in length. The bird is endangered over most of its range, particularly because it is so coveted as a pet. Its loud squawk and rainbow-colored feathers are quite distinctive.

PRIME VIEWING   Carara National Park, Corcovado National Park, and Piedras Blancas National Park.

Resplendent Quetzal

Scarlet Macaw

SCIENTIFIC NAME   *Pharomchrus mocinno*

WORTH NOTING   Perhaps the most distinctive and spectacular bird in Central America, the **resplendent quetzal,** of the trogon family, can grow to 37cm (15 in.). The males are distinctive, with bright red chests, iridescent blue-green coats, yellow bill, and tail feathers that can reach another 76cm (30 in.) in length. The females lack the long tail feathers and have a duller beak and less pronounced red chest.

PRIME VIEWING   High-elevation wet and cloud forests, particularly in the Monteverde Cloud Forest Preserve and along the Cerro de la Muerte.

SCIENTIFIC NAME   *Fregata magnificens*

WORTH NOTING   The **magnificent frigate bird** is a naturally agile flier, and it swoops (unlike other seabirds, it doesn't dive or swim) to pluck food from the water's surface—or more commonly, it steals catch from the mouths of other birds.

PRIME VIEWING   Along the shores and coastal islands of both coasts. Often seen soaring high overhead.

Magnificent
Frigate Bird

Montezuma's
Oropendola

SCIENTIFIC NAME   *Psarocolius montezuma*

WORTH NOTING   **Montezuma's oropendola** has a black head, brown body, a yellow-edged tail, a large black bill with an orange tip, and a blue patch under the eye. These birds build long, teardrop-shape hanging nests, often found in large groups. They have several distinct loud calls, including one that they make while briefly hanging upside down.

PRIME VIEWING   Low and middle elevations along the Caribbean slope, and some sections of eastern Guanacaste.

SCIENTIFIC NAME   *Ajaia ajaja*

WORTH NOTING   The **roseate spoonbill** is a large water bird, pink or light red in color and with a large spoon-shape bill. Also known as *garza rosada* (pink heron). They were almost made extinct in the United States because their pink wings were sought for feather fans.

PRIME VIEWING   Low-lying wetlands, both fresh and salt water, along both coasts.

Roseate Spoonbill

Cattle Egret

SCIENTIFIC NAME   *Bubulcus ibis*

WORTH NOTING   The **cattle egret** changes color during breeding: A yellowish buff color appears on the head, chest, and back, and a reddish hue emerges on the bill and legs. They are usually seen anywhere there are cattle, hence the name, but can also often be found following behind tractors.

PRIME VIEWING   Throughout the country.

SCIENTIFIC NAME *Cochlearius cochlearius*

WORTH NOTING The midsize **boat-billed heron** (about 51cm/20 in.) has a large black head, a large broad bill, and a rusty brown color.

PRIME VIEWING Throughout the country, near marshes, swamps, rivers, and mangroves.

Boat-Billed
Heron

Laughing Falcon

SCIENTIFIC NAME *Herpetotheres cachinnans*

WORTH NOTING The **laughing falcon** is also known as the *guaco* in Costa Rica. It gets its name from its loud, piercing call. This largish (56cm/22-in.) bird of prey's wingspan reaches an impressive 94 centimeters (37 in.). It specializes in eating both venomous and nonvenomous snakes but will also hunt lizards and small rodents.

PRIME VIEWING Throughout the country, most commonly in lowland areas, near forest edges, grasslands, and farmlands.

SCIENTIFIC NAME *Amazona farinosa*

WORTH NOTING Called *loro* or *loro verde* this large, vocal parrot is common in lowland tropical rainforests on both coasts. Almost entirely green, it has a touch of blue on the top of its head, and small red and blue accents on its wings. *Loro* means parrot, and *verde* means green, so you and locals alike may confuse this parrot with any number of other local species.

PRIME VIEWING Lowland rainforests on the Caribbean and Pacific coasts.

Mealy Parrot

Scarlet Rumped Tanager

SCIENTIFIC NAME *Ramphocelus costaricensis*

WORTH NOTING With a striking scarlet red patch on its backside, this is one of the most commonly sighted tanagers in Costa Rica. It is known locally as *sargento* or *sangre de toro*. For true ornithologists, a recent reclassification has divided the Costa Rican scarlet rumped tanagers into two distinct species, Passerini's Tanager, which is found on the Caribbean slope and lowlands, and Cherrie's Tanager, which is found along the Pacific slope and lowlands.

PRIME VIEWING   Throughout the country, in lowland and mid-elevation areas.

SCIENTIFIC NAME   *Pandion haliatus*

WORTH NOTING   These large (.6m/2 ft., with a 1.8m/6-ft. wingspan) brownish birds with white heads are also known as *gavilan pescador* or "fishing eagle." In flight, the osprey's wings "bend" backward.

PRIME VIEWING   Lowland coastal areas and wetlands across Costa Rica; they can be seen flying or perched in trees near water.

Osprey

Pygmy Owl

SCIENTIFIC NAME   *Glaucidium brasilianum*

WORTH NOTING   Unlike most owls, this small (about 38cm/15 in.) grayish brown or reddish brown owl is most active during the day.

PRIME VIEWING   Low and middle elevations along the north Pacific slope, in both wooded areas, as well as forest edges and farmlands.

SCIENTIFIC NAME   *Campylopterus hemileucurus*

WORTH NOTING   The largest hummingbird found in Costa Rica, the violet sabrewing shines a deep purple when the sun strikes it right. Its beak is long, thick, and gently curving.

PRIME VIEWING   Mid- and higher-elevation rain and cloud forests countrywide.

SCIENTIFIC NAME   *Turdus grayi*

WORTH NOTING   In a country with such a rich variety of spectacularly plumed bird species, this plain brown robin is an unlikely choice to be Costa Rica's national bird. However, it is extremely widespread and common, especially in the central

Violet Sabrewing

Clay-colored robin

valley urban areas, and has a wide range of pleasant calls and songs. Known locally as the *yiguirro,* it has a uniform brown coat, with a lighter brown belly and yellow bill.

PRIME VIEWING   Low and middle elevations nationwide, especially in clearings, secondary forests, and amid human settlements.

AMPHIBIANS

Frogs, toads, and salamanders are actually some of the most beguiling, beautiful, and easy-to-spot residents of tropical forests.

SCIENTIFIC NAME   *Bufo marinus*

WORTH NOTING   The largest toad in the Americas, the 20-centimeter (8-in.) wart-covered **marine toad** is also known as *sapo grande* (giant toad). The females are mottled in color, while the males are uniformly brown. These voracious toads have been known to eat small mammals, along with other toads, lizards, and just about any insect within range. They also have a very strong toxic chemical defense mechanism.

PRIME VIEWING   In forests and open areas throughout Costa Rica.

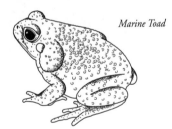

Marine Toad

Mexican Burrowing Toad

SCIENTIFIC NAME   *Rhinophrynus dorsalis*

WORTH NOTING   The bloblike, 7.6-centimeter (3-in.) Mexican **burrowing toad** will inflate like a blowfish when frightened. It often has a single red, orange, or yellow line down the center of its brown or black back.

PRIME VIEWING   Pacific lower-elevation forests and moist grasslands and farmlands.

SCIENTIFIC NAME   *Agalychnis callidryas*

WORTH NOTING   The colorful 7.6-centimeter (3-in.) **red-eyed tree frog** usually has a pale or dark green back, sometimes with white or yellow spots, with blue-purple patches and vertical bars on the body, orange hands and feet, and deep red eyes. This nocturnal amphibian is also known as the gaudy leaf frog or red-eyed tree frog.

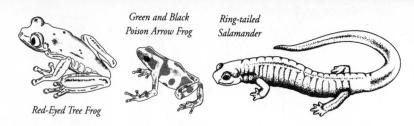

Green and Black Poison Arrow Frog

Ring-tailed Salamander

Red-Eyed Tree Frog

PRIME VIEWING   Low- and middle-elevation wet forests throughout Costa Rica. This is a very beautiful and distinctive-looking frog that you will certainly see on T-shirts and postcards if not in the wild.

SCIENTIFIC NAME   *Dendrobates auratus*

WORTH NOTING   Also called the harlequin poison-arrow frog, the small **green and black poison arrow frog** ranges between 2.5 and 4 centimeters (1–1½ in.) in length. It has distinctive markings of iridescent green mixed with deep black.

PRIME VIEWING   On the ground, around tree roots, and under fallen logs, in low- and middle-elevation wet forests on the Caribbean and southern Pacific slopes.

SCIENTIFIC NAME   *Bolitoglossa robusta*

WORTH NOTING   This midsize black salamander can grow to 13cm (5 in.), and is distinguished by its namesake yellow to orange ring near the upper portion of its tail.

PRIME VIEWING   Middle and higher elevation wet forests across Costa Rica.

REPTILES

Costa Rica's reptile species range from the frightening and justly feared fer-de-lance pit viper and massive American crocodile to a wide variety of turtles and lizards. *Note:* Sea turtles are included in the "Sea Life" section below.

SCIENTIFIC NAME   *Boa constrictor*

WORTH NOTING   Adult **boa constrictors** (*bécquer* in Costa Rica) average about 1.8 to 3m (6–10 ft.) in length and weigh over 27 kilograms (60 lb.). Their coloration camouflages them, but look for patterns of cream, brown, gray, and black ovals and diamonds.

PRIME VIEWING   Low- and middle-elevation wet and dry forests, countrywide. They often live in rafters and eaves of homes in rural areas.

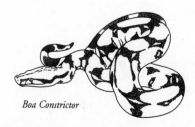

Boa Constrictor

Fer-de-Lance

SCIENTIFIC NAME *Bothrops atrox*

WORTH NOTING Known as *terciopelo* in Costa Rica, the aggressive **fer-de-lance** can grow to 2.4m (8 ft.) in length. Beige, brown, or black triangles flank either side of the head, while the area under the head is a vivid yellow. These snakes begin life as arboreal but become increasingly terrestrial as they grow older and larger.

PRIME VIEWING All regions.

SCIENTIFIC NAME *Clelia clelia*

WORTH NOTING This bluish black, brown, or grayish snake grows to 2.4m (8 ft.) in length. While slightly venomous, this snake has rear-fangs and is of little danger to humans. In fact, it is prized and protected by locals, since its primary prey happens to be much more venomous pit vipers, like the fer-de-lance.

PRIME VIEWING Open forests, pastures, and farmlands across Costa Rica.

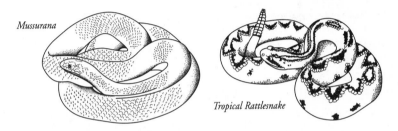

Mussurana

Tropical Rattlesnake

SCIENTIFIC NAME *Crotalus durissus*

WORTH NOTING Known as *cascabel* in Costa Rica, this pit viper has a triangular head, a pronounced ridge running along the middle of its back, and (of course) a rattling tail. It can reach 1.8m (6 ft.) in length.

PRIME VIEWING Mostly found in low elevation dry forests and open areas of Guanacaste.

SCIENTIFIC NAME *Phyllodactylus xanti*

WORTH NOTING Spotting the 6.8-centimeter (2½-in.) **leaf-toed gecko** is easy—it loves to be around buildings and other areas of human activity.

PRIME VIEWING Common on the ground and in the leaf litter of low- and middle-elevation forests throughout the country.

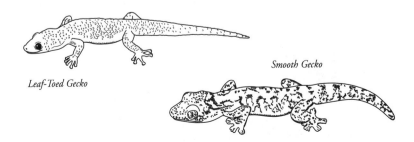

Leaf-Toed Gecko

Smooth Gecko

SCIENTIFIC NAME   *Thecadactylus rapicauda*

WORTH NOTING   The **smooth gecko**'s autonomous tail detaches from its body and acts as a diversion to a potential predator; it grows back later in a lighter shade.

PRIME VIEWING   Low-elevation wet forests on the Caribbean and southern Pacific slopes, as well as in urban and rural residential environments.

SCIENTIFIC NAME   *Iguana iguana*

WORTH NOTING   **Green iguanas** can vary in shades ranging from bright green to a dull grayish-green, with quite a bit of orange mixed in. The iguana will often perch on a branch overhanging a river and plunge into the water when threatened.

PRIME VIEWING   All lowland regions of the country, living near rivers and streams, along both coasts.

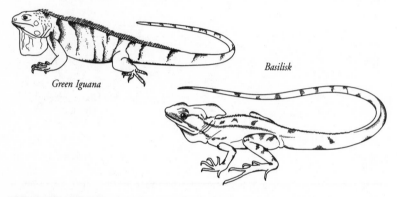

Basilisk

Green Iguana

SCIENTIFIC NAME   *Basiliscus vittatus*

WORTH NOTING   The **basilisk** can run across the surface of water for short distances by using its hind legs and holding its body almost upright; thus, the reptile is also known as "the Jesus Christ lizard."

PRIME VIEWING   In trees and on rocks located near water in wet forests throughout the country.

SCIENTIFIC NAME   *Crocodylus acutus*

WORTH NOTING   Although an endangered species, environmental awareness and protection policies have allowed the massive **American crocodile** to mount an impressive comeback in recent years. While these reptiles can reach lengths of 6.4m (21 ft.), most are much smaller, usually less than 4m (13 ft.).

PRIME VIEWING   Near swamps, mangrove swamps, estuaries, large rivers, and coastal lowlands, countrywide. Guaranteed viewing from the bridge over the Tarcoles River, on the coastal highway to Jacó and Manuel Antonio.

American Crocodile

SCIENTIFIC NAME   *Sphenomorphus cherriei*

WORTH NOTING   This small, brown lizard has a proportionally large head and neck, and short legs. A black stripe extends off the back of its eyes and down its sides, with a yellowish area below.

PRIME VIEWING   Common on the ground and in leaf litter of low- and middle-elevation forests throughout the country.

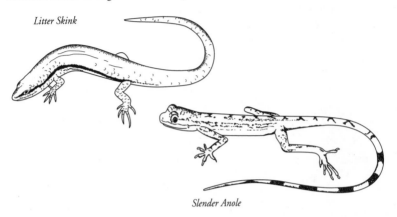

Litter Skink

Slender Anole

SCIENTIFIC NAME   *Anolis (norops) limifrons*

WORTH NOTING   This thin, olive-colored lizard can reach 5.1cm (2 in.) in length. There are some 25 related species of *anolis* or *norops* lizards.

PRIME VIEWING   Lowland rainforests nationwide.

SEA LIFE

Boasting over 1,290km (780 miles) of shoreline on both the Pacific and Caribbean coasts, Costa Rica has a rich diversity of underwater flora and fauna.

SCIENTIFIC NAME   *Rhincodon typus*

WORTH NOTING   Although the **whale shark** grows to lengths of 14m (45 ft.) or more, its gentle nature makes swimming with them a special treat for divers and snorkelers.

PRIME VIEWING   Can occasionally be spotted off Isla del Caño, and more frequently off Isla del Coco.

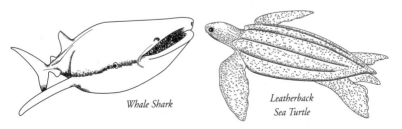

Whale Shark

*Leatherback
Sea Turtle*

SCIENTIFIC NAME   *Dermochelys coriacea*

WORTH NOTING   The world's largest sea turtle (reaching nearly 2.4m/8 ft. in length and weighing more than 544kg/1,200 lb.), the **leatherback sea turtle** is now an endangered species.

PRIME VIEWING   While these large reptiles do nest off Tortuguero, their prime nesting site in Costa Rica is Playa Grande, near Tamarindo.

SCIENTIFIC NAME   *Lepidochelys olivacea*

WORTH NOTING   Also known as *tortuga lora,* the **olive ridley sea turtle** is the most common and popular of Costa Rica's sea turtles, famous for its massive group nestings, or *arribadas.*

PRIME VIEWING   Large *arribadas* occur from July through December, and to a lesser extent from January through June. Playa Nancite in Santa Rosa National Park and Playa Ostional are the prime nesting sites.

Olive Ridley Sea Turtle

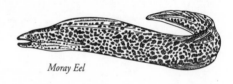

Moray Eel

SCIENTIFIC NAME   *Gymnothorax mordax*

WORTH NOTING   Distinguished by a swaying serpent-head and teeth-filled jaw that continually opens and closes, the **moray eel** is most commonly seen with only its head appearing from behind rocks. At night, however, it leaves its home along the reef to hunt for small fish, crustaceans, shrimp, and octopus.

PRIME VIEWING   Rocky areas and reefs off both coasts.

SCIENTIFIC NAME   *Megaptera novaeangliae*

WORTH NOTING   The migratory **humpbacked whale** spends the winters in warm southern waters and has been increasingly spotted close to the shores of Costa Rica's southern Pacific coast. These mammals have black backs and whitish throat and chest areas. Females have been known to calve here.

PRIME VIEWING   Most common in the waters off of Drake Bay and Isla del Caño, from December through April.

SCIENTIFIC NAME   *Tursiops truncates*

WORTH NOTING   Their wide tail fin, dark gray back, and light gray sides identify **bottle-nosed dolphins.** Dolphins grow to lengths of 3.7m (12 ft.) and weigh up to 635 kilograms (1,400 lb.).

PRIME VIEWING   Along both coasts and inside the Golfo Dulce.

SCIENTIFIC NAME   *Manta birostris*

WORTH NOTING   **Manta rays** are the largest type of rays, with a wingspan that can reach 6m (20 ft.) and a body weight known to exceed 1,361kg (3,000 lb.). Despite their daunting appearance, manta rays are quite gentle. If you are snorkeling or diving, watch for one of these extraordinary and graceful creatures.

PRIME VIEWING   All along the Pacific coast.

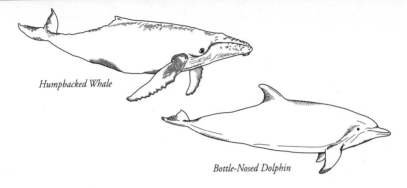

Humpbacked Whale

Bottle-Nosed Dolphin

SCIENTIFIC NAME *Diploria strigosa*

WORTH NOTING The distinctive **brain coral** is named for its striking physical similarity to a human brain.

PRIME VIEWING Reefs off both coasts.

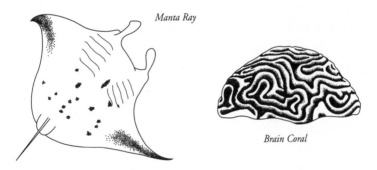

Manta Ray

Brain Coral

INVERTEBRATES

Creepy-crawlies, biting bugs, spiders, and the like give most folks chills. But this group, which includes moths, butterflies, ants, beetles, bees, and even crabs, includes some of the most abundant, fascinating, and easily viewed fauna in Costa Rica. In fact, there are nearly 500,000 recorded species of invertebrates in Costa Rica, with more than 9,000 species of butterflies and moths alone.

SCIENTIFIC NAME *Morpho peleides*

WORTH NOTING The large **blue morpho** butterfly, with a wingspan of up to 15 centimeters (6 in.), has brilliantly iridescent blue wings when opened. Fast and erratic fliers, they are often glimpsed flitting across your peripheral vision in dense forest.

PRIME VIEWING Countrywide, particularly in moist environments.

SCIENTIFIC NAME *Atta cephalotes*

WORTH NOTING You can't miss the miniature rainforest highways formed by these industrious little red **leafcutter ants** carrying their freshly cut payload. The ants

Blue Morpho

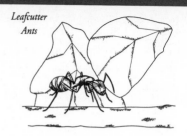

Leafcutter Ants

do not actually eat the leaves, but instead feed off a fungus that grows on the decomposing leaves in their massive underground nests.

PRIME VIEWING   Can be found in most forests countrywide.

SCIENTIFIC NAME   *Nephila clavipes*

WORTH NOTING   The common Neotropical **golden silk spider** weaves meticulous webs that can be as much as .5m (2 ft.) across. The adult female of this species can reach 7.6 centimeters (3 in.) in length, including the legs, although the males are tiny. The silk of this spider is extremely strong and is being studied for industrial purposes.

PRIME VIEWING   Lowland forests on both coasts.

Golden Silk Spider

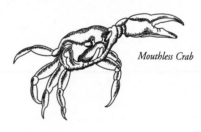

Mouthless Crab

SCIENTIFIC NAME   *Gecarcinus quadratus*

WORTH NOTING   The nocturnal **mouthless crab** is a distinctively colored land crab with bright orange legs, purple claws, and a deep black shell or carapace.

PRIME VIEWING   All along the Pacific coast.

SCIENTIFIC NAME   *Grapsus grapsus*

WORTH NOTING   Known simply as *cangrego* or "crab," this is the most common crab spotted in Costa Rica. It is a midsize crab with a colorful carapace that can range

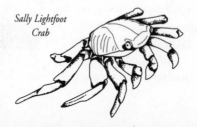

Sally Lightfoot Crab

from dark brown to deep red to bright yellow, with a wide variation in striations and spotting.

PRIME VIEWING   On rocky outcroppings near the water's edge all along both coasts.

2 Flora

TREES

Despite the cliché to the contrary, it's often a good thing to be able to identify specific trees within a forest. I've included illustrations of the leaves, flowers, seeds, and fruit to get you started.

SCIENTIFIC NAME   *Ceiba pentandra*

WORTH NOTING   Also known as the kapok tree, **ceiba** trees are typically emergent (their large umbrella-shape canopies emerge above the forest canopy), making the species among the tallest trees in the tropical forest. Reaching as high as 60m (197 ft.), their thick columnar trunks often have large buttresses. Ceiba trees may flower as little as once every 5 years, especially in wetter forests.

PRIME VIEWING   Countrywide.

Ceiba

SCIENTIFIC NAME   *Enterolobium cyclocarpum*

WORTH NOTING   The **guanacaste** tree is one of the largest trees found in Central America, and gives its name to Costa Rica's northwestern-most province. It can reach a total elevation of over 39m (130 ft.); its straight trunk composes 9 to 12m (30–40 ft.) of the height (the trunk's diameter measures more than 1.8m/6 ft.).

PRIME VIEWING   Countrywide.

Guanacaste

SCIENTIFIC NAME   *Ficus aurea*

WORTH NOTING   This parasitic tree gets its name from the fact that it envelops and eventually strangles its host tree. The *matapalo* or **strangler fig** begins as an epiphyte, whose seeds are deposited high in a tree's canopy by bats, birds, or monkeys. The young strangler then sends long roots down to the earth. The sap is used to relieve burns.

PRIME VIEWING   Primary and secondary forests countrywide.

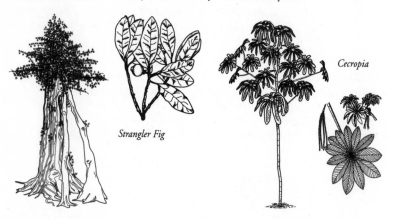

Strangler Fig

Cecropia

SCIENTIFIC NAME   *Cecropia obtusifolia*

WORTH NOTING   Several **Cecropia** (trumpet tree) species are found in Costa Rica. Most are characterized by large, handlike clusters of broad leaves, and a hollow, bamboolike trunk. They are "gap specialists," fast-growing opportunists that can fill in a gap caused by a tree fall or landslide. Their trunks are usually home to Aztec ants.

PRIME VIEWING   Primary and secondary forests, rivers, and roadsides, countrywide.

SCIENTIFIC NAME   *Bursera simaruba*

WORTH NOTING   The bark of the **gumbo limbo** is its most distinguishing feature: A paper-thin red outer layer, when peeled off the tree, reveals a bright green bark. In Costa Rica the tree is called *indio desnudo* (naked Indian). In other countries it is

Gumbo Limbo

the "tourist tree." Both names refer to reddish skin. The bark is used as a remedy for gum disease; gumbo limbo–bark tea allegedly alleviates hypertension. Another remarkable property is the tree's ability to root from its cut branches, which when planted right end up, develop roots and leaves, forming a new tree within a few years.

PRIME VIEWING Primary and secondary forests, countrywide.

FLOWERS & OTHER PLANTS

Costa Rica has an amazing wealth of tropical flora, including some 1,200 orchid species, and over 2,000 bromeliad species.

SCIENTIFIC NAME *Cattleya skinneri*

WORTH NOTING The **guaria morada** orchid is the national flower of Costa Rica. Sporting a purple and white flower, this plant is also called the "Easter orchid" as it tends to flower between March and April each year.

PRIME VIEWING Countrywide from sea level to 1,220m (4,000 ft.).

Guaria Morada

Heliconia

SCIENTIFIC NAME *Heliconia collinsiana*

WORTH NOTING There are more than 250 species of tropical heliconia, of which more than 40 are found in Costa Rica. The flowers of this species are darkish pink in color, and the underside of the plant's large leaves are coated in white wax.

PRIME VIEWING Low to middle elevations countrywide, particularly in moist environments.

SCIENTIFIC NAME *Psychotria poeppigiana*

WORTH NOTING Related to coffee, **hotlips** is a forest flower that boasts thick red "lips" that resemble the Rolling Stones logo. The small white flowers (found inside the red "lips") attract a variety of butterflies and hummingbirds.

PRIME VIEWING In the undergrowth of dense forests countrywide.

Hotlips

Red Torch Ginger

SCIENTIFIC NAME   *Nicolaia elatior*

WORTH NOTING   Called *bastón del emperador* (the Emperor's cane) in Costa Rica, the tall **red torch ginger** plant has an impressive bulbous red bract, often mistaken for the flower. The numerous, small white flowers actually emerge out of this bract. Originally a native to Indonesia, it is now quite common in Costa Rica.

PRIME VIEWING   Countrywide, particularly in moist environments and gardens.

SCIENTIFIC NAME   *Gunnera insignis*

WORTH NOTING   The **poor man's umbrella,** a broad-leaved rainforest ground plant, is a member of the rhubarb family. The massive leaves are often used, as the colloquial name suggests, for protection during rainstorms.

PRIME VIEWING   Low- to middle-elevation moist forests countrywide. Commonly seen in Poás National Park and Braulio Carrillo National Park.

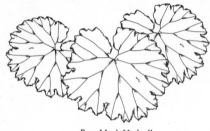

Poor Man's Umbrella

Index

See also Accommodations index, below.

ACCOMMODATIONS